Vanbrugh

by Kerry Downes

A. ZWEMMER LTD

Published by A. Zwemmer Ltd, 76–80 Charing Cross Road, London WC2
ISBN 302 02769 6
Printed in Great Britain by Lund Humphries, London and Bradford

J.W.W. and L.R.W. in Memoriam

Contents

List of Plates

List of Text Illustrations

Abbreviations

Note: year dates are given New Style throughout unless otherwise noted.

Account Book	Vanbrugh's Account Book (printed here, Chapter 12)
Beard	G. W. Beard, *Georgian Craftsmen*, 1966
BIHR	Borthwick Institute of Historical Research, University of York
BIHR (Yarburgh)	Yarburgh papers in the above
BM	British Museum, London
Bodl.	Bodleian Library, Oxford, Western MSS.
Chandos	C. H. Collins Baker and M. I. Baker, *The Life and Circumstances of James Brydges, Duke of Chandos*, Oxford, 1949
Colvin	H. M. Colvin, *Biographical Dictionary of English Architects 1660–1840*, 1954
CRO	County Record Office
CSP Dom	*Calendar of State Papers, Domestic*
CSP Col	*Calendar of State Papers, Colonial*
CTB	*Calendar of Treasury Books*
CTP	*Calendar of Treasury Papers*
DCR	Registers of the Dutch Church, London (Guildhall Library MS.7381, to 1601, MS.7382, from 1602)
Denizations	*Denizations and Naturalizations 1603–1700*, ed. W. A. Shaw (*Huguenot Society*, XVIII, 1911)
DNB	*Dictionary of National Biography*
Downes (1959)	K. Downes, *Hawksmoor*, 1959
Downes (1966)	K. Downes, *English Baroque Architecture*, 1966
Downes (1969)	K. Downes, *Hawksmoor*, 1969
Downes (1971)	K. Downes, *Christopher Wren*, 1971
Elton Drawings	H. M. Colvin and M. J. Craig, *Architectural Drawings in the Library of Elton Hall* (Roxburghe Club), 1964
English Homes	H. A. Tipping and C. Hussey, *English Homes*, IV, ii, *The Work of Sir John Vanbrugh and His School*, 1928
Foster, *Grantees*	*Grantees of Arms . . . between the years 1687 and 1898 . . . collected . . . by . . . Joseph Foster* (*Harleian Society*, LXVII–LXVIII, 1916–17)
Foster, *Oxon.*	J. Foster, *Alumni Oxonienses*, Oxford, 1891
Gent. Mag.	*Gentleman's Magazine*
Godfrey	W. H. Godfrey and others, *The College of Arms*, 1963
Green	D. Green, *Blenheim Palace*, 1951
Guildhall	Guildhall Library, London
Harl. Soc.	*Harleian Society Publications*

Hessels III	J. H. Hessels, *Ecclesiae Londino-Batavae Archivum*, III, 1897
Hessels IV	J. H. Hessels, *Archives of the London Dutch Church*, 1892
HMC	*Historical Manuscripts Commission* Reports and Calendars (with name of collection or number of report)
King's Works	H. M. Colvin, ed., *The History of the King's Works*, 1963–
Lees-Milne	J. Lees-Milne, *English Country Houses, Baroque*, 1970
Le Neve	P. Le Neve, *Pedigrees of the Knights* (*Harleian Society*, VIII, 1873)
Luttrell	N. Luttrell, *A Brief Relation of Historical and State Affairs*, Oxford, 1857
Moens	W. J. C. Moens, *The Marriage, Baptismal and Burial Registers . . . of the Dutch Reformed Church*, Lymington, 1884
Palladio	A. Palladio, *I Quattro Libri dell' Architettura*, Venice, 1570
Parentalia	C. Wren, *Parentalia*, 1750
PRO	Public Record Office, London
PROB	Probate Documents of the Prerogative Court of Canterbury, now in the PRO, transferred from Somerset House. The Registered Copy Wills (PROB 11) are in a sequence of numbered volumes, in which a folio (fol.) consists of 4 or 8 leaves
Returns II, III	*Returns of Aliens* (*Huguenot Society*, x, parts ii, iii, 1903, 1907)
RIBA	*Catalogue of Drawings in the Royal Institute of British Architects, London*
RO	Record Office
Rosenberg	A. Rosenberg, 'New Light on Vanbrugh', *Philological Quarterly*, XLV, 1966, pp.603–13
SOED	Shorter Oxford English Dictionary
Survey of London	London Survey Committee, afterwards Greater London Council, *Survey of London*
V & A	Victoria and Albert Museum, London
Venn	J. and J. A. Venn, *Alumni Cantabrigienses*, Cambridge, 1922–54
Vit. Brit.	C. Campbell, *Vitruvius Britannicus*, 1715–25
Walbrook Register	Register of St Stephen Walbrook, London (Guildhall MS.8319, printed in *Harleian Society, Register Series*)
Webb	*The Complete Works of Sir John Vanbrugh*, IV, *The Letters*, ed. Geoffrey Webb, 1928
Whistler	L. Whistler, *The Imagination of Vanbrugh and his Fellow Artists*, 1954
Whistler (1938)	L. Whistler, *Sir John Vanbrugh*, 1938
Wren Soc.	*Wren Society Publications*, 1923–43

Preface

This book has expanded with an irony not inappropriate to its subject. It was intended originally to combine a short survey of accepted knowledge about Vanbrugh's architecture with an attempt to restore the balance in the reputation of two great men, in which Vanbrugh has suffered from Hawksmoor's gain. It soon became clear, however, that rather little knowledge of Vanbrugh could be considered 'accepted'. He was a man of many accomplishments, and while I hope it is clear that he became foremost an architect it is inevitable that the discipline of the history of art spread into others less familiar to me. My excuse for three detailed chapters on his family is the abundance of hypothetical, unsubstantiated or erroneous statements in the previous literature.

The acuity of my wife's instinct for stones unturned, or ready for turning again, is shown by the whole second part of the book, which embodies the results of our joint researches. We count ourselves fortunate in being able to use many of the difficult original documents before these were replaced by even more difficult photographic copies. While our discoveries might have been summarized with the idea of eventual fuller presentation, the architect's account book seemed so important as to alter the whole balance of the work, especially as this unique document came to our notice when we knew how to solve many of its puzzles. Again, in view of Vanbrugh's stature and variety, the opportunity itself of publishing the account book in full seems to me adequate justification for doing so.

An author's debts are many and diverse, but the greatest are to those persons on whom in some way the book's very existence depends. First then to John Fleming and Hugh Honour, under whose editorship in another series the first part was originally drafted. Had it been planned at the outset as part of the larger work now presented, it might have been different but not, I think, better. When the development of the material seemed to me finally so momentous as to involve a change to another series, they generously acquiesced in the transfer. Laurence Whistler, whose name will always be justly associated with Vanbrugh, has over many years been unsparing with information, with moral support, and more recently with encouragement to undertake a subject which has been very much his own. For over a decade Margaret Whinney taught me at the Courtauld Institute in the field to which Vanbrugh belongs; subsequently and for longer as a friend she sustained a lively interest in the field. Sadly she did not live to fulfil the wish she had expressed to read this book in proof. I would also acknowledge here the past privilege of illuminating conversations with the late Geoffrey Webb, whose edition of Vanbrugh's letters has been my almost daily reading over several years, and whose insight into the period and into the psychology of the artist were both remarkable and humane. In more material respects my particular gratitude goes to Desmond Zwemmer for his ready support at critical moments; to Mr George Howard, who has long been generous with facilities and with information about the buildings and documents at Castle Howard, and to His Grace the Duke of Marlborough who has allowed me exceptional facilities for research and photography at Blenheim.

Many friends, colleagues and others previously unknown to me have answered my questions and offered me information. The sections on Vanbrugh's gardens were sketched for, and benefited from, a colloquium on garden history held at the Courtauld Institute in August 1973. Although my research on Vanbrugh has been independent of that as a contributor to the *History of the King's Works*, I have had the privilege of access to the relevant volume of the latter in proof. Particular thanks are due to Alan Bean (on documents), Patricia M. Butler (on Suffolk), Howard Colvin (on many things), Timothy Connor (on Grimsthorpe and Houghton), Trevor Dannatt (on Greenwich), Katharine Fremantle (on Thornhill), G. B. Greenwood (on Walton and Esher), Bernard Harris (on plays and Vanbrugh's son), John Harris (on many things), Edward Hubbard (on Cheshire), Roger Quarm and Neil Rhind (on Greenwich matters), Raymond Richards (on Cheshire), John Rowntree (on Scarborough), Frank Simpson (on pictures), Norman Summers and Keith Train (on Nottinghamshire), T. E. Conway-Walker (on Esher), and Peter Willis (on gardens and on Seaton Delaval). The owners of buildings and documents have been liberal with permission to study and reproduce them. Among the many institutions which have helped my wife and myself we should like to thank especially the staffs of the Guildhall Library, the Goldsmiths', Mercers' and Skinners' Companies, London, Mr Reginald Winder of Hoare's Bank, John Hayes and Richard Ormond of the National Portrait Gallery, Julian Watson of the Greenwich Local Collections, John Hopkins, Librarian of the Society of Antiquaries, and last but not least the staff of the Borthwick Institute of Historical Research, University of York. We hope that those many helpful persons not singled out for mention will accept our thanks nonetheless.

The last stage in writing a book is one which, if well done, leaves no trace in print: the final copy for the printer. This was the work of our friend Marion Smith, who instead of a holiday came to stay, and in the minimum of time and with the greatest skill and co-operation produced from a series of overworked drafts an impeccable typescript complete to the last footnote.

It was not originally foreseen that this book would appear in the two hundred and fiftieth anniversary year of Vanbrugh's death, but we should like to think that the tribute would be acceptable to him.

Department of Fine Art
University of Reading
September, 1975

Acknowledgements

Pl.118 and Fig.11 are reproduced by gracious permission of Her Majesty the Queen.

Drawings and other works are reproduced by permission of the following: The Warden and Fellows of All Souls College, Oxford, Pl.83; the Earl of Ancaster and the Lincolnshire Archives Committee, Pls 92, 94, Fig.18; Bodleian Library, Oxford, Pls 55, 74, 82, 108, Fig.8; British Museum, 25, 34; British Library Board, 90, 107, 112, 113, 114, 149; The Duke of Marlborough, 50; The Trustee of the Martin Collection, London Borough of Greenwich Local History Library, Pl.111; National Portrait Gallery, Frontis., Pl.1; The Duke of Portland, Pl.18; Sir Richard Proby, Pls 106, 109, 110, 156, Figs 1, 6, 7, 13(B); Public Record Office, Pl.146; Sir John Soane's Museum, Pl.24; Society of Antiquaries of London, Pl.105; Victoria and Albert Museum, Pls 20, 21, 48, 70, 86, 93, 133, Figs 5, 20; The Provost and Fellows of Worcester College, Oxford, Pl.134.

Documents in Chapter 12 and the Appendixes are printed by kind permission of the Bodleian Library, the Borthwick Institute of Historical Research, University of York, the British Library Board, The Marquess of Cholmondeley, Leicestershire County Record Office (Hanbury Deposit), the Public Record Office, and the Victoria and Albert Museum.

The following credits are also due: *Country Life*, Pls 11, 37, 38; A. F. Kersting, Pl.51; National Monuments Record, Pls 22, 33, 35, 39, 45, 144, 148; *The Studio*, Pl.36; Warburg Institute, Pls 97a, 98, 100, 101; G. Zarnecki, Pl.16. Fig.4 is reproduced by permission from Richard Leacroft's *Development of the English Playhouse* (Eyre Methuen Ltd).

Introduction

Vanbrugh, Sir John, Kt 1714; architect and dramatist, Comptroller of H.M. Works since 1715 (re-appointed), Surveyor of H.M. Gardens and Waters since 1715, Surveyor, Greenwich Hospital since 1716. *b* Jan. 1664, *s* of Giles Vanbrugh of London and Chester, and Elizabeth, *d* of Sir Dudley Carleton of Imber Court; *m* 1719, Henrietta Maria, *d* of Col. James Yarburgh of Heslington Hall, York; one *s*. Capt. Earl of Huntingdon's Ft Regt, 1686; political prisoner in France 1688–92; Auditor, Duchy of Lancaster, Southern Divn, 1693–1702; Capt. Lord Berkeley's Marine Regt, 1695–1702. Comptroller of Works 1702–13; Carlisle Herald 1703; Clarenceux Herald 1704–25 (nominated Garter 1715–19); Commissioner for building new churches 1711–15. Founder and architect, Queen's Theatre, Haymarket, 1703. *Plays include* The Relapse, 1696; The Provok'd Wife, 1697; The Pilgrim, 1700; The Confederacy, 1705. *Architectural works include* Castle Howard, 1699; Blenheim, 1705; Kings Weston, 1711; Grimsthorpe Castle (in progress); Claremont, 1715; Eastbury, 1718 (in progress); Seaton Delaval, 1719 (in progress); Temple at Castle Howard, 1725 (in progress). *Recreations*: politics, staying in country houses, listening to music, writing letters. *Address*: H.M. Office of Works, Scotland Yard; Vanbrugh Castle, Greenwich; Vanbrugh House, Whitehall. *Club*: Kit-Cat.

[*Died 26 March 1726*]

This is what might have appeared in *Who's Who* if that publication had existed in 1726. It is intended to introduce Vanbrugh rather than to give a precise – or even a totally straight-faced – account of his activities.

Overleaf will be found tables, supplementary to the family trees on pp.129–37, designed to show how Vanbrugh was related to a number of important figures; only persons relevant in some way are included. In two cases (Lords Huntingdon and Willoughby) he acknowledged kinship, but Lords Carlisle and Bindon were among his patrons and other noblemen were his associates; Vanbrugh was undoubtedly aware of the existence rather than the details of these connections.

In these tables, which have been compiled from Collins's *Peerage, Harleian Society* Visitations and Pedigrees and other standard printed works, typographical conventions are used as follows: *ITALICS* for forebears of approximately equivalent generation; **BOLD** for the Carletons (Vanbrugh's mother's family); ROMAN CAPITALS for his friends, patrons and associates. Mention is made of membership of the Kit-Cat Club.

Kinship in Vanbrugh's Patrons and Associates

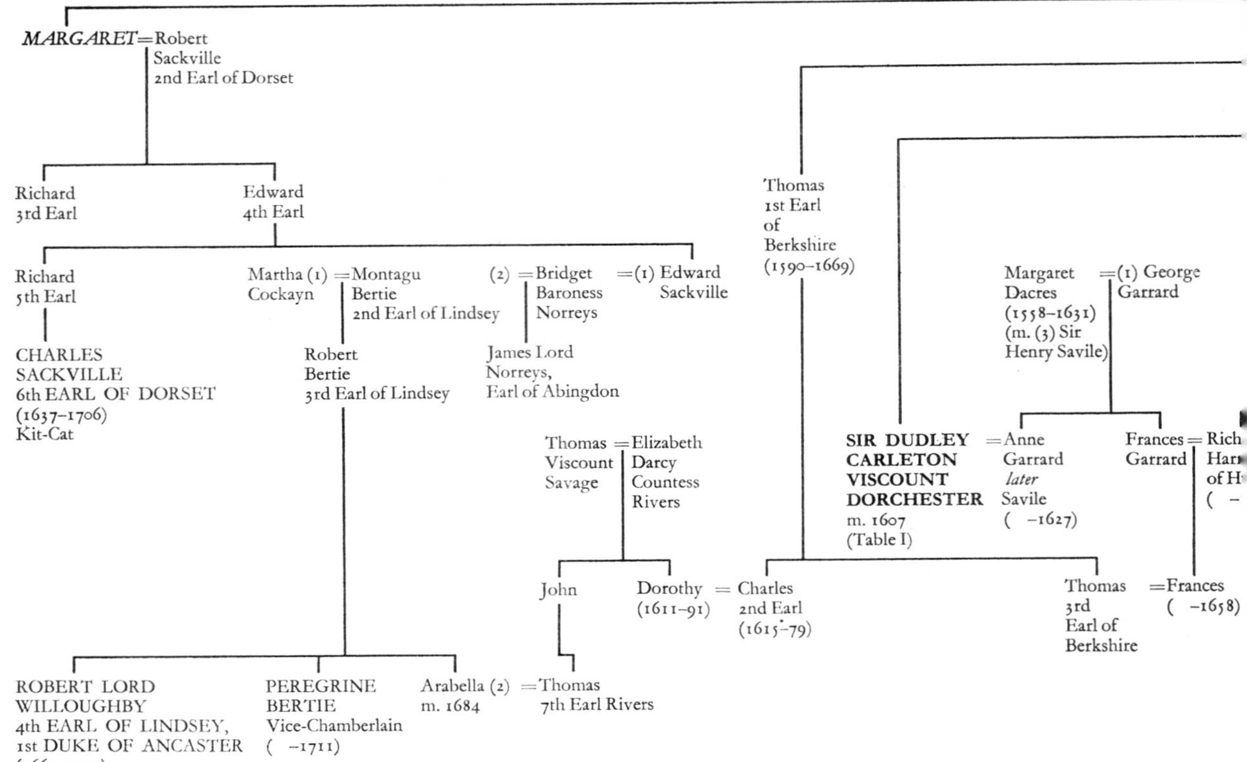

(A) Howard and Bertie connections

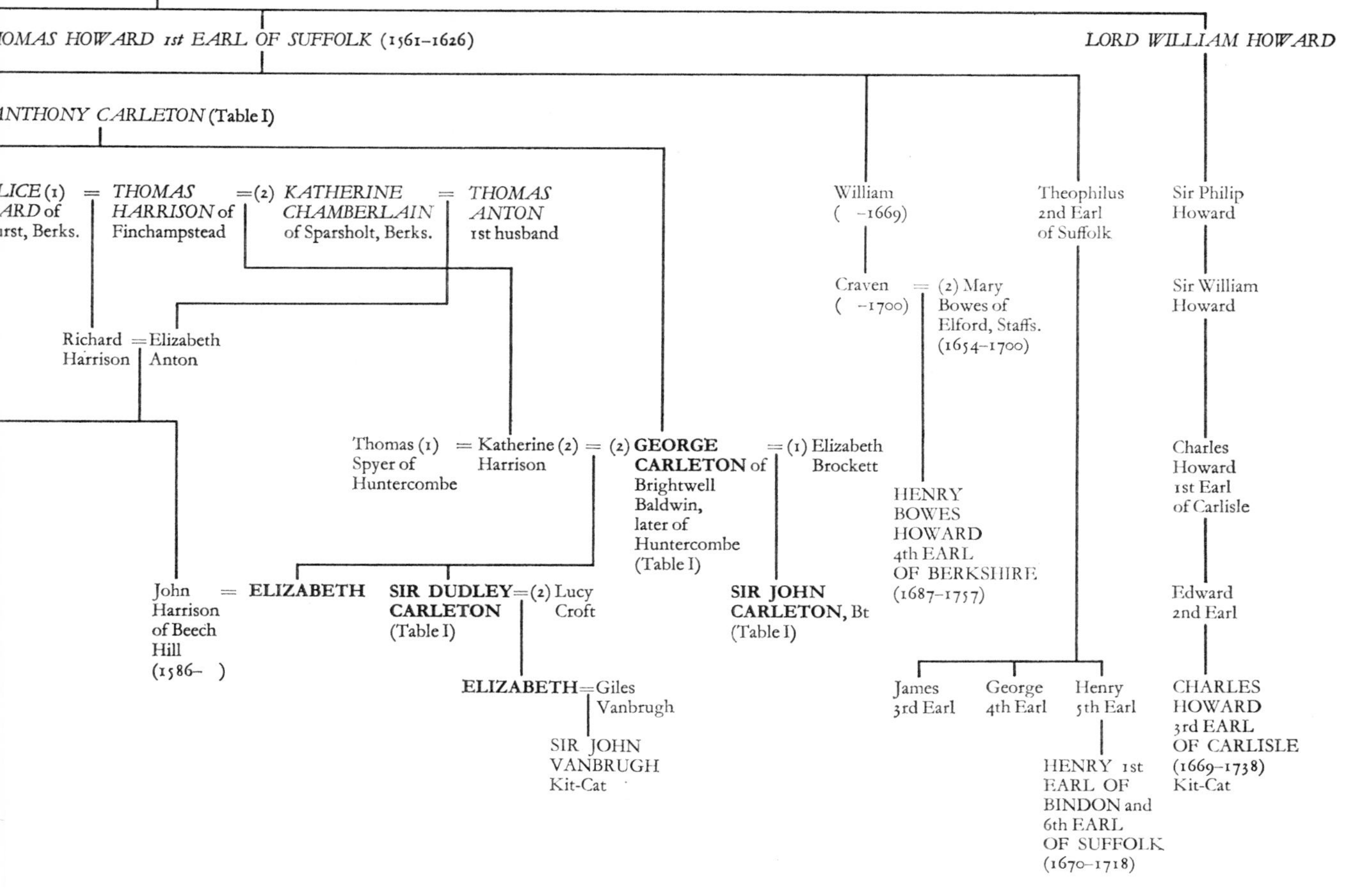

homas Howard 4th Duke of Norfolk (1536–72)
HOMAS HOWARD 1st EARL OF SUFFOLK (1561–1626)
LORD WILLIAM HOWARD
ANTHONY CARLETON (Table I)
LICE (1) ARD of urst, Berks.
THOMAS HARRISON of Finchampstead
(2) KATHERINE CHAMBERLAIN of Sparsholt, Berks.
THOMAS ANTON 1st husband
William (–1669)
Theophilus 2nd Earl of Suffolk
Sir Philip Howard
Craven (–1700)
(2) Mary Bowes of Elford, Staffs. (1654–1700)
Sir William Howard
Richard Harrison
Elizabeth Anton
Thomas (1) Spyer of Huntercombe
Katherine (2) Harrison
(2) GEORGE CARLETON of Brightwell Baldwin, later of Huntercombe (Table I)
(1) Elizabeth Brockett
Charles Howard 1st Earl of Carlisle
HENRY BOWES HOWARD 4th EARL OF BERKSHIRE (1687–1757)
John Harrison of Beech Hill (1586–)
ELIZABETH
SIR DUDLEY CARLETON (Table I)
(2) Lucy Croft
SIR JOHN CARLETON, Bt (Table I)
Edward 2nd Earl
ELIZABETH
Giles Vanbrugh
James 3rd Earl
George 4th Earl
Henry 5th Earl
CHARLES HOWARD 3rd EARL OF CARLISLE (1669–1738) Kit-Cat
SIR JOHN VANBRUGH Kit-Cat
HENRY 1st EARL OF BINDON and 6th EARL OF SUFFOLK (1670–1718)

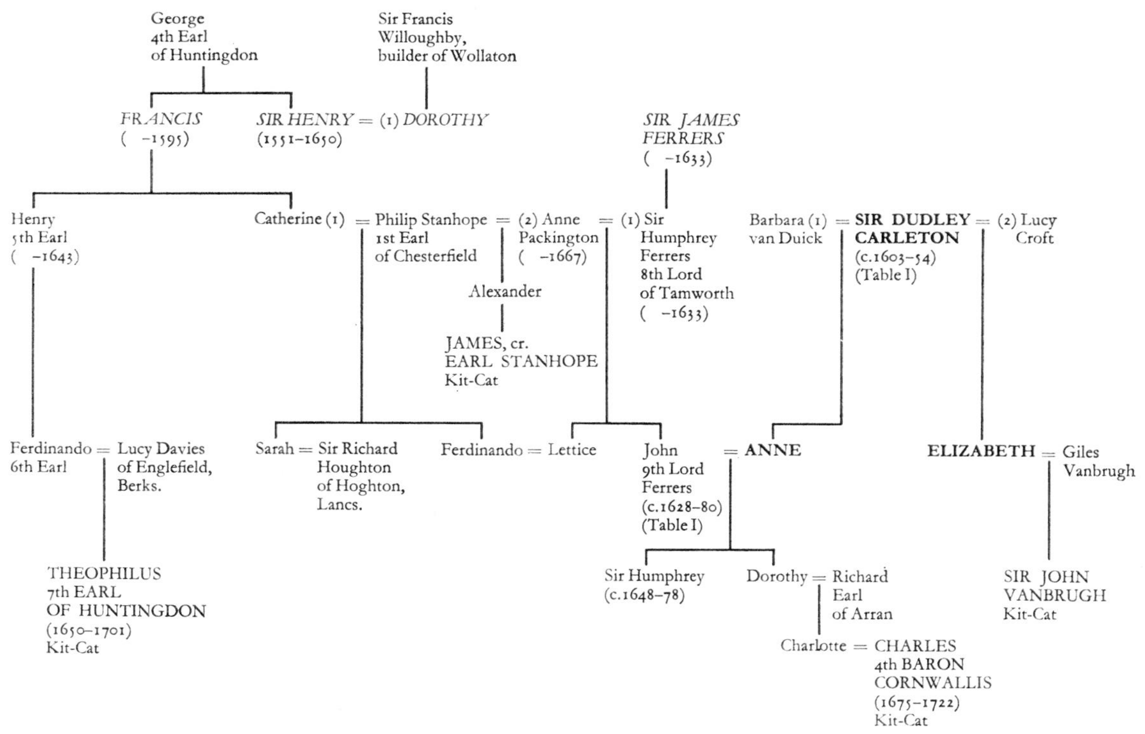

George 4th Earl of Huntingdon
Sir Francis Willoughby, builder of Wollaton
FRANCIS (–1595)
SIR HENRY (1551–1650)
(1) DOROTHY
SIR JAMES FERRERS (–1633)
Henry 5th Earl (–1643)
Catherine (1)
Philip Stanhope 1st Earl of Chesterfield
(2) Anne Packington (–1667)
(1) Sir Humphrey Ferrers 8th Lord of Tamworth (–1633)
Barbara (1) van Duick
SIR DUDLEY CARLETON (c.1603–54) (Table I)
(2) Lucy Croft
Alexander
JAMES, cr. EARL STANHOPE Kit-Cat
Ferdinando 6th Earl
Lucy Davies of Englefield, Berks.
Sarah
Sir Richard Houghton of Hoghton, Lancs.
Ferdinando
Lettice
John 9th Lord Ferrers (c.1628–80) (Table I)
ANNE
ELIZABETH
Giles Vanbrugh
THEOPHILUS 7th EARL OF HUNTINGDON (1650–1701) Kit-Cat
Sir Humphrey (c.1648–78)
Dorothy
Richard Earl of Arran
SIR JOHN VANBRUGH Kit-Cat
Charlotte
CHARLES 4th BARON CORNWALLIS (1675–1722) Kit-Cat

(B) Hastings and Ferrers connections

Part I
The Architecture of Vanbrugh

Chapter 1

Vanbrugh's House

On the evening of 4 January 1698 a maid is said to have left some linen to air before the hearth in one of the hundreds of rooms that made up the rambling Palace of Whitehall. On this occasion the common but risky practice was disastrous: the linen caught fire, then the room, and then the building. By next morning London correspondents were reporting to the country the nearly total loss of the Palace, its Tudor and Caroline state-rooms, its theatre, and the new range of private apartments built by Sir Christopher Wren and finished only ten years before, including the elaborate Popish chapel designed for James II. The Queen's Building overlooking the river, which was even more recent, was gutted. The lodgings over towards St James's Park, known collectively as the Cockpit, survived and so did the administrative buildings, including those of the Office of Works, in Scotland Yard to the north. Of the palace proper, little to speak of was saved beyond the Banqueting House of Inigo Jones and the three gateways from Whitehall street into the palace and out towards Charing Cross and Westminster. William III was chesty and preferred the drier atmosphere of Kensington, only coming to Whitehall on council days. He was aware that 'Whitehall' was synonymous with government, but the King's Works were subject to a chronic shortage of money, and the King decided to shelve Whitehall, Narcissus Luttrell tells us, 'till the parliament provide for the same' a special vote for rebuilding. William was not a popular figure and it was for fear of something worse, the return of James II from exile in France, that the majority of Englishmen wished to keep William, their first constitutional monarch, on the throne. It was from Whitehall that Charles I had stepped to his execution for high treason in 1649, and amid the allegations in different quarters that the Whigs, or the Jacobites, had started the fire deliberately, the site was surveyed by Wren, and some attempt was made to clear up and make safe the ruins. That was to be all. William decided to press on with Wren's modernization of Hampton Court as a counterpart of Versailles.

Three years after the fire the Treasury confirmed a grant from the King to John Vanbrugh, then a successful writer of comedies, aged thirty-seven, to build a house for himself at his own expense, but using brick and stone from the ruins, on the site of the Vice-Chamberlain's lodgings.[1] In subsequent years other gentlemen followed suit and the old palace was buried for ever under select eighteenth-century residences, some of which survive as government offices.

The grant afforded a dwelling-place, within hailing distance of the official – if not

[1] CTB 1700–01, p.48; PRO T27/16/324; *Survey of London*, XVI, 1935, pp.168–71. Vanbrugh's house stood on what is now the north side of Horse Guards Avenue, about 70 yards from modern Whitehall.

actual – residences of the Surveyor and other officers of the Works, for a recent convert to architecture who was not connected with royal building. Wren as Surveyor was able to recognize in others artistic talents very different to his own, and he may have encouraged Vanbrugh's advancement in architecture. It is certain that in 1700 he knew more of the extent of Vanbrugh's talents than we do now, through the intermediacy of his assistant Nicholas Hawksmoor who, as we shall see, was working for Vanbrugh elsewhere. Another contact was Vanbrugh's cousin William, Secretary to Greenwich Hospital and an officer of the Royal Household. The location of Vanbrugh's house was a delicate matter of etiquette; it also confirmed Wren's fears that a new Whitehall Palace was out of the question, and in his words it offered 'a precedent for more of this nature.' Wren felt bound to ask for instructions from the Treasury on grounds of precedent, because his orders had been 'not to permit any new Foundacions in his Majestys Palaces', and because the warrant did not limit either the amount of materials or the ground site at Vanbrugh's disposal. Thus it was on 1 March 1701 that the Treasury informed the Works that a house might be built on a plot not exceeding 64 feet square.

The Vice-Chamberlain, on the site of whose official residence Vanbrugh built his new house, was a friend, and distantly a relative, of the architect. Vanbrugh's connections with the Bertie family, of whom the principals were Lords Willoughby of Eresby and Earls of Lindsey, and later Dukes of Ancaster, can be traced, albeit imperfectly, throughout his adult life, and in 1692 he quoted, and did not deny, a statement by the English Ambassador to Paris to the effect that 'I had been at the Hague in my Lord Willoughbys Company; That I was his Relation, and that (as he was pleas'd to say) I lead all the Bertue family, wch way I wou'd.'[2] Lord Willoughby was then Robert (d. 1723), son of the 3rd Earl of Lindsey, whom he succeeded in 1701. The 3rd Earl's second son, Peregrine (d. 1711), was appointed Vice-Chamberlain of the Household early in 1694.[3] He is several times mentioned in Vanbrugh's letters either by name or as 'The Vice',[4] and was described in 1694 as Mr Vanbrugh's intimate friend;[5] the choice of site for the house may thus not have been fortuitous.

Vanbrugh's house was unique (Pl.24). He appears to have designed it himself. It was very small, of two storeys with the roof hidden by a parapet, and it was squat on the ground. It looked at its neighbour the Banqueting House as a sparrow might look at a swan, and was unkindly likened by Swift – whose imagery has stuck to it – to a goose pie, which was presumably a square one. Vanbrugh had no ground lease for the property until

[2] Appendix B (2).

[3] Luttrell, III, p.271 (20 Feb. 1694). Warrant 14 April 1694 (CTB 1693–6, p.580).

[4] Webb, pp.5, 17, 25, 51.

[5] Appendix C. While there were several Mr Vanbrughs at that date, it is reasonable to assume that John is understood in the light of his later references to Peregrine. The latter must have been the Peregrine, 'son to the late earl of Lindsey', who in August 1690 'upon a wager run the Mall in St James Park 11 times in less than an hour' (Luttrell, II, p.98). The Peregrine of the previous generation was nearly sixty and less likely to have run six miles: 'Old Peregrine' is mentioned by Vanbrugh in 1699 (Webb, p.5).

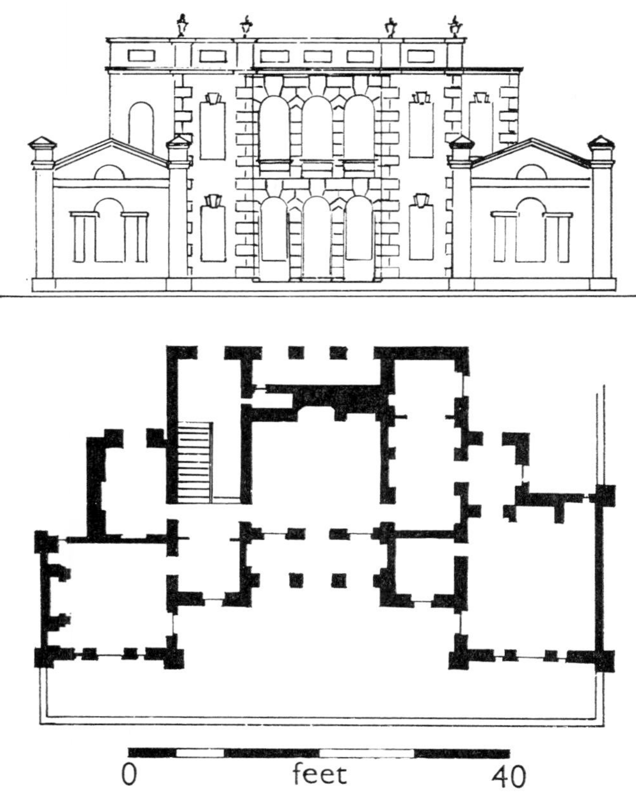

1 Vanbrugh House, Whitehall. Plan and elevation. From a drawing at Elton Hall (112).

1719 when, newly married, he himself enlarged the house.[6] He then added the wings, with Venetian windows, which projected in front to form a small court. It is clear from a plan and elevation which come from his office (Fig. 1) and were probably made at the time of the enlargement, that the banded rustication of the stucco in the centre bays is Vanbrugh's own. The drawing made for Sir John Soane shows the effect of alterations in the 1790s, but gives a better idea of the house in three dimensions than old photographs, for before its demolition in 1906 the house had suffered further disfiguring alterations. Originally it was a well thought out small house for a professed bachelor, conveniently planned within the framework of its symmetrical shape and central loggia and entrance hall. A second loggia at the back looked over what can only have been a tiny garden and obliquely to the right towards the Strand and the City. The only external departure from symmetry is

[6] In August 1718 Vanbrugh petitioned for a lease, having had no legal title previously (CTB 1718, p.519). Bricklayer's bill paid 17 Aug. 1720; fee for passing the lease, 12 Nov. (Account Book, ff.32v, 33v). The house remained in the family until 1793 when Edward Vanbrugh sold it to the Hon. Charles Stewart. The character of a goose pie is obscure. Working backwards from Swift's comparison, it would appear to be rectangular rather than round, like what is known in the trade as a 'raised pie.' It was also large; in an unfinished and undated play, *A Journey to London*, Vanbrugh presented a country family who on arrival in London were robbed of their hand baggage, including the 'great goose pie' which was snatched from under the arm of the cook. Another feature of goose pie may have been an assortment of ingredients: according to the *Oxford English Dictionary* it was made of 'goose, etc.' and there is an aptly derogatory use of the term in a letter of the Earl of Mar in 1718. Writing about a design made for him by an Italian architect, full of 'trifling gimcrack insignificant ornaments, worthy of nobody but Vanbruge', he says that the Italian 'has made a goose pie of my plan and on it raised a modern Gothick superstructure of an order of his own' (HMC Stuart VI, p.162). Mar may have referred to Swift's poem.

likely to have been the small room projecting from the middle of the right-hand side, which according to the longer of Swift's two lampoons contained a privy.[7]

In elevation the house was more remarkable, in fact quite unlike any previous town or country house. That it was detached, and thus not a 'town house' in our modern estate agent's sense, is not surprising since instead of being in a street it was on an open site in the former palace yard. Even so, the conventional formula would have been a regular elevation in one plane with identical bays of rectangular windows except for one, in the middle or otherwise, containing the doorway; in a freestanding house the same pattern would continue along the sides, and the storeys would be separated by horizontal mouldings roughly at upper-floor levels. Only a grand and expensive, and thus probably large-scale, house would depart from this formula. Vanbrugh, on the other hand, achieved a kind of grandeur on a small scale, by treating the middle three bays of his symmetrical elevation as a unit, in which the divisions between them are much less marked than the divisions from the end bays. This is done first of all by the absence of mouldings round the arches of the ground-floor loggia and first-floor windows, and secondly by making the side bays project, by emphasizing the projections with quoining and by giving them openings that are different in shape and size and have prominent sills and triple keystones.

Swift was too concerned with ridicule, or too insensitive to the qualities of architecture in general and those of sculptural architecture in particular, to appreciate the worth of Vanbrugh's novelty. We can no longer tell how the side walls were treated before the enlargement, but it must have stood free and foursquare and gaunt and uncompromising in its proportions near to a perfect cube, with its surfaces punctured rather than adorned by arches and windows. Swift also made play of the smallness of the house in comparison with one like Blenheim; he did not understand monumentality enough to realize that it is neither synonymous with nor dependent on largeness.

Vanbrugh's house in the ruins of Whitehall made common knowledge in the metropolis what was already known to his acquaintances: that he was seriously concerned with the practice of architecture. How this happened is one of the crucial questions of late seventeenth- and early eighteenth-century English architecture, and one which must be examined with some care and detail in order to understand Vanbrugh's achievement. It is unlikely that the full story will ever be known, and contemporaries were surprised, not to say puzzled. Swift wrote in 1706:

> Van's genius, without Thought or Lecture
> Is hugely turn'd to architecture.[8]

Enough of Van's genius was visible by then at Castle Howard and in the footings of Blenheim to explain the word *hugely*. Formal instruction was not available, and *lecture* thus means study by reading, and for Swift it was clear that Vanbrugh was prepared for those great enterprises by neither study nor premeditation. An examination of the sequence and timing of events leading to his architectural conversion shows this view to be over-

[7] 'The Epilogue behind, did frame
A Place not decent here to name'
(*V-'s House*, 1708). The standard modern edition of the poems is by H. Williams, Oxford, 1937. A chancery suit of 1702 confirms that 'rustic quoins and panels' in brick were original (PRO C5/314/25).

[8] *The History of Vanbrug's House*, 1706.

simple, but it remains true that while we may choose to interpret the little we know of Vanbrugh's first thirty-five years in the light of his later career in architecture, there is nothing in our knowledge of his earlier life from which to predict the later.

John Vanbrugh was born in January 1664 in the parish of St Nicholas Acons in the City of London, the fourth of nineteen children, and the eldest son to survive into adulthood. His father, Giles, was a City merchant, born in England and of Flemish Protestant origin; his original business was in the cloth trade, and he had many family and commercial connections in the City. Giles was a man of some culture, and from a letter of his, written in an educated hand, we learn that he spent three years in France and Italy 'for pleasure and improvement' including a year in Rome; there he caught the germ of a scheme, elaborated after the Popish Plot, to 'liberate' the contents of the Vatican Library in the service of Protestantism.[9] John's mother Elizabeth and her sister Dorothy were both daughters of Sir Dudley Carleton who was the nephew of Viscount Dorchester; John also claimed the 7th Earl of Huntingdon as his kinsman. Giles Vanbrugh and his family may have left London during the Plague of 1665 or after the Great Fire of 1666, but Giles was still in business in London in February 1667;[10] some time in that year they moved to Chester, where Giles acquired and managed a business in sugar refining and confectionery.[11] Chester was a garrison town and a port for Ireland, America and the West Indies; hence the relevance of the sugar trade. It was also deeply provincial; however, the recognition of his mother's lineage alone would have sufficed, when John grew up, to allow him to move easily and congenially among the landed and titled classes when he met them. His education could have been in Chester, but it was very common to send boys away either to school or to a tutor (often a parson).[12] All we know is that he wrote a good hand. It would be natural for the son of a prosperous merchant with many family connections among London merchants to start in employment with one of them, and indeed a John Vanbrugg was working for Giles's cousin William Matthews, in the London wine and brandy trade, in about 1681. But Matthews went bankrupt the following year, and it is clear from John's subsequent life that commerce was not his choice.[13] Yet some trace of early training in the world of business appears in the carefully kept accounts which survive for the last ten years of his life.[14]

The story that Vanbrugh went to France in 1683 to study architecture seems to be entirely fictitious.[15] But when he was just twenty-two he took up the traditional alternative avocation of the upper middle class, the king's shilling. On 30 January 1686 he was commissioned in Lord Huntingdon's Foot Regiment, although when the promise of adventure looked unlikely to be fulfilled he resigned: that summer the regiment was

[9] See p.164 and Appendix A.

[10] See p.165.

[11] See p.165.

[12] There is no evidence that he went to school in Chester; he is not in G. D. Squibb's list of scholars compiled for the King's School there (copy in Chester City RO). The school at Ashby-de-la-Zouch had Huntingdon associations and was founded by the 3rd Earl. Could the 7th Earl's help to Vanbrugh (n.16) have been in this direction?

[13] See p.146.

[14] See p.174.

[15] See p.126. A reference in 1725 (Webb, p.170) to his having begun his days in a French prison would seem to confirm that there was no previous study visit.

posted to Guernsey, and such postings were commonly for life without the prospect of relief.[16]

In 1687 Vanbrugh was already involved in the affairs of the Bertie family. James Bertie, Earl of Abingdon, had been elected High Steward of Oxford, and at his installation on 16 September 1687 the freedom of the City and bailiff's places were given to Robert Lord Willoughby, Peregrine Bertie, Charles Bertie, John Vanbrooke and other members of his retinue.[17] For Vanbrugh the honour was a brief one, for he was one of those removed from office by order of James II on 16 February 1688.[18]

In July 1689 John's father died, leaving him one-seventh – the eldest son's share – of the estate. By that time John had been several months in a French prison. The official French version of the time was that he was arrested at Calais in the summer of 1690, as he was preparing to leave France without a passport in time of war, but from his own account that must have been a statesmanly fiction.[19] He had been arrested two years earlier for talking about William of Orange, and used as a hostage in exchange for a French spy, and since he was neither a celebrity nor a spy the negotiations were fruitless. In 1691 he was moved, at his request and his own expense, from Calais to Vincennes; nevertheless his treatment subsequently deteriorated sufficiently for him to begin a campaign of complaints to Louis XIV which finally resulted in his transfer, in February 1692, to the Bastille. Besides the higher tone and better administration of this fortress, the move gave him the benefit of renewed attention to his case in London, and in November 1692 he was finally released on surety as part of an exchange of political prisoners; he returned to England in April 1693.[20] On 3 May he resumed an appointment apparently made while he was in prison, as Auditor for the Southern Division of the Duchy of Lancaster; the Chancellor of the Duchy was his friend Robert Bertie.[21] Vanbrugh had been with him in Holland shortly before his arrest in France,[22] and the young nobleman may have felt some personal responsibility for Vanbrugh's misfortunes abroad, and obtained the appointment as compensation. The post was a sinecure, which Vanbrugh held until 1702, but we next hear of his commission at the end of 1695 as a captain of marines, and he did

[16] He wrote to the Earl of Huntingdon as his kinsman on 28 Dec. 1685, acknowledging previous help and asking for employment (Rosenberg, pp.603–4). He was commissioned ensign in Huntingdon's Regiment on 30 Jan. 1686 (CSP Dom 1686–7, p.20) and resigned in August (C. Dalton, *English Army Lists*, II, p.67).

[17] M. G. Hobson, *Oxford Council Acts 1665–1701* (*Oxford Historical Soc.*, N.S.2, 1939), p.191, 12 and 16 Sep. 1687. For the Bertie family in general see Arthur Collins, *The Peerage of England*, and *Harl. Soc.*, L, 1902, pp.129–31.

[18] Hobson, op.cit., p.196.

[19] He was probably arrested before 18/28 Sep. 1688. See Appendix B (2).

[20] See p.247.

[21] Robert Bertie, Lord Willoughby, succeeded as 4th Earl of Lindsey 1701, created Duke of Ancaster 1715, died July 1723: 'my Old Friend & Ally . . . is at last gone' (Webb, p.150). Vanbrugh was one of the trustees of his will (PROB 11/596, fol.81). The appointment from 1693 to 1702 is given by R. Somerville, *Office Holders in the Duchy . . . of Lancaster from 1603*, 1972, p.71. But Lady Vanbrugh's papers (BIHR, Yarburgh) include not only a warrant of enrolment of 11 May 1693 but two earlier documents also: a warrant of 23 March 1689 appointing Tobias Legros to the post, and a declaration of the same date by Legros that he is only the deputy of 'John Vanbrough of [blank].' Robert Bertie had been appointed Chancellor of the Duchy on 21 March 1689 (Somerville, op.cit., p.3). Legros held several offices in the Duchy and his appointment in 1689 is recorded (ibid., p.71).

[22] See p.12. Willoughby was perhaps the 'mylord' mentioned by Barbezieux in connection with Vanbrugh (Appendix B (3) [vi]). In March 1688 Willoughby and Peregrine Bertie had been planning to meet in Paris (HMC Lindsey, p.50). No record appears to exist of any passports for them or for Vanbrugh.

not resign from the army until 1702.[23] He remained all his life very much the old soldier, both in his admiration for the Duke of Marlborough and in the imagery of his architecture (Pl.41). However, there is no evidence that he saw action, and perhaps his attitude would have been different if he had. Certainly his duties were not so exacting as to prevent him from an activity of greater significance for him and for us, and from 1698 he was on half-pay which left him virtually free.[24] Early in 1696 he had seen Colley Cibber's comedy, *Love's Last Shift*, at the Theatre Royal in Drury Lane; by April he had completed and offered a sequel, and the staging on 26 December of *The Relapse, or Virtue in Danger*, launched his career as a writer of comedies. It was followed within weeks by *Aesop*, a string of fables begun before *The Relapse* and adapted from Boursault's *Esope à la Ville*. Then in May 1697 came *The Provok'd Wife* at the rival theatre in Lincoln's Inn Fields; this was to be his best play and is still the basis of his reputation in literature. It was apparently constructed from sketches he had made in the Bastille, a circumstance which indicates that thought and probably lecture and perhaps practice preceded *The Relapse*.[25] His best dialogue springs from the page with a naturalness that it shares with his letters to his closest friends. His situations are funny, and his plots are well turned. But he cannot have supposed that writing could be made to pay; if he acted it was not on the stage, and in effect he was a talented amateur in the theatre. He was a professional in the routines of army life which gave him subsistence of a sort, companionship, a measure of free time and, as routines may do, a kind of security as opposed to the adventure he failed to find when he was a decade younger and for which his taste must have been dulled by four years' confinement. He had few responsibilities, although one was to his widowed mother who late in life moved from Chester to London and Surrey.[26] His quick eye missed none of the comicalities of life in the metropolis, either for his own amusement or that of his audience. Besides his long friendship with Willoughby and his brother, he had a large circle of friends, many of them persons of substance and influence. He had few enemies. The Duchess of Marlborough was one; although she believed he might be of use to her, she considered his architecture extravagant, and she was suspicious of his clubman's charm and probably jealous of his admiration for and access to the Duke, the passion of her life. That the architect William Talman was another enemy is even easier to understand. Talman was a difficult character at any time; as Comptroller of Works from 1689 he attempted to discredit Wren, the Surveyor and his superior, and in private practice he

[23] Lord Berkeley agreed to exchange a captain for Vanbrugh from Lord Carmarthen's Regiment 15 Aug. 1695; Vanbrugh was said to have been at sea with Carmarthen the previous year (CSP Dom 1695, p.46). Vanbrugh's commission appears as John Brooke on 31 Jan. 1696 (PRO SP44/168, p.171). The John Brook and Brooks who appear in Col. Beveridge's and Col. Farington's Regiments are not Vanbrugh, and the Capt. Vanbrugh in Beveridge's Regiment who killed his colonel was John's cousin Dudley (see p.161).

[24] CSP Dom 1698, p.380. Being on half-pay amounted to being on the reserve. On 10 March 1702 Vanbrugh received a new commission in the new Earl of Huntingdon's Foot Regiment (PRO SP44/168, p.390) which he must have resigned almost at once on appointment as Comptroller of Works (see p.34).

[25] Voltaire (*Lettres Philosophiques*, XIX) says that Vanbrugh wrote a play in the Bastille. Cibber (*Apology for his Life*, ed. 1750, p.177) says that Lord Halifax had heard read a draft and asked Vanbrugh to rewrite it for the Lincoln's Inn Fields Theatre. Vanbrugh's *Vindication* (*Works*, I, 1927, p.207) says *The Provok'd Wife* was 'writ many years ago, and when I was very young.' The origin of *The Relapse* is known, so that cannot be the play written in prison. Vanbrugh's *The Country House*, adapted from Dancourt, tells us nothing about his houses; apparently first performed at Drury Lane 18 Jan. 1698. W. B. van Lennep, *The London Stage 1660–1800*, I, Carbondale, 1960.

[26] See pp.51, 166.

earned a reputation for arrogance and exorbitance which contributed to his decline and is most fully recorded in a letter of Vanbrugh's of 1703 which lists those clients who suffered 'vexation' at his hands.[27] He had more personal cause to dislike Vanbrugh since the latter supplanted him, as we shall see, not only at Castle Howard in 1699 but also, three years later, in the post of Comptroller. Later in life the antipathy between Vanbrugh and the incompetent Surveyor William Benson must have been entirely mutual. John Anstis of the College of Heralds, who was dislikable, hated him for his attitude to heraldry and from personal rivalry.[28] Swift, as a Tory and a cleric, had two grounds on which to attack the Whig playwright who in Sir John Brute in *The Provok'd Wife* appeared to have made fun of the clergy.[29] His lampoons on Van's house hit its architect hard and squarely, but he must have respected Vanbrugh; in 1710 he described him as 'a good natured fellow' and in 1727 he put into print an apology for his 'Railery' at 'a Man of Wit, and of Honour.'[30]

Vanbrugh's friends, however, were of more significance as well as more numerous than his enemies. We are well informed about many of his later friends because they figure in his correspondence, engaged him as architect, and were mostly members of the Kit-Cat Club, whose unminuted deliberations over the claret and the celebrated mutton pies of Christopher Cat held the key to many of the unsolved riddles of early eighteenth-century English architecture. This most famous of the clubs of its time grew up during the later years of William III, with the particular aim – besides its general social one – of working to ensure the Protestant succession of the House of Hanover after the death of William and Anne. By 1700 it included most of the prominent Whigs, and especially ennobled Whigs, of the day. At that time its meetings were held in a London tavern run by the maker of the mutton pies, from the abbreviation of whose name it took the title of Kit-Cat. In 1703 its secretary, the publisher Jacob Tonson, bought a house at Barn Elms between Putney and Barnes, and the series of portraits of the members painted by Sir Godfrey Kneller were hung there; the club sometimes met at Barn Elms, but meetings became less frequent, and by 1720 there were none.[31] Over the two decades of its active life, the members included the writers Addison, Congreve and Steele, soldiers like the 1st Earl Stanhope, the 2nd Earl of Scarbrough and Viscount Cobham, the physician and poet Sir Samuel Garth, the lawyer Lord Somers, diplomats such as Charles Montagu, Earl and later 1st Duke of Manchester, and financiers such as the other Charles Montagu, 1st Earl of Halifax, founder of the Bank of England and inventor of the National Debt. Nearly half the members were courtiers or politicians, and two of those, with Cobham, Scarbrough and Lord Manchester were Vanbrugh's patrons: the 1st Duke of Newcastle and Lord Carlisle. There were also

[27] Printed in *Country Life*, CXII, 1952, pp.1651–2, and in Whistler, pp.35–8.

[28] For Anstis see A. R. Wagner, *Heralds of England*, 1967, pp.319–79; *Harl.Soc.*, CXV–CXVI, 1964, *passim*; CTP 1715–19, pp.241–3, 324–5, 330.

[29] Vanbrugh's reputed anti-clericalism rests on a partial reading of the Brute scene. For the record, his mother's uncle, Herbert Croft, was Bishop of Hereford; his brother-in-law Thomas Hesleden, and his half-sister's husband and son, Dudley and Theophilus Garencieres, were parsons.

[30] Swift, *Journal to Stella*, 7 Nov. 1710; *Miscellanies in Prose*, 1727, Preface.

[31] National Portrait Gallery, *Catalogue of Seventeenth-Century Portraits*, 1963, pp.398–403. K. M. Lynch, *Jacob Tonson, Kit-Cat Publisher*, Knoxville, 1971. National Portrait Gallery, *Kneller Exhibition*, 1971. It is possible that the alterations at Barn Elms mentioned by Vanbrugh to Tonson (Webb, pp.7–8) were designed by him. He did not, however, design the room added later to house the Kit-Cat portraits.

figures of lighter weight, and membership of the club did not guarantee universal amity; what united them was Whiggism. Vanbrugh was no churchman although, unlike some of the club, his morals were fairly conventional and without scandal; his most important public belief was his commitment – secular rather than solely political – to the Whig philosophy. The Whigs were, ultimately, the political descendants of the Roundheads; less crudely, they were the party of the Glorious Revolution of 1688 which had allowed James II, King by Divine Right, to escape with his life and had installed William, his nephew but half Dutch, and Mary, his daughter, on the throne of England. They were united above all in opposition to the Tories, but by the accession of Queen Anne in March 1702 they were well drilled as a party and had well-defined and more positive qualities. Broadly speaking, they were the party of the army, the self-made, the yeomen in the south and east of England, the City men and the financiers (whose support had been vital to William and Mary and would be so to Marlborough's war in the reign of Anne), and Dissenters of every kind (barring Roman Catholics) from Quakers and Deists to libertine aristocrats like the Duke of Wharton. The nub of Whig political theory was the limitation of the power of the Crown, but perhaps even more important were their principles on religion (the rights of nonconformists) and economics (a financial policy based on money and on public borrowing, not on land). This last principle was crucial, for the economic distinctions between Whig and Tory were more meaningful than those of social class. The Tories included most of the country gentry and country clergy, and not only the great hereditary landowners, but also their family servants, tenant farmers and their employees; not surprisingly Whig historians came to identify Whiggism with progress. In the reign of Queen Anne, party government as we know it did not exist; the Queen, whose views were consistently Tory, fought for the right to choose her ministers independently of allegiance to either party or to neither, and while until 1710 Parliament had a Whig majority the chief ministers, in the early years of her reign, were none of them Whigs. The great age of Whig power came after the accession of George I in 1714, and in that age Whiggism came to embrace also the moral philosophy of Shaftesbury and, in consequence, a philosophy of the arts. We shall need to examine the significance of the latter for Vanbrugh in a later chapter; here we are concerned with the situation at the time of his conversion to architecture around the turn of the century. There were two principal figures in the story of that conversion. One was his fellow Kit-Cat, five years his junior, Charles Howard, 3rd Earl of Carlisle, who will be considered in this chapter; the other was his fellow architect, three years his senior, Nicholas Hawksmoor, who will be considered in the next.

The Pyramid at Castle Howard (Pl.45) was built in 1728 by Hawksmoor for the Earl to commemorate the founder of the Carlisle estates five generations earlier; its conical inner chamber contains a bust of Lord William Howard (1557–1640), third son of the 4th Duke of Norfolk, whose marriage to Elizabeth Dacre brought him large properties in Northumberland, Cumberland and around Henderskelfe Castle in the North Riding of Yorkshire. Lord William's great-grandson Charles received a Viscountcy from Cromwell, but reverted on the latter's death to the support of the Crown and was created Earl of Carlisle by Charles II; his son the 2nd Earl sat in the Commons as a Whig before succeeding in 1685. His son Charles succeeded in turn as 3rd Earl in 1692; the following year

Henderskelfe Castle, which had recently been modernized and which belonged to his grandmother, was seriously damaged and partly gutted by fire.[32] In the late summer and autumn of 1698, Carlisle spent a considerable time at Henderskelfe; at that time John Barker was paid for a survey of the estate (perhaps the estate map traditionally dated 1694)[33] and on 10 October Carlisle's grandmother leased the castle to him from the following March. It must have been during 1698 and the beginning of 1699 that his thoughts turned seriously away from public life and towards rebuilding, settling in Yorkshire and developing forestry and agriculture. Such aims, however, were of necessity long term; he was still active in London in November 1701 when, on the resignation of Sidney Godolphin, King William appointed him his chief minister as First Lord of the Treasury. He held this office for six months, that is to say, into the beginning of the reign of Anne. Moreover, he was in charge of her coronation on St George's Day, 23 April 1702, in his capacity as Deputy Earl Marshal during the minority of his cousin the 7th Duke of Norfolk.[34] There may have been personal reasons for his decision for early retirement, but the development of the Henderskelfe estate and the building of the most expensive English country house of its date were not the undertakings of a man tired of life and activity. The positive results of Carlisle's retirement are still visible, and his intentions are made clearer by literary evidence. He was given to placing inscriptions on his estate, and one set up on the great obelisk in 1731 starts with a verse:

If to perfection these plantations rise
If they agreeably my heirs surprise
This faithful pillar will their age declare
As long as time these characters shall spare
Here then with kind remembrance read his name
Who for posterity perform'd the same.

The prose that follows credits Carlisle both with the house, outworks and monuments and again with the plantations of the estate, which were seen more as an investment than as the creation of an ideal landscape, a practical policy which in England can be traced back to the encouragement and publicity of John Evelyn on behalf of the Royal Society in the reign of Charles II, and perhaps to the Puritan ethic of prosperity. Carlisle's intentions are further explained in a long poem written by his daughter Anne, Lady Irwin, soon after the obelisk inscription and with sidelong glances both at Virgil's *Georgics* and at the exposition of the tasteful and tasteless developer in Pope's *Epistle to Lord Burlington* of 1731.[35] Its indifferent verses are largely concerned with the representation of landscape, but they also stress the seriousness of Carlisle's retirement, his 'gen'rous Mind, To ev'ry

[32] The destruction appears to have been only partial: see p.46. Information in this section is mostly from Castle Howard MSS, kindly communicated by Mr George Howard.

[33] The map is usually dated on the basis of a coat of arms. But this is so similar to that on another map of 1727 that it is reasonable to suppose the arms were put on both maps at the same time and to relate the earlier map to the payment to Barker.

[34] Carlisle made the 2nd Earl of Essex his deputy in 1703 (Webb, p.8).

[35] The poem (reprinted here, Appendix J) was first discussed by C. Hussey, *English Gardens and Landscapes 1700–1750*, 1967, p.114ff. For the authorship and date see p.263. Carlisle's labours are also described in verse by T. Gent, *Pater Patriae*, 1738. That title, which art-historians generally associate with Cosimo de'Medici, was used both by and, after the Catiline Conspiracy, of Cicero.

Social Act of life inclin'd' and his aim 'To serve Mankind . . . And make those happy who on you depend.'

The scale and majesty of Carlisle's house also represented something more than the personal vanity which shines from Kneller's Kit-Cat portrait; both in its antecedents, and as we shall see, in some of its decoration, it symbolized the political changes of the time. Of the seven signatories to the invitation of 30 June 1688 to William of Orange to take the throne of England, one was the Bishop of London; of the laymen three built themselves remarkable houses. Thomas Osborne, whose string of titles culminated in the Dukedom of Leeds, retired in 1695 to build at Kiveton near Sheffield (Pl.12); this was the most modest of the three, but it had a hall and staircase painted by Louis Laguerre, the best decorative painter before Thornhill.[36] Secondly, the Duke of Shrewsbury commissioned Thomas Archer about 1706 to build at Heythrop a massive block closer than any other English house of the time in scale and in the vocabulary of detail to the palaces of Baroque Rome. Thirdly, most lavish, ultimately most complete and also earliest in inauguration of the kingmakers' houses was the rebuilding, one range of its square courtyard at a time, of the Elizabethan house at Chatsworth by the 4th Earl and 1st Duke of Devonshire. The first range, the south, was begun in 1687, the year before the Revolution, and may thus be seen as an example of the phenomenon that cultural events sometimes anticipate the political changes they are supposed to reflect. Devonshire's first architect was Talman, who designed the south and east ranges and the west terrace, and who probably also designed Kiveton in a less grand idiom. The west front above the terrace (Pl.13) was built in 1700–2 to an anonymous design, and the north front by Archer in 1705–7.[37] Besides its imposing façades set in the valley of the Derbyshire Derwent, Chatsworth contains a magnificent series of original state-rooms with painted ceilings by Laguerre and others. The decoration of the chapel, with a large marble altar-piece and illusionist wall paintings, was directly modelled on the chapels painted by Verrio and built in the 1680s by Hugh May at Windsor for Charles II and by Wren at Whitehall for James II, and this is typical of Chatsworth. It was the first English house to rival in monumentality, in illusionist decoration and in modernity of style in a European context, the royal palaces themselves, although it was more compact in plan than Charles II's Windsor or William's Hampton Court. The precedent set by Devonshire was closely followed at Petworth (possibly also begun before the Revolution) by the 6th Duke of Somerset (a Whig and a Kit-Cat) and at Burley-on-the-Hill (Pl.10) in the later 1690s by the Earl of Nottingham, a staunchly Protestant Tory who was cordial to both James II and William and later sided with the Whigs. Carlisle at Castle Howard was to put all these in the shade.

His first choice of architect was Talman, who in his private practice was the leading country house designer of the 1690s. We know enough of Talman's behaviour to see how he lost the commission, for Vanbrugh later told the Duke of Newcastle what had happened.[38]

[36] E. Croft-Murray, *Decorative Painting in England*, I, 1962, p.252. The attribution of Kiveton to Talman is on stylistic grounds, but the Duke of Leeds does not appear in the list of Talman's vexed patrons (n.27).

[37] Devonshire seems to have liked young architects, which would partly explain why he dropped Talman when the latter became established. I still suspect that Archer was concerned with the west front of Chatsworth.

[38] In the letter of 1703 (n.27).

On his first visit to Henderskelfe Talman was paid fifty guineas and his expenses, but for a second visit Carlisle offered him only thirty; Talman went down and for 'but four days' was given forty. Talman 'refus'd 'em, said he never stir'd under fifty, and so went away'. His subsequent demand for £50 in addition for his designs (perhaps by now having lost the commission) surprised Carlisle, 'having never had anything but two or three little trifling drawings as big as his hand'. Talman took Carlisle to court, and when the case came up in June 1703 Vanbrugh had the satisfaction of giving the evidence on which the jury found in Carlisle's favour. The critical distinction which Vanbrugh drew shows a sound knowledge of the procedures of the time. Leaving aside payment for professional visits, he divided drawings into two categories:

> That for Designs only drawn imperfectly, by way of proposition for a house, nothing ought to be reckon'd, any more than if a shopkeeper shew'd you his goods, which if you buy you pay for, but not for looking on 'em. But that when a Design was chosen and follow'd the Drawings that wou'd be necessary for the carrying on and executing it must be paid for, being things that took up a vast deal of pains and time.

Vanbrugh's intention in writing thus to Newcastle was to dissuade him from using Talman, but the latter's reputation is sufficiently known. At Chatsworth he had acted as both architect and contractor, an unusual arrangement which meant that the patron had to pay the artificers London rates and all second thoughts were extra items outside the contract. In Devonshire's mind the expense and disputes with the workmen were Talman's fault, and his contract was not renewed. Matters were not improved by Talman's ostentatious mode of travel, in a private coach with four horses and two servants.[39]

Our knowledge of how Vanbrugh won Castle Howard, on the other hand, is still sketchy and the fact of it barely credible. Either Vanbrugh was in 1699 an amateur without training or experience, or he was not. If he was, his assets can only have been imagination, a natural eye, good friends and remarkable, not to say excessive, self-confidence. (One of his good friends, Hawksmoor, was to be indispensable in the early years and to carry on the work at Castle Howard after Vanbrugh's death.) If on the other hand he had training or experience, we may speculate on their character, date and location. So far, however, their *existence* remains to be demonstrated, and there is no evidence. No contemporary provides it. Our knowledge of what he did later serves to show how much he was unable to do at the start. It was not a matter of status, for the designing of buildings was as open to any gentleman as it was to any stonemason who could read, add, handle dividers and use a pattern-book. The most important and one of the most beautiful of mid-century houses, Coleshill in Berkshire (Pl.11) had been the work of the gentleman amateur Sir Roger Pratt, whose notebooks are a valuable source for the history of Restoration architecture. But all of Pratt's work is modest in comparison with the scale and complexity of Castle Howard. Vanbrugh somehow convinced Carlisle that he was a better choice than Talman or anyone else, and that must speak as much for Carlisle's remarkable character as for Vanbrugh's, for all their distant kinship.

Vanbrugh's French was good enough for him to deal with the colloquial language of

[39] F. Thompson, *History of Chatsworth*, 1949, pp.48, 58–9.

the French plays which he translated and adapted for the London stage; according to Colley Cibber 'he had a happier Talent of throwing the English Spirit, into his Translation of French Plays, than any former Author, who had borrow'd from them', and while this may say more about his English than about his French, the latter must have been very good.[40] In the Bastille he shared quarters with M. de Saint-Georges and M. de Sainte-Praye, and the genteel tone of the environment is indicated by the reference to him at his release as M. *de* Vanbrugh.[41] But we still do not know what he saw in France, or whether his motive for going there, apparently with Lord Willoughby, was friendship, or adventure, or the chance to see a foreign country. However, the English, while professing a natural detestation of their nearest neighbours, have for long found their country and its products irresistible, and young Vanbrugh had the example of his father's years on the Continent. The places to which he would naturally be drawn, whether he was interested in architecture or not, were Paris, the capital, and Versailles, the seat of court and government and a show-place. In Paris he might well, as a young ex-soldier, have been to see for himself the arcaded court of Libéral Bruant's Hôpital des Invalides, the prototype in function of the Royal Hospital at Chelsea (Pl.16). Versailles by 1690 had become the overall creation of Jules Hardouin Mansart, from the long, regular suave fronts of the palace to the crisp rustication and round-headed windows of the great orangery below the terrace (Pls 14, 15). It happens that these accessible examples are among the relatively few French seventeenth-century buildings that are close to Vanbrugh's in feeling: in their distinction of stone coursing and relief decoration combined with an admission of the heaviness of masonry, and in the Invalides' aqueduct-like deployment of superimposed arcades. But we do not know for certain that Vanbrugh saw them, or, if so, was impressed by them. It is tempting to wonder whether he had time and trust enough to return to France after the Peace of Ryswick (1697), but from a letter of 1719 it is fairly clear that he had not revisited Paris since his release.[42] The general character of French architecture, which is certainly of major importance for the style of Castle Howard, would have been available to him through many engraved works; there, at home, from the books of Jean Marot, Le Pautre and Le Muet and a multitude of topographical prints, he could have absorbed sufficiently the character of French architecture, the accomplished use of the classical vocabulary, the large repertoire of decorative detail, and more specifically the French conception of the wall as a variegated rather than a plain surface, covered with relief decoration of every kind, figurative, abstract and purely architectural (Pl.8). It is worth remembering that Wren, whose major motive for visiting France seems to have been architectural, brought back 'almost all France in Paper',[43] and that Hawksmoor's extensive knowledge of foreign buildings was entirely from printed illustrations.

The identification of stylistic influences on Vanbrugh is only secondary to the more basic question of formative influences: why did he, in his mid thirties, become an

[40] From certain peculiarities of spelling in Giles Vanbrugh's letter (*entreprise, suddain, valeur, fregatt, suffred, adresse*) it is probable that his knowledge of French was considerable; see Appendix A.

[41] Appendix B (3) [xiii, xiv].

[42] In 1719 he told Tonson of a plan to re-visit Paris (Webb, p.112). While confined in the château of Vincennes he must have seen work there by Louis Le Vau (L. Hautecœur, *Histoire de l'Architecture Classique en France*, II, 1948, pp.248–51).

[43] *Wren Soc.*, XIII, p.41.

architect? Changes of vocation in maturity are of two kinds: some are lunatic, and attended by failure and misery. The others, and probably the majority, are more convinced and more intensely driven even than the aspirations of adolescence precisely because they are based on experience and knowledge of self and of the world. They are seldom easy to initiate and carry through, but more often than not they are proved right by history. Vanbrugh was right, and Carlisle also was undoubtedly right to give him the commission for Castle Howard. Vanbrugh's decision may have been influenced by French architecture, or by something nearer home. Two centuries later Louis Sullivan decided in a street near his home in Boston, in his early teens, to become an architect and 'make beautiful buildings out of his head'. Wren's interest, at about thirty, was stimulated by the mathematical and mechanical properties of the art, by its capacity for visible results, by his early interest in drawing, perhaps by some prompting from Charles II, and least clearly and most deeply by chance remarks absorbed in childhood from his father, who was not uninterested in buildings. In one respect the architect and the playwright are alike, for though their media are disparate and the relation of artifice to reality is quite different, both are concerned with the setting and the manifestation of human activity.

Vanbrugh must also have realized in the London of the 1690s that architecture was a more solid and less ephemeral art than comedy – and his buildings look as if intended, to use his own phrase, to stand like a rock for a thousand years.[44] London was as exciting a place for buildings then as at any time in history. The new St Paul's was, except for its crowning dome and western towers, nearly complete and towered in Portland stone more than twice the height of surrounding buildings apart from the rising steeples of Wren's City churches; the choir of the new cathedral was opened in 1697. The Building Acts after the Great Fire had put an end to the construction of timber houses, and in the rebuilt City, and more spaciously in new areas to the west such as Bloomsbury and St James's, the new regular brick-fronted houses were beginning to give London something of the modernity of the best cities of France, Holland and Italy. Elsewhere in nearby country areas Vanbrugh would be aware of buildings of an unprecedented scale in progress or nearly finished: some of his comrades in arms would hope to end their days as Pensioners of Wren's Chelsea Hospital (1682–9) and his cousin William Vanbrugh was concerned with its counterpart for seamen at Greenwich, begun in 1696 and the work of Wren with the assistance of Hawksmoor.

Swift suggested satirically that Vanbrugh watched boys making mud pies and a young miss making a house of cards, and built 'Goosepie' House to show he could do better. The fantasy encloses a grain of truth: the desire to try his hand at what he had seen others doing and the belief that he could do it better. That is all the evidence we have, but it is reasonable to suppose that it reflects the attitude of mind in which Vanbrugh began to talk himself into architecture and Carlisle into employing him. It rings true, too, because his first completed play, *The Relapse*, was written not only as a sequel to Cibber's, but also as a deliberate attempt to make the characters, if less moral, more realistic.[45] Lord Carlisle decided not merely to look on Vanbrugh's goods, but to buy them in preference

[44] Appendix E.

[45] *Short Vindication* (*Works*, I, 1927, pp. 210–11).

to anyone else's. By the winter of 1699–1700 those goods were definite enough for a wooden model to be under construction. In June 1700 it was taken, presumably from Carlisle's Soho house, to Hampton Court to be shown to the King. A month later came the first authorization to Vanbrugh to build in the ruins of Whitehall, and it is difficult not to see a connection. A fictitious account of his rise to stardom would have more detail but it could hardly be better stuff. What happened to the model, and what it looked like, we shall never know; what happened in the designing and building of Castle Howard itself we must now examine in greater detail.

Chapter 2

Castle Howard

Vanbrugh's letter of Christmas Day 1699 to the Earl of Manchester, at that time ambassador in Paris, is a personal and spicy account of recent events in Parliament and among their mutual friends and acquaintances.[1] Near the end is one paragraph about its author, and that paragraph is entirely about its author as architect:

> I have been this Summer at my Ld Carlisle's, and seen most of the great houses in the North, as Ld Nottings: Duke of Leeds Chattesworth &c. I stay'd at Chattesworth four or five days the Duke being there. I shew'd him all my Ld Carlisle's designs, which he said was quite another thing, than what he imagin'd from the Character yr Ldship gave him on't; He absolutely approv'd the whole designe, particularly the low Wings, which he said wou'd have an admirable effect without doors as well as within, being adorn'd with those Ornaments of Pillasters and Urns, wch he never thought of, but concluded 'twas to be a plain low building like an orange house. There has been a great many Criticks consulting upon it since, and no one objection being made to't, the Stone is raising, and the Foundations will be laid in the Spring. The Modell is preparing in wood, wch when done, is to travel to Kensington where the Kings thoughts upon't are to be had.

Certainly from this account one would imagine that the designing and carrying out of Castle Howard was the easiest thing in the world. Yet even at that date, when not a stone had been laid, the technical problems of quarrying, drainage, foundations, masonry, measurement, payment and the co-ordination of different trades, would have been a challenge to an experienced architect. Very soon there would be additional problems. Workmen must have detailed drawings and instructions to follow and someone with a sharp eye to correct mistakes as they arise, which they inevitably do; a good foreman is invaluable here but the responsibility is ultimately the architect's. An early though undated letter from Vanbrugh addressed to Carlisle at Henderskelfe[2] explains the manner in which many of these problems were to be solved:

> I spoak to Mr Hawksmoor about his perticular concern and found him as he us'd to be. so he intended to ask yr Ldship fourty pound a year Sallary & Fifty each journey wch amounts to £100 clear. I hope he'll deserve it, and that all will go to yr Ldships sattisfaction. for I shou'd be very sorry to have meddled in anything shou'd do otherwise.

[1] Webb, pp.4–5.

[2] Webb, pp.6–7, and p.254 where the date of 1700 is proposed. I can see no good reason to alter this date.

Mr Hawksmoor had already, according to this letter, been engaged by Vanbrugh to bargain with the mason and carpenter and had secured the lowest rate at which the work would not be skimped; the arrangement may have been made in consequence of an unfortunate attempt by Carlisle to do his own contracting.[3] Study of a group of drawings for Castle Howard discovered in 1951[4] shows that the elevations at a very early stage were Hawksmoor's work (Pl.20); this is generally agreed among scholars. Whether or not Vanbrugh drew the accompanying early plans is less certain, but it is inescapable that their draughtsmanship shows neither accomplishment nor experience (Pl.21). The dates both of the drawings and of Hawksmoor's introduction to Carlisle depend on argument, but it is clear from the letter that matters had now reached the stage when Hawksmoor's participation should be made official, and that Vanbrugh had already been consulting him unofficially; if the identification of the earliest idea for the house (Pl.18) is correct – and it also is in Hawksmoor's hand – then it is likely that the private engagement of Hawksmoor was Vanbrugh's first practical step towards architecture. Indeed, their meeting was probably the decisive event leading Vanbrugh to that step.

Nicholas Hawksmoor (1661–1736) was three years older than Vanbrugh. From the age of about eighteen he had been first Wren's personal clerk and later his official assistant in a number of enterprises. By the 1690s he was the best trained architect of his day, Clerk of Works at Kensington Palace and chief draughtsman at St Paul's, positions which did not preclude the development of a modest private practice. Although much of its early history is still uncertain, there is no doubt that the masonry and roof of Easton Neston, which he took over at an early stage from Wren, were finished in 1702 (Pl.17). At Greenwich Hospital, where he was initially, from 1696, Wren's personal assistant and then, from 1698, Clerk of Works, there is evidence from drawings and payments that his contribution approached the status of collaboration in design, and while his architectural ideas were bold and inventive, his personality seems to have suited him for the role of right-hand to the master. In the small circle of public building in and around London there would have been several opportunities for Vanbrugh to meet him, but the obvious one was through William Vanbrugh's connection with Greenwich. The meeting can have been no later than the spring of 1699.

The sequence of events has to be reconstructed from sparse documents and from the interpretation of drawings; these two kinds of evidence are interrelated, and will be more clearly presented in a hypothesis than by the series of arguments on which it is based.[5]

Carlisle spent a considerable time at Henderskelfe in the autumn of 1698, before and after the signing of the lease with his grandmother. The first of Talman's two visits was probably during this time. The lease took effect in March 1699; Talman's second visit, of 'but four days' according to Vanbrugh and therefore probably significantly shorter, is likely to have taken place at the end of June. Carlisle was at Henderskelfe again about 20 June 1699, and one of his first actions was to make enquiry of his neighbour, Thomas

[3] See Webb, p.65.

[4] Marquis of Bute's Collection, Sotheby's, 23 May 1951; now V & A.

[5] Based on: Castle Howard MSS, including Thomas Worsley's letter to Carlisle; Vanbrugh to Lords Manchester and Carlisle (Webb, pp.4–7) and Newcastle (see p.18, n.27); Hawksmoor to Carlisle, 1701 (Downes (1959), pp.234–5). Elevation (Pl.18) at Welbeck; other drawings V & A.

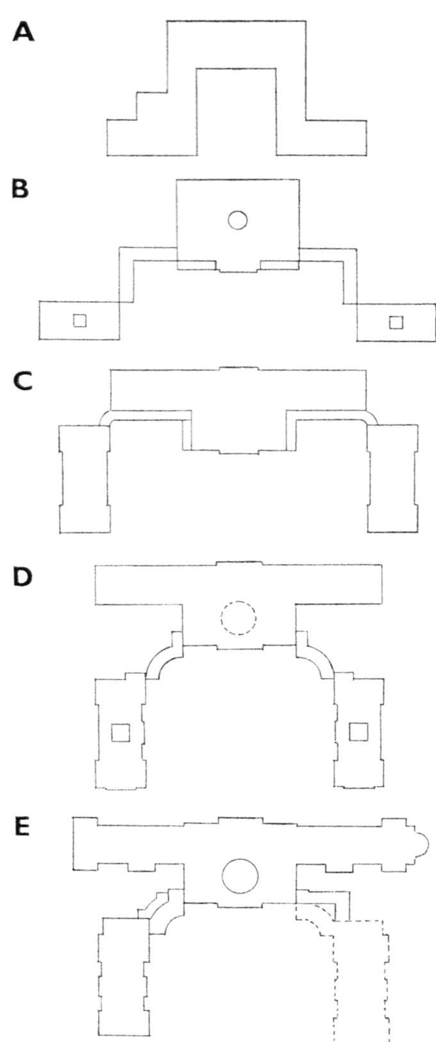

2 Castle Howard. Plans of five stages of the design.
(A) Talman plan. (B) 'Preliminary' design. (C) First design. (D) Second design. (E) as built, from *Vitruvius Britannicus* (1715) with north-west wing (not built) from revised impression (1717).

Worsley of Hovingham, about masons' and carpenters' rates; Worsley replied on 26 June. In view of subsequent events the enquiry was altogether premature, but Carlisle must have been eager to begin building, and his approach to a nearby landowner was perhaps prompted by his first suspicions of Talman's credibility. Vanbrugh was at Henderskelfe some time in the summer, and in his Christmas letter the visit is clearly linked in retrospect with the commission. The gardener George London was also there in July – it was common practice to start the gardens with or before a house – and his two surviving layout plans would have been drawn on his return home. Since one shows Talman's house and the other Vanbrugh's, there may have been a period in the high summer when the two architects were in competition although perhaps not in confrontation. However, London's plan does not show the *first* Vanbrugh-Hawksmoor design.

Worsley's letter refers to lead for roofing and gives the dimensions of Carlisle's house at that stage: the body of the house 106 feet long and 75 feet broad, and the two wings added together 142 feet long by 35 feet broad. These do not fit a house shaped like Talman's (Fig.2A) and what are now designated the 'first' and 'second' Vanbrugh-Hawksmoor plans (Fig.2C, D) have two sets of wings, not one. The dimensions do fit a perspective-elevation among the Welbeck Abbey papers which was endorsed by Margaret Duchess of Newcastle, *Mr Vanbrooks draft of a great house* (the word *great* being inserted) (Pl.18). It is certainly an early drawing, in Hawksmoor's hand, and it was probably sent by Vanbrugh with other drawings to Newcastle in 1703 when the latter was toying with the idea of building and Vanbrugh was, as his letter shows (p.22), in competition with Talman. Moreover, the wings in this drawing (Fig.2B) are unusual in that their length is parallel to that of the central block, as implied by Worsley's setting out of dimensions. London's plans show that Talman's house faced east and west, its forecourt directly approached by a western avenue from the lane to York, and while it is not impossible that Talman or Carlisle himself conceived the change it was Vanbrugh who worked out the decision to turn the house and spread it out along the ridge of the hill, so that the entrance court and hall faced north and all the principal rooms, augmented in later designs by second wings, faced south.[6] The practical advantage of this was the maximum of solar heating, a matter of comfort and economy of which Vanbrugh must have been well aware (p.46). The scenic advantages were perhaps greater: the fine views over rolling country north and south, and the commanding position on the skyline as the house is approached (Pl.7). The placing of the wings in the Welbeck drawing seems to indicate the first idea for a house along the ridge.

That this imposing and logical design was the first can be argued from the three criticisms to which it was open: two of convenience and one of appearance. First, the wings are a long way from the body of the house and the elbow connecting passages appear to be ten-bay open arcades with no direct covered access into the wings. Secondly, the body of the house is small in comparison with either a courtyard house like Chatsworth or such solid ones as Burley-on-the-Hill, or with the final form of Castle Howard. Thirdly, the elevation of the main block is top-heavy, with a giant entablature almost one-third of the total height. The first two deficiencies are remedied by the addition in later plans of glazed corridors (Fig.2C) or of shorter open quadrants with access to body and wings (Fig.2D) or finally by a combination of both (Fig.2E), and also by the attachment of a second pair of wings abutting on to the body and greatly extending the south elevation. In fact from a comparison of dimensions the process looks like one of adding the outlying wings of the preliminary design to the body of the house and designing new larger blocks at right angles to the rest. The third, stylistic criticism is quite in accordance with Vanbrugh's reputation for architectural heaviness, but the excessive disproportion of this elevation confirms the view that it was experimental; certainly the later development of the design shows a progressive decrease in the proportion of the zone above the capitals (Fig.3).

The preliminary design has some other positive features. Exactly what happens at the sides of the central three-bay portico is not clear from the elevation, but its relation to the one-storey colonnades on either side is well managed, considerably better than in what

[6] M. Whinney, 'William Talman', *Journal of the Warburg and Courtauld Institutes*, XVIII, 1955, pp.132–3.

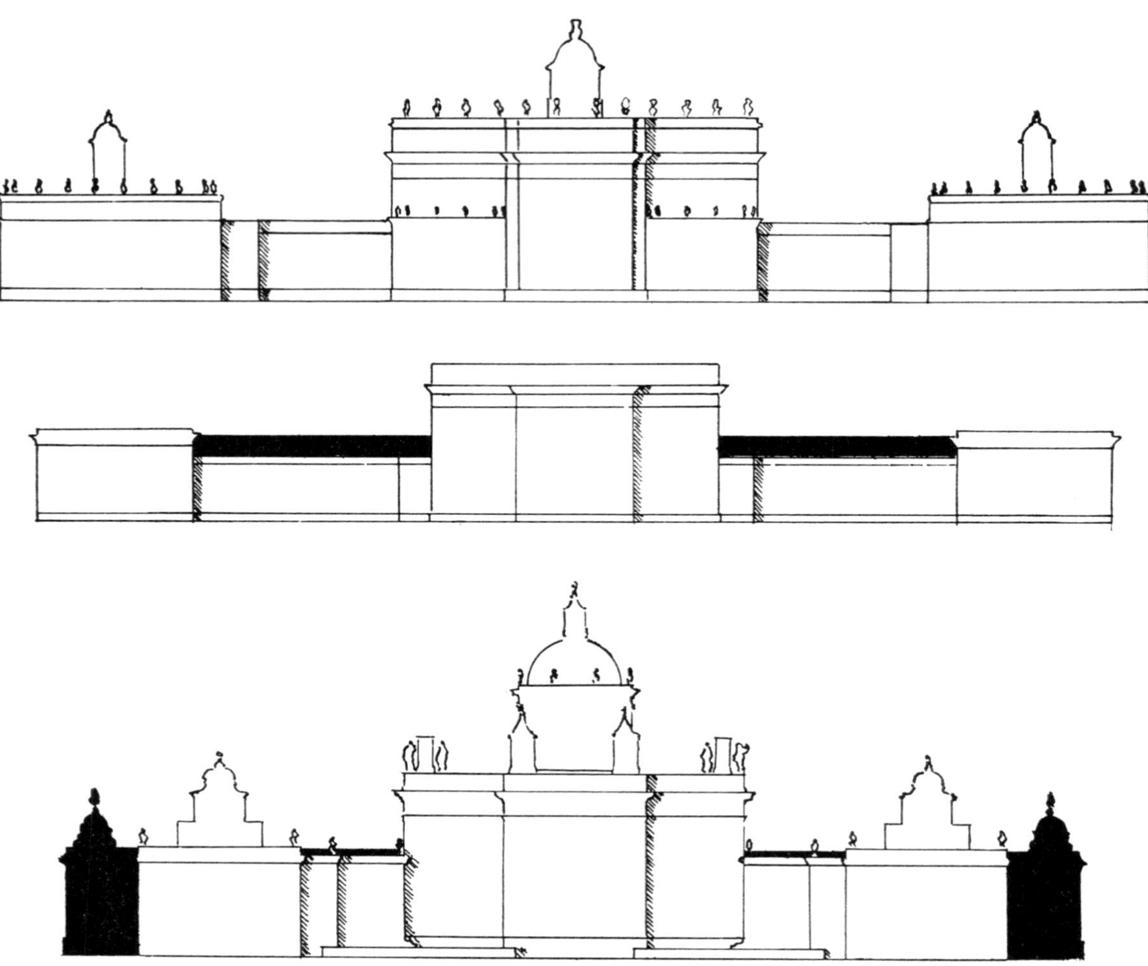

3 Castle Howard. North elevation at three stages of the design: 'Preliminary', first and final.

may be its source, the central block at Chelsea Hospital (Pl.19). The cupola on the skyline is an up-to-date version of a common feature of English houses from Coleshill (Pl.11) almost to the end of the century; it would contain a spiral staircase from the top floor giving access to a viewing platform on the roof. The smaller cupolas on the wings are not new either, and would probably contain a clock and a house bell. Besides their practical function their aesthetic one is considerable, enlivening the skyline from both near and distant viewpoints.

When George London made his park plans, the design of the house had passed from the preliminary through the 'first' to the 'second' stage; we have plans and elevations of both of these. In the 'first' plan, besides the alteration of the wings and their links, the main body has been shortened by about 20 feet, and a corridor has been made almost from end to end of the body-plus-wings (Pl.21). Except for the embryonic sections of corridor which Pratt incorporated into Coleshill, Vanbrugh has usually been credited with the invention of this feature of domestic planning, which at Castle Howard has as much the aesthetic value of a long perspective (Pl.33) as the functional value of an alternative means of access to rooms in sequence. In date the first domestic corridor was at Burley-on-the-Hill, the structure of which was carried out in 1696–8 (p.21). Burley is what the seventeenth century called a 'double pile', that is, two rooms thick, and has a corridor in the middle joining the ends of the main block to the centre rooms. It is short and unscenic beside Vanbrugh's, and the architect is not known; there are stylistic and associational reasons for finding the hand of Wren's scientific and architectural colleague Robert Hooke, as well as some evidence to suggest that Lord Nottingham acted as his own architect.[7] There is thus no way of knowing whether the Castle Howard corridor was influenced by Burley or independent of it. On the other hand, Vanbrugh later told the Duchess of Marlborough that *corridor* was a French word for a passage, and he may have derived the idea as well as the term from France.[8]

It is worth recalling here the houses, all three of them unfinished, which Vanbrugh mentioned to Lord Manchester in his Christmas letter: 'Ld Nottings: Duke of Leeds, Chattesworth', respectively Burley-on-the-Hill, Kiveton (p.21) which was probably Talman's work, and at Chatsworth Talman's new south and east ranges. If their order in Vanbrugh's letter has any significance, he must have seen the first two on the way up and Chatsworth on the way home, and if this were the case then Burley-on-the-Hill could have influenced him in the 'first' plan for Castle Howard. But while that plan gives the impression of ideas somewhat undigested, and might perhaps therefore have been made in the North, its other major feature, absent from the 'preliminary' design, seems to relate to what Lord Manchester had told Devonshire before Vanbrugh arrived at Chatsworth – and that would mean the news reaching him at a remarkable speed. For the 'plain low building like an orange house' suggests to us the south elevation corresponding to this plan (Pl.20) although that is certainly not devoid of the 'ornaments' of pilasters and we cannot tell what the drawings were like which Vanbrugh showed Devonshire; in any case elevations of such precision would probably have been made in London. A partial solution to this chronological dilemma may be found in the way in which the noble gentlemen concerned most probably exchanged information: Manchester's communication to Devonshire was verbal or written and his information from Carlisle may not have been visual either, and it seems most likely that the original point of the communication was nearer to the function than to the appearance of an orangery: the sunshine which was an important advantage in the new long south elevation.[9]

The 'first' plan shows a sort of enclosed verandah linking the north wings to the rest of the house and returning in a curious way along the sides of the centre block, which would surely have given a fussy appearance to the court elevation of the house. In the 'second' plan (Fig.2D) which is the one shown in London's park plan, this feature has been obviated by bringing the north wings much closer to the body of the house – an improvement in

[7] Burley-on-the-Hill was in the charge of John Lumley from 1697 but there is some evidence that the original architect was Robert Hooke (Downes (1966), p.64; Lees-Milne, p.113).

[8] Webb, p.71. Antoine Le Pautre, *Œuvres d'Architecture*, 1652, illustrates a corridor and uses the term. John Evelyn, a frequent coiner of words, refers as 'the corridor above' to the open gallery over the entrance to the Sheldonian Theatre in Oxford (*Diary*, ed. E. S. de Beer, Oxford, 1955, III, p.532).

[9] Remaining imponderables include: (a) Vanbrugh may have shown superseded or variant drawings; (b) no drawings show roof urns except the 'preliminary' one at Welbeck; (c) the Bute elevations are made of pieces pasted together and are not necessarily work done in the studio; (d) drawings were made on site at Kimbolton (p.49); (e) there is no other reason to suppose that Hawksmoor was at Castle Howard as early as 1699.

almost every way. Visually it gives the court height and a feeling of enclosure round a focal point, as we can appreciate today. Instead of the verandah a second corridor has been incorporated inside the north wall of the house with short quadrants to open arcades, and it was not until building had gone some way on the east – perhaps not until about 1709 – that a second glazed quadrant was added behind. The west wing and its link were not built in the 3rd Earl's lifetime or to Vanbrugh's design (Fig.2E).

The 'second' elevations are appreciably closer to the building, although there was at least one further stage in the drawings: the parapet is lighter in proportion, the main block has been lengthened, its base level has been raised (in one drawing this was done by cutting off the wings and pasting them on at a lower level), and different rhythms and surface treatments are established on the two façades, the stonework on the south being plain and that on the north banded. This divergence is extended in the building, where the north front becomes Doric instead of Corinthian; in 1734 Hawksmoor answered criticisms of the disparity with the arguments that the façades had different functions and could not both be seen at one time.[10]

Before the end of 1699 Vanbrugh was sure of the commission for Castle Howard, a model was under construction, stone was being quarried, and foundations were being discussed. By that time, therefore, there were detailed drawings, and work began in the late spring of 1700. It was normal practice to engage artificers when their work was required, and the traditional date of summer 1700 for Vanbrugh's letter introducing Hawksmoor officially into the project (p.26) is probably correct.[11] Vanbrugh had missed Carlisle at Henderskelfe, and had left for Chester before his arrival. He went by way of Lanesborough and Tadcaster, where he wrote to Carlisle. He had talked to the mason and carpenter, who were then on the site, and also with Hawksmoor whom he seems to have left there waiting for Carlisle's arrival; the latter evidently agreed to Hawksmoor's terms. The following year Hawksmoor wrote (26 March 1701) from Yorkshire to Carlisle in London describing favourable progress. The first building work was not on the main block but on the north-east wing (Pl.6); this was the part farthest from the old castle and the church, both of which would ultimately be demolished.[12] Work did not begin on the main block until 1702, and by then the most momentous change in the design must have been made: the introduction of the dome (Pl.38). It is absent from the early drawings. That it was an enormous afterthought is confirmed by the plan of the 'second' design in which the hall, first drawn as a conventional rectangle, was afterwards filled in with the supporting piers for the dome.[13] An ultimately Palladian house plan of a common symmetrical type (p.84) with the saloon behind the hall on the central line, is transformed. The dome is quite different from the roof-top cupolas of earlier houses or of the preliminary design (Pls 18, 11); it is altogether bigger and more solid, of masonry and not of wood, and it is continuous inside with the two-storey hall below, whose four great arches

[10] Hawksmoor to Carlisle (Downes (1959), p.254).

[11] Vanbrugh's letter about Hawksmoor (p.26, n.2). In June 1703 he referred to three years' work (p.18, n.27).

[12] The Ordnance Survey placed the castle site wrongly on the south parterre. The estate map of 1694/8 shows it west of the present west wing (Whistler, Pl.19).

[13] This is evident from close inspection of the plan, in which the additions are not pricked for transfer like the rest. In March 1707 the cupola needed to be added to elevations for engraving (p.35).

and supporting piers provide a combination of structural engineering with a symmetry and a richness and variety of projection new not only in scale but in conception. It is as if the crossing of a great Renaissance church has been implanted into Vanbrugh's house, and while from a distance or from inside the dome is flawless it does not fit very logically on to the exterior at close quarters (Pl.8). There was nothing like this at Chatsworth, and the closest precedent was, significantly, a royal one. The Queen's Staircase at Windsor, built by Hugh May in the late 1670s and destroyed after little over a century, was square in plan with a ceiling in the form of pendentives in the centre of which a large wooden lantern provided overhead daylight illumination. Vanbrugh may have known the top-lit central hall of the Huis ten Bosch in the Hague, but that is a totally painted room. Architecturally the Castle Howard hall may owe something to the domed vestibule to the Painted Hall at Greenwich Hospital, which was on the drawing-board in 1698 and structurally complete in 1702, but the probability of Vanbrugh's knowledge of, and debt to, the Windsor staircase is increased by similarities in use and in decoration. The Castle Howard hall is flanked by staircases from which the hall can be seen through communicating arches. At Windsor the corners of the ceiling were painted with figures representing the Four Elements and the roof of the lantern with Phaeton taking the chariot of the sun; at Castle Howard the Elements would be painted in the pendentives and the dome would show the scene of Phaeton's subsequent fall from heaven. Thus an architectural borrowing is turned into a political comment on the presumption of the absolutist monarchy of Charles II and James II.[14]

By 1702 the elevations had been reworked in detail. On the entrance front the imposition of the more severe Doric order is offset by the remarkable amount and variety of relief decoration – figures and urns in niches, banded rustication and a richly carved frieze – and by the uneven bay rhythms already present in the 'second' design (Fig.3; Pl.8). In size the bays are alternately single and coupled; a very large single bay in the centre has a large glazed area which lights the hall. The division into nine bays corresponds to the number on the garden front. But the single bays have niches instead of windows, and the effect of this is that the façade may also be read as an alternation of large bays of almost equal size: projecting bays without windows and with flanking pilasters, triglyphs in the frieze and statues above the parapet, and recessed bays with windows and a continuous relief in the frieze. The chief changes in the garden front (Pl.31) were the addition of a pediment with a carved tympanum, and a carved frieze of a similar pattern to that on the west front of Chatsworth (Pl.13). The latter was finished in 1702, and while its windows are rectangular and those of Castle Howard are arched, Vanbrugh may have revised his façade in the light of another visit to Chatsworth.

In May 1702 the architect of Castle Howard acquired a new and significant status. Carlisle was surely well satisfied with Vanbrugh's performance and his own choice. His great house was talked about and was beginning to take shape, and Vanbrugh's little house at Whitehall was nearing completion. The accession of a new monarch is a convenient time for changes; Carlisle tendered to Queen Anne his resignation from his short spell at the Treasury, and one of his last acts in office was to secure the dismissal of Talman

[14] For the Windsor staircase see Downes (1966), pp.19–20.

as Comptroller of the Works and the appointment of Vanbrugh in his place.[15] We may well ask how long and how carefully plans had been laid to this end, which was to make Vanbrugh for a decade the most powerful man in English architecture next to the ageing Wren. We may remember that the model of Castle Howard had been shown to the King a couple of years previously, and we may ask, as men must have asked in 1700, why this unusual step was taken. But the questions remain rhetorical, and we should also remember that in the seventeenth and eighteenth centuries a post in the Works was no guarantee of architectural ability or commitment, let alone of genius, and that while to us Vanbrugh's appointment was right, it was not obviously so at the time even to some of those most closely concerned.

The Comptrollership gave Vanbrugh the expectation of a reasonably secure income, although in the monetary situation of the time it far from assured the prompt payment of his salary. He would one day be dismissed, like Talman, but the prospect was better than the military career which he now finally abandoned, and in respect of which he was seeking arrears of pay in July 1702. In fact the appointment corresponds to his wholehearted acceptance of architecture as a career; at the same time it does not mark the summit of his ambition. The possibility certainly occurred to him of succeeding Wren (p.85) and in the meantime he was to add a fourth string to his bow. The post of Clarenceux King-at-Arms falling vacant, it occurred to Carlisle or Vanbrugh that the latter might fill it. This proposal was resisted, although in vain, by the College of Arms, not least because Vanbrugh had made fun of the Heralds in his play *Aesop*. Since no outsider could hold the office, the first step was to make Vanbrugh a Herald; the Deputy Earl Marshal was conveniently able to revive the obsolete title of Carlisle Herald. On 21 June 1703 Carlisle Herald was duly soused with a bowl of wine;[16] the following March he became Clarenceux, with a gold crown, collar of S's, chain, cap, and 'a coat of Her Majesty's arms' in gold on crimson and blue velvet lined with crimson satin.[17] He was surely on the way to a knighthood; yet there seems to have been in the operation little of the seriousness or, historically, the justness of Vanbrugh's incursion into private and public architecture. Carlisle perhaps had his own reasons to welcome a friend in the College of Arms, but Vanbrugh was prompted by the same kind of bravado as had led him to build at Whitehall: at the end of his life he admitted that he had got the post 'in jest.'[18]

In the North, work progressed well under the York masons William Smith and John Elsworth, with visits every summer from the Earl and most years from Vanbrugh and

[15] Vanbrugh's appointment as Comptroller minuted 20 May 1702 (CTB 1702, p.33).

[16] Webb, p.9.

[17] Warrants for his insignia and coat, estimated £185, CTB 1704–5, pp.221, 281. The statement in Godfrey, p.91, that Vanbrugh 'knew nothing of heraldry and genealogy; ridiculed both and neglected official duties' may need some qualification in the light of his conduct in all the other activities he is known to have undertaken. Certainly, as the Account Book shows, the office was lucrative and the opportunities for delegation were extensive, but the fact that his colleague Robert Dale 'lived in his chambers in College' (Godfrey, loc. cit.) should be accounted for by the fact that Vanbrugh had other residences and duties. It is hard to resist the conclusion that among the Heralds, as elsewhere, Vanbrugh incurred disapproval by being (a) different and (b) successful. There is also the assessment of A. R. Wagner, *Heralds of England*, 1967, p.326, as 'possibly the most distinguished man who has ever worn a herald's tabard', even though the appointment was 'incongruous.' 'The real grievance, however, was not simply Vanbrugh's appointment to the College, but his appointment immediately to the second place in it, whereby long established expectations were dashed and promotion throughout the whole body was postponed' (ibid., p.330).

[18] Webb, p.170.

Hawksmoor.[19] By 1706 the latter was preparing directions and dimensions for fitting up the private apartments in the north-east wing for occupation, Carlisle was ordering a set of Soho tapestries from John Vanderbank,[20] and the masons were turning the arches of the cupola. Early in 1707 elevations of the house were being drawn with a view to engraving, a procedure of which today's counterpart would be a feature in the architectural journals.[21] The carving of capitals, friezes, pinnacles, urns, architraves and other mouldings was done partly by the masons, but largely by Samuel Carpenter of York and two Huguenot carvers. Many fine craftsmen were Protestants who had fled from France after the withdrawal of religious toleration there and the revocation of the Edict of Nantes by Louis XIV in 1685; some came through Holland and by sea to Hull, and that is probably how Daniel Hervé (anglicized to Harvey) reached Yorkshire. The other Huguenot, surnamed Nadauld or Nedos, had previously worked at Chatsworth. It was common practice for the architect to indicate in drawings the character and the extent of the decoration he wanted rather than the precise details; these would be supplied, and designed, by the master craftsman concerned, who in some cases was given outline drawings which he filled in with decorative detail in the appropriate areas.[22] In his letter to Newcastle (p.29) Vanbrugh allowed himself satisfied 'in generall' with the design he enclosed, but 'as to the perticulars, I am scarce determined in any thing.' The idea of allowing, indeed expecting, a design to grow to maturity can be found in the work of Wren; it is more strikingly characteristic of Hawksmoor, who must have started many projects in the knowledge, not in the least cynical, that a given design would not be carried out literally. Wherever he derived the idea, this was the basis of Vanbrugh's remark about 'perticulars' and he and Hawksmoor were in agreement. In his letter to Henry Joynes (p.57) who was drawing out the Castle Howard elevations for engraving, Vanbrugh even writes, 'As for the Ornaments on the Top, with the Chimneys on the Main Pile, and the Cupola, I'll get Mr Hawksmoor to Add them' but addition is clearly not the same here as invention since he goes on, 'for I believe you have not the last Designs of 'em.'[23] Nevertheless, at a previous stage, as the early drawings show, these features did need to be added, as and when they were designed. So the ultimate question, beyond why and how Vanbrugh became an architect, is this: what part of the achievement, with which his admirers and his detractors alike have credited him, was in reality Hawksmoor's? The question is more obtrusive in respect of Castle Howard and Blenheim because they have been established from the evidence of drawings and documents as works of collaboration. But when we come to examine the stylistic differences between the independent works of the two masters, and thus to attempt to define the identity and origins of their respective styles, a crucial complication may be found in the fact that Hawksmoor had developed an idiom of his own in the early 1690s before Vanbrugh was at liberty, and that before the end of the decade he was capable of a design as sophisticated as the exteriors of Easton Neston (Pl.17). Yet in the case of Castle Howard the answer is

[19] Accounts (incomplete) at Castle Howard.

[20] Hawksmoor to Lord Carlisle, 2 July 1706 (Castle Howard MSS).

[21] Webb, p.209. For the context of this letter see Appendix D (5).

[22] For example Pl.82.

[23] See n.21.

still relatively simple, firstly because we know that Vanbrugh was learning many things and Hawksmoor is the obvious person to have taught him, and secondly because the formula of collaboration offers a convenient damper to further enquiry.

The handling of detail, whether by inventing it from imagination and memory, or by taking it ready-made from pattern books, depends inevitably on a familiarity which is not gained overnight; certainly every stage of Castle Howard from the first elevations to the finished building shows a degree of control in the placing and the character of detail which precludes the possibility either of its having been left to the craftsmen who determined the particularities or of its having been chosen as one would furnish a house from a mail-order catalogue. It should be evident by now that in 1700 Hawksmoor was capable of such control and Vanbrugh was not, and that even four or five years later Hawksmoor would still have the advantage; in fact our knowledge of the relationship over the building of Blenheim (p.68) confirms these conclusions. At Castle Howard Hawksmoor's letter of instructions of 1706 for the wing certainly conveys such authority that one would imagine him to be in charge, down to such conclusions as 'The Marbles for these Roomes . . . cannot be much varyd from what I here propose.'[24] We also have his annotated drawings for several features, including two undertaken in that same year: the fabric of the dome and the bow-window room which originally formed the west end of the south front (Pl.34) and was destroyed during the completion of the house in the 1750s.

The bow-window room was itself an afterthought, larger and more elaborate than the room already built at the east end of the garden front although that too was topped by two little leaded cupolas (destroyed in the fire of 1940).[25] By 1706 the bow-window room on the east front of Blenheim was under construction; Carlisle saw the foundations there in September 1705 (p.60) and in any case was kept informed of that building's progress. The bow-window at Castle Howard thus may have been added at either his own or his architect's suggestion, and cannot support any argument about authorship. But in both Castle Howard and Blenheim the idea of growth in a design took on a second meaning: growth in sheer size. The introduction of the dome at Castle Howard is the first sign of this, although in practical terms it increased only the weight of masonry and the height of the silhouette. The addition of side courts and ranges to contain kitchens, brewhouse, stables and other offices would, if completed, have nearly trebled the west-east length of Castle Howard; only the eastern side was built (Pl.23), and thereby the length was almost doubled. These courts are absent from the early drawings. Moreover, Castle Howard was to some extent the model for Blenheim (p.61), and was in Vanbrugh's eyes to beoutsh one by it; if side courts had been planned for the earlier house by 1705 they would surely have been emulated at Blenheim. But there they were an afterthought, which makes it probable that the Castle Howard courts were not planned until at least 1706 when the masonry of the main block and the south and north-east wings was nearing completion. Presumably Carlisle originally expected the offices to be concentrated in the north-west wing. The startling increase in area seems to go with the dome, the scenic corridors and the turning of the house to face south; all four are marked by boldness of scale rather than

[24] See n.20.

[25] *English Homes*, Pl.10.

delicacy and intricacy. It is necessary to turn from considerations of style to those of character to see in these features the architect who, as his first essay in the art, undertook a great palace, rather than the architect who, conscious of wheels within wheels in the myriad matters of detail that attend such a work, admitted after a year, 'now I shall wish the conclusion of the work as earnestly as I was for opposing the beginning of it.'[26]

It was with reference to Blenheim that Hawksmoor was to write in retrospect, 'when the Building began, all of them (the Builders) put together, could not Stir an Inch without me'; it was in the same connection that he compared himself to 'a loving Nurse that almost thinks the Child her own.'[27] In happier circumstances these remarks were no less true of Castle Howard, although that house was the creation of three men rather than two. That the large print of Castle Howard was Vanbrugh's is confirmed by every word and action of his that we know; equally clearly Hawksmoor was the indispensable assistant, not in a partnership, but in an executive relationship. In terms other than artistic, the vision as much as the money behind their achievement was Carlisle's, as he was careful to record. It did not occur to him to commemorate his architects in verse or inscriptions, but with a style and an insistence worthy of the Romans he asked posterity to recognize the uniqueness and splendour of what he had made (p.20).

The exterior detail of Castle Howard has received little scholarly attention, and through the action of the elements it is now inevitably less than perfect. It seems unlikely that any specific emblematic programme was intended, but it is nevertheless worth examining how the stone skin of the house changed in character from one part to another. The more severe Doric entrance front (Pls 26, 28) is designed to induce in the visitor the proper gravity of spirit in which to approach the residence of *Carolus Comes Carleolensis*, whose abbreviation is carved as triple C's on the keystone of the upper central window. On the parapet stand four male and four female figures in Antique dress, and four more female figures in niches flank the centre bay of the façade; these statues, which were carved by Nadauld and Harvey in 1709–10 for £14 apiece, are almost without attributes and thus cannot be named, and their number is due to considerations of design and not of symbolism. Higher up, the eight piers of the dome are surmounted by gigantic busts (now re-cut), some with laurel crowns, which suggest, as they were undoubtedly intended to do, the idea of Roman worthies or perhaps emperors. The metopes and intervening sections of the frieze below are carved with military trophies and with shields, both ancient and of a modern curvilinear type which is also to be found on the garden front at Versailles. The end niches of the façade contain urns which by their funerary associations suggest the passage of history. Other relief work on this front, however, is less serious in mood: the middle window is flanked by naked boys with ribbons and garlands, and grotesque busts and masks, their asymmetries carefully balanced with their opposites, grimace from the keystones of the upper windows and niches; Castle Howard, they seem to say, is not all fortress, and its setting is a bucolic one.

The south front is evidently considered as an ornament to the formal garden facing it (Pl.27). The pilasters are fluted and of the richer Corinthian order. The frieze consists of

[26] Hawksmoor to Carlisle, 26 May 1701 (Downes (1959), p.235).

[27] Green, pp.309–10 (2 Sep. 1725, 17 Apr. 1722).

boys blowing conch shells at sea-horses in the centre bays, similar in pattern to those on the west front of Chatsworth (Pl.13), with groups of boys and lions in the outer bays. The pediment, carved with Carlisle's arms and supporters, cannon and other weapons, is again modelled on that at Chatsworth. The three female statues above the pediment appear to hold vegetable attributes. The large relief of Diana on the east end of the garden wing is appropriate to Wray Wood, which it faces, and which Lady Irwin's poem associates with the goddess (p.109).

The frieze on each end of the main block contains a series of small oval windows, while the parapet is raised in the middle into a segmental pediment intersected by a chimney stack. Neither of these features is now very easy to see, but there was some purpose in incorporating them into otherwise plain elevations at an early date when, before the outer courts were designed, they would have been more clearly and widely visible (Pl.5).

The north-east wing (like its pair on the north-west which was intended but not built) lies lower in the hierarchy of building, having no carved ornament except urns on the parapet. The rustication, banded and continued radially over the windows, is a continuation of the basic wall pattern of the main north front; when, in the wing, it is stripped of ornament, its descent is clearly visible, through the wings of the 'preliminary' design (Pl.18) from such French prototypes as the Orangery (Pl.14) or the great stables at Versailles.

The back of the wing, and the base court to the east with its four towers, are again lower in status (Pls 22, 23). The stones are less highly finished, less regularly cut and less closely and smoothly jointed. Yet these structures, which contribute so much to the scenic effect of the whole building at a distance, cannot be considered merely utilitarian at close quarters. They have banded rusticated chimneys. The towers, which are rectangular and not square in plan and designed for staircases, have pyramidal roofs and stand one floor higher than the neighbouring buildings. In the corners of the court are four little single-storey pavilions – bakehouses and such like – finished with leaded cupolas. The passage from the kitchen court into the inner base court is flanked by tall stone drums. While the little cupolas were fairly certainly Hawksmoor's invention the ensemble of blocks and towers is as surely Vanbrugh's. All these elements were built about 1710–11 and probably not designed much before. In other words they belong to the second decade of Vanbrugh's architectural activity; they are later than the exteriors of Kimbolton (Pls 46–9) and their monumental plainness was no longer a novelty for Vanbrugh. The two pedimented archways leading out of the kitchen court to the north were built about 1716, at the same time as the triumphal arch which formerly made the east side of the north court shown in the bird's-eye engraving of 1725 which is generally taken to represent Vanbrugh's final wishes for Castle Howard (Pl.30).[28] The corresponding archway on the west was built in 1722; the northern gate with its four big obelisks was never built, and in 1724 Vanbrugh actually argued against it in an unsuccessful attempt to induce Carlisle to proceed with the north-west wing and west base courts and thus to guarantee the symmetrical completion of the whole house (p.112).

[28] For gateways see Whistler, p.60. The bird's-eye view is to the same plan as that in the re-issue of *Vit. Brit.* I (1717); the 1715 plate is erroneous. The Castle Howard plates often disagree with each other and with the building and are probably early. The bird's-eye does not show the existing arches; the side ones it shows were there in the middle of the eighteenth century. See also p.54, n.39.

One other characteristic decorative feature deserves notice: the exaggerated triple keystone, which at Castle Howard is used at the back of the north-east wing and inside the small courts formed between the two corridors of the main house (Pl.32). This motif embodies one of several forms of over-emphasis which the two architects applied to such parts of elevations as window sills, architraves, parapets and finials. While forms with a family resemblance appear from time to time in Vanbrugh's independent work, this particular type of large fasciated keystone becomes in later years almost a trademark of Hawksmoor, and it would not be surprising to find that its introduction at Castle Howard was due to him. The motif has a basic illogicality in that the keystone, on which the stability of the arched or square opening by definition depends, is prolonged downwards as if it had slipped out of its proper position; when the keystone is tripled and so thickened as to project several inches in front of the wall surface a large part of its mass is without structural function; thus illogicality is compounded by incongruity. The textbook example is the mercurial Giulio Romano's Palazzo del Té in Mantua, but the motif must have reached England through the intermediacy of designs such as the book of gateways published as *Libro Extraordinario* in the most influential sixteenth-century Italian architectural manual, that of Sebastiano Serlio. It is significant that the triple keystone appears prominently in two English buildings which for other reasons were still considered artistic landmarks in 1700: John Webb's King Charles Block at Greenwich of the 1660s, and Talman's south front of Chatsworth begun in 1687. We have already seen that, in terms of prestige and iconography, Chatsworth was a model for Castle Howard; Webb's building stands behind them both as the first Baroque building in England – the first in which liberties taken with the classical vocabulary and language of Roman and Renaissance architecture are based on full understanding, and in which that understanding is applied to the exploitation of the dramatic possibilities of large unit scale and weightiness of appearance.

In historical terms Castle Howard follows from the sequence of the King Charles building and Chatsworth, and leads on to Blenheim, the most ambitious of Vanbrugh's executed works. When Blenheim was begun in 1705, Castle Howard was an uncompleted shell without its dome. Vanbrugh's activities were still increasing towards a range of commitment that would tax the energies of a superman; he was also still enlarging his conception of the nature of architecture. Before turning to a consideration of that most monumental and most controversial building, it is desirable to examine some other aspects of his work during the first decade of the century which have a bearing on Blenheim, on Castle Howard, and on his later work.

Chapter 3

Diversification

Vanbrugh's activity as a dramatist was intermittent, and it lasted only ten years. After his initial successes of 1696–8 he produced no plays until the spring of 1700, when *The Pilgrim* was played at Drury Lane. This was, like the earlier *Aesop* and all his later plays, not an original work at all but an adaptation; *The Pilgrim* was a trimmed and modernized prose version of John Fletcher's play of 1621 of the same name. Further adaptations followed: *The False Friend* early in 1702 at Drury Lane, and *The Confederacy* and *The Mistake* in late 1705 at the new theatre in the Haymarket. These were Vanbrugh's last full-length stage works, and both their date and their close succession are connected with the place of their performance.[1] The London theatres were in bad health: buildings were inadequate, audiences declining, and plays were based on assumptions of a permissive morality which did the stage no credit with the public. Plays were bedecked with what we should call music-hall turns as box-office attractions; at Drury Lane Christopher Rich proposed, in a desperate search for novelty, to put an elephant on the stage, but was dissuaded by assurances that to do so would demolish the building more quickly than his mismanagement was ruining the company. In 1703, however, the rival theatre in Lincoln's Inn Fields was in the worst straits, and a scheme was prepared by its actor-manager, Thomas Betterton, Congreve and Vanbrugh for a brand new theatre in the Haymarket.[2] Vanbrugh was to be both the architect and the financer of the building and was very probably the originator of the whole idea, and while it did not ruin him, the Queen's Theatre, or the Haymarket Opera House as it came to be known, was the most expensive mistake of his life. The intention was to raise thirty life subscriptions of £100 giving free admission to the subscribers. An inscription discovered in 1825 gave the date of laying the foundation stone as 18 April 1704 and the performer of the ceremony as the Duke of Somerset, and we should therefore interpret figuratively the account in a contemporary newspaper according to which one side of the stone was inscribed *Kit Cat* and the other *Little Whig* in allusion to the nickname of Lady Anne Sunderland, the favourite toast of the Kit-Cat Club.[3] But the same source calls the theatre the Temple of the Club, and from

[1] There were a number of revivals of the plays in Vanbrugh's lifetime. *Squire Trelooby*, adapted from Molière by Vanbrugh, Congreve and Walsh (one act each), was first played at Lincoln's Inn Fields on 30 April 1704.

[2] Most of the following section is based on the account of the Theatre in *Survey of London*, XXIX, 1960, p.223 ff. While it does not add very much, Vanbrugh's Account Book shows the extreme complexity of his concerns with the structure, upkeep, management and stock of properties of the theatre which, after several reversals of ownership, he finally sold to his brother Charles in Dec. 1720. The properties and costumes had been an embarrassment to him since at least 1714 (Rosenberg, pp.607–10). In Jan. 1721 the Managers of Drury Lane Theatre finally agreed to buy them from him; the Account Book records payment by instalments until 1726.

[3] *The Rehearsal of Observator*, 5/12 May 1705, quoted in *Survey of London*, p.225.

such evidence it might be expected that the club provided most of the subscribers. However, another contemporary account attacking the scheme contains the lines 'Never [was] Foundation so abruptly laid, So much Subscrib'd, and yet so little Paid' which imply both Vanbrugh's haste and unhonoured promises to him.[4] Of thirty persons known to have agreed to subscribe, less than half were Kit-Cats, and only three are known to have made payments.[5] Indeed the architect, who was negotiating the site in the summer of 1703, told Tonson on 16 June that he expected to be ready for 'business' by Christmas, and although this must mean the business of building and not of staging, the forecast was optimistic.[6] Building occupied most of 1704, a company was licensed in December, and the first performance, of Giacomo Greber's *The Loves of Ergasto*, took place on 9 April 1705.

The initial trouble over financial backing was followed by a series of misfortunes, not to say disasters. The site, where the present Her Majesty's Theatre stands, was too near the western fringe of Westminster to woo a large audience with amenity. Although Vanbrugh designed the theatre with a symmetrical exterior in the expectation of a broad central approach from the Haymarket, the only frontage to that street available at the planning stage was at the north end. He thus had to build the three-bay loggia there (Pl.25) before he managed to acquire the lease of the rest of the frontage in September 1704, and he then decided to retain the houses on the street as an investment. This did not help the architectural prestige of the building, since no more of it could be seen from the street. Inside, however, Colley Cibber tells us that Vanbrugh sacrificed everything to 'a vast triumphal Piece of Architecture' in the form of a grandiose proscenium arch and an excessively high auditorium ceiling; in consequence only one word in ten was audible.[7] For music the defect was judged to be less serious, but the vocal attainments of the Italian singers engaged for Greber's opera did not contribute to its success. Vanbrugh's two productions were intended to boost a flagging season, and had they been audible they might have done so. At the end of the season Congreve withdrew. Quite apart from the drain on Vanbrugh's pocket, architecture was making increasing demands on his time and energies, and he saw the possibility of salvation through the agency of the impresario Owen Swiney or McSwiny. The latter's principal contribution to the arts was to be the commissioning from a number of Italian painters in the 1720s of a series of large allegorical canvases commemorating British worthies of around 1700. Financially that venture seems to have been no more successful than Swiney's conduct of the theatre which had led to his bankruptcy in 1711. Late in 1706 Vanbrugh began a long series of negotiations with Swiney by which the latter was to take control of the theatre. At one point Vanbrugh actually bought out Swiney, but by the summer of 1708 the transfer was complete; after four months exclusively of opera performances the theatre closed early, and alterations

[4] Daniel Defoe, *Review*, 5 May 1705.

[5] A copy in Vanbrugh's hand of an agreement by twenty-nine subscribers of £100 in four stage payments is among the Portland MSS. in Nottingham University Library (MS.Pw 2. 571, f.64). Twenty-five were noblemen and at least thirteen Kit-Cat members. Vanbrugh is known to have received subscriptions of £25 from Newcastle and Carlisle (Whistler, p.39); the 1st Earl of Bristol, who was not a Kit-Cat, records the first three payments in his book of expenses (*The Diary of John Hervey, 1st Earl of Bristol 1688–1742*, Wells, 1894, p.157 f.).

[6] Webb, p.8.

[7] *Apology for his Life*, p.259.

were made to improve the acoustics and probably also the supporting facilities.[8] In June 1708 Vanbrugh wrote to Lord Manchester, 'I lost so Much Money by the Opera this Last Winter, that I was glad to get quit of it: And yet I don't doubt but Opera will Settle and thrive in London.'[9] He nevertheless retained some interest in both the management and the leases until the comprehensive re-settlement of his financial affairs in 1719–20 shortly after his marriage.

Opera in Britain has always been expensive and foreign. The term current in Vanbrugh's day, *the Italian opera*, referred to the origins of the art-form although the singers might be British and the composer of any nationality. From what we know or suspect of Vanbrugh's eye for a setting, his fondness for the large, the dramatic and the extravagant, and his involvement with the London stage, we might imagine all sorts of fruitful connections between architect and man of the theatre. But most of the evidence is to the contrary. His own stage settings were the rooms of houses and his concern as a dramatist is with people and their behaviour. There is no evidence that he designed scenery as some of the leading painters did. It is also extremely difficult to make valid comparisons between the different media of the time. The architect most notably connected with the Italian opera a decade or so later was Lord Burlington, whose tastes in building were opposed in nearly every way to Vanbrugh's. Moreover, whatever homogeneity the art may have attained later, opera in the first decade of the eighteenth century was by all accounts an under-rehearsed artistic mish-mash of speech, recitative and music, of polyglot singing, and of the natural and the artificial; Steele's account in the *Spectator* of the introduction of flocks of sparrows into a painted garden is probably veracious although his subsequent examples of absurdity are patently not.[10] The enthusiasm that produced Castle Howard and Blenheim could extend to such entertainments, but the quality of mind that went into those buildings – whatever Hawksmoor had to do with them – was of a different order.

Externally the Queen's Theatre was unremarkable; the earliest known plan, from the 1770s, shows slight projections in the centre of the long sides (Fig.4) but the east side was only visible from a small courtyard and the west side was obscured by buildings either already existing and adapted or built specially for the use of the theatre. The only elevation to the street was the three-bay vestibule at the north-east corner facing the Haymarket; it was of brick with stone dressings which were probably rather sharper originally than in William Capon's water-colour which was made at about the time the theatre was burnt down in 1789 (Pl.25). The oval windows and perhaps also the other details of the fenestration were carried around the outside. Inside, the auditorium was semicircular, originally with a lofty ceiling under which speech became confused, and a high and deep proscenium arch of half-oval section which must have resembled the slightly later arch which dramatizes the

[8] Cibber (loc.cit.) says it was altered 'two or three years after.' There were no performances 20 May–14 Dec. 1708, then plays were performed again (W. B. van Lennep, *The London Stage 1660–1800*, I, Carbondale, 1960). The literature on Swiney is scattered: see F. Haskell, *Painters and Patrons*, 1963, pp.287–91.

[9] Webb, p.24.

[10] *Spectator*, No.5, on Handel's *Rinaldo* at the Queen's Theatre. The Opera was discussed in several other issues of the *Spectator* and the *Tatler*. Vanbrugh was at least initially a director of the Royal Academy of Music founded in 1719, in which Lord Burlington played a major role, for the encouragement of the Italian Opera (sheet of Minutes of the Court of Directors, PRO LC7/3, ff.71–2).

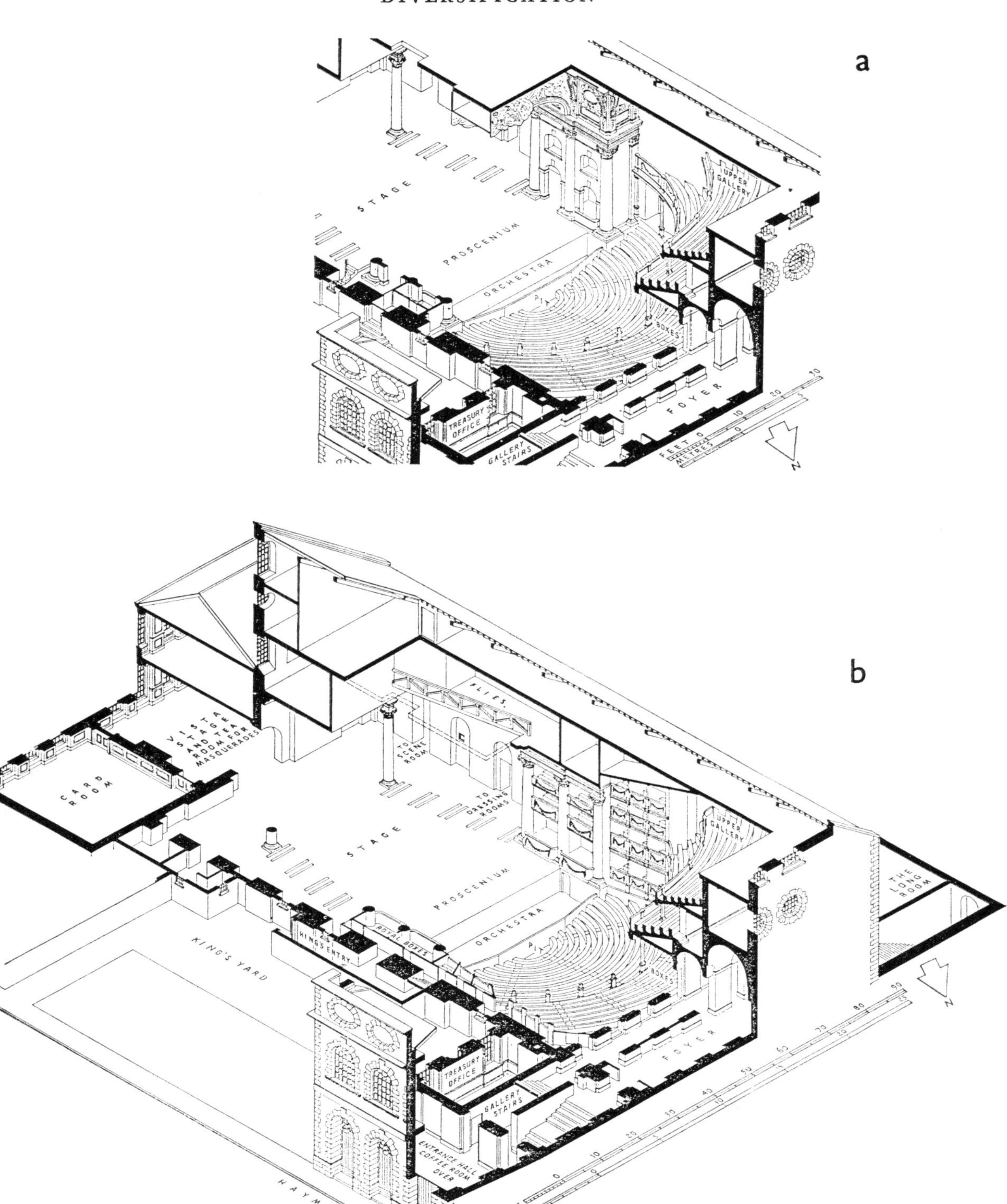

4 The Queen's Theatre, Haymarket. Reconstructions by Richard Leacroft (a) as originally built, (b) after the alterations of 1708.

transition from hall to saloon at Blenheim (Pl.81).[11] The stage had the fixed wings and borders and the extreme depth common to the Baroque theatre; it was deeper from front to back than the auditorium, and the increase in the stalls seating at the expense of the stage in 1782 is typical of the tendency in English theatres towards larger audiences and thus lower costs, rather than elaborate perspectives.

In some of the more spectacular productions of lesser literary or musical merit the scenery and machines were remarkable in complexity and of a high standard. On 22 March 1707 the audience for a revival at the Queen's Theatre of *The British Enchanters* by George Granville, Lord Lansdowne, were treated to additional scenes, 'particularly the intire front prospect of Blenheim Castle, And another Piece alluding to the late glorious Successes of her Majesty's Arms, &c.' We may conclude that the architect was in the house, since he was the author of the after-piece that night, *The Cuckold in Conceit*, and we may assume that he had provided a drawing.[12] We do not know who painted the scenes, but stage work was usually done by the decorative painters whose illusionist halls, staircases and ceilings are one of the features of English Baroque interiors. The scenes for *Pyrrhus and Demetrius*, first given in December 1708, were repainted the following April by 'two famous Italian Painters (lately arriv'd from Venice)'; they were almost certainly Giovanni Antonio Pellegrini and Marco Ricci, who had recently been brought to London by Lord Manchester on his return from an embassy to Venice.[13] From a letter of Vanbrugh it is clear that the Earl's primary purpose was to set them to work at his country house, Kimbolton Castle,[14] but in the event the house, which Vanbrugh was partly rebuilding, was not yet ready for them. They probably therefore worked first in his London house in Arlington Street (destroyed) before going late in 1709 to Castle Howard where Ricci painted a number of overdoors and Pellegrini was to do the most important painted decorations; it is assumed that his employment there was Vanbrugh's idea, and the results contributed in more than one respect to the unique character of Carlisle's house.[15] Since much of the work of that time at Castle Howard was destroyed in the tragic accidental fire of 1940 the most accessible, though not the most striking, of Pellegrini's mural work is at Kimbolton, where he worked about 1711. Fire has reduced the work there also, but the staircase, with a triumphal procession considerably indebted to Mantegna's *Triumph of Caesar* at Hampton Court, has a freshness of technique and bright variety of colours which we associate with a Tiepolo, and which add up to a lightness and gaiety seldom paralleled and nowhere surpassed in England (Pl.40). This is still set in the illusionist convention by which walls and ceiling appear to be altogether open to the infinity of the sky, and architecture other than that provided by the painter hardly exists.

At Castle Howard, where Pellegrini began work in November 1709 and finished in September 1712, the Baroque fusion of painting, sculpture and architecture was replaced

[11] The arch is probably that shown in a scene design in the BM (*Survey of London*, XXX, 1960, Pl.24a).

[12] *The Cuckold in Conceit*, also after Molière; no text seems to have been published. For the state of drawings of Blenheim at this date see Appendix D (5).

[13] *Pyrrhus and Demetrius* adapted by N. Haym from A. Scarlatti, at the Queen's Theatre; *Daily Courant*, 30 March 1709.

[14] Vanbrugh to Lord Manchester, 17 Aug. 1708 (Webb, pp.25–6).

[15] Payments at Castle Howard Nov. 1709–May 1710 (seat on York coach), March 1711–June 1712 (seat on coach); last payment Sep. 1712.

by co-ordination. Castle Howard had a feature common in central Europe but unusual among English houses: two saloons one on top of the other, behind the hall. The other two notable examples of double saloons, Coleshill and Sutton Scarsdale, were both casualties of the twentieth century.[16] Sutton Scarsdale, designed by Francis Smith in the 1720s for the diplomat Lord Scarsdale, was remarkable above all for the Venetian plasterwork in both saloons; Coleshill (p.22) half a century before Castle Howard had two great rectangular rooms superimposed on the garden side, as well as the beginnings of corridors. The High Saloon at Castle Howard was lined with arcades between narrow pilasters and elaborate and very free heads to the doorcases; between these features were a series of Trojan histories painted by Pellegrini. In both the High Saloon and the garden-room below the ceiling was painted with sky and clouds and figures in the centre, enclosed in a curvilinear surround which in the upper room was of stucco (Pls 36, 37) and in the lower was painted to imitate relief.

In the hall (Pls 35, 39) the painting is restricted to certain fields: the side walls and arches of the staircases, parts of the vaulting of the corridors, and above all the pendentives, and the dome which has been rebuilt since the fire and painted by Scott Medd with a replica of Pellegrini's *Fall of Phaeton* so that this one surviving Venetian room can be seen again in something like its original state. These were spaces asking, and perhaps designed, to be filled with painting, but the hall depends no more on painting than on the other components; upon the shapes of the architecture itself, on the rich carving by Samuel Carpenter of soffits, frieze and capitals, and on the stucco overmantel which is probably the work of one of the Italians identified in the accounts only as Plura.

One peculiarity which was later criticized as a solecism is the omission of the architrave, the lowest of the three parts of the entablature, so that the frieze rests immediately on the capitals; this was defended by Hawksmoor, a circumstance which suggests his or Vanbrugh's control.[17] Their hands too can be seen in the Doric alcove, finished in scagliola (an extremely hard-setting composition which can be coloured and polished to imitate marble) which stands opposite the fireplace. Pellegrini undoubtedly started work by offering for approval sketches of what he proposed to paint in the spaces allotted to him, and the free flowing curves and exuberant forms of the overmantel would likewise be designed by the craftsmen who carried it out.

It is difficult to do justice to the lost interiors of Castle Howard, but their unique character raises inevitable, if insoluble, questions about their sources. The High Saloon recalls neither any other Vanbrugh-Hawksmoor room nor any other English interior of 1710–12, which is its date. The elegant curves and angles and the delicate vegetable forms anticipate decoration of the 1730s or 1740s; on the other hand the scrolls of the overdoors are very like those of the hall overmantel and the foliage forms can be picked up in chinoiserie tapestries of about 1700, while the forms of the frieze and the strips between the arches could be paralleled in other rooms at Castle Howard. But the components can be separated out according to their positions more easily than by the trades which contributed to their making, and so the ensemble would appear to be the product of one

[16] Sutton Scarsdale was vandalized in the early 1920s; Castle Howard burnt 1940 and Coleshill 1952, both accidental.

[17] *Walpole Society*, XIX, 1931, p.136.

mind.[18] Did Pellegrini take charge of the whole room, or one of the stuccoists? The room cannot be called Venetian, nor does it resemble at all closely the decorative details invented by the Huguenot with the greatest flair for comprehensive publication, Daniel Marot. Vanbrugh's visit to Hanover in the summer of 1706 could have been timely. He went, in his capacity as herald, with Lord Halifax, to confer the Garter on the Elector's son, the future George II; unfortunately we have no record of what he might have seen in Holland and Germany to account for the Continental feeling of the room. Carlisle himself had been in Padua in 1690, and therefore presumably in Venice also, but we do not know what else he saw in Europe.[19]

No comments of Vanbrugh's survive on the decoration of the interior, but we know he was extremely pleased that the comfort and economy of Castle Howard had fulfilled his predictions to Lord Carlisle; while staying there he was careful to inform at least three other patrons of the success. In October 1713 he wrote to Edward Southwell of Kings Weston that every room was like an oven and that 'in corridors of 200 ft long there is not air enough in motion to stir the flame of a candle.' Even in the hall, he told the elder Craggs a few days later, there was no need to shield the flame in a lantern. While the private apartments in the east wing had been habitable by 1707 Lord Carlisle had continued to use the remains of Henderskelfe Castle until 1712; now after the main pile of the new house had been in use for a year he found that the total household costs were only £100 a year more than previously. This and similar information was for the benefit of the Duchess of Marlborough, for Carlisle had been 'pretty much under the same Apprehensions with her, about long Passages, High Roomes &c.'[20] On a later visit over Christmas 1718–19 he told the younger Duke of Newcastle that, even with freezing weather outside, room windows had to be opened several times a day; 'And so may Nottingham Castle be made, by the same care and Methods.'[21] His references to economy confirm that the methods were more refined than big roaring fires. It is still surprising how easily large early eighteenth-century houses can be warmed if they were well built and are well maintained. Walls like those of Castle Howard, nearly a yard thick, not only insulate but also absorb and retain warmth much as a brick oven does; the absence of draughts speaks for the excellence of the timber and joinery in doors and sash windows. This also was the practical significance of a ground floor so extended 'like an orange house' as to offer a dozen rooms facing south.

The orangery or greenhouse of Vanbrugh's time was remote both in its form and construction and in its function from our modern glasshouses. It was domestic rather than horticultural; its primary function was as a winter-house for half-hardy and exotic plants and shrubs, and its large south-facing windows were designed to make the most of the low sun. But besides the keeping of house-plants on a grand scale it could accommodate the overflow of activities from the house, being by turns a long gallery for walking in bad

[18] Chief craftsmen: William Smith, John Ellsworth, Manger Smith, masons; John Milburn, carpenter; Sabyn, William Thornton, joiners; Samuel Carpenter, Daniel Harvey, Nadauld, 'Mr Tushaine' [Toussaint?], carvers; Bagutti, Plura, Isaac Mansfield, plasterers; John Thorp of Bakewell, marble; John Harvey, Pellegrini and Ricci, painters; John Gardom, ironwork.

[19] Carlisle signed the book for British visitors and scholars at the University of Padua on 1 Jan. 1690 (as Charles Howard of Morpeth: H. F. Brown, *Inglesi e Scozzesi all'Università di Padova*, Venice, 1921, p.172).

[20] Webb, pp.55–7.

[21] ibid., pp.107–9.

weather and, with windows opened and plants carried outside, a summer-house; according to Defoe, Queen Anne often used the Orangery at Kensington Palace as a supper-house, and its elegant exterior brickwork and interior joinery and plasterwork are appropriate to a building in the tradition of the first Trianon at Versailles and the lost Water Gallery for Queen Mary at Hampton Court. An allocation for the building was approved by the Treasury on 17 June 1704, but two months later when one-third of the brickwork had been done the bricklayer's estimate had more than doubled, and the total cost of the work underwent a proportionate escalation. As completed in 1705 the building was thus very different both inside and out from the first proposal, and the only documentary reference to any architect is in a Treasury letter to the Office of Works approving the building 'according to the alteration of the Draft proposed by Mr Vanbrugh.'[22] Traditionally the Orangery has been attributed to Wren as Surveyor and to Vanbrugh because it looked more like the design of a younger generation; the argument that Hawksmoor was responsible, as Clerk of Works at Kensington, carries about equal weight. If we assume that Vanbrugh significantly altered a design which may have been his anyway, then there is a serious likelihood that he was the architect. On the other hand, in 1704 his independent *oeuvre* consisted of the Whitehall house and the Queen's Theatre; Castle Howard, and Blenheim (still to come), cannot, as joint works with Hawksmoor, be used as evidence. The centre-piece of the Orangery, with a lunette set into a segmental pediment above banded columns (Pl.43) can of course be compared with the kitchen gateway of Blenheim (Pl.73) but the latter in its developed form dates from about 1708 and in any case is probably Hawksmoor's contribution. The Orangery is characterized by the combination and permutation of shapes, semicircular and rectangular, blind and open, plane and three-dimensional, to form an intricate system of pattern-relations: one striking example is the way in which the middle attic with its lunette is turned over on its back to form the recesses of the end attics. Such pattern-making is to be found in Hawksmoor's independent works from Easton Neston before 1700 to Spitalfields Church two decades later, and it is not characteristic of Vanbrugh. Moreover, there are affinities in both decoration and feeling between the circular end rooms of the Orangery and the gallery niche of Easton Neston. On evidence of style, therefore, Vanbrugh's case as architect of the Orangery remains not proven, although one document concerns his interest not only in its design but, as Comptroller of Works, in its execution.

Vanbrugh discovered, by asking questions, that the stone-mason working on the Orangery was paid by Benjamin Jackson, the Queen's Master Mason who by the terms of his office was precluded from contracting for royal building. He discovered further that the irregularity was known to Wren, who was not disposed to make an issue of what, in a building of moderate size and mostly brick-built, he considered to be a small matter. Vanbrugh, however, had three reasons to persevere: first, the seriousness which he brought to his office; second, the circumstance that this kind of irregularity and its consequences elsewhere had been his discovery some months earlier; third, personal animus against Jackson, who for many years had been contracting mason to Vanbrugh's enemy and rival William Talman. Accordingly he wrote to Lord Treasurer Godolphin

22 *Wren Soc.*, VII, pp.184–5; PRO Works 6/14, ff.65, 70, 109; PRO T27/17, p.407; CTB 1704–5, p.40.

giving a full account of his enquiries, and this, while giving no indication of concern as designer, is our chief source of information about the incident.[23]

The Earl of Manchester, who was about four years older than the architect, had been one of the first to know about Vanbrugh's work at Castle Howard (p.26), but was already committed to another designer for the remodelling of the central courtyard of Kimbolton Castle. This work, in gauged brick with stone dressings, was probably begun in the early 1690s, and is now thought more likely to be to the designs of Henry Bell of King's Lynn than of the local joiner, William Coleman, who was in charge of the fabric in 1707.[24] Early that summer, while the Earl was ambassador in Venice, the whole of the old exterior south range collapsed, and it was Lady Manchester who asked Vanbrugh's advice. After she had written to the Earl herself, she allowed Vanbrugh to do so; the latter reported that he had taken Hawksmoor down to Kimbolton with him, and that they, with the Countess and perhaps with Coleman, 'all Agreed Upon' a design 'which Differs very much from what Coleman had drawn.' Coleman had not managed to set the door in the middle of the front; this was a defect in the elevation which Vanbrugh solved by an alteration in the plan. Instead of the conventional juxtaposition of drawing-room and bedroom he placed 'a large Noble Room of Parade' between them in the centre of the front, with the door in the middle and on the axis of the garden. 'I wish,' he wrote, 'it cou'd have been made a real Salon, by carrying it up into the Next Story, but that wou'd have destroy'd one of the three Bedchambers Above, which My Lady thinks cannot be Spar'd. 'Twill however be eighteen foot high, which is no contemptible thing.'[25] He then turned to the elevation:

> As to the Outside, I thought 'twas absolutly best, to give it Something of the Castle Air, tho' at the Same time to make it regular. And by this means too, all the Old stone is Serviceable again; which to have had new wou'd have run to a very great Expence; This method was practic'd at Windsor in King Charles's time, And has been universally Approv'd, So I hope your Ldship won't be discourag'd, if any Italians you may Shew it to, shou'd find fault that 'tis not Roman, for to have built a Front with Pillasters, and what the Orders require cou'd never have been born with the rest of the Castle; I'm sure this will make a very Noble and Masculine Shew; and is of as Warrantable a kind of building as Any.

Vanbrugh was anxious to please his patron, far from the scene of operations, and the latter evidently thought one great room enough for any house; in September Vanbrugh was writing to convince him that this was not so, to explain that the ceilings of the new rooms would be too low to be coved for painting as Manchester wished, and, as for the outside, to predict that people would 'See a Manly Beauty in it when tis up, that they did not conceive cou'd be produced out of such rough Materialls; But tis certainly the Figure and Proportions that make the most pleasing Fabrick, And not the delicacy of the Ornaments: A proof of wch I am in great hopes to Shew yr Ldship at Kimbolton.' At that

[23] Webb, pp.11–13. Discussion of this or a subsequent letter, CTB 1705–6, pp.21, 133.

[24] *Country Life*, CXL, 1966, p.614 ff.

[25] Webb, pp.13–26, letters between July 1707 and Aug. 1708.

time Vanbrugh's new south building only extended two bays along the east and west sides (Pl.47). But in March 1708 he foretold 'That your Ldship will two or three years hence find your self under a violent Temptation to take down and rebuild (suitable to this New front) all the Outside Walls round the Castle.' After Manchester's return home in the autumn there are no letters, but by the end of 1710 he not only had been tempted but had yielded, and Kimbolton was well on the way to four new fronts – or almost new. The arched court gateway on the west side was already in existence and the splayed walls that flank it were built on old foundations (Pl.46). The east front is only half Vanbrugh's (Pl.49), for the concealed staircase he designed (Pl.48) was never built. The colossal Doric portico constructed in 1719, the year after the Earl was created Duke of Manchester, was designed by the Florentine Alessandro Galilei and was the only practical outcome of the five years (1714–19) he spent in England in the misguided hope of great commissions.[26] Galilei's most famous later work, the front of the Lateran Basilica in Rome, similarly overbears the building to which it was added.

Both during and after the years of Vanbrugh's work at Kimbolton (1707–10) Hawksmoor was engaged on the building of Blenheim. On the other hand we can point to nothing as Hawksmoor's contribution at Kimbolton; his help may have been technical and perhaps critical, and while he made drawings (the 1710 accounts link him with drawing paper used there and with postage)[27] the invention certainly seems to be covered by Vanbrugh's letters. The formula by which the figure and proportions matter more than the ornaments, of which Kimbolton was to be a particular demonstration, allowed Vanbrugh to dispense with decorative detail; it was in every sense a bold one although, as he acknowledged, he was adapting an idea from an earlier architect. He suspected that the Italians would consider barbarous an architecture almost devoid of the conventional vocabulary of the classical orders as revived and handed on during the Renaissance. To arm his patron in Venice against such criticism, he appealed to the 'castle air', to native tradition, and to the principle which at this time was still almost universally observed, that of symmetry.

The example offered for the 'castle air' is significant both for its modernity and for its relative inappropriateness. Hugh May's pseudo-Norman recasing of the Upper Ward of Windsor Castle in the 1670s indeed consisted of battlemented façades with regular windows of dressed stone. The basic masonry and strength and the historical associations of great age were preserved while giving a more regular kind of monumentality to the exteriors and admitting more light to the rooms within; most of May's work was replaced by the more studied and more romantic nineteenth-century gothicism of Wyattville, and only a few windows survive to show the effect (Pl.44) and how clearly Vanbrugh departs from his model. May's windows are set back well into the wall by a bold surround of concave quadrant section which spans a storey and a mezzanine above; the effect is one which Hawksmoor was to recommend elsewhere on account of 'the beauty it gives the Overture by Receding', that is the exploration of the depth of massive walls and the setting

[26] The north side, one storey lower, was heightened in 1869. Galilei's design, signed *AG*, in the Manchester Deposit, Huntingdon CRO (Lees-Milne, Pl.169). There are no reasonable grounds for questioning this discovery, first made by Ilaria Toesca Bertelli.

[27] Whistler, p.139.

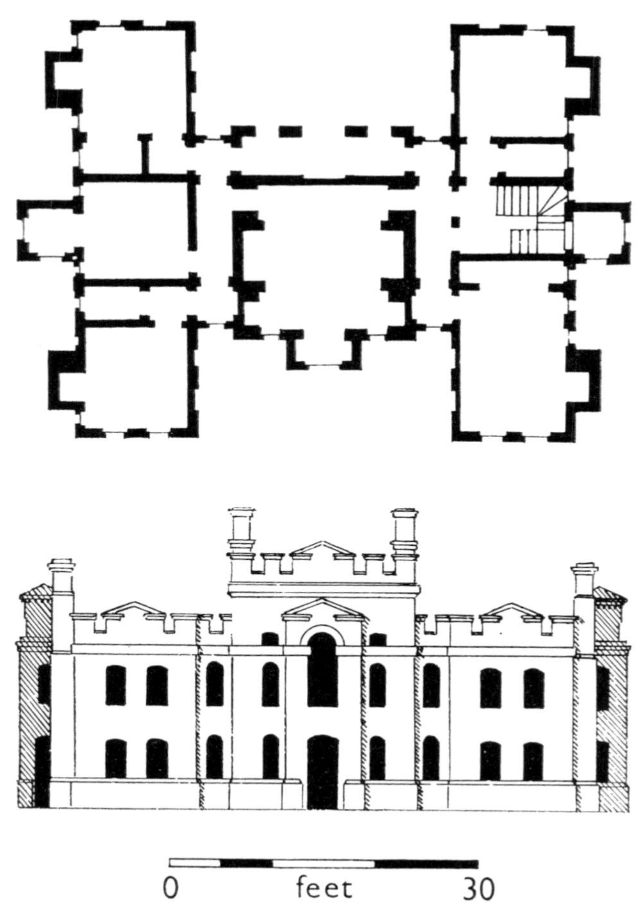

5 Chargate. Plan and elevation. From Vanbrugh's drawings in the Victoria and Albert Museum.

up of highlights and shadows across the surface.[28] The Kimbolton windows on the contrary have simple shallow architraves and the glazing bars are near the front plane of the wall; the relief is restrained, one might almost say delicate, and for all the re-use of old stone the surfaces are smoothly dressed. The massiveness of the building is expressed by broad rectangular areas and by the banded vertical strips which mark the corners and projections. These features show a descent from Vanbrugh's house in Whitehall (Pl.24) while Kimbolton's cousins are the north-east wing at Castle Howard and the Haymarket Theatre (Pls 6, 25).

The 'castle air' was far from precise in Vanbrugh's mind in 1707; it depended more than anything on the element which he did not mention – the battlements – as we can see if we block them from view. In the course of time the idea became for him richer in association and more specific in form, with affinities both in the Middle Ages and in the era of Shakespeare. After Kimbolton it reappeared in his own little house at Esher, which was built in 1709–10 (Fig.5).[29] In the former year he acquired the lease of a brick house with a

[28] May's re-casing of Windsor: Downes (1966), p.17; Hawksmoor's design for All Souls, copying two-storey use, ibid., Pl.545.

[29] Surrey CRO 176/14/2 (Abstract of Title to the Manors of Esher and Waterville Esher and the Mansion House and lands called Claremont, 6 July 1787): Vanbrugh's lease for seventy years from Michaelmas 1709 was indentured on 13 May 1709. The rent was £32 p.a.

60-acre farm there called Chargate, with permission to rebuild it to the same size and standard, and to fell trees to make walks and views. It was in the new house that his mother died on 13 August 1711.[30] At that time he was in serious financial difficulties. In the absence at sea of his youngest brother Philip the arrangement and the expense of the funeral in the neighbouring parish of Thames Ditton fell to John, and three days later he sought an advance from the Treasury 'by reason of the great expense he had bin at . . . in burying his mother.' During 1710–11 he had made unsuccessful approaches to Marlborough for what he considered his proper salary as architect of Blenheim, and in 1713 he told the Duke that his debts still amounted to between three and four thousand pounds. Even earlier, in July 1708, he had tried through Arthur Maynwaring to enlist the Duchess's support; Maynwaring, who informed her but advised her to do nothing, was clear that Vanbrugh's poverty was due to 'his own folly [in] building the play-house, which certainly cost him a great deal more than was subscribed; and his troubles arise from the workmen that built it, and the tradesmen that furnished the cloaths, &c., for the actors.'[31] The money for Chargate was therefore perhaps put up by his mother to provide a country home for them both. In 1654 she had inherited from her father properties at *Claygate* and elsewhere in Thames Ditton parish,[32] but the extent of Carleton and Vanbrugh activities in this part of Surrey at the end of the century is still not entirely clear and we do not know why Chargate was chosen. Vanbrugh wrote a letter from Chargate in October 1710,[33] but he cannot have lived there much. In July 1711 his friend and contemporary the Duke of Newcastle died after a riding accident; his nephew succeeded first as Earl of Clare and then as Duke of Newcastle. A copy of the plan of the house dated 14 August 1711,[34] the day after Elizabeth Vanbrugh's death, may mark her son's first step towards realizing the cash value of the house. At the time of his dismissal from the Comptrollership in the summer of 1713 he chose to live not there but less comfortably in the ruins of Woodstock Manor (p.75), and while late in 1714 he was still described as 'of Chargate', that October he sold the property to Lord Clare.[35] By February 1715 the latter had renamed it Claremont and was employing him on alterations which over several years would add up to a massive enlargement (p.101); our knowledge of the original house depends on drawings from Vanbrugh's office. This little house, with bedrooms no more than 10 feet 6 inches square, was an expanded version of the Goose Pie in Whitehall; again it was symmetrical with a central hall and a triple loggia behind on the garden side. Formally, however, it was considerably more complex. Whether or not it was built on the old foundations, its basic H-plan resembled that of many houses of late Tudor England, and the resemblance was increased by the projecting porch at the front and the square turrets and big chimney flues which broke up the end elevations. Translated into perspective, and with the varied

[30] J. Le Neve, *Monumenta Anglicana*, III, 1717, pp.233–4.

[31] Whistler, pp.145, 238–41; Webb, pp.22, 24; *Private Correspondence of the Duchess of Marlborough*, 1838, I, p.140. For the expense of funerals see p.166.

[32] The properties in Thames Ditton were 'troublesome' and it is unlikely that Mrs Vanbrugh occupied any of them; see p.153.

[33] Webb, p.50.

[34] Bodl. MS. Gough Maps 23, f.39.

[35] Deed between Sir John Vanbrugh of Chargate, Surrey and Thomas Pelham Holles, 1714, relating to land in Leatherhead, Surrey and St Martin-in-the-Fields Parish, London (James Coleman of Tottenham, cat.248, 1903, No.261; also cat.251, 1904, No.352). Sale to Lord Clare, 14 Oct. 1714, see p.100.

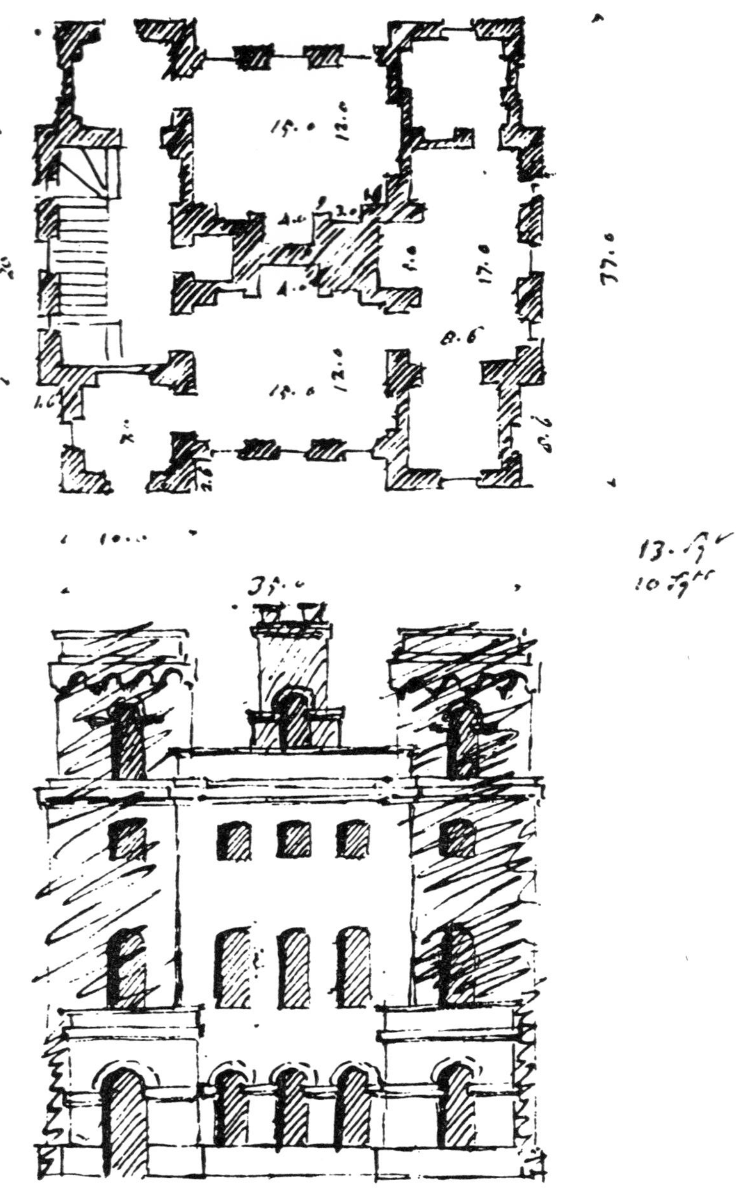

6 Design for a small house. *Elton Hall.*

heights and shapes he gave to its silhouette, Chargate was even more like the crenellated houses of Good Queen Bess's reign, and it is their romantic medievalism and that of Shakespeare's histories (in an age which yet claimed the Renaissance as its model) that informed Vanbrugh's, not only at Chargate but in Audley End, Blenheim, Seaton Delaval and a number of designs for smaller houses (Figs 6, 7). Revivalism of this kind may seem unexpected at the beginning of the Augustan age and after the classicism of seventeenth-century English architecture from Inigo Jones to Wren. The latter found Gothic structural methods useful on occasion, as in the flying buttresses of St Paul's, but its appearance was for him only to be tolerated where the context required it, such as the restoration or augmentation of a medieval building.

7 Design for a small house. *Elton Hall.*

What Horace Walpole called *King James's Gothic* and Vanbrugh's contemporaries *Ditterling* (after the engravings of Wendel Dietterlin) was another matter, although John Evelyn's private taste, rather than what he considered his public taste should be, tended towards the old-fashioned hospitality of mansions of a bygone age.[36] Vanbrugh was in an exceptional position to appreciate the domestic architecture of a century earlier, since he came to architecture not only apparently without conventional instruction, but also after a period of involvement with the stage. Fletcher and Shakespeare, even if considerably 'modernized', were frequently played in Vanbrugh's London, and Dryden's critical writings treat Shakespeare as one whose strength justifies his crudities. Critical opinion was in fact remarkably diverse, and in taking the extreme opposite view and seeing *Othello* as 'none other than a Bloody Farce without salt or savour' Thomas Rymer did more service to Shakespeare's cause than to that of Reason and Rule which he professed to support.[37] Spenser was also considerably appreciated, in particular by the critic John Hughes, who justified Milton's use of old-fashioned words on the grounds that he had taken them from Spenser. In an essay on the *Faerie Queene*, published in 1715, Hughes went further, showing that it was inappropriate to judge that poem by the 'Rules of Epick Poetry, as they have been drawn from the practice of Homer and Virgil' since 'it is plain the Author never design'd it by those Rules'; it was as inappropriate, Hughes significantly wrote, as to judge Gothic architecture by the standards of Roman.[38]

36 H. Walpole, *Anecdotes of Painting*, ed. Wornum, 1888, II, p.54; Aubrey and Evelyn: J. Summerson, ed., *Concerning Architecture*, 1968, pp.5, 34–6.

37 T. Rymer, *Short View of Tragedy*, 1693.

38 J. Hughes, *Of Style*, 1698; *Remarks on the Faerie Queen*, 1715.

The most notable architectural equivalents of Shakespeare and Spenser are the 'prodigy houses' of which the supreme surviving examples are Hardwick and Wollaton (Pl.60). They are still among the most dramatic creations of English art, with their ever-changing silhouettes and massing as we see them from different viewpoints, and with the martial associations potently evoked by their corner towers and turrets and as potently denied by their huge expanses of window glass. Vanbrugh would have passed Hardwick when visiting Chatsworth, and Wollaton is also near a convenient alternative to the Great North Road; Hawksmoor found the latter house in 1731 'an admirable piece of Masonry' with 'some true Stroakes of Architecture' although he regretted its 'Ditterling' strap-work relief decoration.[39]

In 1708 Vanbrugh had made a literal excursion into King James's Gothic; 'All the World,' he told Lord Manchester, 'are running Mad after Building, as far as they can reach' and among them he included Lord Bindon, afterwards 6th Earl of Suffolk, who was 'busy to the Utmost of his Force in New Moulding Audley end.'[40] That Vanbrugh was his architect is confirmed by a petition of John Anstis to the effect that the Earl, as Deputy Earl Marshal, had neglected his promise to nominate him for the office of Garter Herald, 'having about this time employed one Mr Vanbrugh . . . about altering the said Earls Mansion House at Audley End.'[41] The house, which has undergone many alterations, was originally built in 1603–16. It was bought by Charles II from the 3rd Earl and returned to his younger brother, the 5th Earl and father of Lord Bindon, in 1701. Up to that time it had never had a great staircase, although a room at the south end of the hall was intended for one. Vanbrugh replaced the end of the hall with a screen of superimposed arches and built behind it a staircase of two parallel flights (Pl.79). It is now generally accepted that the strapwork ceiling of the staircase, as well as the stone screen, is Vanbrugh's imitation of Jacobean motifs in sympathy – although remarkably restrained – with the ebullient wooden screen of 1605 at the other end of the hall. Architecturally, the combination of screen and staircase to give a variety of views between two spaces of different shapes and purposes, is common to a number of Vanbrugh's houses; in none is the handling more imaginative or more successful.[42]

Some years later, perhaps about 1721, the next Lord Suffolk pulled down a considerable part of Audley End; Horace Walpole was told in 1762 that this was on Vanbrugh's advice, but of this there does not appear to be any other evidence.

[39] *Walpole Society*, XIX, 1931, p.126. Alastair Ward has kindly allowed me to refer to his B.A. thesis (Cambridge 1972) on the occurrence of towers in Late Stuart and Early Georgian houses. Besides Vanbrugh's evident interest in the 'prodigy houses' and the walls of Chester (p.101), he must have known in particular the keep tower of Tamworth Castle, which belonged to his aunt Ferrers (p.152) and, from the start of his architectural career, old Henderskelfe Castle (p.20). A re-reading of Leland's description of Henderskelfe as 'a fair quadrant of stone having 4 toures builded castelle like' (Whistler, p.26) suggests that it was the inspiration for the turreted service wing of Castle Howard (Pls 22,23).

[40] Webb, pp.24–5.

[41] Petition of about 1715 referring to events of 1707–8; Bodl. MS. Rawl. C.335.

[42] N. Pevsner, 'Good King James's Gothic', *Architectural Review*, CVII, 1950, pp.117–22 (esp. p.118); Whistler, p.20, suggests that old material was used for the screen. H. Walpole, *Walpole Society*, XVI, 1928, p.33.

Chapter 4

Blenheim

About Xmas 1704 he meeting casually with the Duke at the Playhouse in Drury Lane the Duke told him he designed to build a house in Woodstock Park and expressed his intention of not exceeding a certain sum, which to the best of Deponents remembrance was 40,000£ and further said he must consult Deponent about the design . . . Viewing a modell which Deponent then had in wood of the Earl of Carlisle's house the Duke said that was the sort of house he liked, only with some alterations and additions as a Gallery &c.

Vanbrugh's account of his preliminary meetings with the Duke of Marlborough, from which these statements are taken, is recorded in a brief of 1720 during the legal action taken against them both by the Strongs, the principal masons of Blenheim, for arrears of payment for work done there.[1] The following year the Strongs won their case to the tune of over £12,000, not from Vanbrugh but from the Marlboroughs; the latter appealed to the House of Lords, who confirmed the judgment but reduced the sum by a quarter. Yet this was not the most acrimonious chapter in the long and stormy history of the building of Blenheim, the most voluminously documented and discussed of Vanbrugh's works. Later in 1721 the Duchess embarked on a counter-suit for conspiracy 'to load the Duke of Marlborough with the payment of the debts due' and to charge 'excessive and unreasonable rates and prices for the same'. The defendants in this vindictive fiasco – for her case was an impossible one and she was widowed the following year worth two millions – must have included every name in the Blenheim accounts from Vanbrugh downwards, 401 altogether.

Marlborough's victory of 3/13 August 1704 at Blindheim on the Danube marked the turning point, although far from the end, of the War of the Spanish Succession; the mood of Queen, Parliament, and (for what they were worth) people was that too great a reward for the victor would be difficult to imagine. After the discussion of various alternatives Queen Anne decided on 18 January 1705 to grant the estate of the Royal Manor of Woodstock to the Duke and his heirs in perpetuity for a peppercorn rent; within two months the grant was enacted by Parliament. If Vanbrugh's later account is to be believed, the Duke anticipated the official decisions in approaching the architect about a house, to be built at his own expense. There was general agreement that the nation's thank-offering extended to an appropriation from the Civil List to pay for Marlborough's house,

[1] Three versions are given in Appendix D (1–3). Most of the surviving drawings are in Bodl.MS.Top.Oxon. a.37*. The building accounts (BM MS.Add.19592–601) were used by Green, 1951 and Whistler, 1954. S. Rogal, 'John Vanbrugh and the Blenheim Palace Controversy', *Jnl Soc. of Archit. Historians*, XXXIII, 1974, pp.293–303, examines the 'terrible waste' of the building of Blenheim from the English Literature scholar's point of view, relying mainly on Webb's publication of the Letters.

although no document could afterwards be found to say so or, more important, to name a maximum cost.[2] In the euphorious year following the great victory it must have seemed inappropriate to question the limits of the royal bounty. Marlborough was fifty-four and looking forward to retirement as soon as he had finished the job in hand. At a time when a bricklayer's labourer earned about £25 a year, Lord Carlisle's house (as distinct from the gardens and the other buildings) cost about £35,000, so it was not unreasonable for a man with Marlborough's self-esteem to contemplate an outlay of £40,000 on his own house. However, by the summer of 1705 when a model had been made and Sir Christopher Wren had been to look at the site, the latter's estimate was between ninety and a hundred thousand pounds, and that was for a house and wings without the side courts later added behind the wings; by 1710 the money paid or owing for the building thus enlarged was twice that sum, and the final cost was nearer £300,000, mostly paid, at length, by the Treasury.[3]

Money was one of the major strands in the tangled knot that became Blenheim; there were others. One was the uncertainty about who was responsible for the whole project. Another was the nature and purpose of the building, which changed during the twenty years of building operations. Then there were the character of Sarah Duchess of Marlborough and the long train of circumstances which led both her and the Duke from absolute favour in 1704 to dismissal and disgrace by 1712. All these difficulties must be considered in turn, although they cannot be entirely separated.

Shortage of money was a chronic condition of government operations in the late seventeenth and early eighteenth centuries, and of government building operations in particular. A vote in Parliament did not automatically ensure a flow of money but only the expectation of it from taxes and other revenues; these were often anticipated, so that either ready money had to be raised by loans or juggling with funds or else credit had to be given by the contractors. The building trade, which was very much a seasonal activity anyway, suffered continually from the fact that the Crown was a slow payer, if eventually a good one. Moreover, since payment was not in figures in a computer but in cash, a shortage of actual money often added to the delay. Money was frequently reported to the Blenheim officials as on its way or about to be sent. The most critical period followed the dismissal of Godolphin from the Treasury in August 1710; with the Tory Harley in his place the future of Blenheim seemed to those on the spot to be in jeopardy, and the workmen were reluctant to extend any further credit. The following month a General Election brought a Tory majority in Parliament. On 10 September it was reported that Strong had laid off most of his men.[4] At the end of the month the Duchess of Marlborough, fearing that the Tories would unload the Blenheim debt on the Duke, brought the season to a premature end by ordering all work to be stopped immediately until money came from the Treasury.[5] There were fears of sabotage: some capitals awaiting setting were broken. Blenheim was caught up in politics, and £7,000 was ordered by Harley less to make the

[2] Webb, p.179; Green, pp.42–4. The allegation in A. Boyer, *History of the Life and Reign of Queen Anne*, 1722, p.169, that the queen ordered Vanbrugh to build Blenheim, is subsequent to the claims and counter-claims of the Marlborough lawsuits.

[3] Webb, pp.199, 31, 50.

[4] Joynes to Hawksmoor, BM MS.Add.19607, f.70.

[5] The Duchess's letter, 28 Sept. 1710; Bodl.MS.Top.Oxon. c.218, f.48.

work safe for the winter – which Vanbrugh judged to be a more cogent argument than hardship among the workmen – than to calm public opinion and to keep a war-weary and disgusted Marlborough in combat.[6]

Responsibility for Blenheim was not solely a financial matter. Vanbrugh had the foresight to obtain a warrant from Godolphin authorizing him as Surveyor (that is architect) of the building on the Duke's behalf, and similar warrants were issued to Henry Joynes as Clerk of Works and later as Comptroller jointly with William Boulter, whom Vanbrugh described as 'a Creature of her Graces.'[7] Blenheim was not in the province of the Office of Works, but its administration, like that of St Paul's, Greenwich Hospital and other major public undertakings, was modelled on the Works and in effect made use of some of the same officers. There was no necessity for such an arrangement, although one might have expected to find Wren, Her Majesty's Surveyor, appointed architect to the project, as he had been to St Paul's and Greenwich. He was capable, as his unrealized projects for a new Whitehall in 1698 show, of designing a palace of true grandeur, his professional status and reputation would have impressed Marlborough, and at seventy-two he was not too old to be asked; he may have been asked, but we have already seen that Marlborough approached Vanbrugh at a very early stage. It was thus as an outsider that Wren gave his estimate and a suggestion for the approach to the house. Vanbrugh and Marlborough moved in the same circles, and Vanbrugh's architecture was as much to the Duke's taste as it was obnoxious to the Duchess. Vanbrugh's warrant specifies that he was the Duke's agent;[8] his official title was Surveyor, and Hawksmoor's, with duties similar to those in respect of Castle Howard, was Assistant Surveyor. In 1716 Vanbrugh resigned for ever, Hawksmoor went with him, and the Duchess, like many a country gentleman but few ladies, became her own architect with the assistance of what she called her 'oracle', a cabinet-maker named James Moore. Three years later she could move the ailing Duke into the east side of the house. But in 1722 she found the completion of the place beyond her capacity, and, lawsuit or no, re-engaged Hawksmoor who, loving nurse that he was to the project, was eager to help in a private capacity. After a further three years he disappeared quietly from the records. In 1731 he visited Blenheim and asked without success to see the Duchess 'only to trye what she wou'd doe.'[9] Vanbrugh 'took Blenheim' in about June 1719, 'not with any affection (for I am thoroughly wean'd) but some curiosity' at the Duchess's plans,[10] but in 1725 neither he nor his lady was allowed, even under the aegis of Lord Carlisle, to set foot there, and the ex-architect was reduced to peering over the wall of the rectory garden.[11]

The purpose of Blenheim was more than domestic. 'Tho' ordered to be a Dwelling house

[6] Whistler, p.239. Vanbrugh told Marlborough that £1000 would have sufficed. Swift, *Journal to Stella*, 19 Aug. 1711.

[7] Text of warrants, Webb, pp.177–8, 182–3. Sarah Marlborough derogatorily called Joynes 'a sort of a Footman' to Henry Wise the gardener but he was already known to the Office of Works in 1700 when, aged seventeen, he was engaged to keep stores at Kensington (PRO Works 5/51, July).

[8] In May 1709 John Smallwell Senior and Junior fitted up presses, a drawing board and writing table in the front upstairs room of Vanbrugh's Whitehall house to make an office for him 'for the Service of Blenheim Castle' at a cost of £12 9s 4d (BM MS.Add.19596, f.44).

[9] Walpole Society, XIX, 1931, p.127.

[10] Webb, p.112. This journey is not recorded in the Account Book.

[11] Green, p.316; Webb, pp.166–7.

for the Duke of Marlborough and his posterity' as Vanbrugh wrote to the Duchess in 1710, it was 'at the Same time by all the World esteemed and looked on as a Publick Edifice, raised for a Monument of the Queen's Glory through his great Genius'[12] and in the same year he told Harley that he looked 'upon it much more as an intended Monument of the Queens Glory than a private Habitation for the Duke.'[13] Marlborough accepted the glory as his due, though in a curiously impersonal way, for the deed not the doer. In Kneller's sketch for a commemorative painting of the reward (Pl.50) and in his written explanation of it, the figures are, at the Duke's wish, allegorical, except that of the Queen, who presents a drawing of Blenheim to a figure of 'Military Merit.'[14] For Vanbrugh, Marlborough was a hero as well as a friend, and the agreement of the two men on the impersonal meaning of Blenheim is significant both for their martial sentiments and for the concept of architecture which was developing in Vanbrugh's mind over the first decade of the eighteenth century. But for Duchess Sarah, Blenheim, progressing from an intractable extravaganza to a 'Monument of Ingratitude' (taking over a phrase Vanbrugh had used to her husband), became finally a personal memorial to the Victorious Duke.[15] To this end were designed and loaded with inscriptions Hawksmoor's triumphal arch at the Woodstock entrance, the 'historical pillar' in the park ultimately designed by the amateur Lord Herbert, and the enormous tomb designed by William Kent and executed by Rysbrack, which fills the house chapel. These were the conventional symbols of prowess which she understood, whereas every stone of the great Bridge and most of the skyline of Blenheim was placed against her judgment. But although she might attempt to overlay in her own way the architectural meaning of the palace, in which she had little interest or understanding, she could not erase it and it is still there to be found.

The Duchess of Marlborough loved above all else in the world the Duke whom, ten years her senior, she had married at the age of eighteen. Her next greatest passion was her own rightness, in judgment (almost devoid of half-tones) and in conduct.[16] She was thrifty, practical, and managing. She told a grand-daughter that 'painters, poets and builders have very high flights, but they must be kept down.'[17] Her rooms were comfortable because she made them so. Marlborough House, which she built at the back of St James's Palace in 1709–11, was deliberately as plain and as unlike Blenheim as possible; her wish was for Sir Christopher Wren (who built few private houses, but plain ones) as architect, but there is good evidence that most of the work was delegated by the Surveyor to Mr Christopher Wren, his son.[18] She was capable of civility to Vanbrugh, and even of sincere compliments, and she was conscious enough of his personality and talents to accept his offices as matchmaker between her grand-daughter and the younger Duke of Newcastle. But the grounds for exasperation existed on both sides. She disliked the vastness, the

[12] Whistler, p.237.

[13] Webb, pp.45–6.

[14] Green, p.298.

[15] W. C. Coxe, *Memoirs of John Duke of Marlborough*, 1848 ed., III, p.143. *Letters of Sarah Duchess of Marlborough at Madresfield Court*, 1875, p.21.

[16] D. Green, *Sarah Duchess of Marlborough*, 1967.

[17] G. Scott Thomson, *Letters of a Grandmother*, 1943, p.134.

[18] *King's Works*, v, 1975, p.37; Downes (1971), pp.123–4.

ornateness, the extravagance of Blenheim. In particular she disliked the Grand Bridge which stood, high and dry over a small stream between two unfinished approach roads; she could foresee no purpose for the 'Bridge in the air' and even hoped that it would crumble away. She was a natural scribbler and communicated her opinions and her wishes freely. During the period of the the building of Marlborough House and her quarrel with the Queen, she wrote constant directions to Joynes and to Tilleman Bobart who had been appointed on the death of Boulter, about the burning of lime in the park, about the order in which work was to be done, about patterns for ironwork, about who was to build the garden wall, about stone, and statues, and extravagance, and Vanbrugh, and the bridge, and 'that ridiculous Court' (the kitchen court), and stopping the work.[19] It was, after all, her house as much as anyone's and she wanted it habitable and comfortable. In her early fifties her energy was boundless. Finally both sides went too far. Vanbrugh had fitted up a *pied-à-terre* in old Woodstock Manor; while assuring her to the contrary he continued to use it. On her side, although the negotiations for the Newcastle marriage were going well, she became impatient, and on impulse engaged a professional broker; at about the same time she sent a long catalogue of Vanbrugh's failings to one of his friends to show to him. Afterwards she claimed that her intention was to 'make them Laugh over a botle of Wine', but to Vanbrugh the combination of events was 'a double Cruelty.' Since Marlborough's stroke she was mistress of Blenheim, and Vanbrugh could serve her no longer.[20]

The Marlboroughs' political and personal circumstances formed the ground bass to all these themes. Marlborough had been a Tory and had joined the Whigs early in the new century on the common ground of complete commitment to the war in Europe. At the end of 1706 the Tory Queen's ministry was predominantly Whig, and early in 1708 the Council and Commons together forced the resignation of Robert Harley, to the Queen's displeasure. But during 1710 the Tories gained ground rapidly; the dismissals of Sunderland in June and of Godolphin soon after, both kinsmen and associates of the Marlboroughs, were followed by the Tory victory in the autumn election and a vicious personal attack on the Marlboroughs by Swift in the *Examiner*.[21] During 1711 Harley, now Earl of Oxford, began secret peace negotiations with France; on the last day of that year Parliament was packed by the creation of twelve new Tory peers, and Marlborough was dismissed on allegations of peculation. The war was costly and it was foreign, and evidence was sought to make him the scapegoat; at the end of 1712 he went abroad into voluntary exile or 'pilgrimage' and the Duchess followed him a few weeks later.

Politics and the press alone might have brought Marlborough down; in the event the fall was the more bitter because personal issues, and the Duchess, were largely involved. They had been on nickname terms with Anne. Sarah and Anne had been friends from childhood; as Queen, Anne appointed Sarah Mistress of the Robes together with other positions of attentiveness and trust. Although Sarah did not know of it for two years, the very foundation year of Blenheim, 1705, saw the beginning of Abigail Hill's influence with the Queen. Abigail had been Sarah's *protégée* and was her cousin as well as Harley's, and it

[19] Bodl.MS.Top.Oxon. c.218 (1708–11).

[20] Green, pp.137–43.

[21] *The Examiner*, No.17, 23 Nov. 1710.

was the latter who converted a petty feminine squabble into political drama. Sarah was partly to blame; she could not allow her sovereign more than one confidante – herself – and her suspicions of the ends to which the rivalry was being directed made her desperate. The rages, reproaches and insults to which she subjected her long-suffering mistress played into the enemy's hands. Her dismissal preceded her husband's by nearly a year and, deprived of her lodgings at St James's, she moved into the barely finished Marlborough House, taking with her even the door fittings. In the new house she dismissed Wren in the belief that she could finish it more cheaply on her own.

The foundation stone of Blenheim was laid on 18 June 1705 by seven gentlemen, one of whom was the architect. Four days later Vanbrugh reported to the Duke that the stone in the park was poor and quarries were being sought further afield.[22] Nineteen quarries altogether were used, from an area of about five hundred square miles, and special stone was also ordered from Portland, Plymouth and Ross-on-Wye.[23] Armies of carters were needed, and in the peak period of building the number of workmen was well over a thousand. The size of the work in itself warranted the employment of officers of the Works, and, as principal masons, of the Edward Strongs, father and son, who had experience of public building on such a scale. The large number of workmen was also a symptom rather than a cause of speed, and they could only be deployed because those in charge knew how to use them. Indeed Marlborough, whose own genius was for the organization between and behind the battles, was the best person to appreciate smooth running in the building of his house.

The Queen's decision was made in mid-January, and by April a wooden model, which like that for Castle Howard has long since disappeared, was ready to go to Kensington for her approval.[24] From mid-April also, workmen were trenching for the foundations of the main house. Thus, even if they were begun about Christmas-time, as Vanbrugh implied, the drawings must have been made in the course of a few weeks. On the other hand, they left a great deal undecided. On 23 June, Hawksmoor wrote instructing Joynes to 'hasten the forming your accounts into the formes I left you to observe'; a month later he was asking for multiple copies of the plan; in one of them 'My Laydy Duchess's appartemt lying next the East you may only put in black lead till I come downe' and two more were to be only pencilled, so 'that when I come downe I may settle the plann of the cellar and Attick Storys.'[25] In mid-August Joynes reported the foundations of the house complete; on 7 September Hawksmoor enquired about those of the linking colonnades and the chapel block, and incidentally wanted to know 'who was with my Lord Carlisle, and how they liked things.' Joynes noted on the back of the letter, 'Duke of Grafton, Lord Carlisle, Lord Kin[g]ston, Ld Martinson, Ld Granvill, Mr Godolphin, Ld Wharton & 2 other gentlemen' – a fairly Kit-Cat party.

The early drawings and the model made from them not only left out many details

[22] Whistler, p.229.

[23] Green, pp.56–9, 127–8.

[24] The model was kept at Kensington: see Appendix D (4).

[25] BM MS.Add.19607 contains letters from Hawksmoor to Joynes and drafts of the latter's replies. MS.Add.19605 contains a similar correspondence mainly between Vanbrugh and Joynes; Vanbrugh's letters are printed in Webb, pp.140, 152, 207–45.

8 Blenheim. Early south elevations. After drawings in the Bodleian Library.

altogether; they represented a building very different in appearance from the final one (Fig.8). According to Vanbrugh's deposition of 1720, he made a design of which Marlborough approved before February 1704/5 when they both went for the first time to see the park and to choose the site.[26] Another account by Vanbrugh implies that the site was chosen before any design was made.[27] However, it was not uncommon for seventeenth-century architects to start with an ideal design and then accommodate it to the realities of the commission, and Vanbrugh's preliminary design for Castle Howard (p.29) was also very probably made before visiting the site. At Blenheim the process of accommodation was complex and took nearly half the five years of the main building campaign. According to the Duke it was Wren's idea to have a model made so as to prevent alterations, and Vanbrugh wrote several times in 1710 that it had been exactly followed.[28] To us that is patently not so, but the Marlboroughs' criticisms of the architect do not include his departures from the model, for two reasons. Firstly, he was careful that one or both approved the changes he made. Secondly, in addition to Vanbrugh's known latitude in respect of 'perticulars', the standards of exactness in these matters were not the same as ours; this can be demonstrated from the colossal liberties which Wren took with the approved design for St Paul's, and, nearer to Blenheim although less spectacular, from the many obvious discrepancies between the drawings of Castle Howard which Vanbrugh himself supplied for Campbell's *Vitruvius Britannicus* of 1715 and the building as it already stood. Very little of Blenheim was *not* changed, but before describing the alterations the architect made it is worth examining the concept with which he started. For that was itself novel enough and in its essentials survives in the plan of the completed house: a house like Lord Carlisle's with such additions as a gallery. Castle Howard, perfectly adapted to its site,

[26] Appendix D (3).

[27] Webb, p.190.

[28] Whistler, p.99; Webb, p.193.

is a long house even without the base courts. Its essentials, in plan, are the hall flanked by staircases, the saloon behind it, the long garden front facing south and the north and south corridors (Fig.2E). All these elements are found in the plan of Blenheim, where the south range, made up of fewer somewhat larger rooms, is slightly longer than at Castle Howard (Fig.9). But Castle Howard has no side elevations. By adding a long gallery at right-angles to the garden range and to the corridors, forming the whole west side of the house, Vanbrugh gave Blenheim a palatial depth as well as breadth, forming a block roughly 190 by 300 feet. The corresponding range on the east was designed for the private apartments. Between these east and west ranges and the corridors are small enclosed courts whose function is to light the inner rooms. Thus in effect the body and wings of Castle Howard are incorporated into a single great block, and the quadrants whose function in the earlier house is one of connection are used in the later one to carve a forecourt out of the north side and to frame the grand entrance. In this way everything was contained within one mass except the chapel and the kitchen. At Castle Howard these had been intended to balance each other at the house end of the north-west and north-east wings; at Blenheim they were first designed in a similar relationship to the main block, lying behind the colonnades which carry on the rhythm – and the small Doric order – of the quadrants and form links to the stable and service blocks to the north (Pl.52).

Neither plan nor north elevation survives from this early period, and our knowledge of the first design depends on south and east elevations and on inference from the subsequent alterations. The house was originally conceived not only much plainer in silhouette, without the roof-top town that grew upon it, but also considerably squatter in elevation, with a Doric instead of a Corinthian order (Fig.8). There was no portico in the centre. Moreover, the hall neither projected forward from the rest nor rose above it into the great clerestory which now provides most of the light and which in 1713 appeared to Lord Berkeley of Stratton like 'a great college with a church in the middle, for the hall looks like one.'[29]

While the elevations of Blenheim were transformed over the period 1705–8 only two significant changes seem to have been made in the plan. The first, which also involved the north elevation, was the most important: four days after the foundation stone was laid Vanbrugh wrote to the Duke that while 'The drawings I sent yr Grace were not (nor cou'd not be) perfect in little perticulars' he had made an alteration 'worth mentioning to your Grace.'[30] This was 'in the first entrance of the House, where by bringing the break forwarder, the Hall is enlarg'd, and from a round, is brought to an Ovall, figure, a Portico added and yet the Room much better lighted than before. And the top of it rises above the rest of the building regularly in the Middle of the four great Pavillions' (Pl.56). The architect went on to express the hope that Marlborough would like this enhancement of the 'Beauty, Regularity and Magnificence of the Building.' The terms 'round' and 'oval' are not to be taken literally – such room shapes would be not only unprecedented but also unique in Vanbrugh's work – but as colloquial approximations to 'square' and 'oblong.' But apart from careless terminology his meaning is clear enough, as he almost casually

[29] J. J. Cartwright, *The Wentworth Papers*, 1883, p.344. Could Lord Berkeley have found a resemblance to Le Vau's Collège des Quatre Nations in Paris, which has a central domed chapel and giant portico, quadrants, and an interwoven small order?

[30] 22 June 1705 (Whistler, p.230).

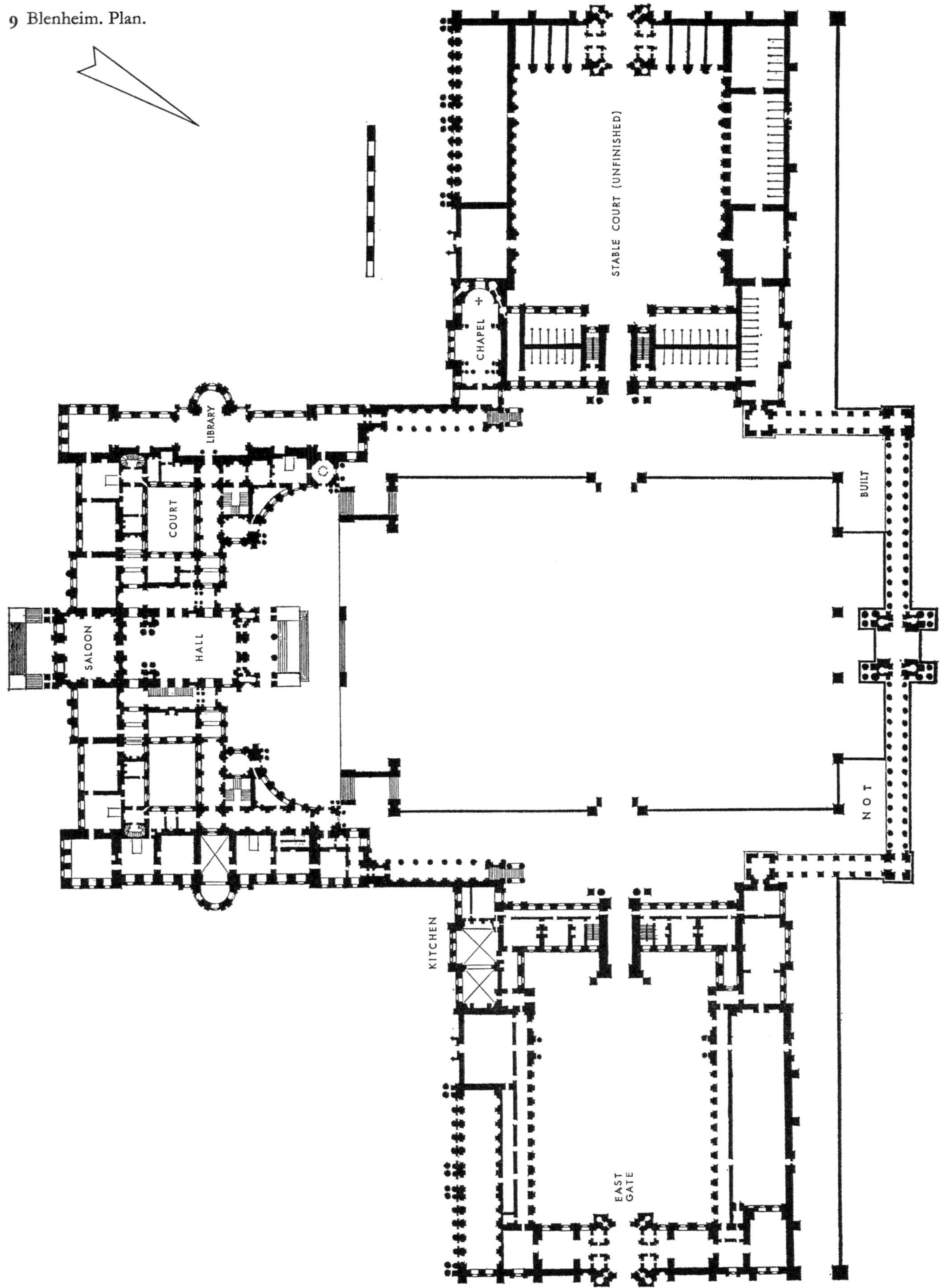

9 Blenheim. Plan.

introduced a change whose effect on the design was hardly less than the introduction of the dome at Castle Howard.

After a month Vanbrugh took the Duchess and Lord Treasurer Godolphin on a tour of inspection and gained their agreement to a second change, which he did not communicate to the Duke until four weeks later. This was 'a Considerable alteration' to the placing of the chapel and kitchen; instead of lying behind the colonnades they were to be included in the stable and service blocks, which Vanbrugh thought would improve 'the Figure both of the Building and Court' and would actually save several thousand pounds.'[31] The further considerable alteration made early in 1708 was not to the house proper but to the offices. Large rectangular courts were now to be built behind the blocks originally designed and partly built.[32] The east or kitchen court was built and completed; Blenheim, like Castle Howard, progressed from east to west and the stable court remained unfinished.

One feature of the western court was to be an orangery facing west with a splendid view over the valley, with 'some of the best Greens, mixed with pictures, Busts, Statues, Books and other things of ornament and entertainment.'[33] In a further letter Vanbrugh calls this room a 'Greenhouse or Detach'd Gallery, for that indeed is what I take it to be, And not a Magazine for a parcell of foolish plants.' The Duchess endorsed this letter, 'The second greenhouse, or a detached gallery I thank God I prevented being built; nothing, I think can be more mad than the proposal, nor a falser description of the prospect.'[34]

If the initial plan provided a sound basis for the development of Blenheim, the early elevations were to be hardly more than sketches. They do show the giant pilasters and columns, the raised central nine-bay torso of the house, the corner towers and varied suggestions for surface treatment and for heroic imagery on the skyline. Allowing for the fact that designs actually followed were usually worn out on the job while superseded ones might be put away and eventually transferred to archives, building began to a design fairly close to the surviving variant drawing (Fig.8B). The porthole basement windows still exist in the towers and in four of the centre bays, as do those along the basement on the court side (Pl.54); in the rest of the garden front, however, the portholes were cut out early in 1707 and replaced by windows with rusticated surrounds to light the basement better (Pl.63). This alteration, which may have been the result of the Duchess's life-long passion for light rooms, was small beside those which accompanied it and were planned in the winter of 1706–7, and which involved the demolition of considerable amounts of finished masonry on the garden front.[35] It now appeared to the architects (and Hawksmoor was as capable as Vanbrugh of such radical afterthoughts) that Blenheim was going to be excessively low, and they decided to raise the order by 6 feet. Since the diameters could

[31] Vanbrugh to Marlborough, 24 Aug. 1705 (Whistler, pp.230–1). Hawksmoor had told Joynes on 28 July that 'the disposition of ye chapell kitchin and colonade is by my Ld Treasurers appoint[men]t quite altered' from that in the mason's hands (BM MS.19607, f.4). On 26 Aug. John Bridges wrote to Sir William Trumbull: 'I hear Captain Van found means to keep fair with the Duchess notwithstanding Sir Christopher Wren's request' (HMC Downshire, I, 2, p.842).

[32] Vanbrugh's long explanation of the courts as convenient (1709), Webb, pp.32–3.

[33] Webb, pp.33, 35, 36.

[34] Webb, p.36.

[35] BM MS.Add.19594, ff.6v, 9v, 29–30: account for demolitions and alterations to south front, February–April 1707. The changes are discussed by Whistler, pp.93–4.

not be changed without complete rebuilding and complete disruption of the bay-system, the extension would have made the Doric pillars disproportionately slender; the only practical solution was to forego the Doric's associations of martial and masculine strength, in favour of the more splendid, and thus not totally inappropriate, leafiness of the slimmer Corinthian order. In fact by fluting the pillars on the garden front and making those towards the court plain the architects achieved, with a single order, something of the contrast of severity and richness that at Castle Howard (p.37) depends on two different orders.

Although work was proceeding in several parts of the palace the hall and its approach on the north lagged noticeably until 1708. Vanbrugh had added a portico in his first major alteration (p.62), but in the absence of sufficiently early plans or elevations it is impossible to say how far it was to project and whether it was to have a pediment. The earliest surviving plan shows a portico of the depth finally built but with all columns instead of the final mixture of columns and square piers.[36] An early section through the saloon and hall, made at about the time the exterior elevation was raised, shows a much shallower portico without pediment, and with the full columns immediately adjacent to the half-columns behind them.[37] The precise form of the portico rather than its provision in principle was settled in 1708, when on 27 April Marlborough wrote to the Duchess, 'I am advised by every body to have the Portico, so that I have writt to Vanbrook to have itt';[38] in July Edward Strong charged for 'making additions &c to Several parts of the foundations on account of the last Designe for the great Hall.'[39]

During 1707 the lanterns of the corner towers were evolved, partly on the drawing-board and partly by trial and error on the site with full-size models which were hoisted up to judge the effect. In 1708 the first lantern, the north-east, was finished; the south-east followed in 1709. In the end Blenheim came to have not four lanterns (or Eminencys as Hawksmoor called them) but eight (Pl.64). Besides the four corners, there are two open cylinders in the middle of the main house which even on the spot are difficult to place; they stand above the ends of the north corridor leading into the bow-window room on the east and the centre of the gallery (Long Library) on the west. Two more lanterns grew out of the modest bell turrets over the office ranges; that on the kitchen side (Pl.73) was completed in 1709 and accompanied by decorative changes in the gateway below it. On the side towards the base court banded piers were added and towards the great court square piers and columns; on both sides windows already existing were obscured by the additions.[40] The support they gave was not structural but visual, for the steady growth

[36] Soane Museum, Wren Drawings Vol. I, 59 (Green, Pl.20, *Wren Soc.*, XII Pl. LIII). This plan was annotated, though not necessarily made, to indicate the disposition of chimneys in the eastern half of the house, and shows an arrangement of columns in the hall different from, and perhaps earlier than, in the section drawings for the hall made in the winter of 1706–7 (p.71). Besides a portico of columns, the plan shows half- and three-quarter-columns at the back of the portico where pilasters were finally chosen. In one plan (Bodl.MS.Top.Oxon. a.37*, f.5) extra coupled columns were added in front of the corners.

[37] Bodl.MS.Top.Oxon. a.37*, f.16 (Whistler, Pl.38). This shows the raised order as Ionic, but with a Corinthian astragal drawn in on one column, and the treatment of the saloon is more tentative than in the design (Pl.82) which is datable before Sep.1707 when it was criticized by Louis Silvestre (Whistler, p.102). The raising of the order was, if not necessarily the cause of the demolitions on the south front, certainly contemporary with the decision to make them. In Sep. 1707 John Smallwell supplied a large wooden model of the saloon, hall and staircase (BM MS.Add.19594, f.77).

[38] Blenheim MSS, E.4.

[39] BM MS.Add.19595, f.61. The springing of the pediment was set by Oct. 1709 (BM MS.Add.19605, f.80).

[40] Mason's account, March 1709 (BM MS.Add.19596, f.22).

of formal complexity and visual metaphor in the detail of Blenheim was both vertical and horizontal, and what had started as base blocks, of a lesser status than the rest, were swept up into the single enormous message of the whole building. These gate towers are sculptural objects, of the same rank as those on the main house, and they were chosen as the site of one of the most explicit allusions to Britannia's might: the British lion mauling the French cockerel on top of the pillars. This is a more graphic image than the finials of the corner lanterns, whose ducal coronets resting on inverted fleurs-de-lis and cannon balls tell the same story (Pl.65). But the biggest of the many carved trophies on the Blenheim parapets is on the middle of the garden front (Pl.61). Vanbrugh had intended to place there a colossal equestrian figure subduing personages emblematic of evil, flanked by an equally colossal British lion and Imperial eagle;[41] these figures appear in the elevation in *Vitruvius Britannicus* 1715 (Pl.59), although they had been superseded. For after capturing Tournai in 1709 Marlborough appropriated from the Porte Royale of the Citadel a colossal bust of Louis XIV flanked by conventional trophies; it was subsequently set up at Blenheim, a perpetual version of the traditional head upon a stake.[42]

Blenheim indisputably succeeds as an emblem of might, whether that of a nation as was intended or that of an individual as it was to be made by Marlborough's widow. Its trophies, cannon-balls, statues, flaming urns and not least its enormous scale show that Vanbrugh and Hawksmoor were fully conversant with the overbearing allegorical language of Wren's Hampton Court and of its model, Versailles. Moreover, in Vanbrugh's mind Castle Howard, which as the personal symbol of one man outshone Chatsworth, was thus to be eclipsed by the impersonal symbol of a nation's achievement. This concept probably had not occurred to him in 1700, and it may only have matured in his mind in parallel with the building of Blenheim; if that is so, then there is, in his repeated remarks in 1710 about the dual purpose of Marlborough's palace, an element of recognition of the way in which his design had grown in stature and in depth of meaning as it rose, through additions and experiments with models and alterations, to monumental reality.

But Blenheim is also architecture, and if it is to be made the centrepiece of a study of Vanbrugh, then the writer should at least argue that it is great architecture. There have always been and will always be those for whom it fails the criterion of artistic value or merit or integrity, either with or without the disclaimer recorded by the Earl of Ailesbury to whom Marlborough showed drawings in September 1705: 'I understand but little or nothing of this matter but enough to affirm (by the plan I saw) that the house is like one

[41] Marlborough was made Prince of Mindelheim on 14 Nov. 1705 and entitled to use the Imperial eagle with his arms; it appears thus in the saloon doorcases. The attic of the south portico was up to the underside of the coping in Oct. 1709 (BM MS.Add. 19605, f.80).

[42] Thornhill's drawing in his 1711 travel diary (V & A, published by K. Fremantle, Utrecht 1975) shows the trophy still *in situ* and confirms that the whole group was taken and re-arranged. Presumably it had to wait after capture for men and tackle to dismantle it, although already on 1 Aug. 1710 Vanbrugh had been 'in hopes Capt: Saunderson wou'd have brought the Busto over with him last time he made' (postscript to letter, Blenheim MSS, B.2.5, not transcribed in Webb, p.42). For Saunderson see p.93. The bust, pedestal and six cases of trophies reached the Office of Works at Scotland Yard in April 1712 (BM MS.Add.19598, f.69). The eleven blocks of marble weighing 30 tons which 'quite ruin'd' Joseph Lamb's boat (BM MS.Add. 19605, f.165) were quite separate, and part of a process of stocking marble which had been of concern to both Vanbrugh and Joynes at least since April 1709 when the Treasury authorized the transfer of eight blocks from Scotland Yard to Blenheim (PRO Works 6/5, pp.6, 108; HMC Portland x, p.98). In March 1710 Vanbrugh wrote, 'there will come a great deal more of that kind very soon, which will quite fill up the Wharf' (Webb, p.236, 14 March 1710, wrongly suggested as 1711). See also BM MS.19605, ff.138, 145; MS.Add.19598, f.68v. It is difficult to see how an estimate of Nov. 1714 should have come to include £1000 for 'The Trophys on the South Front' (MS.Add.19603, f.47) even as a purchase price. The bust weighs 4 or 5 tons.

mass of Stone, without taste or relish.'[43] No such disclaimer came from the Duchess of Marlborough, whose dislike of the building was matched only by her instinct for making homes and her desire to tell the truth to the world. To give Blenheim and Vanbrugh their due is to look at the building and try to understand it, whether by analysis or by intuition. While the north front (Pl.52) is as flamboyant – and can be as unnerving – as a firework display, it has the advantage of permanence, so that what at first may appear disordered can be seen to be coherent and ordered as well as unexpected. Further inspection will show that the building as a whole, taking all the fronts, has greater unity and coherence than Castle Howard, since the same large themes and rhythms run all round it. The big accents are the central torso or core of nine bays and the four corner towers; these are scaled by the giant order in the torso and the block cornice (which implies a similar order) in the towers (Pl.66). They are drawn together by their greater height than the rest, which is further emphasized by the lanterns on the towers and the clerestory in the middle of the torso, and they also share, on both main fronts, a full upper storey of round-headed windows. The rest of the house proper has a lower attic storey with square windows, and these lower parts are tied to the towers and the centre by a small one-storey Doric order which appears fully in the quadrants and linking colonnades (Pl.58) on the north side and by implication in the continuation of its entablature through the middle of the north front and all along the south front (Pl.63) and the two sides (Pl.68). In the corner towers, whose surface is banded, the entablature disappears, but continuity is preserved at the same height by the big labels under the upper windows. There is a further division of level in the quadrants, where the single storey contains a mezzanine with large porthole windows; this division in turn continues in the fronts of the office ranges.

The ensemble is thus made up of simple but differentiated parts linked by common properties; seen as a single huge sculpture it is of the simplest, with a pattern of advance and recession not unlike that in one of the lanterns. The torso of the house, however, is more complex. As at Castle Howard the nine-bay fronts are treated disparately. On the garden side the centre develops logically from the flanking sections, breaking forward from them with a three-bay applied portico forming a second break and with smaller projections in the penultimate bays. The court front on the other hand is marked by interruptions (Pl.52). The flanking sections are actually recessed at the inner ends of the quadrants, so as to leave thin vertical strips of blank wall as punctuation marks either side of the torso. There is a fully three-dimensional portico with the same mixture of square piers and columns as on the garden front and with the middle bay similarly wider than the others. But the bays either side of the portico are *set back* from the rest and are so much wider that the upper window-heads are half-oval instead of semicircular. Further, there is an extra square pier in the angle between the portico and the wall, and the sharp edge made by its outer corner is continued upwards into the clerestory by a buttress; finally the sides of the clerestory and its gable are brought forward over the piers of the portico to form a unique three-dimensional split pediment above the tympanum of the portico (Pls 56, 57).

[43] *Memoirs of Thomas Earl of Ailesbury, written by himself* (ed. W. E. Buckley, Roxburghe Club), London, 1890–1, pp.586–7. Vanbrugh's cousin Sir Thomas Cave visited Blenheim in Sep. 1711: 'after viewing [it] proves a great house with little rooms and less for cost.' He saw 'some foreign Statues and Marbles very curious but not set up' (Margaret, Lady Verney, *Verney Letters of the Eighteenth Century*, I, 1930, p.237).

These prismatic and rectilinear forms are as dramatic in effect as the dome of Castle Howard, but whereas the latter is a simple addition of one shape to another the building blocks of the centre of Blenheim are locked together in every dimension.

In terms of lines and shapes and masses – the stuff of architecture – Blenheim is coherent and forceful. Every detail, however unexpected and however far from the canons of academic imitation of Antiquity, seems to have been thought out; one such detail is the pairs of small columns which frame the quadrants and anchor them to the rectilinear shapes of the building behind them. It is doubtful whether the most sophisticated stylistic analysis would ever succeed in determining the part played by each of the two architects. Even more than Castle Howard, Blenheim is a work of collaboration, and there are several contemporary references to the work as their joint design. Apart from arguments of the kind that apply to the earlier house, it is reasonable to associate with Hawksmoor the complexity and the fondness for diagonals shown in the lanterns and such features as the gate-piers, now known as Hensington Gate, which were made for the east garden within the park (Pl.77); among possible parallels in the following decade they have a great deal in common with some of Hawksmoor's church steeples (Pl.85) and very little with the roof-tops of Vanbrugh's independent houses such as Eastbury (Pl.86). On the other hand, it is not possible to argue from Hawksmoor's authorship of the lanterns to that of the prismatic monumentality of the whole of Blenheim, for three reasons. Firstly because of the difference between the scale of the part and the scale of the whole; secondly because there is a *prima facie* case for Vanbrugh as the author, and finally because Hawksmoor's independent large-scale work (such as his college designs) is structured less by the juxtaposition of large simple shapes and more by variation and complexity in bay rhythms, patterns of fenestration and the relief development of the wall surface. If Swift had modelled Vanbrugh not on card-houses and mud pies, but on a child playing with blocks of wood, he would have been nearer to the truth.

It was Hawksmoor, not Vanbrugh, who tended in the early days to address letters to Joynes at *Blenheim Castle*, and while the term, as with *Castle Howard*, may be little more than a literal translation of the French *château* (of which the seventeenth-century social equivalent is *great house*), it may be asked whether Blenheim has anything to do with the 'castle air' of Kimbolton. One of the hazards of historical study is that only one topic can be pursued at a time, whereas in reality several things are going on at once. Vanbrugh's work at Kimbolton began after Blenheim, but was concurrent (1707–10) with the second half of Blenheim's main period of construction. That Hawksmoor's visual imagination was rich, varied and eclectic can not only be appreciated from looking at his designs, but also demonstrated by collating what he said and wrote about his sources; in Vanbrugh's case this kind of demonstration is not possible, and one of the most fascinating – if to the scholar inconvenient – aspects of his art is the elusiveness of his imagination. Blenheim does show, however, tangible references over a wide range, from nearly contemporary buildings back through the England of a century earlier (p.52) to the Middle Ages. The plan of Blenheim, with its central block with internal courtyards and its progressively widening entrance court flanked by service ranges, grew to resemble the plan of Louis XIV's Versailles – a suitable irony for a monument to Britannia triumphant. On a smaller scale Blenheim's concave court front can be paralleled in the grandest non-royal house in France, Le Vau's Vaux-le-Vicomte (1657–61), which also has the feature of a small order woven into a giant one (Pl.53). Going back in time, the towers of Blenheim are not to be confused in either plan or elevation with the corner pavilions of a great French house; they are not divided internally like *pavillons* into living quarters, and their massiveness as well as their projection in plan associates them with the square bastions of many great English medieval castles.

The portholes too, in the basement and in the upper part of the quadrants, were intelligible at the time – and so was the word – as castellar elements although not exclusively so: Roger North had expected to see gunners in the larger roundels at Hampton Court, and portholes are a feature of certain Romanesque towers.[44] They became one of Vanbrugh's favourite motifs, although they were also used in a different context by Hawksmoor in his Spitalfields church. The most explicit medieval references at Blenheim are certainly in the kitchen court which we know was not conceived until the winter of 1707–8. There are to be found little battlemented turrets (Pls 69, 73) and covered ways which Vanbrugh maintained were purely for utility, but which have double inset arches like those of a Norman church aisle and battlements which sit on the parapet like little vaulting-horses (Pl.71). In all Vanbrugh's castles, historical or literary associations are entwined with the morphology of architectural forms; thus in these covered ways the doorways, which look like nothing so much as portable sentry-boxes, derive clearly from the north and south nave doorways added to Old St Paul's by Inigo Jones.[45] In this context it is perhaps significant that Jones made liberal use of portholes in the strange mixture of Renaissance and neo-Romanesque with which he encased the nave of St Paul's (Pl.72). Finally the east gate, prettied up though it was by Sir William Chambers, is the first of a line of superhuman Vanbrugh gateways (Pls 51, 96). Its military symbolism is that of the cannon-balls at the base of its obelisk-like corner pillars. Yet these pillars, and the tapering shape of the whole gateway, point back for modern eyes to Egyptian pylons which Vanbrugh can hardly have known. The gateway, which became the main entrance to all the buildings and was given a long explanatory inscription by the 9th Duke, had a second practical function: the upper part contained the principal water-storage cistern, filled from the valley by Robert Aldersea's pumping engine (p.73).

In Blenheim also blossomed that indirect medievalism which Vanbrugh took over from the prodigy houses of late Elizabethan and early Jacobean England (p.54). Besides the east and west bow-windows in the plan, those houses account for much of the fantastic clamour of gratuitous masonry of the Blenheim skyline; the cut-out silhouettes of a house like Wollaton (Pl.60) are translated through Hawksmoor's ingenuity into full three-dimensional forms. Moreover, there is some affinity between the clerestoried hall and Wollaton, although Seaton Delaval will be closer to that model (p.104).

After the Duchess stopped the works in 1710, Vanbrugh managed to worry £7,000 out of the Treasury; in consequence the main house and the kitchen court were roofed by the end of the year. Work was resumed in 1711 under the close eye of both the Duke and Duchess, who gave conflicting orders which Vanbrugh attempted to play against each

[44] For Roger North see *Architectural Review*, CX, 1951, p.259.

[45] Hollar's engraving, Pl.72 here; Inigo Jones's design for the doors, RIBA, *Inigo Jones and John Webb*, [32], Fig.28.

other in order to further what he believed to be priorities. These included the Bridge and the finishing touches to the kitchen court: the tower of the stable block would have to wait, and in September 1711 he wrote, 'its a jest to Mention it.'[46] In the end it was built, but the cistern gate on the far west was not. Other efforts were directed inside the house, and by the end of May 1712 when all Treasury payments stopped, the first of the four marble door-cases in the Saloon, designed by Hawksmoor, carved by Grinling Gibbons and inlaid with Marlborough's arms and the Imperial eagle, had been installed (Pl.80). Work was shut down, and only a few men were left to watch the building and save the gardens from ruin. Although roofed, little of the house was ceiled or floored and none of it was habitable.[47] The Treasury had paid £230,000, and about £45,000 was owing. The Marlboroughs returned to England on 2 August 1714, the day after George I's accession, and one of the new King's first acts after his own arrival in September was to reinstate the Duke in his former offices. At the same time Vanbrugh was knighted, officially for his part in the Hanover investiture of 1706.[48] In the financial troubles of Blenheim his pocket had been as badly hit as anyone's, and he had tried to enlist the Duke's help. In 1710 Marlborough had only been able to advise him to wait for 'something lasting' and thus did he keep his promise.

By 1716 a commission had acknowledged the Treasury debt and 'adjusted' it, which meant that for the present one-third of each bill was paid.[49] It was possible to resume work although, on the terms offered, some of the artificers, including the Strongs, refused to return. During 1716 Thornhill painted the apotheosis on the hall ceiling. But relations between Vanbrugh and the Duchess worsened rapidly. The break took the form of Vanbrugh's resignation (p.59), but several weeks previously it was clear to the clerk William Jefferson that the Duchess meant to be rid of the architect.[50] She would make her own arrangements. The gallery was completed as a library in Hawksmoor's second period (1722–5) together with three rooms on the south front. Vanbrugh and Hawksmoor had prepared a design for the Saloon consisting of giant Corinthian pilasters and two storeys of niches containing statues; a drawing of 1707 survives with figures filled in by Gibbons (Pl.82). In 1709 this design was still current, and Vanbrugh was negotiating the purchase of statues by Pietro Francavilla from the Villa Bracci at Rovezzano near Florence, but the sale fell through although the statues were eventually bought in 1750 by Frederick Prince of Wales and are now mostly at Windsor.[51] The Blenheim accounts show that the niches, which appear in the *Vitruvius* plan, were actually constructed, although the wall was subsequently filled in for the illusionist paintings undertaken in 1719–20 by Louis Laguerre, whose rates were lower than Thornhill's. The door-cases were completed to match the first one of 1712.

Thus, apart from some unmistakable chimneypieces in the east rooms,[52] little of the

[46] Webb, p.239.

[47] Plan prepared in 1716 (Green, Pl.68).

[48] Marlborough was Vanbrugh's sponsor (Le Neve, p.511).

[49] Vanbrugh received £800 in March 1716 and the remainder in Aug. 1725 (Account Book).

[50] Jefferson to Joynes, 15 Oct. 1716 (Green, pp.141–3).

[51] Whistler, pp.233–4, 236; Webb, pp.34, 40. For the statues, see *Burlington Magazine*, XCVIII, 1956, pp.77–84.

[52] Green, Pls 54–6.

interior is Vanbrugh's; of the state-rooms he could have been responsible only for the hall, and enough preparatory drawings for that survive to establish that its design was worked out in 1706–7 by Hawksmoor (Pls 78, 81). In one version the side walls are articulated by giant Corinthian columns, in another the middle is occupied by a large and elaborate sculptural overmantel; in one design the superimposed arcades continue round the south side adjoining the Saloon, and in another Hawksmoor tries out different versions of the depressed half-oval finally adopted.[53] This was the room Lord Berkeley of Stratton compared to a church, and its direct descendant is Hawksmoor's St George, Bloomsbury, begun in 1716. Paradoxically it is in this room rather than out of doors that one is aware how coldly and impersonally grand stone can be, and in this atmosphere the miraculous undercutting of Gibbons's capitals (the larger ones composed of fronds of the victor's palm rather than the conventional acanthus) assumes the naturalism of a sub-zero world (Pl.84). The staircases behind the arcades, of which only the eastern was built, were intended to produce a spatial experience similar to that at Castle Howard with views through the arcades across the hall. The combination of screen and stair was indeed one of Vanbrugh's favourite devices, which he used also at Audley End and later at Grimsthorpe (p.121).

Lord Berkeley also noted 'above stairs . . . nothing but lodging rooms enough to lodge an Army.'[54] Hawksmoor, who had shown exceptional ingenuity at Easton Neston in the use of mezzanines to pack in bedroom suites and backstairs around the main living-rooms, also worked out mezzanine suites and staircases in the east side of Blenheim and inside the quadrants although not all of them seem to have been built. The largeness and the Baroque flamboyance of Blenheim have always been open to ridicule; in a letter Pope applied to Blenheim his own phrase 'a labour'd Quarry above ground',[55] and some verses which have been dubiously attributed both to him and to Swift stress the vastness and inconvenience of 'a house but not a dwelling.'[56] Vanbrugh's later correspondence with the younger Newcastle shows that even in a grand house he paid great attention to comfort and convenience, and the north-east wing of Castle Howard is a model dwelling in this respect. If Castle Howard is to be criticized, it is on the extravagance of a plan in which the main house has very few upstairs spaces for bedrooms in relation to the grand suites of the ground floor. Whatever the reason, Vanbrugh's inexperience, or Lord Carlisle's desire for a palace of state rather than a house, or an early but conscious reference to Palladian villas, the increase in bedroom accommodation at Blenheim may have been one of the differences Marlborough wanted between the two houses.

Modern domestic critics comment on the problems of bringing food hot to the table from a kitchen whose odours were to be kept remote from the dining-room. A colourful example of the art of serving occurs in the memoirs of Mrs Kit Welch *alias* Ross, who

[53] Whistler, Pl.38; Downes (1959), Pl.16; *Country Life*, CXIII, 1953, p.353; *Burlington Magazine*, CIII, 1961, p.281.

[54] See p.62, n.29.

[55] A. Pope, *Correspondence*, ed. Sherburn, I, 1956, pp.431–2.

[56] 'Thanks, sir, cried I, 'tis very fine
But where d'ye sleep, or where d'ye dine?'
(*Upon the Duke of Marlborough's House at Woodstock*). Although included in Elwin and Courthope's edition of Pope's *Poetry*, 1882, IV, p.451, the authorship is uncertain. For Vanbrugh's view of Blenheim as a house, see p.93.

served in Marlborough's army first as a soldier and then, when her sex was discovered after a head wound, as a sutler. Even with plenty of salt, her story as recorded by Defoe of a five-mile night journey to the front line with a hot supper shows that at home the problem of good service was not beyond the ingenuity of the time.[57]

Blenheim today stands in the landscape created by Capability Brown in the 1760s, a setting so beautiful and so attuned to the romantic aspects of Vanbrugh's architecture that it is difficult to regret its making or to doubt that Brown improved on what he found. However, in justice to Vanbrugh we should remember how different the setting of his building originally was in three respects: the gardens, the Bridge, and old Woodstock Manor. When Brown laid the turf up to the south front from as far as the eye can see he destroyed the formal parterre, a sort of enormous embroidery of vegetation on which Henry Wise's many workmen had laboured at the same time as the masons on the house. Further away Wise had planted an even larger garden, a hexagonal cultivated 'wilderness' of trees and shrubs and many intersecting paths. It was bounded by a ha-ha, or more accurately in Vanbrugh's terms a ditch and a rampart, with big circular bastions at the corners – and since these can or could be found in other gardens with Vanbrugh connections (p.107), they must have been his idea.[58] That Blenheim today has at least modern formal gardens on the east and west is due to the 9th Duke, who did a great deal in this century to repair the inevitable ravages of time, taste, nature and decay. In 1902 he replanted the great avenue that runs for two miles north from Vanbrugh's unfinished Bridge.[59]

The Bridge (Pls 75, 76) is the most mysterious and the least understood part of all Blenheim. Vanbrugh's complete design is preserved in an engraved elevation (Pl.74) which shows that the centre span was to have been surmounted by tall arcades between corner towers. From its appearance in the engraving a roof joining these arcades would have been structurally impossible; nevertheless the design has rightly been recognized as a free version of Palladio's covered bridge designed for the Rialto, and a version closer to the scale and the Antique associations of Palladio's monumental design than the several toy-like neo-Palladian bridges which sprouted in English eighteenth-century parks.[60] Vanbrugh and Brown between them managed the landscape so well that the Bridge and the valley seem made for each other, as they were. Even without its top storey, even with its bottom 10 or 15 feet submerged in the lake which Brown made by damming up the Glyme, Vanbrugh's Bridge is the finest approach imaginable. But it is not used as an approach, because the avenue leads from Ditchley Gate on the north boundary and visitors have always come through the town of Woodstock. The old Manor stood in line between the town and the north end of the Bridge, near the latter; it was approached by two causeways across the valley, one leading to the town and the other running south-east past the end of Vanbrugh's kitchen court towards Oxford. The visitor taking the causeway from Woodstock would first see the Bridge in elevation

[57] Daniel Defoe, *Life and Adventures of Mrs Christian Davies, usually called Mother Ross*, 1928. The lady ended as an out-pensioner of Chelsea and was buried in the Pensioners' cemetery (C. G. T. Dean, *The Royal Hospital*, 1950, pp.222–3).

[58] The walled kitchen garden survives to the south-east.

[59] Green, pp.203, 204, 205.

[60] Palladio, Book III, pp.26–7.

in the distance and then, after making a circuit of the Manor, find himself near the northern end on the main axis of the house; the Bridge would be in turn scenery and then highway. That must be the way it was conceived when, in April 1706, in a competition with designs and stone models of projects by Vanbrugh, Hawksmoor, Wise and Wren, the Duke chose Vanbrugh's;[61] when in June Bartholomew Peisley contracted for the masonry and Aldersea began to install his pump where the northern arch was to be, to raise water from Rosamond's Well to the house and gardens. But already by 1710 when Peisley turned the great arch the Bridge had been by-passed. It stood 'in the air' as the Duchess said,[62] like a modern motorway bridge built in advance of the road it is to carry. During 1711, as Vanbrugh reiterated that Marlborough wished this work to have priority the Duchess as often denied it. Ten years later the prodigious earthmoving operations were at last complete, and (in Vanbrugh's words) the 'irregular ragged ungovernable hill'[63] under the house had been moulded into approach roads. But the natural way had already been established, by custom and for want of any other, along the town side of the valley and obliquely towards the east gateway. The Bridge could only be scenery, although the Duchess finally gave it a kind of use by placing the Column with its long explanatory inscription in the park to the north of it.

Before Brown made the lake and engulfed the bottom storey of the Bridge, the valley was a marsh traversed by the several strands of the Glyme, a minor tributary of the Thames. When the Duchess accepted the Bridge as a reality, she decided to give it a proper piece of water to cross, and in 1722 engaged William Townesend and the younger Bartholomew Peisley to dig a canal as wide as the centre arch. The necessity of a larger body of water seems never to have occurred to Vanbrugh, and the reason must be that he was satisfied with a land-bridge or what came in the nineteenth century to be called a viaduct. But this was not the only aspect of the Bridge which he left unexplained. It is full of rooms – the Duchess counted thirty-three – some of them with fireplaces and chimneys as if for habitation. He finally told her that when it was finished 'everybody will say, 'twas the best money laid out in the whole design And if at last, there is a house found in that Bridge your Grace will go and live in it.' There are many passages in letters in which he asks anxiously about its progress, and he told the Duchess plainly that while he would defer the projected second greenhouse which he did not love, 'As for the Bridge I do love it.'[64] Indeed, reviewing the last months before his resignation it seems as if he cared more about this than any other part of Blenheim. Did its simplicity, its size and its hidden allegiance to Palladio and Antiquity, make it for him the quintessence of architecture? Did he love it out of growing obstinacy in the face of the Duchess? Was it a gigantic rebus on the word *Brug*, his own name?[65] Was it to form part of a scheme such as

[61] Whistler, p.113; Webb, p.76.

[62] 'Levelling of hills, filling up pricipices & making bridges in the air for no reason that I or any body else can see but to have it said hereafter that Sr John Vanbrugh did that thing which never was don before' (BM MS.Stowe 751, f.150); 'The best thing I have heard since I came to this place is that the bridge in the air is decaying & I hope it will fall, for one may goe under it, but never upon it no more than one can goe into the moon' (ibid., f.205).

[63] Webb, p.30.

[64] Letters, 10 and 27 July 1716 (Webb, pp.71, 74).

[65] Vanbrugh's arms (Gules, on a Fesse, Or, three Barrulets, Vert: in Chief, a Demy Lion. For a Crest, a Demy Lion, issuant from a Bridge composed of three reversed Arches, Or) were granted in April 1714 (Foster, *Grantees*).

Hawksmoor later proposed for the Mausoleum at Castle Howard, an almshouse inhabited by 'aged persons [who] should be the Curators of the Monument . . . and shew it to Strangers with many traditions, and accounts concerning it'?[66] Was it in some way connected in his mind with the old Manor and Fair Rosamond?

This last possibility compounds mystery with mystery. In sentimental history Woodstock was famous for the affair between Henry II and Rosamond Clifford, who to some degree acted out a version of the Tristan legend at Everswell, a property about a quarter-mile west of the Manor and composed of enclosed gardens, pools and chambers; Everswell and the spring which fed the pools later became known as Rosamond's Well, and survived until Brown raised the lake.[67] By the end of the Middle Ages the Manor was a house of considerable size, covering with its walled courtyard an area of about 150 feet radius. After serious damage during the Civil War, it remained a substantial and partly habitable ruin. The origins of Vanbrugh's concern with the building are not clear, but a roof was repaired early in 1708. Further repairs were undertaken; when this came to the Marlboroughs' notice they ordered the repairs to be stopped and the ruins to be demolished. At this point Vanbrugh and Joynes seem to have formed a conspiracy of innocent incredulity, and the practical results were that repairs continued surreptitiously on the more useful parts of the buildings while demolition went on in other parts. Vanbrugh drew a little picture for the benefit of Godolphin and the Duchess, and the latter also received a paper entitled *Reasons Offer'd for Preserving some Part of the Old Manor*.[68] His first reason was historical and sentimental association, and he drew an ingenious parallel between that of Woodstock in the eighteenth century with Henry II, and that of Blenheim in the future with Marlborough, when travellers would be told that 'it was not only his Favourite Habitation, but was Erected for him by the Bounty of the Queen', and so on. And though the Manor was not 'Erected on so Noble nor on so justifiable an Occasion' yet 'it was rais'd by One of the Bravest and most Warlike of the English Kings' and 'has been tenderly regarded as the Scene of his Affections.'

At some time after this, perhaps about 1716, Marlborough decided to put up an obelisk at Blenheim; not in his own honour, for that had been done any way by Carlisle (p.109), but for some thought akin to the original purpose of the place.[69] One of the sites he considered was at the beginning of the avenue; the other was near the old Manor. This he thought 'would please Sr John best, because it would give an opportunity of mentioning that King whose Scenes of Love He was so much pleas'd with.' The Duchess's gloss on this was 'but if there were obelisks to bee made of what all our Kings have don of that sort the countrey would bee Stuffed with very odd things.'

Vanbrugh's second reason for preserving the old Manor was aesthetic. The view from the north front of Blenheim was rather bare and unvaried, and if 'the Habitable Part and the Chappel might Appear in Two Risings' among the trees 'it wou'd make One of the Most Agreable Objects that the best of Landskip Painters can invent.' Thus, just as the further garden to the south, beyond the symmetry of the parterre, was a wilderness of

66 *Walpole Society*, XIX, 1931, p.117.

67 *King's Works*, II, 1963, p.1009 ff.

68 Webb, pp.27–30.

69 Green, p.170.

trees, so might the landscape to the north, beyond the courtyard and the Bridge on the centre line, be varied, irregular, evocative of a past age and ready-made for the artist. Fifty years later such arguments would have won the day, but Vanbrugh's taste for ruins was ahead of his time; asymmetry he himself could only admit in exceptional circumstances. And so the conspiracy continued.

The Marlboroughs had ever more important preoccupations than whether Vanbrugh was diverting precious money to such fripperies. But in the summer of 1713 they were in exile and he himself was in a kind of banishment, having been dismissed from the Comptrollership through a misdirected remark in their support (p.85). Perhaps he felt that loyalty gave him a title. The Manor was greatly improved, and it offered a striking view of the Bridge and the new house; besides, surveillance of the deserted works was no bad thing. Such must have been his thoughts, although for once he appears not to have set them down for the Duchess. But in July 1716 he coolly informed her that it was convenient 'and very pleasant too, altho in the middle of Rubbish', and that he had been using it for three years; he was surprised that she did not know.[70] In September he was building a curtain wall there. It speaks volumes for their characters that his resignation did not come until November. Today a single stone marks the site of the Manor, the last remnants of which were razed in 1723.

70 Webb, p.72. The Account Book confirms what could be deduced from his other activities: that he can only have used the Manor occasionally instead of putting up at Woodstock.

Chapter 5

Establishment

Historical landmarks rarely come singly, but 1715 was a particularly significant year for Vanbrugh. In January he was reinstated as Comptroller, in a newly constituted Board of Works which was intended to assist the ageing Wren. Before the year ended Sir John had started the transformation of his little house at Chargate into the great mansion of Claremont (Pl.118), and also the sequence of designs leading to the commencement in 1718 of Eastbury in Dorset. One of the earliest of these (Pl.86) is among the most attractive drawings from his own hand – a draughtsman's copy also survives – and shows how far he had learned to make drawings that are not only tolerably competent but also pictorial.

Something more indeed needs to be said about Vanbrugh as a draughtsman. The Account Book shows him late in life buying painting equipment, perhaps for heraldic rather than architectural drawing (f.48). On the evidence of the Eastbury drawing (and others) he never drew with the professional neatness of his draughtsman assistants. But a number of observations occur.

First, his handwriting and the *mise en page* of his letters, up to the end of his life, reveal order and discipline which could never justly be called messy. Perhaps therefore in his drawings we ought to ask whether the result is messy, that is, incompetently disordered, or something else.

Secondly, while drawing is different from writing, in this very difference may lie some of the character of his drawings. Even many professional or habitual draughtsmen work on the principle of sketchiness, a kind of impressionism, coupled with a technique not quite adequate to the ideas they wish to express. Vanbrugh may have believed in suggestion as a positive ideal to be attained at the end of the century that produced the drawings of Claude and Rembrandt: both the smoking chimneys and the soft windows of the Eastbury drawing are relevant, the latter also to the visual effect of Kings Weston (p.80). Moreover, he acquired enough ability with a pen to express himself clearly and even dramatically (Figs. 6, 7, 20).

Thirdly, it ought to be less surprising than it is to find Vanbrugh delegating drawing as a process. Delegation – and in particular knowing what to delegate – is part of the success of a businessman, an administrator, and even an architect. The great *entrepreneur* works on the principle that what he cannot do himself he can find and pay somebody else to do. When tidy professional drawings were appropriate there was for Vanbrugh a Hawksmoor, a Joynes, an Arthur to make them, as naturally as there was a Joas Bateman to keep grandfather Gillis's accounts (p.140).

In relation to Blenheim, the Eastbury design shows considerable changes in Vanbrugh's conception of architecture as the art of building. These changes are without doubt partly due to internal causes in the development of his thought, but they are also closely connected with the course of English architecture more generally over most of the second decade of the eighteenth century, which it is appropriate now to examine.

The year 1715 also saw the publication of the first volume of *Vitruvius Britannicus, or the British Architect*, by Colen Campbell, a Scotsman who had arrived in London about 1712. His sumptuous folio volume of engraved plates bore a dedication to George I and an impressive list of subscribers among both nobility and gentry and a number of architects and artificers. Two years later a companion volume followed, with a re-issue of the first, and he produced a third volume in 1725. Campbell's title was undoubtedly intended to pick up earlier published references to Inigo Jones as the English Vitruvius of his time – changed to *British* in the climate of the Act of Union between England and Scotland of 1707, which had helped to direct the progress to the South, of Campbell and other Scottish Whigs. In his first volume Campbell offered plans and elevations of buildings or designs by Jones and his pupil John Webb, Wren (St Paul's and Greenwich), Talman, Vanbrugh, Hawksmoor and Archer and others, as well as several of his own.[1] This wide coverage certainly contributed to the success of Campbell's venture, and thus to the dissemination of his message. In a short introduction of a page and a half he managed to attack recent Italian architecture, naming Bernini, Borromini and Carlo Fontana, and to condemn by implication the emulation in Britain of such foreign extravagances; to praise instead Italian Renaissance architects, above all Palladio, and lastly as proof that 'in most we equal, and in Some Things we surpass, our Neighbours' to put forward 'this great Master', Inigo Jones, whom any impartial judge would admit 'to have outdone all that went before.' In the next breath he complimented the nation on the architects of the time, naming several of those represented in the plates; indeed he could hardly do otherwise since he was indebted to them for drawings. Nevertheless he must have been confident that in the context of his remarks, of his plates, and of the notorious expense of Blenheim in particular, the plates of that house would speak for themselves.

A second factor in Campbell's success, and even more significantly in its effect on architectural taste and patronage, was his timely formula for satisfying a current need. The 3rd Earl of Shaftesbury's *Letter Concerning Design*, addressed to Lord Somers, was written in Italy early in 1712 and, although not published until 1731, was very soon known in England in manuscript. In attacking French taste and influence in the arts, Shaftesbury was clarifying the taste of Whig society; he clearly identified Wren not only with French influence but with a kind of artistic absolutism, and among the disasters resulting from Wren's supposed monopoly over nearly forty years he named St Paul's and Hampton Court, and clearly implied Blenheim and the newly proposed Fifty New Churches which were still on the drawing-board. He prophesied the acceptance of new standards of 'national taste', specifically anti-French, by the 'whole People' of a 'united Britain the principal Seat of Arts.' In the age that invented John Bull, the words *public* and *people* meant for Shaftesbury and his readers the upper middle class and the aristocracy, in whose hands the Glorious Revolution of 1688 had firmly placed the power which three

[1] The others named are Winde, Bodt (Wentworth Castle); Benson, C. Wren (Marlborough House); also the façade, plan and section of St Peter's, Rome. See also R. Wittkower, 'Pseudo-Palladian Elements in English Neoclassicism', *Journal of the Warburg and Courtauld Institutes*, VI, 1943, pp. 154–64.

generations of Stuart kings had considered, as a gift of God, their prerogative.[2] The artistic parallel was close: in place of a court style diffused pyramidally from the Crown itself, Shaftesbury proposed a national style promoted by those enlightened members of society in whom, in Lords or Commons or outside Parliament, the authority of the State was now vested. Theory followed the practice which had begun with the abrogation of royal splendour at Chatsworth (p.21). But Shaftesbury did not attempt to define or describe a national style, and his prescription was negative – un-French, unlike Wren, unlike Blenheim. Certainly there was nothing intrinsically or inevitably Whiggish in Inigo Jones's style or in a revival of it; the reverse ought to have been the case since he had above all been court architect to James I and Charles I. But he was undeniably British and had undeniably adapted Palladio's grave and regular latinity to British needs. Shaftesbury's negative prescription was adroitly and positively filled by Campbell's contribution, carefully filtered, of elements from Jones and from Palladio; moreover, if Jones's connections with an absolutist court were not remembered, Palladio's with Republican Venice rather than papal Rome were not forgotten.

Indeed, it is over-simple to imagine that Palladianism, as the new style came not quite justly to be called, arrived overnight with Campbell's book. The Venetian architect Giacomo Leoni, who reached London in 1713, immediately set about the English translation of Palladio's *Quattro Libri*, and thus worked at the same time as Campbell on a complementary project; when the first part appeared in 1716 it bore the significant date of the previous year. However, interest in Jones and Palladio in preference to the Baroque goes back a little earlier. The first attempt at a direct Jones revival was the calculated plagiarism of William Benson, an ambitious and scarcely scrupulous Whig place-seeker, who in about 1710 adapted John Webb's design for Amesbury, Wilts. for his own house, Wilbury, in the same county. The design, which was included in Campbell's first volume, was more remarkable as a precedent than as architecture, and its construction was slow.[3] Benson's prime claim to notoriety was that in April 1718 he secured through intrigue the dismissal of Wren as Surveyor of Works and his own appointment to that post, in which during a tenure of fifteen months he did considerable damage to the administrative structure of the Works. Vanbrugh was instrumental in Benson's exposure and dismissal, which were not effected before his own position had been placed at risk; his involvement was both personal and official (p.87).

In 1711 John James, a conscientious and capable if uninspired architect who was trained as a carpenter in Wren's circle and who had to his credit translations of Pozzo's *Perspectiva* (1707) and Perrault's *Ordonnance des Cinq Espèces de Colonnes* (1708), canvassed the Duke of Buckingham for an official position so 'that I may once in my life have an Opportunity of shewing that the Beautys of Architecture may consist with the Greatest plainness of the Structure', a demonstration which 'has scarce ever been hit by the Tramontani [those north of the Alps] unless by our famous Mr Inigo Jones.'[4] His opinion appears to have been quite sincere and based as much on reaction to the work of the

[2] Dr John Arbuthnot, *The History of John Bull*, 1712.

[3] Campbell gives the date 1710 for Wilbury, but the house was not completed, to a watered-down design, until about 1725.

[4] Bodl.MS.Rawl. B.376, f.9. In 1712 James published *The Theory and Practice of Gardening*, translated from the French of J. A. Désallier d'Argenville.

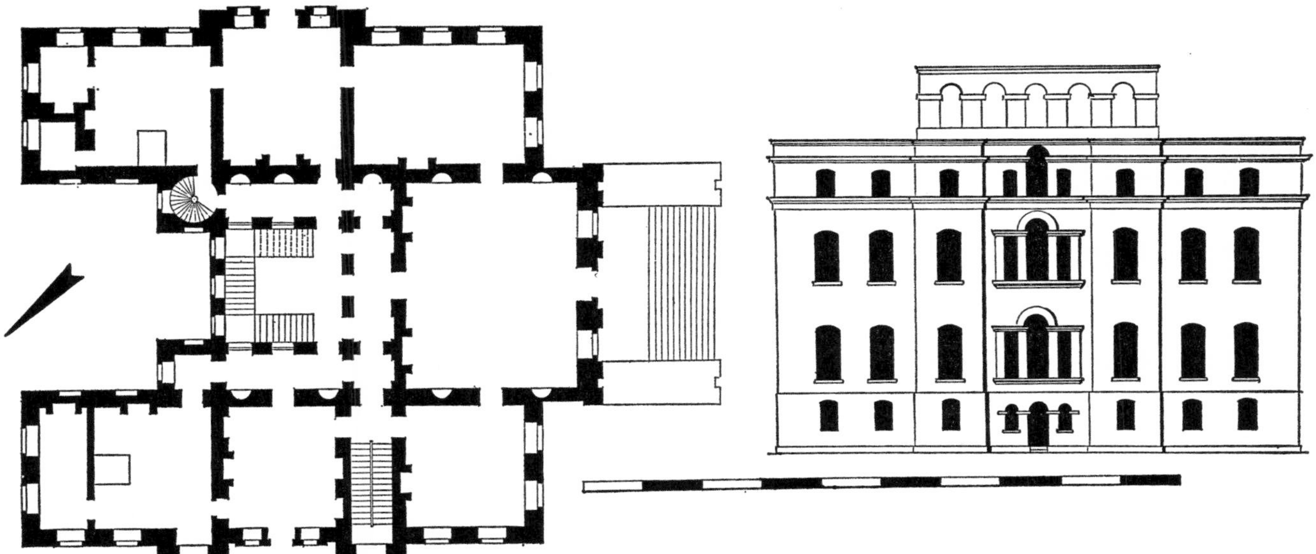

10 Kings Weston. Plan and original west elevation.
After drawings in the Kings Weston Album (Bristol Civic Trust).

previous generation as to Palladian conviction, and it is also significantly concerned more directly with plainness than with Jones; it needs to be understood that these two concepts were distinct and not necessarily concurrent. In fact the 'plain style' as it has recently been called, had been in existence for nearly two decades when James wrote in 1711; moreover, it had been available to Vanbrugh for more than half that time, and in that year he was extending his command of it from the small scale of Chargate to the rather larger masses of Kings Weston, near Bristol, for Edward Southwell. Southwell was a lawyer with Irish connections and Member at times of both the English and the Irish Parliaments; he inherited Kings Weston in 1702 but seems not to have decided to commission Vanbrugh with rebuilding until about 1710. Had he delayed four or five years more his architect might well have been not Vanbrugh but Campbell, who refers to him in *Vitruvius Britannicus* as 'the Angaranno of our age', an allusion to an early patron of Palladio and the dedicatee of his *Quattro Libri*. Campbell is fulsomely discreet about his debt to Southwell, which was perhaps for support for his publication, though Penpole Lodge, one of the Kings Weston garden buildings now destroyed, was at least partly Campbell's work. The new house was finished structurally by 1714 although the interior was still not complete when Southwell died in 1730 and much of what we see now is the work in the 1760s of Robert Mylne who also made additions to the north and east fronts.[5]

Kings Weston is a nearly square block, with a deep recess on the north (domestic) side and projections on the other three sides (Fig.10A). Some of the features of its plan may be due to re-using old foundations, but the simplicity of outline is even more marked in elevation (Pls 88, 91). The entrance portico is reduced in depth to an almost flat application of unfluted Corinthian pilasters, and the crenellated arcade of chimney flues in the centre

[5] C. Gotch, 'Mylne at Kings Weston', *Country Life*, CXXIII, 1953, pp.212–15. The staircase (Pl.87) is basically Vanbrugh's although the glass roof was put in when the original windows were masked by additions. For Penpole Gate see *Architectural History*, x, 1967, p.14, Figs. 28–30.

of the roof is similarly a reduction to simple silhouettes of the rich sculptural forms of the Blenheim roofline. The formal reduction is also applied to the mouldings, of which there are very few. As at Kimbolton, the windows are set near the outer surface of the wall, but here they are closer in feeling to those of Chargate. For with the exception of the east and west centre bays and the lateral ones on the south front they have sills but no architraves. They are thus defined neither by depth of relief, like the windows of Hawksmoor's St Anne, Limehouse, which look as if they have been punched out of the wall (Pl.85), nor by precisely cut mouldings as was the case with almost all major houses from Coleshill (Pl.11) through Chatsworth and Easton Neston (Pl.17) to those of the early Palladians; nor even do they appear as interruptions of a system of banded rustication, as in the wings of Castle Howard and the corner towers of Blenheim (Pl.65). Instead they are more like variations of tone or colour on the surface than changes in the surface itself. The effect over the whole exterior of reddish yellow stone is of a soft wash drawing rather than a pen outline; Vanbrugh was capable of spirited pen sketches, but the analogy with his drawing for Eastbury (Pl.86) may nevertheless be illuminating. He may have found confirmation, if not inspiration, in the schematized elevations which frequent the pages of the *Quattro Libri*.

There has never been any reason to connect Hawksmoor with Kings Weston, or with any other Vanbrugh house begun after Kimbolton. It is clear that from about that time Vanbrugh began to organize his office independently, with other assistants. In 1708 he took over his cousin William's clerk, Thomas Kynaston, and at Christmas sent him down to Blenheim to learn how work was measured.[6] Kynaston may already have worked for Vanbrugh occasionally for some time previously, and it is probable that the latter chose as his clerk someone who showed at least promise as a draughtsman.[7] From about 1715 Kynaston was on the payroll of the Works as Clerk to the Comptroller, or Clerk of Works at Somerset House and the Tower; Benson temporarily deprived him of the last two in 1718–20, but during that period of upheaval Vanbrugh made him Deputy Comptroller.[8] Among other draughtsmen Henry Joynes probably made other drawings for Vanbrugh besides those for Blenheim and Castle Howard (p.35). By 1716 two different hands, neither of them Hawksmoor's, were helping with drawings for Eastbury, but only one other draughtsman is known by name, and only by a single name: 'Arthur' was working for him in 1723.[9] On the other hand Vanbrugh and Hawksmoor remained on good terms until the former's death, and their partnership at Castle Howard may be said to have outlived Vanbrugh, since Hawksmoor carried out his design for the Temple there after 1726. They were also colleagues in the Office of Works, and on numerous occasions Vanbrugh attempted to redress the inequities which affected his old friend both during

[6] 26 Dec. 1708 (Webb, p.223).

[7] In 1719 Vanbrugh said he had employed Kynaston for fifteen years (Webb, p.118). Drawings for Blenheim were made *in situ* in 1709 by Rowney and Andrews (Webb, p.227). The latter was perhaps the John Andrews described as Hawksmoor's 'agent' in 1713 (Lambeth Palace Library, Fifty Churches papers, Box IV, No.3) and his clerk in 1717 (*Greenwich Antiquarian Soc.*, III, No.1, p.17).

[8] *King's Works*, V, 1975, p.59.

[9] Webb, p.83; the letter, there dated 1716, is endorsed *Nov. 1st 1723*. Arthur was Vanbrugh's servant in 1716 (p.183) and was re-imbursed for toll charges in Aug. 1725 (Lady Vanbrugh's Account Book, BIHR (Yarburgh), p.213 – in the section at the back containing Vanbrugh's small expenses).

and after Benson's surveyorship. Hawksmoor's absence from Vanbrugh's private commissions after Kimbolton was not, therefore, due to any rift between them, although it was personal in that neither any longer needed the other. Hawksmoor had never needed Vanbrugh except from a certain diffidence which appears in his behaviour but not in his works; Vanbrugh was able to dispense with Hawksmoor as he gained in knowledge, experience, reputation and outside assistance. Delegation came as easily to him as did delegacy to Hawksmoor; nevertheless there must have been considerable appeal to his artistic rather than his personal self-respect in a style in which he could work without reliance on a mind soaked, as Hawksmoor's was, in 'the delicacy of the ornaments.'

It is not, however, possible to use ornament as a kind of litmus-paper by which Hawksmoor's style (ornamented) could be distinguished from Vanbrugh's (plain); such a procedure is grossly both unjust and untrue. If Castle Howard and Blenheim are as much as half Hawksmoor's work they are still at least half Vanbrugh's, and in his estimation considerably more. Further, they stand in time at the end of a period in which English exterior architecture was particularly concerned, under the influence of France, with surface decoration, and in this respect they follow on from Wren's St Paul's and Hampton Court. Not least, the first reaction to that concern, within Wren's own circle, appears in an early design by Hawksmoor for a commission delegated to him by Wren. The Writing School at Christ's Hospital (1692–5) was destroyed at the beginning of the present century, and old photographs show it to have been less imposing and more domestic than Hawksmoor's preliminary design for which several drawings survive (Pl.83).[10] In them, at a time when Vanbrugh was still confined in the Bastille, there appear the restriction and simplification of mouldings, the prismatic shapes and plain surfaces, of a kind of architecture as unlike anything of Wren's as it is similar to some of Vanbrugh's later buildings. It was Hawksmoor who with extreme literalness put into practice a conception of architecture as solid geometry which Wren had described both in writing (which has come down to us)[11] and undoubtedly in many conversations, but which in Wren's architecture is clothed in a decorative skin. Hawksmoor's attitude to decoration was precise and scholarly, but in his independent works detail does not obscure the basic character of an architecture of masses, of formal rhythms and of blocks of masonry.

His first recognizable contribution to Vanbrugh's architecture was in specific matters of administration and detail; but more fundamentally the 'Vanbrugh manner' itself was Hawksmoor's contribution. We set a high value on innovation, and when it began to appear, a generation ago, that Hawksmoor was in general the innovator of the pair, his reputation began to rise above Vanbrugh's to a degree which is neither just nor supported by the evidence, and at one extreme Vanbrugh's validity as an architect at all was questioned. But while ever since the Renaissance *originality* has been considered commendable, the concept which gives the Renaissance its name is one of *authority*, or what Hawksmoor

[10] For the Writing School see Downes (1959), pp.53–4, Pl.1.

[11] *Tract I* (*Parentalia*, pp.351–68; *Wren Soc.*, XIX, pp.126–8). See J. A. Bennett, 'Christopher Wren: the Natural Causes of Beauty', *Architectural History*, XV, 1972, pp.5–22.

referred to as 'some old father to stand by you.'[12] Architecture as an art uses highly evolved systems of formal language to make permanent settings for diverse human activities; to take an obvious example, a doorway must offer an invitation to enter and often also an indication that entry is restricted or barred. Architecture is therefore especially concerned with the symbolism of shapes and locations and with the establishment of a grammar, syntax and vocabulary around such symbolism. Architecture is also necessarily concerned with stability of structure and with gravity and other natural forces: a doorway must be so designed as not to weaken the structure in which it forms a void interruption. From both linguistic and constructional causes, rules and precedents thus play a significant part in architectural aesthetics. It remains true that any artist worth his salt has a recognizable style, and the deep set windows of Hawksmoor's Limehouse church and the shallow ones of Kings Weston represent two distinct personalities working within the same stylistic area. But it is neither at all uncommon nor invalid for an architect to work creatively within a style which he has taken over virtually ready-made. In the wake of such figures as Michelangelo and Borromini a number of architects indeed could hardly do otherwise. In the early eighteenth century Palladianism was *a priori* a style of imitation, and it was against the growth of specious authoritarianism founded on imitation without understanding that Hawksmoor desired to deploy his 'old father.' Vanbrugh, on the other hand, through both intuition and application, understood completely the style in which he worked and made totally his own.

As an architect Vanbrugh was, like Wren and Jones before him and unlike Hawksmoor (p.27), self-taught. While we know little of the course of his self-education its results are manifest, and to such an extent that we may draw certain conclusions about his motives. It is conceivable that he embarked on Castle Howard in a spirit of adventure, that he considered the Comptrollership initially as a means of subsistence, but his subsequent record is one of commitment of a kind which must be considered both professional and political. The Kit-Cat club owed its vitality to the combination of bonhomie and a common cause. Vanbrugh wrote gossipy letters about a circle of acquaintance as picturesque as the characters in his comedies; the same Vanbrugh also wrote serious letters reminding his political friends of their parliamentary duties. His inquiry into the irregularities in the Kensington Orangery in 1704 (p.47) perhaps owed some of its impetus to spite against Talman's associates, but it has the unmistakable air of a party politician on the scent of a scandal. In October 1703 he became one of the Directors of Greenwich Hospital, whose meetings he attended frequently over many years, and in the summer of 1716 he succeeded Wren as Surveyor to the Hospital.[13] Nearly all the buildings at Greenwich were designed either before or after his connection with it, and the unexecuted projects for a great chapel on the central axis are now known to have been not his but Hawksmoor's; Vanbrugh's role was thus administrative (often examining building accounts) and philanthropic.

[12] Hawksmoor to Lord Carlisle, 7 Jan. 1724 (Downes (1959), p.244). The 'rough guess' of J. Summerson, *Architecture in Britain 1530–1830*, 1953, p.175, is remarkably apt: 'that to Vanbrugh we chiefly owe the daring novelties of composition which are outstanding characteristics of the houses . . . but that it was Hawksmoor who discovered (had, indeed, already discovered) the mode of expression appropriate to these adventures.'

[13] According to Hawksmoor (Downes (1959), p.249) 'Mr Dorrington' got Vanbrugh the Greenwich Surveyorship with an allowance of £200. Dorrington is a surname of the time (See Appendix B, 4) but George Doddington, Lord of the Admiralty (p.114), may well have been meant.

He was likewise an active member of the first Commission for building Fifty New Churches, which operated from 1711 to 1715 and included also Sir Christopher Wren and his son and Thomas Archer. This was the commission which set the pattern for the churches actually built, a quarter of the projected fifty: for the most part they were expensive, ostentatious and self-consciously architectural, and no less than six were designed by Hawksmoor (one of the two permanent surveyors appointed by the Commission) while two were designed by Archer. Rather surprisingly Vanbrugh was not on the second Commission appointed in 1716 by the Whig government of George I and concerned with the practicalities of carrying out a project initiated by the previous government. As an exercise in piety, providing places of worship for the established religion of England in the new suburbs of London and Westminster, the scheme cannot have greatly interested Vanbrugh, although he would have approved of the indirect effect they were intended to achieve of countering the spread of dissenting sects in those areas and thus reinforcing political stability. The fact that the scheme was carried through Parliament by the Tory majority returned in 1710 and was ideologically a Tory and High Church celebration cannot have been at all to his taste. Nevertheless, he recognized the opportunity which the Fifty New Churches Act offered for adorning the metropolis with a series of buildings of an unprecedented Baroque force and grandeur, and his advocacy must have contributed to Hawksmoor's large share of the executed designs. Vanbrugh himself submitted projects for some of the churches, including in November 1714 a design for St Mary-le-Strand in unsuccessful competition with James Gibbs and in May 1715 one for St George, Bloomsbury which was approved, postponed, and superseded thirteen months later by Hawksmoor's. These designs are not extant, but drawings survive for one unnamed church (Pl.70).[14]

However, his major recorded contribution was a long memorandum to the Commission on the design of its buildings. The original manuscript of this in the Bodleian Library is unsigned, and while Hawksmoor has more than once been suggested as its author, the handwriting is without doubt Vanbrugh's (Pl.55).[15] Who composed it is a far more difficult question to answer. The writer places great emphasis on the dignity and visually favourable siting of the churches, on their magnificence and stability, the importance of towers 'for the Ornament of the Towne' and the desirability of a specifically ecclesiastical grandeur, 'the most Solemn and Awfull Appearance both without and within.' At the same time there are many very practical points, such as considerations of visibility, audibility, security from fire, a compromise between good illumination and 'many windows making a Church cold in Winter, hot in Summer', and the avoidance of burials

[14] Vanbrugh's designs are mentioned in Lambeth Palace Library, Fifty Churches Commission Minutes, I, pp.215, 267, 270, 284; Committee Minutes, p.76. The reference on a Hawksmoor drawing of 1714 for St George-in-the-East to 'Mr Vanbrugh in Duke [Street]' is to William, who is recorded there as early as 1699 (*English Homes*, p. xxxi) and in 1711 (HMC Portland v, p.25). From 1711 to 1716 William paid rates there (Rate Books, Westminster City Library, Archives). The books for 1715 and 1717 are missing, but that for 1716 contains both William and, elsewhere in the street, Captain Vanderbrooke, who must be Sir John's brother Charles who shared the house with him from Oct. 1715 (see p.171). The church front (Pl.70) and a side elevation of the same tower are V & A D.104 and 110/1891. They suggest some connection with the tower of Hawksmoor's Christ Church, Spitalfields. See also p.117, n.19.

[15] Bodl.MS.Rawl. B.376, f.351; copy, MS.Eng.Hist. b.2, ff.47–9; see Appendix E and Pl.55. For the handwriting compare Green, Pl.13. Vanbrugh mentions the English cemetery at Surat and gives a sketch of what he imagines to be its appearance; he would have known something about it from his kinsmen in the East India trade.

within the building.[16] Wren also wrote a memorandum for his fellow commissioners,[17] and careful reading shows the two documents to be more similar, Vanbrugh's more practical and Wren's less exclusively so, than it is customary to admit. The Vanbrugh memorandum is in fact laid out with a force and clarity, an awareness of practical problems and an undercurrent of wide architectural experience which read more like Hawksmoor, and an additional argument for his authorship is the writer's opening statement that 'the following Considerations are humbly offer'd to the Commissioners.' Hawksmoor was not a commissioner; Vanbrugh was. Wren's remarks were addressed to a friend on the Commission and contain an acknowledgment that the writer is himself a member. On internal evidence it is thus at least worth asking whether Vanbrugh was putting forward, as he was in a position to do, Hawksmoor's recommendations including the advice that 'necessary dispositions in the usefull part of the Fabrick, shou'd be made consistent with the utmost Grace that Architecture can produce, for the Beauty of it; which Grace shou'd generally be express'd in a plain, but Just and Noble Stile, without running into those many Divisions and Breaks which other buildings for Variety of uses may require; or such Gayety of Ornaments as may be proper to a Luxurious Palace.'

The theory of propriety, that the style of a building should be related to its purpose, is common in Renaissance architectural literature. It underlies much of the eclecticism of Hawksmoor's architecture as well as a number of statements in his surviving letters. Vanbrugh's correspondence tells us rather little about his views on architecture and even less about his reading; the only architectural book he mentions is 'Palladio in French, with the Plans of most of the Houses he built' which he asked Tonson to buy for him in Amsterdam in 1703 and which has been identified as the Paris edition of 1650, translated by Roland Fréart de Chambray.[18] Tonson was evidently successful, for some years later Vanbrugh believed he had left 'the French book of Paladio' in the masons' shed at Blenheim.[19] While for both Vanbrugh and Hawksmoor architecture was a directly visual art, to do with the beholder's eye, on the evidence of their correspondence it is Hawksmoor who appears as the theoretician, and the more likely to have drawn up the memorandum on the churches.

Apart from the dome of St Paul's and the slowing continuation of Greenwich Hospital, Blenheim and the New Churches were in effect the major public building works of the decade 1705–16. None of these projects was directly in the province of the Office of Works, although in artistic terms the 'luxurious palace' of Blenheim was a substitute for

[16] Most of the Vanbrugh family were buried in their vault in St Stephen Walbrook, which was probably concreted over during the repairs of 1850 (W. Thornbury, *Old and New London*, I, 1873, p.560).

[17] *Parentalia*, pp.318–21 (*Wren Soc.*, IX, pp.15–18), wrongly dated 1708.

[18] Webb, p.9 ('there is one without the Plans, but 'tis that with 'em I would have'). The identification was made by Whistler (1938), p.105. The Fréart edition was published by Edme Martin, printed archaistically in a Cinquecento style with blocks from the 1570 Venice edition. The 2nd Earl of Essex, by whom Vanbrugh was 'Souc'd a Herald Extraordinary' shortly before his request to Tonson (Webb, p.9), owned a copy of this edition, which is now in the Fowler Architectural Collection of the Johns Hopkins University, Baltimore, with his bookplate dated 1701 (*Catalogue*, 1961, p.179).

[19] Vanbrugh's report of mislaying the book in 1711: Webb, p.236. Joynes replied (3 March 1711): 'I enquir'd of Kitt Cash about ye French book of Paladio he can't find it, no where here, he supposes either you or Mr. Hawksmoor to have taken it with you' (BM MS.Add.19605, f.131). S. Lang, 'Vanbrugh's Theory and Hawksmoor's Buildings', *Jnl Soc. of Archit. Historians*, XXIV, 1965, p.128, believes that Vanbrugh's proposals for the churches are based on passages in Alberti's *De Re Aedificatoria*, presumably in the French translation of Jean Martin, Paris, 1553. But it is worth making a careful study of Palladio, especially of Book IV (on Temples) in the light of Vanbrugh's remarks.

the rebuilt Whitehall that faded every year further from probability. Vanbrugh's Comptrollership coincided with a period of artistic inertia in the Works, the consequence of economy in Queen Anne's reign and of George I's lack of interest in English life and architecture. The return on the effort Vanbrugh put into the office of Comptroller took three forms: firstly, financial – a regular salary and perquisites; secondly, what is now called job satisfaction, and thirdly the hope, if no more, of artistic achievement of a public and permanent nature.

The financial return was modest and slow to be paid, although the office gave him also official residences in Scotland Yard, Hampton Court, and Kensington, which he was able to let for rent.[20] The Comptrollership placed him at the centre of English architecture, although neither the Castle Howard nor, on his own reckoning (p.57), the Blenheim commission depended on his official status. For a number of years he hoped, with varying degrees of justification, to succeed Wren – who in 1702 was seventy – as Surveyor. His dismissal in March 1713 dashed hopes which were both deeply held and well founded;[21] they must have been resumed at his reinstatement with the establishment of the Board of Works. But when Benson, who had ousted Wren in 1718, was succeeded the following year by Sir Thomas Hewett, hope foundered, and at the end of 1719 he told Tonson that the disappointment was the harder because 'I might have had [it] formerly, but refus'd it, out of Tendernesse to Sr Chr: Wren.'[22]

With the exception of the Kensington Orangery incident we know little about Vanbrugh's first term as Comptroller; his second term, however, is well documented by the minutes of the new Board, at which, until Wren's dismissal, Vanbrugh 'in effect presided.'[23] Between the first minuted meeting of 6 May 1715 and Benson's dismissal in July 1719 he attended 224 out of 250 meetings; his later attendances were fewer, but over the whole period from 1715 to his death the total of his attendances was 383 out of 691 meetings, or sixty per cent; the last was three days before his death.[24] Most of the business was of a routine nature; the more assiduous early attendances can be accounted for at first by his concern for Wren, his hopes for the Surveyorship and his interest in reform; subsequently he was motivated by mistrust of Benson. The decline after 1719 was partly due to periods of ill-health and to periods of absence on private business in the provinces, but in his later fifties he had lost some of the boundless energy of his early architectural career and it was evident to him that the future both of the Works and of English architecture lay in other hands. In June 1715 he was additionally appointed Surveyor of Gardens and Waters; this office, which was a revival of one concerned with gardens held by Hugh May and allowed

[20] Arrangements at the time of the revocation of his patent as Comptroller: CTB 1713, p.178; 1714, pp.29, 199. Details of rents in Account Book.

[21] Vanbrugh wrote to the Mayor of Woodstock on 25 Jan. 1713 of 'the continual plague and bitter persecution [Marlborough] has most barbarously been followed with for two years past' (Webb, p.54). According to the Duchess of Marlborough Vanbrugh's 'want of good Spelling' caused the letter to be 'carried to one Major by which means my Ld Oxford was acquainted with it' (Whistler, p.127, where the event and its sequel are discussed). In the wake of the disgrace of the Marlboroughs the royal warrant was issued revoking Vanbrugh's patent on 31 March 1713 (CTB 1713, p.168). One consequence was the payment in Dec. 1713 of nearly three years' arrears of his salary, amounting to £734 17*s* (ibid., pp.535, 537). For Vanbrugh to Marlborough on his hopes in the Works, see Whistler, p.241.

[22] Webb, p.123. The offer he refused was perhaps made by Carlisle as First Lord in 1715.

[23] Whistler, p.244.

[24] See Appendix G.

to lapse on his death in 1684, was now expanded to include both ornamental waters and the water supply of the royal palaces. The appointment was made during Lord Carlisle's second short term of office as First Lord of the Treasury, and undoubtedly Carlisle was the prime mover. Hawksmoor later reminded him that the post 'was a place yr Lordshp knows was made for Sr John V-.' It was nevertheless rather more than a sinecure, and some documents survive concerning Vanbrugh's administration.[25] In view of his concern with a number of large private gardens (p.107) and Carlisle's own preoccupation with the Castle Howard estate (p.20) the appointment of 'a particular officer in the quality of a surveyor' (as his patent said) was well considered, and not unconnected with moves, in which he was already involved, to reform the Works.

There is no doubt that the establishment which Wren had built up during the last third of the seventeenth century on a basis of individual freedom and responsibility was open to abuse, especially after 1700: in later years Wren, who himself was not beyond cutting administrative corners, had less time and energy for supervision. The widespread allegations of frauds and abuses countenanced if not initiated by him were certainly magnified, and frequently motivated by personal or political jealousies. Nevertheless the case of the Orangery, in which Vanbrugh's pressure on him for action found no response, was undoubtedly not the only example of irregularity in the old man's administration. Late in 1714, while Vanbrugh was out of office and Lord Halifax was at the Treasury, the latter invited his suggestions for the reform of the Office of Works. Vanbrugh's proposals, dated 29 November, included the abolition of several offices and a reduction of the number of clerks, stricter controls on private building within the royal palaces, and measures to ensure the competence of the remaining officers.[26] These proposals, which were intended to save money and increase efficiency, were the product of Vanbrugh's practical experience in the Works. Not all of them were implemented, but by 1718 he at least was convinced that he had considerably improved the economy of the Office.[27] He may also have helped Halifax, by private consultation after his reinstatement as Comptroller, to frame the new orders for the Office issued in the spring of 1715, which among other things constituted the new Board of Works to assist Sir Christopher Wren; another surviving document contains a series of comments on the draft of the order, signed by Vanbrugh on behalf of his colleagues.[28]

Much of this work was undone by Benson who, according to Hawksmoor, 'got more in one year (for confounding the kings Workes) than Sr Christ Wren did in 40 years. for his honest endeavours.' His misdemeanours are well enough documented in the Treasury

[25] Hawksmoor's remark: Downes (1959), p.249. For duties and appointment, CTB 1714–15, pp.550, 691–2. Two letters as Surveyor, Webb, pp.165, 166. See also PRO Works 6/113.

[26] Webb, pp.247–8.

[27] Vanbrugh's belief in his own performance: Webb, pp.96, 104, 115; Whistler, pp.244–5. By careful and specious statistics he also contrived to exaggerate the extent and efficacy of minor reductions in expenditure and thereby, as many a statesman has done since, 'to pose as an economical reformer' (*King's Works*, v, 1975, p.56).

[28] Orders for the Office from Ladyday 1715, CTB 1714–15, pp.493–6; Vanbrugh's comments, Webb, pp.248–50. It is suggested with some plausibility (*King's Works*, v, 1975, p.53) that it was the achievement of the new Board of Works, with Vanbrugh as effective chairman in 1715–17, and not of Wren in the preceding years (Downes (1966), p.7) that 'the Clerks of the Works whatever they may have bin formerly are now required to be well skill'd in all kinds of admeasurement: in Drawing making Plans of the Palaces taking Elevations and competently verst in all parts of Architecture which some among them are to a great degree of Excellence they must be likewise knowing in the goodness choice and value of all sorts of Materialls' (Memorial from Wren, Vanbrugh and other officers to the Treasury, minuted 23 July 1717: PRO T 1/208, No.3).

Papers to show that Hawksmoor's strong censures in letters to Lord Carlisle and Vanbrugh's to Newcastle are not exaggerated.[29] Vanbrugh's last campaign in the Works was with Benson, who attempted to dislodge him a second time from the Comptrollership, but failed owing to the personal support of Vanbrugh by Lord Sunderland as First Lord of the Treasury. The reports by several officers which led to Benson's own dismissal include one in Vanbrugh's hand, from which we learn that 'under Specious pretences of saving money to his Majesty . . . he got Sr Chr; Wren turn'd out, & himself put into his Place; His Brother Lately come from a Merch[an]t in Holland, Clerk of the Workes in the Room of Mr Hawksmoor . . . And his Agent Colen Campbell, chief clerk in the Room of Mr Wren.' Further, that for six months 'no Business was done in the Office', that Benson formulated a specious contract for the upkeep of the palaces very much to his own advantage, that he wrongly certified the House of Lords as dangerous and set up shores and props 'more dangerous to the Buildings than their own decay', and gave other evidence 'of the neglect of his Duty . . . as well as of his Ignorance & Obstinacy.'[30]

But Vanbrugh was finally to be disappointed in his hopes of the Surveyorship which he had refused during Wren's tenure. The history painter James Thornhill, who had pretentions towards architecture, was recommended by the outcast Benson and by the Duchess of Marlborough, neither of whom wished Vanbrugh well. His comment on this move shows how far the architect of Blenheim considered himself not only the rightful successor to Wren, but also, two decades after his own conversion from other avocations, the one properly qualified. He told Newcastle:[31]

> What part my Ld Sun[derlan]d takes, I don't hear said; tho' I think 'tis impossible he can Suffer such a thing to pass. Twou'd be a pleasant Joke to the World, to See a Painter made Surveyor of the Works, in Order to Save money; When all the Small knowledge or tast they ever have of it, is only in the Great expensive part, As Collumns, Arches, Bass reliefs &c which they just learn enough of, to help fill up their Pictures. But to think that Such a Volatile Gentleman as Thornhill, Shou'd turn his thoughts & Application to the duty of a Surveyors business, is a Monstrous project.

Sunderland would be unlikely to promote such a project if its chief advocate was his mother-in-law, but in any case there was another candidate, a Whig like Vanbrugh, eight years his senior, an amateur architect as Vanbrugh had been, and one with friends at court if without great talent; since 1696 he had been Surveyor of Woods North of the Trent; more recently he had first encouraged and then discreetly abandoned Galilei in England (p.49). Thomas Hewett was appointed and received a knighthood the following year. Vanbrugh's next move was to press unsuccessfully for the reversion of the Surveyorship or at least for the confirmation of the Comptrollership for life instead of at the King's pleasure. He also attempted to gain redress for the loss of offices suffered under Benson by Hawksmoor and Kynaston; the latter was successful, but Hawksmoor 'after ten thousand

[29] Hawksmoor's comments: Downes (1959), p.246. Vanbrugh and Benson: Webb, pp.98, 100, 109.

[30] Appendix H.

[31] Webb, p.117.

Assurances . . . of his Friendship to him' received nothing until 1721 when Vanbrugh managed to make him Deputy Comptroller. He was not reinstated as Secretary to the Board until the spring of 1726 when Hewett died a fortnight after Vanbrugh.[32]

Vanbrugh's experience combined with his political orthodoxy and his circle of friends might seem more than a match for such a contender as Hewett, but not everything was in his favour. Allegiances within the Whig party were complex and not necessarily constant. The spectre raised by Shaftesbury, however unreasonable, was still fresh in Whig minds, of Wren as a life-long artistic dictator. There can have been little reason at the time to suppose that elevation to the apex of the architectural profession would have moderated either Vanbrugh's belief in plain speaking or his uncompromising architectural style, and for all his antipathy to the Duchess of Marlborough, Sunderland understood very well the role of both these characteristics in the history of Blenheim. The First Lord would have been less sensitive than we are today to the question of propriety in Vanbrugh's stepping into the shoes of a predecessor whom he had been instrumental in dislodging; on the other hand it is likely that Vanbrugh now suffered, as John Webb had done before him and Hawksmoor still did, from the enduring English distrust of the professional in the higher stages of administration. He came to the conclusion, as he told Carlisle in 1722, that architecture was 'not a Trade I believe for any body to recommend themselves by at Court' and entertained instead hopes of some other benefit from the King 'tho' not as an Architect.'[33] At fifty-eight he had a reasonable life expectancy and several years' start on Hewett. Yet Marlborough's 'something lasting', the knighthood, was to be his first and last significant benefit from the reign of George I. His private commissions during those twelve years were as distinguished as the architecture of the Crown was the reverse. In the earlier years he made three attempts for which plans survive to interest the King in palaces that would bring credit to them both: at St James's, at Kensington and at Hampton Court.

The drawings for St James's include a survey 'as it now is 1712' and plans for a new south range towards the park as well as for a complete rebuilding in stages.[34] One drawing has a reference to the King; thus while the plans may have been made in Anne's reign, they were submitted after August 1714, perhaps soon after, and some are titled in French, the language used between George and his court. The complete project (Fig.11A) some 440 by 340 feet, includes a massive gateway to Pall Mall on the north, similar in plan to the east gate at Blenheim (Pl.51). This is on the main axis of a symmetrical palace and leads into the largest of the nine interior courts; on the far side is a portico fronting an entrance hall which leads to a chapel on the east, a staircase and a proscenium theatre on the west, and southwards to a columned and probably clerestoried hall between the King's and Queen's Sides on the south front. The centre of the south range has an octastyle portico which, like the hexastyle one in the main court, is of Vanbrugh's favourite form with square piers instead of columns set close at the corners. The chapel, with short transept arms on the cross axis and a semicircular apse, is almost identical in plan to those proposed at both Castle Howard and Blenheim (Fig.9).

32 In 1715–16 Hewett was made Surveyor of Woods North and South of the Trent. Vanbrugh and Hewett: Webb, pp.114–15, 117.

33 Webb, p.149.

34 Royal Library, Windsor, Portfolio 58. Unsigned but drawn by a recognizable office hand and inscribed by Vanbrugh.

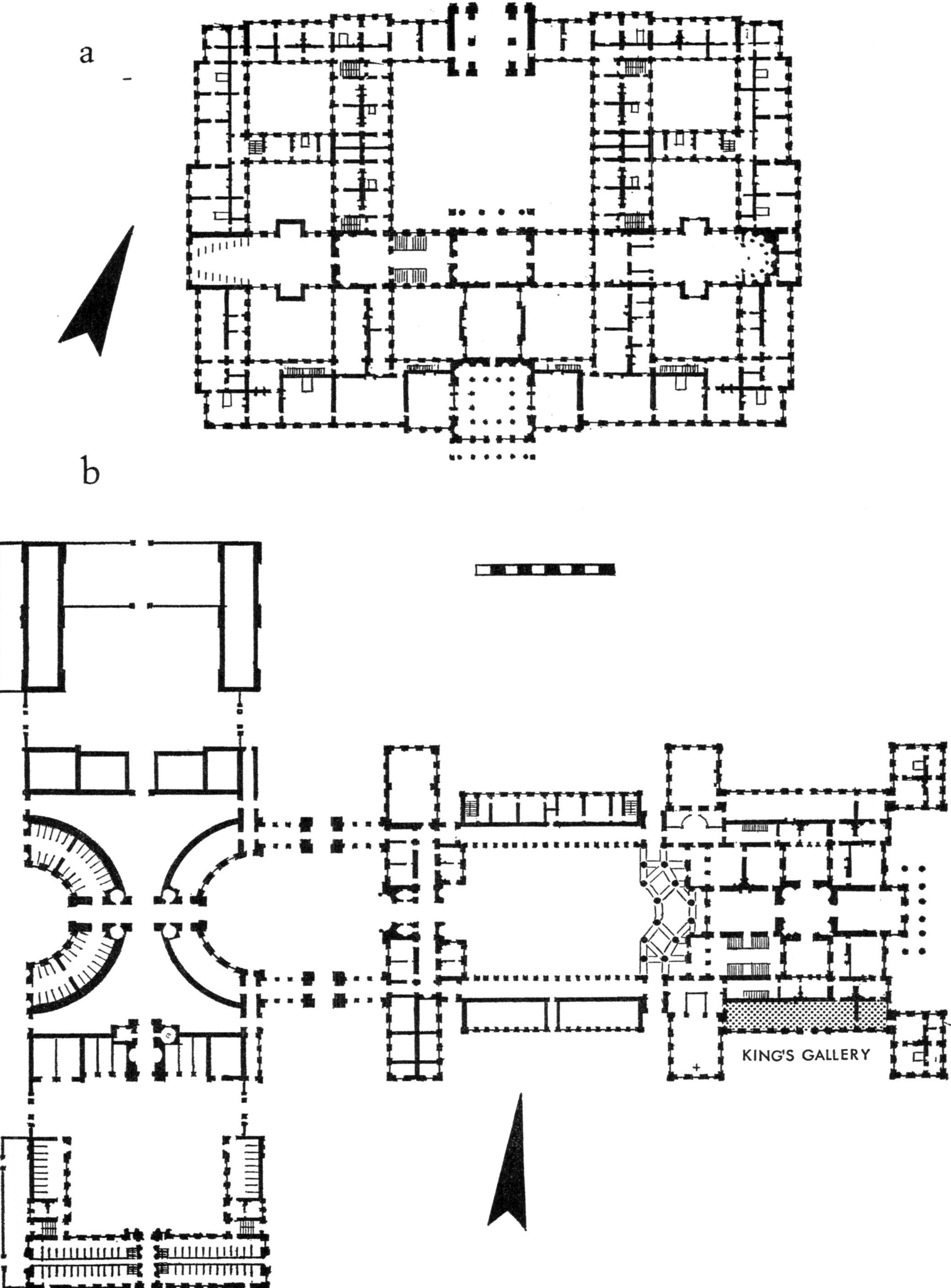

11 Projects for St James's and Kensington Palaces. From drawings in the Royal Library, Windsor Castle.

The Kensington plan[35] is undated but identical in draughtsmanship and anticipates the new inner rooms built in 1718–19 to replace the centre of the original house (Fig.11B). The new central room is to be circular, with large niches on the diagonals, and was probably to be domed.[36] The existing King's Gallery on the south is repeated on the north, and the east front towards the gardens and Hyde Park has a giant hexastyle portico two columns deep and thus similar in extent to the final design for Eastbury (Pl.140). The west side towards a new arcaded base court has a deep vaulted or beamed vestibule on the ground floor; a gallery across this court leads to a second court with north and south gateways and further west a large stable complex. The centre of the stables consists of two semicircular buildings placed back to back and supporting at their conjunction, on the evidence of the spiral staircases on the plan, a massive tower. This proposal bore no more fruit than that for St James's, and the new rooms of 1718–19 appear to have been designed by Benson and Campbell, although Vanbrugh was concerned administratively and made arrangements with Newcastle, as Lord Chamberlain, to convey the wooden model for them to Kensington for the King to see.[37] He also designed the water tower on the palace green (p.123).

At Hampton Court in about 1716 Vanbrugh revived Wren's scheme of 1689 for a court with arcaded wings and corner pavilions on the axis of the Bushy Park avenue on the north of the Great Hall, but this came to nothing.[38] He was also concerned in the same year with the completion of the Prince of Wales's rooms in the north-east corner of Wren's palace; the three small panelled rooms in the corner contain characteristic marble chimneypieces similar to ones at Blenheim and Grimsthorpe (Pls 98–101) and he must also have been responsible for the coved ceiling and handsome chimneypiece of the Music (now Public Dining) Room and the life-size yeomen-herms of the chimneypiece in the Guard Chamber which have a primitive and unclassical boldness worthy of a Jacobean house, and whose nearest parallel in his work is the ruined hall fireplace at Seaton Delaval (Pls 97a, b).

Thus Vanbrugh's architectural success was no greater than his personal advancement, and there is some evidence that his disappointment with the state of his art at court comprehended more than the failure of schemes for individual buildings: of not only administrative but also, prompted by Shaftesbury's *Letter*, stylistic leadership. He could have supplied Shaftesbury's national style, and might have done so if Campbell had not stolen his thunder with *Vitruvius Britannicus*; the fact that his would have been a style largely developed by Hawksmoor is immaterial. The argument depends to a considerable extent on inference from matters already covered in this chapter, and in particular his attitude to architecture as an art, as a profession, and as a political activity, but there are some more

[35] Same portfolio, inscribed 'Dessein general pour Kensington'; another version at All Souls, I, 4.

[36] A similar domed room appears in a design possibly related to Eastbury, about 1716 (Whistler, Pl.71).

[37] References to the model in undated letters, Webb, pp.155–6. The three letters (Nos 151–3) are possibly connected and not in the right order. No.151 can be dated by the reference to the Rev. Ralph Baynes: it is endorsed 'about the living of Swallow in Lincolnshire', and Baynes was instituted under Newcastle's patronage on 23 Nov. 1717 (List of incumbents, Lincs. CRO). A plan of the new rooms (RIBA, *Campbell*, [14]) is marked with the area in Squares, as are many of the house plans in the Elton collection. See also *King's Works*, V, 1975, p.196, n.3.

[38] The plan (now PRO Works 34/32) is redrawn in E. Law, *History of Hampton Court*, III, 1891, p.80, and in *King's Works*, V, 1975, Fig.6C. For the executed work see Webb, pp.73, 77, 154.

substantial pointers. One is the extent to which, in the last decade of his life, a characteristic Vanbrughian style was established for the buildings of the Board of Ordnance while in individual cases the degree of resemblance varies widely. There are particular reasons for his influence in this particular Government department (p.124) but 'Ordnance Vanbrugh' existed simultaneously with the spread of Palladianism and may serve as a model of what might have happened in the Office of Works under his leadership.

A second pointer is the degree of similarity between his later style and Palladianism in spite of their irretrievable differences. One aspect of this similarity was plainness, but another was the change in the direction of Vanbrugh's sources about 1715 or slightly earlier. The Venetian window, an arched light between two upright rectangles, is considered a Palladian hallmark; nevertheless, not a single example occurs in Campbell's first volume. On the other hand, it appears by 1714 in Hawksmoor's work, in Archer's St Paul, Deptford, and probably earlier on the east and west fronts of Kings Weston (Pl.88). The re-orientation is confirmed at the same time in the early design for Eastbury (Pl.86) and more generally by a shifting of Vanbrugh's vocabulary away from France and towards not Baroque but Renaissance Italy.

The final piece of evidence is in another letter which reflects the wisdom of years, written in August 1721 to Brigadier-General William Watkins, Keeper of the King's Roads and a protégé of the Duke of Newcastle:[39]

> Poor Hawksmoor, What a Barbarous Age, have his fine, ingenious Parts fallen into. What wou'd Monsr: Colbert in France have given for Such a Man? I don't Speak as to his Architecture alone, but the Aids he cou'd have given him, in almost all his brave Designs for the Police. A thing I never expect to hear talk'd of in England, Where the Parts of most of the Great men I have Seen or read of, have rarely turn'd to any further Account, Than getting a Great Deal of Money, and turning it through their Guts into a House of Office.

The Police means the general organization of the state, and the brave designs for it were those of Jean-Baptiste Colbert, the archetype of the dedicated and incorruptible public servant. That his service had been to the greatest of absolutist monarchs, Louis XIV, did not diminish Vanbrugh's admiration for him or alter his conviction that such a man would have been good for England. Vanbrugh believed in letting the expert do the job, and it does not sound as if he was convinced by Shaftesbury's parallel between absolutist monarchy and Wren's control of the Works; in any event the latter can hardly have been borne out by his own experience. The difference for him between the Invalides or Versailles or St Peter's and Greenwich or Blenheim was that the latter were built by free men; it was, in the broadest sense, a political difference, not a stylistic one. He thus considered his style and Hawksmoor's perfectly acceptable for Whig Britain, and he had

[39] Webb, p.138. See also Webb, *Baroque Art* (British Academy Lecture), 1947, and K. Downes, 'Vanbrugh and the British Style', *Listener*, XCV, 1 April 1976, pp.407–9.

no doubt that they were capable of finishing the job if they were given the tools.[40] They were not, and English architecture was undoubtedly thereby the poorer – and not necessarily the cheaper. It is to Vanbrugh's private ventures in building and gardening in the reign of George I that we must now return.[41]

[40] Apart from his Comptrollership, Vanbrugh made a number of private incursions into the realm of public works. In Feb. 1718 he applied unsuccessfully for a thirty-one year lease of the quarries at Portland at £20 per annum, on condition that he maintain the wharf, crane and tracks at his own expense and permit quarrying by the Crown (CTB 1718, pp.186, 34). In Oct. 1722 he petitioned for a similar lease of the wharf at Somerset House, which was 'lying at present, in a manner useless, for want of due repair', with similar conditions and reservations, but this was rejected on the grounds that Somerset House might at any time become a royal residence again (PRO T1/240, No.65). The *London Journal* for 16 March 1723 (No. CXC, p.5) carried a note 'that Sir John Vanbrugh, in his Scheme for new Paving the Cities of London and Westminster, amongst other Things, proposes a Tax on all Gentlemens Coaches; to stop all the channels in the Streets, and to carry all the Water off by Dreins and Common Sewers under Ground.' A year later he had hopes, which were not realized, of persuading Lord Morpeth to introduce a paving bill into the House of Lords (Webb, pp.159–60). Shortly before his death Vanbrugh entered in his Account Book (9 March 1726) a payment of £2 2*s*. 'for Carrying about the Paving Petition.' For his concern with Miller the bricklayer, see p.177.

[41] Vanbrugh wrote on 28 Sep. 1713 that he had been at Cholmondeley 'a second Time' and 'concerted a generall scheme for what is left to do' (Whistler, p.242). From the Cholmondeley papers (Cheshire CRO) it appears that the south end of the house had already been rebuilt, and probably designed, by William and Richard Smith. Of the plates in *Vitruvius Britannicus* (which does not mention his name) only the unexecuted design for the north front (Pl.95 here) can therefore be by Vanbrugh.

Chapter 6

Castles and Landscapes

'One may find a great deal of Pleasure, in building a Palace for another; when one shou'd find very little, in living in't ones Self.' This was Vanbrugh's comment, to Tonson in November 1719, on Blenheim three years after his resignation as its architect.[1] At the time he was working on the Great Room at Claremont, the last stage in the conversion of Chargate into a palace for the Duke of Newcastle. At the beginning of 1719 he had married a second cousin of the Duke, and although on this occasion he wrote from Whitehall, he offered his wife's hospitality (with a promise in her own hand 'to neither cheat nor wrangle' at cards) at Greenwich,[2] where he was about to move into the largest and the most remarkable of the houses he built for his own habitation (Pls 102, 103). On 3 March 1718 he bought a ninety-nine year lease from Sir Michael Biddulph of a field and other land near the top of Greenwich Hill between Greenwich Park and Blackheath; there he built Vanbrugh Castle and four other houses, together with outbuildings, gateways, and escarpments on the north where the ground begins to slope down towards the river.[3]

In August 1716 he had succeeded Wren as Surveyor to Greenwich Hospital, but the main attractions of the site on Greenwich Hill must have been social and scenic. Blackheath was on the main London/Dover road. Vanbrugh's neighbours towards Blackheath were to include his friend Brigadier Richards of the Ordnance, the elder James Craggs, the Duchess of Bolton, and the painter Thornhill. Greenwich Park was a favoured spot for seventeenth-century landscape painters, and even now on a clear day there is a fine view, where the trees allow it, north-west over the Hospital towards the City of London and beyond to regions in Middlesex and Essex. Vanbrugh was writing from 'my country morsell' a few days before Christmas 1717,[4] but that was an existing house which he and his brother Charles rented jointly for three years from March 1717 from Sir William Saunderson.[5] A score of subsequent letters are headed from Greenwich, including one of late 1719 from which it appears that in his absence Newcastle 'was pleas'd to Storm my

[1] Webb, p.122.

[2] Webb, p.123.

[3] Vanbrugh's will (PROB 11/608, fol.84). Carter (n.7 below) said in 1815 that the leases were falling due. Vanbrugh paid rates on the field and the Castle site from 1718. The Account Book gives the date of the lease and shows that on 31 Dec. 1719 Vanbrugh agreed to mortgage the Castle to his brother Charles; this appears to date its first completion.

[4] Webb, p.96.

[5] Account Book, 9 March 1717. There is a sketch-elevation showing Vanbrughian proposals for Saunderson's house, *Elton Drawings*, No.129v, Pl. XLa. This house was some way east of the Vanbrugh Castle site, but Saunderson owned more than one. Until Midsummer 1715 he rented a house near the Tilt Yard to Dr Oliver, the Physician to Greenwich Hospital, for £30 per annum (PRO Adm 67/4, 23 June 1715, RIBA E5/7) and it is probably the house that Vanbrugh leased for £40. William Saunderson or Sanderson was a Director of Greenwich Hospital, and Captain of the *Peregrine*, which brought George I to England in 1714; the Captain was knighted on arrival at Greenwich on 18 Sept. (Le Neve, p.511).

Castle yesterday.'[6] But both the Castle and the private residential estate at its gate grew over several years in much the same way as some of the palaces he designed for others. Little more than Vanbrugh Castle itself remains now, although it is possible to form a reasonable picture of the rest. The fullest account is that given in the *Gentleman's Magazine* for 1815 by the antiquary John Carter in his series of historical articles on architecture. Carter's eye was fallible and he attributed to Vanbrugh a house east of the Castle that was only built some years later; his matter-of-fact and literal descriptions, which have the flavour by turns of the architect, the pathologist and the house-agent, can fortunately be amplified by a variety of illustrations ranging from drawings from Vanbrugh's office to photographs and surveys made early in the present century.[7] But Carter, writing at the height of the Picturesque Age, of a group of buildings nearly a century old, was not immune to the 'boldness of parts, and . . . unbounded flow of external decoration peculiar to himself', to 'the romantic knight's peculiar feelings and his peculiar taste', the 'wild luxuriance of his mind', and even to the 'most majestic full-grown oak (coeval with the pile, no doubt of the knight's planting)' in the castle courtyard. It is hard to doubt, also, that Vanbrugh Castle was in the mind of Sir Joshua Reynolds towards the end of his *13th Discourse* (1786) in which he devoted some paragraphs to architecture as an art not imitative, like painting and sculpture, but associative, a topic which he developed almost entirely in relation to Vanbrugh. Although the only works he named are Blenheim and Castle Howard he referred to the delight given by

> . . . whatever building brings to our remembrance ancient customs and manners, such as the castles of the barons of ancient chivalry . . . Hence it is that towers and battlements are so often selected by the painter and poet to make a part of the composition of their landscape; and it is from hence, in a great degree, that, in the buildings of Vanbrugh, who was a poet as well as an architect, there is a greater display of imagination, than we shall find perhaps in any other.

Coming through Greenwich Park or up Maze Hill one would reach first the curtain wall and crenellated gateway of Vanbrugh Castle (Pl.113), but most travellers would approach the estate from the main road through Blackheath and come first to a larger gateway, comprising two habitable towers joined by a half-oval arch, at the south end of what Vanbrugh called 'the field' (Pl.104). Through the gateway the track, sinuous rather than straight, led to a sequence of houses all on the right (Fig.12). The first and third appear to have been similar and probably identical, although Carter dismissed the first as having been considerably altered. These were the two 'White Towers' which Vanbrugh bequeathed to his sisters Victoria and Robina; that on the north is recorded in the corner of one of Buckler's sketches (Pl.107) and that on the south is shown on the right of Sandby's drawing of the gateway. The White Towers were built specifically of white bricks and not of London stocks like the Castle and Vanbrugh House. 'The New White Tower' is also recorded in a plan and elevation from Vanbrugh's office (Pl.110). The

[6] Webb, p.119.

[7] *Gent. Mag.*, LXXXV, i, 1815, pp.326–8, 517–9. Carter wrongly attributed to Vanbrugh the Red House, built for Sir Gregory Page in 1736 and demolished in 1854 (Hasted's *History of Kent, Blackheath Hundred*, ed. Drake, 1886, p.78). The Account Book establishes the dates of Vanbrugh's buildings. See also *London Topog. Record*, IV, 1907, p.23 ff; *Greenwich Antiquarian Soc.*, I, 3, 1912; N. Pevsner, 'Richard Payne Knight', *Art Bulletin*, XXXI, 1949, esp. pp.294–5; *Country Life*, CLIX, 1976, pp.1406–8.

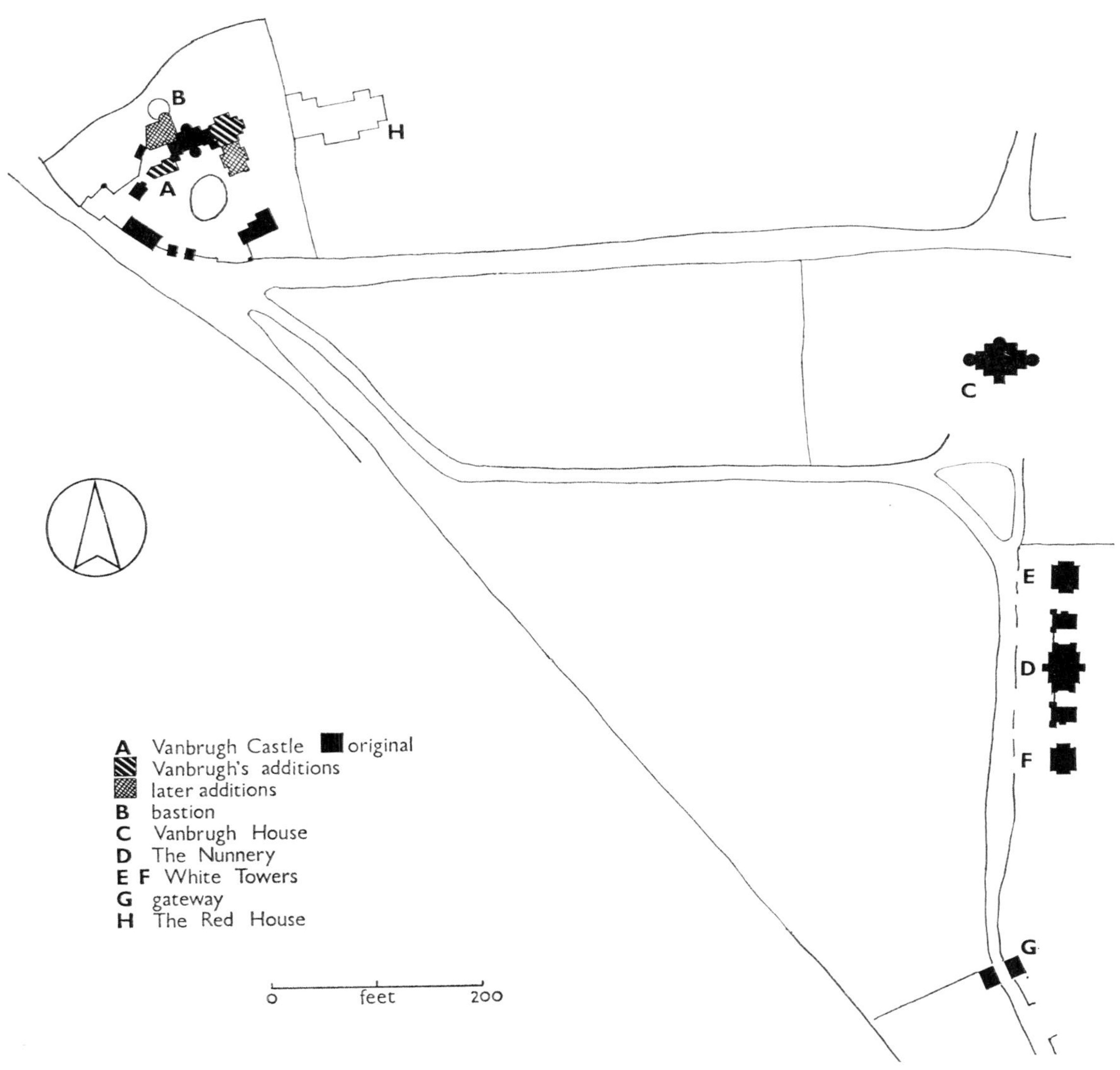

12 Plan of the Vanbrugh Estate at Greenwich.

towers were of three storeys above a basement, with machicolated towers at the ends containing chimneys at one end and stairs at the other. They were entered at the side so that their three-bay fronts presented only windows; their formula of banded rustication and an abrupt change of plane towards the ends was not unlike that of Vanbrugh's original Whitehall house (Pls 111, 24). Between the towers lay a large symmetrical bungalow known as the Nunnery; the name is recorded by the antiquary William Stukeley, who sketched it on 16 June 1721.[8] At either side of the main building a small yard led to an additional building of one room with an attic above (Pls 106, 107). The name suggests a medievalizing joke, in reference to his brother Philip, for whom it was built: he was probably widowed by this time and may have been looked after by his unmarried sisters. It would

[8] Stukeley's drawing, *Society of Antiquaries*, L.C.II, p.23 (Whistler, Pl.91).

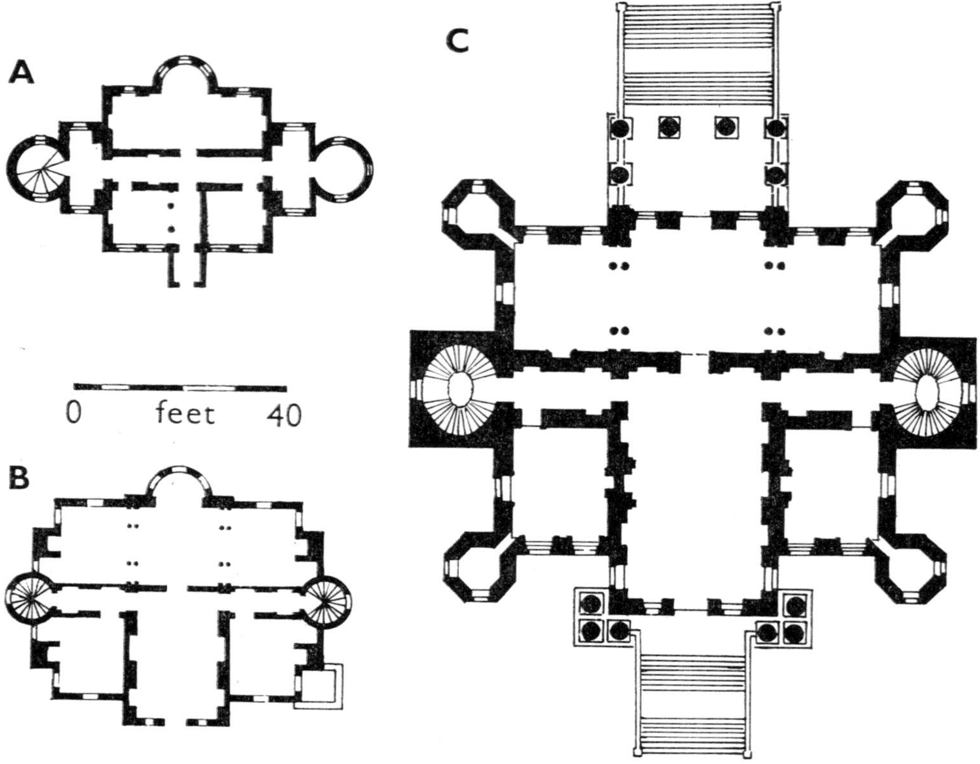

13 Plans of (A) Vanbrugh House, (B) an unidentified project, (C) Seaton Delaval.

appear also to be 'the low house' in which the architect's son was living in February 1743.[9]

Beyond the second White Tower, and facing south instead of west, stood the building variously known later as 'Mince Pie House' or 'Vanbrugh House' (Pl.108). This was built for, and owned by, the architect's brother Charles.[10] It was originally of two storeys above a basement, but by Carter's time an attic had been added to raise it to the height of the round towers at the ends, one of which contained the staircase. The centre of the garden front projected into a bow-window similar to that on the east side of Blenheim, and Stukeley sketched this house in August 1722 because on his previous visit it was not finished. He called it 'Castellulum' (little castle) and it appears to share a common derivation in plan with the most romantic of Vanbrugh's larger houses, Seaton Delaval, which was commissioned in 1719 (p.103). A sketch-plan among the Elton drawings (Fig.13B) is for a house which has stair towers at the sides joined to the hall by a corridor, with a long room occupying the whole of the garden side, divided into three by double screens of columns and opening into a bow window. Seaton is similar in plan but larger in

[9] Charles Vanbrugh's will, PROB 11/740, fol.182. The side yards of the Nunnery had been filled in with extra rooms before J. C. Buckler's drawing of 1823 (Pl.107). This house first appears in the rate books in 1721 and was rented by Philip from the architect from 25 Dec. 1720. The White Towers appear as identical in a naive late-eighteenth-century panoramic view (National Maritime Museum, Charnock's Views, III, p.27: *Greenwich and Lewisham Antiquarian Soc.*, VIII/4, 1976, Pl.VII).

[10] Stukeley's drawing (Bodl.MS.Top.Gen. d.14, f.55, Pl.108) is closer than the Elton drawing (No.167, Pl.109) to what was built. The plan (Fig.13A) is based on G. H. Lovegrove's survey (*Greenwich Antiquarian Soc.*) in the light of Carter's account. The amount of Charles Vanbrugh's debt to Sir John for the house was agreed on 6 Sept. 1722 (Account Book) and it was first rated in 1723.

dimensions (Fig.13C) and with the addition of octagonal corner turrets; a genetic relation with the Elton drawing is implied by the pencilled addition to the latter of a square tower at one corner. The house at Greenwich was smaller than the one in the drawing but retained the same features (Fig.13A).[11] In July 1722 when Vanbrugh's son Charles was nearly two, the architect told Lord Carlisle:[12]

> I fancy your Lordships Godson will be a Professor [of Architecture] for he knows Pillars, & Arches and Round Windows & Square Windows already, whether he finds them in a Book or in the Streets, and is much pleas'd with a House I am building him in the Field at Greenh: it being a Tower of White Bricks, only one Room and a Closet on a floor. He talks everything, is much given to Rhyming, and has a Great turn to dry joking. What these Seeds may grow to, God knows.

Conceivably this could have been a playhouse only big enough for a child. On the other hand, allowing for the inclusion of the staircase it fits the plan and description of the New White Tower. There is one double reference in Vanbrugh's account book to 'Charles's House' and 'Jack's house', and by collating references[13] it is evident that the north tower (or White House), built in 1722–3, was intended for Charles and the southern or second tower, begun late in 1722 and finished in about 1724, was intended for the younger boy, John, who was born in February 1722 but died little more than a year later.[14] Nor was young Charles to fulfil any of the promise of this letter; instead of building or rhyming among his father's professions he chose soldiering and was mortally wounded at Fontenoy on 11 May 1745, when he was yet under twenty-five.[15] In material as well as human terms so short and hidden a life seems to have been totally wasted, especially when we remember that at a similar age his father had got no further than a French prison. And yet, unless the son was a prodigy, the games in the field would seem to have been the father's, and the rhymes and the dry jokes; the father was the inspiration of the little community on Greenwich Hill, and it was when he died that the joy went from it.

Some of the force and quality of that inspiration still comes over to us from the portrait of Vanbrugh, attributed to Thomas Murray, in the National Portrait Gallery (Frontispiece). By comparison with Kneller's Kit-Cat portrait (Pl.1) the sitter is some years older

[11] There was until about 1962 a small house south of Vanbrugh's gateway, known as Beechcroft, which may be related to a drawing (Elton No.127); both are illustrated in *Elton Drawings*, Pl. XIV. As it is not mentioned in the Account Book it may exemplify his influence rather than his hand, but it may be the house which William Pomeroy agreed on 16 April 1726 to build for Lady Vanbrugh (loose sheet in Account Book) and in which, according to her accounts (BIHR (Yarburgh)) she lived from 1728.

[12] 19 July 1722, Webb, p.149. See also Appendix M; p.206, n.227.

[13] Account Book: 5 Sept., 23 Oct. 1722; 21 Jan., 9 July, 5 Aug. 1723; 28 Feb. 1724.

[14] The midwife was paid on 14 Feb. 1722. On 18 June Vanbrugh told Carlisle, 'I am two Boys strong in the Nursery' (Webb, p.146). His godfather was apparently Lord Cobham (Account Book, 1 Jan. 1724). The child had been sent on 19 May 1722 to be nursed at Walton-on-Thames (Account Book) where he died and was buried on 28 March 1723 (Parish Register, Guildford Museum Muniment Room).

[15] Joseph Yorke's account of Charles's death, written to the family servant Jack Jones, was first printed from the original in BIHR (Yarburgh) in *Genealogist*, II, 1878, pp.239–40.

and maturer.[16] Whereas Kneller's architect, a pair of dividers in his hand, gazes confidently into the distance, the later figure looks directly and penetratingly at the beholder. The interpretation of portraits is a risky business but one which portraits invite, and in this case very little imagination is needed. These eyes missed neither the blunders of fools nor the scheming of knaves, political or artistic. But there is warmth as well as shrewdness; these surely are the eyes also that looked at domesticity and found it after all acceptable, at the prattle of a two-year-old and found there the reflection of his own humour. More surely they looked at the young Henrietta Maria Yarburgh and found the traditional but no less genuine refutation of all the confirmed bachelor's arguments. From the letter of Christmas 1699[17] onwards marriage had been a jest, a fate to be avoided. Nineteen years later, to the very day, he gave Newcastle the first sign that it was no longer so, writing from Yorkshire that 'tis so bloody Cold, I have almost a mind to Marry to keep myself warm.' The arrangements must by then have been made, and three weeks later a small party went to York for the marriage; on 24 January 1719 Vanbrugh sent Newcastle the news, adding that Tonson 'will be frightened out of his Witts' by it, for 'I was the last Man left, between him and Ruin.[18] Tonson, in Paris, gave him no cue, and only after five months' silence did Vanbrugh, with as much levity as he could muster, break the news to his old friend.

If the match was more premeditated than the other major steps in his life he was not one to say so; nor, except by opposites, would the conventional jocularity of his letters to associates indicate the depth of his feelings. In our own age it is fashionable to find celibacy incredible, but speculation about the nature and extent of Vanbrugh's sexual experiences serves no useful purpose. The gossip of Lady Mary Wortley Montagu, who at ten had been the toast of the Kit-Cat Club, was as lively as it was ill-informed; in 1713 she told a friend that at the York assembly Vanbrugh's 'inclination to ruins has given him a fancy for Mrs Yarburgh.'[19] Lady Mary thought him ridiculous, but whether *ruin* for him meant Woodstock Manor or, as he used the word to Newcastle, wedlock cannot be established; nor can with certainty the identity of Mrs Yarburgh, but rather than either mother or daughter she was most probably Faith, a maiden aunt of the latter who was then thirty.[20] Certainly five years later Henrietta Maria, the daughter and young enough to be his own, did not find him ridiculous. She already faced the prospect of a long widowhood, although perhaps not as much as half a century; while she appears as a conventional figure of eighteenth-century minor society, on his side at any rate the marriage was for affection and probably for love, and the richer for its being in the late summer of his life. The Murray portrait shows a man who could enjoy capture by a young bride, and since it

[16] National Portrait Gallery, *Catalogue of Seventeenth-Century Portraits*, 1963, p.357, as *c*.1718. A. R. Hood, Eastbourne, sold Christie's, 26 Feb. 1910 (48) with a portrait of Lady Vanbrugh forming a pair; the latter is lost, but may be that reproduced in *Connoisseur*, XLVIII, 1917, p.133, in the collection of John Lane and attributed to Isaac Whood (Pl.2). It was not in the Lane sale, Sotheby's, 1 July 1925, and no dimensions are known.

[17] Webb, p.3.

[18] Webb, pp.107, 111, 112. The marriage took place in St Lawrence's, York, on 14 Jan. 1719. She was of that parish, he was of Castle Howard (*Yorks. Parish Register Soc.*, XCVII, 1935), so Lord Carlisle was perhaps best man (Whistler (1938), p.251).

[19] Lady Mary Wortley Montagu, *Letters*, ed. R. Halsband, I, 1965, p.201.

[20] Faith Yarburgh, baptized Dec. 1683, died 1760, daughter of Sir Thomas and Henrietta Maria Yarburgh (J. Foster, *Pedigrees of the County Families of York*, 1874, II).

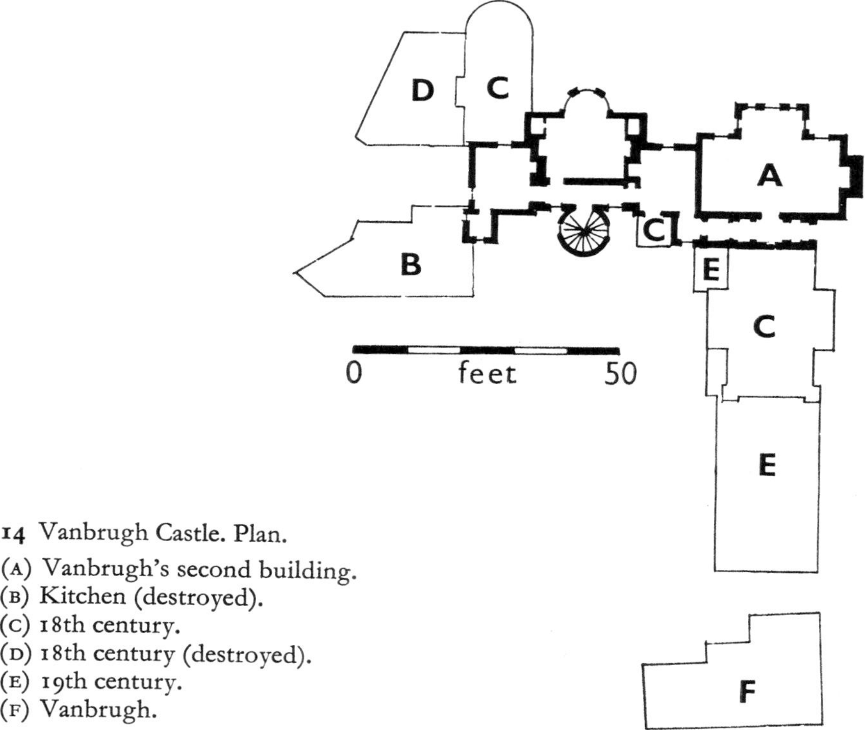

14 Vanbrugh Castle. Plan.
(A) Vanbrugh's second building.
(B) Kitchen (destroyed).
(C) 18th century.
(D) 18th century (destroyed).
(E) 19th century.
(F) Vanbrugh.

appears to have had a pendant portrait of Lady Vanbrugh, it may well have been a wedding picture.[21]

His marriage and the prospect of an heir probably explain the unprecedented final shape of Vanbrugh Castle. The house of 1717 was symmetrical and corresponded to the present court front with a central round staircase tower and square towers at the south corners (Pl.102); on the north side a bow-window room projects on the axis of the stair tower to make the most of the panoramic view (Pl.103, Fig.14).[22] Carter drew a one-storey kitchen to the left of the court with a bell-turret rising out of a pediment (Pl.112). Stukeley's sketch of 1721 (Pl.105)[23] shows this small castle with a gateway at the south-west corner of the court and other outworks; it also shows a low building with semicircular windows or half-portholes which, allowing for perspective, is probably meant to be not in front of the Castle but to the right of it, corresponding to part of the building (F) at the south end of the court. The east side was greatly altered and extended in a pastiche style after the house was bought in 1907 by Alexander Duckham.[24] But Stukeley does not show the

[21] See above, n.16. The portraits are not mentioned in the Account Book; if painted about the time of the marriage they might have been a present from the bride's family. Vanbrugh did pay for the copying of two pictures in July 1720. For Lady Vanbrugh see also p.177.

[22] Elton Drawings, No.104.

[23] Society of Antiquaries, L.C.II, p.23.

[24] *English Homes*, p.191. Carter calls the south porch 'modern.' The bow-ended north-west room, mentioned but not described by Carter, was added in the later eighteenth century and is absent from an engraving by W. H. Toms (BM MS.Add.32364, f.166) titled 'The D. of Richmonds House near Blackheath' (Pl.114). The 2nd Duke (1701–50) rented the Castle from 1734 to 1743 (Lady Vanbrugh's accounts, BIHR). The Duke was the principal backer of Owen Swiney's allegorical paintings, which were originally at Goodwood (see p.41). Philip Vanbrugh's daughter was companion to the Duchess (see p.173).

additional range on the north-east, which must have been built after his visit although, on evidence of style, designed by Vanbrugh (Pl.103).[25] There were no more children, but the enlargement of the house may have been precipitated by the birth or even the expectation of the second boy. Later in 1723, in November, Vanbrugh wrote of his intention to 'move for good' to Greenwich, which meant an appreciable but finite period like a fortnight or a season;[26] with the growth of the estate in the Field he clearly had business as well as pleasure to keep him at Greenwich. In order to enlarge the castle he added a second symmetrical building end-to-end to the first, but in doing so he created a building which is remarkable – and at its date without precedent – in its asymmetry.

No other single feature of the Greenwich houses was new in Vanbrugh's work. The castle concept goes back to Kimbolton and its vocabulary to Chargate. The massing of towers and bastions, of projections and recesses, is common to both Chargate and Blenheim. The plainness of surface, the reduction of mouldings and the Venetian windows treated without architraves or pilasters are found at Kings Weston. The bow-window room and vaulted corridors first appeared at Blenheim and Castle Howard; more generally the inventive planning is characteristic of the small houses from the Goose Pie onwards. What Reynolds called 'the conduct of the background', the feeling for the lie of the land and the relation of buildings to site, goes back to the early days of Castle Howard; the particular form of buildings set in a landscape was developed in the adaptation of Woodstock Manor and no doubt also in the 'picture' of it which he made in 1709 for the edification of Godolphin and the Duchess of Marlborough (p.74). All these features were combined at Greenwich to make an informal sequence of highly formal buildings of varied and unusual styles, set in a landscape. The small scale of the individual buildings and the completeness and informality of the setting were new for Vanbrugh; one reason was that the opportunity was new, but the asymmetry of the completed castle points far ahead to the Picturesque castles of the late eighteenth century. In Vanbrugh's own work it can be linked with the early garden buildings of Stowe, the irregular bastions of Castle Howard (p.102) and the asymmetry of the Great Room at Claremont.

Claremont was demolished in 1769 to make way for the present house, and nothing remains except some garden walls and the Belvedere, a toy castle which mindless vandals of our age have attacked with a literalness which its creator could not have foreseen. In late 1714 the young Newcastle, as Earl of Clare, bought Chargate from him and renamed it Claremont.[27] A book of accounts of the joiner John Smallwell gives some idea of the extent and date of work carried out to Vanbrugh's designs and referred to in his letters to the Duke, at Newcastle House in Lincoln's Inn Fields (which was completely refitted inside from September 1714), at Nottingham Castle (interiors 1719) and at

[25] The Account Book does not always specify the location of work paid for, but the one-storey kitchen described by Carter was probably the kitchen building referred to in a carpenter's bill of 5 Aug. 1723. Further work occasioned the bill for lime on 9 July. The north-east addition appears in Toms's print (Pl.114), and may also be compared with drawings for castellar houses (Figs 6, 7). It does not appear in either the original plan (*Elton Drawings*, No.104) or Stukeley's view of 1721. For the other additions see Fig.14.

[26] Webb, p.82. For the date see p.80, n.9. Eleven days later he wrote from Greenwich of moving 'to Whitehall on Monday next for good' (Webb, p.152).

[27] The Earl agreed to buy Chargate House and its furniture and household goods from Vanbrugh on 14 Oct. 1714, and the copyhold of the estate on 20 May 1715 from Robert Moore (p.50, n.29). The view to the Belvedere from the gardens to the west has been cleared (1976) by the National Trust and some repairs done to the building.

Claremont, which in one account is referred to as Chargett.[28] Building work there must have preceded the joinery, starting in the summer of 1715 with the Belvedere (called the Mount), alterations to the old house, and the construction of two large wings which were fitted up in 1717 and are best recorded in a view of *c.*1750 attributed to J. F. Rigaud (Pl.118).[29] The house stood in front and a little south of the present one, on sloping ground which was cut away to expose the basement storey at the front. Staircases led up to the central block, which was essentially and unmistakably Vanbrugh's little house with the battlements and other picturesque features removed and a pediment added, so that it would stand out by its height and plainness between the long arcaded wings. These extended altogether about 300 feet and were for the most part two rooms deep. Above the roofline stood four squat arched towers, two taller machicolated clock towers, and six linking pairs of chimney-stacks. In 1719–20 Vanbrugh added at the back of the right wing the Great Room, which was about 100 feet long, two storeys high, and bigger than any other single room he built; as it was on the level of the old dwelling-house its upper half, in which the windows were, could be seen over the wing. The practical reason for this glaring asymmetry was that, because of the way the house had grown, there was nowhere else to put it. Nevertheless, it is more credible aesthetically at this date than it would have been ten or fifteen years earlier.

The Belvedere on a small hill behind the house is a rectangular brick building of two storeys with two square battlemented towers on either side; its basic formula is not unlike that of the outer base blocks of Castle Howard (Pls 23, 115). Originally it was glazed and wainscoted. Now its decayed and broken windows have been replaced by black panels, and the trees on the hill have grown so tall as to outreach it, and so dense as to hide it on almost all sides. But one used to be able to climb the tower staircase to an open platform on the roof for an even wider view of the coutryside beyond the gardens (Pl.116). A summer-house with a view was not an innovation, but this particular one may have planted the germ in Vanbrugh's mind of the castle on the hill at Greenwich.

Vanbrugh's medievalism is one stage in the continuous process between the late survival of Gothic architecture in England and its early revival; his inspiration was largely from the stage and from 'King James's Gothic', but he grew up in a Chester that was still largely a medieval walled city. His last recorded visit there was in 1713, and although in later life his annual trips to Castle Howard took him through York, it was to Chester that he referred for the finishing of one of Lord Carlisle's outworks. In 1724 Etty, the clerk of works at Castle Howard, had sent a design for a spire for one of the round towers; Vanbrugh thought this would 'by no means do, a Cap is all that those sort of Towers shou'd have, and I have seen one upon a round Tower on the Walls of Chester that I thought did extreamly well.'[30] He went on to explain that the cap should be 'planted quite even with the top of the Battlements.' Among the buildings which announce to the

[28] BM MS.Add.33442. Vanbrugh inspected Nottingham Castle on 17 Dec. 1718 'In as horrible a day as Storms, hail, Snow and the Divil can make it' (Webb, p.105, misread).

[29] A. P. Oppé, *English Drawings in the Royal Collection at Windsor Castle*, 1950, No.506. A slightly different unfinished view is *Elton Drawings*, No.177. The plan is shown in outline on the garden plan in *Vit. Brit.*, III, Pls 77–8, and in that by J. Roque, 1738. Except for the White Cottage, none of the surviving buildings in the neighbourhood appears in these plans and Vanbrugh's hand must be seen in them with extreme caution.

[30] Webb, p.163.

traveller from York that he is approaching Castle Howard there is a massive curtain wall with towers and bastions, extending to left and right of the road for a total of five-eighths of a mile. None of it would withstand siege, and some of it has not withstood the elements; nevertheless, its winding extent along the contour, its rough construction and its battlemented turrets give a very convincing illusion of a defensive outwork at least partly medieval. If the walls of old Chester were one source of inspiration, the old soldier's nostalgia for fortifications was another, and seventeenth-century stage designs probably a third. In spirit it is closer to the repairing and inhabiting of Woodstock Manor than to Vanbrugh Castle. The Pyramid Gateway, which is the next landmark after the breach in the wall (Pl.124), bears the date 1719, and as the chronology of the outworks appears to proceed outwards the curtain wall will have been built in the early 1720s and Vanbrugh's letter will have related to its completion (Pls 41, 42).

Vanbrugh's inclination to architectural ruins led him, also in 1719, to press successfully for the preservation of a threatened Tudor building as remote from him in time as the works of Robert Adam are from us, but close enough to his own house for him to know it very well in every light of the year. The 'Holbein' Gate of Whitehall Palace had survived the 1698 fire, but was increasingly found to be a hindrance to traffic between the Strand and Westminster. The Treasury was no doubt rather sensitive since Benson's attack on the fabric of the House of Lords the previous year, and Vanbrugh enlisted the help of Newcastle, as Lord Chamberlain, to save 'One of the Greatest Curiositys there is in London' whose construction had 'cost a great Sum of money' and which was 'so well perform'd, that altho' now above 200 Yrs Old, is as entire as the first day.' There were lower and less dignified buildings between the gateway and the Banqueting House, which he suggested should be taken down instead so as to bypass it, and he was even prepared to pay for their demolition himself 'and so put the King to no expence at all.'[31] The reprieve was won – at least until 1759. Eventually it gave way to the transformation of the Whitehall site into a main street flanked by government offices, houses and yards, a transformation in which, ironically, Vanbrugh's application to build his own house had been the first step.

Around 1720 Vanbrugh was concerned with two great houses far from London which have an uncommon measure of the 'castle air': Seaton Delaval and the remodelling of Lumley Castle. Distance meant building by correspondence or by proxy to a greater degree than the less remote houses, and middle age, family commitments and increasing official duties also restricted the number of journeys he made. At the most he visited Seaton three times and Lumley twice, and much depended on local craftsmen and a local clerk of works. Seaton Delaval was gutted by fire in 1822 and, although now roofed, glazed and structurally sound, remains uninhabitable except for the domestic quarters in the kitchen and stable wings (Pl.119). It stands darkly on a plateau above the Northumberland coast within sight of the sea, and it is not unknown to meet a pure sea mist rolling in to engulf the house on an August afternoon. It is a perfect view for a retired sea-

[31] Webb, pp.114–16 (Aug. 1719).

captain, and the house was commissioned by one.[32] In 1717 George Delaval bought the old house from his cousin Sir John Delaval, and in February 1719 expressed the hope of getting the architect of Castle Howard either to alter or to rebuild it. Vanbrugh did not make his usual summer journey to the North in either 1718 or 1719; instead he was at Nottingham in December 1718, spent Christmas at Castle Howard and was in York to be married in January (p.93). Delaval must have engaged him in London and the design must have been made with imagination rather than knowledge of the site. In October 1719 stone was being quarried and a search was in progress in York for oak beams.

The following spring work began on the site and on demolishing the old house; Vanbrugh may well have made his first visit at that time, for he did not attend the Board of Works after 24 February until 7 April. In June 1720 William Etty, who in addition to his valuable service in the later works at Castle Howard acted for a number of architects on houses in the North and was a talented mason, was reported as 'gone to Admiral De Lavalls to lay the foundation of his house.' In February 1721 Vanbrugh sent Seaton papers to Etty, and in August spent some days on the site.[33] The upper part of the north front was building in August 1722 and the shell and roof of the main house were probably finished in 1723 or 1724; in those years Etty paid at least five visits to Seaton, meeting Vanbrugh there on the last occasion, in August 1724. Admiral Delaval was sixty when work began; the architect described him in 1721 as 'very Gallant in his operations, not being dispos'd to starve the Design at all. So that he is like to have, a very fine Dwelling for himself, now, and his Nephew &c hereafter.' In comparison with Castle Howard or Eastbury, Seaton is on the small side, but Admiral Delaval clearly wanted the best possible house for its size. Both the pleasure and the completion were left to the nephew, for the old man died in June 1723 after a fall from his horse. Captain Francis Blake Delaval was helped in the completion by a remunerative marriage in 1724. The north-east ground floor room next to the hall was being wainscoted in 1727, and the figures 1721 and 1729 scratched on the balustrade of the north-west tower suggest that the house was finished at about the latter date.

Much of the interior was finished after Vanbrugh's death in March 1726 and we do not know how much work was done from drawings supplied by him. In those parts executed in masonry his intentions can be read or reconstructed with some probability, while on the north front the details of the Doric order, with an enriched echinus and rosettes on the neck, and of the metopes, are derivatives of the north front of Castle Howard and may have been worked out by Etty (Pls 28, 29). But in planning and in the exterior in general this building can still be seen, like Vanbrugh Castle but on a larger scale, to combine in

[32] Many of the Seaton Delaval papers were lost or damaged through bad storage or fire. A few are at Seaton and some in the Northumberland CRO (NRO 650); others, in Newcastle Public Library, were used by J. Robinson, *The Delaval Papers*, 1888–9 (first published as articles in the *Blyth Weekly News*). Vanbrugh's movements can to some extent be gauged by the record of his Board of Works attendances (Appendix G). The Northumberland CRO has a letter from James Mewburn to Delaval at his house in Stratton Street, Piccadilly, 22 Jan. 1722. The account in the same collection from Mr Vernbergh relates to picture frames and cannot be connected with the architect. The best historical account is still that by H. E. Craster in *History of Northumberland*, IX, 1909.

[33] Beard, p.52; Webb, pp.130, 137. The Account Book does not record a journey in the spring of 1720, but there is an analogous case the previous year of a journey known from another source (p.57, n.10); if Vanbrugh travelled with his patron he would have had no significant expenses to record. Alternatively, having made the winter trip to Yorkshire two years before, he may have ventured as far as Northumberland in Dec. 1720 when a journey of thirty-five days is recorded without destination. In 1721 he was in 'the North' from 6 July to 2 November.

one rich fabric all the threads of Vanbrugh's earlier architecture (Pls 120–2). The Venetian windows, which also occur in the Castle, are here unambiguously Italianate in form. The octagonal corner towers and the banded masonry of the square lateral ones are his most literal evocations of the 'castle air' while in plan the resemblance to a medieval keep is even more marked. In silhouette and in three-dimensional massing Seaton is the closest to the prodigy houses of a century earlier like Hardwick and Wollaton (p.54) and the resemblance to the latter is increased by the device of a two-storey hall with a full attic storey above it. From the attic of Seaton the Delavals could look out to sea as Francis Willoughby of Wollaton looked, with a drier eye, over the city of Nottingham. (By a coincidence they both looked also over coalfields, though whereas Willoughby's coal helped to pay for his mansion the cousin from whom George Delaval bought the Seaton estate was penniless and the eighteenth-century family's money came from careers, marriage and inheritance.)

In planning the interior of the house Vanbrugh retained absolute symmetry of left and right but moved the staircases from positions flanking the hall, as at Blenheim, to the side towers, as first suggested in the smaller plan already discussed (Fig.13). They are oval in plan and the steps are cantilevered from the walls. They rise the full height of the house from basement to attic, and they are connected on each floor by a transverse passage. They are illuminated on each landing, and at the top each tower has Venetian windows on three sides. In this way the formula of the medieval keep staircase, an interminable and gloomy convolution, is transformed into an open spatial experience of grandeur and broad lucidity (Pl.126). At the summit of such an experience it is probable that Vanbrugh intended the attic to be a single great room the full depth of the house, as at Wollaton, and that the partitioning into bedrooms, which in one case divided a window, was a later alteration. On the living floor – hardly a ground floor since, as in a Palladian villa, it is a full storey above the office wings – the two-storey hall is lit only from the north and must always have continued the sombre romantic air of the exterior to the deep arcaded north court (Pl.123). It was paved with black and white marble and lined with blind arcades on both storeys, a similar formula to the open ones of the hall at Blenheim. The chimney-piece was carried by two heroic herm figures, bereft of their arms since the fire but still not unlike in mood the yeomen of the Guard Chamber at Hampton Court (Pls 97a, b). In the upper arches were plaster figures representing music, painting, geography, sculpture, architecture and astronomy; they recall an early scheme for the Saloon at Blenheim (Pl.82) and are thus probably part of Vanbrugh's design.

At the south end of the hall, under a balcony with an elegant wrought iron rail, double-leaf doors led to the saloon which was a complete contrast. It was another of Vanbrugh's sunlit south rooms, a single storey instead of two, but nearly three times as wide as the hall, extending the whole width of the house. It was bright instead of dark, to a degree which can now only be imagined, since the carcase of a house never appears as light as one with rendered walls and ceilings; it had a window at each end and seven on the south side.

Screens of Corinthian columns divided this great room, 70 by 121 feet, into three sections; the arches were not structural, the upper walls being carried on much higher brick arches at a higher level which still exist (Fig.15). The tripartite room appears in the

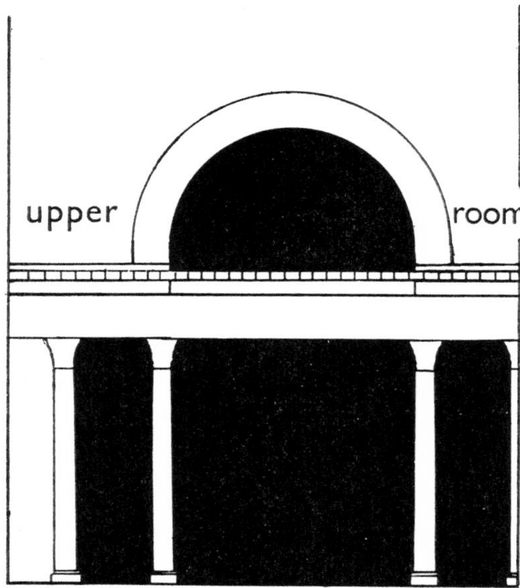

15 Seaton Delaval. Section (reconstruction) through the Saloon.

smaller plan already mentioned, and also in early designs for Eastbury of 1715–16,[34] in both cases with a bow window which was replaced at Seaton by an extremely handsome portico, deep enough to provide outdoor sitting space in clement weather. The fluted Ionic columns of the portico are properly proportioned although for Vanbrugh they seem unusually slender; they combine with the pedimented windows of the Saloon and the Venetian windows of the stair towers (common to all the fronts) to give the garden side an elegance quite different from the rugged character of the court side. At the same time the difference is analogous to that between fronts at Castle Howard, and the portico (Pl.122) looks forward to the classicism of other late Vanbrugh designs (p.113). So completely did he fuse the Gothick castle with the Palladian temple in his south front that in the third quarter of the century it was possible to extend the design to make a south-east wing of six bays plus an eastward bow-window room copied from those designed for Castle Howard. This wing, which reflected an increase in family numbers, is recorded in pictures and prints, some of which show a matching south-west wing that was never built. It contained the drawing and dining rooms described by most writers since the late eighteenth century; it was destroyed in the fire of 1822, although traces of it can still be found east of Vanbrugh's building.[35]

The later history of the Delavals was picturesque and often stormy and violent; they had other houses and Seaton's posthumous reputation is one of not being much lived in and indeed of being uninhabitable. It was remembered in the late nineteenth century as an

[34] Whistler, Pls 63, 65.

[35] The description of the interior is drawn from W. Hutchinson, *View of Northumberland*, 1778, II, and a survey made by John Dobson about 1815, now in the estate office. The plan in *Vit. Brit.* is inaccurate. Hutchinson says the south-east wing was added by Sir John Hussey Delaval, who succeeded in 1752. A fire in that year is said to have been in the north-west wing. Margaret Dobson, *Memoir of John Dobson*, 1885, p.26, says her father was in 1815 'engaged to restore that part of the building which had been damaged by fire, and to add a new wing', but Dobson's drawings show a reduction of the south-east wing by the removal of the bow-window room. She also states that Dobson was again consulted much later in life, and gives an account of his and Lord Strathmore's discomforts in the house.

inconvenient house full of cold air and howling draughts, and Lord Strathmore, who often visited before the fire, always took an extra cloak. This hardly seems the work of the man who made every room in Castle Howard like an oven, but there are several possible explanations of the discrepancy. One is mismanagement of the house, one is the effect of adding an east wing full of chimneys, another is the comparative lack of Vanbrugh's personal supervision of the building, and yet another is the possible effect of the two stair towers; in practice all of them may have combined not only to the discomfort of the occupants, but also to the aggravation of the fire.

Vanbrugh's work at Lumley was a matter of modernizing the fourteenth-century castle for Richard Lumley, who was appointed to the Royal Household in 1714 and entered the House of Lords the following year as Lord Lumley. When he succeeded his father as 2nd Earl of Scarbrough at the close of 1721 he had already engaged Vanbrugh; the architect made his only recorded visit, of 'near a Week', in August 1721, though he is likely to have been there again three years later on the way to or from Seaton Delaval. In April 1722 Lord Scarbrough asked him 'to propose some things for him in order to begin his works there.'[36] Lumley, which stands high above Chester-le-Street, already had the 'castle air' in abundance; Vanbrugh found it 'a Noble thing' and must have appreciated the heraldic and historical decoration added in the late sixteenth century by John, Lord Lumley. During his stay Vanbrugh was able 'to form a General Design for the whole, Which consists, in altering the House both for State, Beauty and Convenience; And making the Courts Gardens and Offices Suitable to it; All which I believe [he told Brigadier Watkins] may be done, for a Sum, that can never ly very heavy upon the Family.' Lawyers were still arguing over the expense of Blenheim, and Vanbrugh was anxious to show that he could save money in private as well as official practice. He did not make Lumley as regular as Kimbolton, but the surviving asymmetries are not immediately apparent. The castle consists of four ranges round a court; under Vanbrugh's direction most of the south side was remodelled to give a sequence of large living rooms on the principal floor with a corridor and staircase on the courtyard side behind them. At the same time the hall, at the south end of the west range, was modernized: the sixteenth-century fireplace and the sculptural ornaments were retained, but what appear to have been four high late Gothic windows were replaced by three deep embrasures which contain two rectangular windows and, in the northernmost, a new doorway and, above them, three oval windows (Pl.127).[37] The outside was extensively refaced and most of the windows, including those in the corner towers, were replaced by sash-windows. The decoration of the new south rooms in wainscot and plaster probably extended into the 1730s and was of a conventional kind for the time. It was probably both executed and designed by York craftsmen and not part of the 'General Design'; the only room with Vanbrughian characteristics is the undercroft of the room in the south-west tower, in which the stones of the regularly spaced square piers are boldly chamfered towards the joints.[38]

How much was realized of the courts, gardens and offices in Vanbrugh's scheme cannot

[36] Webb, pp.138, 142.

[37] *English Homes*, Pl.432. The original window pattern was visible inside the hall in 1972. The castle is now used as a neo-romantic-medieval hotel.

[38] *English Homes*, Pl.435.

now be established. The stable court on the north is basically from the time of the Elizabethan John, Lord Lumley, and the castle has no gardens to speak of. What remains of its setting is the hill-top which Nature provided and the first builder used for strategic ends. The settings of all Vanbrugh's houses have been altered, and it is difficult – sometimes impossible – either to reconstruct their original appearance or to determine his share in them. The presumption that he planted the oak in the courtyard of Vanbrugh Castle, and laid out the serpentine path across the field to the south, is the simplest and the easiest to make and maintain. Moreover, because this was his own house and on a small scale one may argue that this prototype of what planners now call landscaped development was the most authentic Vanbrugh garden; further, that similarities in the setting of other, grander Vanbrugh houses could be taken as evidence of his participation in them.

Participation, however, is not the same as authorship. At Blenheim we know that Henry Wise was in charge of the gardens from the start. At Claremont, Eastbury and Stowe Charles Bridgeman's designs were followed. In each of these the symmetry of the house is carried into its surroundings by walks and regular planted plots. In each of them also, at some distance from the house, irregularity is introduced in one way or another. At Blenheim there was the 'wilderness', the great bastioned hexagonal shrubbery beyond the south parterre, while on the north the sweep of the valley and the ruins of the old Manor offset the symmetry of the bridge and avenue. At Claremont the Belvedere was off the axis of the house, while at Eastbury, the most regular of these gardens, the two sides were diversified. At Seaton Delaval, where no gardener is known, the western avenue from the village is aligned on the side of the main house, so that in order to approach it is necessary to turn off to the left and then make two right turns into the axis of the entrance front.[39] At Seaton too the whole garden was surrounded by a ha-ha, a concealed wall and ditch, with large low bastions at the corners; the ha-ha was a scenic device but technically its origins may be connected with fortifications, and the bastions of Seaton and Blenheim suggest the common hand of Captain Vanbrugh. The Stowe ha-ha was actually fortified with stakes.

At Stowe Vanbrugh proposed alterations, some of which were carried out, to the late-seventeenth-century house, and surely including the surviving north portico which is of his characteristic type (Pls 56, 125). His Kit-Cat friend Sir Richard Temple was one of Marlborough's officers; he was cashiered by the Tories in 1713 but reinstated and created Baron Cobham the following year, and Viscount in 1718. When Vanbrugh visited him at Stowe in June 1719 he was still in commission and later that summer led the successful expedition to Vigo in Spain. The architect found him 'much entertain'd with (besides his Wife) the Improvements of his House and Gardens, in which he Spends all he has to Spare.'[40] Minor improvements had then been in progress for several years, and Vanbrugh had recently started to design garden buildings including the rusticated Palladian one later called the Temple of Bacchus and now destroyed.[41] Shortly after that, in about 1719, Bridgeman prepared a plan for the gardens centred on, and apparently designed to be seen

[39] The south and west avenues were planted in 1721 (Mewburn's letter to Delaval, n.32).

[40] Webb, p.112. The most recent account is in *Apollo*, June 1973. For the staked ha-ha see *Country Life*, CLI, 1972, pp.1254–6.

[41] *English Homes*, Pl.231.

16 Stowe. The Rotondo before alteration. After an engraving in the *Stowe Guide*.

from, Vanbrugh's new Rotondo, an open circular temple which survives in an altered condition south-west of the house (Fig.16). Later in the century the dome was rebuilt to a shallower profile and the original appearance is now best gauged from the replica, perhaps designed by Vanbrugh, at Duncombe (Pl.128).[42] The next reference to Lord Cobham in Vanbrugh's letters is in 1724, the year in which Lord Perceval wrote an account of the gardens from which it is clear that over five years most of the scheme had been carried out.[43] One of the springs of the scheme was an asymmetry, for the old walled garden, and the walk outside it to the south joining what had once been Stowe village to the Roman road from Towcester to Bicester, were at an oblique angle to the axes of the house. Lord Perceval's ascription of the 1719–24 garden to Bridgeman is confirmed by other contemporary evidence, but from the discussion between Vanbrugh and Cobham in 1724 about the setting of Castle Howard (and relayed to Lord Carlisle) it seems probable that neither Cobham nor his architect was disposed to give Bridgeman an entirely free hand: specifically that Vanbrugh not only designed temples at Stowe but also introduced the idea of exploiting the accident of pronounced asymmetry – conceived in the same years as the colony on Greenwich Hill.

Of all the great house parks Castle Howard is exceptional in the degree both of its irregularity and of its anonymity. After George London's early unexecuted plans for canals, avenues and *ronds-points* no major garden designer's name is known, although it is possible that Stephen Switzer's enthusiastic approval of Lord Carlisle's layout in 1718 modestly conceals a share in the design.[44] On the other hand, Lady Irwin's poem (p.20)

42 C. Hussey, *English Gardens and Landscapes 1700–1750*, 1967, pp.143–4.

43 Webb, pp.163–4, 167–8. Bridgeman's perspective is Bodl.MS.Gough Drawings a.4.46; it also shows alterations to the house, not all of which were effected. The south portico was not built, but that surviving on the north is one of the few remnants of Vanbrugh's work. Later in the eighteenth century the house was again considerably altered and enlarged. Otherwise unrecorded visits to Stowe: Account Book, Sept. 1722, Oct. 1723. Lord Perceval's visit: Whistler, pp.182–3.

44 S. Switzer, *Ichnographia Rustica*, II, 1718, p.198.

which attributed everything to her father, may be seen as positive evidence of his personal involvement but not as negative evidence of exclusion, since it makes no mention of Vanbrugh or Hawksmoor as architects, or of any other professional figure. Carlisle was adept, both as a politician and as a landlord, at engaging the right specialist at the right time, and the letters Vanbrugh and Hawksmoor wrote to him indicate the extent of consultation between him and his architects.

The Castle Howard landscape (and it is proper to call it that) grew over nearly four decades of Carlisle's life; it must have grown from such consultation, and it is impossible now to discover which early steps were taken with later ones in mind. A number of decisions were certainly both momentous and generative of irregularity; first the early decision, probably Vanbrugh's, to turn the house round (p.29), which meant that it would be approached sideways. Then the designing of the long straight road west of the house,[45] and the building of the obelisk in 1714 at the junction with the approach avenue (Pl.131); the obelisk was Carlisle's monument to Marlborough but the choice of this form was probably Vanbrugh's. The cross-roads is not at right angles and the obelisk is aligned only to the avenue. The curtain wall further south on the road must have been Vanbrugh's idea, and the Pyramid Gate of 1719 within it (Pl.124). The latter was momentous because it was the first of the hill-top structures, to be followed by Vanbrugh's Temple (p.111) and Hawksmoor's Pyramid and Mausoleum, which extend the aesthetic environment of the house far into the practical one, and which, at one moment seen and at the next hidden by another hill, give the traveller that feeling of being silently observed which is stronger and deeper than the conventional sense of the *genius loci* of many an eighteenth-century garden peopled with classical statues and summer-houses. Near the house the south garden was laid out with regular walks and plots, figures and urns, and beyond it was a rectangular bastioned wilderness of trees studded with small obelisks, essentially that shown in the bird's-eye view of 1725 (*Vitruvius Britannicus* III). But east of the house was Wray Wood, already in Carlisle's youth full of mature deciduous trees, and gradually transformed by irregular 'meander walks', fountains, statues and other delightful objects. This 'paradise', Lady Irwin tells us, was named from Diana's female roe deer, and was not surpassed by the grove of Venus on Mount Idalus (*Aeneid* I) or the forest of Dodona in Epirus, the most ancient oracle of Greece; this contained a magic spring which ignites torches, perhaps the origin of the gilt sculpted flame set up in Wray Wood in 1721. South of the wood lay the old village street of Henderskelfe, which like many a Yorkshire hamlet had straggled along the contour line. The village seems to have become gradually depopulated and ultimately superseded not by the circular model village envisaged on London's plans but by the community at Welburn south of the estate. About 1730 the street became the grassed terrace walk, serpentine and flanked by statues (Pl.9), leading to the Temple, and its last utility before the transformation was probably for carrying building materials to the Temple site.

The eighteenth-century landscape garden was to a considerable extent a Whig creation; this is hardly surprising in an age in which enlightenment and progress were assumed, however mistakenly, to be the prerogatives of the ruling party in a developing two-party

[45] The road was basically a new forest ride and not of Roman origin. It was extended south of Welburn in the 1870s (Hussey, op.cit., p.130).

system.[46] The seventeenth-century formal garden was based on the Cartesian concept of Nature as orderly and regular – Nature as exemplified in the heavenly bodies and the truths of mathematics, so that Wren could identify natural with geometrical beauty. There was a parallel in the minds of men like Shaftesbury or Addison, in the opening years of the eighteenth century, between the Whig liberation of the People from the toils of Absolutism and the liberation of natural forms from the topiarist's shears and the gardener's straight-edge. Vanbrugh was well aware of such parallels, and both Addison and Steele were Kit-Cat members. The surroundings of his buildings were of constant concern; in letters he often mentions house and gardens together. But the English landscape garden was developed by professional writers rather than by professional gardeners or architects. As Surveyor of Gardens and Waters under George I, Vanbrugh brought the same professional administrative attitude to bear as in his Comptrollership, but the innovations of the Stowe and Castle Howard gardens, in so far as they are likely to have been his, came mysteriously, casually and by word of mouth. At least it would be very surprising to find documentary evidence to show that they were of a different order from the house in the Whitehall ruins, the dome of Castle Howard, the Blenheim bridge, Vanbrugh Fields, or his very conversion to architecture.

Lord Carlisle saw the development of agriculture and forestry on his estate as a moral duty, although he did not deny himself the pleasures of being seen to carry out his duty in the grandest possible manner. The great outworks of Castle Howard are unique not in the calibre of their architects but in the combination of several remarkable features: their large scale, the high-contoured landscape in which they are sited, in which views are continually opened up rather than closed; their bold simple shapes which are striking in distant silhouette and close massiveness alike; finally their relative utility. The obelisk marks the turn for the house, the Temple really was a place to spend the afternoon with a good book, a bottle and Ciceronian thoughts. The Pyramid and the Mausoleum are both funerary, and the latter had to replace the old village church for family burial. All have a seriousness quite different even from the later buildings of Stowe, whose associations are largely artificial, exotic and extrinsic. But this landscape of surprises is perhaps the one place in Britain where it would not be surprising to meet a population of wood nymphs, satyrs, goatherds and the rest of Virgil's everyday country characters which Carlisle's poetic daughter attempts to evoke. How near Vanbrugh approached not only the Gothic North but also the warm classical south we have yet to examine.

[46] N. Pevsner, 'The Genesis of the Picturesque', *Architectural Review*, XCVI, 1944, pp.139–46.

Chapter 7

Palladius Britannicus

'I know Sr J Vanbrugh is for a Temple of smooth freestone with a portico each way, and Dom'd over the center, & it woud indoubtedly be beyond all objection, but as yr Lordship desired a drafft of one, made of the common Wall stone, I have done this accordingly.' Thus Hawksmoor wrote to Lord Carlisle on 7 January 1724, enclosing 'Ideas or Scizzas of the Turret at the Corner of Wray wood' alternative to Vanbrugh's.[1] Carlisle wrote a week later to Vanbrugh, who was not well enough to reply until 11 February.[2] In the case of the Temple, or Belvedere, he and Hawksmoor seem to have been in acknowledged competition on equal terms, and Carlisle was of the opinion that rough stone would be cheaper. Vanbrugh predicted that 'when the Estimates come to be made, the first Design I sent, with the 4 Porticos will be found very near (perhaps quite) as cheap, as any Gothick Tower, that has yet been thought of.' But his argument was not only economic: 'My Lord Morpeth [Carlisle's eldest son] about a month ago, View'd all the Designs I had sent, He declared his thoughts utterly against anything but an Italian Building in that Place, and entirely approv'd the first Design' (Pl.129).

This letter crossed with another from Carlisle, who had perhaps in the meantime heard directly from his son. A week later Vanbrugh was 'very glad to find your Ldship at last incline to the Temple with the four Porticos', and pressed his advantage: 'since the Situation requires it shou'd be open to look out every way, were there no Porticos, the sun wou'd Strike in so full, as to make it quite dissagreable, whereas the Porticos will keep the Sun almost always out of it, and yet leave it quite light of the most pleasing kind.'[3] If it was essential to 'husband the Stone' he would not use rustication, 'the whole turn of the Design being of the more delicate kind'; instead he suggested fluting the pillars 'which do's so much disguise the joints, that one may use almost what Stones one will.' A few weeks later Carlisle had 'determin'd upon the four Porticos' and Vanbrugh was preparing instructions for Etty.[4] He proposed to treat the interior simply with 'a Surbase of Wainscote, and then Stucco the Walls quite up to the Cornice. The Ceiling will do very well flat, because it will shape the Room just to a Cube. Or if your Ldship likes it better to show the inside of the Cap, I have no exceptions to it.' In April he was almost ready to post the design, and told Carlisle that 'four doors will give both light and View Sufficient, without Windows, and then there will be Space enough for Chairs; the Table I think (as I have

[1] Downes (1959), pp.243–4 and Pl.87a.

[2] Webb, p.156.

[3] Webb, p.157.

[4] Webb, pp.158–9, 26 March.

mention'd formerly) shou'd stand always fix'd in the Middle of the Room.'[5] He was not happy with the name *Belvedere* because he associated it with 'some high Tower' and he did not altogether exclude the possibility of erecting such a thing at Castle Howard. 'But this Building I fancy wou'd more naturally take the Name of Temple which the Situation likewise is very proper for.'

After April 1724 the project drops out of the correspondence in favour of more urgent matters. One of these was the size and number of the obelisks in the south garden, but the most serious was the question of priority between the northern approach to the house and the commencement of the west wing. Carlisle was in favour of the grand north gateway on the axis of the house, as shown in the bird's-eye engraving (Pl.30); Vanbrugh, with a concern which the future would show to have been only too well founded, believed 'the Wing of so much more weight to the Credit of the House, both in regard to the outside and in, that as far as my Wishes or Opinion may go . . . I give them clearly for the Wing.' He proposed for the moment a pair of causeways ascending the northern slope away from the centre line and curving round to lead into the side gateways already built (p.38). He enlisted the support of Lord Cobham, and of Lord Morpeth 'who (tho' fond of a Gate) approves of it.'[6] In the event neither causeway nor gate nor wing was undertaken, and in December 1725 Vanbrugh was 'sorry to find by a letter yesterday from Mr Etty, your Ldp is going on in the Temple instead of the West Wing';[7] it was left for Robinson later to do his best and worst on that side of the house. In his last surviving letter, however (8 March 1726), Vanbrugh was glad to hear that Etty 'is so far prepared towards the Temple.' At that time work was no further than the basement, since there was still a possibility of enlarging the dimensions from a cube of 20 feet to one of 22 feet, with 'no regard to the Columns, or other parts of the Architecture, which will all do as they stand at Present.'[8] (As executed the interior is a cube of 20 feet, the exterior one of 26 feet.) In June 1726 Hawksmoor was trying to arrange a consultation with Carlisle, Etty and Daniel Harvey about the completion, and it appears that, apart from 'a small alteration in the cap' which he proposed on 1 August, the design of the original architect was followed after his death.[9] The masonry was finished in 1727–8, including unfluted columns and the carving by Harvey of mouldings in the pediments, the vases upon them and the Ionic capitals. The interior, however, was the subject of protracted discussion, and the decoration of walls and cupola eventually carried out in 1737–9 by Francesco Vassali can at most represent to some extent Hawksmoor's design; by that date, with Vanbrugh, Hawksmoor and Etty all dead, Sir Thomas Robinson was Carlisle's principal architectural adviser.

Vanbrugh discussed the provision of windows or niches flanking the doorways within the porticoes, but it was clear that he preferred the walls to be plain and unrelieved and was convinced that the doorways would give enough light for the interior. The concave shells, of a form commonly used for niche heads, on either side of the doorways, were carved by Harvey in 1727; their presence suggests that the walls were originally built

[5] Webb, p.160, 11 April 1724.

[6] Webb, pp.163–4, 21 Nov., 10 Dec. 1724.

[7] Webb, p.171, 16 Dec. 1725.

[8] Webb, p.172, 8 March 1726.

[9] Hawksmoor letters, 21 June, 1 Aug., 3 Sept. 1726 (Castle Howard MSS).

with exterior niches and that the present rectangular windows were an afterthought (Pl.132). This would explain the unusual combination of a window architrave apparently in front of a niche and would suggest that the alteration was made at a late stage in order to give more light. Except at close quarters the effect on Vanbrugh's design is negligible, and the interior is undoubtedly improved.

Annotations on one of Hawksmoor's rejected sketches tell us something of the purpose of the Temple. He marked the four corners as *Bookes, Chimny, Drains* and *A bot wine*, and from an inscrutably learned reference to ancient writers he probably had in mind the precedents of the Younger Pliny's villa at Laurentinum and 'a singular parlour for eating' belonging, according to the antiquary Montfaucon, to Marcus Terentius Varro. It was to be a well-provided summer-house just under half a mile from the house, with views all round – hence the name *Belvedere* – and the views were no less beautiful for presenting the subject and the fruits of Carlisle's own enterprise.[10] Here the description by its designer of a building a century and a half older is singularly appropriate, for it is the formal prototype of Vanbrugh's: 'The site is as pleasant & as delightful as can be found; because it is upon a small hill, of very easy access . . . as it enjoys from every part most beautiful views, some of which are limited, some more extended, & others that terminate with the horizon; there are loggia's made in all the four fronts.'[11] There can be no doubt that Vanbrugh, who had been reading his Palladio for twenty years, was inspired in this case by the Rotonda, or Villa Almerigo, immediately south-east of Vicenza (Pl.130). This, the most famous of Palladio's villas, was the prototype of Campbell's Mereworth and Lord Burlington's Chiswick at almost the same time as Vanbrugh's Temple, as well as two later English villas, and while Vanbrugh's interpretation is much smaller and proportionately taller than any of the others (and consists of a single room) it is the only one in which the scenic peculiarities of the original as described by Palladio are understood and reproduced.

The Temple has the bold simplicity of outline, of *figure* against the *ground* of the sky, common to the outworks of Castle Howard. Its cell is a cube, and its four identical porticoes have a corresponding prismatic clearness of shape. It is not only the last and most consistent of Vanbrugh's essays in the architecture of the 'figure and proportions', it is also the most elegant – his own word was *delicate*, as if in his own mind he had reconciled the figure and proportions with the delicacy of the ornaments (p.48). In the clear North Yorkshire air it has an unexpectedly Mediterranean aspect, entirely and marvellously in harmony with the Virgilian feeling of its landscape setting. In his final tribute to Palladio Vanbrugh came closer to the spirit of the great Italian's Roman gravity, which he had never seen, than did many an architect who had made the Grand Tour.

If Vanbrugh's life is seen as a sequence of conversions (to the army, to the stage, to politics, to architecture, to public service, to matrimony), then the final one was to a personal form of neo-Palladianism that went beyond the quotation of motifs of the early Eastbury design (Pl.86). The Temple was the most literal, and perhaps the finest manifestation of this style but it was not isolated. The last years of his life also saw the definition of

[10] Downes (1969), pp.195–7. B. de Montfaucon, *L'Antiquité Expliquée*, III, 1719; English translation published 1721–2. The Temple was used 'to drink tea in' in 1768 (Viscount Grimston's diary, HMC Verulam, p.236).

[11] Palladio, Bk II. The translation used here is Ware's of 1738 which is more faithful than Leoni's; Vanbrugh presumably used Fréart's French edition although he subscribed to Leoni's (Account Book).

a complete design for the rebuilding of Grimsthorpe in Lincolnshire, only partly carried out, and the construction of the Duke of Newcastle's gallery pew in old Esher church (p.118). The main body of the house at Eastbury also belongs to his last years and indeed to a decade after his death, but the process which led to the final design was a complex one both in terms of the designing of a particular house and in the development of Vanbrugh's later style.

Eastbury, like Seaton Delaval and also Grimsthorpe, was begun for one generation and continued for another. George Doddington bought the estate near Blandford in 1709, but the first firm date after that is 1716, the year given in *Vitruvius Britannicus* to a 'New Design for a Person of Quality' by Vanbrugh (Pls 136, 138–9). Although *new* probably means novel modernity rather than second thoughts in a sequence, it can be argued that drawings for quite different schemes preceded this design, and it is generally agreed that drawings in the Victoria and Albert Museum, of which we have considered one, represent the first idea for Doddington's house and were made by about 1715 (Pls 86, 133). This design shares with Kings Weston the concentration of the ornament in the middle of the elevations, leaving the windows of the end bays without architraves. On the entrance front the centre bay, with Venetian windows in both storeys, is flanked by pairs of Corinthian square piers supporting, above the roofline, colossal urns or finials about twelve feet high. On the garden front the middle five bays enclose a tripartite bow-window room and are articulated by giant pilasters. The projecting bow has windows on the upper storey and on the lower floor three doorways giving direct access by a flight of semicircular steps to the garden. Hawksmoor and Archer were using Venetian windows by 1714 (p.91) and the bow with the flight of steps recalls the circular porch with curved steps in Hawksmoor's St Anne, Limehouse, which was designed in 1714 and which Vanbrugh would have seen as a Fifty Churches commissioner. Above the roof of the Eastbury design he placed open towers built of arches and containing chimney stacks, a derivation from the flue-arcades of the earlier Kings Weston. Probably two towers were intended, over the middle of the house.

The Kings Weston chimneys are related also to a second design, recorded in only two drawings (Pl.134). It has been suggested that this design is several stages later because it introduces the square corner towers found in the final design of about 1718.[12] But it is often impossible, however attractive it may be to the methodical mind, to set out the development of architectural ideas in a single sequence. We make most of our serious decisions by the successive consideration of a number of alternatives, often going over the same arguments more than once, and the designing of buildings is no exception. Assuming that this design was intended for Eastbury, it may be neither later than nor alternative to that with Venetian windows but the earliest of all, since it is closer in feeling to Kings Weston. All the windows are without architraves, and the chimney-arcades are very similar to Kings Weston, although here they are raised above the central clerestory and projected outwards into bastions at the corners; as at Kings Weston also, the portico hardly projects from the block-shape of the house. The corner turrets, with pediments to the main fronts and sloping roofs to the sides, are a sentry-box motif which had already

[12] Whistler, pp.158–9.

appeared in Hawksmoor's repertoire and can be traced back to Wilton, one of the archetypes of English Palladianism. Vanbrugh's portico, of four columns *in antis*, is deeply recessed into the house and would have left the clerestory to provide most of the light for the monumental central hall; the latter would have seemed almost filled by four corner clusters, each of a pier and two three-foot columns. The existing room closest to this in feeling is Hawksmoor's St Mary Woolnoth, which was not designed before 1716, but from what is known of the way the latter's clusters of columns were evolved it is probable that the common source for both architects was their joint design of the clerestoried hall at Blenheim (Pl.81). The hall in the drawing is flanked by an octagonal room on one side and a big circular geometrical stair on the other, lit by windows in recesses of the side elevation; a related sketch shows these recesses to have been arched.[13] It is tempting to wonder whether this design is closer than at first appears to the development of Vanbrugh's Palladianism, for it is possible to interpret the staircase, the arches in the centre of the side elevations, the recessed portico and even the foursquare symmetry and internal divisions of the plan as reminiscences of Inigo Jones's Queen's House at Greenwich. The tall deep arches of the square design and several features of the Venetian window design reappear in the engraved 'New Design' which Campbell dated 1716 (Pls 136, 138–9). The arches appear on all four fronts, the superimposed Venetian windows are moved to the sides, and the garden bow-window is now approached by a horse-shoe outside staircase. The two chimney towers are larger and bolder and enclose circular lanterns which provide the only light for the two staircases flanking the hall. The house now has a projecting entrance portico of four pillars and a large deep forecourt like that at Seaton Delaval, with flanking wings and kitchen and stable courts. This is one of the most extraordinary designs Vanbrugh ever produced, seeming to border on self-caricature; there is, however, no reason to suppose that he or Doddington thought other than seriously of it. Its essence is exaggeration of scale: the colossal arches and the answering ones above the roofline are so large that they conflict both with the scale of the rest of the elevations and with our expectations in domestic architecture. They so demand our attention that the rest of the exterior is totally subordinated to the succession of gigantic accents. The effect is dramatic, bold, and epigrammatic, and it is emphasized by the small round windows on the end elevation. There is an element of the part for the whole, and while there is nothing similar in Vanbrugh's work it represents a phase not uncommon in architects whose work is an exploration of effects of scale and mass. Hawksmoor, in some of his college designs, is the closest parallel in time and place but it is also worth recalling the superhuman scale of Wren's Great Model design for St Paul's of 1673–4.

The wings and service courts were scarcely changed in subsequent stages of the design, except that octagonal rooms (a chapel and an eating room) were added to the house ends of the courts. But the final design of the main building, published in *Vitruvius Britannicus* III in 1725, was the result of considerable alteration to both plan and elevations. In some respects it represents a return to the square design, but while in both outline and detail the latter is close to Kings Weston of about 1710 the final Eastbury design is much

[13] ibid., Pl.68.

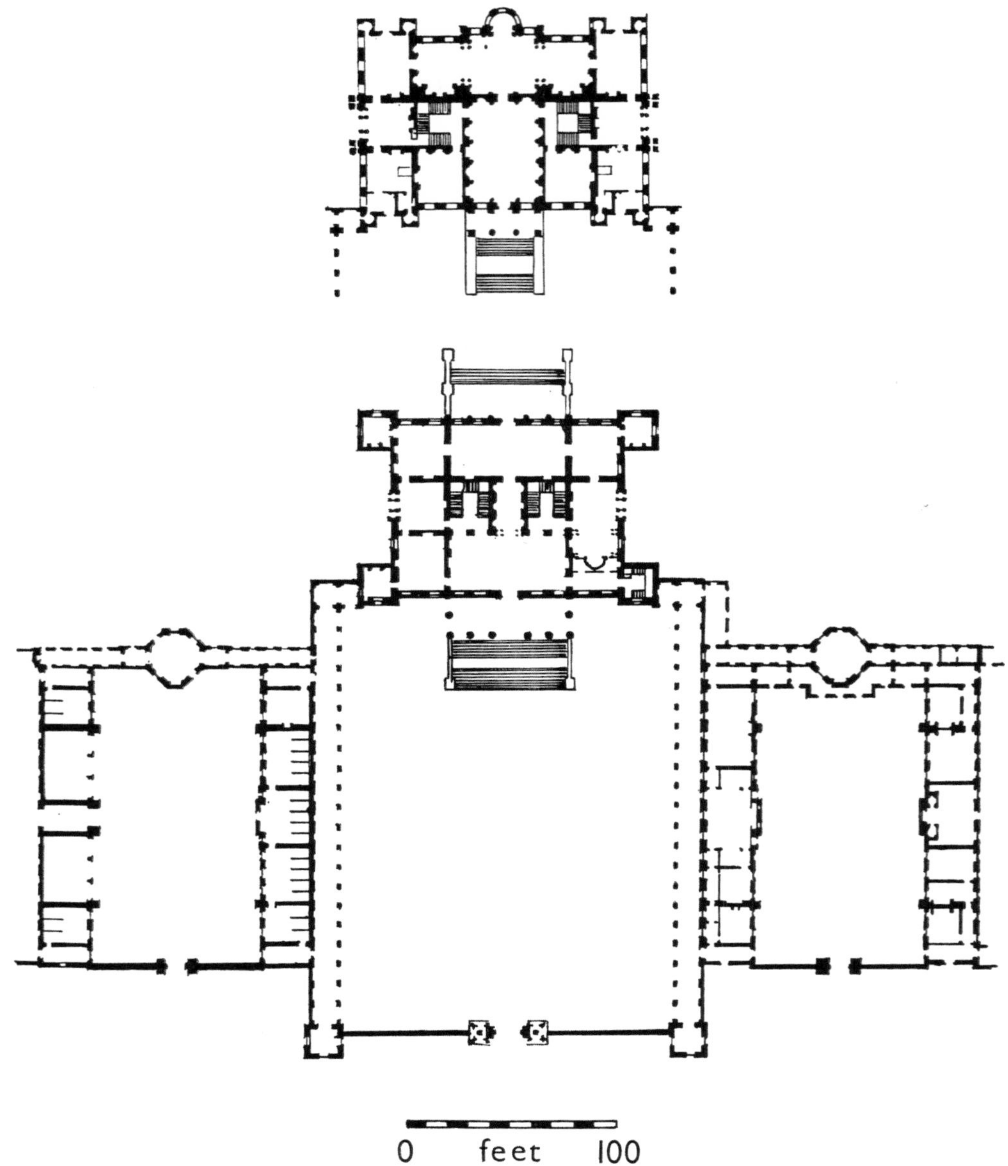

17 Eastbury. 'New Design' and final plans. From *Vitruvius Britannicus*.

nearer to Seaton Delaval of 1719–20.[14] The corner towers end in attics with Venetian windows and round finials very like those at Seaton, and the banded columns of the portico, now projecting and hexastyle, also recall the Delaval house (Pl.140). The substitution of a balustrade for battlements gives the clerestory a new elegance and smoothness of skyline, and besides the Venetian windows there is a further explicit Palladian reference in the block surrounds to the windows of the outer bays. In fact in terms of vocabulary and shape this design appears to be an early Georgian reinterpretation of Wollaton on a scale closer to the original than Admiral Delaval could afford. The area of Doddington's house is in fact reduced from the 'New Design' and the corner towers are

[14] Penultimate design, Whistler, Pl.69; RIBA, *Campbell* [2], 2. A related design exists in a drawing ascribed to James Paine (Whistler, Pl.71).

ingeniously used to retain the overall width in relation to the court. In the plan Vanbrugh made a number of other changes, replacing the tripartite bow-window room by a simple rectangular saloon, turning the staircases round to face the hall, and placing between them a tunnel-like niche-lined vestibule connecting the hall to the saloon (Fig.17). Work began on the forecourt and wings in or before 1718, for Doddington appears to have occupied the kitchen wing before his death in March 1720 and was engaging Thornhill to paint in the octagons the previous year.[15] On the other hand he seems not to have begun the main house, and the date of 1718 given by Campbell may be too early by two or three years. Vanbrugh visited Eastbury in July 1722 and expected the building 'from this time . . . to go on without any Stop.'[16] However, Doddington's nephew George Bubb, who took the name Doddington at his inheritance, seems to have been too busy to do much about building until 1724; after Vanbrugh's death the work was taken over by Roger Morris and completed by him in 1738, without the clerestory and with a pediment over the portico.

Eastbury was shortlived and prodigious and its end was melodramatic. The total cost of house and gardens was about £140,000, or nearly half that of Blenheim. George Bubb Doddington died in 1762, as Baron Melcombe, and the estate passed to Lord Temple. Thirteen years later Temple demolished the main house, unoccupied and unsold, using gunpowder.[17] Most of the wings and courts was gradually demolished, leaving today part of the stable wing as a modest house (Pl.137), with an archway from which grow two mature trees (Pl.135). There are traces of Bridgeman's great garden layout, but nothing remains of the Temple and Bagnio designed by Vanbrugh and recorded in *Vitruvius Britannicus*.[18] The Bagnio or water pavilion, halfway along the right hand edge of the garden, was a two-storey affair with a pedimented Ionic portico above a rusticated room, flanked by plainer wings with Vanbrugh's characteristic plain heavy round-headed windows.

The Temple (Pl.141) was even more Palladian, a hexastyle Corinthian loggia on the axis of the house at the upper end of the garden; apart from the spiral fluted urns above the pediment it would hardly be recognized as Vanbrugh's from the engraving without the authority of Campbell, and the Temple has even been presented as one of the morning stars of Neo-classicism.[19] The hexastyle temple portico was a form of widespread interest to architects in the second decade of the eighteenth century, particularly in relation to churches: Hawksmoor's St George, Bloomsbury, James's St George, Hanover Square and Gibbs's St Martin-in-the-Fields were all under construction early in the 1720s and probably grew out of projects of the previous decade for peripteral temples, notably those by Gibbs

[15] Whistler, p.163.

[16] Webb, p.148. The Account Book records visits in July and Oct. 1723, June 1724 and May 1725, and receipts (from George Bubb Dodington) of £300 (July 1722), £700 (Feb. 1723) and £275 (posthumous, July 1726).

[17] By 1782 he had 'dismantled the park' (*The Torrington Diary*, ed. C. Bruyn Andrews, I, 1934, p.105).

[18] Vol. III, Pls 18–19, dated there 1718. A drawing for the Bagnio is *Elton Drawings*, No.194.

[19] F. Kimball, 'Romantic Classicism in Architecture', *Gazette des Beaux-Arts*, per.6, XXV, 1944, p.95 ff. Vanbrugh's 'anti-Baroque' late style is also over-played in E. Kauffmann's rationalistic survey of *Architecture in the Age of Reason*, 1955. For porticoes and peripteral temples see J. Field, 'Early Unknown Gibbs', *Architectural Review*, CXXXI, 1962, pp.315–19; Downes (1966), p.104. Comparison with Vanbrugh's drawing for a garden building (Fig.20) confirms his authorship of a design for an octastyle peripteral temple (church?) (V & A D.96.1891).

and Campbell for the Fifty New Churches Commission and by Hawksmoor for a colossal university church at Oxford. It is perhaps the scale of Vanbrugh's Temple which places it in this context, separates it from other garden buildings and establishes once again the bold originality of its architect. The floor of this enormous summer-house was fifty feet wide and thirty feet deep. Its columns, which in the elevation are all round whereas in the plan the outer ones are square, were thirty feet high, and the apex of the pediment was fifty-three feet from the ground. Thus the order was as big as the Ionic on the garden front of Seaton Delaval (Pl.122) and almost as big as the applied portico of the garden front of Eastbury itself, facing the Temple a third of a mile away. The portico was the same size as the one Campbell built for the centrepiece of Wanstead House, the first big Palladian mansion (1714–15), and only smaller by three feet or so than Gibbs's portico at St Martin-in-the-Fields. The plates of Campbell's three volumes afford rather arbitrary but not irrelevant comparisons, and they show no other comparable garden building. The architect was, after all, that of the Grand Bridge at Blenheim as well as the Temple at Castle Howard.

The comparisons invited by the scale of the Eastbury Temple suggest that once again Swift had been right: Vanbrugh watched the Palladians at play and believed he could do better. There is no doubt about the classicism of the private gallery pew he built for Newcastle in old Esher Church in 1724–5 (Pl.152).[20] Externally the pew is a square brick addition to the south side of the nave, with its own entrance. It has a plaster fret ceiling and a floor about four feet above the church. The church has been re-seated; when the gallery's white-painted wooden front to the nave stood above box pews it must have looked more comfortable and no less elegant. Nevertheless Vanbrugh's solution, however indebted to classical Italy, was not orthodox. He provided a temple front *in antis* facing into the church and an identical one on the other side of the wall facing into the pew. The columns are structural in that they help to support the joist and the wall above; the double thickness of columns gives a richness and spatial quality similar to, but hardly dependent on, that of some medieval triforium galleries. At the same time Vanbrugh lightened both the appearance and the mood of the temple front by cutting away the architrave and frieze of the order between the pillars, leaving only the cornice.

Grimsthorpe Castle was Vanbrugh's last house and would, if completed, have occupied a place in his *oeuvre* parallel to the Castle Howard Temple. Both designs are remarkable for their Italianate character, and both were made for patrons with whom the architect had been associated for many years. His links with Carlisle went back to Kit-Cat days in the 1690s, those with Robert Bertie, 4th Earl of Lindsey and 1st Duke of Ancaster, even further, for he was the Lord Willoughby who was Vanbrugh's companion in 1688 (p.12). It has not been possible to establish that Vanbrugh actually built for one or other member of the numerous Bertie family either at Swinstead or Eresby, both Bertie estates in Lincolnshire and both retaining traces of demolished great houses. Mystery also surrounds two sets of drawings for a large and a small house among the Ancaster papers

[20] Faculty, 6 Aug. 1724, Vestry consent, 20 April 1725; B. F. L. Clarke, *The Building of the Eighteenth-Century Church*, 1963, p.81 Vanbrugh's letter about a design 'for a Seat in Esher church' is endorsed *Nov. 1st 1723* (p.80, n.9). The pew was subsequently partitioned across the middle for the use of Newcastle and his brother who owned Esher Place.

which probably date, on stylistic evidence, from about 1710.[21] The fact that they were preserved suggests that they were not used even though another may have been, and in view of their long association we cannot assume that payments by Robert Bertie to Vanbrugh in 1711–12 amounting to £57 18*s.* were for professional services. Vanbrugh's closest friendship appears to have been with Robert's younger brother Peregrine (p.12) and it would certainly be surprising if his contemporaries in this proud and propertied family did not employ him earlier and more consistently than in the commission of 1722 for Grimsthorpe. Indeed there is some evidence that work there may have begun several years earlier.

Grimsthorpe was a partly medieval and partly Tudor house round a court, but the north range had been rebuilt in the 1680s in the domestic style of the day. The centre of the range consisted of one enormous two-storey room forty feet by over a hundred with windows on one side, flanked by tower-like projections. A plan at Grimsthorpe is inscribed in Vanbrugh's hand *Principal Floor, as it is now, 1715*,[22] and an elevation for re-casing the north front among the drawings at Elton perhaps dates from this time (Pl.156). It is certainly preliminary to what was carried out, since it shows coupled square piers instead of banded columns and the doorcase has a projecting pediment supported on brackets; nevertheless it belongs in style to Vanbrugh's plainest years, after Blenheim and before Seaton Delaval. Moreover, the centre seven bays, fronting the hall, are closer in the building (Pl.157) to the Elton drawing than to Campbell's engraving of 1725; in the latter the arches formed over the windows by a continuous string moulding are joined by flat horizontal pieces between the windows, whereas in drawing and building the junctions are sharper and almost pointed. The engraving is one of four, representing the plan and north, south and west fronts of an almost complete rebuilding. The 1st Duke died in July 1723 and the following month Vanbrugh was on his way to Grimsthorpe to see the son, 'having the honour of an invitation from him, to consult about his Building; by which I believe he is inclin'd to go on upon the General Design I made for his Father last Winter and which was approv'd of by himself.'[23] Thus the 'General Design' represented by the engravings may have included a new hall front and interior already built several years previously; support for this conclusion is to be found not only in the difference in style

[21] Lincs. CRO, Anc.10/D/3 (Pls 92, 94) and 3 Anc.8/2/25 (Fig.18). It has not been possible to give further confirmation to John Harris's researches (*Architectural Review*, CXXIX, 1961, pp.69–72), but his suggested dating of *c.*1710, based on perforce exiguous evidence, is probably correct. The watermarks of the plan and elevation of the smaller scheme (3 Anc.8/2/25) are very similar to those of two Vanbrugh letters to Marlborough at Blenheim datable 23 Feb. 1711 (D.I.21, Whistler, pp.234–5 as 1710, datable a year later by reference to Travers's letter to the Duke of the same, explicit, date in the same box) and late 1710 (F.I.49, ibid., pp.238–40). Stephen Switzer the garden designer was at Eresby in 1711 (ibid., p.22) and received £305 from Lord Lindsey in 1710–13 (information from Mr Timothy Connor). His stay at Eresby may, however, have been in connection with his work at Grimsthorpe begun in that year (W. A. Brogden, 'Stephen Switzer, *La Grand Manier*', in P. Willis, ed., *Furor Hortensis, Essays in Memory of Frank Clark*, Edinburgh, 1974, pp.21–30). At Eresby today there are remains of seventeenth-century stables, one gate pier of uncertain date about 20 feet high, an avenue leading north to Spilsby, and a sloping site which was terraced, leading down to a large rectangular pool. The house, which may have been still the Jacobean one, was burnt to the ground in 1769. The belvedere or Old Summer House at Swinstead (Pl.117) is of uncertain date. The Engine House and the Rubbing House at Grimsthorpe, drawn by John Grundy, engineer, of Spalding, in 1753 in his *Book Map of the Manor of Edenham* (Lincs. CRO 3 Anc.4/35a) are indeterminately Palladio-Vanbrughian in style.

[22] H. M. Colvin and J. Harris, ed., *The Country Seat*, 1970, Fig.61. See also T. Connor, 'Grimsthorpe Castle', *Archaeological Journal*, CXXXI, 1974, pp.330–3, with analytical plan. The hall at Grimsthorpe, even in its earlier form, may have inspired the Great Room at Claremont of 1719.

[23] Webb, p.151. *Vit.Brit.* (III, Pls 11–14) dates the design 1724 in the text and 1723 in titles. Vanbrugh also visited Grimsthorpe in Dec. 1718 on political business (Webb, p.105), and was there in Sept. 1724 (Whistler, p.246) and Sept.–Oct. 1725 (Account Book).

18 Plan and elevation of a house for the Bertie family. From drawings in the Lincolnshire Record Office.

between the hall front and the rest of the exterior design but also in the abrupt change in mouldings where this front meets the projecting corner towers containing the chapel and the State Dining Room (Pl.155). Moreover the hall chimneypiece (Pl.99) is an almost exact version, though larger, of that in the Duchess's Bedchamber at Blenheim, certainly designed before 1716.[24] The north range was completed, and with it the forecourt with its arcades and little corner towers (Pl.151); considerable further work was done inside the old buildings, but none of it shows Vanbrugh's hand and his great scheme virtually died with him in 1726.

[24] Green, Pl.56.

The hall, entirely carried out in creamy stone, is his most economical great room and perhaps, because of its consistency, his finest (Pl.159). The arcading of the façade is carried all the way round the interior; the niches on the long wall are hollowed out below while in the upper storey they are flat and painted with fictive statues of English kings in brown heightened with gold. At the ends of the hall the arcades are open to reveal on both storeys further arcades beyond them in shadow; further back still are double staircases, leading to galleries on the upper floor (Pl.158). At the stairheads are stone doorcases derived, though not literally copied, from those designed by Michelangelo for the side palaces of the Capitol in Rome and known in England from Specchi's engraving (Pl.160).[25] It is conceivable that Hawksmoor contributed to Grimsthorpe, since his sale catalogue in 1740 mentions drawings 'for the Duke of Ancaster's chapel.' The chapel, however, in the north-west tower, is a mixture of Georgian, early twentieth-century neo-Georgian (in the lower storey) and probably part of the late-seventeenth-century ceiling. Hawksmoor could have provided some of the detailing, but there is little reason to doubt Vanbrugh's authorship of the staircase doorways at the same date as the design of the Castle Howard Temple.

The corner towers and the projected south front have an elegance and an exact sense of the relation of motifs to wall surface which also recall the Temple. While the lowest windows have exaggerated triple keystones and rusticated sides which derive from the south basement of Blenheim the remainder of the detail has the Renaissance Italianate refinement of selection and execution that we have already seen to be within Vanbrugh's capacity. The recognition of this capacity is the more important in view of the resemblance between the south elevation design and Campbell's, published in *Vitruvius Britannicus* for Sir Robert Walpole's house, Houghton in Norfolk (Pls153–4).[26] The resemblance is close enough for the Grimsthorpe elevation once to have been attributed to Campbell, against the evidence of his own published statement. Campbell's Houghton design was made no later than 1722; though his relations with Vanbrugh remained good enough for the latter to supply him with drawings for the *Vitruvius* volume, their contact was very probably limited and formal after Campbell's dismissal from the Works in 1719 in the wake of Benson (p.87). Vanbrugh is more likely to have received early knowledge of the Houghton design through Walpole, to whose house at Chelsea he had made alterations in 1715–16 and with whom he was on intimate political terms in 1720–22.[27] If Campbell regarded the Grimsthorpe design as the sincerest form of flattery, Vanbrugh must have believed, as he had done on earlier occasions, that he could surpass his model; there was

[25] Domenico de Rossi, *Studio d'Architettura Civile*, I, Rome, 1702, Pl.4. The dating of Thornhill's fictive statues after 1722 appears to rest on assumptions about the date of the building. Hawksmoor's sale catalogue has now been published in facsimile by D. Watkin, *Sale Catalogues of Libraries of Eminent Persons*, 4, *Architects*, 1972.

[26] Dated there 1723. Building began in 1722 (H. Stutchbury, *Colen Campbell*, 1967, p.149) although the design was altered in execution.

[27] Appendix L; Webb, pp.63, 127–9, 132, 142–3. In 1723 Vanbrugh and Walpole discussed Houghton (Webb, pp.150–1). In Oct. 1716 Vanbrugh made a journey of eleven days to 'Mr Walpoles' (Account Book) but there is insufficient evidence to connect him with the former stables at Houghton, which Sir Thomas Robinson told Lord Carlisle on 9 Dec. 1731 'are very large and been finished about thirteen years ago [and] are to be pulled down next summer, not only as they are very ill built, but stand in the way of one of the most agreeable prospects you have from the house' (HMC Carlisle, pp.85–6). Robinson, who disliked Vanbrugh and his work, was writing to Carlisle, who liked both, and might be expected to mention any connection with the stables; a similar argument applies to the silence of Horace Walpole (e.g. in *Anecdotes of Painting*) whose knowledge of Houghton was extensive and whose respect for Vanbrugh was strictly moderate.

perhaps also a trace of the outrageous boldness that had led him earlier to build for himself in the ruins of Whitehall, to wrest Castle Howard from Talman, to live in Woodstock Manor and to insinuate himself into the College of Arms. In the last year of his life he 'got leave to dispose in earnest, of a Place I got in jest', selling his office of Clarenceux King-at-Arms to Knox Ward for £2,500.[28]

In the conventional historical sense Vanbrugh had no successors. It is impossible to determine what he would have made of Palladianism if, like Hawksmoor, he had lived another decade. The Vanbrugh school, like the whole English Baroque school of which he was one of the leading figures, was a sporadic manifestation, and traces of his influence can be found in the neighbourhood of most of his major houses. William Wakefield, a Yorkshire gentleman who died about 1730, was credited by contemporaries with the design of Duncombe Park, Helmsley, which was begun about 1713 and has Vanbrughian characteristics; Wakefield, who was certainly eclectic, may also have designed the monumental Debtors' Prison in York (1709) and the almshouses at Linton-in-Craven (1720) which are reminiscent of Vanbrugh at second-hand.[29] Henry Joynes, who after a decade of service at Blenheim became Clerk of Works at Kensington and developed a modest and competent private practice (Pl.150), was Hawksmoor's pupil rather than Vanbrugh's. Nor can Sir Edward Lovett Pearce, the Anglo-Irish Palladian, be called Vanbrugh's follower, although there are family and professional ties between them. Vanbrugh's aunt Mary was Pearce's grandmother, and the presence at Elton Hall of a large number of Vanbrugh sketches among the Pearce drawings, as well as a number of designs which lie stylistically ambiguously between the two, suggests that at some time Pearce worked with his older cousin and carried away some of his drawings.[30] Pearce also marked drawings for the shadowy Arthur who drew for Vanbrugh in 1723 (p.80), and from a study of Pearce's movements the contact must have been some time between 1716 and 1723, a period which embraces the identifiable Vanbrugh drawings in the Elton collection.

The second major source of Vanbrugh drawings is part of a collection bought by the Victoria and Albert Museum in 1891 from a Mr J. Smith, including drawings from about 1708 (Kimbolton) to about 1720 (Eastbury); the drawings for Castle Howard, now in the same museum, and for Blenheim in the Bodleian Library, came through Hawksmoor's or Wren's hands. The album formerly at Kings Weston and bought in 1973 by the Bristol Civic Trust contains no autograph drawings and a considerable number that have no connection with Vanbrugh, but this collection seems to have been made by a mason-designer, perhaps one who worked at Kings Weston after the death of the master mason George Townesend in 1719.[31] Some of the drawings are for Kings Weston and some relate to originals at Elton connected with that house and others; the album contains

[28] Webb, p.170, Oct. 1725; Whistler (1938), p.285; Account Book, 3 July 1725 (as £2500 but with attendant expenses).

[29] Colvin, p.646; Downes (1966), pp.92, 111.

[30] *Elton Drawings*, esp. pp. xxxix–xl. Sir Edward Lovett Pearce was born between *c.*1691 and *c.*1699 (ibid.; M. Verney, *Verney Letters of the Eighteenth Century*, I, 1930, pp.260, 262; T. U. Sadleir, 'Sir Edward Lovett Pearce', *Journal of County Kildare Archaeological Soc.*, x/5, 1927, pp.231–44). In 1740 the young Charles Vanbrugh showed Baron Bielfeld 'all the designs of his father' but apart from the fact that this cannot have been literally true it would not be surprising to discover that what he saw was a collection of engravings. See Appendix M.

[31] K. Downes, 'The Kings Weston Book of Drawings', *Architectural History*, x, 1967. The loggia (Pl.89) has a family likeness to a project in the Newcastle MSS. (BM MS.Add.33064, f.276, Pl.90 here) which may be for 'a Seat for the Water side at Claremont' mentioned in Vanbrugh's letter of 28 Aug. 1724 (ibid., f.247; Webb, p.162).

19 Kensington Palace. The Water Tower. After a wood-engraving in the *Gentleman's Magazine*, 1821.

variant drawings for another of Vanbrugh's Palladian experiments, the north-west loggia at Kings Weston, built about 1719 (Pl.89). The album also contains a number of designs for small houses and bungalows in Vanbrugh's style; on the combined showing of these and similar designs in both Elton and London he could well have designed a complete model town. None of these designs are known to have been executed except one for a Colonel Lambert at Sevenoaks; a few other small Vanbrughian houses existed into the nineteenth century in the Greater London area (Pl.149).[32]

Vanbrugh's immediate influence is to be seen at its most impressive in buildings connected with utility and defence. There is a close resemblance between the Claremont Belvedere, a nobleman's summer-house, and the very practical Water Tower commissioned in 1716 and formerly standing on Kensington Palace Green, or the pump house of 1718 which survives by the Thames under Windsor Castle (Pl.145). Vanbrugh's authorship of the Water Tower (Fig.19) is attested by William Stukeley, who sketched it in 1722.[33] The Windsor pump house, which like the north arch of the Blenheim Bridge housed a paddle engine built by Robert Aldersea, was also Vanbrugh's responsibility as Surveyor of

[32] Hanover House, Peckham (Pl.149); Lord Talbot's house at South Kensington (*Survey of London*, XXXVIII, p.6); Vine Court, Sevenoaks (ibid., pp.23–4, *Architectural Review*, CXV, 1954, p.122; R. Strong, *The Destruction of the Country House*, 1974, Pl.50). A house formerly in London Street, Kingston (on the west corner of the now Queen Elizabeth Road) was, according to Brayley's *History of Surrey* (ed.1878, II, p.237) 'one of the latest productions of Sir John Vanbrugh.' Its 'stack of chimneys' formed 'a turret in the centre of the roof.' Talbot House, *alias* Brompton Park, belonged to the gardener Henry Wise.

[33] In a volume in the Cragg collection formerly deposited in the Lincs. CRO (Cragg 2/20/16, p.5), inscribed *Castellum Aquense Regium apud Kensington Vanbrug invt.* For the Windsor Pump House see PRO Works 6/113, f.4; CTB 1717, pp.361–3; Bodl. Gough Maps 1*, p.23; Colvin, p.516.

Gardens and Waters; a plan and elevation with a costing were made by Thomas Rowland and Thomas Fort. The great kitchen at St James's Palace, built in 1716–17 and still in use, was probably also designed by Vanbrugh (Pl.142). About 1720 Lord Carlisle put up, to his design, Robin Hood's Well near Skelbrooke on the Great North Road (Pl.147), which before the coming of the railways was the first changing place on the road north of Doncaster and had two coaching inns.[34]

His connection with the Board of Ordnance was indirect but pervasive. The Board usually employed its own engineers and designers independently of the Office of Works, and in the early years of George I responsibility for new buildings lay ultimately with Marlborough as Master of Ordnance and proximately with Brigadier-General Michael Richards, Surveyor-General and a friend of Vanbrugh. The Old Pretender's campaign of 1715 gave impetus to a programme of improvement and expansion of military building all over Britain. In January 1719 the mason Andrews Jelfe was appointed architect and clerk of works in charge of all the new buildings of the Ordnance,[35] and his partner in the building business, Christopher Cass, had worked at Blenheim and became Master Mason to the Ordnance. But many of the new buildings were designed before Jelfe's appointment and the similarities between many buildings over a wide area must initially have come from the application of one mind at the highest level. Whether Vanbrugh designed any of them personally cannot be established, and there are certainly different degrees of closeness to his personal style. The closest surviving buildings are at Woolwich, Chatham and Devonport. At Woolwich Arsenal the old Board Room building was constructed in 1718–20 of yellow brick with red brick voussoirs, with an elegant bow window at one end towards the Thames and with portholes and a great central arch which recalls the 'New Design' for Eastbury (Pl.143). At Chatham Dockyard the main gateway (1720) is a larger version of the gate to Vanbrugh Fields, while the Great Store, begun in 1717, has crenellations similar to those of Vanbrugh Castle (Pl.148). At Devonport, where the Ordnance Dockyard was laid out almost as formally and symmetrically as if the harbour were a great park, the surviving stone range of administrative and domestic buildings of the early 1720s at the upper end, now called Gun Wharf Terrace, is unmistakably Vanbrughian (Pls.144, 146).[36]

Vanbrugh died at his Whitehall house on 26 March 1726 after a short illness described as 'a quinsey in the throat' and was buried in the family vault in St Stephen, Walbrook. His will made the previous autumn was not witnessed and its authenticity had to be attested by two witnesses who had known him personally for a substantial time.[37] His

[34] For Robin Hood's Well see Whistler, p.205; HMC Portland VII, p.90; notes by Stukeley (Bodl.MS.Top.Gen. d.14, f.21; MS. Eng.Misc. e.123, ff.59–60) and intermittent correspondence in *Country Life*. The well-head was rebuilt by the Ministry of Works on a new base in the early 1960s after road improvements; one inn stands, converted to a school and since derelict. See N. W. Webster, *The Great North Road*, Bath, 1974, p.88.

[35] PRO W.O.55/490; Whistler, pp.215, 223, 225.

[36] Philip Vanbrugh became Commissioner of Plymouth Dockyard in 1739 (*Gent. Mag.*, IX, 1739, p.328).

[37] The will (PROB 11/608, fol.84) was made on 30 Aug. 1725 and amplified the following day by a codicil and two postscripts, each signed. Although the original autograph will (PROB 1/61) headed 'My will is This' and divided into paragraphs is neatly laid out and written in his customary strong hand, the need for additions and amplifications suggests that it was composed under stress. This is confirmed by the absence of witnesses and by a letter of 4 Sept. 1725 to Lord Carlisle: 'A Distemper has got hold of me, even worse than the Gout, which is an Asthma; at least I have Strong Symptomes of one' (Webb, p.168). The will was verified by George Vanbrugh and John Rogers.

young widow survived him for fifty years and thirty days; his only adult son was killed at Fontenoy in 1745. Several of his cousins and the children of his siblings can be traced into the later eighteenth century, and Edward Vanbrugh who died in Bath on 5 October 1802 was described in the *Gentleman's Magazine* of that year as his immediate descendant; in fact he was the son of the architect's younger brother Charles.

The first collected edition of Vanbrugh's plays was published in 1730 and there were many subsequent editions as well as foreign translations. His architecture had to wait longer for re-appraisal although Blenheim was a showpiece throughout the eighteenth century. For once the reader will be spared Dr Abel Evans's facetious epitaph, which it serves neither truth nor justice to quote. With a better eye for history than for artistic values, Lord Chesterfield in 1766 found the Roman amphitheatre at Nîmes ugly and clumsy enough to have been the work of Vanbrugh if it had been in England.[38] In 1772 Horace Walpole visited Castle Howard and thought it sublime,[39] and the following year Robert and James Adam in the preface to their *Works in Architecture* found his buildings 'so crowded with barbarisms and absurdities, and so borne down by their own preposterous weight, that none but the discerning can separate their merits from their defects.' Nevertheless they saw much to praise in these rough diamonds: novelty and ingenuity, and *movement*, a term 'meant to express the rise and fall, the advance and recess, with other diversity of form, in the different parts of a building, so as to add greatly to the picturesqueness of the composition.' Reynolds's praise in the 13th Discourse (1786) has already been mentioned. A decade later Uvedale Price, while finding Blenheim without rules, praised the uniting there of 'the beauty and magnificence of Grecian architecture, the picturesqueness of the Gothic, and the massive grandeur of a castle.'[40]

The conviction that, while Homer may have nodded, Vanbrugh's artistic licentiousness was as gross as his imagination was original, persisted through the nineteenth century into the twentieth, and it was in the works of architects rather than the words of critics that a new appreciation of Vanbrugh as a builder rather than a painter first appeared. In his 5th Academy lecture (1809) Sir John Soane praised his invention and his 'bold flights of irregular fancy', calling him 'the Shakespeare of Architects.'[41] There is a vein of his massive simplicity hidden in Neo-classicism, and it came to the surface in a few buildings such as the scholarly C. R. Cockerell's Branch Bank of England in Bristol (1844–7). More notably it was taken up by the engineer-builder: by Charles Fowler in the Lower Market at Exeter (1835–6, destroyed 1942) and later by railway architects and by the designers of pumping and other machinery houses which are the direct descendants of Vanbrugh's

[38] 4th Earl of Chesterfield to his son: *Letters*, ed. B. Dobrée, VI, 1932, p.2786. The Earl was writing twenty-five years after his visit to Nîmes in 1741. For a different view of Vanbrugh in 1740, significant less because it is favourable than because it is foreign, individual and thoughtful, see Appendix M.

[39] 'Nobody . . . had informed me that I should at one view see a palace, a town, a fortified city, temples on high places, woods worthy of being each a metropolis of the Druids, vales connected to hills by other woods, the noblest lawn in the world fenced by half the horizon, and a mausoleum that would tempt one to be buried alive; in short, I have seen gigantic places before, but never a sublime one' (H. Walpole to George Selwyn; *Letters*, ed. Mrs Paget Toynbee, VIII, 1904, p.193. 'Gigantic places' is often misquoted as *palaces*. Was Walpole aware of Bielfeld's reference to Blenheim as an entire city, published two years earlier? (Appendix M)

[40] Uvedale Price, *Essay on Architecture and Buildings* (*Essays on the Picturesque*, II, 1810 ed., pp.212–15).

[41] J. Soane, *Lectures on Architecture*, 1929, pp.89–90.

own but, being built for huge steam engines, are on a scale of which he can hardly have dreamed.

The Gothic Revival did nothing to help Vanbrugh's cause, for its codification of medieval architectural styles reinforced the opinion that he worked without rules and also outlawed his attempts at romantic medievalism. The late nineteenth century saw the development of studies of Vanbrugh the playwright, and many of the persistent biographical hares are to be found coursing through the early series of *Notes and Queries*. Repeated requests for the date and place of his birth met with speculative answers, and the story that he studied architecture in France at the age of nineteen is probably based on an amalgam of his father's three years abroad, his own release from the Bastille at the end of 1692 and the suggestion that he was born about the middle of Charles II's reign which was then arithmetically determined as 1672–3. The serious study of Vanbrugh the architect had to wait longer, the recognition that he was more than a wild amateur longer still. Martin Briggs, in the first English book on *Baroque Architecture* (1913) had a little to say about his 'colossal absurdities' and 'megalomania', and only in the 1920s did a new sympathy with Baroque art in general open the way for new attitudes. The year 1928 was crucial, for it saw the publication of Vanbrugh's letters as the final volume of the Nonesuch Edition of his works, and also the appearance of the *English Homes* volume on the Vanbrugh school. Subsequent discoveries in many fields have answered many of the questions raised by those two volumes while posing new ones. We now see him as a rounder and more serious character than the back-slapping figures of his comedies.[42] We can also see that, although they had much in common, he and Hawksmoor were very different both personally and artistically. Because of the strength of what each had to offer, their partnership was one of the most fruitful for their art, and one of the most fascinating for the scholar. The rehabilitation of Hawksmoor in architectural history inevitably altered the balance of our knowledge and our attitudes, but while for a time it might have appeared that Vanbrugh was to suffer in the process the truth must be established that both were remarkable. The solution of factual problems can do no more than provide a framework for attempts to understand the character of the man and his work. But understanding a great man is an activity which never reaches an end and hardly indeed passes beyond a beginning; it is no less rewarding for that.

[42] The reader may gauge the reliability of M. Bingham, *Masks and Façades: Sir John Vanbrugh the Man in his Setting*, 1974, from the ascription (in the frontispiece) of the portrait to Sir *Geoffrey* Kneller. The imputation to Colley Cibber of a firm statement 'that Vanbrugh had studied architecture in France' (p.99) appears to derive from Theophilus Cibber, *Lives of the Poets*, IV, 1753, p.106, that 'in some part of our author's life (for we cannot justly ascertain the time) he gratified an inclination of visiting France . . . His taste for architecture excited him to take a survey of the fortifications in that kingdom.' The younger Cibber goes on to describe how Vanbrugh was arrested in the course of his injudicious sketching with a fulsome account of how his charm gained him 'liberty some days before the sollicitation came from England.' Theophilus, who was Colley's son, was twenty-three when Vanbrugh died, and the *Lives*, published under his name, were mainly compiled by Samuel Johnson's amanuensis Robert Shiels (Boswell's *Life of Johnson*, under 10 April 1776, with Malone's corrective note). It is not therefore reasonable to assume much authority for an account at second or third hand which is in other respects fanciful and which appears to be the first to insert into Vanbrugh's life an incident at Calais involving the painter Hogarth in 1748.

Part II

The Family and Domestic Circumstances of Vanbrugh

In a vituperative letter, part of his unsuccessful campaign to prevent Sir John Vanbrugh's appointment as a Herald, John Anstis referred contemptuously to Vanbrugh's Dutch extraction and argued that it effectively disqualified him from office.[1] Anstis was not the first or the last to promote an imprecision which is not only elementary but also simplistic. The architect's grandparents represented four classes of society: foreign merchants attracted to England by way of trade (Gillis Van Brugh), Protestant refugee merchants (Marie Jacobs, his wife, was born in London of Flemish refugee parents), minor courtiers (Sir Dudley Carleton, nephew and co-heir of Dudley Carleton, Viscount Dorchester, diplomat and friend and patron of Rubens) and the provincial landed gentry (Lady Carleton, Lucy Croft, daughter of Sir Herbert Croft of Croft Castle, Herefordshire). The family into which the architect was born combined in equal measures two well-knit communities: on his mother's side the backbone of seventeenth-century England, Church, army and land, and on his father's side a mercantile and commercial community which had made itself loyally British while retaining strong links in particular with the Dutch Church (Austin Friars) in London.[2]

In 1696 a country visitor to London wrote home to Yorkshire that 'at London I had good company, German and Dutch doctors, travellers, residents, chymists, etc. all countrymen and so acquainted . . . there is all languages spoke, Dutch, German, French, Italian, Latin, Greek and I know not what.'[3] At that moment the thirty-two-year-old Vanbrugh, nominally a soldier, was breaking into the world of the London stage. His ties with the international merchant community were being replaced by those of the Whig nobility who were to be his principal patrons, but the accepted cosmopolitan nature of London at that date was significant not only as a mirror of his own genetic constitution: it was also the social analogue of English architecture in the age of Wren. The eclecticism of Wren and Hawksmoor, and indirectly of Vanbrugh, drew on sources from many countries in Europe, and there are stylistic analogies between their work and that of Jules Hardouin Mansart in France, Hildebrandt and Fischer von Erlach in Austria, and Carlo

[1] To the Duke of Norfolk's mother, 16 March 1703. (A. Wagner, *Heralds of England*, 1967, p.331). The Vanbrughs were of course Flemings.

[2] See in general A. Wagner, *English Genealogy*, Oxford, 1960, and in particular the sections on Flemings, Dutch, Germans and Huguenots (pp.219–29) and on the ways in which names were anglicized – *ad aurem, ad oculum* and *ad sensum* (p.228).

[3] Robert Read to Abraham de la Pryme (*Surtees Soc.*, LIV, 1869, p.279).

Fontana and Juvarra in Italy.[4] In Vanbrugh's lifetime a new wave of British nationalism was to attenuate or even destroy many of the links between Britain and Europe both in architecture and in politics. The study of Vanbrugh genealogy is therefore of importance not merely because it is studiable and a small addition to the sum of historical knowledge, but also because it is part of the background of one of the principal architects of the English Baroque.

Genealogy is a slow and often fortuitous procedure, and in a period as remote as the seventeenth century there are inevitably many gaps in the family tree. Nevertheless a surprising amount of material can be traced, both about the relationships and the activities of many of Vanbrugh's family, and the following three chapters are supplementary to the information tabulated in the family trees on pp.129–37. On his mother's side the families were of sufficient status to interest some of the compilers of English pedigrees. On his father's side we are helped more than anything by the London Flemish Protestants' practice of baptizing their children in the Dutch Church, and of registering the baptismal witnesses, who were usually, though not necessarily, related to the parents. In many other churches, however, the registers were kept very casually; they could be written up some time after the event, and as in some cases there are demonstrable inaccuracies there may be others as yet undetected.[5] It is also unfortunate that the register of burials in the Dutch Church does not begin until 1671.[6]

[4] Fischer von Erlach is supposed, on the basis of a passport, to have visited London in 1705 (H. Aurenhammer, *Fischer von Erlach*, 1973, p.30), Juvarra in 1720. We do not know if Vanbrugh met either, though he can hardly have failed to meet Galilei during his five years in England from 1714 to 1719 (see p.49).

[5] According to James Brydges, Duke of Chandos, 'not one in ten is registered' in the parish of St Andrew, Holborn – referring to baptisms (*Chandos*, p.384). Apart from omission in the first place, there are hazards from loss, damage (especially at the edges of surviving books), unavailability, and travel. A first confinement was often in the home of the maternal grandmother or another relative away from the home parish. The choice of parish for marriages seems often to have been capricious. A death away from home is only likely to be traceable if there is a will.

[6] Guildhall Library MS.7381 contains baptisms and marriages 1571–1601, MS.7382 continues from 1602 and has burials from 1671. The registers, hereafter referred to as DCR, were published in the form of an alphabetical index by W. J. C. Moens, Lymington, 1884 (hereafter quoted as Moens). While this is a valuable adjunct to the registers it abounds in misreadings and is in no sense a transcript; moreover it excludes the names of witnesses. Somewhere in the vast mess of pre-1688 uncalendared Ormonde Papers in the National Library of Ireland there is a letter of Giles Vanbrugh.

Genealogical Tables

I The Family of Sir Dudley Carleton

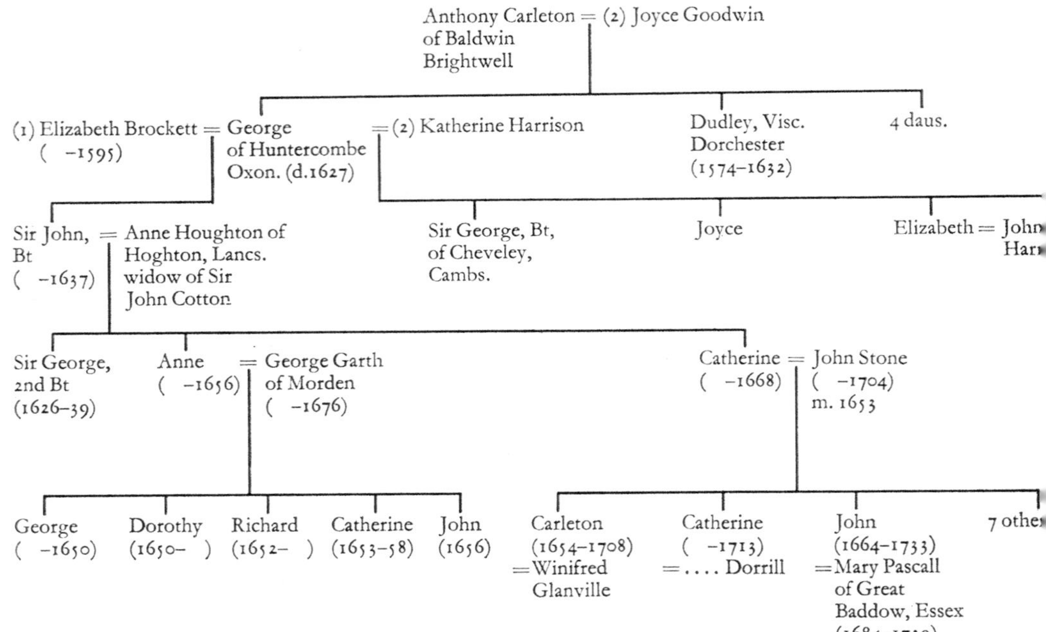

II Lucy Croft and Related Families

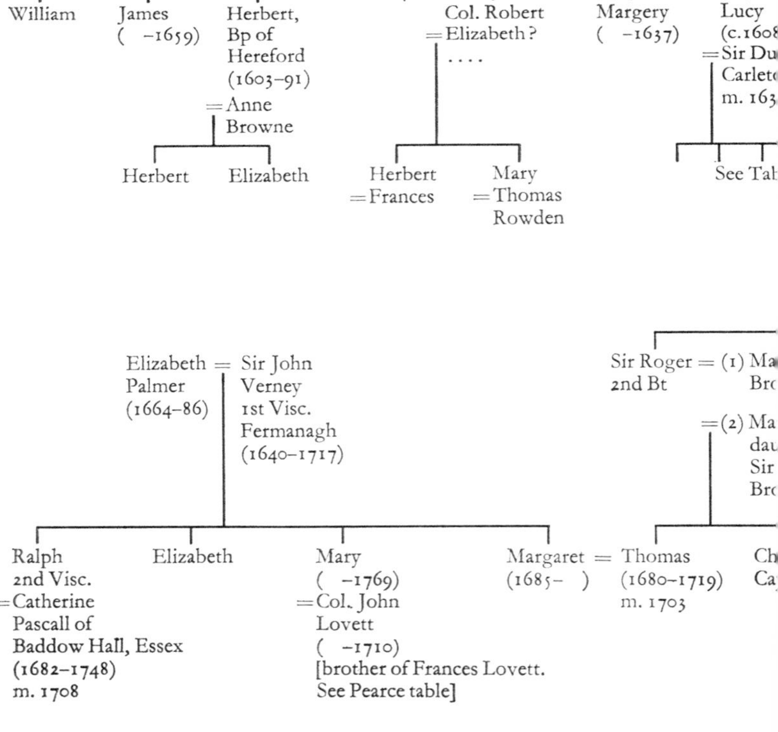

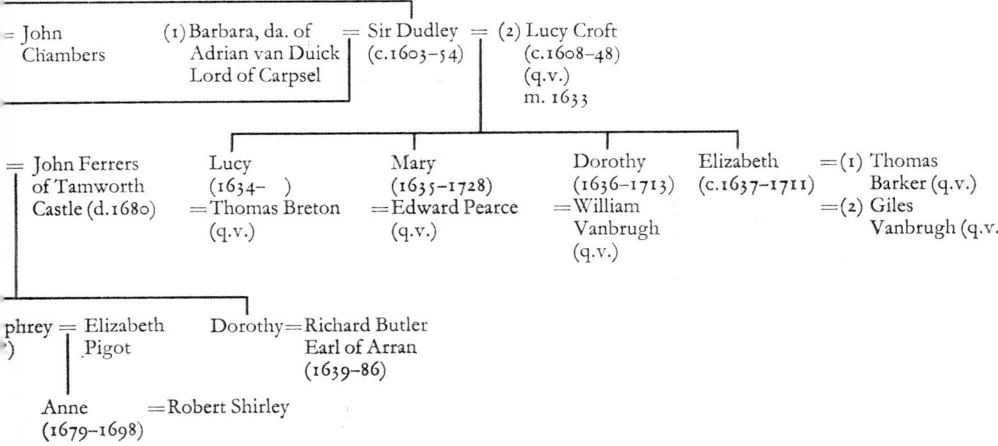

= John
Chambers
(1) Barbara, da. of
Adrian van Duick
Lord of Carpsel
= Sir Dudley
(c.1603–54)
= (2) Lucy Croft
(c.1608–48)
(q.v.)
m. 1633
= John Ferrers
of Tamworth
Castle (d.1680)
Lucy
(1634–)
=Thomas Breton
(q.v.)
Mary
(1635–1728)
=Edward Pearce
(q.v.)
Dorothy
(1636–1713)
=William
Vanbrugh
(q.v.)
Elizabeth
(c.1637–1711)
=(1) Thomas
Barker (q.v.)
=(2) Giles
Vanbrugh (q.v.)
phrey = Elizabeth
Pigot
Dorothy=Richard Butler
Earl of Arran
(1639–86)
Anne
(1679–1698)
=Robert Shirley

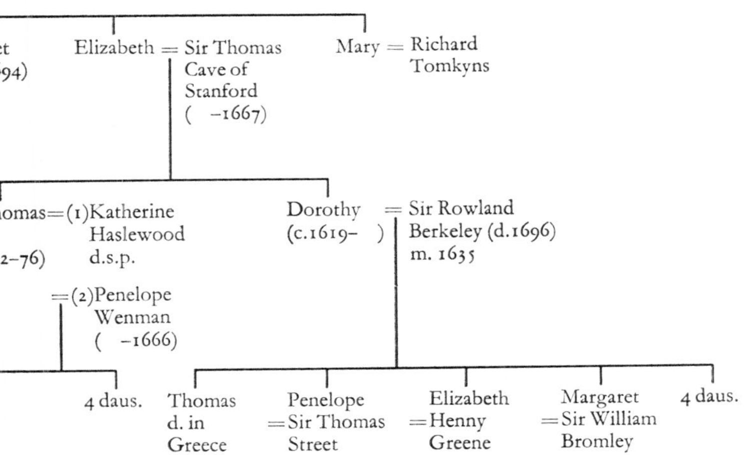

Elizabeth = Sir Thomas
Cave of
Stanford
(–1667)
Mary = Richard
Tomkyns
omas=(1)Katherine
Haslewood
d.s.p.
2–76)
=(2)Penelope
Wenman
(–1666)
Dorothy
(c.1619–)
= Sir Rowland
Berkeley (d.1696)
m. 1635
4 daus.
Thomas
d. in
Greece
Penelope
=Sir Thomas
Street
Elizabeth
=Henny
Greene
Margaret
=Sir William
Bromley
4 daus.

oeth

III Thomas Breton and Lucy Carleton

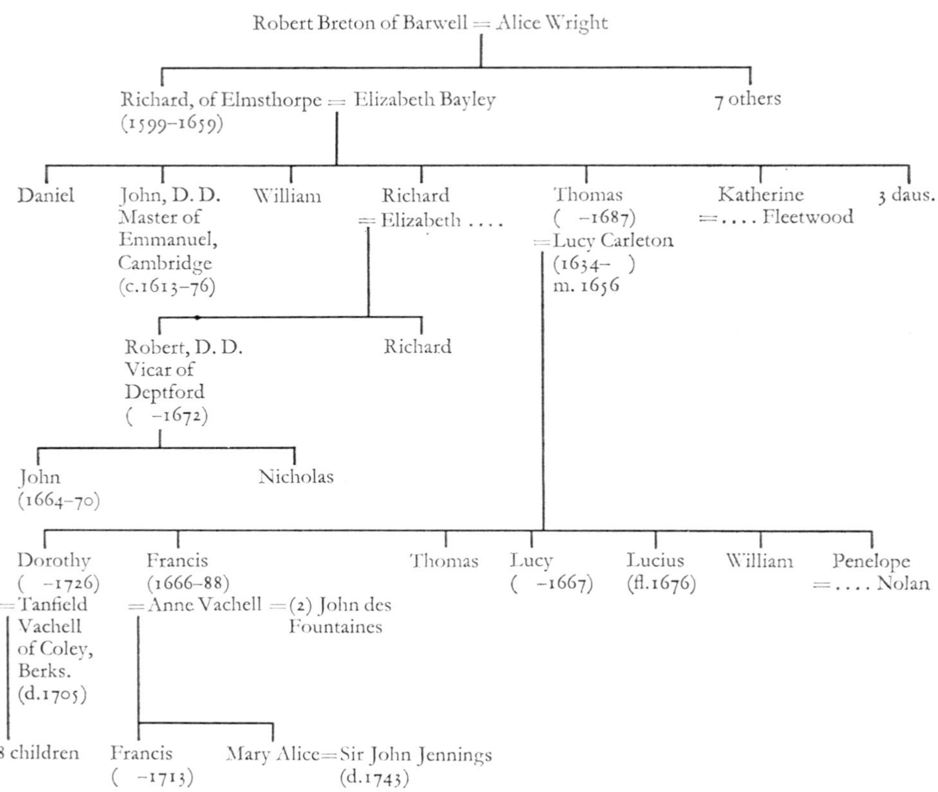

Robert Breton of Barwell = Alice Wright
Richard, of Elmsthorpe = Elizabeth Bayley
(1599–1659)
7 others
Daniel
John, D. D.
Master of
Emmanuel,
Cambridge
(c.1613–76)
William
Richard
= Elizabeth ....
Thomas
(–1687)
= Lucy Carleton
(1634–)
m. 1656
Katherine
= .... Fleetwood
3 daus.
Robert, D. D.
Vicar of
Deptford
(–1672)
Richard
John
(1664–70)
Nicholas
Dorothy
(–1726)
= Tanfield
Vachell
of Coley,
Berks.
(d.1705)
Francis
(1666–88)
= Anne Vachell = (2) John des
Fountaines
Thomas
Lucy
(–1667)
Lucius
(fl.1676)
William
Penelope
= .... Nolan
8 children
Francis
(–1713)
Mary Alice = Sir John Jennings
(d.1743)

IV Edward Pearce and Mary Carleton

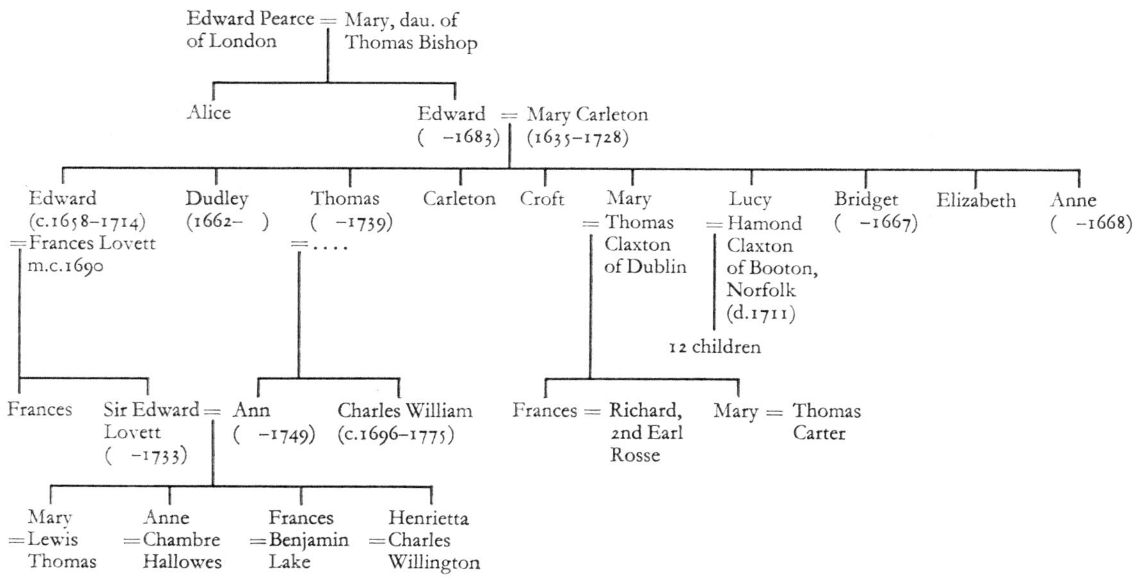
Edward Pearce = Mary, dau. of
of London
Thomas Bishop
Alice
Edward = Mary Carleton
(–1683)
(1635–1728)
Edward
(c.1658–1714)
=Frances Lovett
m.c.1690
Dudley
(1662–)
Thomas
(–1739)
=....
Carleton
Croft
Mary
=Thomas
Claxton
of Dublin
Lucy
=Hamond
Claxton
of Booton,
Norfolk
(d.1711)
12 children
Bridget
(–1667)
Elizabeth
Anne
(–1668)
Frances
Sir Edward = Ann
Lovett
(–1733)
(–1749)
Charles William
(c.1696–1775)
Frances = Richard,
2nd Earl
Rosse
Mary = Thomas
Carter
Mary
=Lewis
Thomas
Anne
=Chambre
Hallowes
Frances
=Benjamin
Lake
Henrietta
=Charles
Willington

V Peter Jacobs(on)

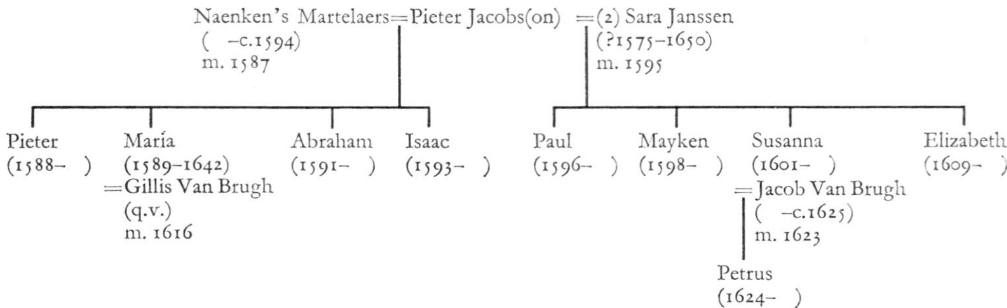

VI Mattheus of Ghent

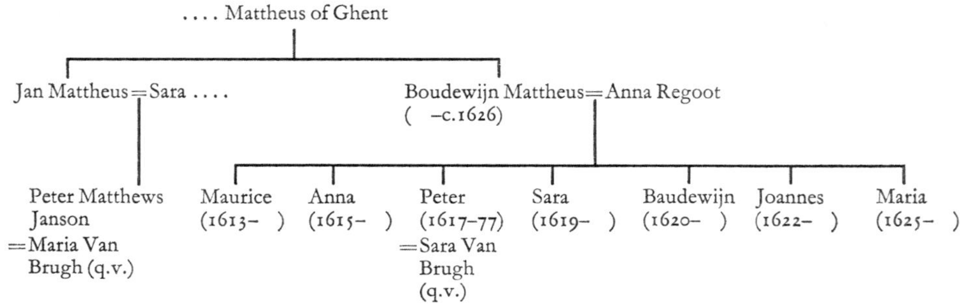

VII Thomas Barker and Elizabeth Carleton

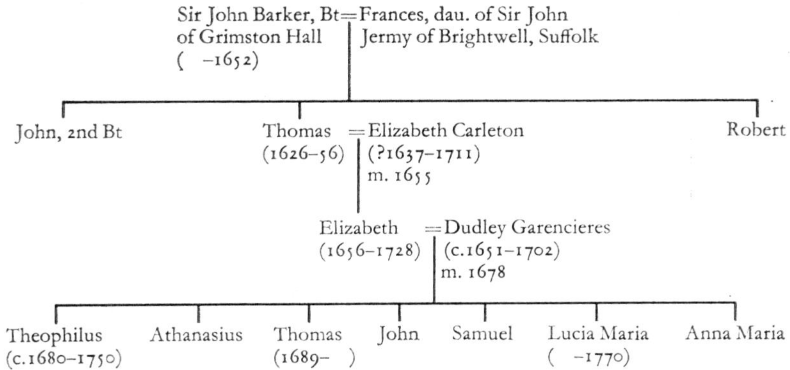

VIII William Vanbrugh and Dorothy Carleton

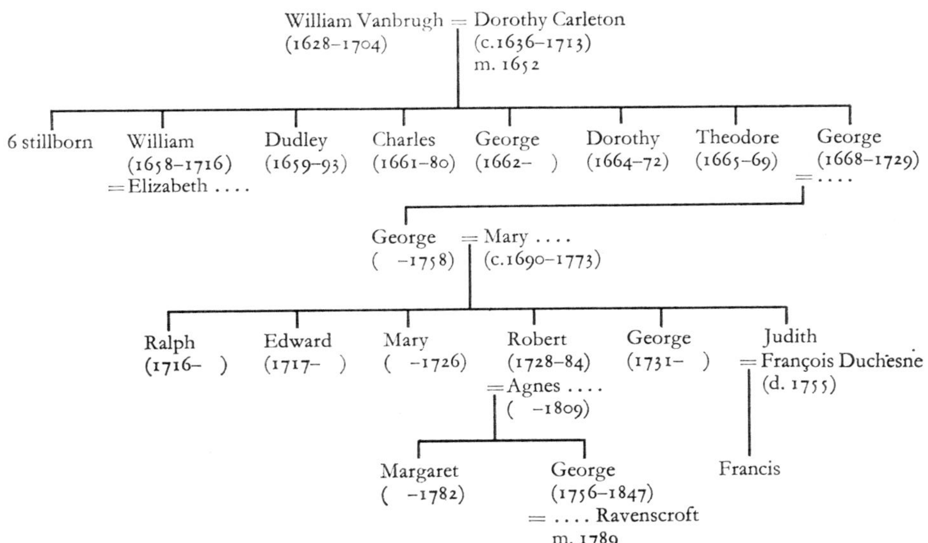

IX Gillis Van Brugh and Maria Jacobs

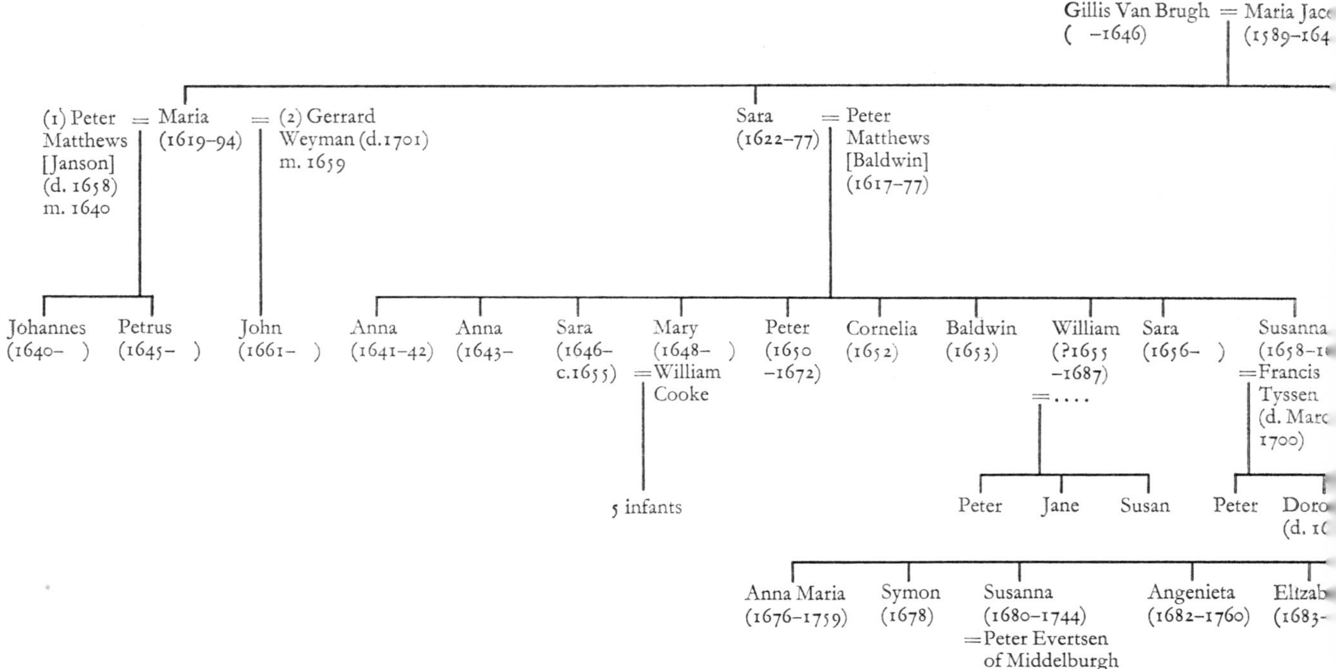

X Giles Vanbrugh and Elizabeth Carleton

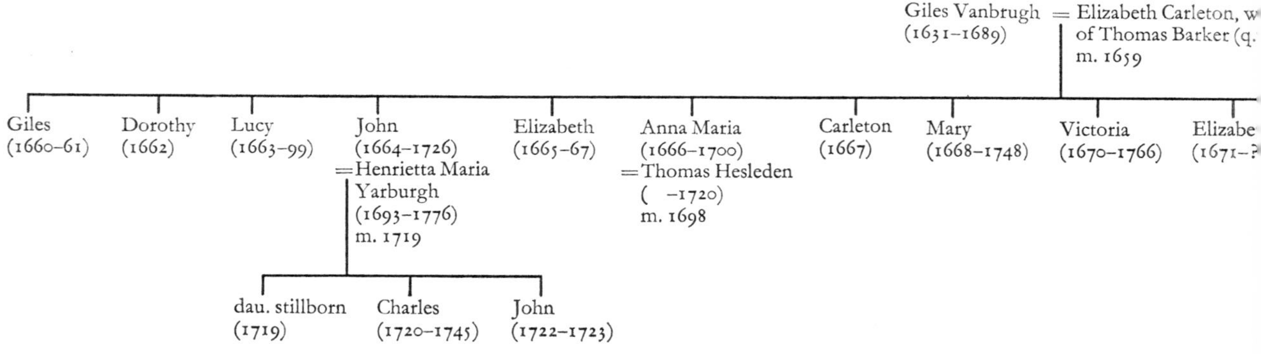

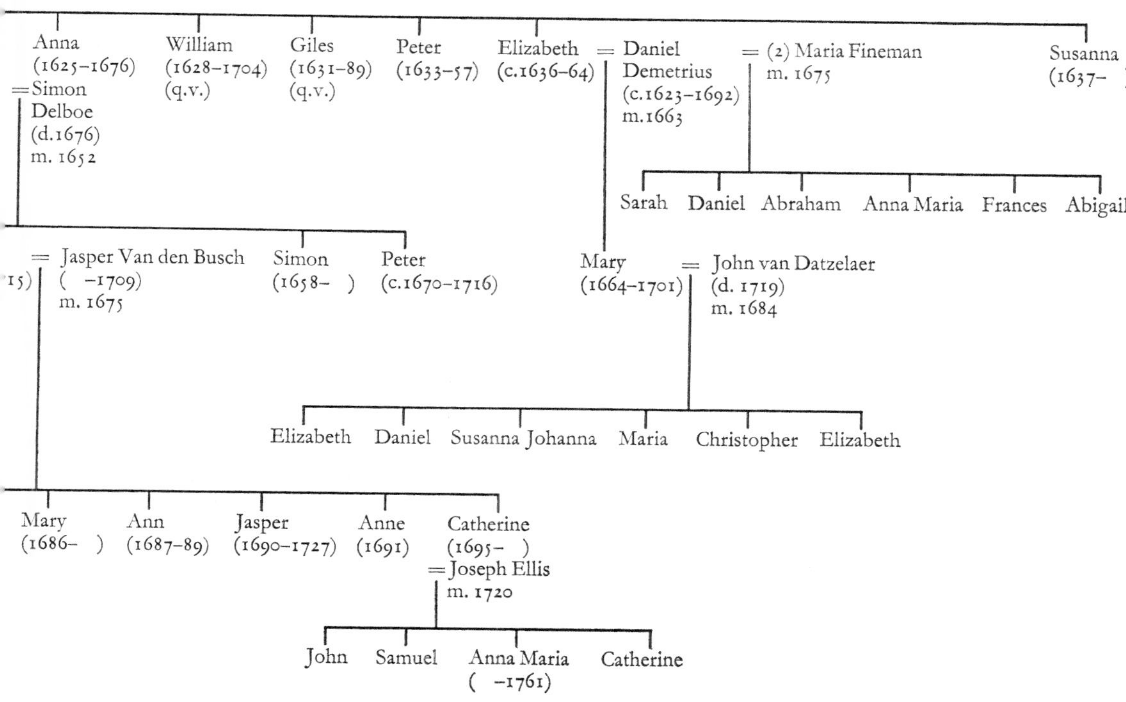
Anna
(1625–1676)
=Simon
Delboe
(d.1676)
m. 1652
William
(1628–1704)
(q.v.)
Giles
(1631–89)
(q.v.)
Peter
(1633–57)
Elizabeth
(c.1636–64)
= Daniel
Demetrius
(c.1623–1692)
m.1663
= (2) Maria Fineman
m. 1675
Susanna
(1637–)
Sarah
Daniel
Abraham
Anna Maria
Frances
Abigail
15)
= Jasper Van den Busch
(–1709)
m. 1675
Simon
(1658–)
Peter
(c.1670–1716)
Mary
(1664–1701)
= John van Datzelaer
(d. 1719)
m. 1684
Elizabeth
Daniel
Susanna Johanna
Maria
Christopher
Elizabeth
Mary
(1686–)
Ann
(1687–89)
Jasper
(1690–1727)
Anne
(1691)
Catherine
(1695–)
=Joseph Ellis
m. 1720
John
Samuel
Anna Maria
(–1761)
Catherine

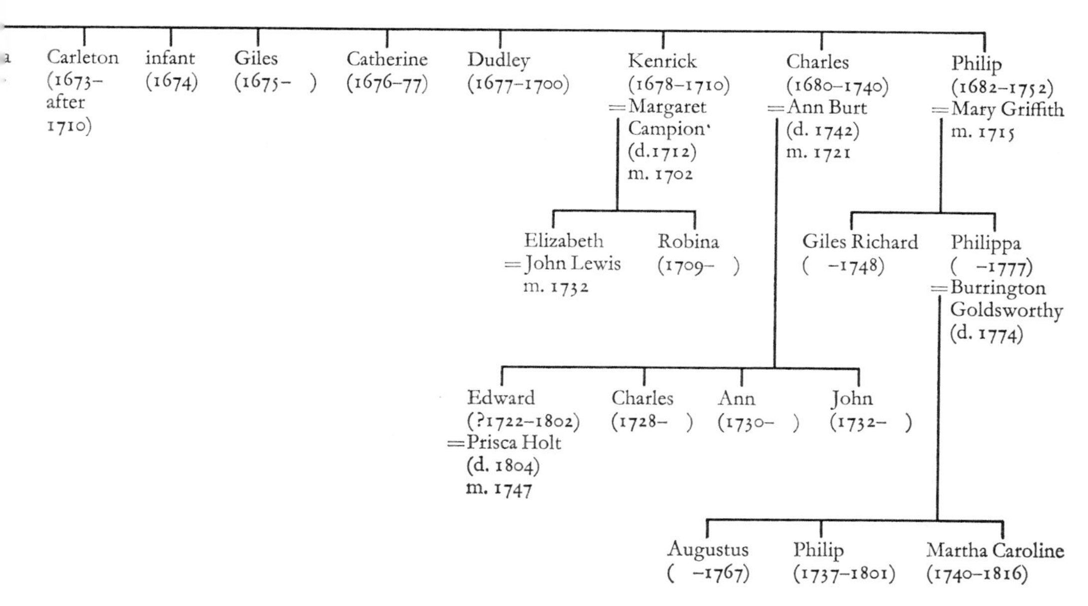
Carleton
(1673–
after
1710)
infant
(1674)
Giles
(1675–)
Catherine
(1676–77)
Dudley
(1677–1700)
Kenrick
(1678–1710)
=Margaret
Campion
(d.1712)
m. 1702
Charles
(1680–1740)
=Ann Burt
(d. 1742)
m. 1721
Philip
(1682–1752)
=Mary Griffith
m. 1715
Elizabeth
=John Lewis
m. 1732
Robina
(1709–)
Giles Richard
(–1748)
Philippa
(–1777)
=Burrington
Goldsworthy
(d. 1774)
Edward
(?1722–1802)
=Prisca Holt
(d. 1804)
m. 1747
Charles
(1728–)
Ann
(1730–)
John
(1732–)
Augustus
(–1767)
Philip
(1737–1801)
Martha Caroline
(1740–1816)

Chapter 8

Giles Vanbrugh's Family

Giles Vanbrugh, the architect's father (1631–89), was the son of Giles or Gillis Van Brugh (d. 1646) and Marie or Maria Jacobs (1589–1642).

Peter Le Neve, who as a herald knew Sir John Vanbrugh well, but seems to have extracted very incomplete information about his family, mentions a John Van Brugghe as praetor of Ypres in 1383,[1] and also records that 'Gyles Vanbrugh fled from flanders in the Duke D'alvas persecution lived in Stevens Wabrook dyed there—day of—1646. buried in a vault there made denizen by King James 1st by letters pat dat 17 Sept.'[2] However, this Gyles (Gillis) did not come to England as a refugee from the Duke of Alva. The marriage took place in the Dutch Church on 10 December 1616 of 'Gillis van Brugh van Haerlem' and 'Maria Jacobs van Londen'[3] and this is confirmed in a return of aliens in London in 1618: 'Giles van Bruggs, merchant, and free denizen, borne at Hardlem, doth acknowledg our soureaigne Lord King James to bee his supreame head and gouernour.'[4] Gillis, like a number of his associates, is usually described as *merchant*, that is to say a wholesaler, and the commodities in which he dealt are not specified. But his son imported linen cloth[5] and his father-in-law Peter Jacobs was a linen wholesaler.[6] It is therefore probable that Gillis dealt in cloth, and this is consistent with his origins. With the fall of Protestant Antwerp to the Duke of Parma on 17 August 1585, Catholicism was re-established there and convinced Protestants were given four years in which to settle their affairs and leave the city. Antwerp was also in economic decline, partly as a result of the Dutch blockade of the port. During the last years of the sixteenth century over 600 families of Flemish textile workers moved from the region to Haarlem; they almost certainly included that of Franchoys Hals and his young son Frans the painter.[7] It is probable that Gillis Van Brugh or his parents were also among their number, and since in 1616 he was established in business and newly married he was perhaps born at about the time of the move from Antwerp to Haarlem in the late 1580s. He probably brought or invited one younger brother to join him: the next entry to him in the 1618 return of aliens is for 'Jacob van Brugges, seruant, borne at Hardlem' and in later generations other

[1] Le Neve, p.511, giving as his source J. B. Gramay the early seventeenth-century Flemish historian.

[2] ibid. Alva, who subdued the Southern Netherlands in 1567 but was defeated and recalled in 1573, is probably a mistake for Parma, who recaptured Antwerp in 1585. In any case Gillis would have been very young, if indeed born, in the time of Alva.

[3] DCR.

[4] PRO SP14/102 quoted from *Returns*, III, p.200. A partial version of this return was published in *Camden Soc.*, LXXXII, 1862.

[5] p.165.

[6] p.141.

[7] S. Slive, *Frans Hals*, I, 1970, p.2.

young relatives acted as servants within the family.[8] His parents must have stayed in Holland; many years later, in 1644, it was reported from Haarlem that 'D. Wijckenburch was married last Tuesday to the sister of our brother Sr. Gilles van Brugh. I believe that he might be induced to come to us if our country [England] enjoyed peace; he would suit us very well, all the more because he speaks English. What do you think of borrowing him for six months?'[9] (England was two years into the Civil War, and it is not known whether the loan was made or why Wijckenburch was thought so useful.) Jacob Van Brugh's line was short. He was denizated on 27 January 1623[10] and in March he married Susanna Jacobson.[11] She was a daughter of Peter Jacobs and his second wife Sara, born 8 March 1601 and the half-sister of Marie, Gillis's wife.[12] Jacob's son Petrus was baptized at the Dutch Church on 11 January 1624.[13] When Susanna stood proxy at the baptism of Gillis's daughter Anna on 1 May 1625 the clerk changed her name from *uxor* to *vidua Jacob van Brug*; neither the widow nor the son is recorded later.[14]

Gillis's marriage in 1616 is the first record of his presence in London; the following year he was named in lists of Dutch Church members as a merchant but not a denizen, and living in Thames Street (Teamstreet) with his wife Mary, 'borne here',[15] and on 18 September 1617 his denization was entered.[16] In 1621 he was probably still in Thames Street, which traverses Dowgate Ward[17] but about 1624 he moved a little way farther from the river to Walbrook Ward,[18] where he ultimately owned three houses.[19] In March 1624 he was one of twenty-six foreigners to receive a royal pardon for various unspecified transgressions since 1620.[20] In 1630 he became one of the Elders of the Dutch Church,[21] and it was in this capacity that he visited Holland in 1637 to deal with some property.[22] He was a frequent witness to baptisms in the Dutch Church, including children of Baldwin Matthews (25 August 1622), Jacob Van Brugh (11 January 1624), Abraham Baert (10 October 1626, 7 October 1627), Philip Matthews (6 January 1628), Paul Ganne (20 September 1629), Andries de Boterdrooge [Drybutter] (14 March 1637) and Peter Matthews (3 November 1640, 12 September 1641, 3 September 1643, 18 September

[8] Return of aliens (above n.4). For other servants see p.146 and 147.

[9] Timotheus Cruso at Haarlem to Cesar Calandrinus in London, 23 June 1644 (Hessels III, p.1934).

[10] *Denizations*, p.32.

[11] Allegation for Licence, Bishop of London's Office, to James Van Brugge of St Laurence Pountney, merchant, and Susan Jacobson of St Margaret, New Fish Street, daughter of Peter Jacobson of the same, merchant; at St Margaret's (*Harl. Soc.*, XXVI, 1887, p.121). Registers for this date do not survive.

[12] See p.140.

[13] DCR. The witnesses were Peter Jacobs and Maria the wife of Gillis Van Brugh.

[14] ibid. A Peter Vanbroke is recorded in London in 1695 (below, Ch.10, n.22).

[15] *Returns*, III, pp.151, 165.

[16] *Denizations*, p.24 (Giles van Burgh, born beyond the seas). The date (in the Patent Roll) is one day after Le Neve's (above, n.1). Denization was from the king, an act of prerogative or executive; naturalization from Parliament, an act of legislature.

[17] Lay Subsidies, 1621, Dowgate Ward (*Returns*, III, p.239). On the same page is a 'Giles Vanbrookhon.'

[18] Lay Subsidies, 1625 (ibid., pp.291 (St Laurence Pountney Ward, i.e. Parish), 295 (Walbrook Ward)). In Jan. 1636 he had lived in Walbrook Ward for eleven years (CSP Dom 1635–6, p.154).

[19] 'Bought of Sir John Sidley'; his will, below, n.29.

[20] *Egidio Vanbrugh*, 19 March 1624 (Hessels III, p.1305).

[21] Moens, p.209.

[22] 'Our brother Van Brugg' (Hessels III, pp.1752, 1757). Other references or signatures as elder, ibid., pp.1680, 1811, 1818, 1820, 1864, 1929, 2019.

1645).[23] His own children were baptized in the Dutch Church, but he was also attending St Stephen, Walbrook by 1628, when he was churchwarden there.[24] In that year he also sought naturalization, but the bill did not pass beyond the committee stage.[25] On 7 July 1642 he buried his wife 'in the cloyster north in his vault which he purchased of this parish';[26] this vault was later to receive his own body and those of many descendants and their spouses down to the widow of his great-grandson Edward Vanbrugh in 1804.

Besides his three houses in Walbrook Gillis appears to have acquired a country property in the Surrey parish of Battersea, and in 1641 he was stated to have lived there for most of the year.[27] In 1644 the physician Sir Theodore de Mayerne prescribed for him.[28] He made his will on 2 February 1646[29] and was buried in his vault on 21 June.[30] By his will money, goods and merchandise previously lent to his sons William and Giles (although not of age) 'to make them a stocke' was left in equal shares to them and their younger brother Peter who, like their brothers-in-law, became successful merchants. Gillis left £50 to the Elders and the same sum to the poor of the Dutch Church. His book-keeper towards the end of his life was Joas Bateman (1620–1704), a native of Hazebrouck in Artois who was later naturalized and became the father of Sir James Bateman (d.1718) of the Bank of England and the South Sea Company.[31]

Gillis Van Brugh's father- and mother-in-law were Pieter Jacobs or Jacops or Jacobson and his first wife.[32] In the 1618 return of aliens Jacobs stated that he was born 'at Antwerpe in the Dukedome of Brabunt' and was 'of the Dutch Church, and dwells heer five and forty years',[33] which reasonably places his arrival in 1573. In 1576 he was living in Duke's Place, Aldgate, with two servants; by 1582 he was in the parish of St Ethelburga, Bishopsgate.[34] On 28 February 1587 at the Dutch Church he married Naenken s'Martelaers of Oudenaerde, and their first child, Pieter, was baptized there on 25 February 1588.[35] Three more followed: Maria (23 November 1589, married Gillis), Abraham (17 January 1591) and Isaac (1 April 1593).

Between 1589 and 1595 he subscribed to the Dutch Church students' fund.[36] He was probably the owner of more than one house, and thus the same Peter Jacobs who with his

[23] DCR. A complete search of the register might produce others.

[24] Walbrook Register.

[25] *Denizations*, p.42.

[26] Walbrook Register.

[27] Certificates of residence to prevent double taxation, 1641: PRO E115/397/22 and 125 (Giles Vanbrigge merchant and alien), E115/440/128 (that Giles Vanbrigge is the same 'for anything they know to the contrary mentioned in the Roll by the name of . . . Giles Vanbrooke.') He was not an alien but his accent may have been against him.

[28] Bodl.MS.Ashmole 1447, ix, art.23.

[29] PROB 11/199, fol.60, proved 6 March 1647.

[30] DCR.

[31] Le Neve, p.463, on information from Sir John Vanbrugh.

[32] See below, n.35. If it seems unlikely that Gillis's wife bore her last child at the age of forty-eight it is not impossible. It is less probable that Gillis married Maria, daughter of Willem Jacobs, baptized at the Dutch Church 21 Dec. 1613 and otherwise unknown. Besides business connections, the record of baptismal witnesses confirms the relationship between Gillis and Peter Jacobs.

[33] *Returns*, III, p.186 (*Peter Jacobson*).

[34] ibid. II, pp.164, 243 (1576, 1582 *Peter Jacob*).

[35] DCR (both as *Jacops*). No later reference is certainly to the son.

[36] *Returns*, II, pp.207, 209, 211, 212.

wife was again recorded in Duke's Place in October 1594.[37] In the Subsidy list of 4 July 1595 'Adrian, ye wief of Peter Jacob, per poll' is listed separately as dead.[38] This name is possible to reconcile with Naenken, but Marie Jacobs's mother had been dead some time: Isaac was born on 1 April 1593, and on 21 April 1595 Pieter Jacobs was married for the second time, to Sara Janssen of London.[39] They had three or four children: Pauwels (Paul, 1 July 1596), Mayken (16 July 1598), Susanna (8 March 1601)[40] and probably after a gap of eight years, Elizabeth (9 November 1609).[41]

In 1601 Peter Jacobs, 'seller of Cloth by great borne at Andwerpe', was harassed and arrested by an informer, 'uppon pretence that he retailleth lynnen cloth and other wares which he in no wise doth not.'[42] On 11 September 1604, perhaps to obviate such incidents, Peter Jacobsen, subject of the Duke of Brabant, born at Antwerp, became a denizen.[43] In the Subsidy list for June 1609 he was described as *stranger* (but not *alien*) and exempt, as twice assessed, from payment in the parish of St Peter-le-Poer; two years later he was assessed in the same parish,[44] very near to the Dutch Church. By 1617 he was in Pudding Lane, Billingsgate, with his wife Sara and two children; Maria was by then married and some of her siblings must have died.[45] Peter was still there in 1621 when his neighbour was Philip Jacobson, certainly his brother,[46] and later one of the king's jewellers.[47] In March 1624 a pardon was granted, among others, *Petro Jacobs*.[48] He witnessed baptisms of children of his brother Philip (20 October 1607, 18 January 1610, 10 March 1616), Gillis Van Brugh (26 July 1618, 28 November 1619) and Jacob Van Brugh (11 January 1624).[49] He died before 25 February 1636 when his widow Sara witnessed a baptism.[50] In 1638 she was living in the house of Gillis Van Brugh with her two daughters, the

[37] ibid., p.468.

[38] ibid., p.476.

[39] DCR. For the Janssens see below, p.142.

[40] ibid.

[41] ibid. This last could have been a grandchild, son of Peter, born 1588, but the latter is more likely to have died in childhood as no other references to him have been found.

[42] Hessels III, pp.1057–8, 1071.

[43] *Denizations*, p.6.

[44] *Returns*, III, pp.129, 133. St Peter's was then probably in Bishopsgate Ward. The next entry is Giles de Hertocke.

[45] ibid., p.152 (Dutch Church list). Identity is confirmed by the next entry, Gillis de Hertoge. He was a surgeon (ibid., p.148) and perhaps lived in the same house as the Jacobsons.

[46] ibid., p.238 (Lay Subsidy). Both were denizated together and identically described (see n.43).

[47] Philip is so described in the Visitation of London, 1633–4 (*Harl. Soc.*, XVII, 1883, p.5). He is called son of Jacob Jacobson and Anne, daughter of Philipp de Croyer, both of Antwerp. He married, 6 Nov. 1604 at the Dutch Church, Elizabeth, daughter of John (Hans) van Sold(t), who had been baptized there on 7 July 1588 (DCR). Philip's children were: Philip (20 Oct. 1607, died); Elizabeth (8 Sept. 1608, died); Philip (18 Jan. 1610, in the East Indies at the time of the Visitation); Anna (15 Dec. 1612, married before the Visitation to Joce (Joos) van Le-ent of Haarlem); Elizabeth (21 Dec. 1613, married before the Visitation to Abraham Beard (Baert) of London. On the evidence of ages, baptisms and witnesses' names she was his second wife and probably married late in 1630); Johanna (13 Dec. 1614, died); Joanna (10 March 1616, Jane in the Visitation); Maria (11 Oct. 1618, died); Jacobus (31 Oct. 1619, James in the Visitation); Johannes (8 Oct. 1622, died before 1633); Paulus (21 Dec. 1623, Paul in the Visitation); Maria (12 Feb. 1626, Mary in the Visitation).

[48] See above, n.20.

[49] DCR.

[50] ibid., Abraham, son of Abraham Baert. She was also witness to children of Philip Jacobs (21 Dec. 1613, 8 Oct. 1622), Gillis Van Brugh (28 Nov. 1619, 10 Feb. 1622), Andries de Boterdrooge [Drybutter] (14 March 1637) and Peter Matthews (Baldwin) (21 June 1646).

half-sisters of Gillis's wife.[51] In 1648 she subscribed £1 to the distress fund for the Dutch Church at Colchester[52] and, as Maria Vanbrugh's stepmother, she was probably the Mrs Jacob buried in the family vault on 12 April 1650.[53]

Maria Van Brugh, *née* Jacobs, bore Gillis twelve children: Maria (baptized 26 July 1618, died); Maria (28 November 1619, married Peter Matthews Janson); Sara (10 February 1622, married Peter Matthews Baldwin); Willem (4 March 1624, died); Anna (1 May 1625, married Simon Delboe); Willem (8 April 1627, buried St Stephen Walbrook 25 July 1627); William (baptized St Stephen Walbrook 25 September 1628, married Dorothy Carleton); Giles (St Stephen Walbrook 27 April 1631, married Elizabeth Carleton, parents of the architect); Peter (8 September 1633); Elizabeth (11 February 1636, married Daniel Demetrius); Susanna (16 March 1637); James, whose burial only is recorded (St Stephen Walbrook, 20 August 1639).[54] The mother died in 1642, no doubt leaving much of the care of the family to her stepmother.[55]

Of the eight children known not to have died in infancy, four daughters married merchants (Maria Matthews, Sarah Matthews, Anna Delboe and Elizabeth Demetrius);[56] Susanna, the fifth daughter, is unaccounted for.[57] The three sons became merchants with their father's help. William and Giles married sisters, daughters of Sir Dudley Carleton,[58] while Peter, who was only thirteen when his father died, was resident in Smyrna in 1654 when he made his will.[59] He left over £3000 to members of the family and it is unlikely that he married. The will was proved on 8 March 1658 and he was buried in the family vault on 28 May;[60] the delay suggests that he died abroad.

Gillis wrote with pride in his will of the good portions he had given his daughters Maria and Sarah,[61] and he seems to have taken some care over the education of at least two of his sons. He made a small legacy to Peter's tutor, Mr Hermanns, and while Giles's three years in Europe for 'pleasure and improvement' can be dated to the 1650s – he was only fifteen when his father died – his handwriting in later life denoted a good education: it is notably similar to that of his close contemporary Sir Christopher Wren.[62]

Maria Van Brugh (1619–94) married firstly Peter Matthews Janson. *Jansen* was a common surname in the London German and Netherlandish communities, but Janson in this case

[51] Hessels III, p.1786.

[52] ibid., p.2135.

[53] Walbrook Register.

[54] All at the Dutch Church unless otherwise stated (DCR, Walbrook Register). Giles is called son of 'Gyles Vanbrugh marchaunt and margarett his wife' but the register is notably careless about names. Giles was born on 19 April 1631, eight days before his baptism, according to his own account in 1676 (see p.165, n.82).

[55] See above, n.51. Maria witnessed baptisms of Petrus, son of James Van Brugh (11 Jan. 1624) and children of Baldwin Matthews (16 Jan. 1625), Abraham Baert (25 Nov. 1639) and Andries Droogboter [Drybutter] (15 March 1640).

[56] See below. Peter Matthews Janson's will, 19 Feb. 1658 (PROB 11/274, fol.114) was witnessed by William and Giles Vanbrugh, Peter Matthews Baldwin, Simon Delboe and Joseph Alport, servant (who also witnessed Anne (Vanbrugh) Delboe's will in 1653 (see below, n.124).

[57] She was alive and single when her sister Anne made her will in July 1653 (see p.146, n.123).

[58] See pp.184, 164.

[59] PROB 11/275, fol.193. On 22 Aug. 1688 Luttrell (I, p.456) reported the earthquake and fire at Smyrna in which 'most of the English factory' [i.e. warehouse] was destroyed with 1000 bales of cloth.

[60] Walbrook Register.

[61] See above, n.29.

[62] Autograph letter of 1678 (PRO SP29/408, No.105). Printed here, Appendix A. For Giles's travels see p.164.

seems to indicate in the Netherlandish fashion that Peter's father was Jan Matheus, who was married to one Sara before 1619 when she was witness by proxy to a baptism.[63] Sara is likely to have been Peter's mother although the place and date of his birth are unknown. He was old enough to marry Mary Van Brugh by 1640: a son, Johannes, was baptized on 3 November 1640 and another, Petrus, on 18 September 1645.[64] By 1654 there were no surviving children of the marriage.[65] In 1648 he gave £3 to the fund for the Dutch Church at Colchester.[66] His will (19 February 1658) describes him as merchant of the parish of St Laurence Pountney, and he left property in St Laurence Pountney Lane, in Battersea and elsewhere.[67] He was buried in the vault of his father-in-law on 26 February 1658.[68]

His widow married secondly Gerrard or Garret Weyman who came to London in 1656 from Amsterdam.[69] He was naturalized in June 1657[70] and by 1664 was a deacon of the Dutch Church.[71] The banns of marriage were called in April 1659,[72] and the marriage articles were dated the same month.[73] A son, John, was baptized on 10 February 1661 at St Laurence Pountney;[74] they lived in property owned by Peter Matthews Baldwin and William Vanbrugh;[75] that property was sold, presumably burnt out in the Great Fire, in 1668.[76] By 1681 they lived in Thames Street in the parish of All Hallows the Less, where their neighbour was Jasper Van den Busch;[77] in November 1691 John Vanbrugh addressed a letter there for his mother, their sister-in-law.[78] Mary was buried in her father's vault on 26 November 1694;[79] her will (8 July 1691) mentioned her marriage settlement of £3000 and named Jasper Van den Busch as residuary legatee.[80] Gerrard made his will in 1695, when he had retired to Lambeth, leaving his property to Jasper.[81] He was buried in

[63] To the baptism of Sara, daughter of Bauduyn Mattheus, 31 Jan. 1619 'loco Sarae uxoris Jan Mattheus' (DCR). Baldwin Mattheus (Matthews, below, p.144) was probably Jan's brother.

[64] DCR.

[65] Peter Vanbrugh's will (n.59) mentions children of his other sisters.

[66] Hessels III, p.2133.

[67] PROB 11/274, fol.114.

[68] Walbrook Register, 'Mr Peter Mathewes Jeanson.'

[69] Recommendation from the church in Amsterdam, 19 Oct. 1656 (Hessels IV, p.67, No.925). Also spelt Gerrit, Wayman, Weymans.

[70] *Denizations*, p.78; son of Gerard Weymans.

[71] Moens, p.212.

[72] Register of St Laurence Pountney (Guildhall MS.7670).

[73] According to her will (PROB 11/476, fol.122).

[74] See n.72.

[75] H. B. Wilson, *History of St Laurence Pountney*, 1831, p.209.

[76] ibid. (30 Oct.) Matthews and Vanbrugh had bought it on 20 Nov. 1646 (ibid., p.208). The two merchants were among a group of subscribers who (according to its frontispiece) made possible the publication of Thomas Fuller's *Pisgah – sight of Palestine and the Confines thereof*, 1650, an illustrated folio compilation of the ancient topography of the Holy Land.

[77] Vanbusche: Guildhall MS.9801. They are adjacent entries in the assessment.

[78] See Appendix B (1).

[79] Walbrook Register.

[80] PROB 11/476, fol.122.

[81] PROB 11/459, fol.30.

the Vanbrugh vault on 30 January 1701, and from the terms of their wills it is unlikely that any children survived them.[82]

Sara Van Brugh married Peter Matthews Baldwin. As with her brother-in-law Peter Matthews Janson, the last name is that of the previous generation, and the action of Jan Mattheus and his wife as baptismal witnesses to four of Baldwin Mattheus's children confirms the supposition that Jan and Baldwin were brothers and the two Peters first cousins.[83] There is some inconsistency in the records of Baldwin or Boudewyn Mattheus, but the balance of probability is that they all concern a single individual, who came from Flanders by way of Haarlem and the cloth trade. In 1618 Baldwin Mathew stated that he was born in Ghent, was a merchant and free denizen and a member of the Dutch Church living in Billingsgate Ward, and had been in England for twelve years.[84] But only six years earlier, in July 1612, the Dutch Congregation received a recommendation from the church in Haarlem for Boudwyn Mattheus and his wife Anna Regouts (Regoot, Regaud) who were then living in St Clement's Lane near the church of that name, he being a thread-twister by trade.[85] Two children were baptized at the Dutch Church, Mauritius (Maurice, 5 September 1613) and Anna (30 April 1615)[86] and were also registered at St Clement's, Eastcheap.[87] In 1617 the couple had moved two or three hundred yards to Crooked Lane, where Boudewyn appears as a merchant not yet a denizen, with two children,[88] probably Maurice and Peter, who was baptized at the Dutch Church on 23 March 1617 and was to marry Sara Van Brugh.[89] Later in 1617 Baldwin Mathewes, 'born beyond the seas', was denizated, and the following year he appears to have moved a little to the east, to the neighbourhood of Eastcheap.[90] In 1621 and 1625 he was in the same area, and his neighbours included Peter and Philip Jacobson.[91] Further children were baptized at the Dutch Church: Sara (31 Janauary 1619), Baudewijn (2 July 1620), Joannes (25 August 1622) and Maria (16 January 1625); Anna Matthews was not yet widowed on 1 May 1625 when she was a witness,[92] but on 2 December 1628 she married Paulus Ganne of Leyden[93] by whom she had two children, Johannes (20 September 1629) and Maria (12 September

[82] It is not possible to identify the Gerret Weijman who, with others, 'caused a tumult' in the Dutch Church in 1703 (Hessels III, p.2760).

[83] Anna (30 April 1615), Sara (31 Jan. 1619), Baldwin (2 July 1620) and Johannes (25 Aug. 1622).

[84] *Returns*, III, p.186.

[85] Hessels IV, p.12 (No.119).

[86] DCR.

[87] *Harl. Soc., Register Series*, LXVII–LXVIII.

[88] Dutch Church lists (*Returns*, III, pp.151, 165).

[89] DCR. Anna, the first child, may have died. In a list of defaulters to the restoration fund of the Dutch Church, at a date after 1634, Mawerice and Pieter Matheus are deleted with the explanation *Jonge Luyden* (young people); Hessels III, p.2917).

[90] See above, n.84.

[91] *Returns* III, pp.238, 293 (Lay Subsidies) under St George and St Margaret (1621) and St Andrew [Hubbard] (1625). This suggests a location in Eastcheap near Gracechurch Street.

[92] DCR.

[93] ibid.

1630).[94] He died in or before 1640,[95] and Anna sought naturalization under her maiden name.[96] She remained an active member of the Dutch community for some years.[97]

Peter Matthews Baldwin was, as already mentioned, baptized on 23 March 1617. In 1657 he became a freeman of the Mercers' Company, 'by redemption £50', an agreed form of admission without apprenticeship.[98] He was five years older than Sara Van Brugh, who married him before she was eighteen. Their first child, Anna, was baptized on 12 September 1641[99] and buried in the Vanbrugh family vault on 27 October 1642.[100] The record of subsequent children is incomplete, since the family moved several times and some were not taken to the Dutch Church. A number died at birth or in infancy and were buried in the Vanbrugh vault, but they cannot be correlated with the recorded baptisms and the Walbrook register does not differentiate between the Matthewses. The wills of Peter Vanbrugh in 1654[101] and of Peter Matthews himself (27 February 1677)[102] indicate the children then living, and the following list is based on all these sources. A second Anna was baptized on 3 September 1643[103] but is not mentioned in 1654 and thus must have died. Sara (21 June 1646)[104] was alive in 1654 but died soon afterwards. Mary (1 September 1648) grew up to marry William Cooke, gentleman, before 1671;[105] five of their children were buried in the Vanbrugh vault.[106] Peter (13 November 1650)[107] was buried in the vault on 20 July 1672, dying in his final year of apprenticeship to his father.[108] Cornelia (16 May 1652)[109] and Baldwin (30 September 1653)[110] died before 1654. Sara having died since then, the next child (12 September 1656) was given her name.[111] William's birth date is not known, but it must have preceded and not followed Sara. He would thus have been about sixteen when apprenticed in turn to his father, then Warden of the Mercers' Company, in January 1671.[112] Susanna (14 March 1658)[113] was one of four children mentioned in her father's will in 1677. Mary had been given a

94 ibid.

95 She is called a widow at the baptism of Johannes Mattheus [Janson], 3 Nov. 1640 (DCR).

96 The bill reached committee stage 25 June 1641 (*Denizations*, p.63, Anne Regaud).

97 She witnessed baptisms in the families of Lucas Jacobs (17 March 1616, 20 March 1625); Gillis Van Brugh (4 March 1624, 1 May 1625); Peter Matthews Janson (3 Nov. 1640) and Peter Matthews Baldwin (12 Sept. 1641, 3 Sept. 1643, 18 Sept. 1645 and 14 March 1658) (DCR).

98 Records of the Mercers' Company. They were originally silk-mercers, and dealt in the more expensive fabrics.

99 DCR.

100 Walbrook Register; also registered in St Martin Orgar (*Harl. Soc., Register Series*, LXVIII).

101 See above, n.59.

102 PROB 11/354, fol.51.

103 DCR and St Martin Orgar (n.100).

104 ibid. (both).

105 St Martin Orgar only. The husband is named in her father's will.

106 Sara Maria (14 Oct. 1671); Mary (22 April 1672); William (20 Nov. 1673); Matthew (18 April 1674); unnamed (27 Oct. 1677) (Walbrook Register).

107 St Martin Orgar only.

108 Seven years from May 1666 (Records of the Mercers' Company).

109 DCR and St Martin Orgar.

110 St Martin Orgar only.

111 St Laurence Pountney (Guildhall MS.7670).

112 Records of the Mercers' Company.

113 DCR only.

dowry; Sara was now left his 'sute of hangings of flower Potts which were made at Mortlack and are in the biggest Parlour of my new dwelling house'; his estate was divided equally between her and two others 'yet unadvanced', William and Susanna.[114] William never became a freeman, and seems to have used and lost his inheritance in a different trade. For in 'about 1676' and subsequent years he 'did drive a trade' in partnership with John Vanhattem, merchant in wines and brandies. Since Vanhattem is said to have received the profits and Matthews to have paid the expenses it is not surprising that the latter went bankrupt in 1682. His uncle, William Vanbrugh, was appointed trustee by the court, and claimed against Vanhattem. The latter denied any debt to Matthews, and the outcome is not known. However, in accounts attached to Vanbrugh's suit and Vanhattem's reply[115] John Vanbrugg is called Matthews's 'servant' in about 1681 'at ye Whiteheart' (probably the White Hart near St Botolph's, Bishopsgate) and in charge of considerable sums of cash. In 1695 Carleton Vanbrugh was servant to his cousin Jasper Van den Busch[116] and there can be little doubt that the future architect was for a short time involved in the wine trade as assistant to his unfortunate cousin. William Matthews was buried in the Vanbrugh vault on 2 December 1687;[117] by his will made on 8 November he made his sister Mary Cooke sole executrix and left his estate to be divided equally between his three children Peter, Jane and Susan.[118]

Susanna Matthews married the London merchant Francis Tyssen in about September 1678 when she was about nineteen and he about twenty-five.[119] Two children were buried in the Vanbrugh vault: Peter (4 August 1679)[120] and Dorothy (baptized at the Dutch Church 15 May 1681, buried 15 August). Susanna was buried there on 16 September 1685; her husband then married Maria Western and had further children who, from 1688, were baptized at the Dutch Church.[121]

Anna Van Brugh witnessed children of Andries Drogeboter [Drybutter] (12 December 1647) and Peter Matthews Baldwin (16 May 1652).[122] In August 1652 she married Simon Delboe, who was probably a Huguenot or Walloon.[123] The parties to the marriage contract were, besides the spouses, Timothy Crusoe,[124] William Vanbrugh, Peter Matthews Janson and Peter Matthews Baldwin. On 22 September 1671 Simon Delboe made a will, as he was about to go to the East Indies, intending 'to abide for some time there.' He

114 n.102.

115 PRO C6/295/60, 28 July 1683. In 1690 Mark Haughton, a business partner of Matthews, replied to a suit brought by William Vanbrugh as a result of the bankruptcy (PRO C9/114/96).

116 See p.147.

117 Walbrook Register.

118 PROB 11/390, fol.6. He was then of the parish of St Bride, Fleet Street.

119 Allegation for marriage licence, 24 Sept. 1678, Vicar General's Office (*Harl. Soc.*, XXIII, 1886). At St Mary-at-Hill, his parish; hers was St Swithin. As her parents were dead her elder brother [William] gave consent. Francis Tyssen was the son of Francis Tyssen senior who was born in Flanders, came to England after 1646 and was naturalized in June 1657 (*Denizations*, pp.71, 78); Hessels III, p.2024 (letter from Flushing 18 Sept. 1646); buried in the Dutch Church 23 March 1699 (DCR).

120 Walbrook Register, 'Peter Aisson.'

121 DCR, Walbrook Register. On 21/31 Dec. 1679 Mrs Susanna Tyson received the Sacrament in St Mary Abchurch parish (Hessels IV, p.113, no.1612).

122 DCR.

123 Contract described in her will (PROB 11/352, fol.151) made 21 July 1653 when expecting her first child.

124 Timotheus, son of Timotheus Cruso, was baptized at the Dutch Church 25 March 1621 (DCR). The elder Timotheus wrote from Haarlem about Gillis Van Brugh's sister (above, n.9); he may have held some trusteeship for Anna.

referred to a bond, with Thomas Breton[125] and Francis Lodwicke, merchants, to the East India Company. After making provision for the maintenance of his son Simon (who was about thirteen) he divided his estate between his three children Ann, Simon and Peter. Simon senior died in Siam; his will[126] was proved on 4 November 1676 by Ann, who had married Jasper Van den Busch; his wife's will, made 23 years previously, was proved, also by Ann Van den Busch, on 23 December 1676. The maintenance of Simon junior, born about 1658, led him in 1683 to an M.A. at Trinity College, Cambridge.[127] Peter Delboe was born about 1670; in 1695 he was a bachelor of twenty-five living in the house of his brother-in-law Jasper Van den Busch.[128] By his will made 17 January 1716 in the parish of St Margaret Lothbury[129] he was buried on 26 January in the Vanbrugh vault[130] near his sister and brother-in-law Ann and Jasper, buried there in 1709 and 1715.[131] He left everything to his Van den Busch nephews and nieces. Ann Van den Busch's will (12 April 1714) describes her as of London, but from the appendage to it of a grant of administration to her daughter Anna Maria (1 December 1715) it is evident that she moved with her family to Southwell, Notts., in the last months of her life. The Southwell connection is more conveniently dealt with in a later chapter;[132] it remains to describe here the London family of Jasper Van den Busch, merchant.

A Jasper van de Bosche wrote from Middelburgh to the London Dutch Church in 1670,[133] but it is in any case probable that our Jasper was a fairly recent immigrant when in December 1675 he married Ann Delboe at All Hallows the Great.[134] On 6 April 1677 Jasper, born at Flushing, the son of John Vanderbussche, was naturalized.[135] Eleven children were born to Jasper and Ann; most of them were baptized in the parish of All Hallows the Less, in which the family lived at least until 1695. In 1692 the household included six children and four servants;[136] three years later there were six children, Carleton Vanbrooke (who was then twenty-two) and two others described as servants, and Peter Delboe, described as bachelor, aged twenty-five.[137] The children named in the 1695 list can be correlated with baptismal records:[138] Anna Maria (8 October 1676, died at Southwell 1757); Susanna (11 August 1680, buried at Southwell 1744); Angenieta or Ann

[125] Related by marriage (see p.155).

[126] PROB 11/352, fol.137.

[127] Pensioner 1676, aged eighteen (Venn).

[128] City of London RO, Marriage Tax Assessment 1695, All Hallows the Less, p.2.

[129] PROB 11/550, fol.24. Proved by his niece Anna Maria Van den Busch.

[130] Walbrook Register, 'Peter Delbrow in Danbrogue Vau.'

[131] ibid., 'Jasper Vanberbush in ye Vault' (20 May 1709); 'Vanderbush in Vanbruggs Vault' (21 Jan. 1715). Jasper's death was also registered at All Hallows the Less (Guildhall MS.5160/2).

[132] See below, p.167.

[133] Hessels IV, p.90, no.1262. Earlier Van den Bos(s)che references in England are probably to another family.

[134] Register (Guildhall MS.5159).

[135] *Denizations*, p.117. In a number of Chancery cases Jasper is described as *alias Vandergoes*; this was probably his mother's surname.

[136] City of London RO, Assessment Box 8, MS.24, Dowgate (East), 1692.

[137] Above, n.128. Peter Delboe was perhaps in partnership with Jasper, since in a Chancery suit of 1693 both are described as *mercator* (PRO C54/4772, no.38).

[138] At All Hallows the Less (Guildhall MS.5160/2) unless otherwise stated.

Geneta[139] (5 February 1682, died at Southwell 1760); Elizabeth (25 March 1683); Mary (14 February 1686) and Jasper (13 August 1690 at the Dutch Church,[140] died at Southwell 1727). Four children died in infancy;[141] the last child, Catherine, was baptized on 17 November 1695 and also moved to Southwell. In 1681 Jasper was a Deacon of the Dutch Church and in 1699 an Elder; in 1702 he was one of those agreeing to dine together every three months.[142] In January 1703 he appears to have been in Port Royal, Jamaica, where a licence was granted him to administer the will of Mary Weyman: her husband, executor and residuary legatee Gerrard Weyman had died in 1701 leaving Jasper as his heir and executor.[143] Jasper died, as already related, in May 1709.

William Vanbrugh (1628–1704) succeeded as head of the family on the death of Gillis in 1646. He was then eighteen, and may already have spent some time with his father's relations in Haarlem;[144] this would explain the recommendation in 1644 from the church in Haarlem to the Dutch Church in London of Wilhelmus van Brugge, *young man, of London*.[145] William took on, as eldest son, the administration of the vault in St Stephen, Walbrook,[146] and in later years he went to law on a number of occasions on behalf of other members of the family.[147] On 21 January 1652 by marrying Dorothy, third daughter of Sir Dudley Carleton and Lucy Croft,[148] he established family links for the first time with a society outside the London foreign merchant circle.

The early attempts of William and Dorothy at building a family were tragic: by November 1656, when Dorothy was still under 21, William had carried to the vault six infants, most of them premature.[149] Two successful confinements followed: both William (baptized 1 January 1658) and Dudley (born 6 July, baptized 13 July 1659) grew to adulthood.[150] Shortly afterwards William was successful enough to be able to live mostly in the country, first of all at Morden in Surrey, where most of the village was owned by George Garth, whose wife was a cousin of Dorothy Vanbrugh.[151] By 1664 the Vanbrughs had a house with fifteen hearths[152] but already in August 1659 one of their maidservants

[139] These, the most credible spellings, are from her will (PROB 11/864), fol.111) and that of Peter Delboe (n.129).

[140] DCR.

[141] Symon (burial only, 13 Sept. 1678); Ann (baptized 24 Aug. 1684, died); Ann (7 Aug. 1687, buried 13 May 1689) and Anne (11 Nov. 1691 at the Dutch Church, buried 8 Dec. at All Hallows).

[142] Moens, pp.210, 212; Hessels III, p.2726.

[143] Above, nn.80, 81.

[144] See p.138.

[145] Thus indicating that London was his return rather than outward destination (Hessels IV, p.52, no.700; 18 Oct. 1644). Four months previously William's aunt had married in Haarlem (above n.9).

[146] References in the register to 'Mr Vanbrugh' (variously spelt) can be shown to indicate William. Until *c.*1674, when the post-Fire church was well under construction, 'the vault' meant the Vanbrugh vault; after that date it means the common vault, and the family one is specifically named each time.

[147] Against Peter Drybutter, 1669 (estate of Cornelius Beard, PRO C6/187/119); against Thomas Breton, 1675, (on behalf of Lucy Breton (C10/181/61); against John Vanhattem, 1683 (C6/295/60).

[148] See p.153, n.7.

[149] Walbrook Register: child, 30 Nov. 1652; stillborn children 9 Aug. 1653, 20 May 1654, 29 March and 15 Dec. 1655, 19 Nov. 1656 (baptized 13 Nov.).

[150] ibid. Curiously these two sons are attributed in the register to William and *Mary*. But Dorothy is named as the mother of all the later children, registered elsewhere, and these must be further instances of the laxity of the Walbrook clerks.

[151] Below, p.154.

[152] Hearth tax, 1664 (*Surrey Record Soc.*, XVII, 1940, with additional information on p. lviii).

was buried at Morden.[153] In 1661 Dorothy probably produced twins, Charles (baptized at Morden on 4 August,[154] buried at Walbrook 2 February 1680[155]) and an unchristened child buried on 7 August.[156] On 29 November 1662 a George was baptized at Morden;[157] in this year William was listed as a member of the Dutch Church 'tot Morton' and the following year his 'constant habitation' was certified to be there.[158] A daughter, Dorothy, was baptized in 1664 and lived eight years,[159] and a son, Theodore, lived from 1665 to 1669.[160]

By 1668 William and his family had moved to Walton-on-Thames, where on 5 November a second George was baptized,[161] and where in 1669–70 William was taxed on fourteen hearths.[162] The nature of his stock is obscure, and his residence half a day's journey from the City suggests that he was a merchant venturer. This company, which was run from Holland, undertook and financed foreign enterprises: unfortunately for historians hardly any records of its activities have survived.[163] In 1694 William was in Ireland but we do not know on what errand.[164] The purchase of country houses in northern Surrey was already a common practice among the industrious merchant class, but it is neither difficult nor unduly fictive to picture William in middle age and later, taking a carriage or a boat up to London on important business of a nature known at the time to few, to attend another coffin, or to visit his lawyer, until, an 'Aiged Gentelman died heare & Buryed in London', he made his last journey on 1 March 1704 to 'his own Vault.'[165] His widow followed him on 20 May 1713.[166]

Giles Vanbrugh (1631–89) married Dorothy Carleton's younger sister Elizabeth; as parents of the architect and numerous other children their subsequent life is more appropriately considered in a later chapter.[167] The short career of Peter (1633–57) has already been described.[168] Elizabeth (1636–64) married Daniel Demetrius, merchant, of St Laurence Pountney, in May 1663.[169] He was born about 1623 in Dordrecht, the son of Daniel Demetrius; it is not known when he came to England but he was naturalized between 1656 and 1660.[170] Their daughter Mary was baptized at the Dutch Church on 3

[153] Morden Registers 1634–1812 (*Parish Register Soc.*, XXXVII, 1901).

[154] ibid.

[155] Walbrook Register.

[156] ibid., 7 Aug. 1661.

[157] Above, n.153.

[158] Hessels III, p.2463; PRO E/115/398/43.

[159] 27 Aug. 1664 (above, n.153). Buried at Walbrook 22 Nov. 1672.

[160] 31 July 1665–13 Feb. 1669; same places and references.

[161] Walton-on-Thames register, Guildford Museum Muniment Room.

[162] PRO E179/258; again *c.*1674 E188/496, m.21v).

[163] Merchant venturers often belonged also to the Mercers' or another Company. See J. M. Imray, 'The merchant adventurers and their records', in F. Ranger, ed., *Prisca munimenta, studies presented to A. E. J. Hollaender*, 1973, p.229f.

[164] Below, p.160.

[165] Walton-on-Thames register (n.161); Walbrook Register; both 1 March 1704.

[166] Walbrook Register. For Dorothy see further below, p.160. For their adult children see below, pp.159–62.

[167] Below, pp.164–72.

[168] Above, p.142.

[169] Allegation at Vicar-General's Office (*Harl. Soc.*, XXXIII, 1892, p.83).

[170] He was about forty and a bachelor according to the marriage allegation. His origin is given in the naturalization papers (*Denizations*, pp.74, 77).

April 1664.[171] Within the year Elizabeth died, and was buried in her father's vault on 22 September.[172] On 14 June 1675 Daniel married Maria Fineman of Dordrecht, who probably came to England about 1668;[173] between 1678 and 1687 they took several children to the Dutch Church, one of whom, Abraham, was executor in 1755 to Anna Maria Van den Busch.[174] Daniel was buried, from St Catherine Cree into the Vanbrugh vault, on 29 July 1692[175] as he desired in his will, although the condition made there that his second wife should also rest there was not observed.[176] Mary Demetrius grew up to marry John van Datzelaer (Vandatchelaer) of St Mary Abchurch on 1 January 1684 in her parish of St Catherine Cree.[177] He was born in Wageningen (Gelderland), the son of Derick van Datselaer, and naturalized in July 1678.[178] Six children were baptized at the Dutch Church: Elizabeth (6 February 1687, buried in the Vanbrugh vault 12 April); Daniel (18 July 1688); Susanna Johanna (25 February 1691); Maria (17 April 1693, buried from St Catherine Cree into the vault on 15 August); Christopher (24 September 1694, not alive in 1695);[179] Elizabeth (9 August 1696).[180]

The indexes to the probate records of the Prerogative Court of Canterbury also reveal an otherwise unknown group of relationships. On 30 September 1681 Seth Vanbrugg of London, merchant, made his will and died shortly afterwards.[181] He left, in the event of his dying in the house of Michael Godfrey, money to him and his wife, children and servants.[182] But he made other specific bequests to Jasper Vandenbusche, his executor (£50 and money for a mourning ring), to Gerrard Weymans and his wife (for mourning rings) and to William Matthews, his cousin, as well as to other persons not known to be related to Gillis Van Brugh: Philip Saffre and Christopher Deynoot. The latter, however, was also given money for a ring, and at the baptism of his son Daniel in the Dutch Church on 26 July 1676 one of the witnesses, though only as a proxy, was Brother Pieter Matthews.[183] After these detailed bequests the residue of Seth's estate was to be divided between his eldest brother John Vanbruggen living in Utrecht, his brother Giles Vanbruggen, and his eldest sister's daughter Katherine Bent. The associations in the first part of the will

171 DCR; also registered at St Laurence Pountney (Guildhall MS.7670). The witnesses were the father's brother Joannes (Jean) Demetrius and the mother's elder sisters Mary Weyman and Sara Matthews. See n.176.

172 Walbrook Register; also registered at St Laurence Pountney.

173 Recommendations from the Walloon Church of Dordrecht, 23 Sept. 1668 and 14 Aug. 1675 (Hessels IV, pp.86, 100, Nos 1202, 1424). Maria witnessed a baptism on 22 Oct. 1671 (DCR). The date of the marriage is given in Daniel's will (below, n.176).

174 Below, p.168, n.112. The children were also registered at St Catherine Cree (Guildhall MS.7889).

175 ibid. and Walbrook Register, 'Danniel Demetryus.'

176 Will, originally in Low Dutch, 5 June 1685, PROB 11/411, fol.149. It identifies John Demetrius as his brother. Daniel's widow lived to be a witness by proxy on 7 Oct. 1717 (DCR).

177 Guildhall MS.7889.

178 *Denizations*, p.121.

179 The 1695 London inhabitants' list (*London Record Soc.*, II, 1966) only gives John and Mary (parents), Daniel and Susanna in the parish of St Mary Bothaw.

180 DCR; Walbrook Register; Guildhall MS.7889.

181 PROB 11/368, fol.148; proved 15 Oct. 1681. He wished to be buried 'in some parish church within three days (but not sooner) after my decease.'

182 Probably Michael Godfrey the Elder, son of Sir Thomas Godfrey of Hoddyford, Kent; Freeman of London; merchant in Bush Lane (1677 London Directory, Guildhall Library). Married Anne Mary Chamberlain. Died 1689, aged sixty-four, buried in St Swithin. Brother of Sir Edmund Berry Godfrey.

183 i.e. Peter Matthews Baldwin; DCR.

are so numerous as to imply a relationship between Seth and his brothers and sister and the family of Gillis. The latter left siblings and perhaps parents in Haarlem. One sister married there in 1644[184] and three otherwise unknown Van Brugs were witnesses by proxy to children of Gillis: Henneken to Maria (28 November 1619), Williem to Sara (10 February 1622) and Anna to Anna (1 May 1625).[185] An uncle William would also explain why Gillis gave his first three male children that name. It is tempting and perhaps worthwhile to speculate whether John of Utrecht, Seth and Giles were sons or grandsons of Williem and nephews of Gillis.[186] Seth was *of London* in 1681 and must have come over, like Van den Busch, Weyman and others, in one of the later migrations. Gillis's sons William and Giles were in Surrey and Chester; Peter, and by 1677 three of their sisters, were dead.[187] Maria, now Mrs Weyman, was the closest relative in London, and Jasper Van den Busch seems to have acquired something of a filial relationship to the Weymans in the absence of surviving children of their own.[188] It would be natural for a recent arrival to cultivate their friendship, while setting up his business, perhaps as a junior partner, with an outsider such as Michael Godfrey.[189]

184 See p.139.

185 DCR.

186 Or conceivably, if he survived and his mother took him back to Holland, sons of Petrus son of Jacob (above, p.139).

187 Nothing is known of the last sister, Susanna.

188 They were also neighbours. See above, p.143.

189 It should by now be apparent that there is no connection, as is sometimes stated, between Gillis Van Brugh's family and John and James, twin sons of John Van Bergh, who although only nineteen were trading in their own name as linen merchants by special licence in 1663 (CSP Dom 1663–4, p.192; CTB 1660–7, p.486). The architect has also on occasion been confused with his cousins Dudley, George and William Vanbrugh and with the distinct persons Verbruggen and Brook.

Chapter 9

Elizabeth Vanbrugh's Family

William and Giles Vanbrugh, brothers, married Dorothy and Elizabeth Carleton, sisters. Whereas the collateral ramifications of Gillis Van Brugh's family are primarily of interest in building up a general, though detailed, picture of the Anglo-Netherlandish merchant community, those of the Carletons involve matters of rank, of estate and of specific kinship with noble families, and for this reason it is necessary to examine the many immediate roots as well as the branches of their family. On the other hand, since many of the persons involved were historically more important for what they were than for what they did, the essential information about them can frequently be found in published sources, and can be contained in the form of a family tree; thus only the more complex or significant relationships need elaboration in this chapter.

When Sir Dudley Carleton made his will in February 1654 he was a widower for the second time and, like his distinguished uncle and namesake who had died as Viscount Dorchester in 1632, had no male children.[1] He had, however, five daughters living. The eldest was Anne, born about 1625 of his first wife and already married in 1649 to John Ferrers of Tamworth Castle.[2] To her he left an inlaid cabinet, his signet ring, and his property in Holland where he had been His Majesty's Resident. He made only these bequests to her because with her dowry they amounted to 'more than an equall portion with the Rest of her Sisters.' The other four sisters were all by his second wife. They are only mentioned all together once in the will, and the custom in testamentary documents of listing children in order of birth, combined with what he says about three of them, allows some conclusions about their ages. He married his second wife Lucy Croft in 1633:[3] Lucy, whom he called the eldest daughter, must have been born in 1634 since Mary, 'my second Daughter by my last wife', was baptized on 24 July 1635.[4] From the mention of all four together, Dorothy must have been the third, and she was probably born about

[1] Sir Dudley Carleton of Brightwell Baldwin, born 21 March 1574. Knight 1610. Ambassador to Venice 1610–15, the Hague 1616–25, Paris 1625–8. Baron Carleton of Imber Court 1626, Viscount Dorchester (Oxon.) 1628. Principal Secretary of State from Dec. 1628 until death in Feb. 1632. Married (1) Anne Savile, *née* Garrard (2) Anne, widow of Paul, Viscount Bayning of Sudbury, Suffolk.
Sir Dudley Carleton, Knight 1 March 1630, buried at St James, Clerkenwell, 9 March 1654 (*Harl. Soc., Register Series*, XVII). Will (PROB 11/239, fol.341) proved 22 March. His executor was William Vanbrugh.

[2] She was buried 5 May 1715 in Westminster Abbey, aged about ninety (*Harl. Soc.*, X, 1875, p.282).

[3] Allegation for marriage licence, Faculty Office of the Archbishop of Canterbury, 8 Feb. 1633; he about thirty, of Imber Court, Surrey, she twenty-five (*Harl. Soc.*, XXIV, 1886, p.26).

[4] Register of St Martin-in-the-Fields (Westminster City Library, Archives).

July 1636 with a small margin of latitude.[5] Elizabeth, 'my youngest daughter', was probably born the following year.[6]

To Lucy he left £1100 upon marriage or the age of twenty-one, with another £400 on condition (with complicated provisions as to the time and occasion of its fulfilment) that she conveyed to Edward Bellamy, fishmonger of London, The Ray and other estates at Walton-on-Thames, Surrey, which were the subject of an indenture between Sir Dudley and Thomas Carleton of London, mercer,[7] and Bellamy.[8]

To Mary he left £1500 upon marriage or the age of twenty-one. To Elizabeth he left tithes from lands at Claygate, Albrook [Arbrook] and Chaddesworth in the parish of Thames Ditton, Surrey, and annuities of £100; since he expected these investments to 'prove troublesome' he also left £800 to Elizabeth. To Dorothy he left £20 for a mourning ring and to William Vanbrugh, her husband and his executor, £500. She would already have had a substantial sum as dowry. His linen was to be divided equally among these four daughters, and Lucy, Mary and Elizabeth were to receive maintenance until they married or came of age. The residue of his estate was to go to Elizabeth.

Sir Dudley was the third son of George Carleton, elder brother of Viscount Dorchester.[9] It would appear that the greater part of the Carleton lands went to Sir Dudley's elder brothers John and George and that his estate was chiefly in money and goods. It is significant that he disposed of Imber Court at Thames Ditton in 1649, the year after his second wife died:[10] with no sons to succeed him his prime concern would have been to provide for his three unmarried daughters. Of their faces we know nothing, but their fortunes were certainly adequate to find them husbands. Lucy married Thomas Breton, a London merchant, Mary married Edward Pearce, gentleman and probably a merchant, and Elizabeth married first a lawyer, Thomas Barker of Freston, Suffolk, and after his death her brother-in-law Giles Vanbrugh. Thomas Carleton, who was presumably their cousin, was already a merchant, and it was perhaps through connections in Surrey[11] that the Carleton girls made their alliances with Breton, Pearce and the Vanbrughs. Sir John Vanbrugh's biographers have always stressed the importance of Lord Dorchester as his mother's great-uncle, and with reason in a society far more conscious than ours of title and lineage: his aunt Ferrers, who like all four of her half-sisters lived into old age, wished to be buried in Westminster Abbey near Dorchester's monument.[12]

Through their father and uncles the Carleton sisters were connected with many county families, and the value of these connections may yet prove not to be confined to social

[5] For physiological reasons less than twelve months between successful live births would be unusual. In the study of baptismal registers it is notable how often prolific families return to the font in the same month in most years. Even so, Dorothy must have married before she was sixteen; her youth may explain the succession of unsuccessful pregnancies which ensued (above, p.148).

[6] Again perhaps in the summer. She first married in 1655 (below, p.157).

[7] Described in his will (PROB 11/326, fol.43) as of Carshalton. Witnessed Dorothy Carleton's marriage to William Vanbrugh there, 1651 (p.148) and buried there 19 March 1668 (Registers, Surrey CRO).

[8] This paragraph summarizes about a page and a half of Carleton's will.

[9] This George actually died before the Viscount, in 1627, so that George's three sons were heirs to them both.

[10] O. Manning and W. Bray, *History and Antiquities of Surrey*, I, 1804, p.459.

[11] Dorothy Carleton married William Vanbrugh at Carshalton (p.148).

[12] Monument by Nicholas Stone, 1640. Anne Ferrers was about ninety (above, n.2). For another example of pride in descent from Lord Dorchester see p.154.

historians and compulsive readers of Debrett. Examination of the family trees on pp.129–37 reveals both the survival of a remarkable amount of information and the existence of numerous gaps in the information, especially in respect of the daughters of families and the birthplaces of children. More of these deficiencies may yet be remedied; it has only recently been possible to establish how (pp.6–7) the architect came to claim kinship with the 7th Earl of Huntingdon[13] and to imply kinship with Lord Willoughby.[14] We may yet discover where Elizabeth Vanbrugh and perhaps Giles stayed during the Great Plague and Fire years 1665–6. It was through Anne Garth, daughter of Sir Dudley Carleton's half-brother John (d. 1637), that William and Dorothy Vanbrugh went to Morden about 1659,[15] and Thomas Breton and his wife Lucy Carleton were also there in the winter of 1665–6 when their son Francis was baptized in Morden church.[16] The following year Lucy at any rate was in Norfolk, where a daughter, Lucy, was buried in Norwich Cathedral.[17] But the movements of Giles and Elizabeth in this period are unknown.[18]

The effects of the disasters of 1665–6 are difficult to over-estimate, although recovery was fast. At St Stephen Walbrook, for example, there were no baptisms in 1667 and only five in the next three years, but from 1671 the number returned to its pre-Fire level, with the important difference that most of the old family names had been replaced by new ones. Giles Vanbrugh's migration to Chester was thus typical, if the distance he went was exceptional. Another example is offered by the Stones of Brightwell Baldwin. By the marriage in 1653 of Anne Carleton (Garth)'s sister Catherine to John Stone (1626–1704) of Upp Hall, Herts., the Stones, who were also a London family, succeeded to the Carleton estates at Brightwell Baldwin. John Stone commissioned a remarkable composite monument in Brightwell church, of black, white and grey marble, with flaming urns in niches and inscriptions, for himself, his wife (d.1668) and several members of the family. Her inscription records that her father, Sir John Carleton, Bt, was 'nephew, and of the elder house, to Sir Dudley Carleton, Viscount Dorchester.' Below, a panel commemorates John Stone's grandfather John and his father Sir Richard, who died in 1640 and 1660 respectively and were buried in St Stephen, Coleman Street, London; their graves were destroyed in the Fire and the 'memorial transmitted with their family to this place.'

Sir Dudley Carleton's first wife, the mother of Anne Ferrers, was Barbara van Duick. His second marriage in 1633 was to Lucy, daughter of Sir Herbert Croft of Croft Castle, Herefordshire, and Mary, daughter of Anthony Bourne of Holt Castle, Worcestershire. By the marriage of Lucy's younger sister Elizabeth the Carletons became connected with the Caves of Stanford, Leics., and two generations later with the Verneys of Claydon, a family whose unwillingness to discard any piece of manuscript has left us with a remarkable

[13] p.15.

[14] Above, pp.6–7, 12.

[15] p.148.

[16] 1 Feb. 1666, Morden register (*Parish Register Soc.*, XXXVII, 1901). Although the Plague was worst in London it was not confined to the City.

[17] 20 Sept. 1667 (F. Blomefield, *History of Norfolk*, 1806, IV, p.10).

[18] p.164.

collection of seventeenth- and eighteenth-century family papers.[19] Lucy's eldest brother Herbert (1603–91) was Dean (1644) and after the Restoration (1661) Bishop of Hereford. In his youth, at the English College in St Omer, he was converted to Catholicism,[20] but he returned to the Church of England under the influence of Bishop Morton of Durham. Burnet considered him devout but of no discretion in his conduct, and Pepys called him 'a great gallant, having 1500£ per annum patrimony.'[21]

Lucy Carleton, the eldest daughter of Sir Dudley's second marriage, married Thomas Breton on 5 February 1657.[22] Her marriage portion was £1500 (the sum of her father's conditional and unconditional bequests), and in return her husband was, within three years, to lay out £4000 on a freehold property within 120 miles of London. These details come from a Chancery suit brought in 1675 by William Vanbrugh, his brother-in-law, because despite pressure he had not in the intervening eighteen years made such a purchase, and as his wife was likely to outlive him her future security was in danger.[23] Breton's answer to the suit was that he was still looking for somewhere suitable. After a further twelve years' procrastination Breton made his will, and charged the assiduous William with the task of himself buying an estate for Lucy.[24] Thomas Breton was successful and rich, and besides enterprises and estates of his own in about 1677 he inherited the manor of Wallington, Herts., from his brother John Breton, Master of Emmanuel College, Cambridge.[25] Thomas was born in Barwell and went to school in Hinckley in Leicestershire,[26] and he left to his son Francis a library of books. He had a collection of plate with the arms of the 2nd Duke of Buckingham which must have come to him in settlement of debts.[27] He had also engaged in the far eastern trade, and in 1673 was still involved with others in litigation over a trading voyage to China and Surat promoted by them more than ten years previously as a joint stock.[28]

Breton's reluctance to buy an estate for Lucy may have been due to his business interests, but a significant sidelight on the matter comes from a court case after his death.[29] Lucy had four children who lived to adulthood: Francis, William, Penelope and Dorothy, but Mr Breton 'having lived many years separate from his lady, did not think fit to acknowledge William and Penelope as his children.' This explains why his will referred to them as children of his wife and why he left them ten shillings each. It is not known who their father was, whether Lucy married him after Breton's death, or where she went to live. In his account book Vanbrugh called her 'Aunt Breton', but he also called Penelope

[19] F. P. Verney and M. M. Verney, *Memoirs of the Verney Family during the 17th Century*, 1904; Margaret Lady Verney, *Verney letters of the 18th Century*, 1930.

[20] His father (d. 1622) was a Catholic apologist who in 1617 took the Benedictine habit at Douai (DNB).

[21] Pepys, *Diary*, 17 March 1667; DNB; Will, PROB 11/405, fol.117.

[22] St Nicholas, Cole Abbey, Register (Guildhall MS.5686). She was then of St Stephen, Walbrook.

[23] PRO C10/181/61.

[24] PROB 11/392, fol.125 and 167. 28 April 1687, proved 4 Feb. 1688.

[25] T. Clutterbuck, *History of Hertfordshire*, III, 1827, p.596. Thomas was principal executor of John Breton's will (PROB 11/352, fol.110, PROB 11/355, fol.105 (sentence).

[26] According to his will.

[27] According to the will of his son Francis (1688) the Duke's money in his possession was over £13,000 (PROB 11/392, fol.103).

[28] HMC 9th Report, II, p.32.

[29] Josias Brown, *Reports of cases in Parliament*, V, pp.51–4 (*The English Reports*, II, 1901, pp.527–9).

'Pen Breton' after her marriage,[30] and habitual names in families often outlive their legal exactness.

Mary Carleton was married to Edward Pearce of Fulham and Whitlingham[31] by 1657, for their son Edward (later Major-General, died 1714) was born the following year.[32] Both he and his younger brother Lt-General Thomas Pearce were distinguished soldiers and first cousins of Sir John Vanbrugh. Edward married about 1690 Frances, daughter of Sir Christopher Lovett who came from Liscombe, Bucks, but, after going to Turkey in his youth as a merchant venturer, had by 1660 settled in Blind Quay (now Lower Exchange Street) in Dublin as a linen-merchant.[33] (Her brother, Colonel John Lovett, bought the Eddystone Rock and built the second lighthouse there, opened in 1708 in place of Henry Winstanley's washed away five years earlier. It was soundly constructed but largely of wood and burned down in December 1755.)[34] The son of Major-General Pearce and Frances Lovett was Sir Edward Lovett Pearce, the architect, who was through Mary and Elizabeth Carleton Sir John Vanbrugh's cousin at one remove. They seem to have had some architectural contact, and although from Pearce's executed work he can hardly be called a pupil or follower it is possible that Vanbrugh's example introduced him to the idea of architecture.[35]

Mrs Mary Pearce outlived her husband[36] and ultimately retired to a house in the Lower Close in Norwich. In 1718, when the land belonging to Whitlingham had been let, the house was advertised for rental as 'still to be disposed of with all the garden ground courtyard stable.' It contained 'an handsome hall or parlour six good chambers and other conveniences fit for a gentleman.'[37] She was presumably the object of an expedition to Norwich about May 1719 by three of her nieces, Elizabeth, Victoria and Robina Vanbrugh, to whom Sir John Vanbrugh gave £13 10*s*. for their expenses;[38] the occasion does not seem to have been a marriage, a funeral or a decade anniversary. Mary attained the age of ninety-three; on 9 July 1728 she dictated a brief will 'for want of time to write more largly', leaving everything to the possession and discretion of her surviving son Lt-General Thomas Pearce.[39]

Dorothy and Elizabeth Carleton have already been mentioned, and their children are discussed in the next chapter.[40] Elizabeth's first marriage, however, was not to a Vanbrugh,

30 Account Book, ff.15, 35v.

31 Edward Pearce, gent., of Parson's Green, Fulham, and W[h]itlingham, now a suburb of Norwich (F. Blomefield, *History of Norfolk*, v, 1806, p.456). The Pearces made an indenture over Whitlingham in 1668 with Herbert Croft, Bishop of Hereford (p.155) and John Ferrers (p.152) according to his will (n.36).

32 Pensioner at Caius College, Cambridge, 23 June 1675 aged seventeen; schooled at Norwich (Venn).

33 Margaret Lady Verney, *Verney Letters of the 18th Century*, 1930, I, pp.138, 347–8.

34 ibid., pp.192, 205, 362–3. Col. Lovett (d.1710) took as his second wife Mary Verney in 1703.

35 Sir Edward Lovett Pearce returned to Ireland in 1726 as a disciple of Lord Burlington, and died there in 1733. His principal work is the Old Parliament House (now Bank of Ireland) in Dublin. See *Elton Drawings*, p.xxxviii; T. U. Sadleir, 'Sir Edward Lovett Pearce', *Journal of County Kildare Archaeological Soc.*, x, 5, 1927, pp.231–44; M. J. Craig, 'New Light on Jigginstown', ibid., xv, 1, 1971, pp.50–8.

36 He died in 1683; will (PROB 11/374, fol.109) made 11 Nov. 1682. Codicil (mourning money for Thomas Breton) 14 April 1683. Proved Nov. 1683. He left land in Norfolk, two houses on London Bridge and stock in the East India Company.

37 *The Norwich Gazette*, 2 Jan. 1718. Whitlingham remained in the family.

38 Account Book, ff.25, 25v.

39 Norfolk CRO, Consistory Wills, 43 Thacker.

40 pp.159–72.

and her husband and their descendants therefore conclude this chapter. Thomas Barker of Freston, Suffolk, was born in 1626, the second son of Sir John Barker, Baronet, of Grimston in that county. From Cambridge he was admitted to Gray's Inn in 1645.[41] In January 1655 he applied to marry Elizabeth Carleton at St Andrew's, Holborn,[42] but in May 1656 he died, leaving his widow with an infant daughter, Elizabeth. He left most of his estate to his younger brother Robert, his executor and a barrister.[43] He provided £2000 to be held in trust for the daughter's majority or marriage, and an income for her upbringing. His widow was to receive £36 a year in lieu of rent on a farm at Walton[44] and presumably she was well enough served by what Sir Dudley Carleton had left her.[45] Perhaps she went with her child to stay with Dorothy, at that time her only married sister, and thus met Giles Vanbrugh on his return from Europe. In 1659 they were married,[46] and Elizabeth Barker grew up as the elder half-sister to their children and moved with them to Chester after the Great Fire. In 1678 at the age of twenty-two she married Dudley Garencieres at St Oswald's, Chester; he was about five years older,[47] and was probably the son of Theophilus de Garencieres (1610–80), M.D. (Caen and Oxford).[48] Dudley went to Westminster School and Trinity College, Cambridge. In 1677 he became Rector of Waverton, Cheshire and a minor canon of Chester; he was later Prebendary, and Rector of Handley. He was buried in Chester Cathedral on 8 April 1702.[49] Five of his sons went to the King's School in Chester.[50] His will mentions properties in Suffolk which were to be sold to provide for the maintenance of his son Theophilus at Oxford, his son Athanasius to the end of his apprenticeship, and the younger children. His executors were his widow, John Vanbrugh and their mother, and the will was witnessed by Mary Vanbrugh (John's sister), Samuel Taylor and Jona[than] Robinson.[51] Samuel Taylor had other connections with the Vanbrughs. In 1700 John, about to spend 'at least a Week' in Chester, asked for letters to be sent to him in Taylor's care,[52] and in 1703 Taylor applied for a renewal of a lease originally made in 1686 of 'a parcel of land called the Salt Grasse near the Starting Stone' which he had taken over from Giles Vanbrugh.[53]

Athanasius Garencieres seems to have lived in Sir John Vanbrugh's household about 1719–21, when with the family servant John (Jack) Jones he witnessed a number of

41 Baptized at Grimston 31 March 1625. Admitted Pensioner, Pembroke College, Cambridge, 13 April 1642; Gray's Inn 6 Feb. 1645. Buried at Grimston 15 May 1656 (Venn).

42 Banns 13–27 Jan. 1655 (Guildhall MS.6668/5) but no record of the marriage there. She was of St Stephen's, Walbrook.

43 PROB 11/255, fol.197, made 25 Feb. 1656 ('sick but of good and present memory'), proved 15 May.

44 Freston, Grimston and Walton are all now in or on the outskirts of Felixstowe.

45 In Dec. 1655 she obtained new administration of her mother's will (PROB 11/247, fol.246).

46 See p.164.

47 Allegation for Licence, Faculty Office of the Archbishop of Canterbury (*Harl. Soc.*, XXIV, 1886, p.142). Alleged by Peter de Garencieres of Westminster.

48 Foster, *Oxon.*; DNB.

49 Venn; Chester Cathedral Registers (*Parish Register Soc.*, LIV, 1904).

50 G. D. Squibb's list of scholars (Copy in Chester City RO).

51 Will 13 March 1702, proved 1 June 1703 (Cheshire CRO). There is a deed of conveyance of 11 Dec. 1703 in the Ipswich and East Suffolk CRO (GC15:52/6/11–13) by which Theophilus's executors sold to Henry Pelton, butcher, of Walton, Suffolk, two cottages at Walton Street, for £20 19*s.* (formerly at the Soc. of Genealogists, HP1/22).

52 Webb, p.7.

53 Chester Assembly Book 3 (Calendar in Chester City RO), ff.7v, 105v. *The Norwich Gazette*, 29 Nov. 1718, carried an advertisement for wines, brandy and punch to be sold in Norwich by 'Thomas Baker, who buys all his wine of Samuel Taylor Esq.'

documents.[54] He is also mentioned several times in the Account Book. Vanbrugh paid interest to his half-sister (*Sis: Garencieres*) on a bond for £300, which he finally discharged on 7 April 1724, only to replace it by a note for £80, of which he repaid £20 the following 27 February.

Theophilus took Holy Orders, went to Chester in 1708 and in 1721 became Vicar of Scarborough and later also of Stainton-in-Cleveland where he was buried in 1750.[55] From 1723 he was also Master of the Grammar School at Scarborough. In 1724 Vanbrugh tried unsuccessfully to obtain for him, through the influence of the Duke of Newcastle, the Prebend of Southwell. It was in itself worth £7 a year, or 'Nothing. Yet so it is, We desire, we may have it; because, We are a Youngish Man,[56] of good Bodily Fortitude, and our mind, not so harrass'd by Our Care of Souls, but that we hope we may Out Live, two certain Elderly Persons; which, if we do, This same Nothing, may prove worth Something at last.'[57] Some of his relatives were in Southwell,[58] but the chief attraction was the capital fee on each re-leasing of the Prebend House, in which the Prebendary did not live. In answers to the Archbishop of York in 1743 the parson stated that he rented a house because the vicarage at Scarborough was too small for his family, though he had a study, and often slept, there.[59] In 1728, whether or not through his cousin's connection, he was made chaplain to the Duke of Ancaster. The same year he published *General Instructions, divine, moral, historical, figurative etc., showing the progress of religion from the creation to this time and to the end of the world.* He seems to have been prosaic but pious: he told the Archbishop that he had refused Communion to very few, 'and to those, because I had just reason to think that they came to it more for the sake of getting a part of the money at those times collected than out of a due sense of their duty, which I believe made them come to that solemn institution in a more serious and devout manner afterwards.'[60]

[54] Agreements about the Haymarket site, 17 Oct. 1719, 13 Oct. 1720 (PRO LR1/282, ff.142, 190); agreement with Thomas Miller, brickmaker, 9 June 1721 (BIHR (Yarburgh)).

[55] *Gent. Mag.*, XX, 1750, p.525 (died 21 Oct. 1750). Mrs Elizabeth Garencieres seems to have died about Nov. 1728 when Lady Vanbrugh paid 'Mr Garrencers' (Theophilus) the remaining £30 of Sir John's £80 note; the following May her annuity was, in accordance with Sir John's will, transferred to her daughter Lucia Maria (Lady Vanbrugh's Account Book, BIHR (Yarburgh)).

[56] Born about 1680.

[57] Vanbrugh writing from Scarborough, 23 Aug. 1724 (and a previous letter of 10 July; Webb, pp.161–2).

[58] See p.167, and N. Summers, *A Prospect of Southwell*, 1974.

[59] *Yorks. Archaeol. Soc.*, LXXV, 1929, pp.133–5.

[60] ibid. Dudley had published a *History of Christ's Sufferings* (London, 1697) and his father a number of works including *Angliae Flagellum* (London, 1647) which acquired a quite unfounded reputation on the basis of a belief that it was about rickets; in fact it concerns pulmonary phthisis (DNB).

Chapter 10

The Vanbrugh–Carleton Families

The previous two chapters have dealt with Sir John Vanbrugh's elders and some of their descendants; this one is devoted to his closer associates, his first cousins by his uncle William and his own brothers and sisters, and to the later, and as far as is known, the last, members of the Vanbrugh line.

After a succession of failures, Dorothy Vanbrugh bore William at least seven live children, three of whom reached adulthood; when Giles Vanbrugh made his will in 1683 he had thirteen children living. These sixteen can be described as of the architect's generation according to birth, but not according to date, since their births span the twenty-three years from 1658 to 1681. Nevertheless it is among them that his most direct contacts are to be found. We know more of some than of others, and it is evident that a number of them were remarkable characters even if their imprint on history is far smaller and fainter than that of their illustrious and versatile companion.

The eldest, the first surviving child of William and Dorothy, was William, baptized on 1 January 1658 at St Stephen's, Walbrook.[1] This was the cousin to whom Vanbrugh referred once in a letter,[2] who appears in many official documents of the time, and who as 'Mr Vanbrugh' managed on occasion to confuse the compilers of the Calendars of State and Treasury Papers.[3] In spite of his active, if minor, public career, Cousin William has managed to elude researches to a degree. It is no doubt accidental that we have found records of neither his marriage nor his burial nor, if there were any, the births of children. But it is hard to forgive him for dying intestate in 1716 at the age of fifty-eight: we might expect him as a lawyer to have been more careful, although more cynically we might imagine that debt was not the only good reason for his not doing so.[4] Peter Le Neve described him as of Walton-on-Thames and Whitehall;[5] he inherited his father's house at Walton and when he died Sir John, as principal creditor, probably acquired at least a share in the

[1] Walbrook Register. He may thus have been born in Dec. 1657.

[2] Webb, p.223.

[3] The confusion between William and John varies among the volumes with the expectations of the compiler, including 'Sir William Vanbrugh' in CTB, 1716, p.555, for Sir John.

[4] He does not appear in the registers of the Temple Church, St Martin-in-the-Fields, St James Piccadilly, St Margaret Westminster (of which his Administration calls him a late resident), the Chapels Royal (PRO RG8/110) or Walton-on-Thames. His Administration (PROB 6/93, f.34) is to Sir John, described as his principal creditor; his widow is named as Eliza[beth]. Venn gives his death as 20 Nov. 1716; on the following day Sir John was at Walton (Account Book), but the Treasury chose Peter Nicols to succeed him on 19 Nov. (CTB 1716, p.45).

[5] Le Neve, p.512.

house.[6] William was admitted to Trinity College, Cambridge on 14 September 1674 and received his M.A. by the King's direction the following year; on 31 May 1676 he was admitted to the Inner Temple.[7] In 1694 he obtained letters of administration of the estate of his younger brother Dudley, their father being in Ireland.[8] On 31 May 1695, in the Guildhall, at the second meeting of the Commission for building Greenwich Hospital, he was appointed its secretary, being proposed by John Evelyn.[9] His involvement with Greenwich was, like Evelyn's, philanthropic, and he was concerned with payments for clothing, as agent to the former Lord Lovelace's Regiment in Ireland.[10] It may have been on similar business that he visited the Netherlands in 1695 and 1697.[11] The fact of Evelyn's recommendation speaks for his capability. By 1698 he was Deputy Comptroller of Accounts of the Treasurer of the Chamber.[12] In November 1701 a move was made to appoint him Comptroller in place of Hugh Chudleigh, who was to have £100 a year until he found another post; there was some objection to this arrangement, for two months later William was to have £100 a year until the Comptrollership should become vacant, meanwhile remaining Deputy.[13] His patent as Comptroller, at £150 a year, was finally issued on 7 November 1707 with effect from the previous Michaelmas.[14] He was subsequently one of the commissioners for stating William III's debts.[15] In February 1715 he petitioned for the renewal of his patent, which he obtained in May; on 23 November 1716 a patent was issued to his successor.[16] He was not buried in the family vault. The grant of administration to his cousin John, 'creditori principali', rather than to his widow suggests that he was in financial difficulties, but while he cannot have lived on £150 a year we do not know other sources of income. He was presumably, with his brother George, the principal beneficiary after the death of their father, who made no will either;[17] their mother must have been the Dorothy Vanbrugh who witnessed Mrs Elizabeth (the architect's mother) Vanbrugh's will on 13 May 1707[18] and was buried in the family vault on 20 May 1713.[19]

If the younger William had little to leave besides the house at Walton, it would be understandable that there were no financial ripples after his death in Sir John's account

[6] See above, n.4. No financial transaction is recorded in the Account Book, but besides its evidence of subsequent visits Sir John's second son was nursed and buried at Walton (above, p.97) and in 1724–5 'Mr Vanbrugh, K[nigh]t' was described as a resident (Bishop Willis's Visitation, *Surrey Archaeol. Colls.*, XXXIX, 1931, p.101).

[7] Venn.

[8] See p.161.

[9] *Wren Soc.*, VI, p.30; Evelyn, *Diary*, 31 May 1695. It was as Secretary to the Greenwich Grand Committee that the Treasury Lords sent an apology to William for absence on 15 Oct. 1695 (CTB 1693–6, p.1409). William is the Mr Vanbrugh referred to in an anonymous letter in the V & A (Appendix F here).

[10] CTP 1557–1696, pp.89, 151, 312.

[11] Passes to go to Holland, 14 June 1695; to Holland or Flanders, 7 Oct. 1697 (CSP Dom 1694–5, p.494; 1696, p.418).

[12] CTB 1697–8, p.78 (13 April 1698).

[13] ibid. 1700–1, p.112 (18 Nov. 1701); 1702, p.120 (17 Jan. 1702).

[14] ibid. 1706–7, p.483. See also Appendix L.

[15] ibid. 1702, p.947; Luttrell, VI, p.314; CSP Col 1708–9, p.535.

[16] CTP 1715–19, p.178; CTB 1714–15, p.522; 1716, p.561.

[17] Administration, PROB 6/81, f.53v.

[18] PROB 11/524, fol.248.

[19] Walbrook Register.

book. The identity of his widow Eliza (almost certainly a clerk's abbreviation for Elizabeth) is uncertain and puzzling, and it would be both neat and plausible to suppose that she was Sir John's sister (born 1671), the Sister Betty of the Account Book, who begins to figure in his finances in August 1717 or nine months after William's death. Some mystery also attaches to her, for Sir John left her out of his will though she outlived him.[20] He left £20 each for mourning to his sisters Mary, Victoria, Robina, his half-sister Elizabeth Garencieres, and his brothers Charles and Philip, and Lady Vanbrugh recorded on the last pages of the Account Book the payments to the sisters. On 20 June 1726 she 'pd sister Mary Elizabeth & Robina £20 Each for mourning' and added, as if to dispel some doubt not necessarily the same as ours, 'Memorandum I gave Sister Betty hers.'[21] It is also neat and plausible to suppose the identity of either or both these Elizabeths with the Mrs Elizabeth Vanbrugh, widow, who died in Southwell at the end of 1730. The Southwell registers are defective for this period, and the information comes from a Cheshire diary, which confirms that this Elizabeth had been brought up there.[22]

Dudley Vanbrugh was born to William and Dorothy on 6 July 1659 and baptized at St Stephen's, Walbrook a week later.[23] Nothing is known of his life until the age of twenty-six, when he was an ensign in Sir Edward Hales's Foot Regiment (June 1685).[24] In February 1689 he was captain in Colonel Beveridge's Foot Regiment.[25] Late in 1692 there took place the unfortunate incident in which romantic writers have attempted to involve the architect: on 22 November Luttrell reported that 'Ostend letters say, Collonel Beveredge of the Scots regiment being at dinner with Captain Vanbrook of the same, words arose and swords were after drawn, and the collonel was killed, having given abusive language to the captain first and shook him.'[26] Dudley was court-martialled but acquitted, on grounds of provocation, on 13 February 1693; five months later, on 29 July, he fell mortally on the field of Landen.[27]

The third brother, George, was baptized at Carshalton on 5 November 1668.[28] When he made his will on 28 March 1728 he was of London, merchant, and in ill health, but he survived until October 1729[29]. His sole heir and executor was his 'true and most faithful servant John Rogers' and the will mentions, besides money and stock-in-trade, personal

[20] PROB 11/608, fol.84. Elizabeth is not mentioned among Vanbrugh's siblings in Le Neve, p.512.

[21] 11 April, 20 June, 27 July 1726.

[22] G. P. Crawford, 'The diary of George Booth and Katherine Howard his daughter of Broughton near Chester 1707–1764' (*Chester & N. Wales Archit., Archaeol. & Historic Soc.*, N.S., XXVIII, 1, 1928, p.48). Katherine Howard was born in 1672 and thus a contemporary. She also noted Sir John's death (p.34). For Elizabeth Vanbrugh in Southwell see p.169. Other unidentified figures are Elizabeth Vanbrugh, spinster, who was involved in an attempted land deal by George Vanbrugh in 1708 (p.162) and Elizabeth, wife of Peter Vanbroke, living in St Leonard, Foster Lane parish in 1695 (*London Record Soc.*, II, 1966, p.300).

[23] Walbrook Register. Among its many errors the mother of both William and Dudley is given as Mary.

[24] C. Dalton, *English Army Lists*, II, p.35. Subsequent references pp.101, 144, 163; CSP Dom 1687–9, p.279.

[25] Dalton, III, p.53. Subsequent references CSP Dom 1689–90, p.464; 1691–2, p.344.

[26] Luttrell, II, p.621.

[27] Dalton, III, p.53. Administration, PROB 6/70, f.77. Warrant for payment of arrears to his executors, 7 June 1694 (CTB 1693–6, p.643).

[28] Carshalton Registers (Surrey CRO). The other children were Charles (baptized Morden 4 Aug. 1661, buried St Stephen Walbrook 2 Feb. 1680), George (baptized Morden 29 Nov. 1662, died before Nov. 1668), Dorothy (baptized Morden 27 Aug. 1664, buried 22 Nov. 1672) and Theodore (baptized 31 July 1665, buried St Stephen Walbrook 13 Feb. 1669). Nothing is known of the family between 1665 and 1668. (Walbrook Register; Morden Parish Register (*Parish Register Soc.*, XXXVII, 1901).

[29] PROB 11/633, fol.285, proved 14 Oct. 1729. Buried at St Stephen Walbrook 17 Oct. (Walbrook Register).

estate in Great Britain and Portugal. George was in the wine and spirit trade. In 1709 he and two other London merchants applied for permission to reduce to proof some brandy imported by them from Portugal; four years later he was one of a number of merchants granted a similar permit to reduce brandy and rum.[30] On two occasions Sir John paid him for wine,[31] and he authenticated Sir John's unwitnessed will.[32] In 1708 he tried to buy the lease of an estate of two messuages, a toft and a close at Manningford Bruce, Wilts., but although he claimed to have been admitted to the reversion for himself and Elizabeth Vanbrugh, spinster, he was unable to obtain the title to the land. In March 1710 he went to law about it, but the outcome is unknown,[33] although ten years later he paid, through Sir John, expenses for a suit with the same defendant.[34] He does appear also to have acquired a home in or near Wiltshire, for on a journey to Eastbury in 1724 the architect recorded payment to his servants, which indicates that he stayed there.[35] The unmarried Elizabeth mentioned in the Chancery suit is unidentified.

The last surviving Vanbrugh was the Reverend George, Rector of Aughton, Lancs. (1756–1847). Sir John's great-nephew Edward Vanbrugh referred to him as his kinsman,[36] and in 1813 he published a cantata, *Lysander*, under the architect's name instead of that of his own grandfather, George.[37] These two references are sufficient to identify him as a descendant of Gillis Van Brugh, and thus by elimination as a descendant of William (1628–1704) and of one of his sons, William (1658–1716) or George (1668–1729); since it is not known whether that George married, or whether his brother had any children, there remains an uncertain link in the family line, and it is marginally possible that the composer was the son of neither but of another son of the elder William of whom we have no archival records.

Of the song-writer himself we are somewhat better informed. The Music Room at the British Museum has a number of printed songs and collections of vocal and instrumental music by George Vanbrugh, none of which is dated but with suggested dates in square brackets between 1710 and 1735.[38] He is presumably to be identified with the 'George Vanbrugh, or Ghentbrugh', bass and song composer, among the Duke of Chandos's resident musicians at Cannons about 1720.[39] George was 'of the precinct of Christ Church Canterbury' when he made his will in 1756;[40] he was not in Holy Orders, but he was buried in the cathedral cloister yard on 16 October 1758,[41] and a reasonable conclusion is

[30] CTB 1709, p.392; 1713, p.397. He does not seem to have been a freeman of the Vintners' Company.

[31] Account Book, 7 June 1720, 24 April 1722.

[32] PROB 11/608, fol.84. The original, bearing George's bold, round and slightly irregular signature on the accompanying certificate, is PROB 1/61.

[33] PRO C9/347/7 and 10. No references to George Vanbrugh or the property could be found in the Wilts. CRO.

[34] Account Book, 21 Oct. 1720.

[35] ibid., 29 June 1724.

[36] In his will, PROB 11/1382, fol.785.

[37] The Rector's mother Agnes died at Aughton in 1809 and he may have found the piece in her papers afterwards.

[38] B.M. *Catalogue of Old Music*, p.102. The best account of George as a composer is by Gerald Hendrie in F. Blume, ed., *Die Musik in Geschichte und Gegenwart*.

[39] *Chandos*, p.133.

[40] PROB 11/842, fol.351.

[41] Canterbury Cathedral Register (*Harl. Soc., Register Series*, II).

that he was a member of the cathedral choir. His widow Mary was buried in Chester Cathedral on 24 March 1773, aged eighty-two.[42] He had left everything to her, and on her death to their daughter Judith, who was the widow of François Duchesne (died 1755) and had a son, Francis.[43] George and Mary had other children, and at least one son, Robert, outlived them. Ralph (9 March 1716) and Edward (24 June 1717) were baptized at St Michael-le-Querne.[44] A daughter, Mary, was buried at St Margaret Moses on 30 December 1726.[45] A George was born on 14 February 1731 and baptized on 2 March at St Dunstan-in-the-West.[46] His elder brother Robert was born on 31 July 1728 and baptized there on 19 August.[47] He went to school first at Sedbergh[48] and then from 1742 to 1746 at Eton on a scholarship.[49] After St John's, Cambridge he was ordained at Canterbury in 1752.[50] He was curate at Aldingham and Dent in Yorkshire and then in 1768 became Master of the King's School in Chester.[51] From 1776 he was Rector of Buckland, Glos., and from 1780 a minor canon of Chester.[52] He died in February 1784 at Hartford, Hunts.[53] His wife, Agnes, outlived him and died in 1809 at Aughton, near Ormskirk, Lancs., where their son, also George, was Rector.[54] He was born in 1756; after going to Cambridge he became a minor canon of Chester at the same time as his father.[55] In 1786 he became Rector of Aughton, where he remained until 1834; in September 1812 he was made one of the King's Preachers in Lancashire,[56] and in 1825 a Prebendary of Wells. In 1824 the Vicar of Audley, Thomas Garratt, dedicated to him *The Pastor,* a rambling and pious exercise in Wordsworthian verse which, although the author says that George was his model, makes no specific references that tell us anything about him. His will tells us rather more.[57] He resigned the living of Aughton in 1834 and lived thereafter at Waterloo on the coast near Liverpool. His worldly property was 'by the blessing of God . . . very considerable', and he had no 'very accurate knowledge of the exact amount of my property . . . by reason of my limited expenditure it is continually increasing.' Besides provision for the poor of Aughton and for his tomb in the church there,[58] he made monetary bequests of over £45,000. As already

42 Chester Cathedral Register (*Parish Register Soc.*, LIV, 1904).

43 Judith Vanbrugh married François Duchesne at St George's Chapel, Hyde Park Corner, on 4 June 1747 (*Harl. Soc., Register Series,* XV). Duchesne's will, proved 1 April 1755, refers to his wife Judith and son Francis and gives his address as St James, Westminster (Middlesex CRO, Archdeaconry Wills, 1747–55, Vol.19, p.1149).

44 Baptized 11 March 1716, 7 July 1717 (*Harl. Soc., Register Series,* XXIX).

45 ibid., XLII.

46 Guildhall MS.10349.

47 ibid.

48 *Sedbergh School Register 1546–1895*, 1895, p.144.

49 Eton College records state that he was the composer's son.

50 Venn.

51 Cheshire CRO, EDA 1/6, f.52; 1/7, ff.93v, 94.

52 Cathedral Register, 12 July 1780 (*Parish Register Soc.*, LIV, 1904).

53 *Gent. Mag.*, LIV, 1784, p.235.

54 ibid., LXXII, 1809, p.187 (25 Jan. 1809, aged 83). Her first name is given in the burial record of their daughter in Chester Cathedral, 25 April 1782 (*Parish Register Soc.*, LIV, 1904). In a codicil to his will George stated that 'my late Mother's family was much connected with Sedbergh.'

55 Above, n.52.

56 *Gent. Mag.*, LXXXII, ii, 1812, p.287.

57 PROB 11/2065, fol.882.

58 By J. S. Westmacott, 1866.

mentioned, he published his grandfather's cantata believing it to be by Sir John Vanbrugh. In March 1789 he had married a Miss Ravenscroft at Chester;[59] they are not known to have had any children. The will mentions his 'late cousin Samuel Wayman Wadeson of London, attorney' and the residuary legatee was presumably George's godson, the Reverend Robert Vanbrugh Law, Rector of Christian Malford, Wilts.[60] With him William Vanbrugh's line died out.[61]

Giles Vanbrugh's male line had ended with the death of his grandson Edward in 1802, and it is now appropriate to return to Giles's youth, to enumerate his children and to deal in more detail with those who grew up. At some time after his father's death Giles continued his education by travelling abroad in France and Italy 'for my Pleasure & Improvement.' He was away for 'above 3 years' and spent one of them 'at Rome, where I had the opportunity of taking notice of many things relating to that Citty.'[62] He was back in England before 1659 when he married, and his travels can be approximately dated by his signature in the register kept for British visitors to the University of Padua: on 22 January 1655 he signed as *Giles Vanbrook Anglo-Londinensis*.[63] On 15 October 1659 he married his sister-in-law Elizabeth Barker, *née* Carleton, at All Hallows, London Wall.[64] They settled in the parish of St Nicholas Acons, which abuts among others on those of St Laurence Pountney and St Martin Orgar. A son, Giles, was born on 6 October 1660, baptized eight days later[65] and buried in the vault at Walbrook the following 31 March.[66] A second child, Dorothy, born on 14 February 1662 and baptized on the 20th, was buried on 27 September.[67] Perhaps as a result of these misfortunes the third child, Lucy, was christened in the house the day she was born, 11 February 1663.[68] Nothing is known of her except that she died in Southwell in 1699.[69]

The next child of Giles and Elizabeth was baptized on 24 January 1664, again in the house and thus was perhaps born that same day.[70] This was the eldest surviving son, the subject of this book, and at this point alone nothing more needs to be said about him. In 1664 Giles was a Deacon of the Dutch Church.[71] The last child to be christened at St Nicholas Acons was Elizabeth, born on 7 January 1665 and baptized on the 18th.[72] She was buried in Chester on 27 November 1667.[73]

The whereabouts of the family later in 1665 and until June 1667 are unknown, although

59 *Gent. Mag.*, LIX, 1789, p.275 ('lately' in March).

60 Not Essex as the will says.

61 Violet and Irene Barnes took the stage name of Vanbrugh at the suggestion of Ellen Terry (DNB).

62 Letter to the Bishop of London, 1678 (below, Appendix A).

63 H. F. Brown, *Inglesi e Scozzesi all'Università di Padova*, Venice, 1921, p.160.

64 Guildhall MS.5085.

65 W. Brigg, *The Register Book of the Parish of St Nicolas Acon 1539–1812*, Leeds, 1890.

66 Walbrook Register, 'a youngue Child of Mr Giles Van Bruggs.'

67 Brigg, op.cit.; Walbrook Register, 'a young child of Mr Giles Vanbroge.'

68 Brigg, op.cit.

69 p.167.

70 Brigg, op.cit.

71 Moens, p.212.

72 Brigg, op.cit.

73 Holy Trinity Register.

it is a reasonable supposition that they left London after early reports of the Plague. Some time in the earlier half of 1666 Anna Maria was born, for there is no other gap into which she can be fitted.[74] She married in Southwell in 1698 and died in 1700.[75]

Giles was probably in London in February 1667 when he was one of several City merchants petitioning for the release of goods from the Customs; his concern was 65 ells of linen.[76] In June 1667 Elizabeth at least was in Richmond, Surrey, for a son, Carleton, was baptized there on 6 June.[77] By the autumn the family had moved to Chester, where the boy born in Richmond was buried on 13 October.[78] There Giles set up in the parish of Holy Trinity in a business which is usually described as sugar-baking but which included the refining of sugar. Chester, as a port with developing links with the New World, was as logical a situation for sugar processing as Liverpool, which superseded it, still is today.[79] Giles became a respected member of the Chester community, and several times he appears in the diary of Sir Willoughby Aston.[80] They met at a coffee-house in the city and discussed books, and subsequently they dined together. In 1685 Aston consulted Giles and Mr Kenrick about apprenticing his son Willoughby to an India Merchant. Giles is mentioned in Tong's life (1716) of the Dissenter, Matthew Henry, as one of a number of Anglican citizens who, notwithstanding their orthodoxy, also attended Henry's weekday lectures.[81] Giles perhaps derived a fundamentalist streak from his London Dutch upbringing, and indeed there is at least a touch of religious fanaticism in the letter he wrote to the Bishop of London at Christmas 1678. Even in the aftermath of the Popish Plot it seems an extraordinary scheme to take a commando force from Ostia to Rome in order to scale the walls of the Vatican and carry away the contents of the Library.[82]

On 25 October 1683 Giles made his will,[83] leaving to his widow the household goods and furniture, excepting plate, and what was due to her from his estate 'according to ye Contract of Marriage.' The rest of the estate, of whatever kind, was to be sold and divided into fourteen equal parts of which John, the eldest son, was to receive two and each of the other twelve children living one part. As far as we know all were still alive when he was buried on 19 July 1689,[84] comprising Lucy, John, Anna Maria and ten of the twelve born after the move to Chester. The full list, from the register of Holy Trinity, is as follows: Mary (born 3 November 1668, baptized 19th); Victoria (baptized 25

[74] See p.153, n.5.

[75] p.168.

[76] PRO T51/10, p.357. The English ell is a yard and a quarter.

[77] Richmond register (*Surrey Parish Register Soc.*, I, 1903).

[78] Holy Trinity Register. Elizabeth (b.1665) was buried on 27 Nov.

[79] According to local tradition Vanbrugh's refinery was the building formerly in Weaver Lane known as the Sugar House. See J. Davies, 'Sir John Vanbrugh in Chester', *Cheshire Life*, Dec. 1958, p.55.

[80] Not, as suggested by R. Richards, *Old Cheshire Churches*, 2nd ed. Didsbury, 1973, p.805, the architect Vanbrugh. 'Mr Vanbrugh' is mentioned in the diary on 15 Feb. 1682, 2, 4, 11 May 1683, 6, 7 Aug. 1685 (Liverpool RO, MD 172–3).

[81] Whistler (1938), pp.16–17.

[82] See Appendix A. On 20 Sept. 1676 Giles wrote to William Lilly the astrologer (1602–81) about a dangerous direction of his nativity expected in 1678 (Bodl.MS.Ashm.423, f.253). According to the letter, his brother (William Vanbrugh senior) was a friend of Lilly; both lived at Walton-on-Thames.

[83] Cheshire CRO.

[84] Holy Trinity Register.

January 1670); Elizabeth (baptized 4 May 1671); Robina (baptized 22 September 1672); Carleton (baptized 18 September 1673); an infant buried unnamed on 31 August 1674; Giles (baptized 3 September 1675); Catherina (baptized 9 October 1676, buried 22 March 1678); Dudley (born 21 October 1677; baptized 25th); Kenrick (baptized 21 November 1678); Charles (baptized 27 February 1680) and Philip (baptized 31 January 1682).[85]

From Giles's will it appears that the family house was part of the estate to be sold. His widow was assessed for the Poor Rate in 1690 but not thereafter and it is probable that she moved away altogether.[86] She made her will on 13 May 1707, when she was 'of London', and left everything to her youngest son Philip, to 'perform whatsoever I have expressed in writing with my own hands.'[87] When she died four years later Philip was on the high seas and administration was given to John, the alternate whom she nominated.[88] It was thus to him that the task fell of burying her at Thames Ditton, and of settling her affairs at a time when his own were financially far from stable.[89] Three days after the funeral he was seeking an advance on his Blenheim salary, 'by reason of the great expense he had bin at . . . in burying his mother.'[90] Since she died at his house at Chargate in the parish of Esher[91] she may have been living there, and indeed it is possible that the house had been built for their joint use and with her financial help.[92] In the absence of her written instructions many questions about the family are likely to remain unanswered, but it is possible that she expressed a wish to be buried at Thames Ditton because it was the parish in which, at Imber Court, she had spent some of her childhood.

[85] ibid.

[86] Extracts from churchwardens' accounts, Holy Trinity (Chester City RO, 761); 'Madm Vanbrugh.' In later references she is variously 'of Chester' and 'of London.' The fact that John Vanbrugh wrote to her care of Gerard Weyman her brother-in-law in 1691 suggests, but does not establish, that she was in London then (see p.143).

[87] PROB 11/524, fol.248. Witnessed by Dorothy Vanbrugh and Mary Smith.

[88] ibid. The second alternate was their sister Robina.

[89] The extant registers of Thames Ditton do not cover the period, and the burial is known from J. Le Neve, *Monumenta Anglicana* III, 1717, pp.233–4.

[90] Samuel Travers to Marlborough (Whistler, p.145). Vanbrugh's comment on Marlborough's funeral in 1722 was that 'this Idle Show will be gone in half an hour, and forgot in Two days' whereas a mausoleum 'wou'd have been a Show, and a Noble one, to many future Ages' (Webb, p.148). Wren wrote in 1711 of 'the Fashion of the Age to solemnize Funerals by a Train of Coaches (even where the Deceased are of moderate Condition)' (*Wren Soc.*, IX, p.15). The zenith of bourgeois funerals appears to have been that in November 1717 of Francis Tyssen, Vanbrugh's kinsman by marriage (the third of that name), which led the Earl Marshal, Lord Suffolk, to insert a notice in the *London Gazette* (No.5592, 19/23 Nov.) after a report in the *Post Boy* of 14 Nov. Tyssen's body 'lay in state at Goldsmiths-Hall in so grand and compleat a manner as had not been seen before' and a week later 'was carried in great procession with four of the King's Trumpets, etc. with a led horse in a velvet caprizon and all the trophies proper to a gentleman on that occasion to Hackney where he was interr'd.' (Tyssen incidentally was not a Goldsmith and the hall must have been hired.) Further, the officers of the College of Arms were willing 'to direct and marshal the said funeral . . . but the manner in which the body was set forth and also had a led horse, trumpets, a guidon and six penons with a coach of state being insisted upon . . . (all [of] which far exceeded the quality of the deceased, he being only a private gentleman) the said officers refused to give their attendance . . . although of right they ought to have borne the trophies proper to the degree of the defunct . . . the same were carried by improper persons in so very irregular and unjustifiable manner that not any one of the said trophies was carried in the right place.' This 'licentious liberty' was of late not uncommon; it was, the Earl Marshal concluded, 'not only an open violation of the several established rules & orders heretofore made for the enterments of all degrees but highly tends to the lessening of the rights and honour of the nobility and gentry and more especially when the funerals of ignoble persons are set forth by them with such trophies of honour as belong only to the peers and gentry of this realm.' Travers's remark is the only evidence we have of the expense of Mrs Vanbrugh's funeral, and it is not easy to reconcile with the choice of a sleepy Thames-side village. He would, however, have needed ready cash for such items as mourning gifts in the family. Costly funerals were not very new: in 1639 Lord Dorchester's widow wished to be buried at Gosfield, Essex, 'with a moderate Solempnitie' which she defined as not exceeding £500 (PROB 11/179, fol.4).

[91] J. Le Neve, loc. cit.

[92] Above, p.51.

The younger children at least would have left Chester with their mother. Mary, who though not the eldest was almost twenty-one when her father died, may have remained in Chester; on the other hand she may have been in the household of her great-uncle, Herbert Croft, Bishop of Hereford; it was the custom of the time for unmarried women to act as ladies' or children's companions in other branches of a family, and the Bishop made bequests to his four Carleton nieces and, alone among their children, to Mary.[93] She probably died in Chester, after a long life, for she was buried in Holy Trinity churchyard on 2 March 1748.[94] Two months later a Cheshire diarist sent her maid 'to see a wonderful thing I heard of in Trinity Church, a tree grown upon Mrs Mary Vanbrugh's coffin, the sexton opening the tomb to mend something on it; many hundreds flock to see it with wonder; it is above ½ yd high & has 8 stalks & like pods on, to grow so, since March she was buried and no rain or air; it is a strange thing thought by many and slighted by some.'[95]

Mary and her three sisters were born in succession within the space of four years, and while we know nothing of their personalities it is probable that there was quite a strong bond between them. With the possible exception of Elizabeth they did not marry. Their brother John kept in touch with them all and borrowed money from them at interest in the period covered by the Account Book. The visit to Norwich of three of them in 1719 has already been mentioned,[96] and their mother and her sisters seem likewise to have kept in touch with each other. Mary Vanbrugh lived to be eighty; Victoria, who died in London in December 1766, was nearly ninety-seven,[97] and Robina, who moved to Southwell in 1745, died there in her eighty-seventh year.[98] Elizabeth probably died there also, in December 1730, but that is only one of the mysteries involving that town and the Vanbrugh family.

In 1789 a traveller found Southwell 'a well-built clean town such a one as a quiet distressed family ought to retire to',[99] and this impression has today by no means disappeared from the area around the Minster. It became a Cathedral only in 1884, but in the middle ages the Minster had been a collegiate church with the regional influence and most of the other attributes of a cathedral including a late fourteenth-century palace belonging to the Archbishop of York. In Vanbrugh's time there were a number of clergy and there was a school attached to the Minster. We have no idea what magnetism there was to draw three of his sisters and a whole family of his cousins there, although once one or two had settled there it is understandable that others followed.

John Vanbrugh's elder sister Lucy died in Southwell and was buried at the Minster on 18 April 1699.[100] Anna Maria was there in 1698, when at the age of thirty-two she

[93] Will, PROB 11/405, fol.117. Mary is described as his cousin but in the context this must be his great-niece; the term was used to cover many relationships. She was in Chester in March 1702 when she witnessed Dudley Garencieres's will (p.157).

[94] Holy Trinity Register. The Diary of Katherine Howard (above, n.22), p.74, says that she died at 4 a.m. on 29 Feb.

[95] ibid.

[96] See p.156.

[97] Walbrook Register, 30 Jan. 1767: 'Mrs Victoria Vanbrugh, in their family vault in the north ile by the screen door, aged 98 years, brought from Tower Hill, St Katherine Court.' Her death on 24 Dec. 1766 was noted in *Gent. Mag.*, XXXVII, 1767, p.95.

[98] Buried at the Minster 11 June 1759 (Minster Register).

[99] *The Torrington Diary*, ed. C. Bruyn Andrews, IV, 1938, p.142.

[100] Minster Register: 'Mrs Lucy Vanbrug.'

married Thomas Hesleden, schoolmaster and cleric.[101] She died, however, at Hatcliffe, her husband's living, in January 1700,[102] and this, as far as we know, was the end of the first Southwell connection.

In the second half of 1714 their first cousin Ann Van den Busch[103] moved from London to Southwell with her family, although when she died in December she was buried in the Vanbrugh vault in London.[104] Since her late husband Jasper had inherited the Weymans's estate[105] it is hard to believe that they were, in John Byng's phrase, a distressed family,[106] and we do not know how their son Jasper and their four daughters subsisted in Southwell. Young Jasper died in 1727[107] intestate; the administration was to his second sister Susanna.[108] She subsequently married Peter Evertse(n), physician of Middelburgh, and made her will and died there.[109] She was nevertheless buried at Southwell on 22 October 1744, and two other sisters were buried there on 4 May 1757 (Mrs Anna Maria Vandenbush) and 4 June 1760 (Mrs Angenetta Vandenbush).[110] The youngest sister, Catherine, married Joseph Ellis early in 1720,[111] and their daughter, also Anna Maria, was buried there on 7 October 1761.[112]

Meanwhile two other Vanbrughs moved to Southwell, sisters of the architect. In 1745 Robina made a new will there; her sole heir was her half-sister's daughter Lucia Maria Garencieres, who also died in Southwell in 1770.[113] Robina asked that 'If I dye at Southwell I will be buried by my two sisters'; otherwise she was to be buried in any parish in which she died. Her sister Lucy had been buried at Southwell in 1699;[114] her half-sister Garencieres appears to have been buried somewhere else unknown, and the latter's son Theophilus Garencieres failed to get the Prebend of Southwell in 1724.[115] The second

[101] Son of Thomas Hesleden of Bracken Bottom, Horton-in-Ribblesdale, Yorks. B.A. 1685, M.A. 1688 (Cantab.). Ordained 1686 when he was of Southwell. Master of Grammar School 1685–97 (W. A. James, *Schools of Southwell*, 1927, pp.18–19). Rector of Barnoldsby and Hatcliffe, near Grimsby, 1697–1715 (Venn). Married at Southwell or Gonalston (Allegation for licence, 11 Oct. 1698: *Index Library*, LVIII, 1930, *Notts. Marriage Licences*, 1). By his will (Lincs. CRO wills 1720/5, no.172) he made small bequests to Ralph Baynes, Rector of Swallow, Lincs., under the patronage of the Duke of Newcastle at the prompting of Sir John Vanbrugh (see p.90, n.37).

[102] Hatcliffe Register (Bishop's Transcripts, Lincs. CRO). Buried 17 Jan. 1700. Hesleden remarried, to Catherine –, buried 10 [Dec.?] 1719 (ibid.); he died 30 Aug. 1720, buried at Hatcliffe (ibid.).

[103] Daughter of Anna Van Brugh and Simon Delboe, widow of the elder Jasper Van den Busch.

[104] p.147. Her will, made on 12 April 1714 (PROB 11/549, fol.246) calls her 'of London' but the administration attached (1 Dec. 1715) refers to 'testamento Annae Vandenbush olim de civitate London. sed apud Southwell in com Notts viduae defunctae.'

[105] p.143.

[106] Above, n.99.

[107] The transcript of the Southwell register in the Minster Library gives 'Mr Vanderburgh', 8 Oct. 1727, but this must be an easy misreading of Vandenbusch.

[108] PROB 6/104, Feb.

[109] PROB 11/735, fol.245; translated from Low Dutch.

[110] Southwell Register.

[111] Allegation for licence, 19 Feb. 1720, at Gonalston or Thurgarton (*Index Library*, LX, 1935, *Notts. Marriage Licences*, 2).

[112] Southwell Register. Anna Maria Van den Busch's will (PROB 11/834, fol.376) made Anna Maria Ellis executrix 'of all which relates to me hereabouts', i.e. in Southwell, and Abraham Demetrius of London executor of 'all my effects which he has been so kind as to manage'; the probate letters call him previously her agent. Did the sisters live in absence on the proceeds of a City enterprise? Anna Maria Ellis died at Oxton, Notts. (will PROB 11/881, fol.456).

[113] 26 Aug. (Minster Register).

[114] See p.167.

[115] Webb, pp.161–2; above, p.158.

sister intended by Robina must therefore be Mrs Elizabeth Vanbrugh, widow, whose death at Southwell was recorded on 1 January 1731 in a Cheshire diary, who must therefore have been of the Chester family, whose maiden and married names must have been Vanbrugh, who must be the Sister Betty of Sir John's Account Book, whom for some reason he omitted from his will although she outlived him,[116] whose own will has not been traced, and who even more unaccountably is omitted from Le Neve's admittedly incomplete attempt at a Vanbrugh pedigree.[117] In February 1726 Elizabeth Vanbrugh of Southwell, widow, signed or renewed a lease for twenty-one years of the Archbishop's Palace 'commonly called or known by ye name of ye Courthouse and all that court adjoining by ye said messuage lying within or encompassed by ye old walls of the demolished Palace in Southwell' together with portions of the garden.[118] The premises appear from eighteenth-century views to have been large but ramshackle, and the rent was £4.[119] She was probably the Mrs Vanbrug who in 1722 had requested and obtained permission to build over land overlooking the Minster churchyard and belonging to the Chapter.[120]

Sir John Vanbrugh left to his sisters Robina and Victoria the choice of the two White Towers at Greenwich, but they do not appear ever to have lived in them.[121]

After these four sisters, the remaining children of Giles and Elizabeth to grow up were brothers. Carleton (b. 1673) went into trade, and there are a few documentary references to him. In 1695 he was in the household of his cousin Jasper Van den Busch as a servant.[122] In July 1702 certain proposals made by him and Simon Clement were referred to the Prince's Council.[123] In 1709–10 he was involved with others in the transfer of crown money from Ireland through Bristol to London; one of the others was John Sansome, late Collector of Customs at Bristol, who had 'absconded much in debt to the Queen', but Carleton Vanbrugh's part in the affair is not made clear.[124] He was evidently not a brilliant businessman; in 1706 he was buying, for £250, comprehensive rights in a very large tract of New Hampshire in America,[125] but the vendor never managed to secure the title to the land or Carleton the right to buy it.[126]

Of Giles (b. 1675) nothing at all is known, but since there is no record of his burial in Chester it is probable that he at least outlived his father.

Dudley (b. 1677) had leanings to study or the Church, and matriculated at Merton

[116] See p.161.

[117] Le Neve, pp.511–12.

[118] BIHR, CC AB3/9, Granges Notts. V(47), Lease no.13.

[119] BIHR, BP Dio 2, Archbishop Sharpe's MSS Vol.2, p.185.

[120] Chapter Decree Book, 19 April 1722 (kindly communicated by Dr Norman Summers). Sir John sent tea to Southwell in March 1724 and fans and handkerchiefs in Jan. 1725 (Account Book, ff.50v, 55).

[121] PROB 11/608, fol.84. The Robina Vanbrugh, spinster, who was a party to two land deeds in Soho in 1740 may be Robina the daughter of Kenrick Vanbrugh (p.170).

[122] p.147.

[123] Prince George of Denmark; CSP Dom 1702–3, p.201.

[124] CTB 1709, p.45; 1710, pp.219, 253; 1711, p.596; 1712, p.337.

[125] PRO C54/4952, no.11: indenture 31 Aug. 1706 with Thomas Allen of London.

[126] CSP Col 1708–9, pp.1–2, 40–1, 53, 138–9, 156, 186, 239, 244, 435–6; 1710–11, pp.9, 31, 43, 123–4, 271, 280. On 14 July 1702 Carleton Vanbrugh deposited £47 10*s.* 3*d.* at Hoare's Bank, but the following day he withdrew it (Hoare's Bank archives).

College, Oxford in 1694, gaining his B.A. in 1697 and M.A. in July 1700, but he died shortly afterwards and was buried in the college chapel in September.[127]

Kenrick (b. 1678) was probably named after the Kenricks of Chester.[128] In 1705 he was appointed Correspondent for the Irish Commissioners of Revenue; he was to reside in London and correspond with officers in England about illegal and contraband trade with the East Indies.[129] His will made on 5 October 1709, when he was of St Martin-in-the-Fields, refers to dangers of seas and wars, and he died in Spain the following year; the probate letters refer to him as Captain.[130] In January 1702 he had married Margaret Campion, daughter of Elizabeth Campion of St Anne's, Soho.[131] His widow died two years after him,[132] leaving two daughters, Elizabeth and Robina. From references to them in Sir John's Account Book it appears that their aunts helped to bring them up.[133] On 28 September 1732 Elizabeth married John Lewis, skinner,[134] who became a Freeman of the Skinners' Company in 1745.[135] By that time Elizabeth had probably died, as in 1741 the will of her aunt Ann (wife of Charles Vanbrugh) referred not to her but only to her sister Robina.[136] Ten years later her uncle Philip Vanbrugh left £50 each to the two youngest children of 'my deceased sister [*sic*] Elizabeth Lewis' and it is to be presumed that he made a mistake for *niece* in the heat of the moment.[137] His previous bequest is to 'my sister [*sic*] Wilkinson and her husband' which suggests that Robina married a Wilkinson after 1741. In January 1740 John and Elizabeth Lewis assigned to Robina Vanbrugh of St Martin-in-the-Fields a moiety of properties in Dean Street, Frith Street and Coventry Street, London, and in March Edward Sanderson and Robina Vanbrugh assigned to Elizabeth Cotton properties in Dean Street and Frith Street.[138]

Charles and Philip Vanbrugh (born 1680 and 1682) were very young when John left home, and by the time they grew up he had lived the most picturesque part of his life. They must have remained very much the younger brothers to him, and in the 1720s, after they had made successful careers in the Navy, they were involved in his colony at Greenwich.[139] Charles was appointed 3rd Lieutenant on the *Ranelagh* on 14 December 1702;[140] by 4 April 1707 he was Commander of the *Dispatch*, and on 21 February 1709

127 Foster, *Oxon*.

128 See p.165.

129 CTB 1705–6, p.253.

130 PROB 6/86, March; PROB 11/532, fol.48. Administration passed from his widow, who died in March 1712, to her mother.

131 Allegation for marriage licence, Vicar-General's Office (*Lambeth Palace Library*), 26 Jan. 1702. No record at St Margaret's, Westminster.

132 See n.130.

133 Account Book, ff.7, 11v, 18v, 25v.

134 At St Michael, Paternoster Royal (Guildhall MS.5145).

135 3 Sept. 1745; records of the Skinners' Company, giving his father as John Lewis of Kensington, gardener.

136 PROB 11/721, fol.312. For Charles and Ann Vanbrugh see below.

137 PROB 11/804, fol.242.

138 Westminster City Library, Archives Dept., Deeds, 96/12 and 13.

139 See p.95. In 1689–90 Philip Vanbrooke, gentleman, of Datchet, Bucks., was charged with recusance (*Bucks. Sessions Records*, ed. William le Hardy, I, Aylesbury, 1933, pp.319, 328). Susan Salmon, widow, and others, were charged again on later occasions in 1690–91. It would be prudent to dissociate this reference from the staunch Protestant family with which we are dealing, unless there was some mistake at the time. Datchet registers (Bucks. CRO) reveal nothing.

140 PRO Ad 6/7, f.66. There is an index to commissions and warrants, on the whole accurate, in the Round Room, 6/109, etc.

Captain of the *Faversham*.[141] He was subsequently Captain of the *Sorlings*,[142] and it was in this ship that he was involved in the spring of 1714 in the illegal transport of liquor in the West Indies from the French colony of Martinique to the British one of Barbados. It is unlikely that he was the only master to engage in such irregularities, which were against the Anglo-French agreement of 1686 restricting colonial trade of each country to its own colonies, and he does not appear to have received the reprimand requested by the French.[143]

In 1715–17 Charles shared with Sir John a house in Duke Street, St James's, on which he paid rates in 1716;[144] thereafter they shared Sir William Saunderson's house at Greenwich for three years.[145] In July 1719 he was 'coming home through France', and sent Sir John an account of the public speculation there in the Mississippi Company.[146] In June 1721 he married Ann Burt; he was then of St Martin-in-the-Fields.[147] At that time Sir John was building a house for him at Greenwich, which he bought on a lease from the architect on completion at the end of 1722.[148] Charles and Ann had at least four children, of whom only the eldest, Edward, survived childhood. He was born about 1722–3, perhaps the child at whose christening Sir John gave five guineas on 14 June 1722.[149] Charles seems to have been back at sea in November 1733 as Captain of the *Cornwall*.[150] In June 1740 he was elected M.P. for Plymouth, 'on a petition against John Rogers Esq., Sitting Member.'[151]

In 1738 Charles occupied 37 Sackville Street, Piccadilly;[152] after his death in 1740 this and the Greenwich house were taken over by his widow, and after her death in 1742 by their son Edward.[153] The latter married Prisca Holt in 1747;[154] as his nearer and remoter cousins died he came gradually to be the main inheritor of Vanbrugh estates and mementoes. He and his wife moved to Bath, where they led a fairly social life. In 1773 he wrote to the architect's widow that 'fresh people pour in upon us every day . . . evening amusements are . . . thick upon the back of another.'[155] Fanny Burney in 1780 called him 'a

141 PRO Ad 6/9, f.60; 6/10, f.34.

142 7 July 1710, 14 Dec. 1714 (PRO Ad 6/11, f.56; 6/12, f.11).

143 CSP Col 1712–14, pp.367–8, 375–9.

144 'Captain Vanderbrooke' (see p.83, n.14).

145 Account Book.

146 Webb, pp.112, 114.

147 Allegation for licence, Bishop of London's Registry, 26 June (Guildhall MS.10091/58, f.652). She was the daughter of Edward Burt of the same parish, who gave his consent as she was over twenty but under twenty-one. Charles may have been the Captain Vanbrugh who occupied 19 Queen Anne's Gate in 1722–3 (*Survey of London*, x, 1926, p.116).

148 See p.96.

149 Account Book. According to a note on his mother's will (PROB 11/721, fol.312) he was twenty-five before 13 Feb. 1749; he was eighty in 1802 (below, n.157). Three other children were baptized at St James, Piccadilly: Charles (2 July 1728); Ann (13 May 1730) and John (8 Feb. 1732) (Registers in Westminster City Library, Archives Dept.).

150 PRO Ad 6/14, f.154v, 23 Nov. 1733.

151 *Gent. Mag.*, x, 1740, p.37.

152 *Survey of London*, XXXII, 1963, p.353.

153 Charles Vanbrugh buried in the family vault 9 Nov. 1740. Will, PROB 11/706, fol.310. Ann Vanbrugh buried in the vault 20 Sept. 1742 aged forty (Walbrook Register). Will, PROB 11/721, fol.312, proved 22 Oct. 1742.

154 Allegation for licence, Bishop of London's Registry, 21 Oct. 1747, at St Bartholomew-the-Great (Guildhall MS.10091/87, f.566). She was between twenty and twenty-one; her father, Rowland Holt, was dead and her mother Elizabeth gave consent.

155 BIHR (Yarburgh), 20 Oct. 1773.

good sort of man.'[156] He died on 5 October 1802 at 6 Brook Street, Bath, and was buried in the family vault.[157] His widow was buried there in March 1804.[158]

Philip, the youngest of Giles's family, went to sea as a volunteer in the *Deal Castle* (12 June 1696).[159] He became Captain of the *Speedwell* on 27 November 1710[160] and of a succession of ships thereafter, until in June 1739 he was appointed a Commissioner of the Naval Dockyard at Plymouth[161] which he gave as his residence in his will.[162] In December 1704 he applied to marry Mary Griffith of Arnold, Notts., but they did not marry until 1715.[163] We know that two children, Giles Richard and Philippa, followed quite soon, although the dates and places of birth of neither are known. However, we can follow them in later life. From the plan of the house Sir John built for Philip in 1719–20 at Greenwich,[164] and the absence of any further mention of his wife, it is probable that she had died by then. This is his only known land base, and he probably relinquished it entirely on his appointment to Plymouth; it would appear to be 'the low house' in which the architect's son was living in 1743.[165] From June 1738 to June 1739, when he went to Plymouth, Philip was Governor of Newfoundland.[166] In 1749 he was appointed a Commissioner for the Navy.[167] He died on 25 July 1753,[168] survived only by his daughter Philippa, to each of whose four children he was able to leave £1000.[169] Neither he nor any of his family were buried at St Stephen, Walbrook.

His son Giles Richard went to sea first of all in 1732 as a volunteer in the *Edinburgh* under his father;[170] early in 1734 he followed his father to the *Burford*.[171] In 1745 he became a captain[172] and was a member of a court martial on Captain Norris of the *Essex*.[173] He died in 1748 as Captain of the *Antelope*, unmarried, and his father received letters of administration.[174]

156 *Diary and Letters of Madame D'Arblay*, ed. Charlotte Barrett, 1876, I, p.272.

157 *Gent. Mag.*, LXXII, 1802, p.1065, calling him 'an immediate descendant of the celebrated Sir John Vanbrugh'; Walbrook Register, 14 Oct. 1802, as aged 80. Will, PROB 11/1382, fol.785.

158 Walbrook Register, 16 March 1804, aged seventy-seven. Will PROB 11/1406, fol.218.

159 PRO Ad 6/4, f.6.

160 PRO Ad 6/11, f.84.

161 *Gent. Mag.*, IX, 1739, p.328. The references to Commissioner and Captain Vanbrugh in the Verney papers (above, n.33), II, pp.181, 218, are probably to Philip.

162 PROB 11/804, fol.242, made 11 Jan. 1752.

163 Allegation for licence to marry at Arnold or Lambley, she aged eighteen (*Notts. Marriage Licences*, II, *Index Soc.*, LX, 1935). Marriage at Arnold, 24 July 1715 (W. P. W. Phillimore, *Nottinghamshire Marriages*, XIII, 1910).

164 See p.95. The house was already known as the Nunnery in 1721 when William Stukeley drew it. Present to Philip's children, 12 July 1720 (Account Book).

165 His will, PROB 11/740, fol.182. From the collection of receipts in Lady Vanbrugh's account book (BIHR (Yarburgh)) the house appears to have been let to Lord Perceval after her son's death in May 1745.

166 *Gent. Mag.*, VIII, 1738, p.325; IX, 1739, p.328.

167 ibid., XIX, 1749, p.237 (30 May).

168 ibid., XXIII, 1753, p.344.

169 Will, PROB 11/804, fol.242. The executor was his nephew Edward.

170 PRO Ad 6/14, ff.111v, 112.

171 ibid., ff.160, 161.

172 PRO Ad 6/16, p.492.

173 *Gent. Mag.*, XV, 1745, p.365.

174 PROB 6/123, June.

Philippa was companion to the Duchess of Richmond,[175] probably in the early 1730s, when she was in her teens. In 1723–4 the Duke of Richmond occupied a house on Maze Hill, Greenwich, lower down than Vanbrugh Castle; from 1734 he occupied the Castle itself.[176] Philippa had married Burrington Goldsworthy of Down House, Dorset, by about 1736.[177] Horace Walpole found her in 1743 'a pert, little, unbred thing'; she was then about to go with her children to live with her father at Plymouth.[178] Burrington, to whom Edward Vanbrugh referred as 'the old gentleman' in 1773,[179] died the following year, Philippa in 1777; both were buried in Bath Abbey.[180] Of their children, Augustus died in 1767;[181] Philip and Martha Caroline were both associated with the court of George III. Major-General Philip Goldsworthy was Equerry to that king, who held him in high regard. Fanny Burney found him 'a man of but little cultivation or literature' but with a dry humour which he often used against himself.[182] Martha Caroline was sub-governess to the young princesses and the object of universal affection at court. She died in 1816 and was buried with her parents;[183] Philip wished to be buried in Salisbury Cathedral.[184] These last descendants of Giles and Elizabeth Vanbrugh figure in the pages of both Fanny Burney and Mrs Delaney, and thus it is possible to form the impression that we have met them in a way that is not possible with those of their forebears whose memory is only retained in official documents. Fortunately records of both kinds exist for the greatest member of the Vanbrugh family.

[175] H. Walpole, *Letters*, ed. Mrs P. Toynbee, I, 1903, p.120. The Duchess was born in 1706, married at thirteen but did not live with her husband until 1722.

[176] Rate Books 1723–4, Greenwich Libraries Local Collections. In 1734, according to Lady Vanbrugh's account book (BIHR (Yarburgh)) the Duke leased Vanbrugh Castle.

[177] Philip, their son, was born about 1737.

[178] Walpole, op.cit., p.324.

[179] Above, n.155.

[180] Bath Abbey Registers (*Harl. Soc., Register Series*, XXVIII), 19 Jan. 1774, 18 Jan. 1777.

[181] Administration to his father, PROB 6/143.

[182] *Diary and Letters of Madame D'Arblay*, 1876, II, p.190.

[183] Will, PROB 11/1580, fol.254.

[184] Will, PROB 11/1352, fol.28. Proved 28 Jan. 1801.

Chapter 11

Vanbrugh's Accounts

The Account Book published here for the first time is part of a collection of papers which came to the University of York with Heslington Hall, which had been the family home of Lady Vanbrugh. The papers now in the Borthwick Institute of Historical Research, University of York, include various miscellaneous documents concerning Sir John Vanbrugh, his widow and their son Charles, and two account books which probably owe their preservation at Heslington initially to the fact that both were used by Lady Vanbrugh; both had also been used by her husband. He used principally the one published here, which was taken over by his widow for about half a year; he also used a second book to record small day-to-day expenses from February 1722, and in April 1738 Lady Vanbrugh started again at the other end of the book, continuing until 1757. This is known as Lady Vanbrugh's Account Book, while the one with which we are dealing is known as Sir John Vanbrugh's Account Book.

Vanbrugh's accounts are virtually complete from January 1715 to his death in March 1726, but there are two gaps. The first is between ff.4 and 5, in the centre of the first signature: here four or eight pages, covering the period from 25 January to 18 August 1715, have been lost. The second gap is between ff.14 and 15, where one page has been torn out with the loss of the period from 2 April to 6 June 1717. The first gap covers, among other events of interest, a journey to the North which is known from his correspondence.[1]

Vanbrugh described the book as a journal of all receipts and payments and other transactions, to be copied annually into another book, the 'Green Book' (f.4). This is lost, and it is only possible to speculate whether it started some years earlier, and whether it was divided into credit and debit pages; the book we have is indiscriminate in the same way as the left-hand columns of a modern bank statement, recording both types of entry in chronological order. Until the end of 1725 each entry in the book is ticked (for editorial reasons these ticks have not been transcribed) as an indication that the entry has been transferred to the Green Book; this operation was doubtless the occasion for remedying various mistakes in the record such as entries duplicated or made out of sequence.

Vanbrugh's description shows that he intended the book to represent every transaction, of whatever kind, every penny he received or paid or gave. Whether he kept to that intention, whether he reserved certain items to be recorded only elsewhere, and what his reasons were if he did, cannot be ascertained; however, the care and literalness with which

[1] Webb, p.243. Vanbrugh's account in the archives of Hoare's Bank is singularly uninformative. Between Nov. 1714 and May 1715 he deposited and withdrew a total of £819 in bank notes. The period is not covered by the Account Book.

he made the entries, and their wide range and variety, suggest that omissions were accidental. If certain items we expect to find are wanting, some other explanation must be found. Yet certain classes of possible omission must be considered.

The first is that of journeys. We know from other sources of one journey of several days' duration which is not mentioned at all in the book: on 1 July 1719 he had recently returned from a visit to Stowe and Blenheim.[2] The explanation may be that, as both friend and patron, Lord Cobham paid all his incidental expenses and there was thus nothing to record. If this is so, there may be other cases: for example we should expect Vanbrugh to have visited Seaton Delaval in the spring of 1720, since work on the new house began that year and he was absent from the Board of Works between 24 February and 6 April.[3]

A second class is that of payments for architectural services. There are a number of quite large payments of this kind in the book, but there are none from Lord Carlisle, for whom Vanbrugh worked more or less continuously throughout his career, and none from Robert Bertie, 4th Earl of Lindsey and 1st Duke of Ancaster. It is true that the main house at Castle Howard had reached in 1712 the stage not of completion but of being habitable, Lord Carlisle moving in during the summer. This is the kind of occasion on which, to judge both from common sense and from other examples in the Account Book, a considerable payment to the architect would have been in order; but it is before the beginning of the book. It might alternatively be supposed that the pages missing between ff.4 and 5 were removed not because they were the centre of a signature but because they were of some special significance; this is more likely to be the case with the leaf missing between ff.14 and 15, which has been roughly torn out. On the other hand, a hypothesis that payments from Lord Carlisle were recorded only on the pages lost from the book is neither helpful nor very probable. If Vanbrugh were paid for the house in 1712–13, he might not expect further payment until some other stage was reached more definitive than the completion of wall bastions, obelisk parterres and such-like – and no such stage was reached in his lifetime. Then we should expect at least a payment soon after his death such as that recorded (f.64) from Doddington. However, a decade later, Hawksmoor's widow had to submit a bill to Carlisle of what was due to her late husband, and subsequently a letter explaining the basis on which the bill was computed.[4] At that stage Carlisle was evidently a reluctant payer, and it is conceivable that a similar process occurred between him and Lady Vanbrugh at some time in the gap between the two account books; on the other hand, Hawksmoor's relationship with Carlisle was always on a different footing from Vanbrugh's. The simplest hypothesis, however, and one which does not absolutely exclude those already suggested, is that the normal monetary reward was replaced by Carlisle's special position as Vanbrugh's patron. His patronage extended to Vanbrugh's establishment as a Herald and as an office-holder in the Royal Works, and brought about the rapid rise, through the Castle Howard commission, of an architect previously quite unknown. It is not inconceivable that he may have lent Vanbrugh money at a critical time; if that were so, there might be little in the way of fees. Vanbrugh's letter to Carlisle discusses not his pay but that of Hawksmoor, who was to receive £40 a year

[2] Webb, p.111.

[3] Appendix G.

[4] Downes (1959), pp.266–9.

and £50 for each journey.[5] Similar reasoning perhaps applies with Vanbrugh's oldest friends, the Berties, although the extent of their patronage is unclear and the only record in the book is the repayment to Peregrine Bertie's executors of a considerable loan (f.9).

A further class of omission comprises a few entries, not in themselves duplications, which Vanbrugh made and then deleted. While one concerns a hall bench (f.49v) they are mostly connected with persons and thus in an area in which it might equally well be realistic or impertinent to expect some delicacy or even secrecy. Thus on f.11v there is a deleted note of an annuity arranged by Vanbrugh with Mary Helps, one of his servants. There are several mentions of a person who is recorded only by a cypher (Pl.3); the forms are not consistent enough to identify as shorthand. Less open to speculation is the deletion on f.43v of a fee to Lord Ancaster's keeper for venison.

It is also a matter for speculation whether there was some other kind of account book, since we know of three kinds already: domestic (the book taken over by Lady Vanbrugh), comprehensive (the Account Book) and the Green Book. As the son of a merchant family Vanbrugh probably acquired early and as a matter of course the inclination and habit of keeping careful accounts, and while he was working for his cousin William Matthews he had to do so.[6] While he evidently eschewed a commercial career the Account Book reveals complex, if small-scale, financial manoeuvres in his last ten years, including mortgages, rental and investment arrangements with his brothers and sisters; some of the latter may have depended on such arrangements for part of their income.

The entries in the Account Book give a remarkable picture of the Vanbrugh household, including the cost of many everyday items and services: students of inflation will note changes in the price of hay over the period. The names of servants are recorded, with their wages and gratuities, but surnames are not always given; thus we are no nearer to identifying Arthur, who appears intermittently between 1716 and 1725 and who worked as a draughtsman in 1723.[7] Jack Jones remained in the service of Lady Vanbrugh. His position was one of trust and responsibility; on occasion he witnessed his master's signature, and it was to him that Joseph Yorke sent the news of young Charles's death in 1745.[8] Both Arthur and Jack were thought to have musical talents, and payments are entered for instruments and lessons for them.

Vanbrugh recorded the duration, the incidental expenses and sometimes the destination of his journeys, which varied from two or three months in the North to a few hours' absence. They include visits to Walton-on-Thames, where there was some sort of accommodation,[9] and to Esher, where he, like Jacob Tonson, had a room at his disposal from the Duke of Newcastle.[10] On the other hand no indication is given of movements between his customary residences in Whitehall, Duke Street in 1715–16 and Greenwich from Lady Day 1717. The domestic expenses of Duke Street and of the house rented at Greenwich

[5] Webb, p.6.

[6] p.146.

[7] p.80.

[8] pp.157, 97.

[9] p.159.

[10] p.194, n.148.

from Sir William Saunderson were shared with his brother Charles until May 1718 and settled at the end of the year.

Marriage inevitably changed and complicated the domestic situation. The entry on 31 January 1719, when Vanbrugh started to write 'Given to Mrs Yarburgh' and remembered that she was newly become Lady Vanbrugh (f.24), was followed by the acquisition of apparatus for the playing of card games and the taking of tea. The female servants were augmented, and in due course a nurse was added. The increasing attentions of physicians and surgeons are accounted for partly by Vanbrugh's increasing years, partly by maternity and partly by Lady Vanbrugh's somewhat uncertain health: she was bled from time to time. From small indications in her own later accounts and elsewhere, we may infer that she was sensitive, sociable, lively and pretty, with no more education than was thought proper for Yorkshire girls of her time and background. Her chief interests, to judge from expenditure, were friends, clothes, and theatre, young Charles, and after his tragic death on the field of Fontenoy in 1745, religion. She did not care much for Vanbrugh's houses, for within a month of his death she had contracted with Mr Pomeroy, who seems to have acted as factotum in that uncertain period, to build her a small house; the agreement is preserved among loose papers in Sir John's Account Book. She moved out of the Castle at once and let it, although she kept on the house in Whitehall.

Certain concerns recur through the ten years of the Account Book, including the salaries of Vanbrugh's several offices, usually received months or even years late, the taxes, fees and gratuities payable on them (almost any substantial exchange of money involved a tip to the cashier), the payment of rates and taxes, and fees received for services nominal or actual as Clarenceux Herald. The accounts also cover outlay on and income from investments in property and shares. Vanbrugh constantly revised the arrangements for income from the Haymarket Theatre and the houses and other properties on the remainder of the site. Among his family his brother Charles was principally involved, but there was also the succession of arrangements with his sisters, already mentioned. Vanbrugh derived rent from other properties. There were his official houses at Kensington, Hampton Court and Scotland Yard and (as Surveyor of the Hospital from 1716) at Greenwich. There was also the bungalow he built and rented to his brother Philip on the Greenwich site; the house he built for Charles was sold outright to the latter. Vanbrugh had shares in the South Sea Company, which continued to pay after the Bubble, and in the Chelsea Waterworks and the Copper Bubble of 1720. On 9 June 1721 he entered into partnership with Thomas Miller of Fulham, who the following year patented an improvement in the manufacture of bricks, tiles and lime.[11] The white bricks used for the building of the White Towers at Greenwich were made by Miller, and were evidently valued by the architect, but there is no other indication whether Vanbrugh considered the association mainly of financial or of architectural importance.[12]

Of Vanbrugh the architect the accounts tell us most directly about the estate at Greenwich, making possible a reconstruction of the sequence of events that is considerably fuller and more secure than is possible from the sum of other evidence; indeed most other sources

[11] Agreement, 9 June 1721, between Thomas Miller of Fulham and Sir John Vanbrugh (BIHR (Yarburgh)). Millers' patent, No.440, 30 March 1722, for burning bricks evenly hard (Patent Office).

[12] For Vanbrugh's public enterprises see p.92, n.40.

now assume a confirmatory role. The accounts leave a great deal unspecified, since bills are often simply for materials or workmanship; thus, while the Greenwich houses can now be securely and individually dated, the various enlargements and alterations to Vanbrugh Castle are still obscure.

The Account Book necessarily contains many regular or repeated payments. Some of the most significant entries, on which conclusions in the preceding chapters of this book depend, are referred to there, and a separate index to the accounts is provided on p.234, but it is hoped that the complete transcript will be of sufficient interest to students of Vanbrugh, and indeed of the early eighteenth century in general, to be read in its entirety. In the matter of annotations a middle course has been attempted between over- and under-explanation.

Two pages of the Account Book are reproduced on Pls 3 and 4; these will give some idea of the editorial alterations which are inevitable in preparing for the press anything other than a complete photographic facsimile. The aim has been to preserve as far as possible the form and the sense of the original, while removing some ambiguities, amplifying some abbreviations and where possible simplifying the problems, and thereby the cost, of typesetting. The principles and procedures adopted are detailed below.

PAGINATION The modern folio numbers are retained and are used in the index (pp.234–41). Rectos or versos not mentioned are blank.

DATES The style of dates in January-March has been retained. Dates repeated at the heads of pages have been omitted. The form '$17\overline{14}$ / 15' has been reduced to '1714/15'; similarly, in order to keep date figures in line, the form '1715 / Augt: 18' has been changed to '1715 Augt: / 18'

ACCOUNTANCY CONVENTIONS Most pages have ruled columns; these have been omitted, as have the *£ s d* signs at the head of each page, the £ sign before each amount, and the colons (:) occasionally placed between the numbers. The use of a dash (–) instead of zero has been followed; in the original a zero (0) usually indicates an altered amount. In single items within multiple entries such as journeys, the original style has been followed. Most entries start with a date or a small dash; as an aid to clarity missing dashes have been tacitly supplied. Vanbrugh used both *Rec'd* and *Recd*: the latter has been used as the difference is not always clear.

ALTERATIONS Vanbrugh's emendations have been accepted and insertions above the line have been brought down. Deleted words or passages have been omitted, except where they add materially to the general or particular understanding. In such cases they are printed in italics and annotated.

SPELLING The original spelling has been transcribed as faithfully as possible, although even with long experience it is possible to find ambiguous readings in eighteenth-century manuscript, especially of proper names. Two specific problems of transcription are the use of the thorn (*y* for *th*) and the very frequent abbreviation of words with superior final letters. Some authorities regard the literal transcription of *ye* as barbarous and ignorant, but Vanbrugh's intermittent use of the archaic form is a component of his orthography, the preservation of which does no harm and brings the reader nearer to a view over the shoulder of the writer.

ABBREVIATIONS The same argument applies to the abbreviations, but it must be said that the inclusion of a large number of superior letters adds to both the difficulty and the expense of every operation in producing the book. Moreover, since not all such abbreviations are readily intelligible there is a need for further explanation. In the present case a compromise has been adopted. The omissions and their forms are of more significance than the distinction – which it is not always possible to establish – between letters written on the line and those written above it. All superior abbreviations have therefore been brought down and printed in the same type-size. In many cases where the sense is clear (e.g. the names of months) they have not been expanded. Where omitted letters have been supplied they appear within brackets [ ], and it may be assumed that all other uses of [ ] are explained in notes. Blanks in the original are not always annotated.

CAPITALS Vanbrugh was also inconsistent, as was the custom, in distinguishing capital and lower case initials, and in the case of letters such as *C* and *S*, in which size rather than form indicates the use of a capital, the distinction has been observed as far as possible.

PUNCTUATION This has been copied as accurately as possible, but the original is seldom regular. On occasion Vanbrugh used a dash as an emphatic equivalent for a period (.); in such cases a period has been substituted, as being closer to the sense of his orthography.

The same general principles apply in the Appendixes.

Chapter 12

Journal of all Receipts, Payments and other Transactions, 1715–26

[f.4]

January ye 1st 1714/15

Journal of All Receipts Payments and other Transactions.
To be transcrib'd fair into the Green book annually

Memd: That all receipts and Payments of money due to me or from me to Others, to this day Jan: ye 1st. 1714/15 will be entred in the Old book mark'd A and nothing in this Book, but what shall become due from this Time.[1]

Memd: I have accepted of Mr Swinys Resignation of his Lease of the Playhouse[2] as on the 10th of May last, to wch time having settled the Account between us (wth Mr. Sexton his Agent, he himself being in France) I paid him part of the Ballance, and Sign'd a note to him payable at Michaelmass next, of £125. for the remainder, which is in full, of All Accounts between him and me. The Surrender of his Lease is only by a Writing sent from France; the lease it self being lock'd up with things of his at Leyden as likewise a Mortgage he had upon the Playhouse for £1000. But I have his Receipts for the Whole Sum Written upon the Counterpart or annex'd to it.

[f.4v]

Memd: I have let the Vaults under the Playhouse to Mr Maes and Partners, for £30 a year, the Rent to commence from December ye 25th 1714.

May ye 10th 1715. I took up my Sis[te]r Garrencieres[3] Mortgage for £600 on the Playhouse (of which at Severall times there had been £300 of the Principal paid her) and gave her a Bond for the remaining £300. Sign'd by my Brother Charles and myself the Interest to Commence June ye 25th 1715.

I mortgag'd the Playhouse to my Brother Charles for £2500. the Int[erest]; to Commence June ye 25th 1715.

I let the Chocolate Room &c[4] to Mr Bowden, for £60. a year, to begin from Michaelmass 1714.

1714/15 January		[£	s	d]
14	pd Godston[5] the Farrier a bill in full	1	2	4
15	pd for the Highways on the Playhouse acct: to Christmass last	–	15	–
–	pd Jack Jones[6] a Qrs. wages, to Christ[ma]s last	2	10	–
22	pd a Bill at the Cooks in Charles street	1	5	9
24	pd monsr: Buher[7] for a long Periwig & a tyed one	8	–	–
–	Recd from the Heralds Colledge on Lady Cartwrights acct: & Kn[igh]ts fees[8]	5	16	10
25	pd Mr Aires[9] in full of a bill for Coales	11	–	–

[f.5][10]

1715 Augt:				
18	Recd fee[11] for the Marquiss of Clare & Duke of Newcastle	7	11	8
–	Recd my share of £40. for ye Queens funeral[12]	5	5	6
19	Recd Rent from Bowden on Account	20	–	–
–	Recd 4 Knights fees	3	17	4

[1] Italic paragraph deleted.

[2] The Queen's Theatre in the Haymarket. See p.41, and *Survey of London*, XXIX, 1960, p.223 ff. Swiny, as a bankrupt, was obliged to live abroad.

[3] Vanbrugh's half-sister (see p.157).

[4] Part of the Haymarket site.

[5] Later Goulston (f.25v).

[6] Stayed in the service of Lady Vanbrugh after Sir John's death.

[7] Later Buhet (f.15).

[8] Fees payable to a Herald upon ennoblement or knighthood. See in general A. R. Wagner, *Heralds and Heraldry in the Middle Ages*, 1939.

[9] Later Ayres (f.6).

[10] Several pages missing before numeration.

[11] Thomas Pelham Holles, Duke of Newcastle, creator of Claremont.

[12] Herald's fee for attendance at Queen Anne's funeral.

		£	s	d
22	Paid Potter the Carpenter in full of a Bill	27	19	–
24	Paid Amy Broad in full for Wages &c[13]	4	10	–
–	Recd Rent for the Playhouse of Mr Heydegger,[14] Since January ye 1st on the foot of £12:10:– a day being 30 Days	375	–	–
31	pd Mr Wooley[15] ½ a years ground Rent to Midsummer 1714	25	–	–
–	pd for entring my Patent for Comptroller,[16] at the Excheqr	1	–	–
–	pd fee at the Treasury for reference to the Survey[o]r: Gen[era]ll: of a Petition for renewing the Lease in the Haymarket[17]	1	1	6
Sept				
6	pd for work done in the Vaults at the Playhouse a Bill to John Street plummer	–	19	4
–	pd ditto to Wm Prince Bricklayer	3	6	4
–	pd Mr Portales for 12 bottles of St Lawrence	2	2	–
–	Recd of Mr Portales ½ a years rent for the Vaults under the Playhouse to Midsumr. last	15	–	–
–	Recd at the Office of Works for Two months & 7 days due at ye end of March last	50	9	–
10	pd Mrs Wood for a Black velvet Cap	1	1	6
20	Recd from the College 2 Knights Fees	1	18	4
–	From ditto, ¾ salary From Mid[summe]r: 1714 To Ladyday 1715	30	–	–
–	pd Fees and Taxes for ditto	8	17	2
–	pd John Porter &c for Bottles, Corks &c	2	1	10

		£	s	d
–	pd for a lining to a Rich Wastcoat	1	15	–
23	pd Hodges ye Joyner, for Work done at Duke Street[18]	1	17	10

[f.5v]

		£	s	d
29	pd Sisr: Garencieres a Quarters Int. due this day	3	15	–
30	Recd Rent from John Darwell[19] half a year from Ladyday last to Mich[aelma]s	3	–	–
Octr				
5	pd Poors Tax for ye Playhouse half a year to Michs: last	7	10	–
8	Recd of Mr Fryar[20] for half a years Rent due at Midsumr. last	20	–	–
12	Recd From Lady Thomas in full for Rent for Hampton Court House,[21]	30	–	–
14	Recd from the Heralds Colledge for Coronation[22] Fees and Largess for Peers	66	3	11¼
–	pd for 14 Muslin Neckcloaths	7	–	–
–	pd Bowcher in full of a Bill for Horses Meat[23] Hyre &c	66	5	2
–	Recd for a little Bay Mare	5	–	–
–	Gave to Mr Gildon[24]	1	1	6
–	Gave to Hartley[25]	1	1	6
18	pd Hodges ye Joyner for a Bedstead for James[26]	–	12	–
–	Memd. I Let a Lease to Chaffey of the Stables in Market Lane[27] for 21 years at £6. a year Rent, to Commence from Ladyday last			
31	Recd from Chaffey half a years Rent for the Shed & Stable. due at Michs: last	8	2	6
–	pd Walter Evans a Bill for Oyl & Powder[28]		9	6
Nov:				
1	pd Jefferys[29] the Butcher a Bill	4	19	10

13 Servant. Only mention.

14 John James Heidegger, (*c.*1659–1749), manager of the Opera 1708; later in partnership with Handel.

15 William Wooley, ground landlord of part of Haymarket site (*Survey of London*, XXIX, 1960, p.224).

16 Reinstated Jan. 1715.

17 Granted 1716 (*Survey of London*, vol. cit., p.225).

18 See p.171.

19 Tenant of part of Haymarket site.

20 Tenant of one of the Haymarket houses (f.28v).

21 Official house as Comptroller (CTB 1713, p.178).

22 George I.

23 Grass, hay and straw (f.19v).

24 Charles Gildon, *The Complete Art of Poetry*, 2 vols, 1718.

25 See below, 15 Nov.

26 James Wood, servant.

27 West side (back) of the Haymarket site.

28 For wigs.

29 At Walton (f.15v).

		£	s	d
–	pd Shirley[30] the Waterman a Bill	1	11	–
4	pd John Wilkins a Bill for paving in the Haymarket	3	14	–

[f.6]

		£	s	d
8	pd to Mr Sexton, in part of a Note for £125 wch I sign'd to Mr Swiny for the Ballance of the Acct: between us	50	–	–
–	pd for bedding for James	4	2	6
10	pd Mr Ayres, a bill in full for Coales	18	8	–
–	pd for oates, hay and Straw	8	15	–
15	pd for 2 pair of buckskin britches for James and Will[31]	2	3	–
–	pd for a pair of Coach horses	40	–	–
–	Given the servant		7	3
–	pd an arrear of Taxes, due in 1694, for my Place of Auditor of the Dutchy of Lancaster[32]	5	–	–
–	pd a Quarter at Hartleys,[33] to Michs: last	1	1	–
16	pd Mr Bonfoy[34] for 19 ells of holland at 7s. ell	6	13	–
29	pd for 12 trusses of hay	–	15	–
30	pd Green the Brewer a bill in full	5	–	–
Decr.				
1	pd Bowcher, a Bill for horse meat	24	–	–
6	pd Mr Sly, a Bill for hatts	5	4	6
8	Recd a Qrs Rent for Greenwich house to Lady day last[35]	1	5	–
10	pd for 24 Trusses of Hay	1	8	–
–	pd John Shortland a bill for Stable utensils	–	14	2
15	pd James Wood ½ a years wages to Christmass next	5	–	–
20	pd Mr Collivoe[36] for insuring Pictures &c	12	11	–
–	pd House Bills, this year	118	18	9¼
–	pd Servants Bills of disbursments	14	1	9
25	pd Sisr: Gar[enciere]s: a Qurs: Interest due this day	3	15	–
–	Given to servants, &c	8	14	7

[f.7]

1715/16 Jan: January ye 1st 1715/16

		£	s	d
21	pd for horses meat on ye Road, in the Bath Journey[37]	4	4	9
–	pd ye eating bills in the Inns, in dto	5	18	9
–	pd ye Farrier in dto.	1	4	2
–	pd for mending & greasing ye Calesh[38] in dto:	–	14	6
–	pd Servants Allowances for drink in dto.	1	8	–
–	pd for meat fire &c at the Bath	12	4	5
–	pd Servants Allowances there for drink	5	12	–
–	pd horse meat there	14	3	3
–	Given the servants in the Inn	–	15	–
22	pd for 36 Trusses of straw	–	18	–
24	Recd from Scullard,[39] a Qrs: Rent, to midr: last	7	10	–
–	Recd at the office of Works, a Qrs. Salary as Comptroller, due at Midr. last	76	6	2
–	Recd at dto: a Qrs: Salary as Surveyr: of ye Gardens[40]	100	–	–
–	pd Wm: Wall, Shoemaker a bill in full	–	16	6
–	pd Sisrs: Mary, Victoria and Robina, half a years Int: and annuity, due ye 10th & 20th of Novr: last	39	–	–
–	pd Sisr: Betty, for things bought for Niece Bin[41]	3	19	–
25	pd Grimsby ye Sadler, a Bill in full	10	17	6
–	Recd of Parson Garrencieres[42] in full of £15 lent	5	–	–
26	pd for 3 Qrs & 4 bushells of oats	2	17	6
–	pd at Hartleys a Qr: to Christs. last	1	1	–
–	Bromes for ye stable[43]	–	1	–
30	pd Bowcher in part for horse hyre	15	–	–
–	Recd from Coll[one]l: Godolphin[44] In full for a years Rent to Christs: last	53	15	–
31	pd White ye Taylour, in full of a Bill	24	–	–

30 At Walton (f.7v).

31 Will Curtis, servant.

32 See p.16.

33 Bookseller (*Chandos*, p.19). Quarterly subscription.

34 Draper.

35 Official house as Surveyor to the Hospital.

36 See f.18.

37 The seal of fashion was set on Bath by Queen Anne's visit in 1702–3.

38 Calash, a light carriage with low wheels and a removable folding hood (SOED).

39 Tenant of one of the Haymarket houses (f.28v).

40 Patent 15 June 1715 (CTB 1714–15, p.550).

41 Orphan daughter of Kenrick and Margaret Vanbrugh (p.170).

42 Theophilus (p.158).

43 Brooms.

44 Sidney (d.1732); Auditor of the Principality of Wales. Tenant of Vanbrugh's official house in Scotland Yard (CTB 1714, pp.29, 199).

Feb.

1 pd Mrs Davis at the Bull head in Clar-market[45] a Bill in full	1	18	–
2 pd a Bill at the Kings arms	6	13	10
[f.7v]			
3 Recd half a years Exchegr Salary to Midsr: last[46]	13	13	9
– pd fees for Dto	1	6	5
4 Recd 1 Nights Rent from the opera	12	10	–
11 Recd dto:	12	10	–
13 Pd Land Tax for the Playhouse, ½ a year to Michs last	11	5	–
14 pd White the Taylour on acct:	25	–	–
15 pd Jack Jones ½ a years Wages to Michs: last	5	–	–
– pd Sisr Gars: a Qrs Int: due at Chriss: last	3	15	–
16 Recd 1 Nights rent from the Opera	12	10	–
– Pd for Ten Quarters of Oates at 14s pr Qr.	7	–	–
– Recd a Baroness fee[47]	1	1	8
– pd for a load of Hay	2	6	–
21 Recd 1 Nights rent from the opera	12	10	–
22 pd for a Load of Hay & 24 trusses of straw	3	–	–
24 Recd one Quarters salary as Clar[encieu]x: to midr: last	10	–	–
– pd fees for a Qrs Salary as Clarx.	1	5	–
25 pd the Scavenger for a Year, due at L.day last	3	3	–
– pd for Stringing a Dulcimer	–	10	–
– pd for a New Sword & Belt	4	15	–
– pd for horse meat out of Town one night & a bait[48]	–	11	–
– pd for Lace for 4 shirts	6	–	–
28 pd for horse meat out of Towne two nights	–	19	8
March			
3 Recd 1 Nights Rent from the opera	12	10	–
9 Recd one third of my Blenheim arrears[49]	800	–	–
10 Recd Half a years Rent for ye Playhouse Vaults to Chriss: last	15	–	–
– pd Pattison for a sett of Calesh Wheeles	4	–	–
– pd Bowcher in full	1	3	6
– pd Mrs Howell Washerwoman a Bill	6	6	4
– pd Mr Middleton[50] a Bill	5	7	–
– pd Mrs Gibbert[51] a Bill	3	7	–
– Recd 2 Nights Rent from the Opera	25	–	–
16 pd Shirley ye Walton Waterman a Bill	1	2	6
– pd Jefferies ye Butcher Two Bills	10	6	–
– pd Trophy money for ye year 1714[52]	–	2	6
17 pd for a pair of Buckskin Britches for Arthur[53]	1	1	6
– pd for things sent to the Bath	2	3	–
– pd for 2 dozen of Hay & 3 doz: of straw	2	10	–
– Recd 2 Nights Rent from the opera	25	–	–
[f.8]			
22 pd Saunders[54] a Bill in full	12	12	–
– pd Haslam[55] a Bill in full	10	3	2
23 pd the Executors of Mr Peregrine Bertie[56] In full Discharge of Principal & Interest of three Bonds	676	13	8
– pd Middleton Chairmaker a Bill in full	6	10	–
24 Recd one nights Rent from the Opera	12	10	–
1716[57]			
29 pd Sisr: Gars: a Quarters Int: due a Lady day last	3	15	–
April			
3 Spent in a Journey to Blenheim, being out nine days. Meat & Drink &c £5. 16. 2. Horse meat £5: 10: 6	11	6	8
– pd for mending Mr Nappers road there	–	18	–
4 Recd one nights Rent from the Opera	12	10	–

45 Clare Market, off Portugal Street, south of Lincoln's Inn Fields.

46 Vanbrugh's salary from the Office of Works came from three sources: (i) The Exchequer (recorded in PRO E403); (ii) The Wardrobe (Livery money); (iii) allowances from the Paymaster of Works, which had come to make up the bulk of the remuneration.

47 College of Heralds.

48 Food for travellers, or especially horses, on a journey (SOED).

49 As Surveyor. See p.70. For the other two-thirds, see f.58v.

50 Chairmaker (f.8).

51 Or Guibert? (f.62v).

52 A tax on householders for incidental expenses connected with the militia (SOED).

53 See p.80, n.9.

54 Brewer (f.13).

55 Hosier (f.53).

56 See p.12. Vanbrugh's old friend probably lent him money in an early period of hardship.

57 Old style new year.

–	Recd half a years Rent for Greenwich house due at Michs: last	2	10	–
7	Recd Rent from Brandish,[58] One Year and Three Quarters to Michs: last	21	–	–
–	pd Brandish a Bill	1	16	3
–	allow'd Taxes to ditto. to Michs: last	1	4	8
–	one night and a Bait out of Towne Mans meat £–: 7: – Horse meat £–: 16: 3	1	3	3
–	pd for a Load of Hay	2	9	6
9	pd Wheatley ye Walton Baker a Bill	1	9	6
10	pd for a Quar[te]r: of oates maps & brooms	1	9	4
12	pd The Minister of St James, to Ladyday last	1	–	–
–	pd Will: Curtis half a years wages to Lady day last	2	10	–
–	pd Co: Anna Vandebuss[59] a years Int: due at Chris: last	5	–	–
–	pd Mary Helps[60] in full for Wages to L.day last	18	3	–
–	pd to ditto. in Discharge of a Bond, Principal & Int	23	6	–
16	pd Shirley ye Waterman a Bill	1	2	6
18	Recd Rent from Mrs Rice,[61] a year due at Lady day last	18	–	–
–	allow'd Taxes to ditto. a year: to ditto	1	7	4
–	Recd from ditto, on acct: her Brothers arrear of Rent being £32:–:– for which she is Liable	1	–	–
–	Recd Rent from Sylvester[62] half a year to Michs: last	3	–	–
–	pd for Horse meat out of Towne 2 nights	–	18	6
–	servants meat ditto	–	5	–

[f.8v]

18	pd for a Flute for Arthur	–	15	–
19	Recd a Quarters Salary at the Board of Works, to Michs: last	179	3	6
–	pd Taxes as Comptroller half a year to Michs: last	10	10	6
21	Recd Three Nights Rent from the opera	37	10	–
25	Recd Rent from Chaffee[63] half a year to Lady day last	8	2	6
27	Recd from the Heralds College[64] Grant of Arms to Reneu £15:–:– Ditto. to Wowen £30:–:– Ditto. to Hoadley £30:–:– Ditto. to Hurt £30:–:– Confirmation to Newnham £10:–:– Ditto to Peares £10:–:– Assignment of Arms to Ld Carteret £20:–:–	145	–	–
–	Allow'd Gratuitys & Entrys in the Earl Marshalls Book	12	18	6
–	Recd Fee for Lord Parker[65]	1	6	–
28	Recd Two Nights Rent from the opera	25	–	–
–	pd at Hartleys a Qr: to Lady day last	1	1	–
30	pd for 4 bushells of oates & 2 brooms	–	7	8
May				
1	pd for a load of Hay at 8s a Truss	2	14	–
–	pd for 28 Trusses of Straw at 5 p Truss	–	11	8
2	Recd one Nights Rent from the opera	12	10	–
–	pd Sisr: Mary ½ a years Int: and Annuity to the 10th & 20th Inst:	13	–	–
3	pd for teaching Jack Jones &c on the Dulcimer	1	6	–
–	pd for 10 Qurs of oates and 2½ Qrs of Beans	9	12	6
5	pd Rogers[66] for a new Long Periwig	5	–	–
7	Horse meat out of Towne 3 nights	1	11	6
–	servants meat	–	7	6
10	pd Jack Jones ½ a Yrs Wages to Lady day last	5	–	–
–	pd his Bass Viol Master	1	12	3
–	pd Horrobin the Shoemaker a bill in full	1	16	–
–	Recd Two nights rent from the opera	25	–	–

58 Tenant of one of the Haymarket houses (f.28v).

59 Anna Maria Van den Bush (1676–1757), eldest daughter of Jasper, and Ann Delboe, Vanbrugh's first cousin; probably managing the Southwell household after her mother's death. See p.168.

60 Servant.

61 Tenant of one of the Haymarket houses (f.28v).

62 Unidentified. Continues until Michaelmas 1720.

63 Chaffey.

64 Peter Renew, London; John Wowen, London; Benjamin Hoadley, Bishop of Bangor; John Hurst, Welbury, Herts.; Lewis Newnham, Northaw, Herts.; Major-Gen. Thomas Pearce, Whitlingham, Norfolk (p.156); Baron Carteret (Foster, *Grantees*). Details of grantees are taken from this source, whose spelling has been followed except in obvious cases of misreading.

65 Baron Parker of Macclesfield. Lord Chancellor 1718–25; resigned after impeachment for corruption. See n.272. Persons for whom fees were paid have been identified by reference to the *Complete Peerage; Complete Baronetage*; W. A. Shaw, *The Knights of England*, 1906; J. Le Neve, *Fasti Ecclesiae Anglicanae*, continued by T. Duffus Hardy, Oxford, 1854.

66 Cf. *Chandos*, p.201.

		£	s	d
[f.9]				
11	pd James a Qrs wages to Lady day last	2	10	–
–	pd Arthur Half a years Wages to Lady day last	2	10	–
–	pd Mary 7 months wages to ditto	2	18	–
–	pd Mrs Yeomans,[67] on Acct: of Brickwork done by her deceasd husband In the Haymarket	100	–	–
14	Recd 4 nights rent from the opera	50	–	–
–	pd Mr Wooley a years Ground Rent to Midr: 1715	50	–	–
21	Journey to Blenheim &c. being out of Towne, 11 Nights. mens meat £3:19.6 Horse meat £4.5.6 Given to servts in private houses £1.12–	9	17	–
23	Recd Rent from Scullard half a year due at Christmass last	15	–	–
–	allow'd to ditto. Taxes to Michs: last	3	7	10
	allow'd To ditto. towards some repairs	2	–	–
–	pd for a Peice of Doily stuff[68] for a Suit	2	3	–
–	pd for Silk lyning for dto:	2	19	6
–	Recd from the Wardrobe by Composition for Sr Henry St George's Coat, wch he gave me for having officiated for him[69]	50	–	–
–	Recd from dto: Composition for my own coat	50	–	–
–	Gave the clark and servant there	1	4	–
25	pd White the Taylor on acct:	21	10	–
28	pd Mr Alexander[70] for a Laid Cordebeck[71] Hatt	–	17	–
29	pd for a Load of Hay	2	8	–
30	pd Mr Harding[72] for 20 Gall: of Ale	1	6	8
31	Recd Rent from Fryar ½ a year to Chriss: last	20	–	–
June				
2	Recd Two nights Rent from the opera	25	–	–
–	pd Sisrs: Victoria and Robina a ½ years Int: & Annuity, to the 10th & 20th of May last	26	–	–
[f.9v]				
7	pd for new Buttons & mending a black suit	–	8	–
9	pd my Brother Charles In full for Int: due at Lady day last	112	10	–
–	Recd from dto: in full for Dyet for himself & servants, wth all other demands to Ladyday last	105	11	6
–	pd Subscription to Browns book of Medals[73]	1	–	–
–	pd poors Tax for the Playhouse ½ a yr due at Lady day last	7	10	–
10	pd for the High Ways in the Playhouse acct: to Christ: Last	–	15	–
–	one night out of Towne at St Albans			
–	Horse meat	–	17	–
–	Servants meat &c	–	13	9
15	Horse meat out of Towne 2 Nights	1	–	–
–	Servants	–	5	–
16	pd for a Load of straw	1	–	–
21	Two nights Rent from the Opera	25	–	–
–	Horse meat at a Bait	–	5	–
27	Pd James a Quarters wages to Midr: last	2	10	–
28	pd Mr Soley a Bill for passing a Lease from the Crown, to make up the Term in the Haymarket fifty years[74]	47	18	6
–	pd Fine for ditto	200	–	–
July				
4	pd my Sisr: Gars: a Quarters Int to Mids: last	3	15	–
–	Recd Rent for Greenwich house half a year to Midr: last	2	10	–
–	out of Towne 14 nights at Blenh[ei]m: & Mr Dodingtons:[75] Horse meat	5	5	6
–	Servants &c	6	9	10
[f.10]				
12	Out of Towne at Windsor. 1 Night, 5 horses			
–	Horse meat	–	12	6
–	Servants &c	1	3	–
16	Out of Towne at Hampton Court 4 horses 1 Night			
–	Horse meat	–	10	6
–	Servants &c	–	9	–
–	Recd from the Heralds College			
–	2 Viscounts fees	3	5	–
–	6 Barrons fees	7	16	–
–	2 Barronets fees	2	3	4
13	pd Ayres a Bill for Coales	16	11	–

67 Widow of Thomas Yeomans. See *Survey of London*, XXIX, 1960, pp.224–5.

68 A summer woollen fabric (SOED). See also f.21v, Doily's.

69 Garter Herald, died Aug. 1715 (Godfrey, p.56). Vanbrugh subsequently acted as Garter until ousted by Anstis, but was never confirmed in the office.

70 Cf. Alexandra (*Chandos*, p.201).

71 Caudebeck, a kind of woollen hat (from Caudebec, Normandy) (SOED).

72 Later Hardy (f.10v).

73 Not identified.

74 See n.17.

75 Eastbury. See p.114.

Recd for a nights Rent from the opera being a Charity 6 5 –

– pd for 30 Trusses of Hay at 1s. 6d p Truss 2 5 –

20 pd Mr Bridges[76] a Bill in full 60 3 –

– pd Land Tax for the opera house, half a year to Lady day last 11 5 –

– pd at Hartleys, a Qr: to Midr: last 1 1 –

21 Recd for Attendances at Greenwich[77] a year and three Qrs: to Lady day last 25 – –

– pd to Mr Sexton in full of a Note Sign'd to Mr Swiny for £125 on the Ballance of the acct: between us 75 – –

23 pd Jack Jones a Qrs: Wages to Midr: last 2 10 –

Augt:

20 pd: Window Tax for the Playhouse, a year to Lady day last 1 10 –

– pd: My Sisr: Gars: on acct: of Principal 20 – –

– Recd of Mrs Sells:[78] on acct: of Rent 11 13 8

– Recd ½ a years Excheqr: Salary to Chrs: last 13 13 9

– pd Fees for ditto 1 6 7

Sep

29 Recd half a years Salary from the Office of Works. to Chriss: last 364 12 –

– pd: Taxes & Gratuitys for dto: 45 5 10½

[f.10v]

29 Paid Will Curtis ½ a Yrs Wages to this day 2 10 –

– Spent In a Journey to the North. being out 2 months & 3 days six Horses £23.10.6 Meat & Drink £21.13.3 Casual Expences £20.17.4 66 1 1

Octr.

10 pd Billinger ye Carrier[79] a Bill in full 2 11 2

12 pd Sisr: Gars: Qrs Int: to Michs: last 3 15 –

18 Spent in a Journey to Blenheim and Mr Dodingtons.[80] being out 14 days Six Horses £6.18.10 Meat & Drink £6.06: – Cassual Expences £–.17.4 14 2 2

19 Recd of Mr Bradley, in full for an arrear of Rent for Kensington house[81] 6 – –

20 out of Towne at Greenwich a Bait. Four Horses £– 4: 6 Servants £– 2: – – 6 6

21 out of Towne at Esher[82] one day Four Horses £– 13. – Servants £– 3. 6 – 16 6

23 pd Mr Burton for Horses standing at Livery 7 – 2

– pd Mr Hardy a Bill for Ale 2 13 –

24 pd at Hartleys a Qr. to michs: last 1 1 –

Nov:

2 Spent in a Journey to Mr Walpoles[83] being out 11 days. six horses. £3:11.6 Meat &c £3.5.6 Casual Expences £2:9: – 9 6 –

[f.11]

8 Recd Rent from Sylvester half a Year to Lady day last 3 – –

– out of Towne one day. 5 horses: £– 15:3 Servants £– 4:6 – 19 9

– pd Robinson[84] the smiths Executors, a bill in full 5 10 –

9 pd: Jefferys the Butcher 2 Bills 14 12 –

– Recd Rent for Scotland Yard house Three Quarters due at Michs: last 40 6 3

10 pd Mary Ruffle for Corn for ye Horses 5 – 6

– pd John Bowcher for Hay and straw 3 16 6

13 pd White the Taylour, in full of a Bill 14 8 –

– Charges in qualifying for Surveyr: of Greenh:[85] – 15 –

14 Recd Rent from Chaffee. half a year due at Michs: last 8 2 6

15 Pd Walter Evans, a Bill for Powder 1 4 6

– Recd from the Heralds College ½ a year Salary to Christs: last 20 – –

– allow'd Fees for ditto 2 – 4

– Pd Taxes as Clarx: 3 Qrs: to Christs: last 6 3 4½

– Memd: One Payn a Joyner, having an Excheqr: order of my mothers, No 5051 of Ten pounds a year, on the 99 years annuitys, for Security of £100, lent

76 Woollen draper? (f.53). See also n.90.

77 As Surveyor to the Hospital.

78 Tenant of one of the Haymarket houses (f.28v).

79 Bellinger of Woodstock (f.18).

80 Eastbury.

81 Vanbrugh's official house as Comptroller of Works.

82 Claremont (p.100).

83 Probably Houghton, Norfolk. See p.121, n.27.

84 Probably Thomas Robinson, who made gates for New College, Oxford, 1711 (Beard, p.181).

85 Hospital.

		£	s	d
	I accounted with him to Midr: last discharging Principal & Int: and the said Order is entred in my name at the Excheqr: the annuity to commence from Middr: last[86]			
19	Pd James a Qrs: Wages, to Michs: last	2	10	–
–	pd Mrs Ruffle a Bill for Corn for ye Horses	10	7	–

[f.11v]

		£	s	d
21	One night out of Towne at Walton[87] four horses £– 9.6 Servants, Ferry &c £– 15 –	1	4	6
–	Rent for Greenwich house, a Quarter to midsr: last	1	5	–
–	Recd for Blenheim Prints	6	16	–
23	pd Land Tax for the Playh: ½ a Yr to Mich: last	22	10	–
–	Recd Rent from Bowden in full to Michs: last past	50	–	–
24	pd Charles Osborn for 2 pair of Buckskin Britches for James & Will	2	3	–
–	pd Wheatly the Walton Baker a bill	–	10	–
27	Pd Sisr: Mary for half a years Int: and annuity, to ye 10th & 20th Inst:	13	–	–
–	pd dto: for Niece Bin[88]	10	–	–
–	pd Mrs Stevens[89] a bill for Shoes	–	19	6
28	pd for a Load of Hay & a Load of straw	4	2	6
30	Recd from Sergeant Bridges,[90] as Executr: to Sr Harry St George[91] In full of what was due to me from Sr Harry	37	–	–
–	pd Mr Bridges a Bill in full	56	14	–
–	*pd Mary Helps a Quarter*[92]			
	Memd. I Recd a hundred pounds at Midsummer last from Mary Helps, to pay her Ten pounds a year for life[93]			

[f.12]

Dec:

		£	s	d
5	Recd from Scullard on Acct of Rent	10	15	–
–	Recd of Monsr: Portalles, half a years Rent for the Vaults in the Haymarket, to Midsummer last	15	–	–
6	Recd a Quarters Salary from the Office of Works, to Midsr: last	179	5	–
–	pd Taxes and Gratuitys for ye Same	25	19	7
8	pd Arthur half a years Wages to Michs: last	2	10	–
–	pd Mary half a Years Wages to dto:	2	10	–
12	pd for Marchants Water,[94] at the Haymarket a year, due at Lady day last	4	–	–
18	pd Sisr: Garens: on Acct: of Principall	25	–	–
20	Recd from the Heralds College, ½ a Years Salary, to Midr: last	20	–	–
–	allow'd Fees for dto:	2	4	6
25	Recd a years Rent from Mr Addison for Kensington house[95]	50	–	–
26	pd Jack Jones ½ a years Wages due today	5	–	–
–	pd Burton a Bill for Horses at Livery	7	15	6
–	Recd on Acct: of Rent from the opera	25	–	–
–	one night out of Towne 4 Horses £– 9. 4 Servants £– 3:	–	12	4
27	pd James a Qrs: Wages, to Chriss: past	2	10	–
–	pd for a Load of Hay	3	6	–
–	pd Sisters Victoria and Robina, half a years Int: and annuity to the 10 and 20th of Nov: last past	26	–	–
–	pd for 3 Livery hats	1	16	–
–	Recd from the College: Fee for a Confirmation	10	–	–

[f.12v]

		£	s	d
–	Paid House Bills this year	107	18	9¼
–	pd: Servants Bills of Disbursemts:	17	10	–
–	Given to Servants &c	8	3	9
25	Pd: my Brother Charles three Qrs: Int: to Christs: now past with £500 of ye Principal	612	10	–
–	Recd from dto: in full for Dyet for himself & servants to dto:	75	–	–
–	Recd of dto: for 3 Qrs: of a year stable Hyre due this day	12	–	–
–	For Housekeepg & Rent in Duke Street since October ye 13th: 1715	115	2	5

86 Exchequer annuity, sold by Vanbrugh on 13 Jan. 1720 (f.29).

87 Probably in connection with cousin William, dead within the previous few days (see p.160).

88 See n.41.

89 Or Stephens (f.15).

90 William Brydges, Sergeant of the Temple (*Chandos*, p.34).

91 See n.69.

92 Deleted.

93 Deleted.

94 Printed form of agreement, 27 Jan. 1707, between Hugh Marchant of Marchant's Water Works and John Vanbrugh, to supply water to six tenements in the Haymarket (BIHR (Yarburgh)).

95 Probably Joseph Addison, writer, Secretary of State and Kit-Cat; married the Countess of Warwick, 3 Aug. 1716; a Kensington resident for some years. Vanbrugh obtained the Board of Works's permission to let the house to Mr Addison on 13 Feb. 1716 (PRO Works 4/1, p.93).

[f.13]

1716/17 Jan. January ye 1st 1716/17

		£	s	d
3	Paid Saunders the Brewer a Bill	19	16	–
–	Memd: I have let the Opera house to Mr Heydegger at £400 pr annm to begin from Michs: last[96]			
5	Recd of Monsr: Portailles half a years Rent to Chriss: last	15	–	–
–	Recd on Acct of Rent from the Opera	12	10	–
8	pd Mary Darwell a bill for washing	3	12	2
–	pd dto: for Bedding for ye Stables	5	6	–
–	pd John Youle, for an Iron bar to a Chimney at the Playhouse	–	7	10
–	Recd of John Darwell in full for old arrears of Rent	21	–	–
–	Recd of dto: a years Rent to Michs: last	6	–	–
–	Recd half a years Excheqr: Salary to Midr: last	13	13	9
–	pd Fees for Dto:	1	16	9
12	Recd on Acct. of Rent from the Opera	12	10	–
–	pd Mr Woolley a years Ground Rent to Midsr: last	50	–	–
18	pd Hardy a Bill for Ale	2	13	–
19	pd for a Load of Hay & a Load of straw	4	16	–
–	pd The Farrier a Bill	27	14	–
23	Recd on acct: of Rent from the Opera	12	10	–
26	Recd on dto:	12	10	–

[f.13v]

		£	s	d
29	pd Trophy money for ye year 1715	–	2	6
Feb.				
1	Recd Rent from Fryar. ½ a Yr. to Midr: last	20	–	–
–	Pd for a Load of Hay	2	8	–
4	Recd a Quarters Rent from Bowden to Christs: last	12	10	–
–	pd a Bassviol Master for Jack Jones	1	1	6
5	Recd on Acct of Rent from the Opera	12	10	–
–	pd a Quarter at Hartleys to Christs: last	1	1	–
–	pd Coz: Anna: Vandebuss a Years Int. to Christs: last	5	–	–
7	pd Mr Ayres a bill for Coales	8	14	–
9	Recd at Greenwich for Salary as Surveyr: and for attendances, to Michs: last	44	6	8
–	given the Treasurers Clerk	–	2	6
–	Recd on acct of Rent from the Opera	12	10	–
11	pd Mrs Ruffle a bill for Corn	6	18	6
–	pd Poors Tax for the Playhouse half a year to Michs: last	7	10	–
16	Recd on acct of Rent from the Opera	12	10	–
19	Recd from the Heralds College Fee for the Duke of Portland[97] & one Baronet	9	19	4
21	Recd on the Excheqr: annuity half a year to Christs: last	5	–	–
–	pd for entring the order for dto:	–	2	6
22	pd Mrs Stevens a Bill for Shoes	1	7	–
–	Out of Towne at Kensington Two horses Six nights £1.3.– Servants drink .3: –	1	6	–
23	Recd on acct: of Rent from the Opera	12	10	–
25	pd Burton a Bill for Horse meat	9	2	–

[f.14]

		£	s	d
25	pd Shirley ye Waterman a Bill	1	14	8
–	pd Jeffereys the Butcher a Bill	5	–	9
–	Memd: Robert Griffin came to me the 20th Inst: for five pds: a year Wages. & a Livery			
–	Memd. I sign'd a Bond the 5th Inst: to Mr Heydegger, in trust for John Potter, for £600. To enable him to Give Security to Potter for £300. by making over Part of the stock of the Opera house to him, wch Part is recited in the said Bond			
March				
2	Recd on Acct: of Rent from the Opera	12	10	–
5	pd Langhorne,[98] ye Framemaker a bill	–	17	–
9	Memd: I Sign'd a Lease this day to Sr Wm. Saunderson, for his House at Greenwich, for three years Certain, four more if I desire it; or to purchace it out at £800. The Rent £40 pr Anm to commence from Lady day next[99]			
–	pd the attorney for drawing the lease	1	–	–
–	Recd on Acct: of Rent from the Opera	12	10	–

[f.14v]

		£	s	d
12	Out of Towne 2 Nights 5 horses £1.7.1 Servants £.6.	1	13	1
14	Pd for a Load of Hay	3	9	–
–	Recd from the Heralds College Fees for the Duke of York,[100] An Irish Viscountess, and 2 Barronets	11	11	10

96 Eighteen months earlier than stated in *Survey of London*, XXIX, p.225.

97 6th Earl, created 1st Duke.

98 Later Langthorne.

99 See p.93.

100 Prince Ernest Augustus (1675–1728).

–	Recd on account of Rent from the opera	12	10	–
16	Recd from ditto	12	10	–
–	Recd for a Bay mare	2	3	–
–	pd: for a Diaper[101] for Napkins, from Uttoxeter	2	8	–
19	pd. the sadler a Bill	5	12	6
–	pd for 12 pints of Lisbon White[102]	–	12	–
22	Recd a Quarters Salary from the Office of Works, to Michs: last	178	4	2
–	pd Taxes & Gratuitys for dto: to dto:	26	11	11½
23	a Bait at Greenwich 2 Horses £–:2:– Servants £–:4:–	–	6	–
25	Rent from Bowden a Qr: to this day	12	10	–
27	Rent for Scotland yard house half a year to Lady day last	26	17	6
–	pd White the Taylor on acct:	20	–	–
–	pd Will: Curtis ½ a years wages to Lady day last	2	10	–
30	Recd on acct of Rent from the opera	25	–	–

April

1	Out of Towne 1 night. 5 horses £–:12:– Servants &c £–:13:–	1	5	–
2	Recd Rent from Scullard to Michs: last	11	15	–
–	allow'd taxes to dto. to Lady day last	4	10	4

[f.15][103]

June

6	Recd on acct: of Rent from the Opera	37	10	–
–	Recd from the Heralds College, Fee for Lady Hodges's Funeral[104]	10	–	–
–	Allow'd Mr Mawson[105] for attendance at the said Funeral for me	2	–	–
7	pd Mrs Stevens a Bill for washing, to the 3d of May last past	6	15	9
–	Recd half a Years Salary as Surveyr: of Greenwich Hospll, and half a years attendances to Lady day last	115	–	–
–	Given the Treasurers Clerk	–	2	6
12	Out of Towne 4 Nights & 3 baits			
–	2 horses	1	2	6
–	Servants	–	9	–
–	Given to Aunt Breton[106]	16	2	6
13	pd John Hudson for 2 frocks for James and Will[107]	1	4	–
–	pd Siss: Mary, Vic: and Robina, for ½ a year Int: & annuity to aprill last	39	–	–
–	Pd. to Mr Bobart at Woodstock to discharge Severall Bills for Work and Goods at the Old Manour[108]	96	5	5
19	Pd Mr Billinghurst on acct:	50	–	–
21	pd Mr Langthorn a Bill for framing Prints	3	4	6
–	pd Mr Weeks, Mercer a Bill	8	18	10
22	pd Iremonger the Coachman a Bill in full	6	2	6
–	Recd Rent from Sylvester, 3 Qrs. to Christs: last	4	10	–
–	pd Buhet for a Long Wigg	6	9	–
24	Recd Rent of Bowden in full to this day	15	–	–
27	pd Mrs Stephen's a Bill for Shoes	1	12	–
30	Out of Towne. 2 horses a Bait	–	2	–

July

1	Recd of Mrs Sells in full for Rent to Lady day last was twelve months	15	6	4
–	allow'd her for Taxes to Lady day last	2	12	8
–	pd her a Bill	1	8	–

[f.15v]

3	pd Taxes for the Playhouse half a year to Lady day last	22	10	–
–	Recd on acct: of Rent from the opera	12	10	–
7	Bait at Twittenham[109] 2 Serts. £– 2:– 4 horses £– 4:–	–	6	–
8	Dto.	–	6	–
–	Pd Mr Hardy a Bill for Ale	2	13	4
10	Recd a Quarters Salary from the Office of Works, to Christs: last	178	9	4
–	pd Taxes & Gratuitys for dto. to dto.	25	19	7
11	pd James Wood a Quarter Wages to Midr: last	2	10	–
–	pd Jefferys the Walton Butcher Two Bills to midsr: last	12	6	9
–	pd Taxes as Clarx: to midr. 1716	9	19	5½
12	pd Seigr: Leoni in part of five Guineas Subscrib'd for Palladio's Architecture[110]	3	4	6
16	pd Window Tax for the Playhouse a year to Lady day last	1	10	–

101 For table linen, with a diamond pattern shown up by reflection (cf. damask) (SOED).

102 Wine.

103 Leaf torn out before numeration.

104 Widow of Sir William Hodges, Bt, of Cadiz and Middlesex; died 25 April 1717. For attendance at funerals see p.166, n.90.

105 Charles Mawson, Chester Herald; resigned 16 July 1720 (Godfrey, p.125).

106 Lucy Breton (see p.155).

107 Servants, James Wood and Will Curtis.

108 Tilleman Bobart, Comptroller at Blenheim. For the Old Manor see p.74.

109 Twickenham.

110 Giacomo Leoni. Published with the date 1715. See R. Wittkower, *Palladio and English Palladianism*, 1974, pp.79–86.

–	Recd Rent for Greenwich house ½ a year to Chriss: last	2	10	–
21	Out of Towne one Night 3 Serts £. 6– 3 horses £. 7.9	–	13	9
24	Recd Rent from Scullard half a year to Lady day last	15	–	–
30	Pd Mr Bonfoy for a p[ie]c[e]: of Cambrick[111] £2:–:– for 12 Napkins & a Table Cloath £2:7:6	4	7	6
31	Recd Rent from Fryar ½ a year due at Christs: Last	20	–	–
–	pd at Hartleys a Quarter to Midsr: last	1	1	–

[f.16]

31	From the Heralds College, Grants of Arms, to Meyer, Granger, Decker Wilson, Colbatch, Astell, Batt, and a Confirmation to Humfrey and Sawbridge[112]	140	–	–
–	pd Gratuitys &c	12	10	8
–	From the Heralds College half a years Salary, to Christs: last	20	–	–
–	pd Taxes for a Year to Dto	13	18	7½
–	pd Fees for the half years Salary	2	4	–
Augt.				
3	pd Sisr: Gars: a Quarters Int: to Midr. last	2	16	3
5	pd Thompson, Haberdasher, for a Hat for Griffin[113]	–	13	–
–	out of Towne 2 Baits	–	9	–
–	Given Sisr: Mary	10	15	–
–	pd Sisr: Robina for Int: & Annuity to the 10th & 20th of Octor: next	13	–	–
10	Given Sisr: Betty	21	10	–
15	Out of Towne at Hampton Court & Windsor, at severall times 13 Nights, 4 Horses £3:10:6 1 Saddle horse 7 nights £ :10.6 Servants eating £2:9:–	6	10	–
–	my own eating 2 nights	–	13	–
16	pd Mr Presgrave	4	6	–
–	Recd Excheqr: Salary half a Year to Christs: last	13	13	9
–	pd Fees	1	16	9
27	pd Stevens the Shoemakers Bill	1	12	6
Sept:				
3	Out of Towne at Hampton Court 4 nights 3 servants £1:10:– 3 Horses £1:14:6	3	4	6

[f.16v]

4	pd Arthur in full for Wages to Midr: last	1	5	–
–	pd Sisr: Gars: on Acct: of Principall	5	–	–
–	pd for a Hat	–	18	–
–	pd Jack Jones in full for Wages to Midr: last	5	–	–
5	pd John Hook a Bill for Bricklayers Work done at Whitehall	8	14	–
Nov:				
9	Spent in a Journey to the Bath being out 63 days vizt: House Bills upon the Road £14:19:8 Horses upon the Road £8:11:2½ House Bills & Lodging there £56:5:6 Horses there £19:8:11 Physitian there £10:15 – Appothecary there £8:15:–	118	15	3
–	Given Jack Jones to send his Mother	1	1	6
–	Building at Dean Jones's[114] & elsewhere	3	5	–
–	Other odd expences	7	8	10
–	pd Robert Griffin in full for wages	3	10	–
–	pd for Hyre of 2 Coach Horses	7	15	6
11	Pd Mr Hesledens Int:[115] money to ye first of may last	4	4	–
13	Recd from the Office of Works, a Quarters Sallary to Lady day last	175	17	–
–	Given the Clark	–	5	–
–	Given the Paymasters man	–	5	–
–	Allow'd Taxes to Lady day Last	25	14	7
–	Recd Rent from Fryar ½ a Year to Midr: last	20	–	–
15	pd Rogers for a Periwig to Tye	5	–	–
20	pd Marchant for Water a Year to Lady day last	4	–	–
21	Recd from the Heralds College, a Quarters Salary to Lady day last	10	–	–
–	pd Taxes for ditto £3:19:2 Fees £1.2:	5 2	2	[*sic*]
–	pd at Hartleys a Quarter due at Michs last	1	1	–
26	pd White the Taylor in full of a Bill	12	18	–

111 Fine linen originally made at Cambrai (SOED).

112 Sir Peter Meyer, London and Holstein; John Grainger, Westminster; Sir Matthew Decker, Bt, of Dutch extraction; Thomas Wilson, Stratford-le-Bow; Sir John Colbatch, Westminster and Dr John Colbatch, Middlesex; William Astell, Everton, Beds.; Christopher Batt, Kensington; Sir William Humfreys, London and Wales; Elizabeth Fisher, wife of Jacob Sawbridge.

113 Robert Griffin, servant.

114 Barzillai Jones, Fellow of All Souls and Dean of Lismore. As a non-juror he lost preferment; he was disliked but entertained by the Duchess of Marlborough, for a time as domestic chaplain. In August 1722 Vanbrugh gave him lavender drops (f.42) and also a letter with a note for £100 from the new Duchess, Henrietta, to buy mourning for the Duke (Green, pp.154, giving his reply, and 269). As he answered from Bath, that may have been the destination of Vanbrugh's journey recorded on 3 August. Vanbrugh refers to the Dean in 1716 (Webb, p.79) but another reference to 'Jones' (p.83) is of 1723 (see p.80, n.9) and probably to his servant Jack.

115 See p.168.

– pd Tonkeson, Taylor in full of a Bill	10	15	–
– pd Poors Tax for the Playhouse half a year to Michs: last	10	–	–

[f.17]

Nov.

2 pd Mr Bonfoy for 38 Ells of Holland for Shirts	14	5	–
28 pd Land Tax for ye Playhouse half a year to Michs: last	15	–	–
– Recd Rent from Scullard half a year to Michs: last	15	–	–
– allow'd Taxes to ditto	1	10	–
– Recd Excheqr Salary a Qr to Lady day last	6	16	10
– Fees for ditto	–	18	3
– pd Sisr: Garens: ½ a years Int. to Christs: next	5	12	6
– pd Barnard, a Bill for Oyl & Powder	1	–	–
– pd Mrs Ruffle a Bill for Corn and Stable Utensils	6	18	8
– pd Mr Chaffey a Bill for one load of Hay, and ½ a load of straw	3	15	–
– pd ditto a Bill for a Load of Hay And a Load of Straw	2	15	6
29 pd Siss: Mary and Vict: half a years Int: and annuity to October last	26	–	–
– pd Burton a Bill	1	18	–

Decr.

5 Pd a Bill at the Inn at Greenwich for Horse meat &c	3	11	7
7 a Bait at Esher. 4 Horses £–9.9 Servants £–2.–	–	11	9
10 Recd from the office of Works, a Qrs: Salary to Midr. last	175	16	2
– Given the Clerk	–	5	–
– To the Paymasters man	–	5	–
– allow'd Taxes to Mid: last	18	5	2½
– allow'd towards fees at the Treasury	–	7	3¼
13 pd Mrs Ruffle for 10 Quarters of Oates	7	15	–

[f.17v]

18 pd Brockwell at Greenwich, a Bill for Horse meat	8	11	–
– pd Mr Hardy a Bill for Ale	4	–	–
19 pd White the Taylor on Acct:	20	–	–
24 pd the Exrs: of John Hook a Bill in full	12	2	–
27 Recd of Coll: Godolphin for three Qrs Rent to Christs. last	48	6	–
– Recd half a years Salary as Surveyr of Greenwich Hospitall, and half a years attendances, to Michs: last	117	–	–
– Given the Treasurers Clark	–	5	–
30 Recd from Greenwich Hospitall allowance for houserent half a year to Christs: last past	15	–	–
31 pd Will Curtis, in full for Wages to Christs: last past	3	15	–
– pd Walter Evans a Bill for Powder	1	6	11
– pd for Lace for 12 Shirts	13	–	–
– pd House Bills this year	138	3	8¾
– pd Servants Bills of Disbursments	13	3	9½
– Given to Servants	11	15	3
– Spent in Small things	18	16	5
– pd my Brother Charles a years Int to Christs: last	120	–	–
– Recd from dto: for a years Dyet for himself & Servants	100	–	–
– Recd from dto. for a Years Stable Rent to Christs: last	16	–	–
– Recd from dto: Towards Rent for Greenh: house, for 3 Qrs. due at Christs: last	15	–	–
– Spent in Duke Street from Christs. to Ladyday when the Family remov'd to Greenwich	50	–	–
– House Bills at Greenwich from Ladyday to Christs: last	104	9	8
– spent there in settling, Furnishing &c to dto: time	57	7	–

[f.18]

1717/18 Jan: January ye 1st: 1717/18

2 pd Mrs Yeomans on Acct:	105	–	–
– Recd Rent from Chaffey, a year to Michs: last	16	5	–
– Recd from the Heralds College Fees for Lord Stanhope, Baron & Viscount £2:18: – Lord Longvill, Earl £2:3:4 Elton, Baronet £1:1:8 Jackson, Lock & Bull. Knights £2:18:–[116]	9	1	6
– pd Chaffey for a Load of Hay	2	5	–
3 pd Stevens, a Bill for Shoes	1	1	–
– pd Mr Hales in full for Plumbers Work at the Playhouse &c	150	–	–
8 Recd Rent from Mr Portailles to Christs: last	52	10	–
– pd Prince the Bricklay[er], for some jobs at Mr Portailles	–	11	4
10 pd Sanders the Brewer a Bill in full	32	3	6
13 pd Paulden, Taylour a Bill	2	10	–
– pd Mr Ayres for Coales in full	19	16	–
15 pd Bellinger, ye Woodstock carrier a Bill	1	13	–
16 pd Mr Collivoe a Bill for mending Pictures	9	9	–
– pd for Nine Muslin Neckcloaths	3	–	–
18 pd Mr Wooley ½ a year Ground Rent to Christs: last was 12 Months	25	–	–
24 Recd One years Excheqr annuity, to Christs: last	10	–	–
– Rd. from Mr Heydegger on Acct of Rent	100	–	–
– pd James Wood half a yrs wages to Christs: last	5	–	–

116 James Stanhope, Baron and Viscount Stanhope (1673–1721); Kit-Cat. See also n.131. Talbot Yelverton, 1st Viscount de Longueville, created Earl of Sussex 1717. Sir Abraham Elton, Bt, of Bristol. Sir Philip Jackson, Sir John Lock, Sir John Bull, Turkey merchants.

[f.18v]

21	pd at Hartleys. Christs. Quarter	1	1	–
31	Pd: Sisr: Mary for Little Bins[117] Dyet to Michs: last	10	–	–
–	pd Coz: Anna[mari]a. Vandebuss one years Int: due at Christs: last	5	–	–
Feb.				
5	pd for a Load of Hay to Chaffey	2	6	–
6	Recd from the Heralds College in Lieu of a New Collar	6	3	6
12	pd the Minister of St James's a year to Lady day next	1	–	–
–	pd for the Highway a year to Christs: last	–	15	–
12	pd Wm Salter a Bill for Chairs	3	13	–
13	pd Middleton a Bill for Chairs	8	8	–
14	pd Mr Billinghurst on Acct:	50	–	–
–	Out of Towne. a Bait. 4 horses £–:4:6 Servants £–:5:6	–	10	–
–	Recd from Mr Heydegger on Acct: of Rent	100	–	–
15	pd Will Curtis in full for Wages £–:12:6 Gave him over £1:1:–	1	13	6
17	pd Mr Tonson on a Subscription for Mr Priors Works[118]	1	1	–
19	pd Mr Woolley half a years ground Rent to midr: last	25	–	–
20	pd Mr Wetherhilt[119] on Acct: of Plaisterers Work done at the Haymarket	20	–	–
27	pd Poors Tax for the Playhouse, a Quarter to Christs: last	5	–	–
March				
3	pd Trophy money for the Playhouse	–	2	6
–	Memd: I took a Lease from Sr Mich[ae]ll. Biddulph at Greenwich, of a Field & Other Grounds, at the Rent of Sixteen Pounds a year for 99 Years.			
–	pd Mr Fuller for drawing the Lease	3	3	–
6	Recd from the College, Fee for the Duke of Wharton[120]	4	6	8

[f.19]

10	pd Dorothy in full for Wages	4	5	–
17	pd Chaffey for Hay & Straw	5	4	–
15	Recd from the Heralds College in Lieu of a New Chain and for two old Badges	31	12	–
–	pd fees at the Jewell office £3.3– Gave the maid there £ :2:6	3	5	6
19	Recd from Mr Cook of Cirencester[121] in full, upon giving up his Deputation	4	–	–
–	Given on a Subscription for Mons: Pillionier[122]	2	2	–
–	pd for Insuring Greenwich House £5:11:4 gave the clerk £– 2.2	5	13	6
26	Recd from Mr Rice[123] half a years Rent to Michs: last	9	–	–
–	allow'd Taxes to ditto	3	1	1
31	pd Mr Richards at the Wine Cellar a Bill	3	3	10
–	Recd of Mr Heydegger on Acct of Rent	100	–	–
April				
2	Recd of Coll. Godolphin a Quarters Rent to Lady day last	15	15	–
3	Recd Rent from Fryar, ½ a year to Chrs: last	20	–	–
9	Paid Mr Hargrave[124] on acct: of painting work at the Playhouse &c	31	10	–
–	Recd of the Marquiss of Lindsey[125] for Wine	14	–	–
–	pd for 3 pair of Buckskin Britches	3	15	–
–	pd Mrs Ruffle a Bill for Corn &c	16	–	–
10	pd Fee at the Wardrobe for a New Coat	1	–	–
–	pd for Ribons to it, & to the Porter	–	2	6
–	pd Jeffereys the Butcher a Bill in full	1	9	10
–	pd Shirley, Waterman a Bill in full	1	2	4
–	pd Fees for Venison at Woodstock	3	–	–
19	pd Sr Wm Sanderson, in full for one years Rent, due at Lady day last past	40	–	–
24	Recd Rent from Sylvester, half a year to Midsr: 1717	3	–	–
25	pd James Wood a Qrs: Wages to Lady day last	2	10	–
–	pd Chaffey, for a Load of Hay	2	[?	?]

[f.19v]

25	pd Middleton a Bill	2	5	–

117 See n.41.

118 Matthew Prior. Folio ed. 1718.

119 Josiah Wetherill. Perhaps son of Robert Wetherill (Beard, p.171).

120 Philip, 1st Duke (1698–1731).

121 Not identified.

122 François de la Pillonnière, controversialist. *Défense des Principes de la Tolérance*, London 1718.

123 Haymarket.

124 William Hargrave of St James's, born about 1670 (BM MS.Add.19617, f.179). Vanbrugh to Joynes, 15 Sept. 1711: 'Mr Hargraves Wife will send him downe Pelegrinis Colour for Priming the Salon' (Webb, p.239).

125 2nd Marquess; 2nd Duke of Ancaster in 1723.

		£	s	d
–	pd Haslam a Bill	7	2	6
–	pd John Darwell for Washing £5 –:4 and a Bill for disbursments £3:1:–	8	1	4
–	Recd of John Darwell for a year and ½ Rent due at Lady day last	9	–	–
28	Out of Towne one Night	–	11	6
–	Recd from Mrs Sells on Account	10	–	–
–	pd at Hartleys. Lady day Quarter	1	1	–
–	Recd Excheqr. salary, a Quarter to Midr: last	6	16	10
–	pd Fees for dto:	–	18	3
May				
8	pd White the Taylor on Acct:	15	–	–
–	pd the Scavenger, a year, to Lady day last	3	3	–
16	Recd Livery money for the years 1714, 1715: 1716[126]	25	8	–
–	allow'd Fees at the Wardrobe (Doorkeepers included)	2	3	–
–	Fees for the Debenters, at Mr Edd: Dummers[127] (including the Debentr. for 1717)	1	1	–
22	pd Mr Tonson for Binding Bleaus Atlas[128] & for Echards 3 Volls: of ye English History[129]	15	15	–
24	pd Sisr: Garencieres, half a Years Int: to midr: next	5	10	–
26	pd Natll: Brockwell a Bill for horse meat at Greenh: vizt: Saddle Horses Grass £4.8:– Hay & Straw for ye Coach horses £9.9:6	13	17	6
–	Recd From Greenh: Hospital half a years Salary as Surveyr to Lady day last £100:–:– Attendances to dto: £12:–:–	112	–	–
–	Gave ye Treasrs: Clerk	–	5	–
29	Recd from the Earl of Hertford in ful for two years Rent for My house at Hampton Court	100	–	–
–	Gave his Servant that brought the money	–	10	6
–	pd Stevens the Washerwoman a bill	5	14	2
–	pd Mr Chaffey for Hay & Straw in Augt: last	3	18	–
–	pd dto: for a Load of Hay	2	8	–
–	Recd Rent from Chaffey half a year to Lady day last	8	2	6
30	pd Mr Bridges upon acct:	42	–	–
–	pd Seigr: Lioni[130] on the delivery of the 3d book of Palladio, he having recd 3 Gs. before	1	1	–

[f.20]

		£	s	d
June				
5	Out of Towne 2 nights. Servts &c £– 14: 6 Horses £1: 4: 6	1	19	–
6	Recd from the office of Works, a Qrs Salary to Michs: last	174	19	2
–	Given the Clerk 5s To the Paymasters man 5s	–	10	–
–	allow'd Taxes to Michs last, & Fees at ye Treasy	18	12	10
–	pd Stevens a Bill for Shoes	–	14	–
7	pd Mr Billinghurst on acct:	52	10	–
10	Given Sisr: Betty	10	10	–
17	out of Towne, one night and a Bait. horses £–11.7 Servts £–4:6	–	16	1
18	Recd Rent from Scullard ½ a year to L[ady]day last	15	–	–
–	allow'd Taxes to ditto time	1	10	4
–	pd Window Tax to ditto time	1	10	–
–	Recd from the Heralds College, Fee for Earl Stanhope[131]	2	3	4
–	Recd from dto: Fee for Sr Brook Bridges[132]	1	1	8
–	pd John Hudson, for frocks	1	5	–
19	pd Land Tax for ye Playhouse, ½ a year to Lday last	15	–	–
–	pd Wallis the Taylour a Bill	–	15	–
20	pd Mr Billinghurst on acct:	50	–	–
July				
4	Out of Towne 8 Nights 6 Horses £3:8:8 Servts &c £3:–:11	6	9	7
–	pd Sisr: Mary, Victoria and Robina, in full for half a years Int. & Annuity to April last	39	–	–
–	pd Mr Wray a bill for Linnen	2	3	11
–	pd Mr Sparks, a bill for Kitchen utensils	2	10	10
–	pd Mr Oram in full for Malt	2	16	–
–	Recd From my Brother Charles for Pewter Ale and Corks	6	13	6
9	Recd Rent for the Vaults and Chocolate house in the haymarket half a year to Midr: last	45	–	–
–	pd Mr Portailles &c a Bill for Wine	11	5	6
10	From the College, Fees for Earl Cadoghan & Viscount Cobham[133]	6	14	4
15	From Dto: Fees for Knighthood of the Duke of York, Prince			

[126] Paid at the Wardrobe. See n.46.

[127] Edmund Dummer, Clerk of the Great Wardrobe.

[128] Joan Blaeu, *Atlas Major*, Amsterdam (11 vols, Latin, 1662; 12 vols, French, 1663; 9 vols, Dutch, 1664).

[129] Laurence Eachard, *The History of England from the First Entrance of Julius Caesar*, 1707–18.

[130] Leoni (n.110).

[131] 1st Earl, previously Baron and Viscount (n.116).

[132] Sir Brook Bridges, Bt, of Goodneston, Kent.

[133] 1st Earl Cadogan (1672–1726). Richard Temple, 1st Viscount Cobham (1675–1749); Kit-Cat.

Day	Entry	£	s	d
	Frederick, The Duke of St Albans & the Duke of Montague[134]	3	17	4
–	From dto: Knight[hoo]d: fees for Caswell & Jacobson[135]	1	18	8

[f.20v]

Day	Entry	£	s	d
15	From the Heralds College, Fees for Lord Cowper, Earl & Viscount[136]	3	15	10
–	From dto: Grants of Arms, to Conduit Hyde, Gratwick, Beachcroft, Perry Mackarell, Ket & Townsend, neat money[137]	86	4	4
–	From dto: 3 Barts: fees, vizt: Chaplain Tench and St John[138]	3	5	–
–	From dto: 2 Knts: fees. Jones and Penrie[139]	1	18	8
–	From dto: Grant of Arms for Hall[140]	15	–	–
–	From dto. grant of arms for Halsey[141]	27	7	–
–	pd Gratuitys &c	3	18	–
–	From the Heralds College, fee for an Alteration in Halseys Arms[142]	1	1	6
–	From dto: a Qrs: Salary to Midr: 1717	10	–	–
–	Allow'd Fees & Taxes	3	18	3
–	From dto: rec'd Out of the Fees appropriated by my Lord Marshall for defraying the Charges of the suit with Mr Anstis[143]	169	11	–
–	pd on acct: of the said suit a Bill of disbursments to Mr Le Neve[144] £18:3:– Given the attorney Genll. £10:15:– pd Sollicitor Troughtons bill £7:10.6 pd Mr Stebbing[145] a bill of Disbursments £113:2:6 pd Sollicitor Cardell on acct £20:–:–	169	11	–
–	Recd my Share of the said Fees remaining	33	9	–
21	Out of Towne 6 nights. 6 Horses £2:14:3 Servts: &c £2:17:7 Other expences £1:9:6	7	1	4
–	pd Mr Hesleden one years Int: to ye 1st of May last	3	10	–
22	pd Richd: Oliver for Bricks in full	15	15	–

[f.21]

Day	Entry	£	s	d
25	Recd from the Duke of Newcastle, in full of all demands, a Bond for[146]	400	–	–
–	pd To Mr Tho: Churchill by Assign[men]t of the Duke of New: Bond for the Use of the Execu[tri]x of Mr Smalwell[147] Joyner: Upon Acct: of Work done at the Playhouse in the Haymarket	400	–	–
29	pd Godfrey, the Coachmaker on Acct:	40	–	–
30	Recd Rent from Brandish, a year and half, to Lady day last was twelve months	18	–	–
–	allow'd Taxes to ditto time	1	10	–
–	pd at Hartleys Midr: Quarter	1	1	–
Augt.				
2	pd Sanham the Greenwich Farrier in full	2	–	–
4	pd Wigzell, the Greenwich Corn Chandler in full	19	10	4
6	pd Williams, Cornchandler a Bill	8	3	2
12	pd Mr Hargrave, Painter, in full	31	10	–
13	pd Mr Billinghurst, on acct of Work done at Chargate[148]	50	–	–

[134] Garter installation: Duke of York (n.100); Prince Frederick Lewis, nominated but not created Duke of Gloucester; 1st Duke of St Albans, 2nd Duke of Montagu.

[135] Sir George Caswell and Sir Jacob Jacobson of the South Sea Company.

[136] 1st Earl Cowper, Viscount Fordwich.

[137] John Conduit, Westminster; John Hyde, Hyde, Hants.; William Gratwick, Ham, Sussex; Samuel and Joseph Beachcroft, London; Samuel Perry, Goodman's Fields, Middx.; John Mackarell, Norwich; Elizabeth Kett, London; Robert Townsend, Coggeshall, Essex.

[138] Sir Robert Chaplin, Bt, South Sea Company. Sir Fisher Tench, Bt, Low Leyton, Essex. Sir Francis St John, Bt, of Longthorpe, Northants.

[139] Sir Thomas Jones, Secretary to Society of Antient Britain. Sir Henry Penrice, LL.D., Admiralty judge.

[140] John Hall, Mayor of Norwich.

[141] Edmund Halsey, Deadmans Place, Surrey.

[142] The same.

[143] About the post of Garter Herald. See A. R. Wagner, *Heralds of England*, 1967, p.319 ff.

[144] Peter Le Neve, Norroy Herald 25 May 1704; died 24 Sept. 1729 (Godfrey, p.114).

[145] Samuel Stebbing, Somerset Herald 31 May 1700; died 21 Aug. 1719 (Godfrey, p.160).

[146] See next entry, and Vanbrugh's letter to Forbes, 4 July 1718 (Webb, p.99).

[147] Senior.

[148] Claremont. Vanbrugh had a pied-à-terre there, where John Smallwell put up shelves in 1715 and a lock 'on Sr John's door at the Lodge' in 1718 (BM MS.Add.33442, ff.73, 91v).

		£	s	d
–	out of Towne one night & a bait 6 Horses £–:15:– Serts: £–:4:6	–	19	6
–	pd Foubert, a Bill for Wine	1	1	6
19	pd Jane Wright for Carriage of Bricks &c[149]	20	19	–
21	Out of Towne one night 4 horses £–:11:– Serts: £–:10:8	1	1	8
27	Recd a Qrs Excheqr Salary to Michs: last	6	16	10½
–	allow'd Fees for dto:	–	18	4½
28	Out of Towne one Night. 4 Horses 12.2 Servts. –4.2	–	16	4
30	pd Mr Billing[hurs]t: in full for Work at Chargate	15	13	8
Sept:				
4	pd Mr Cardell in full of Two Bills	7	15	–
–	Rd of Mr Hoare one years Rent for a slaughter house in Market Lane due at Midsumr: last[150]	6	–	–
6	pd Mr Billinghurst on acct: for work done at Greenwich	50	–	–

[f.21v]

		£	s	d
9	Out of Towne 2 nights, 4 Horses £1:2:6 Servts: £:8:6	1	11	–
10	pd Mrs Stevens a Bill for Shoes	–	18	–
14	out of Towne a bait. 2 Horses £– 2:6 Servt:1	–	3	6
15	Recd from the Office of Works, one Qr to Christ: last	176	19	6
–	pd Taxes to dto:	18	12	9½
–	Given the Clerk	–	5	–
22	pd for 6 Muslin Neckcloaths	2	14	–
–	pd for 2 dozen of Rhenish wine	3	–	–
24	Out of Towne one Night. 2 Horses £–4– Serts £– 2.4	–	6	4
26	pd Mr Barret on Acct: for Bricks	50	–	–
–	Recd from the Heralds College a Qrs Salary to Michs: last	10	–	–
–	Fees for dto:	1	2	6
29	pd Int: to Sisr: Gars: a Quarter due this day	2	15	–
Oct.				
1	Recd of Mr Heydegger on acct: of Rent	50	–	–
–	pd Mr Bonfoy for Cambrick for 9 Handkers:	2	5	–
2	pd Poors Tax for the Playhouse ½ a year to midr: last	10	–	–
–	pd Mr Blunt for a Coach horse	20	–	–
–	given his man	–	5	–
7	Out of Towne 5 Nights. 5 Horses £2:14:6 Serts: £1:5:	3	19	6
–	Rent from Sylvester ½ a year to Christs: last	3	–	–
–	pd John Mason, for Six Knives & Forks	3	6	–
–	pd Mr Wetherhilt Playsterer in full of all accts	50	–	–
–	pd Josh: Huddleston on acct: of Carpenters Work done in the Haymarket	25	–	–
10	pd James Wood ½ a Yrs Wages to Michs: last	5	–	–
–	pd Mr Barret on Acct: for Bricks	50	–	–
17	Out of Towne 8 Nights 5 Horses £3:13:– Servts £3: 8.4	7	1	4
21	Out of Towne 1 Night 4 Horses £–:16:6 Serts: £–6–	1	2	6
23	pd at Doilys[151] for a White Quilt £2:–:– a Coarse Table Cloath £–:3:6 3 Coarse Towells £–:2:6	2	6	–

[f.22]

		£	s	d
25	pd Mr Billinghurst on Acct: of work done at Greenh:	10	10	–
27	pd My Lady Biddulph, for half a years Rent due at Michs: last	8	–	–
28	pd Mr Billinghurst on Acct: of Work done at Greenwich	50	–	–
–	pd at Doilys for Stuff for a Suit £2:–:– Lyning £1:18:–	3	18	–
29	Recd Rent from Scullard half a year to Michs: last	15	–	–
–	allow'd taxes to dto: £1:10– and repairs of Casements £ :5–	1	15	–
–	pd White the Taylor in full of a Bill	16	5	–
–	pd for a New Belt without ye Buckles	–	12	6
Nov.				
7	pd Mr Vallance for a Tyed Wigg	7	7	–
10	Out of Towne 7 nights 5 Horses £3.4.8 Servants £3.17.8 Servants at the Duke of Ancasters[152] £1.12.6	8	14	10
–	pd Mr Carr for a Ty'd Periwigg	5	15	6
12	pd Stevens a Bill for Shoes	1	11	6
–	Recd from Mrs Sells on Acct of Rent	10	–	–
14	pd Mr Hardy, a Bill for Ale	10	13	4
17	pd Mr Godfrey, Coach Maker on Acct:	21	–	–
	Memd: I agreed this day with Mr Godfrey, to keep the Calesh as well as the Chariot, for fifteen pounds a year, to begin from Christs: next			
–	Recd from Coll: Godolphin, half a years Rent, to Michs: last	31	10	–
19	pd Mrs Yeomans on acct: of Brickwork at the Playhouse	50	–	–
–	pd The Land Tax at Greenh: for 12 Acres on May[153] hill, half a year to Michs: last	–	11	4

149 At Greenwich (f.22v).

150 West side of the Haymarket site.

151 Doily's in the Strand (*Chandos*, p.19).

152 Grimsthorpe.

153 Maze.

		£	s	d
–	pd Fees to Mr Cholmley[154] for a Report to the Treasury	4	4	–
–	Recd from Mr Heydegger in full Rent to Michs: last as likewise an old arrear of £20	70	–	–

[f.22v]

		£	s	d
20	pd Mr Woolley ½ a years Rent to Christs: last	25	–	–
–	pd for Marchants Water at the Playhouse a year to Lady day last	4	–	–
–	pd Mr Mallory a Bill for Livery Lace	16	7	–
24	pd Mrs Wright at Greenh: on acct: for Carriage of Bricks	10	10	–
	Memd. I this day cancell'd the Mortgage of the Playhouse to my Br Charles (on wch remain'd due to to him £2000: Principal) paying to my Sisrs: Victoria Betty & Robina £250: each, (out of his money according to his Order) and Sign'd a Bond to him for the Remaining £1250. The Int: to Commence from Christs: next			
	Memd. I also took up & Cancell'd the Bonds my Said Sisters had from me, and Gave them new ones, for £400 each, the Int to commence from Christs: next			
28	pd Mr Castell for Silk for a Gown & Scarf	6	14	–
Dec.				
2	pd dto. for Velvet & Lineing for a Cap	–	18	–
–	pd Mrs Wright at Greenh. in full of a Bill for Carriage of Bricks	11	4	9
6	Recd of Mr Hill for Hay & Grass at Greenh:	5	–	–

[f.23]

		£	s	d
9	pd Mr Richards, Pewterer[155] a Bill	10	10	–
–	Recd Rent from Sylvester a Quarter to Ladyday last	1	10	–
10	pd Tax for the Playhouse, ½ a year to Michs: last	15	–	–
31	Recd of my Bro: Charles for Dyet & Lodging for himself & Servants 5 months to the end of May last	41	15	–
–	Recd of ditto, Rent for the Stable 3 Qrs. to Michs: last	12	–	–
–	Recd of ditto. his Share of Rent for Greenh: house to Christs: last past	20	–	–
–	pd to ditto for Principal & Int. of a £2000 mortgage to Christs: last past	2100	–	–
–	Recd of ditto, upon Bond	1250	–	–
–	Recd ½ a years Salary at Greenh: to Michs: last	100	–	–
–	pd My Sisters Victoria, Eliz: and Robina in full discharge of the Principall of three Bonds for £100 each	300	–	–
–	pd ditto, in full for Int: and annuitys, to Christs: last past	37	6	–
–	Recd from ditto upon Bond, each £400	1200	–	–
–	pd Sisr: Mary in full for Int: and anuity to Christs: last past	13	–	–
–	House Bills this year in Towne	139	16	¾
–	Servants Bills of Disbursments	28	9	2
–	Spent in Small things	20	3	9
–	Given to Servants	7	3	–
–	pd House Bills at Greenwich	171	14	6
–	Spent in Other things relating to the house there	79	9	3

[f.24]

1718/19 Jan: January the First 1718/19

		£	s	d
1	Recd from Mr. Heydegger on Acct:	250	–	–
–	Recd upon the Excheqr: annuity for one year	10	–	–
30	Recd Rent from Fryar ½ a year to Midr: last	20	–	–
–	Out of Towne 46 nights Eating £23:13:3 Horses £18:2:2 To Servants £7:8:3 Extra[ordinar]y: Charges[156] £14:15:10	68	19	5
–	pd for things for Solomon & Will[157]	–	5	6
–	allow'd Mrs Floyds Expences	3	–	–
–	Wine to Sisr: Gars:	–	12	–
31	pd Poors Tax for the Playhouse ½ a year to Christs: last	10	–	–
–	pd Jack Postillion a Qrs Wages to ditto	1	5	–
–	*pd to Mrs Y*[158] Given my Wife	52	10	–
Feb.				
4	pd James, ¼ a Yrs Wages to Christs: last	2	10	–
5	allow'd fees at the Excheqr.	–	18	3
–	Recd a Quarters Excheqr Salary to Christ[mas] was 12 months	6	16	10½
7	pd a Slaters Bill at Greenwich	5	12	–
–	Paid Sisr: Betty	10	–	–
–	pd for a Tea Table £2:10:– Cups £1:7:– Pot £–:10:– Lamp &c £1:17:– Spoons £1:8:–	7	12	–
10	Recd from Mr Heydegger on acct:	100	–	–
12	pd Int: to Sisr: Gar. a Qr: to Christs: last	2	15	–

[154] Perhaps connected with his application to lease the Portland quarries (p.92, n.40).

[155] Cf. *Chandos*, p.197.

[156] Wedding expenses.

[157] Will Curtis. Solomon (ff.33, 36v, 42, 55v) was apprenticed on 25 Aug. 1722 but died at the end of March 1725; the other entries are for medical attention. There was a Solomon Garencieres in the next generation.

[158] Italic words deleted.

		£	s	d
11	pd Cozn: Vandebuss a years Int: to Christs: last	5	–	–
17	Recd from Mr Heydegger on Acct:	25	–	–
16	pd Trophy money for the year 1717	–	2	6
–	pd at Gumblys[159] for a Table & Glass	4	8	–
–	pd for Table Boxes £1:1:– for 2 sconces £ :3:–	1	4	–
–	pd for Tea, and Potts &c	1	10	6
18	pd Mr Spight of York, for the Hyre of a Coach[160]	13	18	–
–	pd for a Card Table	1	10	–

[f.24v]

		£	s	d
20	pd for a Guilt pan & Tongues for ye Tea Table	2	2	–
21	Recd from Greenh: Hospital attendance money to Michs: last	14	–	–
–	given Mr Walpoles Clark[161]	–	5	–
–	pd Hook the Bricklayer on acct:	10	–	–
24	pd Harrison the Joyner a Bill	1	18	6
26	pd Mr Billinghurst on acct: for Work done in the Haymarket	80	–	–
–	Recd of Mr Heydegger, in full for Rent to Michs: next	25	–	–
28	pd Saunders the Brewer a Bill in full to Chrs: last	17	6	6
March				
7	Given my Wife	52	10	–
10	Recd Rent for Greenh: house, a Year, to Midr: last	5	–	–
17	pd Mr Vallance for a New Periwig	7	7	–
18	pd the Minister of St James's, to Lady day next	1	–	–
23	pd Monsr Portailles a Bill for Wine	3	5	–
26	pd Jack Postillion a Qrs wages to this day	1	5	–
Aprill				
2	pd My Lady Biddulph, for half a years Rent to Lady day last past	8	–	–
–	pd for Delfware & Tea	–	17	6
–	pd Sisr: Garencieres a Quarters Int: to Lady day last, & £5 on acct of Principal	7	15	–
6	pd Morris, a bill in full for 20000 of Bricks	14	–	–
–	Recd of Monsr: Portailles half a years Rent for ye Chocolate Roome & vaults to Christ last	45	–	–
–	pd for a pair of half Jack boots, for the Postillion	1	3	–
–	pd for a Looking Glass	1	15	–
8	Recd Rent from Sylvester, ½ a year to Michs. last	3	–	–
–	pd Sigr: Haym[162] on a Subscription of 5 Gs. for a book of medals &	3	4	6
–	pd Mr Ayres a Bill for Coales, to Christs: last	20	1	–
8	pd Dr Bateman	1	1	–
–	pd Mr Hesleden a years Interest to Mayday next	3	10	–
9	pd Collinson, Upholsterer a Bill	2	–	–
–	pd the Scavenger a year	3	3	–
10	to Dr Bateman	1	1	–
11	To dto:	1	1	–
–	To Dr Chamberlain[163]	1	5	–
12	To Dr Bateman & Dr Chamb	2	2	–
13	To Dr: Bateman	1	1	–
–	Given Mr Jacob[164] for his Book	1	1	–

[f.25]

		£	s	d
14	To Mr Martin[165] for bleeding	–	10	6
–	To Dr Bateman	1	1	–
–	Recd for 8 Nights selling fruit at ye Playhouse[166]	8	8	–
18	pd for Guillm's display of Heraldry[167]	1	10	–
20	Recd Rent from Fryar, ½ a yr to Christs: last	20	–	–
23	Out of Towne one night	–	10	8
24	Recd Rent from Scullard, a Qr: to Chr: last	7	10	–
25	pd Mr Billinghurst on acct: for work at Greenwich	25	–	–
–	pd Brockwell at Greenh: for Hay, Straw & Grass	19	8	4
–	pd the Land Tax for Maze hill, ½ a year to L.day last	–	11	4
27	pd James Wood a Qrs: Wages to Lady day last	2	10	–
–	pd the Washerwomans Bill	8	–	–

[159] Eliza Gumley, glassware (*Chandos*, p.198); John Gumley supplied mirrors at Chatsworth in 1703 (F. Thompson, *A History of Chatsworth*, 1949, p.157).

[160] For the wedding.

[161] Galfridus, brother of Sir Robert Walpole (died 7 Aug. 1726), Postmaster General and Treasurer of Greenwich Hospital. A rather involved letter dated 21 Feb. 1728 from John Whormby to Charles Vanbrugh Esq., (Cambridge Univ. Library, Cholmondeley (Houghton) MSS, Correspondence, No.1598) explains a supposed discrepancy in the accounting of Vanbrugh's Greenwich salary 1717–19. The Account Book records the correct sequence of payments from Michaelmas 1717 to Michaelmas 1725, except that on f.55 he wrote *quarter* for *half*. Lady Vanbrugh's Account Book (p.50) records on 1 April 1731 the receipt of £100 'from Mr Gal. Walpoles executors being money due to Sr John.'

[162] Nicolo Haym, *Del Tesoro Britannico . . . overo il Museo Nummario; The British Treasury*; both London 1719–20.

[163] Hugh Chamberlain (1664–1728), male midwife, in succession to his father (DNB).

[164] Giles Jacob, author of numerous compendia on legal matters, also *The Compleat Sportsman*, 1718.

[165] Later *Monsr.* Martin (f.29v).

[166] Payment for trading franchise.

[167] John Guillim, *A Display of Heraldrie*, 1610; 5th ed. 1678–9.

– pd Tax for the Highways at the Haymart: a year to Lady day last   – 15 –
– pd for a Reference at the Treasury   1 1 –

May

1 Rd. Rent from Col: Godolphin ½ a year, to Lady D last   31 10 –
– pd Edward Cliff, Smith, a Bill   1 16 –
– pd Tax for ye Playhouse ½ a yr to Lady day last   15 – –
– pd Sarah Godwin, a Yrs Wages to Chrs: last   4 – –
– Given her over   – 4 –
– pd Mr. Bridges in full of a Bill   32 12 –
4 pd Wigzell at Greenh: a Bill for Corn   19 8 –
6 pd Huddleston, on acct: of Carpenters work at ye Haymart   15 – –
– Recd from the Heralds College Fees for Lord Sherwood, Vicount £1:12:6 Sr Lambert Blackwell & Sr Adolphus Oughton. Barts: £2:3:4 Sr Jo. Fellows Bart: £1:1:8 Sr Patrick Strahan Sr Jo: Askew Knts. £1:18:8 Duchess of Munster Barroness & Countess £7:16:–[168]   14 12 2
9 pd Mr Richards. Pewterer a Bill   – 12 –
10 pd Sisr: Vic: a Qrs. Int. &c to Lady day last   10 – –
– To dto: for her Journey   5 5 –
11 pd Mrs Graham for 10 ells of Holland £2:15:– for a Yard of Lace £2:18:–   5 13 –
– pd Jack Postillion a Qrs Wages to Christs: last   1 5 –
15 Out of Towne 4 Nights. 5 Horses £1:15:– Farrier &c £ :4:–   1 19 –
– meat and Lodging   4 11 8
– other Expences   0 16 –
– Tea cups   1 6 6
16 To Dr Bateman   1 1 –
18 To Monsr: Lioni, for ye 4th Book of Palladio   1 1 –

[f.25v]

18 Recd from the Heralds College Fees for [blank]   16 5 –
20 Recd of Brandish on acct: of Rent   5 5 –
20 pd for Cloaths for Niece Bin to this day   11 1 –
– pd Sisr: Gars: on acct: of Principall   10 – –
– pd Sisr: Robina for ½ a yrs Int & anuity to Midsr: next   20 – –
– pd Sisr: Betty for ½ a yrs Int: to dto: 10 – –
– Given her   10 – –
– Given her & Sisr. Bin for their Journey to Norwich   8 10 –
21 Recd Rent from Scullard a Qr: to Lady day last   7 10 –
– allow'd Taxes to dto: 1 10 4
– pd Window Tax for ye Playhouse a yr to Ladyday last   1 10 –
22 Recd of Mr Secretary Craggs[169] in full for Rent for Hampton Court house   50 – –
– pd Mary Whitwood a Years wages due the 12th of March last   5 – –
– pd for Cloath for Towells   – 8 –
– pd for a Fire Shovell Tongs. &c   – 15 6
– pd for a pair of Candlesticks   – 10 –
– pd for Lamps   1 5 –
– pd for Patty pans   – 5 –
– pd for Juggs, Basins, pans &c   – 9 6
– pd for Pyrmont Water[170]   1 13 –
27 pd Mr Sly a Bill for Hatts   3 15 –
– pd Goulston the Farrier in part of a Bill   20 – –
– pd Mr Doily for Stuff for a Coat   – 16 6
– pd Mr Chaffey a Bill for Hay & Straw   22 18 9
– Recd of ditto a years Rent due at Ladyday last   16 5 –
28 pd White the Taylor on account   20 – –
– pd for a Lottery Ticket   3 2 6
– for a Trunck   – 10 –

June

9 Out of Towne 7 nights. 4 horses   4 12 0
13 pd Mrs Wright a Bill for Carriage of bricks &c   12 17 –
16 Recd for a Gold Snuff box   8 11 –
– pd for 20 Ells. of Holland for sheets   4 – –
– pd for 10 Ells for 3 Shirts   2 15 –
18 pd Stevens the Shoemaker a Bill in full   2 16 –

[f.26]

19 Recd from the Office of Works a Qrs. Salary to Lady day was twelve month   174 17 8
– pd Taxes as Compt: to dto: 18 5 7½
– Gave ye Paymasters Clark   – 5 –
– Recd for a Coach horse   10 10 –
– Given my Wife   10 10 –
– pd Hook the Bricklayer on acct: 10 10 –
– pd for a Doily Table Cloath   – 4 6
20 pd Mrs Ruffle a Bill for Corn, to Christs: last   10 17 –
23 pd Mr Bonfoy a Bill for Table Linnen   8 11 –
– pd John Brookes at Greenwich on acct: for Lime   26 5 –

[168] 1st Viscount Sherard of Stapleford. Sir Lambert Blackwell, Bt, of Sprowston, Norfolk, diplomat. Sir Adolphus Oughton, Bt, of Tachbrook. Sir John Fellows, Bt, of Carshalton, South Sea Company. Sir Patrick Stra(c)han of Glenkindy, Barrack Master General in Scotland. Sir John Askew, Sheriff of Wilts. Baroness von der Schulenberg, George I's mistress, Duchess of Munster and later of Kendal.

[169] James Craggs the Younger (1686–1721), Secretary of State.

[170] Bad Pyrmont, Principality of Waldeck, popularized by George I. Cf. *Chandos,* p.111.

		£	s	d
–	Given a Gratuity for ye Copy of a Deed	2	2	–
–	pd Mr Tonson for Priors Works[171]	1	10	–
July				
2	To Mr Brown ye Surgeon	5	5	–
–	pd Mr Scott a Bill for Bricks	26	18	–
–	pd Monsr: Dorigny.[172] in full for a set of the Cartoon prints	3	3	–
7	pd James Wood a Qrs Wages to Midr. last	2	10	–
–	out of Towne 2 Nights 3 Horses £– 17.4 Servt £–5:	1	2	4
8	Out of Towne 2 Nights 3 horses £–14:– Servant £–3–	–	17	–
13	Recd half a Years Salary as Surveyr of Greenh: Hospitall, to Lady day last	100	–	–
–	Recd attendance money to ditto	11	–	–
–	Gave Mr Walpoles Clark	–	5	–
15	pd Huddleston the Carpenter in full	23	2	–
17	pd Godfrey, Coachmaker on acct:	10	10	–
18	pd Rent for Greenwich House, a year, to Lady day last	40	–	–
20	pd Savage the Plumber on Acct. for Work done at Greenwich	21	–	–
	Memd: I let my house at Hampton Court to Mr Fort,[173] for £50 a year; to commence from midsumer last			
–	Recd one years allowance towards Rent at Greenwich to Lady day last	30	–	–
–	Gave the Clark	–	2	6
23	pd Barret on Acct: for Bricks	50	–	–
–	pd The Tayler at Greenwich a Bill	3	–	–
Augt:				
6	pd Poors Tax at the Playhouse half a year to Midr: last	10	–	–
–	pd for Lace for three Shirts	3	7	6

[f.26v]

		£	s	d
6	From the Office of Works a Quarter due at Midsr: 1718	175	16	–
–	Gave the Paymasters Clark	–	5	–
–	pd Taxes a Qr to Midr: 1718	17	12	1
–	pd for Christs: Gratuity	–	7	4
8	To Dr Chamberlain & Midwife[174]	4	9	–
11	pd Mr Billinghurst on acct: for Work at Greenwich	25	–	–
13	Recd of Mrs Heard for one years Rent due at Midsumr: last	6	–	–
–	pd Sisr: Mary for half a years Int. & annuity to midr. last	13	–	–
17	pd Int: to Sisr: Gar: a Quarter to Midr: last	2	10	–
21	pd the Minister of St James's a year to Lady day last	1	1	–
–	pd Customs and other Charges for half a pipe[175] of Mountain Malaga	9	9	–
22	pd Sisr: Victoria, one Qrs. Int. & annuity to Midr. last	10	–	–
25	pd Mr Wooley a Years Ground Rent to Christs: last	50	–	–
–	Recd Rent for Kensington House. a Year & half to Lady Day last	90	–	–
–	Recd from the Heralds College half a years Salary to Midr: 1718	20	–	–
–	pd Taxes & fees	7	12	6
–	From dto fee for Earl Coningsby[176]	2	3	4
Sept.				
2	Out of Towne 8 Nights. 3 horses £1 9.7 Serts: &c £2.3.5	3	13	–
4	pd Marchant for Water a year & quarter to Midr: last	5	–	–
–	pd Mr Kynaston,[177] for his Disbursments at Hartleys for the four last Quarters to Midsr last	4	4	–
–	pd Mr Lowe, for 20400 of White Bricks	42	17	–
8	Out of Towne 2 Nights 2 Horses £–10.7 Servts: £–2.6	–	13	1
12	pd James Ewin Tayler	–	9	–
–	pd John Handcase in full for Wages	2	10	–
–	Given him over	–	5	–
16	pd John Darwell a Bill for Washing	4	5	–
–	pd Ditto for Small disbursments about the Playhouse &c	1	5	–
–	Recd of ditto one year's Rent to Lady day last	6	–	–

[f.27]

		£	s	d
17	pd Mary Whitwood in full for wages	2	10	–
–	Given her over	–	7	6
18	pd Sarah Hook in full	6	6	–
19	pd Mr Billinghurst on acct: for Work at Greenh:	20	–	–

[171] See n.118.

[172] Nicolas Dorigny (1658–1746) began work in 1711 on a set of engravings after the Raphael Cartoons of the Acts of the Apostles, then in the gallery built for them at Hampton Court. The set was published in 1719 with a dedication to George I. Three years later Dorigny published ninety heads from the Cartoons, dedicated to the Prince of Wales.

[173] Thomas Fort, Clerk of Works at Hampton Court.

[174] 'I have been two days at Claremont, but not en Famille, a Bit of a Girle popping into the World, three months before its time' (11 Aug. 1719; Webb, p.116).

[175] A pipe is usually two hogsheads or 105 imperial gallons (SOED).

[176] Thomas Coningsby, 1st Earl Coningsby.

[177] Vanbrugh's clerk (see p.80).

– Out of Towne 1 night 3 Horses. £–6:–6 Servt £–:1:–6 — – 8 –
24 Out of Towne 3 nights 5 Horses £– 4: 6 Serts: £–12:– — – 16 6
– Given to Serts: at Sr John Jennings[178] — 3 4 6
25 pd Mr Richards a Bill for hatts — 8 17 –
28 pd Elias Wood Lime Man On Acct. — 15 15 –
– pd Davis the Waterman a Bill — 1 16 3
– pd for a Gold Watch Chain — 6 – –

Octr.

5 Out of Towne one night two Horses &c — – 5 11
7 pd Mrs Clark for Camlet[179] from Norwich — 17 11 –
– pd at Hartleys, Michs: Qr last — 1 1 –
8 pd Mr Sly for a Hatt — 1 1 –
24 Out of Towne 15 days 5 Horses £9:12:– Servants &c £16:2:– — 25 14 –
26 Out of Towne one Night 4 horses £–:10:10 Servts: £–:2:6 — – 13 4

Nov:

3 pd Poors Tax at Greenh: a year to Lady day Next — 3 8 –
4 Recd from the office of Works, on acct: of Michaelmass Qr. 1718 — 150 – –
5 Recd from the Heralds College, half a Years Salary to Chr: last — 20 – –
– allow'd Taxes & Fees — 7 12 6
– Recd Towards Rent at Greenh: half a year to Michs: last — 15 – –
– Gave the Clark — – 2 6
6 pd Int: to Sisr: Gars: a Quarter to Michs: last — 2 11 3
7 pd The Executors of Baldwin, Coachmaker in full — 47 9 –
10 Recd Excheqr Salary a year to Christs: last — 27 7 6
– allow'd Fees — 3 2 9
11 pd Sisr: Vict. a Qrs: Int: to Michs: last — 10 – –
16 pd Mrs Wright on acct: for Carriage of Bricks — 10 10 –
– Recd Rent for the Field at Greenh: ½ a year to Michs: last — 2 10 –
20 pd Wall ye Shoemaker for 2 pr of Shoes — – 14 6
– Given Charity — 1 1 –
– Out of Towne one night two Horses — – 7 –
21 Recd Rent from Fryar a Qr. to Lady day last — 10 – –
– pd Unwood [?] a bill for Sugar — 4 7 –
25 pd Mrs Ruffle on Acct: — 10 10 –
– pd James Wood a Qrs Wages to Michs: last — 2 10 –

[f.27v]

Dec.

5 Recd of Mr Heydegger on Acct: of Rent for This year, beginning at Michs. last — 52 10 –
7 Recd Rent from Monsr; Portales half a year to Midsumr: last — 45 5 –
– pd to ditto. a Bill for Wine — 14 13 6
8 Recd from the Office of Works, in full of Michs: Quarter 1718 — 28 4 –
– Gave ye Paymasters Clark — – 5 –
– pd Taxes a Qr: to Michs 1718 — 11 19 6
– pd on a Subscription to Mr Addisons Works[180] — 1 1 –
– Given Charity — 1 1 –
14 Out of Towne one night & a bait 2 horses £– 6.8 Sert £– 1.6 — – 8 2
– Gave my Wife — 26 5 –
17 pd Goulston the Farrier a Bill in full — 21 10 6
– pd in part of the Sadlers Bill — 8 8 –
19 pd on the Subscription to the Academy of musick[181] — 10 – –
21 pd for the Highways at Greenh: a year to Christs: next — – 9 –
– Recd from Mr Heydegger on Acct: for Rent — 52 10 –
22 pd Hutchinson in full for Shoes — 1 7 –
23 pd Lady Biddulph ½ a yrs Rent, to Michs: last — 8 – –
26 pd Mrs Wright in full of a Bill for Carriage — 11 18 –
28 pd Sanham the Greenh: Farriar a Bill in full — 1 18 –
30 pd Knight the Slater a Bill for Work at Greenh: — 4 7 6
31 pd James Wood a Quarters wages to Christs. last — 2 10 –
– Gave him over — – 2 6
– pd Martha Bowles a Years wages to ye 13th of Feb: last, and gave her over 5s. in all — 4 10 –
– pd John Westbrook for Wages due at Christ: past — 1 11 –

[178] Newsellsbury, Herts. Sir John Jennings (1664–1743), admiral, Governor of Greenwich Hospital 1720. Vanbrugh's cousin by marriage to daughter of Francis (d.1688) Breton.

[179] Camlet, originally costly Eastern fabric, subsequently substitutes made of various combinations of wool, silk, hair; latterly of cotton or linen (SOED). A Mrs Clark was housekeeper to Vanbrugh's aunt Mary Pearce of Norwich (p.156, n.39). The journey recorded on 24 October was to East Anglia: on 5 November Vanbrugh wrote that he had been recently at Culford, which is north-west of Bury St Edmunds (Webb, p.120) and was the seat of Lord Cornwallis (1675–1722), a Kit-Cat member.

[180] Quarto edition, Tonson, 1721.

[181] The Royal Academy of Music was founded in the middle of 1719 as a subscribing body for staging Italian opera at the Haymarket Theatre. Lord Burlington was the chief mover, subscribing (like the Dukes of Newcastle and Chandos) £1000. The musical directors were Handel, and Bononcini who was later replaced by Ariosti (see n.394). By 1729 the Academy was bankrupt, in spite of continual calls on the subscribers, and partly through a change in public taste and the success of the *Beggar's Opera* in Jan. 1728. Vanbrugh is not among the subscribers listed in PRO LC7/3, f.63, but as a Director he attended meetings on 30 Nov. and 2 Dec. 1719 (single sheet of minutes, ibid., f.71).

– pd Sarah. a years wages to Chrs: past & gave her over 4s. 4 4 –
– pd Taxes for the Playhouse, $\frac{1}{2}$ a year to Michs: last 18 15 –
– pd The Washerwomans Bill 13 7 –
– pd Coz: Garencieres a Bill[182] 7 7 –
– pd the Powder Bill 3 12 –
– pd Poors Tax for the Playhouse $\frac{1}{2}$ a year to Christs: last 10 – –
– pd White the Tayler on acct: 25 – –
– pd Sanders the Brewer a Bill in full 12 16 –

[f.28]

31 pd my Brother Charles in full for Principal and Int: of a Bond for £1250 1312 10 –
– pd House Bills this year, in London and Greenwich 292 19 –
– Other things at Greenh: not entred in particular 48 2 11
– Servants Bills of Disbursments 37 3 $7\frac{3}{4}$
– Spent in Small Things 17 16 1
– Recd of my Brother Charles, on a Mortgage at Greenh: 2000 – –
– pd Sisr: Robina for $\frac{1}{2}$ a years Int: & Annuity to Christs. last past 20 – –
– pd: Sisr: Betty for a $\frac{1}{2}$ years Int: to ditto 10 – –
– pd them both, in Discharge of their Bonds of £400 each 800 – –

[f.28v]

December 31st: 1719

Memd On the 6th of October last I sign'd Leases to John Potter Carpenter of 5 houses in the Haymarket; before inhabited by; Fryar, Scullard, Rice, Sells and Brandish.

The Leases are for ye 1st. house pr Anm.	£20	–	–
ye 2nd	£13	–	–
ye 3d	£13	–	–
ye 4th	£13	–	–
ye 5th	£17	–	–
	£76	–	–

The Term 46 years, 2 months & 20 days, to Commence from Midsummer 1719.
The Rent to Commence from Christs: 1719 Free of all Taxes whatever.
Memd. On the 7th of October last I sign'd an Instrument to my Brother Charles in Trust for my Sisters, Elizath: And Robina, wherin I make over for their use for Life, the Abovesaid Rents of £76 p Anm: in consideration of £400. Each, Rec'd from them.
Memd: on the last day of December 1719 Having discharg'd A Bond to my Brother Charles, for £1250, I Borrowed of him £2000, for Security of which I Mortgaged to him the Castle &c at Greenwich.

[f.29]

1719/20 January ye 1st: 1719/20

Recd of my Sisrs: Betty & Robina for Rents in the Haymarket made over to them for their Lives 800 – –

Jany.

9 Out of Towne 1 Night. 4 horses £– 9.10 Servts. £–3.2 – 13 –
13 Recd Int: on the Excheqr Annuity to this day 10 7 1
– Recd for the Sale of the said Annuity at $21\frac{1}{4}$ yrs Purchace 212 10 –
– pd Charges on the Sale – 6 6
14 pd Mary Ward in full for Wages 1 15 5
16 pd Barret on Acct: for Bricks 50 – –
15 pd at Hartleys a Qr: to Chrs: last 1 1 –
19 pd Mr: Bonfoy a Bill for Linnen 15 – –
22 Recd Salary at Greenh: $\frac{1}{2}$ a year to Michs: last 100 – –
– gave the Treasurers Clark – 5 –
– pd Mr Wray a Bill for beer & Ale 5 12 –
– pd Mrs Ruffle in full of a Bill for Corn 12 8 –
25 Recd of Coll: Godolphin, in part of Rent due 45 – –
– pd Mr Groves,[183] on acct: for Carpenters work done at Greenh: 50 – –
26 pd Middleton a Bill 3 19 –
– pd Cox the Upholsterer a Bill 26 5 –
28 pd for a pair of Buckskin britches for John Westbrook 1 1 –
– Recd on Acct: of Rent from Mr Heydegger 95 – –
Memd: I this day sign'd a Mortgage of the Buildings &c on Maze hill[184] to my Brother Charles for £2000. the Int: to Commence from ye 1st of Jany. last
29 To Dr Johnson[185] 1 1 –

Feb.

1 Out of Towne one night. 2 Horses &c – 6 –
5 pd for Stuff for a Gowne for Martha[186] 1 10 –

[182] Athanasius (see p.157).

[183] James Grove.

[184] This marks the initial completion of Vanbrugh Castle.

[185] Later Johnston (f.29v).

[186] Martha Bowles.

– pd for Cloath for Towells, &c	1	17	–
6 pd Savage, the Plumber on Acct:	21	–	–

[f.29v]

8 pd Mathews the Plumber on Acct for Work done at Greenh:	21	–	–
– pd Sisr: Victoria; a Quarters Int. to Chrs: last	10	–	–
– pd Sisr: Mary half a yrs: Int: to Chrs: last	13	–	–
12 pd Atha[nasiu]s: Garencieres a Bill	1	18	–
– pd Sisr: Garencieres on acct of Principall £5. The Remainder now due on the Bond for Principal being £200	5	–	–
14 To Monsr: Martin for bleeding my Wife	–	10	6
16 pd Coz: Vandebuss a Yrs Int: to Christ: last	5	–	–
23 pd Mr Birch the Appothecary a bill	–	18	8
– Given Seigr: Lioni, on the Delivery of his last Book, being over and above my Subscription	1	1	–
25 Memd. I this day Sign'd a Lease of the Chocolate House & Vaults, to Mr Portalles for 3 Years & half to Commence from Christs: last, at £90 a Yr.			
– pd Mr Haym, on the Subscription for his Book of Medals, ye 2d. Vo.[187]	1	1	–
26 Recd from Mr Heydegger on Acct of Rent	100	–	–
27 pd Mr Gilham on Acct: of Joyners work at Greenwich	72	–	–
– pd Mrs Wright on acct:	10	10	–

March

1 pd Francis Beale a Bill for Bricks	10	2	–
– To Dr Johnston	1	1	–
2 Recd from Mr Heydegger in full for Rent to Michs: next	100	–	–
3 Charges on Qualifying	–	12	–
4 pd Trophy money for ye year 1718	–	2	6

[f.30]

March

4 pd Gale the Upholsterer a Bill	28	7	–
11 pd Mr Brooks on acct for Lime	21	–	–
– pd for mending the Calesh at Greenh:	1	–	–
– pd Land Tax, for the Field &c on Maze hill a Year; to Lady day next	1	2	8
14 out of Towne 2 Nights. 2 horses. 11s Servants 3–	–	14	–
15 pd Mr Edes a bill for Bricks	–	8	9
16 pd My Sisr: Garencieres ½ a Years Int: to Lady day next	6	1	6
– pd Mr Pemble,[188] apothecary at Greenh: 2 Bills	3	4	6
– pd Davis ye Waterman a Bill	1	11	6
17 pd Mr Demetrius[189] for 4 peices of Tapistry	18	–	–

April

1 pd Mr Hesleden a yrs Int: to May next	3	10	–
2 Recd half a years allowance towards Rent at Greenwich, to Lady day last	15	–	–
– Gave the Clark	–	2	6
– pd James Wood. a Qrs. Wages to Lady day last	2	10	–
– pd Cuffs the Ipswich Hoyman for freight of Bricks &c	1	13	–
– Recd Fee for a Grant of Arms to Taylor[190]	15	–	–
– Gratuity to Mr Hesket[191]	1	1	–
4 Recd Fee for a Grant to Frampton[192]	15	–	–
– Gratuity to Mr Green[193]	1	1	–
– pd Sr Wm Saunderson in full for Rent	40	–	–
– To Dr Johnston	1	1	–
5 Recd Fee for a Grant to the Bishop of Bristol[194]	15	–	–
– Gratuity to Mr Hare[195]	1	1	–
– pd Mr Groves on account	50	–	–
6 pd John Westbrook a Qrs: Wages to Lady day last	1	5	–
7 pd Mr Barret on acct: for Bricks	50	–	–
– Recd Fee for a Grant to Wise[196]	15	–	–
– Gratuity to Mr Bound[197]	1	1	–
8 pd at Hartleys a Qr: to Lady day last	1	1	–
– Recd Fee for a Grant to Pearce[198]	15	–	–

187 See n.161.

188 Later surgeon.

189 Probably Abraham of Laurence Pountney Lane, born 24 Nov. 1680 (DCR) to Daniel and Maria; executor to Anna Maria Van den Bush 1755 (p.150, nn.173–4).

190 Joseph Taylor, Sandford, Oxon.

191 John Heskett (Hesketh), Lancaster Herald, resigned 18 May 1727 (Godfrey, p.139).

192 Matthew Frampton, M.D., Oxford.

193 James Green, Bluemantle Poursuivant, 24 June 1719–4 Sept. 1737 (Godfrey, p.200).

194 Dr Hugh Boulter.

195 John Hare, Richmond Herald, d.14 May 1720 (Godfrey, p.147).

196 Henry Wise, H.M. Master Gardener, Brompton Park.

197 John Bound, Rouge Croix Poursuivant, d.March 1721 (Godfrey, p.215).

198 Nathaniel Goldson Pearce, London.

Day	Entry	£	s	d
	Gratuity to Mr Mauduit[199]	1	1	–
–	Recd Rent for the field ½ a year to ladyday last	2	10	–
8	Given to Nieces Van.[200]	10	10	–
9	pd Wood, a Bill in full for Lime	16	5	–

[f.30v]

Day	Entry	£	s	d
11	pd Mr Carey, a Bill for Port Wine	4	17	6
15	pd Trout at Greenwich, a bill for Hay, Straw & grazing to Christs: last	19	17	6
–	pd Window Tax at Greenh. a yr: to Lady day last	1	10	–
16	pd Steel, Joyner a bill	1	11	6
–	pd Mrs Wright, in full of a Bill for Carriage of Bricks &c	4	6	6
18	out of Towne 1 Night 2 horses	–	6	6
25	Recd Rent from Sylvester 3 Qrs to Midr: last	4	10	–
–	Recd Rent for Kensington House, a year to Lady day last	60	–	–
–	pd on the Subscription to the Academy of Mus[ic]k	10	–	–
26	Recd of Mrs Wiseman of Cambridg,[201] in full discharge of all demands	10	–	–
27	pd Mallory a Bill for Livery Lace	14	12	–
–	out of Towne a Bait, 2 horses	–	7	6
28	pd the Scavenger a year to Lady day last	3	3	–
–	Re'd Fee for a Grant to Paggen[202]	15	–	–
–	Gratuity to Mr Hare	1	1	–
29	pd Mr Portailles a bill for Wine	3	18	–
–	Recd of ditto half a years Rent to Christs: last	45	–	–
–	pd a Plumbers bill for work at dto:	1	5	–
30	pd Joseph Roberts. a Bill for Turf	1	11	6
–	pd Mathews the Plumber in full of a Bill	8	1	9
–	pd dto: in full of an other Bill	4	15	3
–	pd Mr Wetherhilt on Acct: for work at Greenwich	21	–	–

May

Day	Entry	£	s	d
2	pd Elizh: Ransford in full for Wages &c	2	12	6
–	pd Mary Rooth in full for dto: to Midr: next	5	5	–
–	To my Wife for Sheets &c	15	15	–
–	pd Sisr: Vic: a Qrs. Int: & Anuity to Lady day last	10	–	–
7	pd Coz: G. Vanbrugh[203] for disbursmts: of his for Wine &c	9	12	–
–	pd for a Carpet	3	10	–
–	Recd of A B	57	12	0

[f.31]

Day	Entry	£	s	d
15	To Dr Chamberlain	1	1	–
–	Recd Fee for a Grant to Nicolls[206]	15	–	–
–	Gratuity to Mr. Bound	1	1	–
–	Out of Towne one night. 2 horses	–	6	10
16	Given	1	7	–
21	pd Athas. Garencieres a Bill	3	3	–
–	pd Mrs Wright in part of a Bill	10	10	–
24	To Mr Tonson on a Subscription for Miltons Works[204]	1	1	–
–	Pd at Doileys for Stuff for Two Suits	3	10	–
–	Out of Towne one Night & a bait. 4 horses	–	17	2
26	pd Mrs Ruffle on Acct: for Corn	15	15	–
27	pd for the Highways a year to Lady day last	–	15	–
–	pd Mrs Stevens Washerwoman in full	11	1	–
30	pd for Two Carpets	8	–	–
–	Recd of my Bro: Charles, on Acct: for the Purchase of the Playhouse[205]	2406	–	–

June

Day	Entry	£	s	d
2	Recd for a Grant to Pulse[206]	15	–	–
–	Gratuity to Mr Green	1	1	–
4	pd for Asses milk	5	6	–
–	Two Knights fees	1	18	8
–	pd upon Two Subscriptions in the South Sea[207]	2000	–	–
6	Recd for a Grant to Merry[208]	15	–	–

199 Piers Mauduit, Windsor Herald, resigned 3 Dec. 1726 (Godfrey, p.176).

200 Robina and Elizabeth, orphans of Kenrick (see p.170).

201 See f.35v: ? Thomas Wiseman, painter, later J.P. and Mayor of Cambridge. Monument in St Andrew the Great (1693–1764).

202 Peter Paggen, Wandsworth.

203 George Vanbrugh, wine merchant (see p.161).

204 *Poetical Works*, quarto, 1720.

205 *Survey of London*, XXIX, 1960, p.225.

206 John Nicoll, Colney Hatch, Middx.; James Pulse, Westminster.

207 Mid-June 1720 was the high point of the South Sea Company speculation or Bubble. The crash came in the autumn with a suddenness that surprised all but the luckiest or canniest speculators. While there were many cases of hardship and some of ruin, some of the losses were no more real than the gains which preceded them and existed only in promises. The South Sea Company remained in existence to pay dividends on the annuity granted by the Government as interest on the payment of the National Debt. See J. Carswell, *The South Sea Bubble*, 1961.

208 Capt. John Merrye, Whitby, Yorks., Barton, Derbys., and London.

		£	s	d
–	Gratuity to Mr Mauduit	1	1	–
–	Recd for a Crest to [blank]	5	–	–
–	Gratuity to Mr Mauduit	–	7	–
–	Recd for a Grant to Ongley[209]	15	–	–
–	Gratuity to Mr Bound	1	1	–
–	pd the Minister at Greenh: for Easter offering	1	1	–
9	pd the first paymt: on a Subscription for two Volumes of the Monasticon[210]	1	1	–
11	pd for a Hogshead of Cyder	3	17	–
20	Out of Towne 4 horses 1 Night & a Bait	–	16	–
25	Out of Towne a Bait 4 horses	–	5	6
–	Dto	–	6	–
26	pd James Wood a Qrs wages to Midr: last	2	10	–
30	pd for a Night Gowne & Sash	2	7	–
July				
2	Recd for a Grant to Lamborn[209]	15	–	–
–	Gratuity to Mr Hesket	1	1	–
–	pd Land Tax for the Playhouse a yr. to L.day	15	15	–
–	pd Poors Tax for dto a year to Midr. last	10	–	–
–	pd Barret for Bricks on account	50	–	–

[f.31v]

		£	s	d
–	pd Sisr: Gars: a Qrs: Int: to Midr: last	2	10	–
2	pd Mr Hysing for Copying two Pictures[211]	6	6	–
–	pd on Acct: of the Copper Bubble[212]	250	–	–
12	Out of Towne 9 Nights: 4 horses Horses £3:18.9 Servts &c £3:15.10 Horse hyre £1:5:–	[8	19	7]
–	Given Brother Phill's Children[213]	1	11	6
14	pd for things sent to the Children at Heslington[213]	2	10	–
–	pd. Sisr: Victoria, in full discharge of her Bond for £400. Principal & Intrest	410	–	–
–	Given her	9	–	–
–	pd for running of 6 Neckcloaths	–	6	–
–	Recd for a Grant to Raper[214]	15	–	–
–	Gratuity to Mr Green	1	1	–
16th	pd John Westbrook in full for Wages to Michs: next £1.5 Given him for his Old Coat £–:5:– Given him over £–:4:–	1	14	–
20	Recd for a Grant to Dominic[215]	15	–	–
–	Gratuity to Mr Mawson	1	1	–
21	pd at Hartleys a Qr: to Midr: last	1	1	–
–	Recd from the Heralds College Fees, for the Duke of Dorset Duke of Bridgewater & Marquiss of Brackley Viscount Falmouth & Baron Boscawen Viscount Limington & Baron Wallop Baron Ducie 3 Barronets 2 Knights[216]	24	5	2
24	Out of Towne one Night 4 horses Horses 7.6 Sert 3	–	10	6

[f.32]

		£	s	d
25	To Lord Aylmer's Bardgmen[217]	1	3	6
–	pd Loss on Insurance of the Playhouse this last time	8	14	1
28	Recd from the Board of Works a Years Salary to Michs: last	713	15	–
–	Allow'd Taxes &c to dto	71	18	–½
–	gave ye Paymasters Clark & Servant	1	11	6
–	pd the Sadlers Bill in full	3		
–	pd Mrs Wright for Carriage of bricks in full of a Bill	6	1	–
–	pd Wallis the Gardener	1	7	–
30	pd Mr Groves on Acct:	50	–	–
–	pd Mrs Wright for Carriage a Bill in full	8	7	–
–	pd Lady Biddulph for half a years Rent to Lady day last	8	–	–
–	pd Daws the Smith on Acct:	10	–	–
Augt:				
3	pd White the Taylor in full of Two Bills, to ye last of December 1719	40	10	6
–	pd Hardy, a Bill for Ale	6	18	8
4	pd: Halbout, for putting up bells at Grh:	2	17	6
6	pd: for 2 dozen of Delf Plates &c	1	–	6
–	Recd for a Grant of Arms to Roberts[218]	15	–	–
–	Gratuity to Mr Green	1	1	–

209 Sir Samuel Ongley, London. Richard Lamborn, Greenwich.

210 (Dugdale) John Stevens, *The history of the Ancient Abbeys, etc.*, 1722–3.

211 Hans Hysing, born Stockholm 1678, died London 1752/3. Came to London *c.*1700 worked with, and followed the style of, his compatriot Michael Dahl. In 1721 he married a Frances Breton (both of St Anne, Soho) at St Benet, Paul's Wharf (*Harl. Soc., Register Series*, XXXIX). She may have been related to Vanbrugh.

212 The year 1720 had seen a mania for new commercial schemes, serious, preposterous and ultimately satirical. Credit and the joint stock company were new inventions. Vanbrugh seems to have been fairly cautious in investment. See Carswell, op.cit.

213 Phil's children: Giles Richard and Philippa Vanbrugh (see p.172). Heslington was Lady Vanbrugh's family home.

214 William Raper, Oundle, Northants.

215 Andrew Dominick, Great Marlow, Bucks. and Stratfieldsaye, Hants.

216 1st Duke of Dorset (1688–1765); Kit-Cat. Scroop Egerton, 5th Earl of Bristol, Marquess of Brackley and 1st Duke of Bridgewater. Hugh Boscawen, Baron of Boscawen Rose and Viscount Falmouth. John Wallop, Baron Wallop and Viscount Lymington, later 1st Earl of Portsmouth. Matthew Ducie Moreton, Lord Ducie, Baron of Moreton, Staffs.

217 1st Baron Aylmer; Governor of Greenwich Hospital 1714–20.

218 John Roberts, Stepney and Radnorshire.

		£	s	d
8	Recd for two Grants, to Surman & Bodicoate[219]	30	–	–
–	Gratuity to Mr. Hesket	2	2	–
–	pd: on a Call of 4 pr Cent to the Copper bubble	40	–	–
–	pd Mr Wood in full of a Bill for Lime	33	4	–
–	pd ye Keepers for a Buck from Haland[220]	1	1	–
10	Recd of John Darwell a years Rent to L.day last	6	–	–
–	Out of Towne 1 night 2 Horses & Servts:	–	7	–
–	Recd of my Bro: Charles on Acct. of the Purchace of ye Playhouse	200	–	–
–	pd at the Copper office upon a Transfer	–	11	8
13	pd Mr Billinghurst on Acct. for work at Greenwich	50	–	–
–	pd for 15 Flasks of Claret	1	17	6
16	pd Clark the Painter for work done at Greenwich on Acct.	10	10	–
17	pd Mr Billinghurst & Partner in full for Work done at the Theatre in the Haymarket	52	12	–
	[f.32v]			
17	pd Mr Billinghurst and Partner in full of Two Bills for Work done at Whitehall. vizt. £48:18:$7\frac{3}{4}$ £7:16:10[221]	56	15	$5\frac{3}{4}$
29	Out of Towne 12 Nights 4 Horses Horses £5.2:9 Servants £1:11:– Smith £–:2:6 Sadler £–:7:6 Given to Serts: £1:16:– Horse hyre £1.5:–	10	4	9
–	Recd from the Heralds College $\frac{3}{4}$ a yrs Salary to Michs: 1719	30	–	–
–	allow'd Taxes & Fees	11	8	9
	Sept:			
2	Charity	1	1	–
3	pd on a Parish Assessment at Greenwich	–	8	–
5	pd Rivers[222] the Gardener a Bill	1	6	6
7	Recd for a Grant of Arms to Burdu[223]	15	–	–
–	Gratuity to Mr Mawson	1	1	–
–	Recd for Two Grants to Lansdel & Fisher[224]	30	–	–
–	Gratuity to Mr Green	2	2	–
–	pd Mr Barret on account for Bricks	50	–	–
–	pd Mr Arbunot a Bill for Looking Glasses	3	16	–

		£	s	d
–	pd Mr Vallance for a Periwig	7	7	–
–	pd Mr Bonfoy a Bill	20	14	–
–	pd Mr Ayre a Bill for Coals	28	15	–
–	pd a Bill for Mum[225]	1	15	–
9	pd Mr Booth a Bill for Smiths Work	5	1	–
10	pd Sisr: Gars: for a Qrs: Int to Michs: next	2	10	–
–	pd at Greenh: for 60 Flasks of French Wine & 3 Galls: of Brandy	8	14	–
–	pd Fee for a Buck from Haland	1	1	–
12	pd Mr Weeks, Mercer, a Bill	6	3	–
–	Recd Excheqr Salary $\frac{3}{4}$ to Michs: 1719	20	10	$7\frac{1}{2}$
–	allow'd Fees for Dto:	2	14	9
–	pd for a New Belt	1	1	–
17	pd a Joyners Bill for a Table &c	1	5	–
–	pd Barret on Acct: for Bricks	50	–	–
–	pd Fees &c for 2 Bucks from ye Duke of Ancaster	1	11	–
20	pd Mrs Ruffle upon Account	10	10	–
–	pd Mr Amory, Upholsterer upon Acct:	12	12	–
21	pd Mr Bennet for 18 Gallons of Port	5	13	–
	[f.33]			
22	pd Barret in full of Two Bills for Bricks	52	18	–
30	pd Poors Tax at Greenwich: $\frac{1}{2}$ a year to Michs next	1	6	8
	Octor:			
1	pd Mr Malthus,[226] 2 Bills	23	6	–
3	Out of Towne a Bait 2 horses & Serts:	–	3	8
4	Recd from the Board of Works one Quarter to Christs: last	181	8	–
–	Allow'd Taxes to dto:	17	12	1
–	Gave the Paymasters Clark	–	5	–
7	Recd of my Brother Charles, in full for the Purchase of the Playhouse, and other things adjoining to it, as describ'd in the Conveyance	3975	–	–
–	pd to my Brother Charles, in full discharge of a Mortgage of Two thousand pounds, upon My House &c at Greenwich	2075	–	–
–	Pd on a Subscription into the Bank of £2000 15 pr Ct:	300	–	–
–	pd for four hundred pounds, Southsea stock	1050	–	–
8	pd Wheler the Farrier at Greenh: a Bill	0	7	6

219 Robert Surman, London; Thomas Bodicote, London.

220 The Duke of Newcastle's estate at Halland, near East Hoathley, Sussex. Vanbrugh's thanks, Webb, p.100.

221 Additions to Vanbrugh's house.

222 Richard Rivers at Greenwich.

223 Thomas Burdus, Middx.

224 John Lansdell, Chamberhouse, Berks. and Halstead, Kent. Elizabeth Fisher (n.112).

225 A beer originally brewed in Brunswick (SOED).

226 Daniel Malthus, Apothecary to the King's Person. Premises in Pall Mall 1716 (CTB 1716, p.427).

		£	s	d
	pd Mrs Wright for Carriage of Bricks, a Bill	22	10	6
–	pd Window Tax at Greenh: ½ a Year to Michs:	–	15	–
–	Recd half a years Salary as Surveyr: of Greenh: Hospitall, to Ladyday last	100	–	–
–	Recd half a years attendance money to ditto	11	–	–
–	Gave Mr Walpoles Clark	–	5	–
–	Recd half a years allowance for Rent to Michs: last	15	–	–
–	Gave the Clark	–	2	6
10	pd Wigzell, Corn Chandler a Bill	20	4	–
–	pd the Washerwoman, 2 Bills	8	–	–
12	pd Rogers on Acct: for Bricks	43	10	–
14	pd at Hartleys a Qr: to Michs: last	1	1	–
–	pd Solomons Surgeon And Nurse	10	13	–
15	pd Mr Bennet a Bill for 22 Galls: of Port	7	15	10
18	pd: for freight of 5500 Bricks from Maidstone	1	13	–
20	To Mrs Jefferys the Midwife[227]	3	9	–
–	Recd fee for a Grant to Du[cie][228]	15	–	–
–	Gratuity to Mr Bound	1	1	–
–	pd Mary Jones for Wages in full	2	2	–
21	pd Pluckington the Hampton Court Waterman b[il]l	–	18	4
22	pd Daws the Greenh: Smith on Acct:	5	5	–
–	pd Mrs Ruffle in full of Two Bills to the 3d of March last	20	19	3
–	pd Rivers the Gardner a Bill	2	8	4
–	pd Mr Brown a Bill for Glaz'd Tyles	19	–	–

[f.33v]

		£	s	d
–	Recd of My Co: George Van. to pay Mr Cardells Bill upon the suit with Busfield[229]	15	4	–
–	pd Mr Cardells Bill for the Suit with Busfield	15	4	–
26	pd Godfrey Coachmaker on Acct:	25	–	–
28	pd Davis a Bill	2	–	6
–	Recd Fees for Grants to Barber & Meads[230]	30	–	–
–	Gratuity to Mr Green	2	2	–
31	pd Chaffey on Acct:	25	–	–

Nov:

		£	s	d
1	pd for freight of 6000 Bricks from Maidstone	1	16	–
–	pd Mr Wetherhilt on account	10	10	–
2	pd Mr Halls assignees a Bill for Beer & Ale	8	12	6
–	pd To the Executors of Sr Cha: Hobson, in full discharge of a Bond of £373:6:10½ to Jo: Warren & Company[231]	297	12	6
–	pd Knight the Slater, a Bill for work at Greenh:	3	13	6
5	pd Mrs Ruffle on acct.	10	10	–
8	pd James Wood in full for Wages & given him over	3	13	6
–	pd Mr Wooley a years ground Rent to Christs: last	50	–	–
10	pd Leignes for a New Periwig	5	15	6
12	Recd of Mrs Smith on Acct: of fruitmoney in 1718	6	6	6
–	Recd of Mrs Sells on Acct: of Rent	5	–	–
–	Recd of Mrs Crawford in full for fruitmoney to Michs: last	54	12	–
–	pd for Passing a Lease of my House in Whitehall	38	11	2
–	Recd Fee for a Grant to Webster[232]	15	–	–
–	Gratuity to Mr Mawson	1	1	–
–	Charity	1	1	–
–	pd Rivers the Gardener a Bill	9	18	2
14	Recd Fee for a Grant to Hall[233]	15	–	–
–	Gratuity to Mr Warburton[234]	1	1	–
16	To Dr Johnson	1	1	–
–	Fee to Mr Reeves	1	1	–
17	Fee to Mr Bunbury	2	2	–
–	Given to Mr Mills. Attorney to Anstis[235]	1	1	–
19	pd Mr Crowley[236] at Greenh: a Bill	5	2	8
–	Churching[237]	–	1	6
22	pd Banister the Sword Cutler a Bill	–	15	–

227 Charles Vanbrugh's birth cannot have been more than a few days earlier. On 21 Oct. 1725 his cousin Frances Norcliffe (n.245) wrote a letter to him (BIHR (Yarburgh)) in reply to one from him about his fifth anniversary.

228 Supporters (see n.216).

229 See p.162, n.33.

230 John Barber, London and East Sheen; Thomas Meads, Holborn.

231 Sir Charles Hopson, Master joiner, died 6 April 1710; his son John, master-joiner, died 9 June 1718; John Warren, wrought-iron worker (Beard, pp.177, 182).

232 Sir Thomas Webster, Bt.

233 John Hall, haberdasher of small wares, London and Horton Hall, Bucks.

234 John Warburton, Somerset Herald 24 June 1720; died 11 May 1759 (Godfrey, p.160).

235 See n.143.

236 Coal merchant (f.59v).

237 The thanksgiving of women after childbirth, commonly called the Churching of Women (Book of Common Prayer). See n.227.

		£	s	d
–	pd for 2 Sconces[238]	–	8	–
–	pd Roger Instip a Quarters Wages	1	10	–
–	Given Mrs Darwell	1	3	–

[f.34]

		£	s	d
22	pd to the opera on a call of 5 p Ct:	10	–	–
23	pd Mrs Ruffle in full of a Bill	13	7	–
24	Recd Fee for a Grant to Blandy[239]	15	–	–
–	Gratuity to Mr Bound	1	1	–
25	pd: Roger Instip in full discharge	1	1	–
–	pd: John ye Coachman in full discharge	1	1	–
–	pd ann goundry a Bill for Asses Milk	5	6	–
–	Recd Fee for a Grant to Champion[240]	15	–	–
–	Gratuity to Mr Green	1	1	–
–	pd Mrs Hawkins a bill for Quilting &c	5	12	6
–	pd for Holland for Pillow Cases	1	15	6
–	pd for a Lock	–	1	6
–	pd for a fire Screen & stands	1	7	–
–	pd for Holland for Shirts	5	10	–
–	pd for Lace for ditto	3	10	6
–	pd for a Hood for Nurse	–	4	6
–	pd Mrs Ashcrofts a Bill, for Nursery Trade	12	19	6
–	pd for a Silver Pan and boat for dto:	2	16	–
–	pd for More of dto:	1	12	9
–	pd Mrs Ashcrofts a Bill for More of dto:	24	4	–
–	pd Thomasin[241] Row her Wages	1	10	–
–	pd Amory the Greenh: Upholsterer on Acct:	10	10	–
–	pd: Gale Upholsterer on Acct:	21	–	–
–	pd for China Ware	2	10	6

Dec:

		£	s	d
1	pd Monsr: Perrott a Bill for Wine	12	2	–
30	Out of Towne 35 Nights. 5 horses. £7:4:1 Servants £9:5:4 Given to Servants £7:18:– Guides £–:7:– Tolebarrs £–:5:5 Farriers £–:14:10 Horse Hyre £2:2:– Surgeon for James's Leg £1:12:6 Poor £–:3:–	29	12	2
–	pd the Hampton Court Watermans Bill	–	6	11
–	pd Land Tax for the Playhouse to Michs: last	18	15	–
–	pd Walter Evans a Bill for Powder	2	18	–
–	Given Dr Clark, for Easter Offering to Easter last	1	1	–
–	pd Sisr: Garencieres a Qrs: Int: for £200 to Christs: last	3	–	–
–	pd Sisr: Robina, three Qrs: Annuity to Michs: last	15	–	–
–	pd Sisr: Vic: a Qrs Annuity to Michs: last	5	–	–
31	Recd of Mr Chaffee one year & ½ Rent to Michs: last	24	7	6
–	pd: Sisr: Mary a Qrs Annuity to Michs: last, and half a Years Int: to Christs: last	8	–	–

[f.34v]

		£	s	d
31	pd Sarah Jones a Yrs Wages to Chrs: last past	5	5	–
–	House Bills this Year, in London & Greenh	261	17	8½
–	Candles Tea & Small Parcells of Wine, Brandy &c	16	14	11½
–	Servants Bills of Disbursments	51	2	–½
–	Spent in Small things	18	18	3
–	Given to Servts: and Christmass boxes	5	16	–

Memd: I made a Lease to John Potter Carpenter, of Five Houses fronting to the Haymarket, for the Term of 46 yrs: 2 Months: 20 days To Commence at Christs: 1719. The Rent Seaventy Six pounds pr Anm: Rent Charge. And afterwards, made over the said Rent, to my Siss: Eliz: and Robina, for their Lives, in considera[tio]n: of Two bonds they had from me, of £400 each. The Rent to commence to them, from Chrs: 1719.

Memd: I sold the Playhouse (with some Tenements adjoining) to my Brother Charles, for £8581 – Which he has paid me. But the said Playh: still stands Charg'd with Three annuitys to my Siss: Mary, Victoria & Robina of £20 pr Annm: each and £2000. Settled on my Wife in marriage.

Memd: I Let the Stable &c in Scotland yd to Mr Archer, for £16 a a year the Rent to begin from

[f.35]

1720/21 Jany January ye 1st 1720/21

		£	s	d
2	pd Monsr. Leoni on a Subscription for Albertis Architecture[242]	1	1	–

[238] Candelabra.

[239] John Blandy, Letcombe Bassett, Berks.

[240] Peter Champion, St Columb Major, Cornwall.

[241] A common girl's name at the time.

[242] Published 1726, delivered 14 June (f.63v).

6	Recd Fee for a Grant of Arms to Watson[243]	15	–	–
–	Gratuity to Mr Green	1	1	–
–	pd Contribution for Wine at Mr Heydeggers	2	2	–
–	Recd from the Executors of Mrs Heard in full for a year and Qrs: Rent, to Michs: last	7	10	–
–	pd for 3 doz. of french wine at Greenh:	4	2	–
7	Recd Rent for Kensington house 3 Qrs to Chr. last	45	–	–
–	pd: Mr Jodrell a Bill	7	12	9
8	Recd from the Managers of Drury Lane Playhouse, in part of £1000 they have agreed to pay me for the Stock carryed from the Haymarket[244]	100	–	–
–	Given Mr Swiny	25	–	–
–	To my Wife	30	–	–
–	pd: for Lace for Mrs Norcliffe[245]	5	–	–
9	Recd Fee for a Grant to Neal[246]	15	–	–
–	pd Gratuity to Mr Mauduit	1	1	–
10	Recd Rent from Sylvester 3 Qrs: to Lady day last	4	10	–
–	pd for Coach Grease at Greenh:	–	7	6
11	pd Mr Meuth, a Bill for Coales	21	18	–
12	pd Coz: Anna: Vandebuss, a Yrs Int: to Chrs: last	5	–	–
–	pd for a Corral & String[247]	1	19	6
14	pd: Mr Gillam[248] on Acct:	30	–	–
16	pd: Land Tax at Greenh: 3 Qrs: for the Castle and Field	2	–	–
17	pd Mr Billinghurst on Acct:	26	5	–
18	pd: Fletcher ye Greenh: Taylor a Bill	1	1	–
19	pd: Mr Harrison for Beer at Greenh: to Chrs: last	4	–	–
20	pd Trout at Greenh: a Bill to Christs: last	15	7	6
21	pd Mrs Mrs [*sic*] Wright a Bill	16	13	–
–	pd My Lady Biddulph ½ a Yrs: Rent to Michs. last	8	–	–
[f.35v]				
23	Recd Rent for Greenh: House a year to Midr: 1719	5	–	–
27	pd Sanders the Brewer a Bill to Chrs: last	13	19	–

–	Recd Fee for a Grant to Tucker[249]	15	–	–
–	Gratuity to Mr Green	1	1	–
28	pd Rivers the Gardener a Bill for Work in the field house[250]	11	6	–
30	pd Hutchinson a Bill for Shoes in full	2	9	–
–	Out of Towne one night & a bait 4 horses & Serts:	–	11	–
Feb.				
3	pd Goulston the Farrier in part of a Bill	10	10	–
6	pd Poors Tax a Qr at the Playhouse to Michs: last	5	–	–
–	Sent to A[un]t: Breton a Token[251]	5	–	–
14	Recd Fee for a Confirmation to Baker[252]	10	–	–
–	Gratuity to Mr Mauduit	–	14	–
–	Fees to Councill	7	7	–
15	pd Mr Hoyes for a New Periwig	7	7	–
–	pd for a Black Velvet Cap	1	3	–
16	pd Davis the Waterman a bill to Chr: last	1	1	–
18	pd Wilson the Glazier a bill to dto:	1	16	7
19	Recd Rent from Mr Portalles ½ a year to Midsr: last	45	–	–
–	Recd a Fee from the Treasurer for Ailsbury County Hall[253]	10	10	–
23	To Surgeons for Cupping &c	1	11	6
27	pd the preacher assistant at St James's to Lady day last	1	–	–
March				
2	pd Wm Westhorp a Bill for freight of bricks	1	3	–
5	Recd of my Bro: Charles, a Qrs Int: for £2000 to Christmas last	25	–	–
14	pd: James Wood a Qrs Wages, to Ladyday next	2	10	–
18	pd: Tax for the Highways at Greenh: for ye year 1720	–	9	–
–	Recd Rent for the Field at Greenh: ½ a year to Michs: last	2	10	–
20	pd: Land Tax for the Castle a Qr to Lady day next	–	10	–
–	pd: dto: for the Field	–	3	4
21	Recd from Mr Wiseman of			

243 Jonathan Watson, Westminster.

244 See Rosenberg, pp.608–10.

245 Lady Vanbrugh's aunt Mary Norcliffe, widowed 1720, or first cousin Frances (1700–70), married Sir John Wray 1728.

246 Henry Neale, London. See Webb, p.127.

247 A toy of polished coral (SOED).

248 John Gilham, joiner.

249 William Tucker, Coryton Hall, Devon.

250 The Nunnery (p.95).

251 See p.155.

252 Judith and Elizabeth, daughters of Thomas Baker, London. See also Webb, p.127.

253 Vanbrugh was asked to adjudicate between designs by Brandon and Harris, and chose the latter. According to the schedule attached to a report of 1731 he received a fee of £21 (*Records of Bucks.*, XII/1, 1927, pp.iv, viii).

	Cambridge for a year, to Lady day next[254]	5 – –	
23	Sent to Pen Breton[255]	2 2 –	
–	pd Robert Emery in full for Wages	1 13 4	
27	Recd Rent from Sylvester ½ a Year to Michs: last	3 – –	
–	Recd Rent from John Darwell ½ a Year to Michs: last	3 – –	
–	pd a Bill for paving before John Darwells door	– 9 –	
–	pd Tho: Bensted for Carriage of 5000 bricks from Maid[ston]e.	1 10 –	
30	Recd from the Managers of Drury Lane Upon Acct:	100 – –	
–	Gave the Treasurer there	– 5 –	
31	pd Trophy money for the Playhouse for the year 1719	– 2 6	
–	pd Sisr: Gars: a Qrs Int to Lady day last	3 – –	

April

1	R'd of my Brother Cha: a Qrs Int: for £2000, to Lady day last	25 – –
–	pd Tho: Bond for a Beer Stand	– 9 –
–	Pd: Mr Groves upon Account	31 10 –
–	Recd. ½ a Years Allowance for Rent at Greenh: to Lady day last past	15 – –
–	Gave the Clark	– 2 6

[f.36]

3	Pd Mr Billinghurst on Acct:	40 – –
–	pd Poors Tax at Greenh: for the Castle and Field ½ a year to Lady day last	1 6 8
–	Out of Towne 1 night 2 horses	– 5 6
4	pd Window Tax for the Castle, ½ a Yr: to Lady day last	– 15 –
–	Given [cypher][256]	1 3 –
–	pd: An Assessment for repairing a Bridge by Maidstone	– – 11
–	pd: Mr Stafford, a bill for Mum	1 15 –
–	pd: Sarah a years Wages to	4 – –
–	Gave her to buy a Gowne	1 10 –
–	dto: to Martha	1 10 –
–	pd Nurse, on acct: of Wages	2 10 –
–	To Dr Johnston at twice	2 2 –
–	pd for a Silver Cup	– 16 3
–	pd for Riband for a Cap	– 3 –
–	To Mr Martin, for twice bleeding my Wife	1 1 –
–	pd: Mr Blight, for a Tea Kittle	– 12 6
6	pd: Rivers the Gardner a Bill for Work at the Field house	7 18 8
–	pd: ditto, two Bills, for work at the Castle	8 13 5
7	pd: Dawes the Smith upon acct:	5 5 –
–	pd: Brookes in full for Lime	15 15 –
–	Recd from the Southsea house ½ a years dividend for £400. Stock to Christs: last	20 – –
10	Out of Towne, one night, 2 horses	– 5 6
13	Recd Fee for a Grant to Nash[257]	15 – –
–	Gratuity to Mr Green	1 1 –
17	pd: Brand the Cooper at Greenh: a Bill	3 11 6
21	Recd Fee for a Grant to Normoor[258]	15 – –
–	Gratuity to Mr Hesket	1 1 –
22	pd Daws the Smith upon Acct:	10 10 –
24	Recd Salary at Greenh: half a year to Michs: last	100 – –
–	Recd for attendances to ditto	10 – –
24	Recd of Coll: Godolphin, in full for Rent to Christs: last past	68 – –
–	Recd of ditto, for a Qrs: Rent to Lady day last	15 15 –
–	Gave his Man	– 2 6
27	pd the Sadler a Bill in full	5 8 –
–	pd Ryland the Plumber a Bill	1 13 6
–	pd Mr Haslam a Bill to Christ: last	16 1 6
29	pd Mr Groves upon Acct:	50 – –
–	pd Mr Gilham upon Acct:	50 – –

[f.36v]

29	pd Rivers the Gardner a Bill for work at my Brother Phils:[259]	14 4 9½
–	pd dto: a Bill for work at the Castle	2 16 10
–	pd Nurse in full of wages ½ a year to the 20th Inst:	4 10 –
–	pd for a Gowne for Mrs Bishop	2 – –
–	pd for a Coat for Charles[260]	1 – –
–	pd for three pair of Servants Sheets &c	1 16 –

May

1	pd My Lady Biddulph ½ a Yrs: Rent to Lady day last	8 – –
3	pd: to the Executor of Mr Hesleden,[261] for one years Int: due the 1st of this Inst:	3 16 –
8	pd: for a Peice of Indian	

[254] See n.201.

[255] Penelope, daughter of Vanbrugh's aunt Lucy Breton but not acknowledged by Thomas Breton (see p.155). She signed *Penelope Nolan* in 1707 (HMC House of Lords, n.s. VII, p.38).

[256] See p.176.

[257] James Naish, Holborn.

[258] William Northmore, Cleve, Devon.

[259] The Nunnery.

[260] The child.

[261] Brian Hesleden of Bracken Bottom, sole executor. Thomas Hesleden died 30 Aug. 1720 (see p.168, nn.101–2).

		£	s	d
	Damask, and a Peice of Lutstring[262]	8	17	–
–	pd: for Lace for Shirts &c	2	6	9
12	pd: the Scavenger at the Playhouse for half a year to Michs: last past	1	11	6
–	pd: Mr Billinghurst upon Acct:	21	–	–
–	Recd from the Heralds College Prince of Wales Installation Fee £6:13:4 Sr Luke Schaub Knt: £–:19:4 Earl Castelton £2:3:6 Sr Oswald Moseley Sr Wm Chapman Sr Wm Sanderson Sr Wm Codrington Barts: £4:6:8 Barron Clinton £1:6:8[263]	15	9	6
18	pd: Window Tax for the Playhouse for half a year to Michs: last	–	15	–
–	pd Middleton a Bill	1	8	6
–	pd Solomons Nurse	4	–	–
–	To Dr Chamberlain	1	1	–
–	pd Mr Gale upon Acct:	21	–	–
–	To Mr Martin for bleeding my Wife	–	10	6
19	pd Mr Mallory a Bill for Lace	12	18	–
–	pd Will Cocker in full for Wages	–	16	–
–	To Dr Chamberlain	1	1	–
20	To dto:	1	1	–
–	pd: Scott a Bill for Bricks	17	12	–
21	To Dr Chamberlain	1	1	–
–	To Mr Martin	–	10	6
–	To Solomons Doctor	1	1	–
23	pd Mrs Ruffle a Bill in full to Christs: last	7	3	–
24	Pd Mr Towers for 3 dozn: of Rhenish	5	8	6
26	Recd of Mr Fort one years Rent for Hampton Court house to Midsummer last	50	–	–
29	Recd Rent for Greenh: house a Year to Midr: last	5	–	–

[f.37]

		£	s	d
30	pd Mr Chaffee; in full of a Bill, to Christmass last past	28	11	9
31	pd Mr Godfrey, Coachmaker in full of a Bill	30	–	–
–	pd Mr Black a Bill in full for Ale to Christs: last	4	–	–
–	pd ditto, in full of an other Bill since	4	–	–
–	pd to the Opera, on a Fourth Call[264]	10	–	–

June

		£	s	d
1	Recd from my Brother Charles half a years Int: for £2000. to Michs: next	50	–	–
–	pd Neve the Clockmaker a Bill	1	1	–
4	Out of Towne one night 4 horses	–	11	–
12	pd: the Minister at Greenh: for E. offering, to East: last	1	1	–
–	pd: Poors Tax at Greenh: for the Castle, a year to Ladyday last, on ye foot of 16d in the pd	2	–	–
–	To Dr Slare[265]	1	1	–
13	pd: Wood; Lime Man, on account	21	–	–
–	Recd: Fee for a Grant to Cooper[266]	15	–	–
–	Gratuity to Mr Mawson	1	1	–
17	pd: the Fifth Call to the Opera	10	–	–
25	To Dr Slare	1	1	–
–	pd for a dozen of China plates & 6 basons	1	11	–
–	pd for a japan Salver	–	6	–
–	for a straw hat &c	1	5	6

July

		£	s	d
4	pd: Rivers the Gardener a Bill	3	3	–
–	pd: Daws the Smith in full of Two Bills	7	4	11
–	pd: Mr Billinghurst upon acct:	100	–	–
–	pd: Mr Groves upon Acct:	50	–	–
–	pd: Mr Gilham upon Acct:	50	–	–
–	pd: Mrs Wright a Bill	24	8	6
–	pd: for a Perspective Glass, Pocket book &c	1	1	–
–	pd: for things for the Children at Heslington	1	–	–
5	pd Mr. Barrat upon Acct:	71	–	–
–	pd. Mr Dalton a Bill for Plumbers work	15	–	–
–	pd: Sisr: Mary half a years Int: to Midsr: last £3:–:– and gave her £3:10:–	6	10	–
–	pd: Mr Savage on Acct: for ditto[267]	25	–	–
–	pd Hutchinson a Bill for Shoes	3	16	–
–	pd: Sisr: Gars: a Qrs Int to Midsr: last	3	–	–
–	pd: Coz: Garens: a Bill	23	3	10
–	pd: a Bill for Lamps	3	3	–
–	Recd Rent from Mr Portalles, a Quarter to Michs: last	22	10	–
6	pd Davis two Bills, in full to this day	2	8	–
–	pd King the Washerwoman a Bill	3	19	6

[f.37v]

6th: pd Mr Wooley, for three Qrs Ground Rent to Michs last when

262 A kind of glossy silk fabric (SOED).

263 Sir Luke Schaub, Hanoverian. 1st Earl Castleton. Sir Oswald Mosley, Bt, of Rolleston, Sheriff of Staffs. Sir William Chapman, Bt, of London. Sir William Saunderson, Bt (see p.93, n.5). Sir William Codrington, Bt, of Dodington, Glos. Lord Clinton, later 1st Earl Clinton.

264 Subscription, Royal Academy of Music.

265 Later Slaar (f.40).

266 John Cooper, Trowbridge.

267 Plumber's work: the previous entry is an insertion.

		£	s	d
	my Brother took Possession of the Playhouse	37	10	–
–	Recd from the office of Works a Quarter to Lady day was twelve months	176	15	6
–	allow'd Taxes to ditto	17	12	–
–	Recd for the Bank Subscription sold out	350	–	–
–	pd James a Qrs wages to Midsr: last	2	10	–
–	pd Daws for a Horse	5	–	–
–	pd Nurse	3	11	6
12	pd the Farrier on Acct:	5	5	–
26	pd White the Tayler on Acct:	26	5	–
–	Out of Towne, in a journey to the North, from July ye 6th. 1721. to November the 2d. following being 119 days. Horses £17:–:8 Eating £32:5:5½ Given to Servants £26:–:– Farrier £2:4:4 Washing £6:–:10 Horse Hyre £15:7:– Harness maker £1:9:5 Pocket money & small necessary expences £12:13:3 Appothecarys Bills, for Sick Servts. £3:17:– Carriage of things from & to Londn £2:11:9	119	9	8½
–	Things bought at York a Coat &c for the Lad £3:1:8 a Damask Table Cloath £1:15:– Muslin for a dressing Table £–:12:– Snail water[268] £–:19:– Palsy drops £–:17:6 Tea £–:4:– Stockings for Taffy £–:4:– Knives & forks £1:4:– A New Periwig £4:4:– Mounting a Wigg £–:7:6 a pair of Stockings £–:7:6 Shoes & Gloves £–:7:6	14	3	8
Augt				
2	pd Mr Gale, upholsterer, in full	23	–	–
3	pd: to Coz: Gars: towards the Charge of a Patent to Miller the Brickmaker[269]	20	–	–
Sept:				
6	pd to ditto on Acct: of his Mothers Principal	10	–	–

[f.38]

		£	s	d
Nov:				
3	Recd from the office of Works three Qrs: Sallary to Christmass last	537	8	–
–	allow'd upon the New Tax of 6d pr pound	13	8	9
–	Land Tax ¾ to Chr: last	48	15	–
–	Given the Paymasters Clark. 15s. & his man 5s.	1	–	–
–	Recd Excheqr: Salary a year and Qr: to Christs: 1720	34	04	4½
–	allow'd Fees & civil list Tax	5	5	3
–	pd Mrs. Constantine a Bill for Lace, for Miss Roses Head, and my Shirts	5	9	–
4	pd for a Load of Hay	2	–	–
–	pd for a Load of Straw	–	15	–
9	Recd Fee for a Grant to B [blank]	15	–	–
–	Gratuity to Mr Green	1	1	–
–	pd: At Hartleys, for Chrs: Lady day, Midsr: & Michs: Quarters last	4	4	–
10	pd: Bensted the Hoyman, for freight of 7000 Br[ic]ks: from Maid[stone]:	2	2	–
11	pd: Mrs Wright in part of a Bill for Carriage of bricks	21	–	–
–	Recd for three Qrs: attendances at Grh: to Midsr: last	14	–	–
–	Recd three Qrs: Salary to ditto	150	–	–
–	Gave the Clark	–	5	–
–	Recd ½ a years Rent, to Michs: last	15	–	–
–	Gave ye Clark	–	2	6
–	Recd Rent from Mr Portailles, a Qr: to Christs: last	22	10	–
15	pd. James a Qrs: wages, to Michs: last	2	10	–
–	pd Two Calls to the opera, one of 4 pr Ct. & one of 5	18	00	–
18	pd: Mr Godfrey in part of a Bill	50	–	–
–	pd: James a Qrs: Wages to Chrs: next	2	10	–
–	pd: Andrew in full for Wages to Michs: last	2	2	6
–	Charity	–	5	–
–	pd: My Lady Biddulph ½ a Yrs: Rent to Michs: last	8	–	–
–	pd: Nurse in full for a years Wages, to the 20th of Oct: last	3	10	–
27	pd: Wood, Lime Man, in part of a Bill	21	–	–
–	pd: Loxam: a Bill for Glaziers Work in full	17	9	–
–	pd: Wallis the Gardener a Bill for Work done at Sr Wm Saundersons Garden	4	19	–
–	pd: Tax for the Highway at Greenh: a year to Chrs:	–	9	–
29	Recd of Mr Dorrel[270] ½ a Years Rent for the field at Greenh: being to Lady day 1721	2	10	–
Dec.				
2	pd: Mansfield[271] the Plaisterer a bill in full	17	17	–

[f.38v]

		£	s	d
6	pd: Langthorn ye Framemaker a Bill	2	1	–

268 Made by boiling snails in barley-water or tea-water, said to be wonderful for a cough (Mrs Delaney's *Letters*, III, p.477).

269 See p.177.

270 Agreement, 27 March 1719 with Thomas Dorrell, to have use of the herbage for grazing a cow for £5 a year (BIHR (Yarburgh)). First payment (without name) Michaelmas 1719 (f.27).

271 Isaac Mansfield, d.1729 (Beard, p.168).

		£	s	d
–	pd: for things for Charles	1	4	–
–	Recd from the Heralds College Sr Nathan Gold Knt £–:19:4 Sr George Watson dto £–:19:4 Sr George Sanders £–:19:4 Viscount Ewelm £1:12:6 E: of Mackelsfield £2:3:4 Vist: Harcourt £1:12:6 Vist: Torrington £1:12:6 Baron Byng £1:6:– Baron Lechmere £1:6:– Bisp: of Sarum £–:18:– Bisp: of Gloucester £–:18:– Bisp: of Hereford £–:18:–[272]	15	4	10
–	Rd: from the Southsea House, for half a Yrs dividend of £400 Stock, to Midsr: last	16	–	–
7	Pd for a Load of Hay	2	2	–
10	pd: Sisr: Gars: on acct: of Principall	10	–	–
12	pd: Tax for the High ways, ½ a year to Michs: 1720	–	7	6
–	pd: The Preacher Assistant at St James's ½ a yr: to ditto	–	10	–
13	pd: Barret on Acct: for Bricks	50	–	–
–	pd: Rogers in full for Bricks	46	–	–
15	To Dr Chamberlain	1	1	–
16	To ditto	1	1	–
–	To the Surgeon	1	1	–
17	To Dr Chamberlain	1	1	–
18	To dto:	1	1	–
18	Memd: My Brother Charles this day Transferr'd £400 Stock in the South Sea Company, to me, it having been bought in his name. I Likewise accepted Stock at £300 for Two third Subscriptions, one of which was in my Wifes Name the other in my own.			
–	pd: for a Transfer at the Southsea house	–	11	9

[f.39]

		£	s	d
18	pd: Ath: Garrencieres, on Acct: of his Mothers Principall	10	–	–
28	pd: Mrs Ruffle a Bill in full to this day	22	17	5
23	pd: Mr Billinghurst on Account	50	–	–
–	pd: Mr Groves, in full of his Bills, and all demands to this day	152	2	–
27	For a load of Hay	2	–	–
–	Recd from my Bro: Charles a Qrs Int: to Christs: last	25	–	–
–	House Bills at London & Greenh:	176	18	3
–	Wax Candles, Tea, & Small Parcells of Wine & Brandy	12	13	2
–	pd Servts bills of Disbursmts.[273]			
–	Spent in Small things	12	5	–
–	Given to Servts. & Christs: boxes	3	19	6

[f.40]

1721/22 Jany: January ye 1st: 1721/22

		£	s	d
4	Recd Rent from Mr Portales ½ a year to Midsummer last	45	–	–
–	pd: ditto, a Bill for Wine to Christs: last	16	–	4
–	Newyears Guift to Miss Phil[274]	–	10	6
6	pd Land Tax for the Castle at Greenh: a year to Lady day next £2:13:4 ditto for the field £–:13:4	3	6	8
–	pd Davis a Bill to this day	1	1	–
12	pd: Mr Kettle for 3 dozen flasks of French wine	4	10	–
13	pd: Mr Meuth a Bill for Coales	8	12	6
–	pd: Pluckington ye Hampton Court Waterman a Bill to ys. day	–	2	4
15	pd: Goulston, Farrier, in full of a Bill to Christs: 1720	14	–	–
17	pd: an eighth Call to the opera	10	–	–
–	To Kens Daughters[275] for Newyear Guifts	1	1	–
–	pd: Sisr: Mary ½ a years Int: to Christs. last	3	–	–
18	Charity to the Poor of St Martins	1	1	–
–	pd: two years & ½ Excheqr: Rent for White[ha]ll: house, to Michs: 1722	25	–	–
–	fee for ditto	1	13	4
–	pd for a Load of Hay	2	–	–
–	pd. Mr Kettle for two dozn: of french Claret	3	–	–
20	pd Mrs Wright in full of a Bill	10	2	3
–	pd Gilham on Acct.	25	–	–
25	To Dr Slaar	1	1	–
26	pd: a Bill for freight &c of 1¾ Chaldron of Coales from Bawtry	2	2	3
29	pd Savage the Plumber on Acct:	25	–	–
–	Given Sisr: Bin	10	10	–

Feb.

		£	s	d
2	pd. Rivers the Gardener a Bill	7	7	11
–	pd Sanders the Brewer a Bill to Christs: last	10	2	6
3	Rd: Rent for the House at Greenh: a Yr: to Midsr. last	5	–	–
5	pd Clark the Painter in full	6	6	–
–	Recd from Greenh: Hospital, one Qrs: Salary to Michs: last	50	–	–
6	pd: Middleton a Bill in full to this day	2	14	–
9	Rd: from the Office of Works half a Years Salary to Midsumr: last	345	5	7
–	allow'd upon the new Tax of 6d pr Pound	8	17	1

[272] Sir Nathaniel Gould, Director, Bank of England. Sir George Walton and Sir George Sanders, Captains, R.N. Baron Parker, Viscount Parker of Ewelm and Earl of Macclesfield (see n.65). 1st Viscount Harcourt. 1st Baron Byng of Southill, Beds. Viscount Torrington. 1st Baron Lechmere (married Elizabeth, daughter of 3rd Earl of Carlisle). Richard Willis, Bishop of Salisbury. Joseph Wilcocks, Bishop of Gloucester. Benjamin Hoadley, Bishop of Hereford (from Bangor, see n.64).

[273] No amount.

[274] Philippa, his niece.

[275] See n.200.

		£	s	d
–	pd Land Tax ½ a year to Midsr: last	34	10	7½
–	Treasury & Exceqr Gratuitys	–	14	5
–	Given the Paymasters Clark 10s.6 & his man 5s.	–	15	6
13	pd: Mr Barrat in full of a Bill	72	13	–
–	pd: for a Load of Hay £2 & a Load of Straw 13s.6.	2	13	6
14	Recd from Mr Fort Rent one yr: to Midr. last	50	–	–

[f.40v]

		£	s	d
14	pd Mr Wray, Draper, in full of a Bill	4	18	6
–	To the Midwife & Nurse keeper[276]	4	12	–
–	pd for things sent to Mrs Pitts	1	1	–
–	pd for things for Charles. Vizt a Night Gowne £– 13 Frocks £1:4:– a Coat £1:7:6 flannel for Pettys £– :7:10 Pins £–:2:6	3	14	10
15	pd: the Powder Bill to Christs: last	2	2	–
16	pd. White the Taylor, a Bill in full to Christs: last was Twelve month	28	3	–
17	pd: Mr Gilham in full	57	–	6
19	pd: Coz: Garencieres a Bill in full	9	11	6
–	pd: to ditto Intrest for his Mother to Chrs: last	5	14	–
22	pd Mr Chaffey a Bill in full to Christs: last	16	–	6
–	Recd for Kensington house, a Year to Christs. last	60	–	–
24	pd Mr Browne a Bill for Glazd Pantyles. in full	17	17	–
–	Recd Fee for a Grant of Sr Jn: Lake's Arms, to Martin[277]	15	–	–
–	Gratuity to Mr Green	1	1	–
–	pd: Richards for Hatts to Christs: last	12	–	–
27	pd: Ayres a Bill for Coales. to ditto	14	5	6
–	pd: Gosling a bill for Candlesticks &c.	1	1	–
28	To my Wife	30	–	–
–	pd: Mr Valliant for a Book of Architecture	5	9	–
–	To ditto, on a Subscription to the Collosseum[278]	1	1	–

March

		£	s	d
2	pd Wigzell Corn Chandler one Bill for a year from Jany: 1st: 1719/20 to Jany: 1st 1720/21	17	15	8
–	pd ditto, for the next year	14	5	6
3	pd: Nurce, a Qrs wages to	3	10	–
5	pd: Wood, in full of a Bill for Lime	24	4	–
–	pd Fletcher ye Greenh: Taylor a Bill	1	1	–
–	pd: Harrison the Brewer a Bill in full to Chrs: last	5	2	6
9	pd: Godfrey Coach Maker upon Account	25	–	–
10	pd: for a Load of Hay	2	2	–
–	pd: Mr Bonfoy a Bill	10	14	–
–	pd: for a Watch sent to Bro: James Yarburgh[279]	4	10	–
15	pd: Leigne for a New Periwig & altering an old one	6	6	–

[f.41]

March

		£	s	d
15	Recd Fees from the College Bishops of Winchester Norwich Durham Bangor £6:6:8 Earl of Pomfret £2:3:4 Sr Richd: Manningham Knt: £–:19:4[280]	9	9	4
–	Rd Salary from ditto a year and Quarter to Christs: 1720	50	–	–
–	Allow'd Taxes & Fees	18	12	11
–	allow'd the Secretary for entering 38 Grants of Arms in the Earl Marshals book at 5s each	9	10	–
17	pd John Owen a Quarters wages, to Ladyday next	1	10	–
–	pd the Greenh: Upholsterer in full of a Bill	7	8	–
20	To Dr Slaar	1	1	–
–	pd the Greenh: Upholsterer in full of an other Bill	10	5	–
–	pd Mr Robinson, Appothecary at Greenh: a bill in full to Christs: last	11	–	–

April

		£	s	d
5	To Dr Slaar	1	1	–
–	Recd of my Bro: Charles a Qrs Int: to Ladyday last	25	–	–
–	Recd, of the Managers of Drury Lane Playhouse on acct:	125	–	–
–	pd Mr Ashcroft alias Reade, a bill in full	10	–	–

276 Second son, John (Jack).

277 Sir John Leake, Essex and Sussex, to Stephen Martin-Leake (afterwards Garter King of Arms).

278 In 1735 Paul Vaillant of London issued a catalogue of French books available (BM *Catalogue of Printed Books*); 'a Book of Architecture' cannot be identified, but it was expensive and could conceivably have been the rare first edition of Fischer von Erlach's *Entwurff Einer Historischen Architectur* (Vienna, 1721), or the three volumes of Rossi's *Studio d'Architettura Civile* (1702–21, cf. Hawksmoor's sale catalogue, lot 155, 'A Book of Architect per Rossi'); this was a work of importance for Grimsthorpe (see p.121, n.25). 'The Collosseum' is probably Carlo Fontana, *Anfiteatro Flavio*, The Hague 1725. The Account Book does not mention *Vitruvius Britannicus*, for all three volumes of which Vanbrugh was a subscriber (1715, 1717, 1725).

279 Brother-in-law. See *Survey of London*, XXIX, 1960, p.225.

280 Charles Trimnel, Bishop of Winchester. Thomas Green, Bishop of Norwich. William Talbot, Bishop of Durham. Richard Reynolds, Bishop of Bangor. 1st Earl of Pomfret. Sir Richard Manningham, M.D., of London.

Day	Entry	£	s	d
9	Paid Mr Mallory a Bill in full for Livery Lace	11	9	–
14	Recd Livery money for 1717. 1718.1719	25	8	–
–	Paid Fees at the Wardrobe £2:10:9 Gave Mr Woodeson £1:1:–[281]	3	11	9
–	Recd for half a years allowance for house rent at Greenh: to Ladyday last	15	–	–
–	Gave the Clark	–	2	6
16	pd Sisr: Garencieres. ½ a Yrs Int: to La:day last	2	14	–
–	pd: Mr Dennis[282] ½ a Guinea for the first paymt: of my Subscription to his Works	–	10	6
17	pd: James Ewins Taylor for mending a black Suit	–	10	–
–	pd: for Lace, Combs &c for the Children	1	2	–
19	pd Mr Barrat on Acct: for Bricks	50	–	–
–	pd for a Load of Hay 2 Gu[inea]s: a Load of Straw 15	2	17	–
20	pd Couzen Vanbrugh[283] in full for Wine	14	2	–
26	pd Mr Vokins, for Stuff for a Suit	6	6	–

[f.41v]

Day	Entry	£	s	d
28	pd: Wood the Lime Man on Acct.	21	–	–
–	pd: Mr Graham appothecary a Bill in full	4	12	–
29	*Given* [cypher][284]	*1*	*3*	–
30	pd: Mr Kettle a Bill for Wine	2	5	–
–	pd: Sayer the Brasiers bill	1	14	–
–	pd: Nicholson ye Pewterer a Bill	–	19	–
–	pd: for a pair of Steel Snuffers	–	5	–

May

Day	Entry	£	s	d
11	Recd of Coll: Godolphin, a years Rent to L.Day last	63	–	–
–	pd Mr Stanton, Surgeon	5	5	–
19	pd Window Tax for the Castle at Greenh: a yr to Lady day last	1	10	–
–	pd: Nurse Winter	1	1	–
–	Charges in Sending the Child Jack to Walton[285]	–	7	6
30	pd: Jones the Bricklayer a Bill	3	3	–
31	pd: Mr Tonson, in full of the subscription to Mr Addisons Works & for binding them[286]	1	16	–

June

Day	Entry	£	s	d
7	Out of Towne. 5 Nights. Horses & horse hyre	3	9	3
–	Servants &c	3	–	4
11	pd: at Doileys for Stuff for a Suit	2	2	–
–	pd: at ditto, for Stuff to Hang a Closet	1	16	–
–	pd: for Silk for a Gowne, for Lucy Gars:[287]	4	–	–
12	To Sr Hans Sloan[288]	1	1	–
–	For a Load of Hay	2	2	–
–	To Mr Martin, for bleeding my Wife	–	10	6
–	pd for China Ware	–	13	–
14	Given at Brother Charles Christening	5	5	–
–	To Sr Hans Sloan & Dr Slare	2	2	–
19	pd Mrs Wright in part of a Bill	15	15	–
20	pd: James a Qrs Wages, to Midsummer next	2	10	–
21	pd My Lady Biddulph ½ a Years Rent to La: day last	8	–	–
–	pd for Spirrit of Lavender	–	12	–
23	Recd Salary at Greenwich ½ a Yr: to Lady day last	100	–	–
–	Recd at Ditto for Attendances to ditto	9	–	5
26	pd Sisr: Mary ½ a years Int: to Midsr: past	3	–	–
28	pd: Mr Hesleden a years Int: to Mayday last	3	10	–
–	pd: Barratt on Acct:	100	–	–
30	pd: Sister Garencieres, on Acct: of Principall	30	–	–
–	pd: Wood in full of a Bill for Lime	21	–	–

July

Day	Entry	£	s	d
3	pd: Nurse Higgs in full for Wages &c	4	10	6
4	Recd from my Bro. Charles a Qrs Int: to Midsr: last	25	–	–
5	pd: for a Mare	6	11	–
–	Recd of Mr Dodington upon account[289]	300	–	–
6	To Dr Slare	1	1	–
7	pd Mr Billinghurst on Account	50	–	–
9	Recd for a Horse	3	3	–
–	pd: for China Ware	2	8	6
–	pd: My Wife	15	–	–
10	pd: Mr Bennet for half of a Party Wall at Greenh:	20	7	5

281 ? John Woodeson of the Privy Seal Office.

282 John Dennis, critic. 2nd ed. of *Select Works*, 1721; *Original Letters, Familiar, Moral and Critical*, 1721.

283 George.

284 Entry deleted.

285 See p.97.

286 See n.180.

287 Lucia Maria Garencieres (d.1770), daughter of Elizabeth Barker and Dudley Garencieres and sister of the Rev. Theophilus. Sir John left her £10 for mourning and an annuity of £10 after her mother's death.

288 Sir Hans Sloane, M.D., F.R.S. (1660–1753), Physician to Queen Anne and George II. His collections became the nucleus of the British Museum.

289 For Eastbury (see p.117).

12 Out of Towne 2 nights. 5 horses[290] 1 2 6
– pd for a Scritore[291] 1 11 6
14 pd the minister at Greenh: his Easter offering 2 2 –

[f.42]

14 Gave the Clark of the Parish Church at Greenh: for last year and this – 10 –
15 pd: things for Charles 2 07 –
– pd for Two peices of Peelings[292] 2 10 –
16 pd: Mrs Wright, in full of a Bill for Carriage 14 14 –
– pd: for Muslin and Blue Stuff for dressing Tables 2 – 6
– pd: for Stuff for Wastcoates – 7 10½
– pd: for 4 Large China plates – 4 –
17 Recd from the office of Works, half a years Salary, to Christmass last 360 2 4
– pd: on the Tax of 6d p Pound 9 – 0¾
– pd: Land Tax ½ a year to Chr: last 36 11 3
– Given the Paymasters Clark – 10 6
18 pd: Mr Bridges a Bill to Christs: 1720 35 9 –
– pd: The Washer Woman a Bill to June ye 5th. 1722 9 6 11½
– pd: the Powder Bill to Midsr: last 1 7 –
– pd: On a Subscription to Monsr: Desaguilliers' book[293] 1 1 –
21 pd: Savage the Plumber, in full of all Accts: 79 8 –
24 pd: Richd: Rivers, two Bills for Trees &c 5 7 6
– pd: ditto, for one year keeping the Garden, & courts ending at Midsummer last 4 – –
– pd: Mr Trout a Bill in full for Hay, Straw & Grass, to Christs: last 13 7 –
25 pd: Mr Pratt a Bill for Bricks, in full 16 12 –
– pd: Hutchinson Shoemaker, a bill in full 2 17 6
– To Dr Johnston 1 1 –
26 pd: Mrs Alsop, a bill for Livery Stockings – 15 6
– pd for Lavender Drops for Dean Jones – 5 –

Augt:

3 Out of Towne 8 Nights. 5 Horses £3:13:9 Servants £5:4:1 Guides &c £1:18:6 10 16 4
– pd for Scissors at Salisbury & a Razor 1 3 6
6 To Dr Slare 1 1 –
8 pd: Rivers the Gardener upon Acct: 10 10 –
– pd: for a Load of Hay 2 2 –
10 Given Mr Swiny 25 – –
– pd Langley the Joyner, a bill in full for Sashes 6 6 –
18 pd Nurse Wintour on Acct: 4 10 –
– pd for Stuff for a Suit 2 19 –
– pd: Ben Dolly, for making a Seat at Walton 1 10 –
– 2 Horses at Walton 9 nights 2 9 9
25 pd: Mr Collivoe a Bill for Picture Frames &c 4 15 –
– pd: to Bind Solomon Prentice 7 7 –
28 To Dr Johnston 1 1 –
30 pd: to an assessment for repairing the County Goale – 3 1½

Sept:

3 Recd Fee for a Grant of Arms to Harwood[294] 15 – –
– Gratuity to Mr Green 1 1 –

[f.42v]

5 pd: Rivers A Bill for Foundations &c at ye White house[295] 1 17 4
– pd Ditto for digging up the Coach Way in the Field 25 9 11
– Recd Fee for a Grant of Arms to Smith[296] 15 – –
– Gratuity to Mr Mawson 1 1 –
– pd for Frocks &c for Charles 1 5 –
– pd Scott a Bill for Bricks 58 10 –
– Out of Towne 9 days 2 horses & Saddle horses 2 7 9
– Recd from the Southsea House, one years Dividend for my Stock arrising from Two third Subscriptions, due at Midr: 1721 58 13 4
– Recd from ditto, One years Dividend of my Whole Stock, (that arising from the Subscriptions included And making together £1511:2:2) due at Midsr: last 90 13 2
– Memd: There is likewise £2053:6:8 Stock in the Southsea Books, in my Name,

290 Deleted entry: *a Bait at Esher 4 horses.*

291 Escritoire: writing-desk.

292 Pearling, a kind of lace (SOED).

293 J. T. Desaguliers, natural philosopher, lived at Greenwich. Published *c.*1720 (BM *Catalogue of Printed Books*) a syllabus for his *Course of Experimental Philosophy*, 1734– .

294 Henry Harwood, Crowfield Hall, Suffolk.

295 The north White Tower.

296 Joshua Smith, Runcton and Great Yarmouth, Norfolk.

Day	Entry	£	s	d
	but is only in Trust for the Countess of Coventry[297]			
–	Memd: Having Disburs'd Severall Sum's of money for building Materialls &c for my Brother Charles, and having this day made up all Accounts with him to the 25th of July last, there was due to me upon the Ballance £543:–:6. for which he has given me a note payable upon demand.			
6	Recd of my Brother Charles, in part of the above mention'd note	300	–	–
7	pd: Mr Hargrave a Bill in full	30	5	–
24	Out of Towne 19 days. 6 horses £3:10:– Given Ld Cobham's Servants[298] £5:5:– Eating on the Road £5:18:5	14	13	5
–	pd for a Cloak for Jack[299]	–	18	–
28	Recd Excheqr. Salary, a year to Christs: 1721	27	7	–
–	allow'd Fees for ditto	3	13	6

Octr.

Day	Entry	£	s	d
4	Out of Towne. 2 Nights. 4 Coach horses. 1 Saddle £1:11:8 eating £2:17:–	4	8	8
6	pd James Wood a Qrs. Wages to Michs: last	2	10	–
–	pd Caleb Crompton for 20 Chaldron of Coales	19	10	–
8	pd. Land Tax for the Castle a year to Ladyday next £1:14:– ditto for the Field £–:8:9	2	3	9
–	pd Wiggens the Carpenter on Acct:	25	–	–
–	pd: Poors Rate at Greenh: ½ a year to Michs: last past	1	–	–

[f.43]

Day	Entry	£	s	d
10	pd: Mrs Wright a Bill	18	19	6
13	pd: Mr Carter a Bill for Dressing Tables &c	12	12	–
–	Recd towards House rent at Greenh: ½ a Yr: to Michs: last	15	–	–
–	Gave the Clark	–	2	6
–	pd Wood the Lime Man on Acct:	25	–	–
–	pd: to the Highways at Greenh: a Yr: to Christs: next	–	9	–
15	Recd Fee for a Grant to Mandeville[300]	15	–	–
–	Gratuity to Mr Green	1	1	–
–	pd: for Stuff for Charles Coat	2	17	–
–	pd: for Lawn for his Frock &c	1	–	–
–	pd: for a Cup for him	1	1	–
–	pd: for Holland for 12 Shirts	12	–	–
–	pd: for putting New blades to 12 knives	–	12	–
17	pd: Window Tax at Greenh: ½ a year to Michs: last	–	15	–
18	pd: Mrs Crook a bill for holland	2	17	9
20	pd: Mr Billinghurst on Account	50	–	–
22	pd: My Lady Biddulph ½ a Year's Rent to Michs: last	8	–	–
23	pd: Rivers the Gardener a Bill for Work at *the White*[301] Little Charles house	5	15	–
–	pd: ditto a Bill for digging Foundations at Jacks house[302]	4	04	6
–	pd Freight for 22000 of White Bricks from Miller	4	8	–
26	pd: Mrs [blank] for 18 Trusses of Hay	–	19	–
27	Recd Fee for a Grant to Jackson[303]	20	–	–
–	Gratuity to Mr Green	1	8	–
–	pd Dunning the Brasier a bill	2	3	2
–	pd. for Lavender Drops	–	8	6
–	pd. for Diaper, for Tablecloaths & Napkins	5	5	–
–	pd: John Westbrook in full for Wages to Michs: last	1	13	6

Nov:

Day	Entry	£	s	d
2	To Dr Slare	1	1	–
–	To Mr Pemble for bleeding my Wife	–	5	–
7	Recd from the office of Works, ½ a year to Midsr: last	354	2	8
–	pd: Tax of 6d pr. pound	8	17	1
–	pd: Land Tax, to Midsr: last	30	9	4½
–	Gratuitys at the Treasury & Excheqr	1	1	6
10	pd: Trout a Bill	16	12	–
12	pd: Rivers a Bill for Unloading Bricks	–	10	6
–	pd: Harrison the Brewer a bill	4	10	3
14	pd: Barrat in full of a Bill	65	13	–
–	pd: the 2d paymt: on the Subscription to the Monasticon[304] & 5s for binding	1	6	–
–	pd Mr Hawkins a bill for Mohair	43	15	–
–	pd: Blunt for hyre of a Horse	–	5	–

[f.43v]

Day	Entry	£	s	d
19	pd: Nurse Wintour to ye 25th: of this month	4	14	6

297 Perhaps Anne (1673–1763), widow of 2nd Earl, author of *Meditations and Reflections*, 1707, or Anne (1690–1788), widow of 4th Earl, remarried 1725.

298 At Stowe.

299 Probably Jack Jones.

300 John Mandeville, D.D., Dean of Peterborough.

301 Italic words deleted. The north White Tower.

302 The south White Tower.

303 James Jackson, Woodford, Essex, and Ripon.

304 See n.210.

		£	s	d
21	Given Sisr: Vic:	10	10	–
–	pd: Sisr: Garencieres in full for Interest to Michs: last	4	19	–
–	pd: at Hartleys, a year to ditto	4	4	–
–	pd: for a Refference from the Treasury	1	1	–
–	pd: an attorney, & for Certificates from St James's Vestry	–	12	6
–	pd: for Lighteridge & Porteridge of 20 Chald[ro]n: of Coales	3	–	–
–	pd: Powell for a Load of Hay £2.2– & a Load of Straw £–18–	3	–	–
28	pd: at the Exchequer, for Two Years & half ground Rent for my House in Whitehall	25	–	–
–	pd: Godfrey, Coachmaker on Acct:	25	–	–
Dec.				
1	Recd Fee for a Grant to Potenger[305]	15	–	–
–	Gratuity to Mr Green	1	1	–
–	pd for ½ a Chaldron of Coale sent to Nurse Wintour[306]	–	16	10
–	*To the Duke of Ancasters Keeper, Fee for Venison*[307]	*1*	*1*	–
4	Recd from Mrs Smith, in full of an Old arrear for Selling Fruit at the Opera	5	5	–
–	pd Betty Hawkins in full for Wages to ye 3d. of Nov. last	5	15	6
6	pd: Wiggens on Account	25	–	–
–	Recd at Greenwich half a Years Salary to Michs: last	100	–	–
–	Recd Attendances to ditto	12	–	–
–	Gave the Treasurers Clark	–	5	–
8	pd Williams a Bill in full for Sugar &c	3	2	9
10	pd: Miller in part of a Bill for Bricks	10	10	–
14	pd: Mr Martin for Bleeding	–	10	6
15	pd: Mr Goatley on Acct: for Bricks from Maidstone	15	–	–
–	pd Howard the Dyer a Bill	5	5	–
–	pd: for a Tea Kettle	2	15	–
–	pd for a Velvet Cap	–	18	–
–	pd for Two Shaving Cloaths	1	2	–
–	pd for 7 Table Cloaths and Six Napkins	1	14	6
–	pd: for Pocket handkerchers for Charles	–	5	–
–	pd: for Thread	–	9	3
18	pd: Mr Goodwin a bill in full for Bricks	14	6	–
–	pd: for a Load of Hay	2	2	–
–	pd White the Tayler in full of a Bill for 1721	35	18	–
–	pd: Mr Bridges in full of a Bill for 1721	19	12	–
–	pd: Richds the Pewterer in full	8	4	–
–	pd: Mrs Ackers a Bill for things for Charles	1	10	–

[f.44]

		£	s	d
20	pd: Mr Miller in full of a Bill for Bricks	20	15	6
–	pd: ditto for my half of the Expence in making 38900 White Bricks, being in Partnership with him[308]	20	17	3
–	pd: Charges in passing a Patent for Miller for a New Invention to Burn Bricks.	72	3	8
–	Recd of Miller, being his half of the expence for the Patent	36	1	10
–	Recd Fees for Grants of Arms to Colebrook Ward, Martin and Hallet[309]	60	–	–
–	Gratuitys to Mr Warburton	4	4	–
–	Recd Fees for 12 Knights £11:12:– for ye Bishop of Chichester £–:18:– for ye Barroness of Brentford & Countess of Darlington £6:18:8 For Baron Grahme and Earl Grahme £6:18:8[310]	26	7	4
21	pd: Goulston the Farrier a Bill in full	21	–	–
22	pd: Mr Kettle a Bill for French Wine	3	15	–
–	To my Wife	15	15	–
–	Recd Fee for a Grant to Woolbol[311]	15	–	–
–	Gratuity to Mr Mauduit	1	1	–
24	pd: Ervin the Tayler in Full	13	8	–
–	pd: The Sadler in full	12	1	6
–	pd Daws the Smith in part of a Bill	5	5	–
31	To Dr Slare at twice	2	2	–
–	pd. Rivers the Gardener 3 Bills	8	18	1
–	pd the Greenwich Farrier a Bill	2	6	2
–	pd: James Wood, a Qrs: Wages to Christs: last	2	10	–
–	pd: Sanders the Brewer a bill in full to this day	11	14	–

[305] Richard Potenger, Reading.

[306] At Walton.

[307] Entry deleted.

[308] See p. 177.

[309] James Colebrooke, Southgate; John Ward, Hackney; Matthew Martin, Wivenhoe, Essex; Sir James Hallett, Crewkerne, Som.

[310] Thomas Bowers, Bishop of Chichester. Baroness von Kielmansegge, George I's mistress, Baroness Brentford and Countess of Darlington. Baron Graham of Belford, Earl Graham.

[311] William Woolball, London.

		£	s	d
–	pd Sisr: Mary $\frac{1}{2}$ a years Int: to Christs: last	3	–	–
–	House Bills this year for Eatables	225	19	10
–	Utensils &c for the House use	16	10	10
–	Odd things or petty Expences	33	17	4
–	Soap, Starch, &c relating to washing	8	4	4
–	Wine, Brandy &c in Small Parcells	11	1	8
–	Candles	11	4	7
–	Tea, Coffee &c	4	7	6

[f.44v]

		£	s	d
–	Given to the Boxes of Tradesmens Servants &c	1	5	–
–	Given to Other Servants, besides what is included & entred upon Journeys	7	13	6
–	Petty Pocket Expences	13	11	6

[f.45]

1722/23 Jan: January ye 1st: 1722/23

		£	s	d
1	Newyears Guifts to [cypher] Charles & Jack	2	6	–
–	ditto to Miss[e]s Betty & Bin Vanbrugh[312] at Greenwich	2	2	–
2	pd: for a Load of Hay at Greenwich and a Load of Straw	2	8	–
–	Recd from my Brother Phil: Two years Rent to Christs: last	60	–	–
–	pd Land Tax for his house from Christs: to Lady day 1721 £–:3:4 from Ladyday 1721 to L.day 1722 £1:1:4 from Ladyday 1722 to L.day 1723 £–:14:–	1	18	8
–	pd Brother Phil: for 12 flasks of Claret	1	4	–
–	pd to ditto. for Duty on White wine	1	11	6
–	pd: to ditto for Bottles & Charges	–	12	5
–	pd: the Ninth Call to the opera	10	–	–
10	Recd Fee for a Grant of Arms to Stone[313]	15	–	–
–	Gratuity to Mr Hesket	1	1	–
–	Recd Fee for a Grant to the Bisp: of Chichester[314]	15	–	–
–	Gratuity to Mr Mawson	1	1	–
–	Newyears Guift to Miss: Philly	–	10	6
14	Recd Fee for a Grant to Morley[315]	15	–	–
–	Gratuity to Mr Warburton	1	1	–
–	pd: for two pair of large Sheets	4	11	–
–	pd: Scarlet for dying a Gowne	–	6	–
–	pd: Rivers for a hundred of Ash Faggots	–	18	–
–	pd: for a Load of Hay	2	2	–
21	pd: Wood Lime Man a Bill for Lime usd at the White House	27	12	–
–	pd: Mr Grantham a Bill for bricks, in full	15	–	–
–	pd: Wright a Bill for Carriage	14	11	–
–	Out of Towne 2 Nights 5 Horses	1	7	6
–	pd: Martha Bowles in full for Wages	15	7	6
–	pd: Robinson the Appothecary, in full to this day	13	7	–
23	pd: Barrat in part of a Bill	50	–	–
28	pd: Nurse Wintour in full to this day	3	–	–
–	pd: The Kingston Appothecary Mr Uvedale a bill	8	12	10
–	pd for Coales sent to ditto[316]	–	16	10
30	Rd: Fee for a Grant to Miller[317]	15	–	–
–	Gratuity to Mr Mauduit	1	1	–
–	pd: Mr Van Ruyven a Bill for Chairs &c in full	13	13	–
31	Recd Rent for Kensington house, a year to Christs: last	60	–	–

[f.45v]

Feb.

		£	s	d
1	pd: for painting 2 Draughts of Arms	1	1	–
5	Recd from the College of Arms $\frac{3}{4}$ Salary to Michs: was twelve month 1721	30	–	–
–	allow'd Taxes & Fees to ditto	11	3	7
–	Recd Rent for Greenh: house 3 Qrs. to	3	15	–
6	pd Mr Goodchild[318] a Bill for Linnen	8	8	7
7	Recd Fee for a Confirmation to Hicks[319]	5	–	–
–	Recd Fee for the Countess of Walsingham &c[320]	6	18	8
–	Recd Fee for Earl Ker &c[321]	6	18	8
–	Recd a Knights Fee	–	19	4
–	Recd Fee for a Grant to Woolball[322]	15	–	–
–	Gratuity to Mr Mauduit	1	1	–

312 See n.200.

313 James Stone, Bradbury, Wilts. and London.

314 Thomas Bowers.

315 John Morley, Halstead, Essex.

316 To Nurse Winter; the previous entry is an insertion.

317 Pancefort Miller, London.

318 Cf. *Chandos*, p.201.

319 Henry Hickes, Covent Garden.

320 Petronille Melusine von der Schulenberg, illegitimate daughter of George I.

321 Robert Ker, Earl Ker of Wakefield, created 1722 when about thirteen. Later 2nd Duke of Roxburghe.

322 See n.311.

		£	s	d
8	Recd for a Grant to Heysham[323]	15	–	–
–	Gratuity to Mr Green	1	1	–
11	pd: Mr Beckham, Greenh: Brewer a Bill, to ye 31st dec last	20	1	–
–	pd: Wigzell the Corn Chandler a Bill to ditto	16	5	6
15	pd: Mrs Ruffle on Acct:	20	–	–
–	Recd of my Brother Charles ½ a Yrs Intrest to Christs: last	50	–	–
20	Recd of my Brother Charles on account of a Note from him for £543:–:6	100	–	–
–	pd: Mr Goatley, in full of a Bill for Bricks	20	–	–
21	pd: Prat a Bill for Bricks	31	13	–
–	Recd of Mr Dodington in full for my Pains & Charges about the Building & Gardens at Eastbury, accounting to Midsr: next	700	–	–
–	pd for a Load of Hay in London: £2:8:– & a Load of Straw £1:4:–	3	12	–
26	Recd Fee for a Grant to Neal[324]	15	–	–
–	Gratuity to Mr Stibbs[325]	1	1	–
–	pd: John Westbrook a Qrs Wages to Christs: last	1	5	–
27	Recd Fee for a Grant to Gumley[326]	15	–	–
–	Gratuity to Mr Hesket	1	1	–
28	pd: Mr Graham a Bill in full to Chr: last	8	5	–
March				
1	pd Mr Josiah Wetherhill a Bill in full for Work done at Whitehall	8	17	6
–	pd: Mr Ayres a Bill for Coales to Chr: last	15	–	–
–	Recd from the Earl of Carlisle to buy a Cup for Charles[327]	25	–	–
–	pd for the said Cup	33	12	–
[f.46]				
6	pd Mr Barrat in full of a Bill	104	13	–
–	Recd Fee for a Grant of Arms in a particular manner to Mrs Merry[328]	10	–	–
–	Gratuity to Mr Mauduit	–	14	–
–	pd: Mr Gale, Upholsterer a Bill in full	20	–	–
18	pd: on an Assessment at Greenh: for Parish Uses	1	10	–
–	To my Wife	20	–	–
–	Given John Westbrook	1	1	–
–	pd for a Load of Hay	2	11	–
21	Recd Fee for a Grant to Gardner[329]	15	–	–
–	Gratuity to Mr Green	1	1	–
22	pd: for 6 chances upon Lottery Tickets last year	22	1	–

		£	s	d
–	pd for one Prize	10	–	–
–	Recd for the Prize	19	7	6
–	pd: for a Ticket in the Present Lottery	10	6	6
28	pd: Middleton a Bill	1	16	–
29	Recd of Mr Portalles	45	–	–
–	pd Haslam a Bill to Christs last	5	10	–
–	Recd Last Christmass Dividend from the Southsea, being for ½ a year	45	6	7
–	pd: Wilson the Glazier a Bill	1	18	8
30	pd: Wood Lime Man in full of a Bill	9	16	–
–	pd: Brother Phillip pr 30 pints of Malaga	1	–	2
April				
1	pd: Window Tax for the Castle ½ a year to L:day last	–	15	–
2	pd: Poors Tax for ditto ½ a year to ditto	1	–	–
–	pd: James Wood a Qurs: Wages to ditto	2	10	–
4	pd: a Bill of Disbursments to Nurse Wintour	–	14	1
–	pd: Eliz: Bomber for a Load of Hay	1	18	–
–	Recd of my Brother Charles a Qrs. Int. to Ladyday last	25	–	–
–	pd: the Walton Waterman a Bill to Chrs: last	–	13	3
–	pd: Mr Uvedale a Bill in full	4	4	–
–	pd: the Lady Biddulph ½ a years Rent to L.day last	8	–	–
5	Recd of the Managers of Drury Lane Playhouse on Acct	125	–	–
–	a Bait at Hampton Court. 5 horses	–	4	6
–	pd: White the Tayler in full of a Bill to Christs: last	26	–	–
–	pd: Mallory the Laceman in full to ditto	17	–	–
–	pd: Richardson the Haberdasher in full to ditto	5	15	–
–	pd: Mr Bridges in full to ditto	14	18	–
–	pd: for 2 Pocket Rulers	–	12	–
8	pd: Godfrey Coach maker in full to Christs: last	51	1	–
[f.46v]				
10	pd: Mary Rooth in full for Wages to Christs. last	8	8	–
–	pd Mary Cox in full to ditto	13	13	–
–	pd Sarah Jones in full to ditto	11	11	–
13	Recd from Greenh: Hospital, Allowance for half a years house Rent, to Lady day last	15	–	–

[323] William Heysham, Greenwich, M.P. for Lancaster.

[324] John Neale, Surrey.

[325] Edward Stibbs, Chester Herald, 15 Dec. 1720–10 Jan. 1740 (Godfrey, p.126).

[326] John Gumley, Isleworth.

[327] The Earl was Charles's godfather.

[328] No trace in Foster, *Grantees*, unless Capt. John Merrye (n.208).

[329] John Gardner, Southwark and Jamaica.

		£	s	d
–	Given the Clark	–	2	6
17	Out of Towne two nights 4 horses	1	5	–
20	pd for ½ a Load of Hay & a Load of Straw at Greenh:	2	5	–
–	Things for Charles	–	5	6
–	pd for Holland for Shirt Sleeves	1	6	–
–	pd for Lavender Drops	–	6	6
–	pd Nurse Wintour	4	3	–
–	pd for making a Skreen	–	13	–
–	pd for Quilting a Bed Quilt	–	12	–
–	pd Mr Pringle for bleeding my Wife	–	5	–
24	pd a Bill for Lace for Shirts	5	–	–
26	pd Blake a Bill for Ale to Christ: last	6	–	–
–	Recd from the Office of Works, a Quarter due at Michs. last	179	3	10
–	allow'd for the Sixpenny Tax	4	9	7½
–	for the Land Tax	12	03	9
–	Given the Paymasters Clark	–	5	–
–	pd for Coffee dishes & a China Mugg	–	15	–
30	pd Several things during the Childs Sickness and for his Burying at Walton[330]	8	6	7
–	pd for a Load of Hay £2:14 – one of straw £1:4:–	3	18	–
May				
3	Recd from Mr Fort on Account for Rent	30	–	–
–	Recd for a Mare	5	–	–
–	pd: for a Coach Horse	25	–	–
–	Given the Servant	–	10	6
4	pd: for a Mare	6	6	–
6	Gave Settle the Poet[331]	1	1	–
–	pd: Leignes for Two New Perriwiggs	11	11	–
–	pd: Charges upon ten Shares I Subscrib'd for, in the Chelsea Waterwork[332]	3	10	–
8	pd: Mr Miller the Brickmaker towards Carrying on the project of making White Bricks, being in Partnership with him	10	10	–
9	Recd from Coll: Godolphin a Years Rent to Lady day last	63	–	–
16	pd: Interest to Mr Hesleden, a year to ye 1st of this month	3	10	–
–	Recd for a Grant of Arms & Supporter to the Royal Insurance Comp.	45	–	–
–	Gratuity to Mr Mauduit			

[f.47]

		£	s	d
16	pd Mr Vokins for Stuff & Silk for a Suit	5	5	–
–	pd the Powder Bill to Lady day last	1	13	6
–	pd for a Card Table	3	13	6
–	For a New Coat for Charles			
–	pd for Cheny & a Teaboard	1	14	6
17	Recd for a Coach horse	3	3	–
–	pd the Walton Waterman a Bill	–	7	–
18	pd: Mrs Ruffle in full of her Bill to Christs. last	6	16	6
–	pd: The Washer Womans bill for 10 months to ye 1st Inst:	10	17	4½
–	pd: for Silk for a Morning Gowne	6	16	–
–	pd for Silk for Coach Curtains	1	2	–
24	To Dr Arbutnot[333]	1	1	–
25	To ditto	1	1	–
–	pd John Westbrook his Wages in full	1	17	6
26	To Mr Amyand, for Inoculating Charles[334]	10	10	–
27	To Dr Arbutnot	1	1	–
28	To Ditto	1	1	–
–	To ditto	1	1	–
29	To ditto	1	1	–
–	pd for a Belt	–	12	6
–	for a Load of Hay at London	3	–	–
30	pd Interest to Sisr: Gar: ½ a Year to L.day last	4	10	–
–	To Dr arbutnot	1	1	–
31	pd: Mr Barratt a Bill in full of All Accts	66	15	–
June				
1	To Dr Arbutnot	1	1	–
–	pd For Fringe for a Sash	–	8	–
4	pd Mr Miller Brickmaker, on account towards making Bricks in Partnership	10	10	–

330 Jack. See p.97.

331 Elkanah Settle, poet and playwright (1648–1724). Progressively less successful, obtained a place in the Charterhouse *c.*1718. 'Settle did as well for Aldermen in his time, as John Home could do now. Where did Beckford and Trecothick learn English?' (Dr Samuel Johnson; Boswell's *Life*, 15 May 1776).

332 Incorporated 1722 by Act of Parliament. The main reservoir was in Pimlico, on the site of Victoria Railway Station. A loose paper in the Account Book (numbered f.64A) is a printed notice of change of meeting from 17 to 23 June 1726 and of calls of 20*s.* per share due on 30 June and 10 Aug.

333 Dr John Arbuthnot (1667–1735), one of Queen Anne's physicians. Author of *John Bull* (1712).

334 Claudius Amyand, surgeon to George I and George II. Inoculation by a scratch with a mild form of smallpox was common in Turkey; it was described to the Royal Society in 1713 but popularized a few years later by Lady Mary Wortley Montagu. An epidemic early in 1721 renewed public attention; the Princess of Wales's daughters were treated by Amyand in April 1722. Some deaths ensued and the practice remained controversial. Apart from complete ignorance of the principles and uncertainty of the technique, the practice helped to spread the disease rather than control it. It was superseded late in the eighteenth century by Edward Jenner's method of vaccination, from cow-pox, which conferred immunity. Vanbrugh wrote to Lord Carlisle about the controversy on 18 Feb. 1724 (Webb, p.158); on 2 March he recorded a double fee to Amyand, perhaps for his wife and himself (f.50v).

8	Recd Fee for a Grant to Cook[335]			
–	Gratuity to Mr Jones[336]			
15	Recd Fee for a Grant to Blythe[337]	15	–	–
–	Gratuity to Mr Green	1	1	–
17	Out of Towne 8 days. 15 horses. all expences	7	2	–
19	pd: Mr Lukin a Bill for Plate, in full	26	11	–
27	pd: for a Load of Hay at London £3:6:– of Straw £1:4:–	4	10	–

July

3	pd: Mr Miller Brickmaker on Acct for making bricks	10	10	–
–	pd: Mr Chaffee a Bill for horse meat	4	5	3
–	Recd from my Bro: Charles. a Qrs Interest to Midsr: last	25	–	–
–	Memd. I let a Coach house & Stable in Scotland Yard to Mr Tho: Rich for £16 a year, to commence from Midsumr: last past			

[f.47v]

5	pd. Tho: Williams a Bill for Casks	1	11	–
6	Recd for Attendances at Greenh: Hospitall to Lady day last	11	–	–
–	Recd Salary at ditto ½ a Year to ditto	100	–	–
–	Gave the Clark	–	5	–
8	Easter offering to the Minister of Greenh: to Lady day last	2	2	–
–	To the Clark	–	5	–
–	pd: Billinghurst on Acct:	10	10	–
9	pd: Wood Limeman a Bill for the Castle	4	–	–
–	pd: Ditto a Bill for the White House or North Tower	7	4	–
–	pd: Ditto a Bill for the South Tower	3	12	–
–	Out of Towne, 2 baits, 5 horses	–	11	10
11	Recd Rent for Greenh: house ½ a Yr. to Mich: last	2	10	–
13	pd: Williams, the Coalman at Greenwich a Bill	4	17	–
15	pd. for a Load of Hay at Greenh:	3	5	–
–	pd: for the Highways at Greenh: a Yr: to Lady day last	–	9	–
19	pd: Richd: Rutland for Brewing	–	7	6
17	Out of Towne 3 days 5 horses	6	5	–
22	pd Rivers in full of a Bill for the Whitehouse	2	6	11
–	pd ditto a Bill for the Castle, for Materials	1	7	6
–	pd ditto a years allowance for keeping the Garden to Midsr: last	4	–	–
–	pd: [blank] a Bill for painting	2	5	6
24	pd: Mr Schaart a Bill for Rhenish wine	5	1	–
25	pd: Mr Miller on Acct: for making white bricks	10	–	–
–	Recd from the office of Works, a Qr: to Chrs: last	177	4	6
–	pd the 6 penny Tax	4	8	6
–	pd the Land Tax	12	3	9
–	Treasury and Excheqr Gratuitys	–	11	–
–	Given the Paymasters Clark	–	5	–
–	pd Thomson the Tayler a Bill for Charles's Pee Jacket[338]	–	10	6
–	pd: Ervin the Tayler a Bill in full	9	9	–
26	Recd Rent from my Brother Phil: half a year to Midsr: last	15	–	–
27	To my Wife	15	15	–
–	pd: my Sisr: Mary ½ a yrs. Intt: to Midsr: last	3	–	–
30	For half a Load of Straw	–	12	–
–	Recd Excheqr Salary a year to Chrs: last	27	7	6
–	allow'd the 6d Tax	–	14	–
–	Fees	3	19	6
31	Recd Fee for a Grant to Chambers[339]	15	–	–
–	Gratuity to Mr Mawson	1	1	–
–	Keeping the Mare 6 weeks and 2 days at 5s a week	–	11	6

[f.48]

Augt:

1	Recd Fee for a Grant to Piper[340]	15	–	–
–	Gratuity to Mr. Green	1	1	–
–	pd for Livery Stockings	–	15	6
–	pd a Bill for Pyrmont Water	2	9	2
–	pd for 3 Gallons of Arrack[341] at Greenwich	–	17	–
3	pd: for keeping the Mare at ye black Lion at Greenh:	–	5	10
5	pd: Wiggens the Carpenter for Work done at *Charles's House*[342] the White House In full of a measur'd Bill £22:–:– a Day Bill £8:–:–	30	–	–
–	pd: ditto a Bill for the Kitchin at the Castle	4	16	–
–	pd ditto a Bill of days Work in severall places	21	–	–
–	pd Bardney a Bill for Pyrmont Waters	3	5	2
6	To Dr Slare	1	1	–

335 Thomas Cooke, Norwich.

336 Philip Jones, York Herald 9 Nov. 1722–9 June 1735 (Godfrey, p.189).

337 William Blyth, Mayor of Norwich.

338 Pee or pea jacket, a short stout coarse woollen overcoat (1725, SOED).

339 Thomas Chambers, London and Derby.

340 John Piper, Ashen, Essex.

341 Properly any Eastern spirituous liquor, especially from the coco-palm (SOED).

342 Italic words deleted.

		£	s	d
–	pd: Gilham a Bill at the Castle	28	10	–
–	pd: Daws in full	9	13	–
–	pd: Mr Billinghurst on Account	80	–	–
–	pd: Wigzell Two Bills for Corn £7:5:10 £10:2:6	17	8	4
9	To Dr Slare	1	1	–
30	Recd of Mr Strickland in full for two years Rent of the Stables &c in Scotland Yard	32	–	–
–	pd for Pencils & Water Colours	–	6	–
–	pd for the Horses at Hampt: Court. a bait in Aprl: last[343]	–	4	6
2	pd: Mr Miller on Acct: for making White Bricks	14	–	–
Sept:				
17	Out of Towne on a Journey[344] to Castle Howard 42 days 5 horses £9:4:9 Turnpikes £–:10:– Eating Bills £13:16:6 Hyre of a Calash from Nottingham &c £5:5:– To Servants in Inns £1:9:– To Servants in private houses £8:3:– Washing, Farryer, Letters &c £4:4:6	42	12	9
Oct				
17	pd Window Tax for ye Castle ½ a year to Michs: last past	–	15	–
–	Out of Towne in a Journey to Ld Cobhams. 16 days 6 Horses £1:19:2 Turnpikes £–:7:2 Eating Bills £3:19:2 Hyre of a horse £2:10:– To Servants in Inns £–:8:3 To Servants at Stowe, and to the Postillion afterwards £6:–:6 Washing, Letters &c £–:19:9	16	4	–
[f.48v]				
19	pd My Lady Biddulph, half a years Rent to Michs: last	8	–	–
–	pd to ditto for Two Loads of Hay	6	–	–
21	Recd Fee for a Grant of Arms, to the Bishop of Norwich[345]	15	–	–
–	Gratuity to Mr Green	1	1	–
–	Recd Salary as Clarx: half a year to Lady day last was twelve months	20	–	–
–	allow'd Fees & Taxes	2	3	–
22	Recd Fee for a Grant to Bird[346]	15	–	–
–	Gratuity to Mr Mawson	1	1	–
–	Recd of Mr Potter £10 he was oblig'd to pay me upon Signing the Lease I made him of Some Houses in the Haymarket	10	–	–
–	pd: To ditto in full of a Bill for Work &c and of all Demands	20	–	–
–	pd: at Hartleys for a year, to Michs: last	4	4	–
24	pd: My Sisr: Gars: ½ a Yrs Int: to Michs: last	4	10	–
25	pd for a Load of Hay at London	3	6	–
–	pd Mrs Ruffle in full for half a years corn to Midsr: last	17	–	–
26	pd: Mr Billinghurst on Acct:	40	–	–
–	Recd at Greenwich Hospitall allowance for House Rent, ½ a year to Michs: last	15	–	–
–	Gave the Clark	–	2	6
–	Given towards the Expences in the Contest about the Church Warden	3	3	–
Nov:				
7	Out of Towne on a Journey to Mr Dodingtons. 12 days 5 Horses £3:19:8 Turnpikes £–:2:8 Eating Bills £3:16:9 To Servants in Inns £–:10:3 To Servants at Mr Dodingtons £–:12:6 To Servants at Mr Merrils £1:1:– Washing Letters &c £–:7:–[347]	10	9	10
–	Given James	–	10	6
9	Brown a Bill for Glaz'd Tyles	3	5	–
–	pd ditto another Bill	3	10	5
18	pd Land Tax for the Castle ½ a Yr. to Michs: last	–	18	4
–	pd Mrs Wright a Bill for Carriage	7	6	–
[f.49]				
20	pd Poors Tax for the Castle ½ a Yr to Michs: last	1	–	–
22	pd James Wood ½ a Yrs Wages to Midsr. last	5	–	–
–	pd for ½ a Load of Straw	–	10	–
–	pd Mrs Gilham a Bill in full	19	17	–
25	pd: the 10th Call to the opera	10	–	–
26	Recd Fee for a Grant to Hankey[348]	15	–	–
–	Gratuity to Mr Green	1	1	–
–	pd for India Dimity[349]	3	3	–
29	Recd from the office of Works a Qrs: Salary to Lady day last	180	15	–
–	pd: the Land Tax to ditto	12	3	9
–	pd: Fees at the Treasury	–	7	4
–	pd: the Six penny Tax	4	10	3
–	To the Clark 5s. & to ye Paymasters Man 2s:6	–	7	6
–	out of Towne one Night 4 Horses	–	15	6
Dec:				
	5th pd: My Sisr: Gar: on acct: of Principal, there remaining now			

[343] Also entered on 5 April (f.46).

[344] Taking in Scarborough on the way and Grimsthorpe on the return journey (Webb, p.151).

[345] John Leng, Bishop of Norwich.

[346] Edward Bird, Westminster.

[347] Mr Dodington's: Eastbury. Mr Merril's: probably Lainston, near Winchester. John Merrill, Deputy Paymaster of the Forces, died 19 Dec. 1734.

[348] Henry Hankey, Cheshire.

[349] Stout cotton fabric with raised stripes and fancy figures, often for beds and hangings (SOED).

		£	s	d
	upon the Bond but one hundred pounds Principal due to her	50	–	–
–	pd: in full discharge of Mr Hesledens Bond for £70	70	–	–
9	pd: for a Load of Hay at London	3	10	–
12	pd: Mr Miller on acct:	6	–	–
–	Recd from the Heralds College 2 Lds Fees £1:18.4 Ld Walpole £2:7:8 Bishop of London £–:18:–[350]	5	4	–
14	pd Billinghurst upon acct:	10	10	–
17	Recd From the Wardrobe, 2 Yrs Livery Money 1720 & 1721	16	18	8
–	pd: Fees for ye Same	–	19	10
–	pd. de la Bourd for a Guilt Sconce	2	10	–
20	pd: Rogers, Brickmaker, a Bill in full	27	–	–
27	pd: Sisr: Mary half a yrs Int: to Christs; now past	3	–	–
28	Recd for attendances at Greenh: Hospital Half a Year to Michs: last	8	–	–
–	Given the Clark	–	2	6
–	Recd Rent for Greenh: House ½ a Yr: to Ladyday last	2	10	–

[f.49v]

		£	s	d
30	To Dr Slare	1	1	–
–	pd Mr Ransom the Glazier in full	9	14	–
–	pd: for Silk for Charles's Coat	4	17	–
–	pd: for Frocks, Stockings & Pins for dto:	2	15	–
–	pd: Wigzell a Bill in full to this day	12	9	–
–	pd: Wheeler the Farrier at Greenh: a bill in full	2	7	–
–	pd: Watson ye Sadler at Greenh: a bill in full	–	13	–
–	pd: Beckham the Brewer at Greenh: a bill in full	14	3	–
–	pd: Bennet the Shoemakers Bill in full	6	16	6
–	pd: Mrs Read a Bill for Shoes for Charles	–	15	–
-	Recd from my Brother Charles ½ a years Interest to Chrs: Last	50	–	–
–	pd: Mr Portalles a Bill for Wine	31	15	6
31	pd: Mr Graham the apothecarys Bill in full	6	6	–
–	pd: Mrs Ruffles Bill in full	9	15	–
–	pd: Middletons Bill in Full	5	5	–
–	pd: Mr Ayres, his Bill, in full	9	–	–
–	pd: Mr Haslams Bill in full	2	19	–
–	pd: Sanders's Bill in full	7	17	–
–	pd: The Powder Bill in full	2	1	–
–	*pd: for a Bench for the Hall at Greenh*[351]	*2*	*10*	–
–	pd: the Sadlers Bill in full	3	–	–
–	pd: Richards's Bill in full	5	14	–
–	pd: Mallorys Bill in full	14	10	–
–	pd: Godfrey the Coach Maker, a Bill in full	54	–	–
–	pd: Mr Bridges a Bill in full	15	15	–
–	pd: Robinson the Greenwich Apothecary in full	5	15	–
–	pd: Hutchinson Shoemaker	6	17	6
–	pd: Rackett the Taylor a Bill in full	19	4	–
–	pd: Mary Rooth a Yrs Wages to this day, & given her over £1.6:–	6	6	–
–	pd: Sarah Jones dto: & given her over £–:16:–	6	6	–
–	pd: Mary Cox dto & given her over £–:12:–	6	6	–
–	pd Betty Hawkins a yr & 2 months to this day, & given her £–:6:6	6	16	6
–	pd Mary Whiffins, a Yr & Qr: to Chrs: last. given her 2s.6d	7	–	–
–	pd: Goulston the Farrier in full	10	15	–
–	house Bills this year for eatables	202	18	4
–	Utensils &c for the House	11	15	5
–	odd things or petty expences	29	13	7½
–	Soap starch, Mangling &c relating to Washing	8	17	4
–	Wine, Brandy, Tea &c in Small parcells	14	6	9
–	Candles	11	12	10½
–	Petty, Pocket expences	5	5	11

[f.50]

1724 Jany January ye 1st, 1724

		£	s	d
1	Recd from Ld Cobham, to pay for Plate formerly order'd for his Godson[352]	120	–	–
–	pd Mr Lukin a Bill for the said Plate in full	120	–	–
6	pd: Wiggens the Carpenter 2 Bills in full of all account	24	–	–
–	pd: Billinghurst on account	25	–	–
9	To Dr Arbutnot	1	1	–
15	To ditto	1	1	–
–	To Dr Slare	1	1	–
–	To Mr: Standfast a Bill for Books	2	3	–
16	To Dr Slare	1	1	–
–	For a Load of Hay & one of Straw in London	4	13	–

Feb.

		£	s	d
8	For a Load of Hay in London	3	9	–
11	Recd of Mr Portalles a years Rent, due at Christs: 1722	90	–	–
19	From the Heralds College, fee for a Grant to Morson[353]	15	–	–
–	Gratuity to Mr Mawson	1	1	–
20	pd: Mr Hargrave a Bill for work at Whitehall	12	4	–

350 Robert, eldest son of Sir Robert Walpole, created Baron Walpole of Walpole, 1723; later 3rd Earl of Orford. Edmun d Gibson, Bishop of London.

351 Entry deleted.

352 Jack, who had died.

353 Richard Morson, London.

		£	s	d
21	Fee for a Grant to da Costa[354]	15	–	–
–	Gratuity to Mr Green	1	1	–
24	pd: Francis the Bricklayer a Bill for Work at the Playhouse	1	12	6
28	Recd from the Southsea ½ a years dividend on £1605 :11 :– stock to Midsummer last	48	3	3
–	Recd from ditto, a quarters annuity on £802 :15 :6 to Michs: last	10	–	8
–	Recd from ditto, on £802 :15 :6. Stock half a years dividend, to Christs: last	24	1	7
–	Recd a Years Rent, for Kensington house due at Christs: last	60	–	–
–	Recd Fee for a Grant to Lintot[355]	15	–	–
–	Gratuity to Mr Mauduit			

[f.50v]

		£	s	d
28	pd Mr Elkin a bill for the Brickwork in the Second White Tower at Greenwich	53	17	–
–	pd ditto a Bill for Work done at Whitehall	17	15	–
29	pd for a Load of Hay in London	3	6	–
March				
2	To Mr Amyand Surgeon[356]	21	–	–
–	To Mr Shipton Surgeon	15	15	–
11	Recd Fee for a Grant to Teale[357]	15	–	–
–	Gratuity to Mr Wyniat[358]	1	1	–
12	pd Rivers a Bill in full	8	11	8
13	To my Wife	15	15	–
–	for a Velvet Cap	–	19	6
–	Playthings for Charles	–	10	6
14	Recd from the office of Works a Quarter to Midsumr: last	177	5	8
–	Paid the 6 penny Tax	4	8	8
–	Paid the Land Tax to Midsr: last	10	16	8
–	To the Paymasters Clark	–	5	–
–	pd: for Tea sent to Southwell[359]	1	3	–
18	pd: Mrs Ackres a Bill	2	10	–
20	pd: my Sisr: Garencieres on Acct: of Principal	20	–	–
–	pd: ditto for ½ a years Intrest to Lady day next	3	11	–
–	pd: Mr Marriot, for six years Rent of a Close at Hampton Court	9	–	–
–	Recd of Mr Fort on Acct; of Rent	25	–	–
21	Recd of my Brother Phil: ½ a Yrs Rent to Christmas last	15	–	–
–	pd: Moor[360] the Gardener for Pinning & Nailing Trees	–	8	8
–	pd: Land Tax for Bro: Phil's house ½ a Yr to Christs: last	–	14	8
–	Recd half a year Salary at Greenh: Hospital to Michs: last	100	–	–
–	Gave the Treasurers Clark	–	5	–
25	pd Rivers in full	1	–	–
28	pd: the eleaventh Call to the opera	10	–	–
–	pd Peter Colton in full for Wages to this day	4	8	–
31	Recd Fee for a Grant to Thompson[361]	15	–	–
–	Gratuity to Mr Jones	1	1	–
28	pd for a Load of Hay in London	3	6	–
April.				
4	pd Land Tax for the Castle ½ a Yr: to Lady day last	–	18	4
–	pd: Wilkins[362] the Plaisterer two Bills in full	22	17	–
6	pd: Window Tax for ye Castle ½ a yr. to Lady day last	–	15	–
7	pd: Billinghurst in full of Work done at Greenwich, to Christmass last past	47	16	–

[f.51]

		£	s	d
8	pd my Sister Garencieres in full discharge of her Bond for £300	80	–	–
–	Recd from ditto upon a Note under my hand	80	–	–
9	pd Lady Biddulph ½ a Years Rent to Ladyday last	8	–	–
–	pd ditto for 2 Loads and half of Hay £7 :2 :6 pd ditto for ½ a Load of Straw £–:12:–	7	14	6
–	pd: John Moor the Gardener a Bill	4	4	–
22	Recd from the Managers of Drury Lane Playhouse on Acct:	150	–	–
24	pd for Stuff and Lining for a Suit	5	15	–
–	pd for Stuff for a Gowne	1	19	–
–	pd for a Load of Hay at London £3 :3 :– and one of Straw £1 :4 :–	4	7	–
25	Recd Int: from my Bro: Charles, a Qr. to Lady day last	25	–	–
29	pd Mr Wood, Clockmaker a Bill	1	16	–
May				
2	pd: Mr Goulding at Greenh: a Bill for 2 Stacks of wood	2	–	–
5	Recd from the Southsea, half a Yrs annuity upon £802 :15 :6. to Lady day last	20	1	–

[354] Leonor, relict of Alvaro Da Costa, Highgate.

[355] Thomas Lintot, Wadhurst, Sussex.

[356] See n.334.

[357] Isaac Teale, Hanover Square.

[358] Charles Whinyates, Richmond Herald 3 Nov. 1722–14 Oct. 1737 (Godfrey, p.148).

[359] See p.168.

[360] John Moor (f.51).

[361] Ralph Thompson, London.

[362] John or Chrysostom Wilkins (Beard, p.172).

	£	s	d
– Recd for a Quarters Rent for Kensington house to Lady day last	15	–	–
– Recd from the Heralds College, a Yrs Salary [to] Lady day 1723	40	–	–
– pd Fees and Taxes	16	19	10
6 Recd Rent from Coll. Godolphin a year to Lady day last	63	–	–
– pd. for Cloath for 6 Shirts, at Mr Bonfoys	6	10	–
– pd for Shirts for Charles, at ditto	–	15	–
– From the Heralds College Fees for 8 Bishops	7	4	–
– Fee for Sr Chaloner Ogle[363]	–	19	4
– Fee for Sr Peter Vandeput[364]	1	1	8
– Fees for Sr Clement Werg Sr John Darnell Sr Moor Molineux Sr James Campbell[365]	3	17	4
11 out of Towne a Night 4 Horses	–	15	10
12 pd. Spark ye Brasier for a Silver'd Cup	2	13	6
13 pd: Mr Hudson[366] for a Picture of Charles £6:6:– For a Copy £3:3:– for a case £–:5:–	9	14	–
[f.51v]			
16 Recd Allowances for Attendances at Greenh half a year to Lady day last	8	–	–
19 pd a Bill for Mum	–	14	6
20 pd: Wood, Lime Man a Bill	1	9	4
25 pd: Mr Crowley a Bill of £34:12:2 of which £29:3.10 is for my Brother Charles	5	8	4
– Lace for 3 Shirts	2	14	–
– Strip'd Holland for a Wastcoat	–	12	6
29 Fee for a Grant to Brown[367]	15	–	–
– Gratuity to Mr Mauduit	1	1	–
June			
1 pd: Pomroy[368] the Joyner in full of five Bills	40	–	–
– pd: Moor the Gardener a Bill	12	3	–
5 pd James Wood, in full for Wages to Midsumr: next and gave him a Qr more	12	10	–
6 pd Taxes as Clarx: 1 yr & ¼ to Ladyday 1723	13	2	6
15 pd: John Moor, Gardener a Bill to this day	8	13	1
– pd: Dr Skerret for his Easter dues to Easter last[369]	2	2	–
– pd the Clark	–	5	–
– Given Mrs Kemp	10	10	–
20 pd a Call of 40s pr Share to the Chelsea Waterwork	20	–	–
29 Out of Towne on a Journey to Eastbury 11 days Six horses £5:2:9 Fruit &c £–:9:6 Turnpykes & Ferrys £–:4:8 Eating Bills £9:–:1 To Servants in Inns £–:16:6 To Servants at Mr Dodingtons £1:–:– Ditto at Coz: Vanbrughs[370] £–:12:6 Washing, Letters &c £–:4:2 Mending the Wheels & Carriage £1:6:3 Horse hyre £1:1:–	19	17	5
30 Recd Salary from the Excheqr. a year to Christs. 1722	27	7	6
– Fees for ditto	2	19	6
– Sixpenny Tax	–	14	–
July			
3 Recd Salary at Greenwich ½ a year to L.day last	100	–	–
– Gave the Treasurers Clark	–	5	–
4 pd for 3 Lottery Tickets	30	–	–
– Cloath for frocks for Charles	2	8	–
– pd for 12 pair of Scizars at Salesbury[371]	1	6	6
8 Recd Rent from Bro: Phillip ½ a Yr. to Midsr: last	15	–	–
– pd: to ditto for 3 Galls: Arrack & 3 of Brandy	3	1	–
9 Recd in full discharge of Brother Charles's Note to me for £543:–:6	143	–	6
[f.52]			
10 Recd of my Brother Charles, Ground Rent for his House at Greenwich, a Year, to Midsr: last	10	–	–
14 pd Chaffee, a Bill for Horse meat	–	18	8
15 pd Mrs Ruffle for a Mare	9	9	–
– pd the Powder Bill	1	14	–
– pd. the Washer Womans Bill	4	1	–
– pd. Mr Des Fontaines, Surgeon	26	15	–
– pd Sisr: Mary ½ a years Int. to midsr last	3	–	–
Augt.			
27 pd My Sisr: Garencieres a Quarters Int. upon a Note for £80 due at Midsr: last	1	4	–
20 pd for a load of Hay & a load of Straw	4	2	–
– pd Williams at Greenwich a bill for coales	4	11	6

363 Sir Challoner Ogle, Captain, R.N. Sir Peter Vandeput.

364 Sheriff of London, Kt 1684.

365 Sir Clement Wearge, Solicitor General. Sir John Darnell, Serjeant at Law. Sir Moore Molyneux of Loseley, Guildford. Sir James Campbell of Edinburgh.

366 Presumably an early work of Thomas Hudson (1701–79).

367 Thomas Browne, London.

368 William Pomroy or Pomeroy, joiner, but used by Lady Vanbrugh after Sir John's death as factotum.

369 Ralph Skerrett (b.c.1681), Vicar of Greenwich 1720–51.

370 George. See p.161.

371 Salisbury was still noted for flannel, drugget and fine white cloth exported to Turkey.

		£	s	d
Oct				
24	Out of Towne on a Journey to the North from July ye 15th to October the 24th following being 101 days. Eating Bills £55:–:– six Horses £36:10:2 Given to Servants in Inns £4.4.3 Given in private houses £16:11:6 Farrier, Smith & Greasing £4.5.4 Washing £3.10.7 Horse Hyre £15.11.6 Turn Pikes and Guides £–.17.3 Appothecary £2.2.– Lodging at Scarborough £2.2.– Pocket money & Small Expences £10.8.4 Carriage to York £1.7.7 Carriage Back £–.19.–	153	9	6
–	Bought Huggaback[372]	4	5	–
–	Lavender Drops, Tea, Spices &c	3	2	–
Nov.				
10	Out of Towne on a Journey to Stowe from October the 27 to Nov: ye 10th. being 15 days. Six horses. Eating £4.8.8 Horses £2.– Serts in Inns £– 11.6 ditto at Stowe £6.3.– Turn Pykes £– 8.–			
[f.52v]				
	Brought over £13:11:2 Washing £–:6:6 Guide, Oyle, Smith &c £–:10:1 a Postillion £–:16:– Board Wages £–:8:–	15	11	9
15	Paid Lady Biddulph half a year Rent, to Michs: last	8	–	–
–	Recd from the South Sea half a years Annuity to Michs: last	20	1	–
–	Recd Dividend on South Sea Stock ½ a Yr, to Midsr: last	24	1	–
17	For a Copy of a Privy Seal, from the Signet office	1	6	–
–	Recd from Mr Fort in full for Rent for Hampton Court House	20	–	–
–	pd Mr Huggins in full for three Years Rent for a Close at Hampton Court, to Michs: last	4	10	–
–	pd: Peter Collton in full for Wages	1	18	–
20	To my Wife	10	10	–
–	pd. Tax half a Year, for ye Castle, to Michs: last	–	16	8
–	Recd from the Office of Works, Salary for July, Augt: Sept: Oct. Nov. Decr: 1723	355	8	10
–	pd The Civil List Tax	8	18	1½
–	pd Fees at the Treasury[373]			
–	pd the Land Tax to Christs: last	21	13	4
–	To the Paymasters Clark	–	10	–
21	pd Robert Guest in full for Wages & gave him £1.1.6	5	8	–
26	pd a Second Call at the Chelsea Waterworks	20	–	–
–	for Silk for a Coat for Charles: Holland, Cambricke	3	7	6
28	pd Mrs Wright in part of a Bill for Carriage of Bricks	10	10	–
30	pd Moor for 4 bills	4	8	6
Dec				
1	pd for a Chest of Drawers	2	–	–
–	pd. Window Tax at Greenh: ½ a Yr. to Michs: last	–	15	–
–	pd Moor the Gardener in full of 3 Bills	9	8	11
–	pd at Hartleys for a year to Michs: last	4	4	–
3	pd: for Advertisements about Greenh: & Hampton Court[374]	1	2	6
–	pd for a Load of Hay at London	2	17	–
8	pd Co: Garencieres a Bill	1	9	6
10	To Mr Martin, for bleeding my Wife	–	10	6
–	Recd for Attendances at Greenh: ½ a Yr. to Midsr: last	6	–	–
12	pd Cleave the Smith 2 bills in full of all Demds.	14	14	–
19	pd for a Load of Hay in London	3	2	–
[f.53]				
19	From the Heralds College fees Arch Bishop of York £1:16:2 Lord Peircy £1:16:8 Sr John Mitchel Bart: £1:1:8[375]	4	14	6
–	Recd from ditto, a Qrs Salary. to Midsr: 1723	10	–	–
–	pd Taxes for dto	1	13	4
27	pd Fees for ditto	1	–	9
–	To Dr Arbuthnot	1	1	–
28	To ditto	1	1	–
29	To ditto	1	1	–
30	pd: my Sisr: Garencieres ½ a Yrs Int: for £80 to Christs: last past	2	8	–
–	Recd for 3 Blank Lottery Tickets	21	16	–
–	Recd a Quarters Salary at the Heralds College being due from the late Queen, at Ladyday. 1714	10	–	–
–	pd Taxes & Fees[376]			
31	pd Wigzell, Corn Chandler at Greenh: a bill in full	10	18	–
–	pd: Mr Metcalf, Brewer at Greenh: a Bill in full	11	3	–
–	pd: Saunders, the Brewer, a Bill in full	8	13	–
–	pd: Mrs Ruffle a Bill in full	26	6	–
–	pd Robinson Appothecary a Bill in full	–	18	–

372 Huckaback towelling.

373 No amount.

374 Houses for rent: see ff.56, 59v.

375 Lancelot Blackburn, Archbishop of York. Algernon Seymour, 1st Baron Percy; later 11th Duke of Somerset. Sir John Mitchell, Bt, of Westshore, Zetland.

376 No amount.

		£	s	d
–	pd Leignes a bill for three New Perriwigs	17	6	6
–	pd: Brown the Sadler a Bill in full	3	15	–
–	pd: Mr Bridges Woolen Draper a Bill in full	20	15	–
–	pd: Mr Ayres a Bill for Coales in full	27	18	–
–	pd: Malory Laceman a Bill in full	12	14	–
–	pd: Racket, Tayler, a Bill in full	42	–	–
–	pd: Hutchinson Shoemaker a Bill in full	3	8	–
–	pd. Richards, Haberdasher a Bill in full	7	13	–
–	pd: Graham Appothecary a Bill in full	10	9	6
–	pd: Haslam Hosier a Bill in full	3	9	–
–	pd: Graham Appothecary a bill in full[377]	10	9	6
–	pd: Wood the Clockmaker a Bill in full	–	7	6
–	pd: Gale the Upholsterer a Bill in full	7	7	–
–	pd: the Greenwich Farrier a Bill in full	1	15	–
–	pd: Goulston the Farrier at London in full	11	11	1
–	pd: Mary Rooth in full for Wages to Chrs: last	6	6	–
–	pd: Sarah Jones ditto	6	6	–
–	pd: Mary Cox to ditto	6	16	6
–	pd Betty Hawkins to ditto	5	16	6
–	pd: Mary Whiffins to ditto	5	15	6

[f.53v]

		£	s	d
1724	House Bills this Year for Eatables	174	14	10½
–	Utensils &c for the House	14	16	5
–	Odd things	18	11	7
–	Soap, Starch, Mangling &c relating to Washing	12	13	1
–	Tea, Brandy, Wine &c in small parcells	9	6	5
–	Candles	11	17	–
–	Petty Pocket Expences	8	14	2
–	Given to Tradesmens Boxes	1	10	–
–	Given to Other Servants besides what is Included in Journeys	8	14	–

[f.55]

Jany: January ye 1st: 1724/5

		£	s	d
1st	To Doctor Arbuthnot	1	1	–
–	Newyears Guift to My Wife	5	15	–
–	To Charles		10	6
–	To Miss Philly		11	6
2	To my Wife	15	15	–
9	pd Rutland for Carriage of Water at Greenh:	–	19	4
–	pd at Greenh: for the Highways, a Yr. to Ladyday next	–	9	–
5	pd: for a Load of Hay in London	3	–	–
11	pd for a Load of Straw in ditto	1	1	–
–	pd Tho: Chambers, Coachman, in full	2	12	6
15	pd Mr Plaistow for 4 dozen french Whitewine	5	9	–
23	Recd a qrs [*sic*] Salary at Gr: to Michs. Last	100	–	–
–	Gave the Clark	–	5	–
–	pd for a Load of Hay at London	3	–	–
24	To Martin for bleeding	–	10	6
–	Stockings for Charles	–	12	–
–	Pins	–	2	–
–	Fans & Handkerchers to Southwell[378]	1	6	–
30	pd: Two years Rent into the Excheqr, for Whitehall House, being in full discharge, to Michs: last	20	–	–
–	pd fees for the same	1	12	8

Feb:

		£	s	d
2	pd Seymour the Brazier a Bill	1	13	10
4	pd: Mr Miller for 12 Bottles of French White Wine	1	4	–
–	To Mrs Holt, earnest, towards teaching Charles to read	1	1	–
16	pd: for a Load of Hay £3 – & ½ a Load of Straw 11.3	3	11	3
–	pd: Benton a Bill for the mares	–	19	5
18	Recd of my Brother Phil: ½ a yrs Rent to Christs: last	15	–	–
–	allow'd to ditto a Yrs Land Tax to ditto	–	13	4
–	pd: the Hampton Court[379] Watermans Bill	–	18	5
22	pd: Mr Protin for a New Perriwig	5	5	–
23	pd Mr Wetherhilt a Bill in full for work done at the Haymarket	9	8	6
–	pd Ditto on account for work at Greenh.	10	–	–
–	Recd from the Southsea, ½ a Years Dividend, to Chrs. last	24	1	6

[f.55v]

		£	s	d
24	Recd from the office of Works, one Quarter, to Lady day last	180	19	8
–	Paid the Sixpenny Tax	4	10	6
–	pd. Taxes to Lady day last	10	16	8
27	pd. my Sisr: Gar. part of an £80 note	20	–	–

March

		£	s	d
2	pd the 12th and 13th Calls to the Opera	20	–	–
4	pd. Mrs Holt, for a Months teaching of Charles to read	1	1	–
–	pd Mrs Wright, in full of a Bill	1	16	6
9	pd: Dorsells the Joyner a Bill	1	4	–
11	pd. for a Load of Hay	3	3	–
16	Rd. Fee for a Grant to Spake[380]	15	–	–
–	Gratuity to Mr Mauduit	1	1	–
21	To Mr Martin for bleeding		10	6

377 Entered twice.

378 See p. 168.

379 Altered from *Walton*.

380 No trace in Foster, *Grantees*.

22 Recd of Mr Portalles, a Years Rent to Christ: 1723 | 90 – –
– pd Ditto, in full for two Bills for Wine | 58 19 8
– pd Balack a Bill for Coarse Linnen | 3 – 7
23 pd: for Holland for Charles | 1 3 6
26 pd: Moor three Bills | 3 10 6
31 pd: Mrs Dewell a Bill for Printing | 1 2 6
– pd. Bromley, a Bill for Green Mill Serge | 12 – –
– Given to bury Solomon[381] | 1 1 –
– pd Howard for cleaning the Yellow Bed | 1 1 –

April

3 pd: Land Tax for Greenh: Castle, ½ a year to Lady day last | – 16 8
– pd for a Ld of Hay £3.3– & a Ld. of Straw £ 17.3 | 4 – 3
9 pd: Towards the Losses by Fire, on Acct: of the Insurance of Sr Wm Sandersons House at Greenh: | 2 11 8
3 pd Sisr. Mary ½ a yrs Int: to Chrs. last | 3 – –
– pd the first payment on a Subscription to Coopers Prints[382] | 1 1 –
12 pd Mrs Ackres a Bill | 2 3 6
14 pd: Rogers a Bill in full for Bricks | 9 – –
17 Recd in full for my House Rent allowance at Greenh: to the time of its discontinuance | 33 15 –
– pd. Coxed, a bill for a Table & Glass | 3 8 –
– pd Clark the Painter at Greenh: a Bill in full | 16 5 7
20 pd Smith for a Load of Hay | 3 3 –
– To Mrs Holt for a Month's teaching, and books | 1 6 –

May

1 pd Moor the Gardener a Bill for Lome | 2 8 –
– pd ditto a bill for pibbles[383] | 3 14 –
3 pd Bromley, a Bill for Green & Red Mill'd Serge | 7 7 –

[f.56]

7 Out of Towne To Walton & Windsor from the 5th to the 7th 3 days. 6 horses Eating £3:16:– Horses £1:15:– Given to Servants £–:18:7 Turnpykes & Ferrys £–:7:1 Smith £–:1:– Hors hyre £–:15:– | 7 12 8
8 pd for a Load of Straw at London | – 18 –
11 pd Will: Bonny in full for Wages to L.day last | 2 2 –
– pd for a Load of Hay in London | 3 1 –
– Out of Towne, on a Journey to Eastbury 7 days. 4 horses. Eating £4.9.8 Horses £2.–.5 Servants £1.7.4 Turnpykes & ferrys £–.2– Smith £– 8.3 Letters &c £– 2.1 | 8 9 9
20 Recd, from the South Sea ½ a Years Annuity to L.day last | 20 1 –
– Memd: I let my house at Hampton Court to Mr Edwards, for £41:10– pr Anm. the Rent to Commence, from Ladyday last
26 pd for 2 Chaldron of Scotch Coal | 3 6 –
– pd Mrs Holt | 1 1 –

June

2 Fee to Mr Reeves[384] | 1 1 –
6 pd: Sr Gregory Page[385] ½ a Years Rent to Lady day last | 8 – –
– Recd from the College, The whole Fee for a Grant to Baker[386] | 30 – –
– Gratuity to Mr Jones | 2 2 –
7 a Night at Claremont, Men & Horses | – 10 8
8 Recd Fees for 3 Kts & 2 Bishps £4.14.4 Sr John Eyles £–.19.4 Bishops of Landaff & Exeter £1.16.2 Sr Jeoffrey Gilbert £–.19.4 Sr Tho. Masters £–.19.4 Sr Conrade Sprengell £–.19.4[387] | 10 7 10

[f.57v]

8 Given Sisr: Ro[bina]. | 10 – –
– pd for a Load of Hay £3:–:– at London & one of Straw 18s. | 3 18 –
10 pd Mrs Newman, for Cleaning 9 Copper Plates | – 15 –
– pd for a Microscope | 1 1 –
– pd Mrs Holt | 1 1 –
12 Recd Attendances at Greenh: ½ a year, to L.Day last | 9 – –
– Given Sisr: Vic: | 10 10 –
13 to Mr Martin for Bleeding | – 10 6
16 pd Mr Goodchild for Cloath for Shirts | 7 10 6
– For Books | – 8 6
– to my Wife | 15 15 –
– pd for Charles's Coat and Lining | 1 14 5

[381] See n.157.

[382] Not identified.

[383] Pebbles.

[384] Perhaps a legal fee, as on f.57v. In an undated letter, possibly of 1704, to Peter Le Neve (Rosenberg, pp.607–8) Vanbrugh refers to the selection by Mr Reeves for a day for their 'swearing.'

[385] Ground landlord of Vanbrugh Castle in succession to Lady Biddulph.

[386] No trace in Foster, *Grantees*.

[387] Sir Joseph Eyles, M.P., Sheriff of London. Robert Clavering, Bishop of Llandaff. Stephen Weston, Bishop of Exeter. Sir Jeffery Gilbert, Baron of the Exchequer. Sir Thomas Masters of London. Sir Conrade Joachim Sprengell, M.D., F.R.S., Physician to William III and George I.

		£	s	d
23	pd: Mr Partridge a bill for Cyder	3	12	–
–	pd March, for a Load of Hay in London	3	14	–
–	Recd from the Office of Works, half a Years Salary, to Michs: last	358	8	10
–	pd The Sixpenny Tax	8	19	3
–	pd The Land Tax	21	13	4
–	pd Gratuitys at the Treasury	–	14	10
–	Given the Paymasters Clark	–	10	–
24	pd Burges at Greenh: a Bill for Hay & Straw	8	14	6
–	pd: Moor a Bill in full	4	9	–
–	pd: Pomroy, on Acct: for Joyners Work at Greenh:	100	–	–
26	pd: Window Tax at Greenh: ½ a Yr. to Ladyday last	–	15	–
–	pd: at Greenh: for 24 Flasks of Claret	2	8	–
–	pd: My Sisr: Mary ½ a Years Int: to Midsr. last	3	–	–
28	pd: John Heath on account of Wages	2	2	–
29	Recd Rent from Coll. Godolphin, a Year to L.day last	63	–	–
–	pd: Winfield for Fencing the Field	1	13	–
30	pd: Crouch for a Tea Table	2	2	–
July				
1	pd: Wood a Bill for Lime	18	16	–
–	pd: ditto a Bill for Flints	1	4	–
3	Recd: Rent from Brother Phillip ½ a Yr. to Midsr: last	15	–	–
–	Pd: Pomroy in full of 5 Bills	100	–	–
	Recd *of Mr Ward*[388] on the Resignation of my office of Clarenx.	2500	–	–
–	pd: Mr Finch, for passing Mr Wards Patent	64	3	2
–	pd: Fee to Mr Reeves for attending the Caveat entred at the Signet office against the Patent	5	5	–
–	pd: Mr Walker ye Soliciter on the same occasion	5	6	10
[f.58]				
3	Gratuity to Mr Jones,[389] the Earl Marshals Secretary	42	–	–
–	pd: him for the Entry of 56 Grants of Arms	14	3	4
–	Recd Salary from the College, a Year and Qr. to michaelmass last	50	–	–
–	pd Fees and Taxes for the Same	13	–	–
–	pd the third Call to the Chelsea Waterworks	20	–	–
5	pd: Clark the Chairmaker for 12 Chairs	12	12	–
31	Out of Towne on a Journey to Lord Cobhams 26 days 16 Horses Eating £7:18:3¼ Horses £4:13:1 Turnpykes & Guides £–:16:11 Smith, Greasing & Oyle £–:16.8 Washing £–:18:6 given to Servants at Ld Berkshires[390] £4:4:– given to Servts at Ld Cobhams £5:5:–	24	12	5¼
Augt:				
2	pd Poors Tax at Greenh: ½ a Yr. to Ladyday last	–	15	–
5	pd. Mr Bromley for 2 pieces more of Green Serge	4	–	–
–	pd Arbunot for a Glass	1	–	–
–	pd Mr King a Bill for Mantua silk sent to Scarborough[391]	4	18	–
6	Recd from the office of Works a Qr. to Christmass last	183	7	8
–	pd: the Civil List Tax	4	11	8
–	pd. The Land Tax	10	16	8
–	To the Paymasters Clark	–	5	–
–	pd Mrs Ruffle a Bill to midsumr:	25	8	–
7	pd. Emery ye Upholsterer a Bill in full	6	–	–
8	To Dr Slare	1	1	–
9	pd: Trout a Bill	5	6	–
–	pd: Ransom a Bill for Glazing the South Tower	10	3	6
–	pd: ditto a Bill for Work at the Castle	3	6	2
–	pd: for Books	1	8	–
–	pd: for a Looking Glass	1	–	–
–	pd: a Bill for Asses milk for Charles	1	–	6
–	pd: Wigzell a Bill in full	4	8	4
12	pd: Dr Skerret his Easter offering, for Easter last	2	2	–
–	Gave the Clark	–	5	–
13	pd Mr Jacob Fonseca for £1500 Southsea Stock	1822	10	–
–	pd: Brokeridge	1	17	6
–	pd: Kemp for a Load of Hay at Greenwich	3	12	–
–	pd: Moor a Bill for work in the Court	1	8	10
–	To Dr. Slare	1	1	–
17	Recd Excheqr. Salary three Qrs. to Michs: 1724	20	10	7½
–	pd Civil List Tax £–:10:6. Fees £2.7.6	2	18	–
–	Recd From the Southsea, ½ a yrs Dividend to Midr: last	24	1	6
19	pd: Wetherhilt on account for work done at Greenh	21	–	–
–	given Mr Jones's Clark	1	1	–
–	pd the 4th Call to the Chelsea Waterworks	20	–	–
[f.58v]				
19	pd Arbunot for a Lookinglass	1	–	–

388 Italic words deleted. See p.122.

389 See n.336.

390 Henry Bowes Howard, 4th Earl (1687–1757); succeeded 1706 as Earl of Berkshire and 1745 as Earl of Suffolk. Seat and tomb at Charlton, near Malmesbury, Wilts. Another seat at Elford, Staffs.

391 Probably to Theophilus Garencieres's family (see p.158).

		£	s	d
20	pd. Kelham for a pair of buckskin Breeches	1	–	–
21	Recd from Greenh: Hospital half a years Salary to Lady day last	100	–	–
–	Given the Clark	–	5	–
18	pd Mr John Colt, for £400. Southsea Stock	491	10	–
–	pd Brokeridge	–	12	6
–	pd Mr Jos: Vere. for £100 ditto	121	–	–
27	pd Mrs Daws, Widdow to the Smith in full	5	5	–
30	Recd from Mr Rich, Rent for Stables and a Coach House in Scotland Yard a Year & half, to Christs: last	24	–	–
–	Recd from the Excheqr. The full arrear of what was due to me from the late Duke of Marlborough, for Salary and Disbursments, to the Time that the Building was Stopped in 1712[392]	1663	10	9
–	Paid Fees at the Treasury and the Excheqr:	145	6	–
–	Gave Mr Woodeson	2	2	–

Sept:

		£	s	d
1	pd Mr Constance[393] for two Busts	1	10	–
3	pd: Wm: Williams a bill for paving the Court at Greenwich	5	9	–
–	pd Mr Anthony da Costa, for one Thousand pounds, Southsea Stock	1236	5	–
–	pd Brokeridge	1	5	–
–	pd for the Highways at Greenh: a Yr. to L.day next	–	9	–
–	pd: a Bill for Asses Milk	1	–	6
7	Out of Towne at Claremont Two days, 3 Horses	–	15	0
–	To my Wife	11	10	–
–	pd: Kemp for a Load of Hay at Greenh.	3	12	–
9	pd: Mrs [blank] for Lace for Shirts	3	7	6
13	pd: Billinghurst upon account	21	–	–

[f.59]

Oct:

		£	s	d
12	Recd from the office of Works a Qr. to Ladyday last	177	16	8
–	pd the Civil List Tax	4	8	11
–	pd the Land Tax	10	16	8
–	Paymasters Clark	–	5	–
14	pd: Land Tax for Greenh Castle ½ a Yr. to Michs last	–	16	8
15	To Dr Slare	1	1	–
–	Out of Towne, on a Journey to Grimsthorp from the 24th of Sept to the 12th of Oct. 1725 being 27 days, Six horses Eating £15:04:8 Horses £5:19:7 Turnpikes & Guides £–:15:3 Smith & Greasing £–:17:8 Washing £–:14:10 Odd things £–:10:8 Servants at Grimsthorp £5:5:–	29	07	8
19	pd Window Tax at Greenh: ½ a year to Michs: last	–	15	–
–	pd John Heath in full for Wages to Midsr: last	2	12	6
23	pd for a Load of Hay at London	3	3	–
25	Recd from the Hospital at Greenwich instead of Coales which were due to me in the year 1724	4	–	–
–	pd: a Parish assessment for this year, to defray some extraordinary expences	–	15	–
27	pd: Poors Tax at Greenh. ½ a year to Michs: last	1	–	–
28	pd: Mr Crowley a Bill in full	5	17	6
30	pd: Sr Gregory Page ½ a Yrs Rent to Michs: last	8	–	–
–	pd: Mrs Wright a Bill for carriage of bricks	6	12	–
–	pd: Kemp for a Load of Hay at Greenh: & 4 Trusses	3	16	–
31	Recd for Two Old Coach Horses	8	8	–
–	Given Jo Heath	–	5	–

[f.59v]

Nov.

		£	s	d
11	To Dr Slare	1	1	–
–	pd Mr Giles of Deptford for Malt & Hops	1	6	–
18	pd Mr Billinghurst upon Account	40	–	–
27	Recd Rent for Greenh House ½ a Yr to Ladyday was Twelve month	2	10	–
–	Recd from the south sea ½ a Yrs any. to Mich last	20	1	–

Dec:

		£	s	d
2	pd Barrat a Bill in full for Bricks	53	–	–
4	pd: Mr Bladwell, Upholsterer, a bill in full	11	12	–
5	pd Black a Bill for ale in full	5	6	8
–	pd: Protin for a New Wigg	5	5	–
–	Recd from Mr Edwards, Rent for Hampton Court house ½ a year, to Michs: last	20	15	–
–	given Seigr. attillio[394] for a Musick Book	2	2	–
8	pd Mr Goodchild a Bill for Shirts & handkers	10	14	6
14	pd Kelham for a pair of Buckskin Breeches for Will[395]	1	1	–

392 For the first instalment see n.49. Vanbrugh's comment, Webb, pp.168–9.

393 Mr Constance, 'figure-maker', was paid in 1736 for two heads at Wrest Park, Beds. (R. Gunnis, *Dictionary of British Sculptors*, 1953, p.112).

394 Attilio Ariosti (b.1666), violinist and composer. In London 1716 and from 1722. Published 1728 by subscription a volume of cantatas and viola d'amore lessons dedicated to George II.

395 Will Bonny.

		£	s	d
17	pd Rogers a Bill in full for Bricks	78	–	–
–	pd Dr Arbuthnot on a Subscription for his Book of Measures, Weights &c[396]	1	1	–
–	pd Brother Charles for 12 flasks of Claret	1	8	–
18	pd for a Load of Straw in London	–	16	6
–	Recd of Brother Phill for 12 bottles of Red Port	1	–	–
23	pd for a Load of Hay at Greenwich	2	9	–
27	To Dr Slare	1	1	–
–	pd Moor the Gardener, a Bill in full	4	12	–
31	To Mr Pemble the Surgeon	4	4	–
–	pd the Farrier at Greenwich a Bill in full	3	15	–
–	Recd for Attendances at Greenh ½ a year, to Mich last	9	–	–
–	pd Mary Routh a years wages to Chrs: last, & gave her £1:6:–	6	6	–
–	pd Sarah Jones ditto, and gave her £–:16:–	6	6	–
–	pd Betty Hawkins ditto, and gave her £–:16:6	5	16	6
–	pd Mary Whiffins ditto, and gave her £–:5:6	5	15	6
–	pd Mary Cox ditto, and gave her 6s.6d	6	16	6
–	pd Robinson the Apothecary a Bill in full	7	–	–
–	pd. Metcalf the Brewer a Bill in full	10	10	–
–	pd Williams a Bill in full for coales	9	7	–
–	pd Mr Crowley ditto	3	5	6
–	pd, Mr Christy for one Stack of wood	1	–	–
–	pd Mr Ayre a Bill in full for Coales	19	18	–

[f.60]

		£	s	d
31	pd the Coach Maker Two Bills, for the years 1724 & 1725	60	–	–
-	pd Sanders the Brewer a Bill in full	8	6	6
–	To my Wife	26	5	–
–	pd Mr Gale, a Bill in full	30	9	–
–	pd Hutchinson the Shoemaker a Bill in full	2	18	6
–	pd Goulston the Farrier a Bill in full	13	2	6
–	pd Middleton a Bill in full	1	7	–
–	pd Mr Bridges a bill in full	7	4	–
–	pd Richards a bill in full	2	10	–
–	pd Wigzell a bill in full	11	17	–
–	pd Haslam a bill in full	1	5	6
–	pd Graham a bill in full	3	16	–
–	pd Mr Portales a bill to this day	64	2	10
–	Recd of ditto for a years Rent Christmas last	90	–	–
–	pd John Heath for ½ years wages due at Christs last	5	–	–
–	pd Tregany the Sadler a Bill in full	10	–	–
–	pd Racket the Tayler a Bill in full	7	7	–
–	pd Willson the Glazier a Bill in full	4	11	–
–	pd Mrs Ruffle a Bill in full	6	12	–
–	House Bills this year, for Eatables	210	14	1
–	Utensils &c for the House	16	5	–
–	Odd things	29	5	5
–	Soap, Starch, Mangling &c, relating to washing	14	–	8
–	Candles	19	2	7
–	Brandy, Wine &c, in Small parcells	1	14	6
–	Tea	7	12	3
–	Petty Pocket Expences	17	6	–
–	Given to Trades mens boxes[397]			
–	Given to Other Servants, besides what is included in Journeys	4	1	–

[f.61]

January the 1st: 1725/6

		£	s	d
4	Recd from the Managers of Drury Lane Playhouse in full for the Stock of Cloaths and Scenes which they had from the Haymarket	200	–	–
9	pd. Miller a Bill in full for Wine	7	8	–
11	pd Weatherhilt, in full of a Bill for Plaistering, of £53:9:7	14	11	3
–	To Mrs Holt	1	1	–
–	pd for a Horace's Metas: for Charles[398]	–	18	–
15	pd Mr Berry a Bill for the new Closet	15	15	–
–	pd for a Load of Hay at London	2	8	–
19	To Dr Hulse	1	1	–
22	To Dr Slare	1	1	–
24	To ditto	1	1	–
28	Recd Rent from Bror. Phil. ½ a year to Chrs: last	15	–	–
–	allow'd Taxes ½ a year to midsr. last	–	6	8
29	Recd Salary at Greenh: Hospll: ½ a Yr: to Michs: last	100	–	–
–	Given the Clark	–	5	–
Feb.				
1	Recd from the office of Works, one			

[396] Dr John Arbuthnot, *Tables of the Grecian, Roman and Jewish Measures, Weights and Coins, reduc'd to the English Standard* (*c*.1705), new ed. 1727.

[397] No amount.

[398] No doubt Ovid's *Metamorphoses*, and, from the cost, Tonson's folio edition of 1717, edited by Sir Samuel Garth, translated by Dryden, Addison, Congreve and others, and illustrated with engravings. Charles had been learning to read for nearly a year, but perhaps only his father would choose such a work as a large print picture book. The Rev. C. B. Norcliffe wrote (*Genealogist*, II, 1878, p.238) of volumes of the Classics owned by Charles including Juvenal and Persius, then extant and presumably (since he was descended from the Yarburghs and had access to documents there) at Heslington. Charles was at Westminster School 1732–6 (G. F. R. Barker and A. H. Stenning, *The Record of Old Westminsters*, 1928, II, p.942).

		£	s	d
	Quarter due at midsumr: last	178	15	8
–	pd The Sixpenny Tax	4	9	4
–	pd Land Tax	10	16	8
–	gave the Paymasters Clark	–	5	–
8	To Dr Monroe	1	1	–
13	To ditto	1	1	–
–	To Dr Slare	1	1	–
19	To Dr Monroe	1	1	–
–	Recd from the South Sea the Dividend from Midsr: to Christs: last, for £3802:15:11 Stock	114	1	7
21	pd Coll. Montague for two Coach geldings	46	–	–

[f.61v]

		£	s	d
19	Paid Mr Tho: Churchill, Executor to Mrs Fifield Deceas'd, who was Executrix to John Smalwell Seigr:[399] deceas'd, The Sum of five hundred pounds, in full of all demands upon me, for Work done by the Said John Smalwell at the Playhouse in the Haymarket and elsewhere	500	–	–
–	Recd from my Brother Charles, for one years Intrest of Two Thousand pounds due at Chrs: last	100	–	–
–	Recd from ditto for a year and halfs ground rent at Greenwich due at Chriss: last	15	–	–
–	Recd from ditto for[400] dozen of Wine			
24	For half a Load of Hay at London	1	5	6
–	For a Load of Straw at ditto	–	18	–
–	pd for Silk for a Coat for Charles	2	8	6
–	To Dr Slare	1	1	–
25	pd Benton, for a Pad, & to the Servant 10s	22	11	–

March

		£	s	d
7	pd Mr Maynard for Ten Quarters of Oates & 10 Bus[hel]s of Bran	8	7	–
8	pd for a Lo 30 Trusses of Hay at London[401]			
9	pd Savage the Plummer, a Bill in full	76	14	–
–	pd Martin for bleeding my Wife	–	10	6
–	pd the 5th Call to Chelsea Waterworks	20	–	–
–	Given for Carrying about the Paving Petition[402]	2	2	–
10	pd Mrs Ruffle a bill in full from Jany ye 1st to March ye 1st	4	17	–
15	pd the 14th and 15th Calls to the Opera	20	–	–
–	Handkerchers and Neckcloaths for Charles		13	–

(*Vanbrugh died on 26 March 1726. His widow continued to use the book until September. Only those items which in some way concern the architect or other foregoing matters are transcribed below.*)

		£	s	d
April 9th	pd the land Tax ½ a year to Lady day	0	16	8
March 26th	given Dr Monroe	3	3	
–	given Dr Slare	3	3	–
April 4th	given Dr Slare	1	1	

[f.62]

		£	s	d
10	Recd for 2 coach Horses	46	0	0
–	Recd for a pad	26	5	0
–	given to the Duke of Ancasters man when he had the Horses[403]	1	1	0
19	pd wingfeild a Bill for levalling & sowing the middle part of the feild	10	0	0
20	for mending the hedges in the feild	0	10	0
–	for a hundred of Bushes	0	6	0
–	Recd for a chariot a calash a traveling caridge for a coach & harness for 4 horses	16	16	–

[f.62v]

		£	s	d
26	Paid Mr Cook for proving the will	6	9	2
29	Paid Mrs Lucya Garancers her Legacy[404]	10	0	0

May

		£	s	d
6	for odd things for the kitchen at the white House	0	15	3
–	Recd of Coll Godolphin in full for rent	63	0	0
10	paid Mr Billinghurst on account	25	0	0
11	paid Clark the Painter on account	2	6	0
–	paid Mr Guiberts Bill	38	16	6
–	pd Sister Tora her Legacy for mourning[405]	20	0	0
21	Recd of Mr Edwards in full for Hampton Court Hous	20	15	0

[f.63]

		£	s	d
[27]	pd for 2 Trunks for miss philly & Charles	0	5	6
–	pd a bill for painting posts & rails in the feild	4	9	0

June

		£	s	d
1st	pd John Heath his wages in full & for keeping the coach & chariot one qr	5	10	0

399 Senior.

400 Blank; no amount.

401 No amount.

402 See p.92, n.40.

403 Apparently the 2nd Duke bought three horses from Lady Vanbrugh.

404 Daughter of Sister Garencieres. £10 for mourning.

405 Victoria.

14	Recd of the Capt for his Hors going in the feild 8 weeks	00	12	10

[f.63v]

–	pd Signior Leoni for delivery of his first book[406]	2	2	0
–	Recd from the office of works one qr Sallery due at Michaelmas 1725	179	13	8
20	pd sister Mary Elizabeth & Robina £20 Each for mourning Memorandum I gave Sister Bety hers	60	0	0
–	Recd 3 years Sallery from the wardrobe	23	11	6
–	pd the sixth call to the Chelsea water works	10	0	0
–	pd my cosen Vanbrugh[407]	34	1	0
–	given Master Ned[408]	0	5	9

[f.64]

July

9	Recd of Mr Dodington what was due to Sr John	275	0	0
–	pd Sister Mary ½ a years intrest to midsumer	3	0	0

[f.64v]

12	Recd from the office of works the xmas qr	183	7	8
27	pd for Binding Signor Leonis Book in blew paper	0	2	6
–	pd Mrs Garenceirs her Legacy for mourning	20	0	0

Augt

6	pd Mr Pomroy a Bill for Plumers work done at the too white houses	2	5	0
–	pd Mr Pomroy a Bill for fencing & paleing Moors Garden	8	17	0

[f.65]

20th pd Sister Tora her Legacy	100	0	0

A loose sheet of notes (numbered as f.60A) includes payments in Lady Vanbrugh's hand:

To Sister Mary[409]	153	0	0
To Sister Bin	100	0	0

406 Alberti (n.242).

407 George.

408 Nephew, Edward Vanbrugh (see p.171).

409 Legacy £50; interest £3; capital £100.

Index to the Account Book

This index to the Account Book refers to folio numbers of the original, not to page numbers of the printed text. Items which are mentioned only in the Account Book are not included in the general index at the end of this book.

Appendixes

Appendix A

Giles Vanbrugh to the Bishop of London, 1678

(PRO SP 29/408, No.105)

My Lord

the Eminent imployment and place yu possess in the Nation, induces mee to this Adresse, and though I am unknowne to yr Lordsh: I hope the occasion of it will bee my Apologye.

My Lord the Horrid plott lately discoverd against his Majestye the Kingdome and protestant Religion and certainly knowne to have been hatch'd at Rome, and cheifly furthred by the Pope himselfe has renew'd in my thoughts, what I have often wish'd and judg'd easily feasible; But I doubted the proposition would have been rejected and thought a little dishonnorable to attaque a prince in his owne Dominions & without a just pretence or provocation. But, that objection being now remov'd, I shall acquaint yor Lordsh. with what I thinke not only warrantable but honnorable, and may much advantage the Protestant religion. It is in short, my Lord, the assaulting the citty of Rome on that side where ye Vatican Palace stands and bringing away the Library. And pray My Lord before yu censure my proposall, I desire yr Lordsh to consider what reasons I have to beleeve the thing not only possible but easy to be Effected.

It was my fortune some years Since to travell into France & Italy for my Pleasure & Improvement, and above 3 years that I was abroad, I spent one year at Rome, where I had the opportunity of taking notice of many things relating to that Citty. The inhabitants are not numerous, about 100,000 of all sorts, religious men and nuns included, of wch I had a list for the 10 preceding years. They are not warrlike, like their Ancestors, but of a poor spirit, kept under by the clergye and prone to their superstitious worship rather than fighting: the citty is of a great Compasse, about 10 miles within the walls, and they built after the ancient manner and weake, excepting towards the Vatican, and no great garrison in the Castle St. Angelo. The city is about 15 miles from the sea, about 5 houres march, so that if the entreprise succeeds, it may bee finish'd in 24 or 30 houres time. And now at this time is the favorablest opportunity, that coul'd be wish'd for; for Sir Jo Narborough has for many months been hovering in those seas and Gone into the Spanish ports for recruits and into other Harbours, without any suspition of the Italian Princes, so that his appearing on the coast of Romagna would give no great alarum, so that a Competent Number might quickly bee landed and without opposition and come upon the citty in the suddainest and most unexpected manner imaginable. I could beleeve if Sr John could spare foure thousand briske active men, well arm'd and provided with scaling ladders and other Instruments, and Bombes especially to fire the citty, in several places at the same time; it might accomplish the Businesse, for the Garrison could in no means resist such a force, nor would stirre out of the Castle; nor could the cittizens in so short a time & such a fright rise in Armes to defend them selves, and much lesse sallie out after them in their Retreat. But, if upon consultation that number bee thought too small and that Sr John cannot safely spare more, there is an opportunity of sending what Number is more Requir'd, out of the disbanded men in Flanders. But, as secrecy is the main hinge of this Exployt, So, great care must bee taken, that not one Romanist officer or soldier slip in amongst them; for, though all were kept secrett till their very landing, yett then one zealous fugitive might poste to Rome, and betray all to ye indangering of many a brave man, and frustrating the whole Design.

My Lord, this is the main I have to say as to ye design, and if it succeed, yr Lordp well knowes the great valeur of those ancient manuscripts (which they have Rob'd the Prince Palatine's library and many others of) and of what benefitt they would bee, towards defending ours and Impugning their own Religion, if they were faithfully printed, or communicated to our learned men. And besides this, my Lord, it would make such an open Breach between us and them, as would occasion a more strict union, and close confederacy between all other Protestant Princes and ours: wch, in these dangerous times it were Good Policy to Endeavour. These are the two cheifest advantages I propose this design for, And, because it would bee dangerous to Lett the soldiers hope to gett much plunder in the citty, they should bee promis'd a good reward before hand, of 10 or twenty thousand pounds, to Incourage their Endeavours, But, if another as great affront might bee propos'd and approv'd of, it were no difficult matter, at the same time to send 8 or 10 fregatts into the Adriatick sea to Ancona and there land and march to Loretto (which is but little distant from the sea) and by surprise take & raze that neast of superstition and bring away all its treasure, which some such madd fellows as were at Mons would make no great bones of. I doubt not 2,000 men might do it. And These two affronts, would questionless bee applauded by all protestant Princes, considering the many great provocations his Majesty has had, and his three famous ancestors who have been often assail'd in publick and plotted against in secrett, and the kingdome suffred much by the late Rebellions fomented by them, and fires contrived by the Jesuiticall Romanists, and yett nothing has been retaliated to them for all their Evill doings. My Lord, I have made bold with this adresse to yr lordsh, although of martiall concern, rather than elsewhere, as to a true protestant and zealous prosecutor of what your Lordsh is convinc'd may conduce to the good of Church & State. If, therefore, yr Lordsh upon Mature Consideration shall judge these designs of that Nature, and shall thinke good now or at a more seasonable time to communicate them to his Majesty immediately or to Prince Rupert first, I shall rest satisfied with the result, which way soever it inclines. But if yr Lordsh think not convenient to meddle in it, I shall consider further what to do, for I must confesse till I know his Majesty is made acquainted with it, and disallowes it, I cannot but think it an honnorable & usefull Attempt; And that, wherein, upon his Majestyes Command, I would Venture my life, and further with my best advice & fortune.

So with all Due Respects I subscribe myself
yr Lordsps Most humble servant
to command
Giles Vanbrugh

28 December 1678
Chester
For the Right Reverend father in God Henry
Lord Bishop of London

Appendix B

Vanbrugh's Imprisonment, 1688-92

The principal documents concerning Vanbrugh's imprisonment in France are his own letters to his mother and to William Blathwayt, in the Finch MSS deposited by the late Lt.-Col. J. R. Hanbury of Burley-on-the-Hill, Rutland, in the Leicestershire Record Office, Cat.No.DG 7 (Nos.1 and 2 below) and the French archival material published by F. Ravaisson, *Archives de la Bastille*, IX, 1877, pp.338–42, 346 (No.3 below). There is also material in the Earl of Ailesbury's *Memoirs* and Sir James Thornhill's travel diary (Nos.4 and 5 below) as well as in State Papers, the Finch MSS (calendared in HMC Finch) and Narcissus Luttrell's *Brief Relation of State Affairs*.

It is evident that there were several attempts to release or exchange Vanbrugh, not always with the same French prisoner. The information from these sources may usefully be summarized in chronological order as follows:

1688

23 Aug.	Luttrell reports Dutch preparations for invasion of England (I, p.457).
27 Aug.	Luttrell reports French preparations: 'tis certain a war must ensue' (I, p.458).
8 Sep.	Luttrell reports French declaration against Holland (I, p.459).
18 Sep. O.S.	Bevil Skelton, James II's envoy at Paris, arrested and sent to the Tower (CSP Dom 1687–9, p.278).

Vanbrugh's second letter implies that he was arrested before these events.

1690

18 Sep. N.S.	The *gentilhomme* proposed in exchange for Vanbrugh sent to Newgate: Vanbrugh to be more closely guarded (Ravaisson, i).

1691

1 Jan. N.S.	William III has several times asked for Vanbrugh in exchange for a French officer. Louis XIV will only exchange him for a *gentilhomme* who has been in custody in London for six months (Ravaisson, ii). Vanbrugh's first letter implies that this is Martin Bertillier, who is next mentioned as being in prison as a suspected spy, 24 Feb. 1691 O.S. (HMC Finch III, p.24).
14 Feb. N.S.	Vanbrugh not to walk about Calais (Ravaisson, iii).
28 Feb. O.S.	Martin Bertellier, in Newgate as a suspected spy, prays the liberty of the yard on grounds of ill-health. Granted (CSP Dom 1690–1, p.285).
27 Apr. N.S.	Permission for Vanbrugh to be transferred to Vincennes (Ravaisson, iv).
10 Jul. N.S.	Chrestien, double agent, had wished Vanbrugh to be at Calais as an exchange in case of Chrestien's capture. Since Chrestien's treachery is discovered, Vanbrugh is to be kept against a man [Bertillier?] sent to England who had been arrested (Ravaisson, vi).
1 Sep. O.S.	Major General Dorrington and Major General Maxwell (No.4 below) in the Tower (HMC Finch III, pp. 245, 406).
20 Oct. N.S.	Vanbrugh offering bail of 10,000 livres, from Joseph Du Livier [who deals with exchange of prisoners from the French side]; to have the liberty of the courtyard at Vincennes (Ravaisson, vii).
26 Oct. N.S.	Vanbrugh's letter to his mother not to be forwarded, since it could embarrass Bertillier (Ravaisson, ix).
31 Oct. N.S.	Opinion that Du Livier's surety of 1500 livres will be regarded by Vanbrugh as a ransom. Not to have the liberty of the courtyard (Ravaisson, x).
9 Nov. N.S.	Vanbrugh writes again to his mother, by way of Sir Daniel Arthur and Gerard Weyman. This letter, which implicates both Bertillier and Joseph Du Livier's cousin Peter Du Livier, who is free in London, reaches Mrs Vanbrugh and is forwarded to Lord Nottingham, Secretary of State (No.1 below).
21 Nov. N.S.	Daily complaints from Vanbrugh to the French King. He is to be well treated (Ravaisson, xi).
9 Dec. O.S.	Warrants transferring Martin Bertillier from Newgate to custody of William Jones, Messenger (CSP Dom 1691–2, p.28).

1692

30 Jan. N.S.	Order to transfer Vanbrugh to the Bastille (Ravaisson, xii), probably as a result of his complaints.
5 Feb. O.S.	Warrant for arrest of Peter Du Livier, London (CSP Dom 1691–2, p.128).
11 Feb. O.S.	Luttrell reports 'Mr Vanbrook, Mr Goddard, and Mr. North . . . clapt up in the Bastile, suspected to be spies' (II, p.355).
15 Mar. O.S.	French merchants recently sent to the Tower 'to be used as Mr. North and Mr. Vanbroke are in the Bastile' (Luttrell II, p.387).
29 Mar. N.S.	Servants of William Blathwayt (Secretary for War) to be seized on arrival at Dunkirk (Ravaisson, p.342).
14/24 Apr.	William III considers Bertillier not an equal exchange for one of Blathwayt's clerks (HMC Finch IV, p.73).
4 May N.S.	[James] D'Ayrolle in the Bastille, arrested in service of the Prince of Orange (Ravaisson, p.343). D'Ayrolle was formerly secretary to Sir William Trumbull at Constantinople (HMC Finch IV, p.209). He later represented Great Britain at Geneva and the Hague. Cf. Webb, pp.21, 258.
10/20 Jun.	Joseph Du Livier complains about his cousin's imprisonment for nearly five months in reprisal for Goddard, Vanbrugh and North, and in particular against 'that most false ungratefull Vanbrugh . . . who has most ungratefully caused all these most false suggestions by his letters which he has since recanted' (HMC Finch IV, pp.221–2).
July	Blathwayt threatens 'very ill consequence to the French Protestants' if D'Ayrolle is not released (ibid., p.314).
26 Aug. N.S.	Vanbrugh writes to Blathwayt a brief account of his imprisonment and the deadlock in exchange negotiations. He suggests Count Marlotte as a suitable and deserving bargaining point (No.2 below).
19/29 Aug.	Nottingham reports a petition for bail from Peter Du Livier (HMC Finch IV, p.405).
23 Aug. O.S.	Maxwell bailed by the Queen (ibid., p.414).
4 Sep. N.S.	Blathwayt to Nottingham: William III, in reply to Vanbrugh's letter of 26 August, is willing to exchange Bertillier for Vanbrugh and others in the Bastille including Marlotte, subject to approval of the Council (ibid., p.416).
2/12 Sep.	Nottingham to Blathwayt: Bertillier *alias* Forvall 'has been a spye for France in most countrys of Europe and came here for the like errand, and for his dexterity in that treacherous art is much valued by the Court of France. The condition of those gentlemen who are imprisoned in France is much to be pittied, there being no colour for such hardship towards them; whereas Forvall may justly be hanged and would at any time redeem any man who might be sent into France upon the like account. Besides, it may be dangerous to those gentlemen to offer Forvall in exchange for them and Marlotte, for tho' Mr. Vanbruck thinks this proposall would be accepted, yet he is not sure of it, and it might give a fair praetext to France to treat them as spyes, tho' hitherto there is no ground for the suspicion, since Forvall certainly is so. But if the King thinks it fitt his orders shall be speedily obeyed' (ibid., p.441).
8/18 Sep.	Blathwayt to Nottingham: further orders concerning Bertillier deferred until the King returns to England (ibid., p.448).
11–12 Sep. O.S.	Joseph Du Livier attempting an exchange of prisoners. Blathwayt reminds Nottingham about D'Ayrolle (ibid., p.453).
28 Sept. N.S.	Passport to Mr Du Livier. 'Le Sr Ayrol', being French, cannot be exchanged (ibid., pp.464–5).
20/30 Sep.	Nottingham insisting on restitution of D'Ayrolle (ibid., p.466).
20 Oct. O.S.	William III arrives in London after delay of three weeks (Luttrell II, pp.577, 598).
22 Nov. N.S.	Vanbrugh released on bail (Ravaisson, xiv).

1693

1 Apr.	Vanbrugh and Goddard, having arrived at Folkstone or Dover, have been arrested. Nottingham writes to the mayors of those towns explaining their predicament and ordering their release and good treatment (CSP Dom 1693, p.89).

1695

10 Feb. O.S.	Bertillier still, or again, in custody (CSP Dom 1694–5, p.388).

1

Vanbrugh to his Mother

(Finch MSS, Box 4946, bundle 6)

Vincens, ye 9th novb: 1691 New Style

Madam.

I have writt yo severall letters, but have had none from you since yrs of ye 24th of July. I find at last, 'tis du Livier stops 'em all, and amongst others, one I writt ten days since to acquaint you wth his Roguery. but he got it stopt at Callis, as I have been inform'd. I send you this in Sr Daniell Arthur's packet upon whom I desire yo to give me credit for thirty pounds, for my mony's gone allmost. I desire you likewise to give to his Corespondants in England the same surety yo gave to Peter du Livier, to the end he may be my Bayl here, for after a great deal of paines, Mr. Porter having procur'd an order from Monsr: de Pontchartrain, to let me have the liberty of the Castle upon du Liviers Bail for a Thousand Pistols, this Rogue has fail'd me saying 'tis true he promis'd me, but that men don't allwayes keep wt they promis. I believe he has writ to his Cozen that I have the Castle, but pray never believe that, till I write you word so. for I am so far from it, that within this month, I am worse us'd every day then other, not by any order of the Court, but purely by du Livier's means, who I find do's me all the mischief he can, upon Bertillers account, for I have now found the whole mystery of this buiseness, & whence it comes yt there is so much stickleing for his Liberty. 'Tis that du Livier is the man upon whom they much rely here, for his intelligence in England, and he had assur'd, yt I shou'd be a sure exchang for any prisoner of State yt might be taken in England, upon this assurance Bertl: ventures over, and now du Livier finds he had not well inform'd himself of me nor my friends, but this he dares not owne to Mr. de Pontchartrain for fear of a reprimand, and so persuades him every day that the thing is ready to be granted. for I can assure you that Mr. de Pontc: has been once or twice upon the point of giving me my Liberty, and du Livier still prevents it, and hinders likwise my having better usage, in hopes the more uneasy I am the more paines my friends will take to deliver me. I can assure you likewise (for he blob'd it out before he was aware, himself) that his Couzen Peter writes him word, that the thing will succeed at last. So you see plainly 'tis du Livier keep's me in prison & can free me when he will. I therfore desire you will first see if my Ld Nottingham will hear of setting Bert: free, and if he gives you a flat deniall; declare to du Livier & Martin, that if they will not immediatly let me come over, you'll sue the bond they gave you for 500£ and declare every perticular of the business to my Lord Nottingham & to the whole world, by wch it will plainly apear that they play the Spys in England. If you do yt, I am fully assur'd they'll let me go; for shou'd Peter du Livier happen only to be sent out of the Kingdom upon ys score, I know it wou'd be a vast prejudice both to himself and his Cozen here. And for my part, I believe he'd hardly come off so well, if the buiseness were expos'd, for it would apear plainly he's a Spy, and not being naturalis'd, he cou'd not come out upon bail as others may. 'Twas to prevent yr suing the Bond, yt du Livier was so civill to me at Callis, for a little before I had threatned him with it. So pray lose no time, but let him see you are resolv'd to sue, and let no excuses put you off, but depend upon what I write to you, that du Livier can free me when he will, without Berts: consent; for Bert: tells yo true, he has no friends; he is a man of no birth, nor never was more then a Lieutenant in a Privateer, he had been before, a Vallet de Chamber. This I know from the English here, who I'm sure are more my friends then his. Do nothing against him in person, for that wou'd do me no good, but pray have no mercy upon du Livier, and you'll find I shall soon be free. If this letter comes to you, I shall be glad on't, for du Livier here, is cruelly affraid I shou'd write you all this, and so do's all he can to get my Letter's into his hands. He writ word to the Governour of Callis, (to prevail wth him to stop my Last letter) that I actually had the Liberty of the Castle, but he ly'd. and if his Cozen sees you ready to sue him, he'll tell you so too, but don't believe him, till I write yo word so. No matter whither there be any likelyhood of recovering the bond or not, let him see you are resolv'd to sue, if it be but to expose him. I have no more to say, but am

Your most obedient Son
J Vanbrug.

To Mrs Vanbrug, at Mr Gerrard
Weyman's hous.
Merchant
In Thames Street
London.

2

Vanbrugh to William Blathwayt Secretary of State for War

(Finch MSS, Box 4948, bundle 12)

Sir

Tho' I have not ye honour of being personally known to you; the unfortunate condition in wch I am, and have been near four years, I hope will excuse my begging yr assistance.

I was arrested Sr about ye time ye Warr broak out, accus'd of speaking somthing in favour of ye enterprize the King was then upon ye point of executing upon England. and the accusation was easily believ'd, upon Mr Skeltons acquainting Mr de Louvois, That I had been at the Hague in my Lord Willoughbys Company; That I was his Relation, and that (as he was pleas'd to say) I lead all the Bertue[1] family, wch way I wou'd. Upon this score, I have been us'd (till of late) with all the rigour upon earth. and nobody cou'd be heard, that offer'd to sollicite my Liberty; 'till at last, One Monsr: Bertiller being ceas'd in England, they have offer'd me my freedome, if I cou'd procure his release. They offer the same to a Son of the late Lord Keeper North, who has been two years prisoner at Thoulon; and to one Mr Goddard, nephew to Sr Samuell Dashwood, who was in the Accademy at Angers before ye Warr broak out, and was there ceas'd on. However, our friends have not yet been able to get this Bertiller releas't, my Lord Nottingham thinking it a dishonnour to the Nation, to be oblieg'd to give a Prisoner of State, arrested in time of Warr, for men that have been ceas'd in time of peace, contrary to what has been practis'd in England towards the French. However, this nicety of honnour, sitts so very hard upon us who are Prisoners; that we shou'd be very glad some medium might be found to put an end to our misfortune. Permit me Sr to name one to you, and to beg the favour of you, to propose it to the King.

There is in the Bastile, one Count Morlotte, his Father was under Tutor to the King, and he himself has had the Honour to be consider'd by him. He was ceas'd about nine years ago; accus'd of serving the King privatly here; and thereupon was condemn'd to death, but his Sentence was reduce't to a perpetuell Imprisonment. He is shut up, in a miserable Dungeon, without leave to see, speak with, or write to any body; no, not so much as his Daughter. However, by an extraordinary means, (my Chamber being near the place where he is) he has inform'd me of his Condition, and beg'd I wou'd engadge some body to Implore ye Kings Protection; since unless his Majesty delivers him, by some suitable Exchange during the Warr; he is sure to pass the rest of his miserable Life, in the malancholy condition he is in.

I perform my promis to him Sr, in giving you this account of his misfortune, and I wish for his sake, as well as my own, that an Exchange might be made between him and Bertiller; wch I hope may be found reasonable of all sides, since they are Prisoners, much upon the same score. I am not yet sure, the French Court will exchange ye Count Morlott, but I believe they wou'd. I therfore humbly beg the favour of you Sr, to speak to the King about it, and if he approuves on't, to give me Commission to propose it here. If the thing happens to be agreed too on both sides, I have good assurance, both Mr North Goddard & my self shall be releas't. As for Monsr: d'Ayrole, I don't doubt but he'll procure his freedome by the same means. So that the ease and fortune, of so many Gentlemen, depending upon the release of one poor Spy, I hope the King will please to put an end to our imprisonment, that our Liberty may be employ'd in his service

I am
Sir
Your most Obedient
humble Servant
J Vanbrug

From the Bastile. ye
26th of August New Stile
1692

[1] Altered from Bartue, a common form.

3
Excerpts from

F. Ravaisson, Archives de la Bastille
IX, 1877, pp.338–42, 346.
The numbering in [brackets] is mine.

Pontchartrain to M. de Laubanie, Commandant of Calais

[i] Versailles, 18 sept. 1690
Le Roi ayant été informé que le gentilhomme français qu'on avait proposé d'échanger contre M. Vanbrugh a été mis dans les prisons de Newgate, S. M. m'ordonne de vous écrire que son intention est que vous fassiez resserrer et garder plus étroitement Vanbrugh, et que vous parvoyiez à sa garde, de manière qu'il ne puisse s'échapper.

[ii] Versailles, 1 jan. 1691
Le roi d'Angleterre a déjà plusieurs fois demandé au Roi la liberté de M. Vanbrugh, qui est prisonnier à Calais, pour obtenir celle d'un de ses officiers qui est retenu à Londres, et comme S.M. ne veut pas qu'il puisse être échangé pour un autre que pour un gentilhomme français qui est pareillement prisonnier à Londres, et que vous savez y être passé depuis six mois, elle m'ordonne de vous écrire de ne point mettre Vanbrugh en liberté, quelques ordres que vous en receviez, que je ne vous aie fait savoir que c'est son intention. Vous pouvez cependant le faire bien traiter, et lui donner tous les secours qu'il vous demandera, parvu qu'ils n'empêchent point qu'il soit bien gardé.

[iii] Versailles, 14 fév. 1691
Sur ce que j'apprends que vous avez permis à M. Vanbrugh de se promener pendant trois jours dans la ville de Calais, j'ai cru devoir vous dire que, de quelque bonne foi qu'il vous paraisse, c'est un Anglais dans la parole duquel il ne faut prendre une confiance si entière. Le Roi m'a donné ordre de vous écrire de le bien traiter, mais, en même temps, S.M. vous a recommandé de pourvoir à la sûreté de sa garde, de manière qu'elle puisse s'assurer qu'il ne s'évadera pas; nous

restant peu de moyens, si cela nous manque, de retirer des prisons d'Angleterre le gentilhomme que vous savez y être passé pour le service du Roi.

[iv] Versailles, 27 avril 1691
Le Roi ayant bien voulu accorder à Vanbrugh d'être transféré de Calais, où sa santé s'altère, à Vincennes, à ses frais, S.M. s'est remise à vous de pourvoir à sa garde, et elle m'ordonne de vous écrire qu'elle vous charge de ne le confier qu'à un homme dont vous soyez sûr, et sur lequel vous puissiez compter; S.M. estimant nécessaire pour son service de le faire garder avec attention pour servir dans la suite à l'échange, ou d'une espèce de représailles du gentilhomme qui était passé par vos soins en Angleterre. Vous trouverez ci-joint l'ordre du Roi pour tirer Vanbrugh des prisons de Calais, et celui qui est nécessaire pour le faire recevoir dans le château de Vincennes. Vous pouvez lui donner le nombre de gardes que vous trouverez à propos.

[v] Versailles, 9 mai 1691
J'ai reçu la lettre que vous avez pris la peine de m'écrire pour m'informer du depart de Vanbrugh pour Vincennes, et que vous me ferez part de tous les avis que vous aurez de la mer; je vous serai obligé du soin que vous en prendrez.

Barbezieux to Pontchartrain

[vi] Versailles, 10 juil. 1691
Vanbrugh a été arrêté à Calais, sur un avis que donna une femme de Paris, que cet homme s'en allait sans passeport, après la déclaration de la guerre, et il a paru, par les notions que l'on a eues depuis ce temps-là, que cet homme avait produit cette femme de Paris à un mylord, et que ce mylord avait fort à cœur la liberté de Vanbrugh. Chrestien, qui s'est trouvé depuis espion double, avait désiré qu'il fût mis dans la citadelle de Calais pour, en cas qu'il fût pris, pouvoir être échangé contre lui. Depuis la friponnerie de ce Chrestien ayant été reconnue, M. de Seignelay a eue ordre du Roi qu'il y fût encore gardé pour pouvoir être échangé contre un homme que l'on avait envoyé en Angleterre par ordre de S.M., et qui avait été arrêté. Depuis la mort de M. de Seignelay, je crois me souvenir que Vanbrugh a été transféré à la Bastille ou à Vincennes, sur un ordre de S.M. que vous avez contre-signé; c'est tout l'éclaircissement que je puis vous donner sur la lettre que vous m'avez fait l'honneur de m'écrire aujourd'hui au sujet de Vanbrugh.

Pontchartrain to M. de Bernaville

[vii] Fontainebleau, 20 oct. 1691
Vanbrugh offrant de fournir une caution qui s'obligera de payer 10,000 livres en cas qu'il s'évade, le Roi veut bien à cette condition que vous lui donniez la liberté de la cour et de se promener. Demandez-lui quelle personne il veut offrir pour caution, afin que je puisse vous faire savoir si elle est suffisante.

[viii] Versailles, 21 oct. 1691
Vanbrugh m'a proposé, pour sa caution jusqu'aux 10,000 réglées par le Roi, M. du Livier, et comme je sais qu'il est solvable, vous pouvez le recevoir et laisser ensuite à de Vanbrugh la liberté de se promener dans la cour que S.M. a accordée à cette condition.

Pontchartrain to Laubanie

[ix] Versailles, 26 oct. 1691
J'ai reçu la lettre qui vous a été remise de Vanbrugh pour sa mère.
J'ai lu la traduction de cette lettre, et comme elle pourrait attirer de l'ennui à M. de Berteillier, qui est le gentilhomme que vous avez fait passer en Angleterre, il ne faut pas l'envoyer, et je la retiens. Le moyen que Vanbrugh a imaginé pour avoir sa liberté peut être bon, et le Roi voudra bien dans la suite y donner les mains, mais il ne convient point encore qu'il paraisse que M. de Berteillier est réclamé au nom de S.M., de crainte que sa liberté ne devînt plus difficile à obtenir par la pensée où on est qu'il a été envoyé en Angleterre pour informer de ce qui s'y passait. Il est même à présumer que Vanbrugh en écrira encore à sa mère, et il ne lui fera plus les mêmes plaintes, S.M. lui ayant accordé la liberté de se promener dans la cour du château de Vincennes qu'il a demandée. Je vous prie, cependant, d'avoir toujours attention à ses lettres, et de défendre à son correspondant d'en envoyer aucunes sans vous les faire voir, et pour l'empêcher de chercher d'autre voie, il faut que vous l'engagiez demander à Vanbrugh qu'il a envoyé celles qu'il lui a adressées.

Pontchartrain to Bernaville

[x] Fontainebleau, 31 oct. 1691
J'ai rendu compte au Roi de la lettre que vous m'avez écrite pour m'informer de la condition sous laquelle M. du Livier consent de se rendre caution de M. Vanbrugh. S.M. n'a point voulu y entrer, et elle m'ordonne de vous dire que son intention est que du Livier s'oblige purement et simplement de le représenter, étant persuadée qu'il regardera les 1,500 liv. qu'il s'offre de payer comme une espèce de rançon qui ne sera pas capable de le retenir, et il faut, jusqu'à ce qu'il ait satisfait à cette condition, le garder ainsi que vous avez fait jusqu'à présent.

[xi] Versailles, 21 nov. 1691
Le Roi reçoit tous les jours de nouvelles plaintes de Vanbrugh, sur les mauvais traitements qui lui sont faits, et il marque en dernier lieu qu'on lui a retranché son entretien et que vous ne lui faites point donner de feu. Comme il n'est point à présent en état de se procurer les secours qui lui

sont nécessaires, l'intention de S.M. est que vous pourvoyiez aux choses dont il peut avoir besoin, et que vous le traitiez bien, de manière qu'elle ne soit plus importunée de ses plaintes.

Pontchartrain to M. de Besmaus

[xii] Versailles, 30 janv. 1692

Le Roi donne ordre de faire conduire à la Bastille Vanbrugh qui est à présent dans le château de Vincennes, pour y être gardé jusques à nouvel ordre, et S.M. m'a commandé en même temps de vous dire que son intention est que vous lui permettiez de se promener et de voir les personnes qui viendront le visiter, voulant qu'il jouisse de toute la liberté qui peut lui être laissée sans préjudicier à la sûreté de sa personne.

Journal of M. du Junca, 1692

[xiii]
Du vendredi, *1er* février, à quatre heures du soir, M. du Poy, officier de la prévôté, a amené et conduit ici, traduit de Vincennes, M. de Vanbrugh, Anglais, qui avait aussi sorti des prisons de Calais, lequel on a mis dans la liberté de la tour de la liberté,[2] avec MM de Poncet de Sainte-Praye, et Saint-Georges, etc.

[xiv]
Du mercredi, 22 novembre, onze heures du matin, M. l'abbé de Lagny a porté l'ordre, etc., pour mettre dans une entière liberté M. de Vanbrugh, Anglais, lequel, pour avoir sa liberté dans Paris, il a donné une bonne caution et une assurance de mille pistoles, en cas d'une évasion, dont M. de Lagny, fermier général, a pris toutes les sûretés qu'il a dû prendre pour cela, et M. de Vanbrugh en sortant est allé dans le moment avec le carrosse de M. de Besmaus voir et remercier M. de Lagny.

4
From *Memoirs of Thomas Earl of Ailesbury*

(London, 1890–1), pp.308–9

During the war in Ireland in 1690, as I take it, two general officers, subjects to Great Britain but major generals in the French Army, were taken prisoners, and lay some years in the Tower (Major General Maxwell and Major General Dorrington) and they being my old friends and acquaintances, I went often to see them. Major General Maxwell, husband then to the Duchess Dowager of Norfolk, had obtained this year 1692 leave to treat for an exchange. He telling it me, I did the same to the Earl of Nottingham, Secretary of State, and I proposed to him to have three English prisoners in France released for the Major General (viz. Mr. North detained at Marseilles just as he was embarking for Turkey by an unhandsome trick, to say no worse of it. Mr. Hampden who had a nephew at Aleppo jealous of Mr. North's outshining him there, and Mr. Hampden gave Mr. North letters for his Nephew, filled with news. The others were Mr. Goddard of Ogbourne in Wiltshire, son-in-law to the steward of my lands there, an Academist at Angers, and Mr. Vanbrook the famous poet since, who composed in the Bastille his most ingenious play 'The Provoked Wife.' He was in a dungeon a considerable time, but the Queen at St. Germains procured him the ordinary liberty of the prison.)

[2] The Tour de la Liberté, one of the towers of the Bastille!

5
From Sir James Thornhill's Travel Notebook 1716-17

back end-paper (V & A)

Mr Janse at Calais, give Sr Jn Vanbrughs humble service, Sr Jn was 3 years Prisoner there in ye ruins of ye Cittadel. When I went to Mr Janse he had 2 young Priest confessing him, but dismisst them & kindly remember'd to Sr John.

Appendix C

E. Smith to Henry Tomlin, 1694

PRO SP 32/5, f.150. The paper is damaged by perforations.

May ye 20th 1694

Mr Tomlin

I receiued yesterday yours of Aprill ye 24th; which was an excuse for the chiding letter you sent me, this comes to bring you a letter for Mr Hobes without troubling my Cosen; you need but send it to Mr Vanb[r]ugh who tis inclosed to, and it will certenly come safe to him; that Gentellman you may hear of by any of Mr Lord Lindsees servants: or elce to be sure by his second son, who is his intimate friend. I admier Mr William Raw dos not anser your letters. this inclosed I desier you wi[ll] seal up, before you send it away: and put a couer [on] Mr. Vanbrughs letter: and as soon as [eve]r you receive this, without a superscription pray do not faile to give it my Cousen tis a letter from her sweet hart, so that I am sure you wi[ll take] a glass of wine to drink his health. you may if you think fit get acquainted your self with Mr Hobes, but do as to that as you please, it may be you think him as ill a man, as my Cousen does, say nothing to her that I have writ to him; but get me soon pray an anser of her Sweetharts letter who you must think like a[ll] men in love is in paine to have an anser.

I am ever

Your asured friend
E Smith

For Mr Henry Tomlin
at Mr Friths over
against the Red Lyon
in Bromley Street
Drury Lane
London

Appendix D

Blenheim: Its Commissioning, Models and Drawings

1 From Vanbrugh's answers in the suit of Edward Strong Senior and Junior, 1718 (BM MS.Add. 38056, f.70)

... about Xmas in the Year of our Lord One Thousand Seven hundred & four his Grace the Duke of Marlborough was pleased to tell this Deft that the Queen haveing been Graciously pleased to Give him the Mannor and parke of Woodstock He the said Duke had thoughts of Building an House there but did not intend to lay out above the Sume of Forty Thousand Pounds in or about the same and desired this Deft to let him see a modell for that purpose And his Grace together with the then Lord Godolphin haveing viewed a Modell which this Deft shewed them His Grace came to a resolucōn to have a House Built there according to such Modell with some Addicōns & Alteracōns and desired this Deft to prepare a designe pursuant to such Resolucōn which this Deft accordingly did and made severall Draughts of such Designe which from time to time were Viewed by his Grace, the Dutchess of Marlborough & the then Lord Godolphin.

2 From Vanbrugh's deposition in the suit of Sarah, Duchess of Marlborough and others v. Vanbrugh, Joynes and others, 1724 (BM MS.Add. 19616, ff.16v-19)

... the Duke meeting defendant abt Christmas One Thousand Seaven Hundred and four told him that the Queen having given him the sayd Mannor and parke he had thought of building a house there But intended not to lay out above Forty Thousand pounds in the same and that he would consult deft therein and ... sometime after the duke sent some persons to Woodstock who viewed the parke and took a plan of such part of the ground as they thought proper to build on and that the Duke and the late Lord Treasurer Godolphin came to defts house and viewed a model of a house he had there and on seeing the same the Duke declared he would have such an house built at Woodstocke with some addicōns and alteracōns and desired deft to prepare a draught thereof which he did and made severall other draughts which from time to time were viewed by the Duke and Dutchesse of Marlborough and the Lord Godolphin and such alteracōns were made by the defendant therein as they directed and ... in February One Thousd Seaven hundred and Four[1] the Duke desired deft to meet him at Woodstocke which he did and they fixt upon the scituation for building the said house and gardens thereto and thereupon men were then imediately sett to worke by the Dukes Order to cut down trees and clear the ground for that purpose and soone after the Dukes returne to London he gave deft Ords as Surveyor of the worke and buildings to goe about to erect such house as before agreed on which at his Graces request and according to such his Orders the deft began and ... his Grace as deft verily beleived being apprehensive that such house and gardens to make them soe magnificent as he was desirous they should be would cost more than he was willing to expend therein the said duke or some others by his privity on his behalfe as defendt beleived applyed to the Queen to prevaile on her to be at the expence thereof and ... the Duke and not the Queen gave Deft Ords for a model in wood to be made of the said intended building and deft accordingly prepared one and it was by the Dukes direccōns placed at kensington where, as deft has heard and believed her Majesty sawe and approved of the same.

3 From Vanbrugh's deposition in the brief of the Duke of Marlborough in the suit of Edward Strong Senior and Junior v. Marlborough, H.M. Attorney General and Vanbrugh, 1720 (BM MS. Add.38056, f.101)

That abt Xmas 1714[2] he meeting casually wth the Duke at the Playhouse in Drury Lane the Duke told him he designed to build a House in Woodstock park and expressed his intencōn of not exceeding a certain sume, wch to the best of Depts remembrance was 40,000£ and further said he must consult Dept abt the design. That some time after ye Duke sent some persons down to View the Park and take a Plan of it wch they accordingly did and after their return having made a Rept to him he sent one of 'em to Dept at his House in Whitehall to let him know ye Duke would come to him yt Morning to discourse wth him abt a design for his intended building and accordingly the Duke came & Lord Treār Godolphin with him and

[1] 1704/5.

[2] Corrected to 1704 in margin.

Viewing a Modell wch Dept then had in Wood of the Earle of Carliles House the Duke said yt was ye sort of House he liked onely with some alteracōns and addicōns as a Gallery &c and concluded yt Dept should prepare a design agreable to those general Resolutions and Dept did prepare one and waited upon his Grace with it at his Lodgings at St James's at wch time Lord Treār Godolphin was with him who both viewed and considered ye same several times that day both before and after Dinner and at last came to a Resolution to look no farther, but fixt on yt design but afterwards several Draughts more Correct were made and from time to time shewn to his Grace who at length vizt in Feb. 1704,[3] desired Dept would meet him at Woodstock to fix upon the Situacōn wch Dept accordingly did & during his stay there the situacōn wch Dept proposed to his Grace was resolved on and men were instantly set to work under ye Conduct of one Mr Wise to open ye Ground cut down Trees &c in ordr to ye laying the Foundation.

4 The model shed at Kensington

(i) Charge of works for Oct.-Dec. 1705 at Kensington, including 'New Shedd there for Joyners to make ye Modells of Woodstock House' £125 11s 5d (PRO Works 6/14, f.109).

(ii) 'Kensington. Ordered that the floor and Chimney of the Modell House be Repar'd, wth a Rail round the modells to secure them from being broke' (Board of Works Minutes, PRO Works 4/1, 27 March 1717).

5 Correspondence relating to drawings (BM MS. Add.19605)

Vanbrugh to Joynes 6 March 170[7]
If you have with you my Lord Carlisle's Papers, You'll oblige me to draw the Two Fronts, pretty exact they being for the Engraver to work from; As for the Ornaments on the Top. with the Chimneys on the Main Pile, and the Cupola, I'll get Mr Hawksmoor to Add them here, for I believe you have not the Last Designs of 'em. Pray send 'em as soon as conveniently you can. (f.18)

Vanbrugh to Marlborough Blenheim, 15 July 1707
I hope in a Weeks time to have Some Drawings ready to send your Grace.
[Blenheim MS.A.2.31]

Joynes to Vanbrugh Woodstock 18 July 1707
I ask your Pardon for promising that wch I have not perform'd, but knowing the prespective will take up some time in Shadowing I have sent it first, not but almost all ye other Drawings are Done, wch shall Speedyly be remitd Sr to you in 4 or 5 Days time, but Sr in this as I have sent there is Sevll. things as I have omittd to put in, for fear of Mistake, wch Sr I hope you would be pleasd to Shew Mr. Hawksmoor to Scetch in what is left out. (f.22)
(*Endorsed*: Concerning Drawing prespective Blenheim &c.)

Joynes to Vanbrugh [22 July 1707]
I shall send you all ye Drawings by next Thursday's Oxford Coach. (f.27)

Vanbrugh to Boulter Hatfield 25 July 1707
I am got this far on my way to York ... Pray do me the favour to tell Mr Joynes I just rec'd the Drawings before I came out of Towne; but he'll Oblige me in getting that of the Generall Plan & Upright of my Ld Carlisles, done against I return out of the North As Likewise the South Front of Blenheim as it is now determin'd; wch Mr Strong can inform him in. (ff.28–9)

Joynes to Vanbrugh Blenheim 3 August 1707
The Drawings Sr. that you mention'd in Mr. Boulters letter Shall be done. I have never a perfect plan of Lds Carlisle of my owne, but Mr. Strongs says he has one *neare ye truth*[4] that he thinks is according to ye latter Designs. I should have sent you Sr ye front of Blenheim to ye Gardens wth ye other papers, but young Mr. Strong sayd you had Carried that front away with you but since he went to London I have found it Amongst his papers. (f.30)

Vanbrugh to Joynes Hendersckelf August ye [1707]
I had yr Letter of ye 3d ... thank you [for the] Drawings you sent, And your promise for the rest. (f.195)

Vanbrugh to Joynes London 18 December 1709
I have the Plan Kit Cash sent, and believe 'tis right. the South Front is likewise come up but I have not yet Seen it ... I have just now rec'd Mr Peisley with Mr Rowney's Draught. I desire Andrews to proceed upon the North Front, to the Same Scale he has done the South.[5] (f.82)

6 Engravings of Blenheim

In June 1709 Nicholas Hawksmoor was paid £45 for 'Copper plates to Engrave the planns of Blenheim house, the East Front and the plann, and Front of the Great Bridge, and mony Disburst to the Engravener for Engraveing the said Fronts & planns respectively' (BM MS.Add.19596, f.61). This is perhaps the single plate, $18\frac{1}{4} \times 23\frac{1}{2}$ in., engraved by H. Terasson and sold by Thomas and John Bowles, showing the south and east fronts, plans of the basement and main floors, and the elevation of the Bridge (Bodl.MS.Gough Maps 26, f.51). The elevation of the Bridge is reproduced here (Pl.74). A larger and tidier version of the

[3] 1704/5.

[4] *neare ye truth* deleted.

[5] See p.80, n.7.

Bridge, with titles in Latin, English, French and Dutch, is in the same collection (unnumbered, between ff.53–4) with the engraved signature *P. van Gunst excudit*. A different impression, signed *M. V dr Gucht Sculp,* is reproduced by Webb, facing p.42, from BM Maps 4781 (1). Contrary to persistent allegations, the Bridge engraving does not appear in *Vitrivius Britannicus*.

Appendix E

Mr Van-Brugg's Proposals about Building ye New Churches

Autograph, unsigned and untitled, Bodl.MS.Rawl.B.376, ff.351–2.
The title is from a contemporary copy, Bodl.MS.Eng.Hist.b.2, f.47.

Since it will perhaps be thought reasonable, that the fifty new Churches the Queen has gloriously promoted the Building of, in London and Westminster; shou'd not only serve for the Accommodation of the Inhabitants, in the Performance of their Publick Religious Dutys; but at the same time, remain Monuments to Posterity of Her Piety & Grandure And by consequence become Ornaments to the Towne, and a Credit to the Nation; the following Considerations are humbly offer'd, to the Commissioners who are Instructed with the direction of them

That amongst the several kinds of Buildings by which Great Citys are Adorn'd; Churches, have in all Ages, and with all Religions been placed in the first Rank. No Expence has ever been thought too much for them; Their Magnificence has been esteem'd a pious expression of the Peoples great and profound Veneration towards their Deitys, And the contemplation of that Magnificence has at the same time augmented that Veneration.

If therefore on one hand it be reasonable to design Churches in such Manner, that the People may both hear what is utter'd by the Minister, and at the same time be so accommodated, as not to be disturb'd in their devotions by one an Other, or by the Inconveniencys of too much heat or cold; So on the other, these necessary dispositions in the usefull part of the Fabrick, shou'd be made consistent with the utmost Grace that Architecture can produce, for the Beauty of it: which Grace shou'd generally be express'd in a plain but Just and Noble Stile, without running into those many Divisions and Breaks which other buildings for Variety of uses may require; or such Gayety of Ornaments as may be proper to a Luxurious Palace.

To form the Churches now to be built, to these two general Propositions, it will be necessary to observe these following Rules.

First. That their Situation may be ever Insulate. This do's not only give them that Respectfull Distinction & Dignity which Churches Always ought to have; but it makes the Access to them easy, and is a great Security from Fire.

2dly. That they may be so plac'd, to be fairly View'd at such proper distance, as is necessary to shew their Exterior Form, to the best Advantage, as at the ends of Large and Strait Streets, or on the Sides of Squares and Other open Places.

3dly. That they may be all Accommodated and Adorn'd with Portico's; no part in Publick Edifices being of greater use, nor no production in Architecture so solemnly Magnificent.

4ly. That they may be form'd for the utmost duration both in respect of the material, the Solidity of their Walls, and the Manner of their Construction: The extraordinary Expence of which is so small, That in a Church of Ten thousand pounds cost, it turns upon five hundred, whether it shall be crippled in a hundred Years, or stand like a Rock a Thousand.

5ly. That for the Ornament of the Towne, and to shew at a distance what regard there is in it to Religious Worship; every Church (as the Act of Parliament has provided) may have a Tower, but to Answer those ends, they shou'd be all of Stone or Brick; High and Bold Structures; and so form'd as not to be subject to Ruin by fire, but of such Solidity and Strength, that nothing but Time, and scarce that, shou'd destroy them.

6ly. That as to the Insides, both for the Accommodation of the Ordinary People, and the Beauty of the Place, they may not be too much crowded with Pews: but that a considerable Space may be left in the Middle Line with decent Forms regularly plac'd for People to repose themselves by Turns.

7ly. That for the Lights, there may be no more than what are necessary for meer use; many Windows making a Church cold in Winter, hot in Summer, and being very disagreeable and hurtfull to the sight. They likewise take off very much, both from the Appearance & reality of strength in the Fabrick; giving it more the Air of a Gay Lanthorn to be set on the Top of a Temple, than the Reverend look of a Temple it self; which shou'd ever have the most Solemn and Awfull Appearance both without and within, that is possible.

8ly. That they may be free'd from that Inhumane custome of being made Burial Places for the Dead. a Custome in which there is something so very barbarous in itself besides the many ill consequences that attend it; that one cannot enough wonder how it ever has prevail'd amongst the civiliz'd part of mankind. But there is now a sort of happy necessity on this Occasion of breaking through it: Since there can be no thought of purchasing ground for Church Yards, where the Churches will probably be plac'd. And since there must therefore be Caemitarys provided in the Skirts of the Towne, if they are ordered with that decency they ought to be, there can be no doubt but the Rich as well as the Poor, will be content to ly there.

If these Caemitarys be consecrated, Handsomely and regularly wall'd in, and planted with Trees in such form as to make a Solemn Distinction between one Part and another; there is no doubt, but the Richer sort of People, will think their Friends and Relations more decently inter'd in those distinguish'd Places, than they commonly are in the Ailes and under Pews in Churches; And will think them more honourably remember'd by Lofty and Noble Mausoleums, erected over them in Freestone (which no doubt will soon come into practice,) than by little Tawdry Monuments of Marble, stuck up against Walls and Pillars. *This manner of Interment has been practic'd by the English at Suratt and is come at last to have this kind of effect.*[1]

Upon the whole it may be worth considering, that since Christianity began, there is but one instance, where the Inhabitants of a City have had so Glorious an Occasion as this, to Adorn both their Religion and their Towne at once. A Resolution taken, and money provided to raise fifty New Churches in so short a time shews so glowing a Zeal, and so Noble a Generosity, that 'twere pitty Posterity shou'd not have an equal opinion of the Politeness of the Age, by finding the Edifices Suitable to what produc'd them.[2]

[1] Marginal note. At this point in the text is a sketch of a cemetery (Pl.55).

[2] There follows a plan of a six-acre plot, titled *Manner of planting the Caemitary*.

Appendix F

Mr Wren to You and Mr Hawksmoor, 1712

V & A D. 108–1891

London Octr. 11th. 1712

Sr

Mr Wren gives his service to you and Mr. Hawksmoor and bid me acquaint you he has made it his businesse to attend every Com[itt]ee since Mr. Hawksmoors absence, and that he has been excused very well, they have had a great many Complaints from severall Parishes, but there was no notice taken of any of them. Mr. Wren is informed (but not positively) that the new Commission will be broke open next Wensday; if so, he dos not doubt but he will be excused, when he lets them know how near home he is, and I beleive Mr. Vanbrugh will speak to the Bp. of St. David's and Mr Clarke and Mr. Aislabie to the same effect. Mr Stebbings gives his service to you and heartily wishes you could contrive to make my Lord Suffolks in your way home. The 100£ bill is at last come to light. Mr. Samll. Garenciers is come to town and thinks of b[esto]wing himself in a Muscovy Ship. I am

Sr

(The signature has been trimmed off this sheet, which owes its preservation to the sketch on the reverse (Fig.20). *Mr Wren* is Sir Christopher's son; the *Mr Vanbrugh* mentioned is William, not John. The *complaints from parishes* appear to relate to the Fifty New Churches Commission, of which John Vanbrugh was a member and of whose committee both he and Hawksmoor were members. The *new commission* rumoured, however, is probably for St Paul's Cathedral, although it is uncertain whether it was renewed at this date. The writer of the letter wrote the Minutes of the Greenwich Hospital Fabric Committee at this time, and, with a break between 4 August 1715 and 17 November 1716, at least until 1720 (PRO Ad 67/4). Vanbrugh did not attend after 14 August 1712 until 30 October, and was normally in Yorkshire with Hawksmoor in the summer. *Lord Suffolk's* is Audley End, where Vanbrugh had designed the staircase about 1708 (p.54). *Samuel Garencieres* was a son of Dudley Garencieres and Vanbrugh's half-sister Elizabeth Barker (p.157). The obvious inference is that the recipient of the letter was John Vanbrugh, while he was celebrating with Lord Carlisle the latter's installation in the new house at Castle Howard. The sketch on the reverse, probably for some sort of garden building, is thus perhaps the first idea for something in the park at Castle Howard, in Vanbrugh's hand.)

20 Design for a garden building. *Victoria and Albert Museum.*

Appendix G

Vanbrugh's Attendances at the Board of Works 1715–26

Compiled from the Minutes (PRO Works 4/1–3)

Present	*Absent*
1715	
May 6,11,12,13,14,16,17	May 18,20
21	24,25
27,30,31	
June 1,2,3,10,13,14,15,16,17,18	June 20,21
22,23,24	25
27,28,29,30	
July 1	July 2
5,6	8
12,13,15,16,19,20	21
27,28,29	
August 5,9,17,23,24,30	
September 2,9,13,19,21,27,28,30	
October 4,5,7,12,17,18,21,25,28, 29	
November 8,9,16,23,26,30	
December 2,6,7,10,13	December 31
1716	
	January 7,10,17
January 26,28	
February 1,3,8,13,14,16,17,21, 22,25,29	
March 7,13,14,21,23,24,26	
April 11,13,18,21,25,27	
May 2,8	May 9
29,30,31	
June 5,6,9,12,13,14,19,22,27	
July [-],11,12,18,19,23	July 27,28,30
	August 2,4,9,16
	September 11
October 3,23	
November 7,8,13,16,19,20,25	
December 5,6,10,13,15,17	
1717	
January 8,9,24,31	
February 7,12,13,14,22	
March 5,6,13,27	
April 2,9,10,12,15,24,26	
May 2,7,8,14,15,16,21	May 29
31	
	June 4
June 5,7,20,21,29	
July 3	July 9
11,17,24	
August 6,15,16,27,28	August 29
September 3,4	September 10
	October 1,12,15,31
November 12,21,27	
December 4,10,12,18	
1718	
January 3,7,10,14,15,28	
February 5,6,11,12,13,14,15	

Present	*Absent*
March 11	
April 2,7,25	April 30
June 6,10,12,17,18,19,25	June 26,30
	July 4
July 8,9,10	16,17
23	30
August 6,7,11,20	
	September 10,11
September 15	
	October 14,22
October 28	
	November 6,7
1719	
February 5,6,9,20,23,24,25	
	March 18
June 10,25	
July 2	July 6
16	
September 4,12,16,25	
October 1,2,7,8	October 22,23
28	
November 4,5,6,7,9,10,18	November 19,20
December 4	December 7
9	15,16,17,23
1720	
January 12	January 13
20,27	
	February 3,9
February 10,17,24	
	March 2,8,9,16,23, 30
April 6,12	April 13,27
May 4,10	May 18
25	
	June 15
June 22,29	
	July 6
	August 9
August 10	24,31
September 7,12,22,28	
	October 5
October 20	22
26	
November 2,8	November 16,23,30
	December 7,13,14
1721	
January 3,10,25	
February 1,14	
	March 1,8,15
March 22	29
	April 5,18
April 26	

Present	*Absent*
	May 9,16,24
June 7,13,14	June 21,28
	July 11,12,19
	August 2,8,9,18,23
	September 6,12,13, 20,29
	October 4,11,14, 23,24,27
	November 14,22, 29
	December 6,13,15, 19,20
1722	
January 24,28	January 9,11,17 31
February 14,28	February 5,7,13
March 7 14	March 13 21,28
April 10,11 25	April 18
May 2 9,23,30	May 8
June 12,13 27	June 6 20
July 10 25	July 4 11,12,18
	August 1,2,8,14, 15,17,22
	September 5,12,27
	October 10,17,23, 31
November 7 14 28	November 9,12 21 29
December 5 12 19	December 11 14
1723	
January 23	January 16
February 20	February 1,6,12,13 27,28
March 12,13,20 29	March 6 27
April 26	April 3,10,24
May 1,8,14,15,22	May 29
June 19,26	June 5,11,12,15
July 24,31	July 3,9,10
	August 6,7,10,12, 13,14,19,21,26,28
September 18,24,25,26	September 4,10,11, 13 30
October 23	October 2,4,5,7,9, 12,16 30

Present	*Absent*
November 13 27	November 12 20 28
December 9,10,11	December 4 18
1724	
January 8	January 14,15,22, 29
February 26	February 5,11,12, 19
March 4,10,11,13,18,25	March 30
April 15	April 1,8 22,29
May 6 13	May 12 20
June 3 17	June 9 24
	July 1,3,8,14,15,17, 18,22,29
	August 1,5,7,11,19, 21,26
	September 2,8,9, 16,23,24,30
October 21	October 2,5,7,14, 15,17 24
November 19	November 4,7,18 25
December 9,16	December 2,8 23
1725	
January 12 20,27	January 13
February 3 17,24	February 6,9
March 3 10,17,24	March 9 31
April 8 14,19,21,28	April 5,6,7 10
May 19,26	May 5,11,12
June 2 23,30	June 1 8,9,11,18
	July 7,13,14,21,28
August 10,11,18	August 4 25
September 14	September 1,8 15,22,29
	October 5,6,8,13 27
	November 3,9,10 24
December 8 15,22	December 1 14
1726	
January 19,26	January 5,11,12
February 24	February 2,8,9 16
March 2 9,16,23	March 8

Appendix H

Vanbrugh's Remarks on the Conduct of William Benson

PRO T 1/216, ff.82–3. Unsigned but autograph [March 1719]

Remarks on the Conduct of Wm Benson Esqr
Surveyr: of His Majesties Works

Art: 1. May 1718
That under Specious pretences of saving money to his Majesty in the Works & Repairs of his Pallaces, He got Sr Chr: Wren turn'd out, & himself put into his Place; His Brother lately come from a Mercht: in Holland, Clerk of the Works in ye Room of Mr Hawksmoor, to ye Pallaces of Whitehall &c, And his Agent Colen Campbell, cheif clerk in ye Room of Mr Wren.

2nd
Novbr: 1718
For ye first 6 Months no Business was done in the Office, nor any Tradesmens Bills stated, wch before that time us'd to be done monthly; And ye Pallaces being in good repair, He forms a Project of keeping them so under pretence of having cost his Majesty & former Crowns for the Ordinary Repairs 28000£ p. Annū: (but wch was not communs: anns: one 3d prt of that sum, but occasion'd by Buildings & Repairs of Lodgings by Warrants from ye Treasury call'd Extraordinarys) for ye sum of 12000£ pr Annum, imposing on ye King & ye Lords of the Treasury a Pretended Contract in ye Names of ye Kings Mason, Carpenter & Bricklayer, who were to declare a Trust to his two foremention'd Instruments B. Benson & C. Campbell, but realy in Trust for himself; by which 1000£ pr Month was to be receiv'd of ye Treasury for 4 years, of wch ye said Mason, Carpenter & Bricklayer was not acquainted till ye Contract was ripe, & then they were told by this new Surveyr that they should have each of them sallaries of about 200£ pr Annū: Each, for the use of their Names, wch was either for Bribes or Hush money.

3d This Contract was accordingly sign'd by the 3 Workmen to Commence from ye first Instant, in which it is expressly said that all doubts or disputes should be settled by 3 Persons one to be chosen by ye Lords of the Treasury, One by ye said Surveyor, & ye 3d by ye Contractors, so that He had 2 Arbitrators against ye Treasurys one, and consequently as little money might be expended as he pleas'd, And by ye same Contract he is made Judge what Buildings are necessary or fit to be repaird, or pulld down & rebuilt, whereby to save himself 50£, He might put the Crown to 500£, And call it Extraordinarys.

4th To make the Contract ye more Beneficial to Himself, The Pallace of Somerset House, wch is most out of Repair is left out, And ye Damages by Fires, Storms &c, are excepted; wch soon show'd ye Lords of ye Treasury ye Fallacy, & for whose Benefitt this Contract was contriv'd.

5th Thereupon their Lordships did not sign their Part of ye Contract, but open'd ye same to new Contractors & severall Able & Substantial Workmen deliver'd in a Proposall to ye Treasury under their Hands, to perform ye same Contract for ye sum of 8000£ pr annū so as their Lordships would appoint some Honest and Able Workmen in ye Room of ye New Surveyor to Judge of their Performance; which proposall expos'd & prevented his intended Fraud.

6th About this time the said new Surveyr Alarum'd the King, Lords, & Commons, with the immediate and imminent danger of ye falling of the House of Lords, Painted Chamber, Court of Requests &c. And by his own Orders were set up Shores & Props, found and reported by ye Ablest Builders & Workmen to be more dangerous to ye Buildings than their own decay:

And altho' the House of Peers made an Order, signd by ye Clerk of ye Parliament to Strike those Shores in their House; He oppos'd & Quarreld with ye Workmen for so doing; wch must be ye effect of his Ignorance & obstinacy if not worse; of wch their Lordships have shown their Resentment.

7th He has now been almost a Year in his Office, & alledges there is a debt of near 5000£ owing to Workmen, And yet neither ye Bills before, nor since his time Adjusted, to almost ye ruining of the Artizans & their Family's, And ye Pallaces left unregarded by him, wch is as full a proof of the neglect, of his Duty as ye foregoing Account is of his design'd fraud, contrary to his Trust, as well as of his ignorance & Obstinacy.

Appendix J

Castle Howard by Anne, Viscountess Irwin (1732)

The authorship and date of this poem are established by references in family correspondence at Castle Howard. On 1 April 1732 Colonel Charles Howard wrote to Lord Carlisle: 'I hope my sister Irwin got the Poem I sent last post; I thought it was very pretty, and not knowing whether it was come down to Yorkshire yet, made me send it' (HMC Carlisle, p.90). On 18 January 1733 Lady Irwin wrote to her father from London with observations on Pope's *Epistle to Burlington* (1731) and *Epistle to Bathurst* (1732) in comparison with *Castle-Howard*, and on the reception of the latter. The letter continues: 'That poem is not so much discry'd here as it was in Yorkshire. I was told this morning in particular by Mr. Hammond, who the world allows a good judge, that the poem was good, and that part of it which relates to your Lordship writ after the manner of the ancients, in a beautiful simplicity. He has no other notion I have any interest in the poem than the relation I bear to your Lordship, and the natural affection I have to the place.'

The subject matter is certainly treated in the knowledge of Pope's *Epistle to Burlington*, but Virgil's *Georgics* might seem to be an obvious source for both ideas and form, even without the quotation on the title page. The line and half-line *At secura quies, et nescia fallere vita / Dives opum variarum* (*Georgics*, II.467–8) occur in a passage about the good fortune of the tenant, which may best be illustrated in Dryden's translation of 1697 (639–58).

Oh happy, if he knew his happy State!
The Swain, who, free from Business and Debate;
Receives his easy Food from Nature's Hand,
And just Returns of cultivated Land!
No Palace, with a lofty Gate, he wants,
T'admit the Tydes of early Visitants.
With eager Eyes devouring, as they pass,
The breathing Figures of *Corinthian* Brass.
No Statues threaten, from high Pedestals;
No *Persian* Arras hides his homely Walls,
With Antick Vests; which thro' their shady fold,
Betray the Streaks of ill dissembl'd Gold.
He boasts no Wool, whose native white is dy'd
With Purple Poyson of *Assyrian* Pride.
No costly Drugs of Araby defile,
With foreign Scents, the Sweetness of his Oyl.
But easie Quiet, a secure Retreat,
A harmless Life that knows not how to cheat,
With homebred Plenty the rich Owner bless,
And rural Pleasures crown his Happiness.

While Idalus appears in *Aeneid* I, Dodona and the Castalian Spring occur in the *Georgics*, and Virgil's description of the Elysian fields in *Aeneid* VI is also mentioned in the poem. Lady Irwin's reading was, however, not limited to a single author: she also mentions Pindar, Hippocrates and Hesiod as writers, the legend of the Hamadryads (which is not in Virgil) and that of St Hubert the medieval hunter. In a number of places she provides footnotes; these have been transcribed exactly. No further annotations have been added, since the main points of relevance of the poem to Lord Carlisle and his estate seem to be clear enough and the classical allusions will gain nothing from being explained to the uninitiated.

CASTLE-HOWARD,
THE
SEAT
Of the Right Honourable
CHARLES Earl of *CARLISLE.*
To whom this POEM is humbly inscribed.

Hic secura quies, et nescia fallere vita
Dives opum variarum

VIRGIL.

LONDON
Printed by E. OWEN in Amen-Corner. Price 1s.

When happy Plenty, the Effect of Peace,
Improves our Arts, makes Sciences encrease;
Then may an humble Muse essay to sing,
And try in tim'rous Flights her tender Wing:
So the gay tuneful Choir, who haunt the Grove,
From the small Linnet to the Cooing Dove,
In Consort joyn, their Melody to raise,
Let this excuse a Genius, where the Heart
Dictates from Nature rather than from Art.

Carlisle, to Thee I dedicate these Lays,
Reject them not because they sing thy Praise:
Envy too soon will raze what here I carve;
For those are censur'd most, who least deserve.
An Eminence in Virtue, Rank, or Pow'r,
Creates new Enemies for ev'ry Hour:

And Flatt'rers too, who gild our weakest Side,
Calling that Honour, which too oft is Pride;
But neither Foe or Flatt'rer is here,
I bring the Tribute of a Muse sincere.

How can I best describe your gen'rous Mind,
To ev'ry Social Act of Life inclin'd.
Numbers from you their daily Bread receive,
Th'afflicted Heart – through you forgets to grieve:
To serve Mankind is your peculiar End,
And make those happy who on you depend.
Your Children, Servants, Friends, this Blessing share,
And feel the Bounty of your constant Care.

Through various Paths to Happiness you've try'd,
But ever follow'd a falacious Guide,
Till from the Court and City you withdrew,
A Life of rural Pleasure to pursue.
Soon you resign'd what others most desire;
Nor cou'd Ambition your cool Temper fire:
The Statesman's Schemes you left to those who durst be great,
And found Joys unmolested in this safe Retreat.
Long may you prove the Sweets of this Recess;
While others aim, you taste true Happiness.
But since an Author by his Works we know,
Better than all the Praise his Friends bestow;
Permit me, tho' unequal, to relate,
The many Beauties which surround this Seat.
Tho' void of Art, and destitute of Skill,
Wanting the Power, I only boast the Will.
Virgil presum'd to paint th' *Elysian* Fields,
To him my Lays, but not my Subject yields.
Had *Mantua's* Bard been bless'd with such a Theme,
He ne'r had form'd a Visionary Dream.
All that Luxurious Fancy can invent,
What Poets feign, what Painters represent;
Not in Imagination here we trace,
Realities adorn this happy Place.

A noble Pile magnificently great,
Not rais'd alone for Beauty or for State;
Conveniency with the two former joyn,
Too oft neglected in a great Design:
To please the Criticks, and give no Offence,
We build by Rule, tho' opposite to Sense.
Here Art and Fancy equally aspire,
Correct like *Virgil*, joyn'd to *Pindar's* Fire
Within it answers what our Wishes form'd,
Finish'd with Taste, with Elegance adorn'd.
A Genius here presides throughout the Whole,
And in this *Folio* we read *Carlisle's* Soul.
Some few perhaps this noble Work condemn,
As what we envy, we too often blame:
So Criticks wear a Jaundice in their Eye,
O'r look all Beauties, and all Faults discry.
Can erring Man perform a perfect Peice,
Even in the happy Times of *Rome* and *Greece*,
When Arts and Sciences excell'd the most;
That Golden Age, which now, alass! is lost,
Criticks were known to plague those *Halcyon* Days,
And censur'd all, but never deign'd to praise.
When *Phidias* and the fam'd *Vitruvius* liv'd,
Small Honour for their Labours they receiv'd;
Antiquity now sanctifies their Name,
With their Cotemp'ries they scarce purchas'd Fame.

And now, my Muse, attempt the verdant Scene,
Whose Views delight o'r vary'd Shades of Green.
Wou'd *Hesiod*, gentle Bard, my Verse inspire,
Would he bestow one Spark of Past'rel Fire;
No other Muse or Goddess I'd invoke,
To Him a Hecatomb shou'd freely smoke:
He best can teach to sing the rural Lays,
Who has so well performed his* Works and Days.
But should the daring Muse the Lawrel seize;
Should she succeed where most she hopes to please;
Here to discribe, exactly to unfold,
Th' Attempt to *Hesiod* wou'd appear too bold,
Some Beauties must be seen, but can't be told.

From ev'ry Place you cast your wand'ring Eyes,
You view gay Landskips, and new Prospects rise,
There a Green Lawn bounded with Shady Wood,
Here Downy Swans sport in a Lucid Flood.
Buildings the proper Points of View adorn,
Of †*Grecian, Roman* and *Egyptian* Form.

These interspers'd with Woods and Verdant Plains,
Such as possess'd of old th' *Arcadian* Swains.
Hills rise on Hills; and to complete the Scenes,
Like one continu'd Wood th' Horizon seems.
This in the main describes the Points of View,
But something more is to some Places due.
As *Helen, Dido*, and the *Spartan* Dame,
Stand foremost in the List of ancient Fame;
While other Beauties not in Story told,
Lie undistinguish'd in the common Mould.

Lead through the Park, where Lines of Trees unite,
And Verd'rous Lawns the bounding Deer delight:
By gentle Falls the docile Ground descends,
Forms a fair Plain, then by Degrees ascends.
These Inequalities delight the Eye,
For Nature charms most in Variety.
When ev'r her gen'ral Law by Arts effac'd,
It shows a Skill, but proves a want of Taste.
O'r all Designs Nature shou'd still preside;
She is the cheapest, and most perfect Guide.

Far in the Park there lies a spacious *Vale,
Form'd to inspire a soft Poetick Tale.
On ev'ry Side with shady Wood 'tis bound,
A Maiden Verdure covers all the Ground.
Hither Saint *Hubert* secretly repairs,
And hears the eager Hunters Vows and Pray'rs.
The flying Deer by sad Experience feels,
The cruel Hounds, close at his tremb'ling Heels,
In silent Tears his last Distress he shows,
Then falls *Actaeon* like to bloody Foes.

Here other Woods and Lawns demand a Place,
Which well an abler Poets Theme wou'd grace:
But such unnumber'd Beauties bless this Seat,
'Twere endless on each diff'rent Charm to treat.
†*Hipocrates* has some where justly said.
That Arts are long, and Nature's Debt soon paid.
Cou'd we the certain *Apothem* reverse;
Were Arts soon learn'd, and distant was the Herse,

* *Vid*. Hesiod's *Poem call'd* Works and Days.

† The *Obelisk, Temple, Mausoleum,* and *Pyramid*.

* Bel Bottom.

† Vita brevis est ars longa.

Then wou'd unrival'd *Carlisle's* Genius shine,
Who has so early form'd this great Design:
But Fate has fix'd the Limits of our Stay,
And while I write, Time gently glides away.

East from the House a beaut'ous *Down there lies,
Where Art with Nature emulating vyes:
Not smoother Surface boast the *Tempean* Plains,
Tho' sung by Poets in immortal Strains:
Not finer Verdure can young *Flora* bring,
Tho' she commands an ever blooming Spring.
Upon this Plain a †Monument appears,
Sacred to Piety and filial Tears.
Here to his Sire did grateful *Carlisle* raise,
A certain Record a more lasting Praise,
Than Volumes writ in Honour to his Name;
Those often die, being made the Sport of Fame:
The Moth, the Worm, and Envy, them annoy,
But Time can only Pyramids destroy.

Beyond this Down a *Building rears its Head,
Sacred to the immortal Vert'ous dead.
The Name of *Carias* noted †King it bears,
Made famous by his faithful Consort's Tears.
Nor was the Structure *Artemisia* rais'd,
With greater Justice more deserv'dly prais'd.
Tho' that a Wonder was by Ancients deem'd,
This by the Moderns is not less esteem'd.
More difficult to please, and more perverse,
Judging more rashly, tho' they know much less.
Here *Carlisle* will thy sacred *Manes* repose,
This solemn Place thy Ashes will enclose.
How will it please thy gentle Shade to view,
Some Ages hence, Oh, may my Prophecy prove true!
Descending from thy Line a gen'rous Race,
Fit to adorn the Camp, or Court to Grace:
Who, after having gain'd deserv'd Applause,
For having bravely serv'd their Country's Cause,
Shall to Ambition rural Joys prefer,
And fix their Happiness and Pleasure here.
So when the *Trojan* *Prince with glad Surprize,
Survey'd the Hero's who shou'd from him rise,
All Dangers and all Labours he despis'd,
So much his noble Progeny he priz'd;
Only to future Prospects cou'd attend,
Since from his Line the *Caesars* shou'd descend.

The Garden now demands my humbly Lays,
Which merits a more worthy Pen shou'd praise.
So far extended, and so great the Space,
Magnificence in ev'ry Part we trace.
Before the House you view a large *Parterre*,
Not crouded with the Trifles brought from far:
No Borders, Alleys, Edgings spoil the Scene,
'Tis one unvary'd Piece of pleasing Green:
No starv'd Exoticks here lament their Fate,
Fetter'd and bound like Pris'ners of State:
Or as *Diogenes* in Tub confin'd,
Wishing like him th' enlivening Sun to find.
'Tis ornamented by the Sculpture's Hand,
Here Statues, Obilisks, and Vases stand.

* *The Down before* Preetty Wood.

† *The Pyramid.*

* *The* Mausoleum.

† Mausolus.

* *Vide* Virgil's Aeneid.

Beyond 'tis circl'd by a pleasant *Grove,
Rais'd from the Family of constant Love:
No boist'rous Storms, nor an inclement Sky,
Which tender Leaves, and springing Buds destroy,
Affect the Sombre Shade you here enjoy;
Perpetual Verdure all the Trees disclose,
Which like true Love no Change of Seasons knows.

Nothing this happy Climate can produce,
Is wanting here for Pleasure or for Use.
The Kitchen Ground all Kinds of Fruit afford,
Which crown with Luxury the tempting Board.
Here blooming *Flora* and *Pomona* reign,
Vertumnus too, who helps the lab'ring Swain,
Have all agreed to show their watchful Care,
That *Aeolus* shou'd this young *Eden* spare.
Let these kind Deities their Charge defend,
While I attempt the promis'd Land t' ascend.

A noble Terrass lies before the Front,
By which into a *Paradise you mount.
Not greater Beauty boasts th' *Idalian* Grove,
Tho' that is sacred to the Queen of Love.
Such stately Trees encircle ev'ry View,
As never in *Dodonas* Forest grew.
Here the smooth Beach and rev'rend Oak entwine,
And form a Temple for the Pow'rs Divine:
So Ages past from ancient Bards we've heard,
When Men the Deity in Groves rever'd,
A Tow'ring Wood superior in its Kind,
Was to the Worship of the God's assign'd:
While *Plebian* Trees, which lowly Shade produce,
Were held unworthy of this sacred Use.

Here broad Meander Walks, each Way surprize;
And if Variety's a Charm we prize,
That Charm this Grove can in Perfection boast,
As Art in copying Nature pleases most.
Gardens of diff'rent Forms delight the Eye,
From whence a beaut'ous Country we discry:
And sure, if any Place deserves to claim,
This Wood with Justice **Belvidere* we name.
Statues at proper Views enrich the Scene,
Here chaste *Diana* and the *Paphian* Queen,
Tho' Opposites in Fame, tho' Rivals made,
Contended stand under one common Shade.
Such Harmony of Soul this Place inspires,
All furious Passions, and all fierce Desires
Are here becalm'd, and Gentleness succeeds,
The certain Parent whence Content proceeds.
Who wou'd not then prefer this pleasing Bow'r,
Since Life is fleeting, and the present Hour
Is all that Fate has put into our Pow'r?
To Riches, Grandeur, Fame, Ambition's Pleas,
Since Peace of Mind gives greater Joy than these:
But how this Wood this Peace of Mind bestows,
This ancient Tale the Secret will disclose.

In Days of Old, when Nymphs in Groves were bred,
And Flocks and Herds by Royal Virgins fed,
A Band of Maids of faultless Shape and Air,
Whose Forms created Love, their Eyes Despair;
Their Lives to chaste *Diana's* Rites avow'd,

* *The Wilderness of Ever Greens.*

* Ray Wood.

* Belvidere *Italian for fine View.*

Shunning the Courtship of the flatt'ring Crowd;
Preferring Solitude and rural Sport,
To all the Pleasures of the *Cyprian* Court.
Their Beauty did not long remain unknown;
A Troop of daring *Sylvans* hardy grown,
Resolve their private chaste Retreat t'invade;
And like the *Sabe'an* Rape, each seize a Maid.

With Secrecy their Purpose they pursue,
Till they beheld the blushing Fair in View.
Then they at once the youthful Train surround,
And bear th' unwilling Sisters from the Ground.
The trembling Maids unite their mournful Cries,
Which reach'd the Virgin Goddess of the Skies.
She to prevent her Vot'ries from Disgrace,
And save 'em from the Rusticks rude Embrace,
To *Daphne's* Fate the lovely Nymphs assign'd,
Who now remain in crusted Bark confin'd:
And to express how much they lov'd the Chace,
Ray Wood the Virgin Huntress named the Place.
This Name denotes the Female of the Roe,
On whom these Maids oft drew the circling Bow,
Pursuing them with an unerring Dart,
Prizing a Deer more than a wounded Heart.
Here they in Secrecy have long remain'd,
We view the Trees, nor know we there's contain'd,
In ev'ry Tree, as ancient Bards relate,
An **Hamadryad's* short precarious Fate:
For when the Tree's destroy'd the Nymph attends,
The *Dryad* sickens, and her Life soon ends.

Diana more to bless her fav'rite Grove,
Added this other Mark of partial Love,
That no unruly Passions shou'd invade
The Breast of those who wander in this Shade:
No jealous Thoughts, nor no corroding Care,
Nor Politicians Schemes shou'd enter here.
If Love sometimes – as Love will oft intrude,
No Place so Sacred can that Pow'r exclude.
The Heav'nly *Venus* only here inspires
All modest Wishes, and all chaste Desires.
Pan and his Wanton Train, the *Dryads* dread,
Presume not on this Hallow'd Ground to tread.
This then explains the Reason, why this Wood
Subdues all vicious Thoughts, and raises only Good.

These Scenes of Beauty having now been view'd,
Here let the Labours of the Muse conclude.
No Praise for what I've writ I vainly claim,
Let *Carlisle* but approve – to me that's Fame:
All I desire is that some gen'rous Bard
Wou'd show the World how much the Theme deserv'd
Do Justice to the Beauties of this Seat,
And like *Appelles* – draw a Piece complete.

FINIS

* *The* Hamadryads *were certain Nymphs, who, according to the Ancients, had the Care and Guardianship of Trees: And they believ'd the Fate of these Nymphs so entirely depended upon Trees, they thought they liv'd and dy'd together.*

Appendix K

Vanbrugh's Letters

This is a complete list of Vanbrugh's known letters, including a few memoranda and reports. After the date are given the addressee, the place of writing (if known) and the best source.

1685			
Dec.28	Earl of Huntingdon	Chester	Rosenberg, p.603
1691			
Nov.9	his mother	Vincennes	Appendix B (1)
1692			
Aug.26	William Blathwayt	Bastille	Appendix B (2)
1699			
Dec.25	Earl of Manchester	London	Webb, p.3 (1)
[1700]	Earl of Carlisle	Tadcaster	Webb, p.6 (2)
1703			
Jun.15	Duke ofNewcastle	London	Whistler, p.35 (1)
Jun.15	Jacob Tonson	London	Webb, p.7 (3)
Jul.13	Jacob Tonson	London	Webb, p.8 (4)
Jul.30	Jacob Tonson	London	Webb, p.10 (5)
[1704]	Peter Le Neve		Rosenberg, p.607
1704			
Nov.9	Lord Godolphin		Webb, p.11 (6)
1705			
Jun.22	Duke of Marlborough		Whistler, p.229 (2)
Aug.24	Duke of Marlborough	London	Whistler, p.230 (3)
1706			
Jan.1	Boulter		Webb, p.207 (1)
Nov.8	Boulter	London	Webb, p.210 (6)
1707			
Jan.11	Boulter	London	Webb, p.208 (2)
[c.Jan.23]	Boulter		Webb, p.208 (3)
Mar.6	Joynes		Webb, p.209 (4)
Mar.7	Boulter	London	Webb, p.209 (5)
Jul.15	Marlborough	Blenheim	Whistler, p.231 (4)
Jul.18	Boulter	London	Webb, p.211 (7)
Jul.18	Manchester	London	Webb, p.13 (7)
Jul.25	Marlborough	London	Whistler, p.232 (5)
Aug.	Joynes	Henderskelfe	Webb, p.223 (24)
Sep.9	Manchester	London	Webb, p.15 (8)
Oct.16	Peter Le Neve		Sold Sotheby's, 26 Oct. 1971 (373)

Nov.11	Boulter	London	Webb, p.213 (9)
Nov.18	Boulter	London	Webb, p.214 (10)
Dec.18	Boulter	London	Webb, p.214 (11)
1708			
Feb.24	Manchester	London	Webb, p.16 (9)
Mar.16	Manchester	London	Webb, p.17 (10)
Mar.22	Manchester	Stevenage	Webb, p.19 (11)
Mar.29	Boulter	London	Webb, p.215 (12)
Apr.1	Boulter		Webb, p.215 (13)
Apr.25	Boulter	Henley	Webb, p.216 (14)
May 1	Boulter	London	Webb, p.217 (15)
May 11	Manchester	London	Webb, p.20 (12)
May 14	anon.		Rosenberg, p.606
[1708]	Vice-Chamberlain Coke		Whistler, p.233 (6)
Jun.19	Joynes	London	Webb, p.218 (16)
Jun.24	Joynes	London	Webb, p.219 (17)
Jul.8	?Arthur Maynwaring	[Blenheim]	Webb, p.22 (13)
Jul.27	Manchester		Webb, p.24 (14)
Aug.17	Manchester	Biggleswade	Webb, p.25 (15)
Sep.14	Duchess of Marlborough	Blenheim	Webb, p.26 (16)
Sep.21	Joynes	London	Webb, p.219 (18)
Sep.28	Joynes	London	Webb, p.220 (19)
Nov.6	Joynes	London	Webb, p.220 (20)
Nov.30	Joynes	London	Webb, p.221 (21)
Dec.9	Joynes	London	Webb, p.222 (22)
Dec.26	Joynes	London	Webb, p.223 (23)
1709			
Jan.13	Joynes	London	Webb, p.224 (25)
Feb.10	Joynes		Webb, p.224 (26)
Feb.17	Joynes	London	Webb, p.225 (27)
May 5	Hopkins		Whistler, p.233 (7)
May 31	?Godolphin	Blenheim	Webb, p.27 (17)
Jun.9	Duchess of Marlborough		Webb, p.28 (18)
Jun.11	Duchess of Marlborough		Webb, p.29 (19)
Jun.11	Duchess of Marlborough		Webb, p.30 (20)
Jul.8	[Memorandum]		Webb, p.32 (21)
Jul.14	Duchess of Marlborough	London	Webb, p.33 (22)
Jul.18	?Lord Ryalton	Blenheim	Webb, p.34 (23)
Jul.25	Duchess of Marlborough		Webb, p.36 (24)
Sep.29	Joynes	London	Webb, p.225 (28)
Nov.1	Duchess of Marlborough	Blenheim	Webb, p.37 (25)
Dec.6	anon.	London	Webb, p.226 (29)
Dec.18	Joynes	London	Webb, p.226 (30)
Dec.20	Joynes	London	Webb, p.227 (31)
[1709]	Travers		Webb, p.38 (26)
1710			
Feb.10	Robert Harley		Whistler, p.234 (8)

Mar. 14	Joynes	London	Webb, p.236 (46)
Apr. 1	Joynes and Bobart		Webb, p.228 (32)
Apr. 28	Marlborough	London	Whistler, p.235 (10)
Apr. 29	Joynes	London	Webb, p.228 (33)
May 6	Joynes	London	Webb, p.229 (34)
May 27	Duchess of Marlborough		Whistler, p.236 (11)
May 27	Duchess of Marlborough		Whistler, p.237 (12)
Jun. 6	Duchess of Marlborough	London	Webb, p.40 (28)
Jun. 6	Joynes and Bobart	London	Webb, p.229 (35)
Jun. 8	Joynes	London	Webb, p.230 (36)
Jun. 24	Duchess of Marlborough	London	Webb, p.41 (29)
Aug. 1	Marlborough	Blenheim	Webb, p.42 (30)
Aug. 31	Duchess of Marlborough	London	Webb, p.43 (31)
Sep. 7	Joynes	London	Webb, p.231 (37)
Sep. 21	Joynes	London	Webb, p.231 (38)
Sep. 22	Marlborough	London	Webb, p.43 (32)
Sep. 30	Marlborough	[Blenheim]	Webb, p.44 (33)
Sep. 30	Lord Poulet	Blenheim	Webb, p.45 (33a)
Sep. 30	Robert Harley	Blenheim	Webb, p.46 (33b)
Oct. 3	Marlborough	Oxford	Webb, p.48 (34)
Oct. 10	Treasury		Webb, p.47 (33d)
Oct. 10	Marlborough	London	Webb, p.49 (35)
Oct. 10	Joynes and Bobart	London	Webb, p.232 (39)
Oct. 12	[Joynes]	London	Webb, p.232 (40)
Oct. 19	Joynes	London	Webb, p.233 (41)
Oct. 25	Joynes	London	Webb, p.234 (42)
Oct. 25	Arthur Maynwaring	Chargate	Webb, p.50 (36)
Nov. 2	Joynes	London	Webb, p.234 (43)
[1710]	Marlborough		Whistler, p.238 (13)
1711			
Jan. 9	Joynes	London	Webb, p.235 (44)
Feb. 17	Joynes	Whitehall	Webb, p.236 (45)
Feb. 23	Marlborough	London	Whistler, p.234 (9)
Mar. 22	Joynes	London	Webb, p.237 (47)
May 17	Joynes	London	Webb, p.237 (48)
Aug. 10	Marlborough	London	Whistler, p.240 (14)
Sep. 11	Joynes	London	Webb, p.238 (49)
Sep. 15	Joynes	London	Webb, p.239 (50)
Sep. 25	Joynes	London	Webb, p.239 (51)
Sep. 30	Joynes	London	Webb, p.240 (52)
Oct. 27	Joynes	London	Webb, p.240 (53)
Nov. 13	Joynes	London	Webb, p.241 (54)
Nov. 22	Joynes	London	Webb, p.241 (55)
Dec. 1	Joynes	London	Webb, p.242 (56)
Dec. 3	Joynes	London	Webb, p.242 (57)
Dec. 27	anon.	Whitehall	Webb, p.51 (38)

1712			
Aug.3	Earl of Oxford		Webb, p.52 (39)
Oct.30	Joynes	London	Webb, p.243 (58)
Nov.4	?Marlborough		Webb, p.52 (40)
Nov.10	[Memorandum]		Webb, p.53 (41)
1713			
Jan.25	Mayor of Woodstock	Whitehall	Webb, p.53 (42)
Feb.21	Earl of Oxford		Whistler, p.128 (15)
Mar.18	Marlborough	London	Whistler, p.240 (16)
Apr.2	[a relation]		Webb, p.55 (44)
Apr.14	Earl of Oxford	Whitehall	Whistler, p.129 (17)
Sep.28	Edward Southwell	Chester	Whistler, p.242 (19)
Oct.23	Edward Southwell	Castle Howard	Webb, p.55 (45)
Oct.29	James Craggs	Castle Howard	Webb, p.56 (46)
Nov.30	[?Lord Chamberlain]	Castle Howard	Webb, p.57 (47)
—	[Lord Chamberlain]		Rosenberg, p.608
1714			
May 29	Marlborough	London	Webb, p.58 (48)
Jul.6	[?Vice-Chamberlain]		Rosenberg, p.609
Aug.13	[?Vice-Chamberlain]		Rosenberg, p.609
Nov.29	Earl of Halifax		Webb, p.247
Dec.27	[Vice-Chamberlain]		Rosenberg, p.610
Dec.7	Lord Wharton		Portland Papers, Nottingham University
1715			
Jan.16	Duchess of Marlborough		Webb, p.60 (49)
[1714–15]	Earl of Clare		Webb, p.61 (50)
Feb.5	Earl of Clare	Whitehall	Webb, p.61 (51)
Feb.9	anon.		Webb, p.63 (52)
Mar.31	Treasury		Webb, p.248
?1715	Tonson		Webb, p.63 (53)
May 3	Joynes	London	Webb, p.243 (59)
May 5	Joynes	Whitehall	Webb, p.244 (60)
May 7	Joynes	Whitehall	Webb, p.244 (61)
[Oct.]	Robert Walpole		Appendix L
Oct.17	Robert Walpole		Webb, p.63 (54)
1716			
Apr.5	Joynes		Webb, p.245 (63)
Apr.19	Marlborough		Webb, p.64 (55)
May 1	Joynes	London	Webb, p.245 (64)
May 25	Marlborough		Webb, p.65 (56)
Jun.12	Duchess of Marlborough	Whitehall	Webb, p.66 (57)
Jun.19	Duchess of Marlborough	London	Webb, p.67 (58)
Jun.30	Duchess of Marlborough	Blenheim	Webb, p.68 (59)
Jul.10	Duchess of Marlborough	London	Webb, p.70 (60)
Jul.13	Duchess of Marlborough	London	Webb, p.72 (61)
Jul.27	Duchess of Marlborough	Blenheim	Webb, p.73 (62)

Aug.3	Duchess of Marlborough	London	Webb, p.75 (63)
Aug.19	Duchess of Marlborough	Castle Howard	Webb, p.77 (64)
Aug.21	Duchess of Marlborough	Scarborough	Webb, p.79 (65)
Sep.27	Duchess of Marlborough	Blenheim	Webb, p.80 (66)
Oct.8	Duchess of Marlborough	London	Webb, p.81 (67)
Oct.–	Duchess of Marlborough	Whitehall	Webb, p.81 (68)
Nov.6	Duchess of Marlborough		Webb, p.83 (70)
Nov.8	Duchess of Marlborough	Whitehall	Webb, p.84 (71)
1716	Marlborough		Whistler, p.242 (20)
Nov.10	Duke of Newcastle	London	Webb, p.85 (72)
Nov.15	Duke of Newcastle	Whitehall	Webb, p.86 (73)
Nov.27	Duke of Newcastle	Whitehall	Webb, p.87 (74)
Dec.15	Bobart	London	Webb, p.89 (75)
—	[Memorandum]		Whistler, p.246 (25)
1717			
Jun.27	Marlborough		Whistler, p.243 (21)
Jun.–	Carlisle		Webb, p.89 (76)
Jul.3	Newcastle		Webb, p.94 (77)
Oct.9	Newcastle	Bath	Webb, p.94 (78)
Oct.14	Treasury	Bath	Webb, p.94 (79)
Dec.21	Newcastle	Greenwich	Webb, p.96 (80)
—	Newcastle		Webb, p.96 (81)
—	Newcastle		Webb, p.97 (82)
—	Newcastle		Webb, p.98 (83)
—	Newcastle	Greenwich	Webb, p.98 (84)
—	anon.		Webb, p.99 (85)
1717			
Nov.	Newcastle	Whitehall	Webb, p.155 (151)
[1717–18]	Newcastle	Whitehall	Webb, p.155 (152)
—	Newcastle		Webb, p.155 (153)
1718			
Jul.4	Peter Forbes	Greenwich	Webb, p.99 (86)
Jul.31	Earl of Sunderland		Whistler, p.244 (22)
Aug.7	Newcastle	Whitehall	Webb, p.100 (87)
Aug.30	Newcastle		Webb, p.100 (88)
Sep.17	Newcastle	Greenwich	Webb, p.101 (89)
—	Newcastle	Greenwich	Webb, p.102 (90)
Sep.–	Newcastle	Greenwich	Webb, p.102 (91)
—	Newcastle		Webb, p.103 (92)
Oct.30	Earl of Suffolk	Whitehall	Webb, p.103 (93)
—	Newcastle		Webb, p.104 (94)
—	Newcastle		Webb, p.104 (95)
Nov.29	Newcastle	Greenwich	Webb, p.105 (96)
Dec.17	Newcastle	Nottingham	Webb, p.105 (97)
Dec.25	Newcastle	Castle Howard	Webb, p.107 (98)
[1718]	Newcastle	Whitehall	Webb, p.154 (149)

1719			
Jan.4	Newcastle	Castle Howard	Webb, p.108 (99)
Jan.12	Newcastle	York	Webb, p.109 (100)
Jan.24	Newcastle	Nottingham	Webb, p.110 (101)
[March]	Treasury		Appendix H
May 5	Newcastle		Whistler, p.244 (23)
Jul.1	Tonson	London	Webb, p.111 (102)
Jul.23	Newcastle	London	Webb, p.113 (103)
Aug.6	Newcastle	Whitehall	Webb, p.113 (104)
—	Newcastle		Webb, p.115 (105)
Aug.11	Newcastle	London	Webb, p.115 (106)
Aug.15	Newcastle		Webb, p.116 (107)
Sep.10	Sunderland or Stanhope	London	Webb, p.117 (108)
—	Newcastle	Whitehall	Webb, p.118 (109)
—	Newcastle	Greenwich	Webb, p.119 (110)
Nov.5	Tonson	Whitehall	Webb, p.120 (111)
Nov.23	Newcastle	Whitehall	Webb, p.120 (112)
—	Stanhope		Webb, p.121 (113)
Nov.29	Tonson	Whitehall	Webb, p.121 (114)
Dec.31	Tonson	Whitehall	Webb, p.124 (115)
1720			
Feb.18	Tonson	London	Webb, p.125 (116)
Sep.15	Newcastle	London	Webb, p.126 (117)
Nov.24	Mauduit		Webb, p.127 (118)
1721			
Feb.2	Carlisle	London	Webb, p.127 (119)
Feb.7	Carlisle		Webb, p.128 (120)
Feb.18	Carlisle		Webb, p.129 (121)
Feb.20	Carlisle		Webb, p.129 (122)
Mar.25	Carlisle	Greenwich	Webb, p.131 (123)
Apr.22	Carlisle	London	Webb, p.132 (124)
May 5	Carlisle	London	Webb, p.133 (125)
May 25	Carlisle	London	Webb, p.134 (126)
Jun.8	Carlisle	London	Webb, p.135 (127)
Jul.6	Carlisle	London	Webb, p.136 (128)
Aug.8	Newcastle	Castle Howard	Webb, p.136 (129)
Aug.20	Brigadier Watkins	York	Webb, p.137 (130)
Sep.20	anon.	Heslington	Unpublished[1]
Nov.16	Carlisle	Whitehall	Webb, p.139 (131)
Nov.18	Joynes	Whitehall	Webb, p.140 (132)
1722			
Feb.11	Newcastle		Webb, p.140 (133)
Feb.13	Duke of Ancaster		Sold Sotheby's, 28 Mar. 1972 (330)
Apr.6	Carlisle		Webb, p.141 (134)
Apr.24	Carlisle	London	Webb, p.142 (135)

[1] Family letter, to be published by Professor Bernard Harris.

May 5	Carlisle	London	Webb, p.143 (136)
May 10	Carlisle	London	Webb, p.144 (137)
May 30	Treasury		Webb, p.145 (138)
Jun.18	Tonson	London	Webb, p.145 (139)
Jun.19	Carlisle	London	Webb, p.147 (140)
Jul.19	Carlisle	London	Webb, p.147 (141)
1723			
Jan.19	Newcastle	Greenwich	Webb, p.150 (142)
Jul.30	Newcastle	Greenwich	Webb, p.150 (143)
Aug.3	?Forbes	Greenwich	Webb, p.151 (144)
Aug.20	Newcastle	Castle Howard	Webb, p.151 (145)
Nov.1	Newcastle	Greenwich	Webb, p.82 (69)
Nov.11	Joynes	Greenwich	Webb, p.152 (146)
Nov.26	Carlisle	London	Webb, p.153 (147)
Dec.22	Newcastle	Greenwich	Webb, p.153 (148)
—	Newcastle		Webb, p.154 (150)
1724			
Feb.11	Carlisle	Whitehall	Webb, p.156 (154)
Feb.18	Carlisle		Webb, p.157 (155)
Mar.26	Carlisle	London	Webb, p.158 (156)
Apr.11	Carlisle	London	Webb, p.160 (157)
Jul.10	Newcastle	Greenwich	Webb, p.161 (158)
Aug.23	Newcastle	[Scarborough]	Webb, p.161 (159)
Aug.28	Newcastle	Castle Howard	Webb, p.162 (160)
Sep.4	Guidott		Whistler, p.245 (24)
Nov.21	Carlisle	London	Webb, p.163 (161)
Dec.10	Carlisle	London	Webb, p.164 (162)
1725			
Apr.26	Treasury		Webb, p.165 (163)
May 4	Treasury		Webb, p.166 (164)
Aug.12	Tonson	London	Webb, p.166 (165)
Sep.4	Carlisle	Greenwich	Webb, p.168 (166)
Sep.11	Carlisle	Greenwich	Webb, p.169 (167)
Oct.25	Tonson	Greenwich	Webb, p.170 (168)
Dec.16	Carlisle	London	Webb, p.171 (169)
1726			
Mar.8	Carlisle	London	Webb, p.172 (170)

Appendix L

Vanbrugh to Robert Walpole, 1715

Cholmondeley (Houghton) MSS, Cambridge University Library, Correspondence, No.759

Sunday

Sr

I hear the Office of the Treasurer of the Chambers, is suddenly to be consider'd by you, in order to some new regulations. I have a very near Kinsman (and one I can't but be much concern'd for) who is Comptroller of that office, which Place was given him by ye Late Lord Godolphin, in recompence for some very great Services he had done. But in the noble Earl of Oxfords Reign, tho' he did not turn him out, he Suffer'd above half the vallue of it, to be sunk. My Kinsman has since apply'd to the Treasury for redress, which my Lord Carlisle found very just and reasonable, and wou'd have done what he desir'd, had the Regulation of the Office in generall, come under consideration before he left the Treasury. I am therefore forc'd to trouble you with my solicitations in this matter, which I am confident you will find as reasonable as Ld Carlisle did. I have no other Friend or Relation upon earth, to teaze you about, So hope I shall not apply to you in this small matter for this one, in Vain. The Paper I here enclose is only to possess you, with his merrit; what he has to apply for, I'll acquaint you with some other time. Pray read this, as you come in your Coach. One reading there, is worth twenty in a Room.

I have conceiv'd about your Room and will bring it to you (I think) on tuesday morning. 'tis an expedient between the Two so perhaps you'll like it.

I am
most humbly and most
truly your Servant
J Vanbrugh

To the Rt. Honble:
Mr Walpole
at Chelsea.

(Walpole was appointed Chancellor of the Exchequer on 12 October 1715, and the Establishment of the Treasury of the Chamber was then under review (CTB 1714–15, pp.298, 731). Carlisle had been First Lord of the Treasury (for the second time) from May to August 1715. The post of Treasurer of the Chamber was not, however, vacant in 1715–16. Vanbrugh's kinsman is his cousin William, who was re-appointed as Comptroller on 18 May 1715 (op.cit., p.522). On 17 October 1715 Vanbrugh wrote to Walpole: 'The inclosed is the second part of what I troubled you with the other day, which I hope you will think a most reasonable application' and then went on to discuss 'an estimate of your fabrick, which comes to £270' (Webb, p.63). While the letter printed here is catalogued as 1716, its most likely date would seem to be in the second week of October 1715. Walpole had, as Paymaster-General, had an official house at Chelsea Hospital since late 1714; Vanbrugh's alterations to it are discussed by C. G. T. Dean, *The Royal Hospital, Chelsea*, 1950, pp.201–4.)

Appendix M

A German View of Vanbrugh, 1740

From a letter of Jacob Friedrich, Baron Bielfeld dated 10 March 1740 (*Letters*, IV, 1770, pp.99–101)

This building [Blenheim] has been severely censured, and I agree that it is not entirely exempt from rational censure as it is too much loaded with columns and other heavy ornaments. But if we consider, that Sir John Vanbrugh was to construct a building of endless duration, that no bounds were set to the expens, and that an edifice was required which shoud strike with awe and surprise even at a distance; the architect may be excused for having sacrificed, in some degree, the elegance of design to the multiplicity of ornament. All the several parts are moreover exactly calculated, all the rules of the art are well observed, and this immens fabric reminds us, on the first glance, of the majesty and state of those of Greece and antient Rome. When we behold it at a distance, it appears not as a single palace, but as an entire city. We arrive at it by a stately bridge of a single arch, and which is itself a master-piece of architecture. I have contracted a very intimate friendship with the son of Sir John Vanbrugh, who has lately obtained a company in the foot guards, and is a young gentleman of real merit. He has shown me, not only all the designs of his father, but also two houses of his building, one near Whitehall, and the other at Greenwich. They are indeed mere models of houses, but notwithstanding their confined situation, there are every where traces of a master to be discovered in the execution. The vulgar critic finds too many columns and ornaments; but the true connoisseur sees that all these ornaments are accompanyd by utility, and that an inventive genius is visible in every part. This architect was likewise author of several comedys, which are indeed wrote in a style that is rather licentious, but at the same time are resplendent with wit and vivacity. So true it is, that genius is not confined to one subject, but wherever exercised, is equally manifest. The son of this able artist inherits the genius of his father; but as it is opportunity that makes a man famous, I doubt whether the war will enable him soon to acquire a name equally celebrated.

List of Works

Most of Vanbrugh's *œuvre* is either over- or under-worked, and this is not the occasion for a *catalogue raisonné* of either buildings or drawings from his office. Most of the surviving drawings are in the V & A, the Bodleian, and Elton Hall, and many are for unidentified projects. The list offered here is deliberately brief, and references are not given for works discussed in the preceding text.

Certain works wholly or partly carried out

Castle Howard, Yorks., 1700–12, the west wing designed by Sir Thomas Robinson 1753–9. Obelisk 1714; Pyramid Gate 1719.

Vanbrugh House ('Goose-Pie House'), Whitehall, 1701. *Destroyed.*

The Queen's Theatre (Opera House), Haymarket, 1704–5. *Destroyed.*

Blenheim Palace, Oxon., 1705–16, concluded by the Duchess of Marlborough with the help of Hawksmoor 1722–5.

Kimbolton Castle, Hunts., re-modelling and re-fronting 1707–10. *East portico by Alessandro Galilei 1719.*

Audley End, Essex, staircase and screen, 1708.

Chargate, Esher, Surrey, 1709–10. *Destroyed.*

Kings Weston, Glos., *c.*1710–14. *Interior finished by Robert Mylne.*

Newcastle House, Lincoln's Inn Fields, interior re-fitting 1714–17. *Rebuilt.*

Claremont, Esher, Surrey (incorporating Chargate), 1715–20. *Destroyed* except the Belvedere, 1715.

Orford House, Chelsea Hospital, alterations 1715.

Hampton Court Palace, completion of north end of east front (Prince of Wales's Rooms, Music Room, Guard Chamber), 1716.

Vanbrugh Castle, Greenwich, 1718–*c.*1721.

Eastbury, Dorset (first design *c.*1715), 1718–38, finished and modified by Roger Morris. *Destroyed.*

Nottingham Castle, interior re-fitting, 1719. *Rebuilt.*

Stowe, Bucks., additions to house, and garden buildings, *c.*1719–24. *Mostly altered or destroyed.* North portico and the Rotondo survive in an altered state.

Seaton Delaval, Northumb., 1720–28. *Main block gutted.*

Vanbrugh Fields Estate, Greenwich, 1719–25. *Destroyed.*

Robin Hood's Well, Great North Road, Skelbrooke, Yorks., *c.*1720. (But the date 1711 was formerly scratched on the fabric.)

Vine Court, Sevenoaks, Kent, *c.*1720? *Destroyed.*

Lumley Castle, Co. Durham, re-modelled south and west ranges, 1722– .

Grimsthorpe Castle, Lincs., north range, 1715?, 1722–6.

Kensington Palace, Water Tower, *c.*1722. *Destroyed.*

Esher, Surrey, Old Church, Newcastle pew, 1723–5.

Castle Howard, Yorks., Temple, 1725–8. *Interior by Francesco Vassali 1739–9.*

Probable attributions carried out

Barn Elms, Surrey, room for Jacob Tonson, 1703. *Destroyed.* (Webb, pp.7–8; it is not certain either that Vanbrugh was responsible or that the room was for the Kit-Cat Club.)

Morpeth Town Hall, Northumb., 1714. *Reconstructed.*

St James's Palace, Kitchen, 1716–17.

Windsor Park, Pump House, 1718.

Duncombe Park, Yorks., Rotondo, *c.*1718.

Somersby Hall., Lincs., 1722 (*Archaeol. Jnl,* CXXXI, 1974, p.314; Whistler, Pl.87).

South Kensington, Lord Talbot's House (Brompton Park, for Henry Wise). *Destroyed.*

Peckham, Hanover House. *Destroyed.*

Kingston, house on London Road. *Destroyed.*

Ordnance Buildings

Of those constructed or begun in a style deriving from Vanbrugh the closest to his inspiration are at Woolwich (1716–20), Berwick-on-Tweed (1717–*c.*1727), Chatham (Great Store 1717– and gateway 1720) and Devonport (*c.*1720–5).

Unexecuted projects for which drawings survive

Welbeck, Notts., *c.*1703 (at Welbeck).

Glympton, Oxon., *c.*1705–10? (V & A) (Pl.93).

Houses for Robert Bertie in Lincs., *c* 1710? (Lincs. CRO).

Design for altar wall, All Souls, Oxford, by 'Mr V.B. & H', 1713 (Ashmolean Museum, Oxford, supplement to Gibbs Collection).

Cholmondeley, Cheshire. Project for north front, *c.*1713 (*Vit. Brit.*, II).

Design for a church (V & A) (Pl.70).

St James's Palace, plans, *c.*1712–14. (Royal Library, Windsor).

Kensington Palace, plan, *c.*1714. (Windsor and All Souls).

Hampton Court, north court, *c.*1716 (*King's Works*, V, p.178).

Sacombe, Herts., plans for house and gardens, *c.*1720? (*Elton Drawings*, No.56; Whistler, p.152; Bodl. Gough drawings a.3.64).

Inveraray Castle, Argyll. Sketches, *c.*1720? (*Elton Drawings*, No.79).

Plan endorsed *Earl of Islay* (Milton of Saltoun papers, National Library of Scotland) in a hand similar to some of the Elton drawings.

Claremont, Surrey. Design for a pavilion, *c.*1724 (BM MS.Add.33064, f.276) (Pl.90).

Projects known from written sources

Welbeck, Notts., lake, 1703 (BM MS.Stowe 748, f.9).

Ickworth, Suffolk, 1703 and 1718 (Whistler, p.37 and note).

Woodstock, Oxon., front of Town Hall, 1713 (BM MS.19605, f.175).

St Mary-le-Strand, London, 1714 (Fifty Churches Commission Minutes).

St George, Bloomsbury, 1715 (Fifty Churches Commission Minutes).

Cannons, Middx., 1715 (*Chandos*, p.121; Webb, p.126).

House for John Hedworth of Chester-le-Street, *c.*1716? ('Explanation of the Design', for Mr Hedworth, Sotheby, 25 Jan. 1955 (459); cf. *Vit. Brit.*, II, pl.88).

Middleton Stoney, Oxon., unspecified work for Henry Boyle, Lord Carleton (Information from H. M. Colvin; cf. Webb, p.167).

Attributions rejected as improbable or impossible

Whitton, Middx. (H. M. Colvin and J. Harris, *The Country Seat*, 1970, p.81); Greenwich Hospital; Kensington Palace, Orangery; Cholmondeley Castle and Church; Compton Verney, Warwicks.; Duncombe Park, Yorks.; Oulton Park, Ches.; Iver Grove, Bucks.; Shotover Park, Oxon.; Aston-by-Sutton Church, Ches.; Vanbrugh House, Oxford. The pyramidal Lock-up at Wheatley, Oxon. was built in 1838. L. Whistler's article in *Country Life*, 10 June 1971, was designed for 1 April.

Bibliography

The literature is, to paraphrase a cliché of Marshall McLuhan, the subject, and a study such as the present one is in itself a guide to what the author has read and how his reading has served him. Those who wish to retrace his steps can do so by way of the notes to the text; the most useful or frequent references will be found, in full and abbreviated form, on pp.xiii–xiv. For those who believe that every serious work should have a bibliography, the following is a guide to the principal printed works.

Source works

C. Campbell, *Vitruvius Britannicus*, 3 vols, 1715, 1717, 1725. The earliest, if unreliable, visual record of Vanbrugh's major works. Facsimile reprint, New York, 1967.

J. Vanbrugh, *Complete Works*, ed. B. Dobrée and G. Webb, 4 vols, 1927–8. Still the reference edition. Vol. IV contains all Vanbrugh's letters then available and an important study of his architecture. Later discoveries (listed in Appendix K) were printed by L. Whistler (1954) and by

A. Rosenberg, 'New Light on Vanbrugh', *Philological Quarterly*, XLV, 1966, pp.603–13.

H. M. Colvin and M. Craig, *Architectural Drawings in the Library of Elton Hall by Sir John Vanbrugh and Sir Edward Lovett Pearce*, Oxford, for the Roxburghe Club, 1964. A private publication, selectively illustrated, of an important and little-known collection of drawings.

There are recent new editions of *The Provok'd Wife* by C. A. Zimansky, 1970, and J. L Smith, 1974, and of *The Relapse* by Zimansky, 1970, and B. Harris, 1971.

Studies mainly of Vanbrugh's architecture

C. Barman, *Sir John Vanbrugh*, 1924. Brief appreciation with a series of photographs by F. R. Yerbury.

H. A. Tipping and C. Hussey, *English Homes*, IV.2, *The Work of Sir John Vanbrugh and his School, 1699–1736*, 1928. Overtaken in many respects by more recent scholarship but still fundamental and irreplaceable as a collection of 'Country Life' photographs.

L. Whistler, *Sir John Vanbrugh, Architect and Dramatist*, 1938. The pioneer biography based on sources then available.

D. Green, *Blenheim Palace*, 1951. History of the design, building and later alterations, drawing on the Blenheim archives and the Marlborough papers in the British Museum.

L. Whistler, *The Imagination of Vanbrugh and his Fellow Artists*, 1954. A linked series of studies incorporating many recently discovered letters and drawings.

More general studies bearing on Vanbrugh's architecture

G. F. Webb, *Baroque Art* (British Academy Lecture), 1947.

J. Summerson, 'The Classical Country House in 18th-Century England', *Journal of the Royal Society of Arts*, CVII, 1959, pp.539–87.

K. Downes, *English Baroque Architecture*, 1966. An attempt to outline the style in which Vanbrugh was one of the protagonists.

C. Hussey, *English Gardens and Landscapes 1700–1750*, 1967.

J. Lees-Milne, *English Country Houses, Baroque*, 1970. Complements rather than supersedes the work of Tipping and Hussey.

H. M. Colvin and others, *History of the King's Works*, V, *1660–1782*, 1975. For the context of Vanbrugh's official career.

R. Wittkower, *Palladio and English Palladianism*, 1974. Posthumous collection of articles including that on *Pseudo-Palladian Elements in English Neo-Classicism*.

Nikolaus Pevsner's articles have been reprinted as *Studies in Art, Architecture and Design*, 1968.

Index

Family names in the Genealogical Tables are not indexed unless they also appear in the text. Minor references to individual members of families are not always separately indexed.

Plates

1 Sir Godfrey Kneller. Sir John Vanbrugh, *c.*1705. *National Portrait Gallery.*

2 Anon. Lady Vanbrugh, *c.*1719?

1722/23	January ye 1st: 1722/23				45
Jan. 1	Newyears Guifts to Sr. Charles & Jack	£	2	6	
	ditto to Miss Betty & Binet Vanbrugh at Greenwich	£	2	2	
2	Pd: for a Load of Hay, & one a Load of Straw	£	2	0	
	Rec'd from my Brother Phil: Two years Rent to Christ: last	£	60	—	
	Pd Land Tax for his House from Christ: to Lady day 1721 £:3:4; from Lady day 1721 to L. Day 1722 £4:1:4; from Lady day 1722 to L. day 1723 £:14:	£	1	18	8
	Pd Brother Phil: for 12 Flasks of Claret	£	1	4	—
	Pd to ditto for Duty on White wine	£	1	11	6
	Pd to ditto for Bottles & Charges	£	—	12	[illegible]
	Pd: the Ninth Call to the Opera	£	10	—	
10	Rec'd Fee for a Grant of Arms to ~~[illegible]~~ Rowe		15	—	—
	Gratuity to Mr Hocker	£	1	1	—
	Rec'd Fee for a Grant to the Bish: of Chichester	£	15		
	Gratuity to Mr Mawson	£	1	1	
	Newyears Guift to Miss: Philly	£	—	10	6
14	Rec'd Fee for a Grant to Morley	£	15		
	Gratuity to Mr Warburton	£	1	1	
	for two pair of large Sheets	£	4	11	
	Pd: Scarlet for dying a Gown	£	—	6	
17	Pd: [illegible] for a hundred of Ash Faggots	£	2	10	
21	Pd: Wood Lime Man a Bill for Lime used at the White-House	£	27	12	
	Pd Mr Grantham a Bill for Bricks, in full	£	15		
	Pd Wright a Bill for Carriages	£	14	11	
	Out of Towne 2 Nights 5 Horse	£	1	7	6
	Pd: Martha Bowles in full for Wages	£	15	7	
	Pd: Robinson the Appothecary, in full to this day	£	13	7	
23	Pd: Barrat in part of a Bill	£	50		
28	Pd: [illegible] Wintour in full to this day; the Kensington Appothecary Mr [illegible] a Bill	£	30	12	10
	Pd for Cakes sent to ditto	£	—	16	10
30	Rd: Fee for a Grant to Miller	£	15		
	Gratuity to Mr Maudit	£	1	1	
	Pd: Mr VanHuyven a Bill for Chairs &c in full	£	13	13	
31	Rec'd Rent for Kensington house, a year to Christ: last	£	60	—	

3 Vanbrugh's Account Book (f.45).

1725/6 Feb. 19	Paid Mr Thos: Churchill, Executor to Mrs Fifield Deceased, who was Executrix to John Smallwell Joyner deceased, the Sum of five hundred pounds, in full of all demands upon me, for Work done by the said John Smallwell at the Playhouse in the Haymarket and elsewhere	£500:—:—
—	Recd from my Brother Charles, for one years Interest of Two Thousand pounds, due at Xmas last	£100:—:—
—	Recd from ditto for a Year and halfe ground rent at Greenwich due at Xmas: last	£ 15:—:—
—	Recd from ditto for dozen of Wine	£
24	For half a Load of Hay at London	£ 1 5 6
—	For a Load of Straw at ditto	£ — 18 —
—	Pd for Silk for a Coat for Charles	£ 2 8 6
—	To Dr Slare	£ 1 1
25	Pd Benton, for a Pad, & to the Servant &c	£ 22 11 —
March 7	Pd Mr Maynard for Tenquarters of Oats & 10 Bu: of Beans	8 7 —
8	Pd for a 20 ~~[struck]~~ 30 Trusses of Hay at London	£
9	Pd Savage the Plummer a Bill in full	£ 76 14
	~~Pd Wealtye for Cleaning my Wat…~~	— 10 6
—	Pd the 5th Call to Chelsea Waterworks	£ 20 —
—	Given for Carrying about the Paving Petition	£ 2 2
—	~~[illegible]~~	
10	Pd Mr Ruffle a Bill in full from Jan 1st to March 1st	£ 4 17 —
	~~Pd the 6th Call to the Chelsea~~	
15	Pd the 14th and 15th Calls to the Opera	£ 20 — —
—	Handkerchiefs and Neckcloaths for Charles	£ — 13 —
April 4th	pd the Land Tax for a year to Lady day	£ 0 16 8
9	March 26th given Dr Mongo…	3 3
	Given Dr Slare	3 3
April 7th	Given Dr Slare	1 1

4 Vanbrugh's Account Book, with his last entries (f.61v).

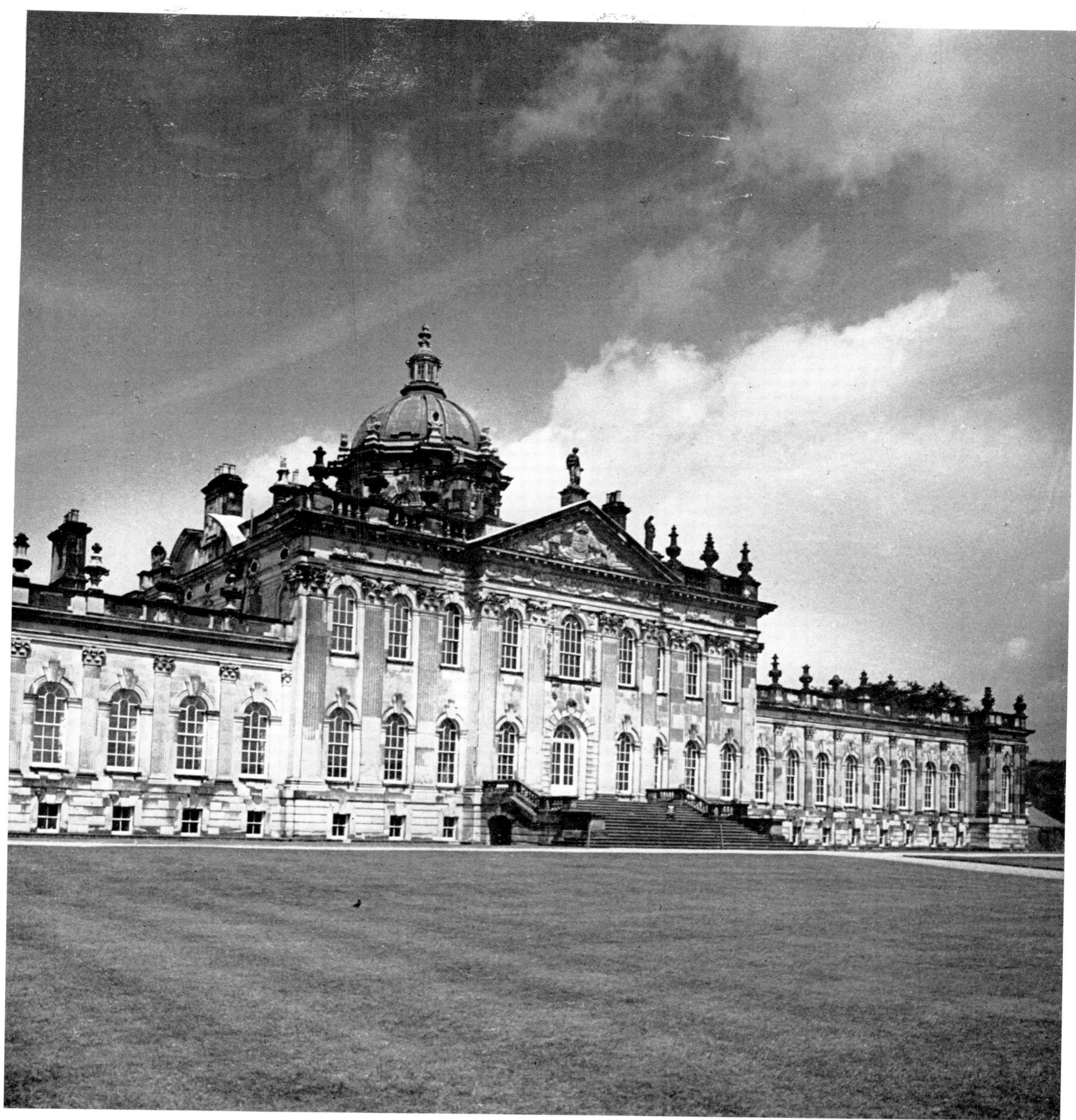

5 Castle Howard, Yorks. South front, 1702–10.

6 Castle Howard. North-east wing, 1700–6.

7 Castle Howard from the north.

8 Castle Howard. North front, main block.

9 Castle Howard from the Terrace Walk.

10 Anon. Burley-on-the-Hill, Rutland. Garden front, 1696–8.

11 Sir Roger Pratt. Coleshill, Berks., 1649–62, *destroyed*.

12 William Talman. Kiveton, Yorks., 1694–1704, *destroyed*. (Engraving by T. Badeslade.)

13 Anon. Chatsworth, Derbys. West front, 1700–2.

14 Jules Hardouin Mansart. Versailles. The Orangery, 1681–6.

15 Jules Hardouin Mansart. Versailles. Centre of garden front, 1678–85.

16 Libéral Bruant. Paris. Hôtel des Invalides. Court, 1670–7.

17 Nicholas Hawksmoor. Easton Neston, Northants. West front, finished 1702.

18 Hawksmoor. Castle Howard. Preliminary south elevation. *Welbeck Abbey.*

19 Sir Christopher Wren. Chelsea Hospital. Portico, 1682–5.

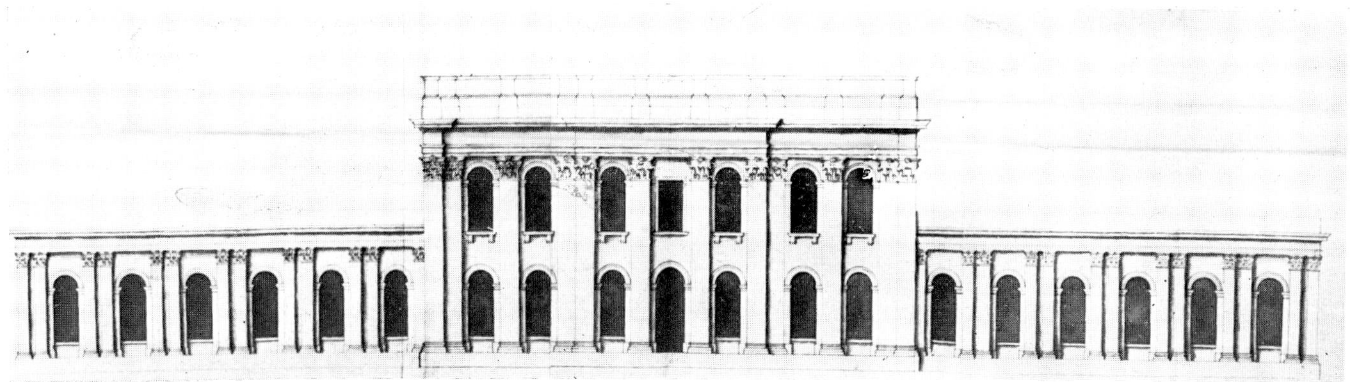

20 Hawksmoor. Castle Howard. Early south elevation. *Victoria and Albert Museum.*

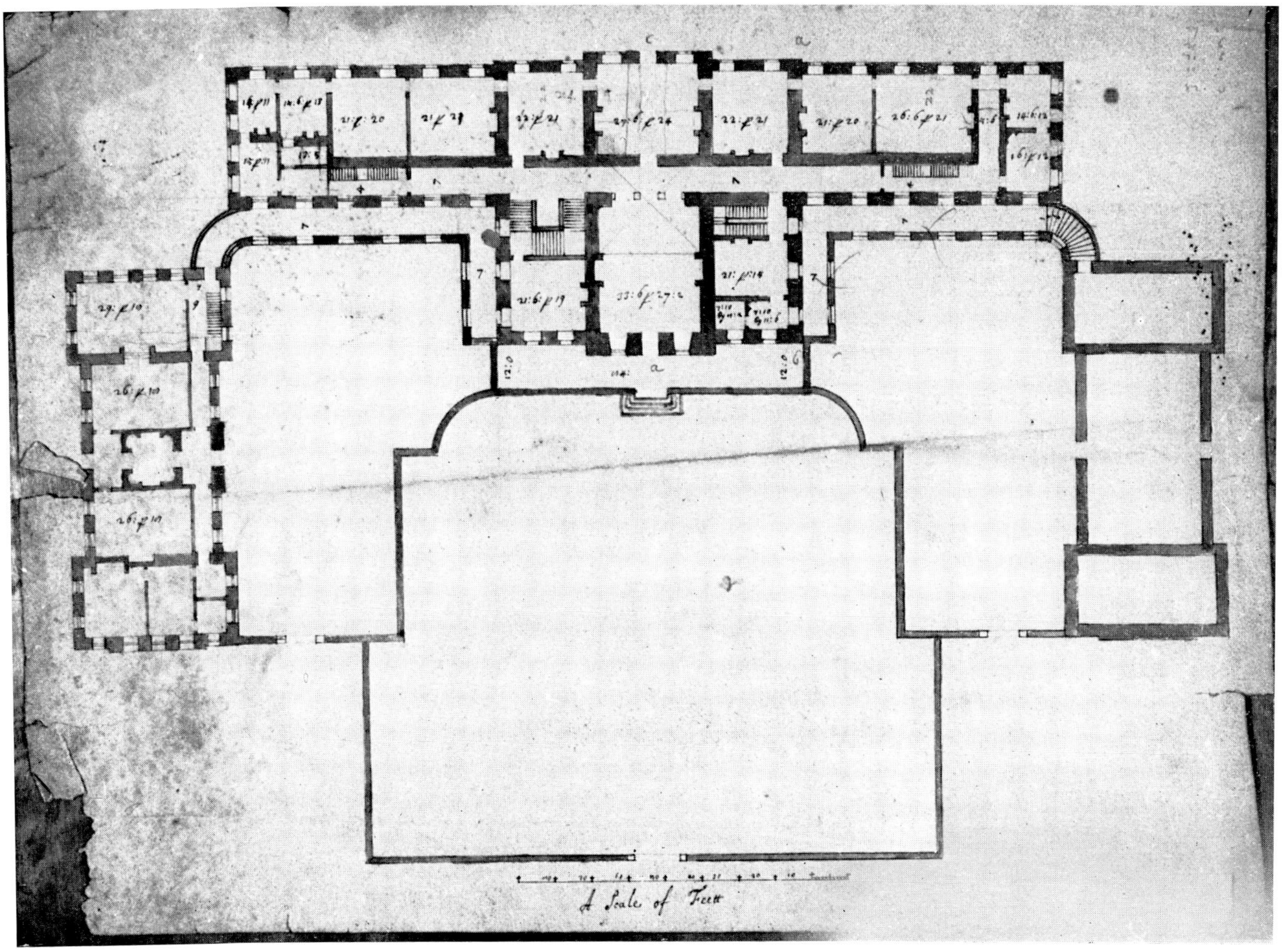

21 Castle Howard. Early plan. *Victoria and Albert Museum.*

22 Castle Howard. Kitchen Court.

23 Castle Howard. Kitchen Court and gates, *c.*1710–16.

24 Vanbrugh House, Whitehall, 1701, *destroyed*. Drawn about 1800. *Soane Museum.*

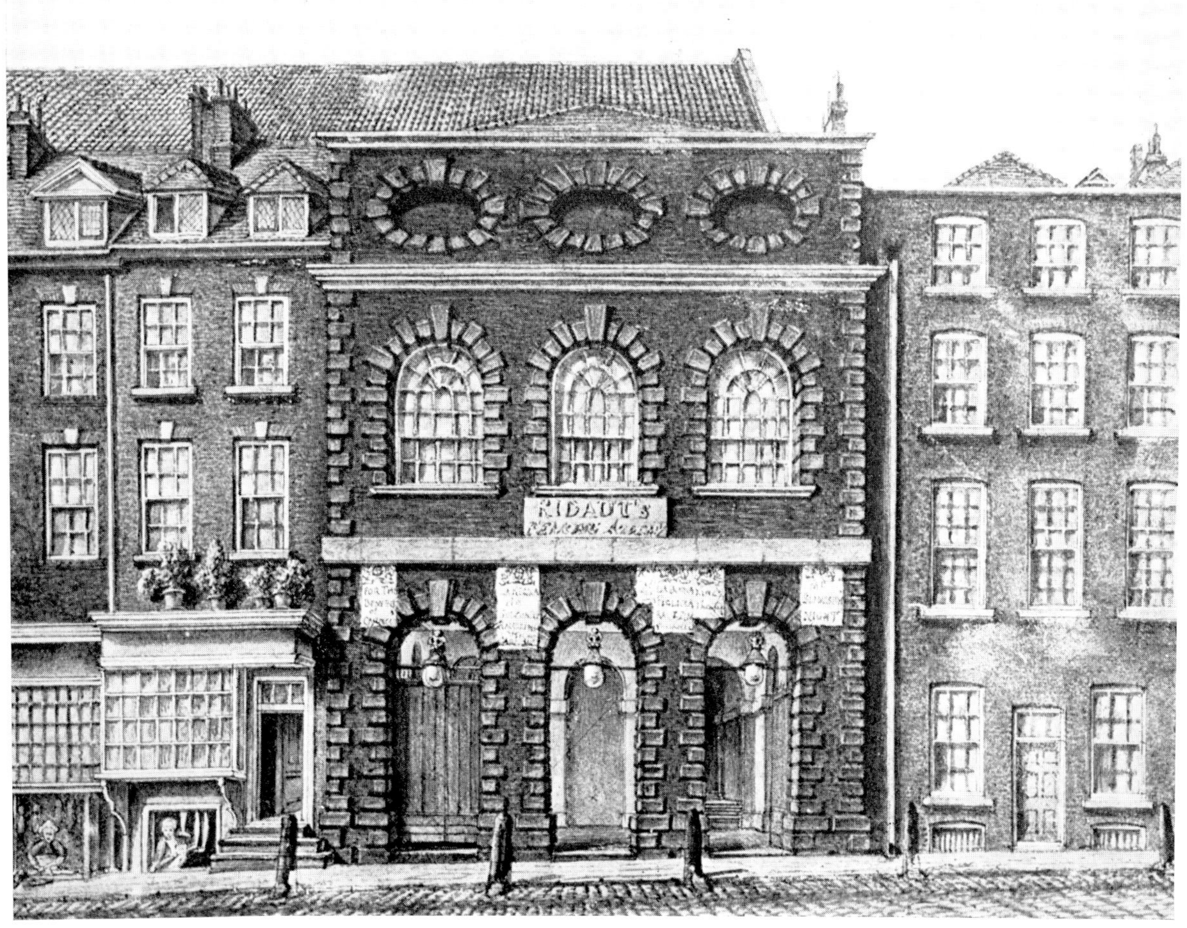

25 The Queen's Theatre, Haymarket. Street entrance, 1704–5, *destroyed*. Drawn by William Capon. *British Museum, Crace Collection.*

26 Castle Howard. Detail of north front.

27 Castle Howard. Detail of south front.

28 Castle Howard. Detail of north front.

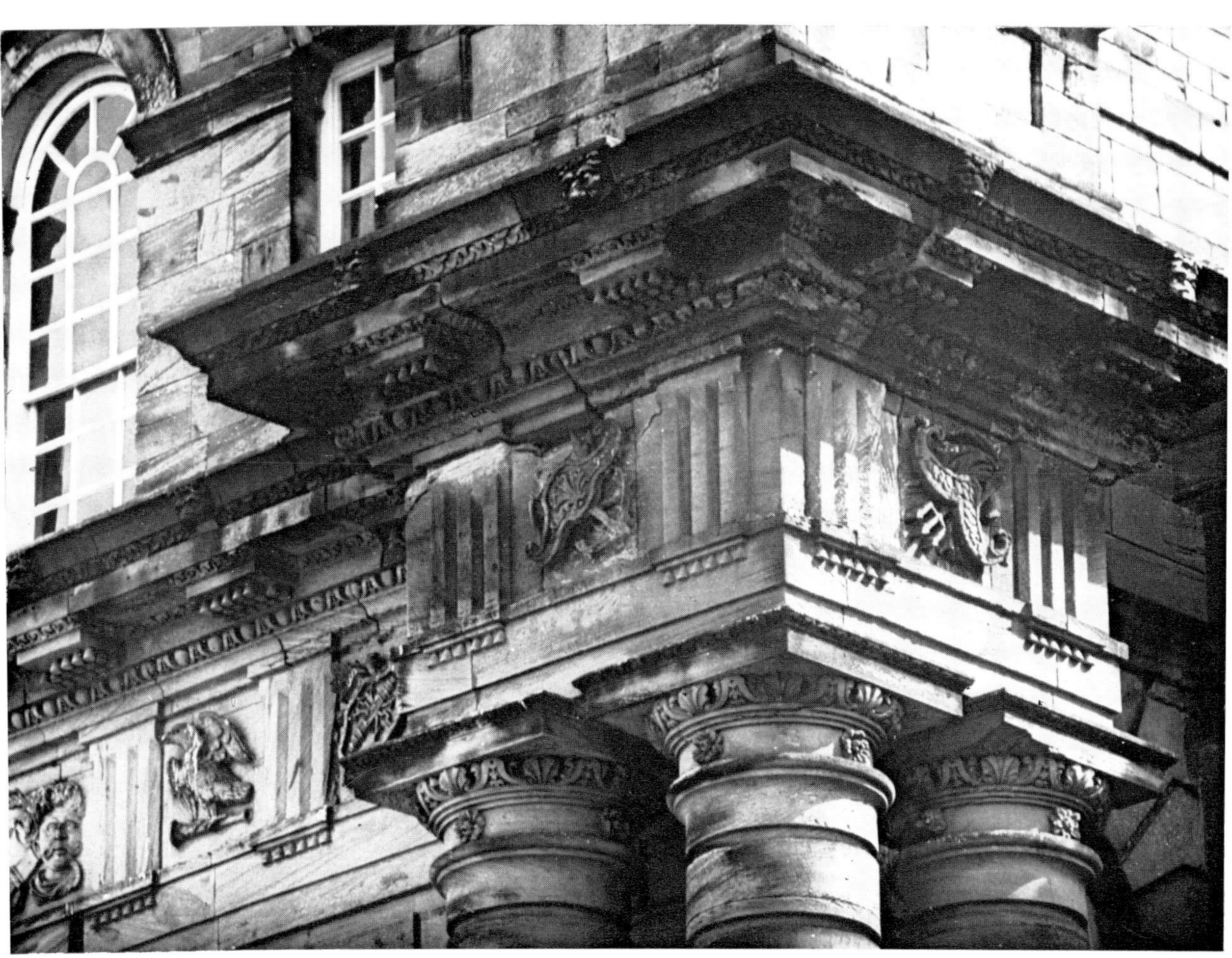

29 Seaton Delaval, Northumb. Detail of north front, 1720–8.

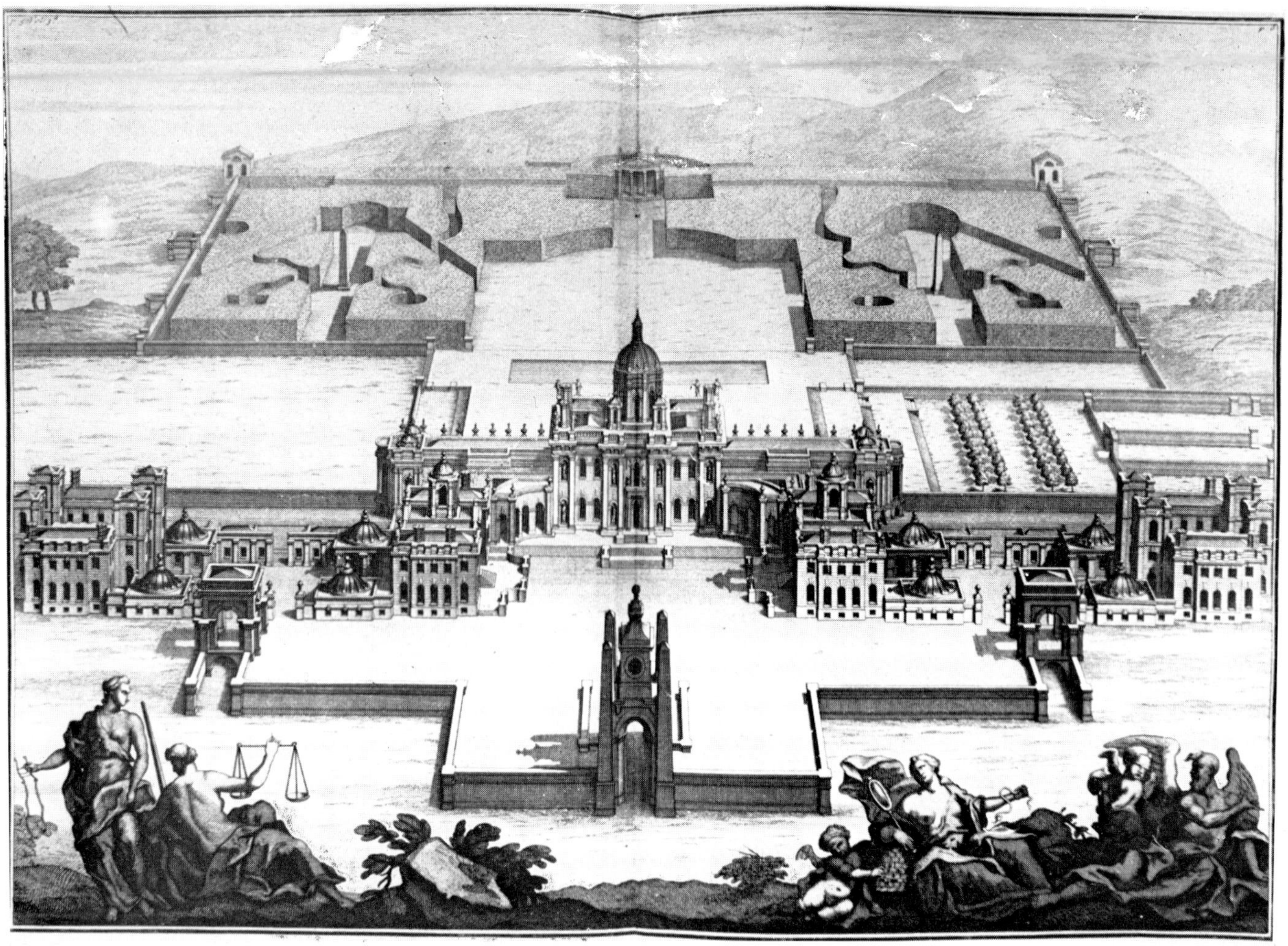

30 Castle Howard as intended. Bird's-eye view. *Vitruvius Britannicus*, III.

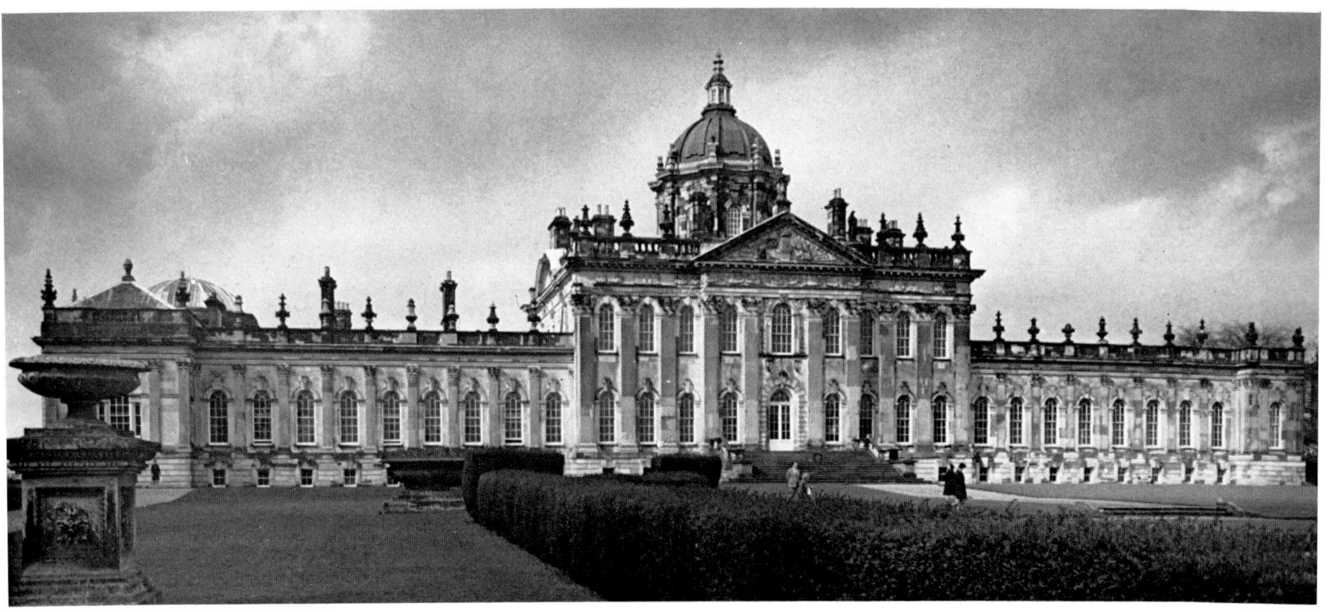

31 Castle Howard. South front.

32 Castle Howard. West internal court.

33 Castle Howard. Corridor.

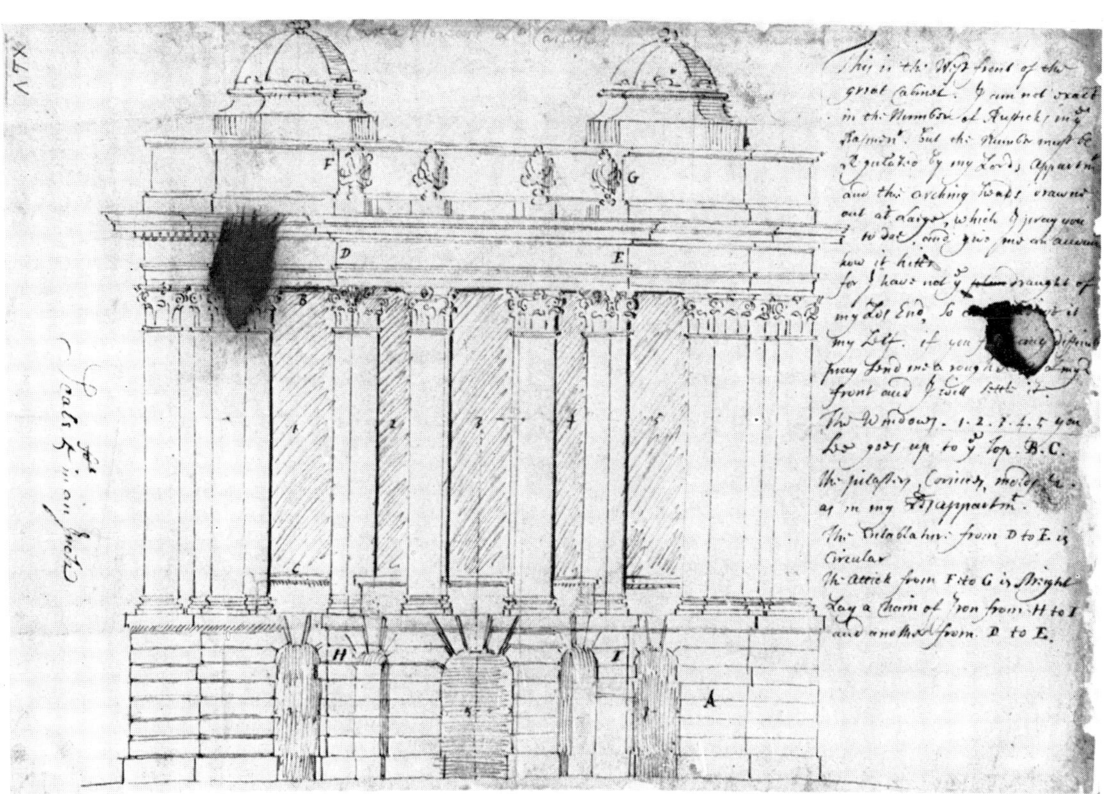

34 Castle Howard. Hawksmoor's drawing for the Bow Window Room, 1706. *British Museum.*

35 Castle Howard. The Hall.

36 Castle Howard. The High Saloon. *Destroyed.*

37 Castle Howard. The High Saloon. *Destroyed.*

38 Castle Howard. Dome and pendentives.

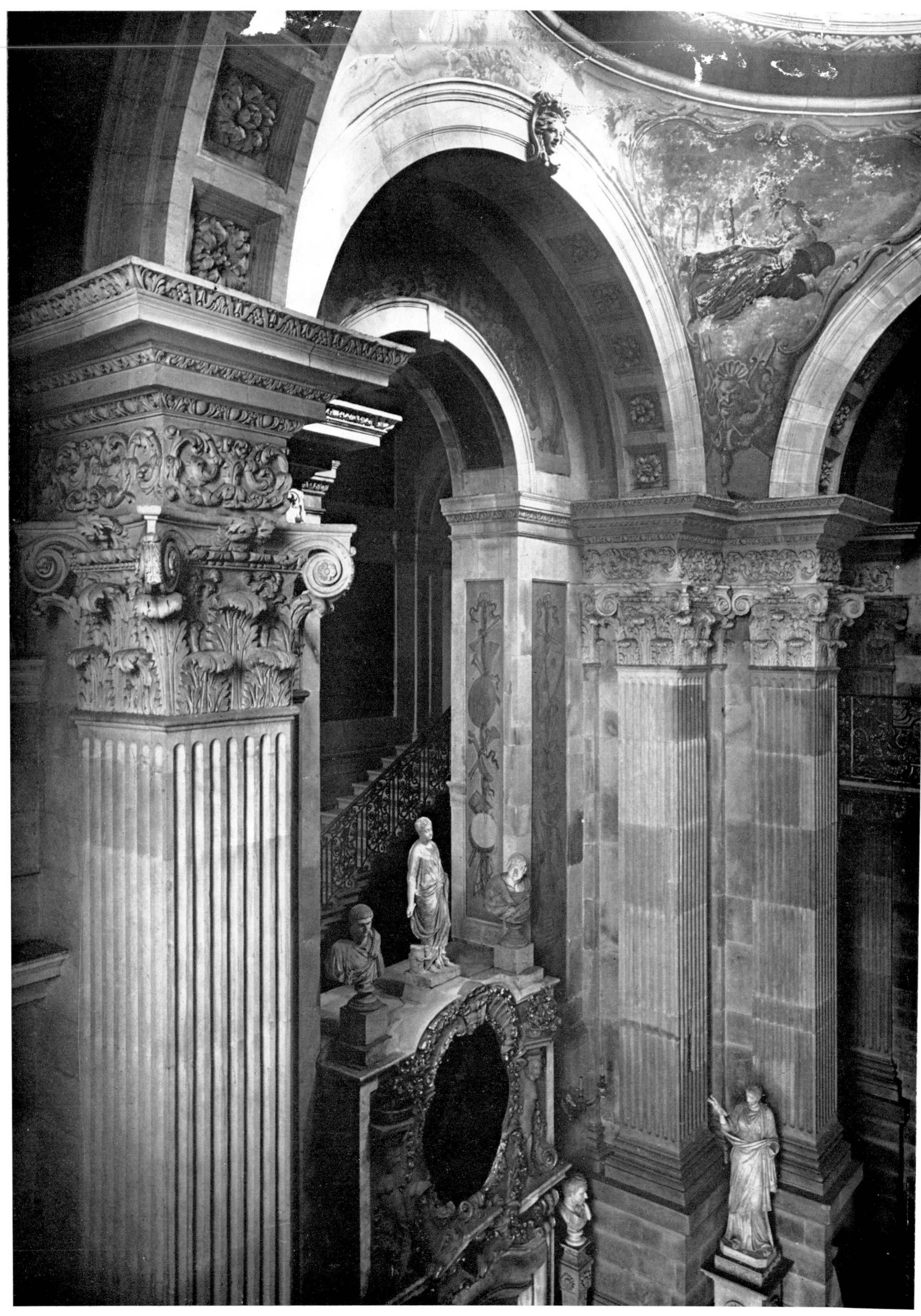

39 Castle Howard. The Hall.

40 Kimbolton Castle, Hunts. Staircase painted by G. A. Pellegrini, *c.*1711.

41 Castle Howard. South-east bastion, *c.*1723.

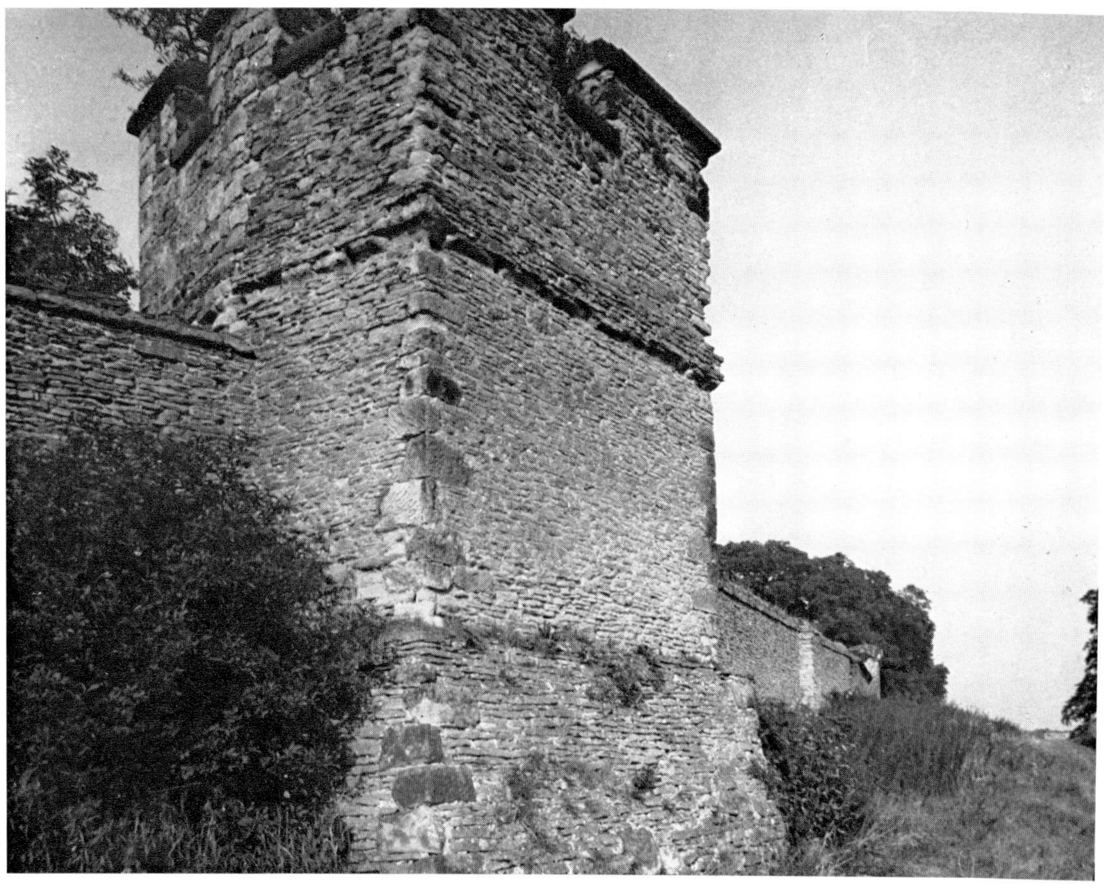

42 Castle Howard. Curtain wall.

43 Hawksmoor. Kensington Palace. Orangery, 1704–5. Detail.

44 Hugh May. Windsor Castle. Window in Henry III's Tower, *c.*1680.

45 Hawksmoor. Castle Howard. The Pyramid, 1728.

46 Kimbolton Castle. West front, 1708–10.

47 Kimbolton Castle. South front, 1707–9.

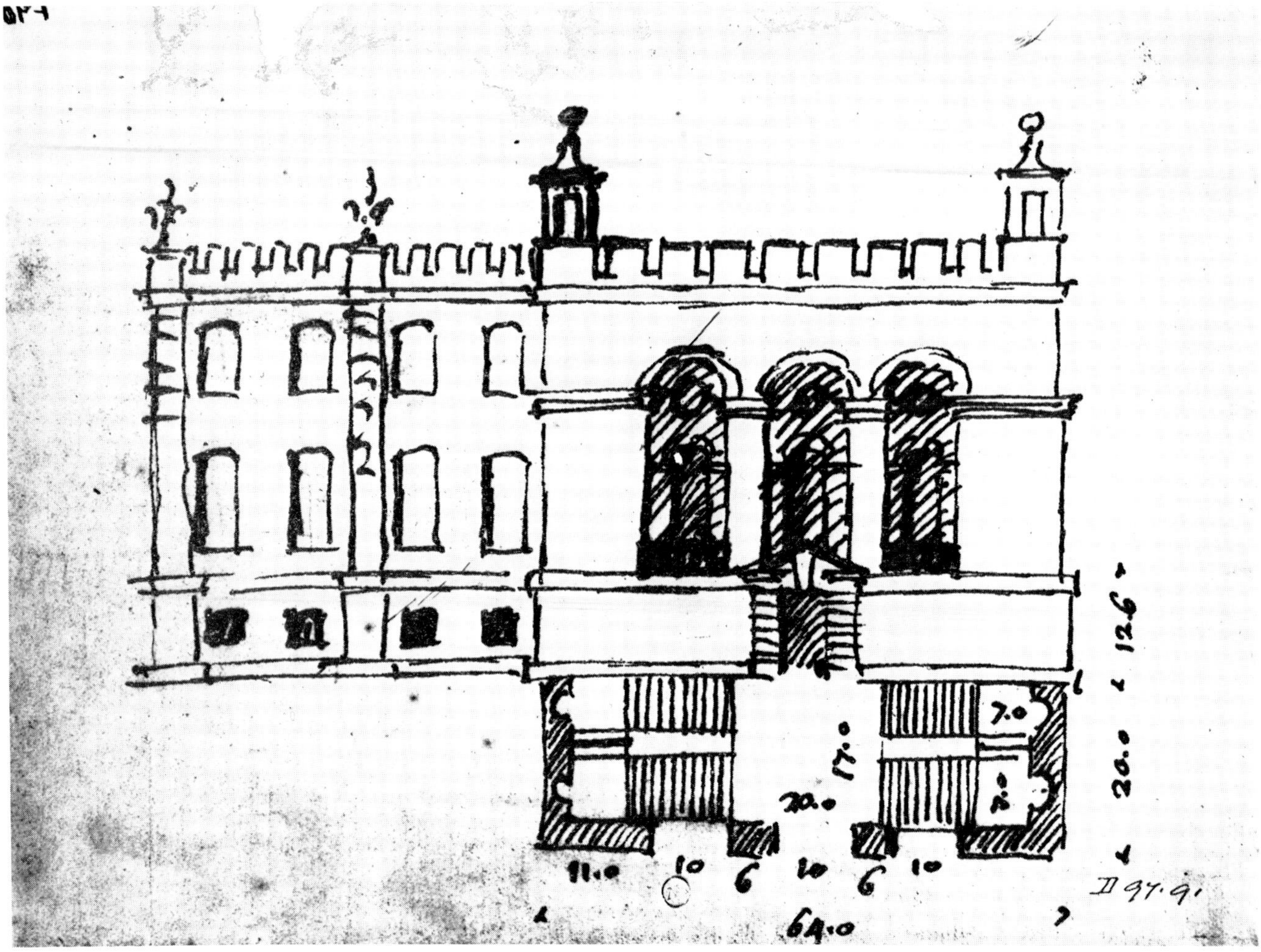

48 Kimbolton Castle. Design for east entrance. *Victoria and Albert Museum.*

49 Vanbrugh and Alessandro Galilei. Kimbolton. East front, 1708–19.

50 Kneller. The Origin of Blenheim. *The Duke of Marlborough*.

51 Blenheim Palace, Oxon. East Gate.

52 Blenheim Palace. North court, 1705–16.

53 Louis Le Vau. Vaux-le-Vicomte, 1657–61.

54 Blenheim Palace. North front.

come into practice,) than by little Tawdry Monuments
of Marble, stuck up against Walls and Pillars.

Upon the whole, it may be worth considering, That since
Christianity began, there is but one Instance, where

55 Vanbrugh's idea of the cemetery at Surat. *Bodleian Library.*

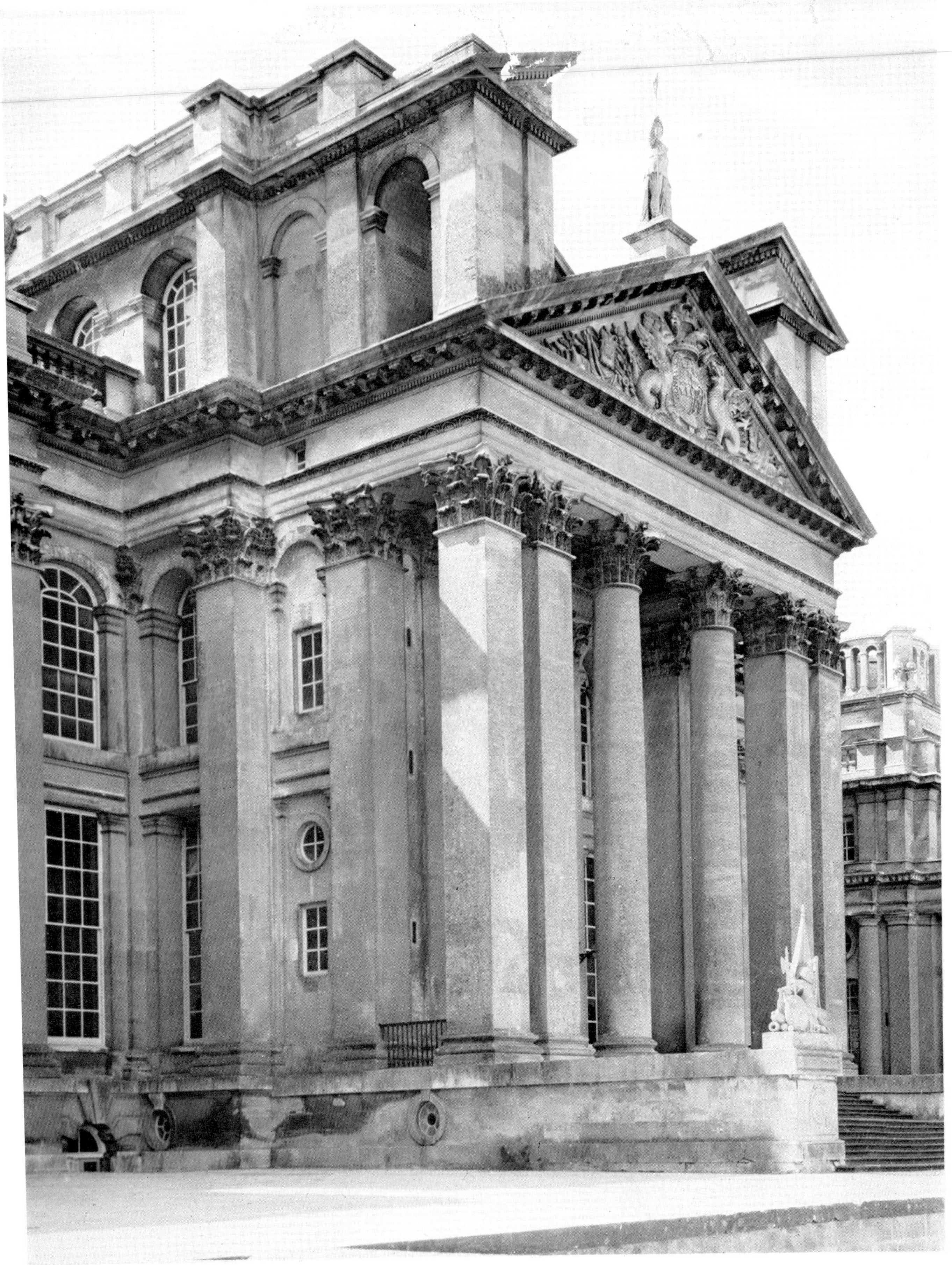

56 Blenheim Palace. North portico.

57 Blenheim Palace. Pediment.

58 Blenheim Palace. Colonnade.

59 Blenheim Palace. South front as projected. *Vitruvius Britannicus*, I.

60 Robert Smythson. Wollaton Hall, Notts., begun 1580.

61 Blenheim Palace. Trophy above south front.

64 Blenheim Palace. South front, centre.

63 Blenheim Palace. South front.

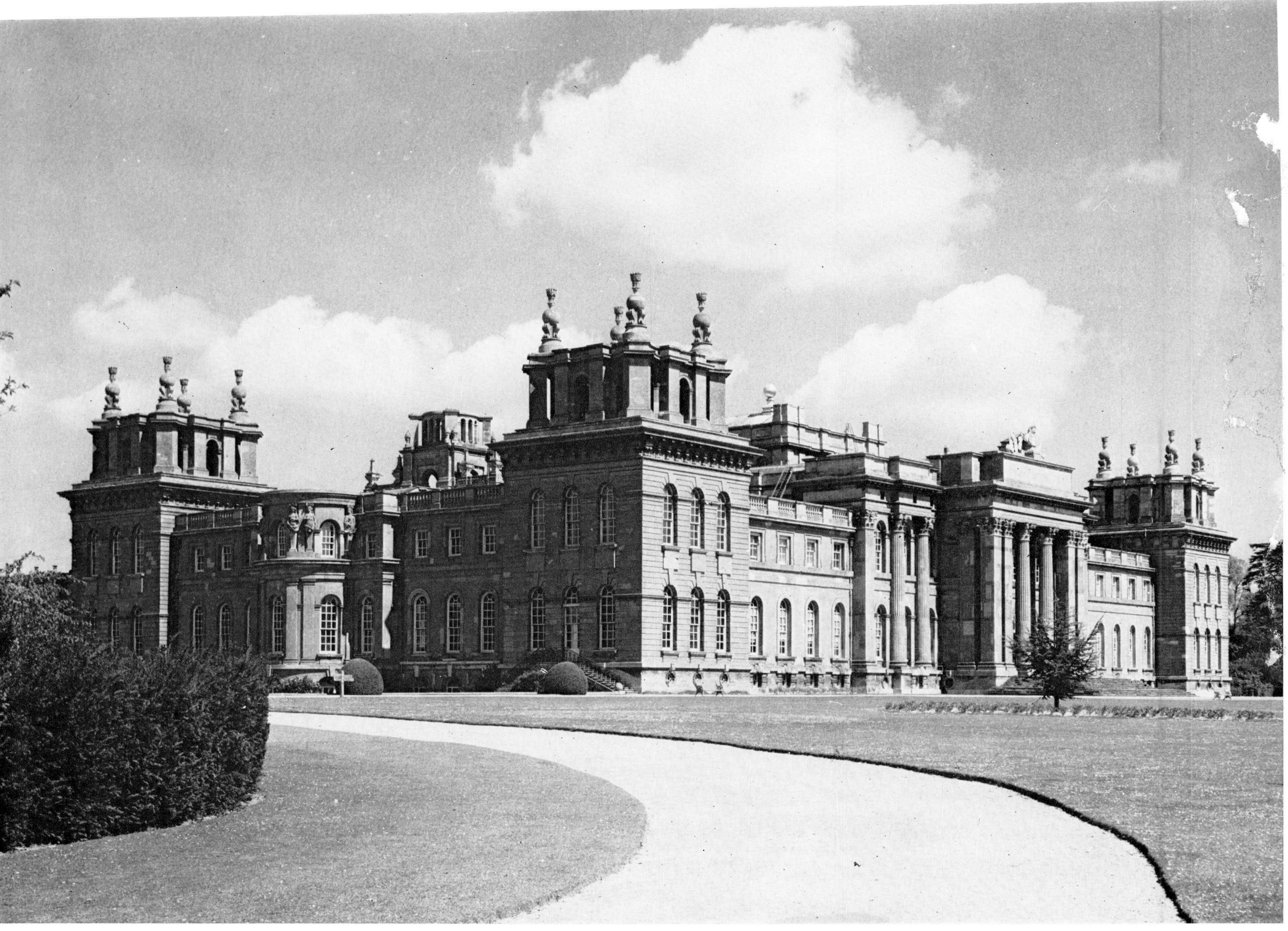

62 Blenheim Palace from the south-west.

65 Blenheim Palace. Corner lantern.

66 Blenheim Palace. Frieze of corner tower.

67 Blenheim Palace. West front. Detail.

68 Blenheim Palace. West front.

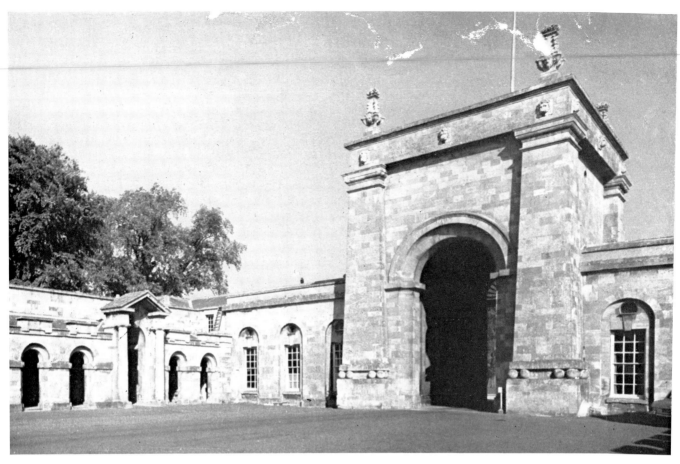

69 Blenheim Palace. Kitchen court.

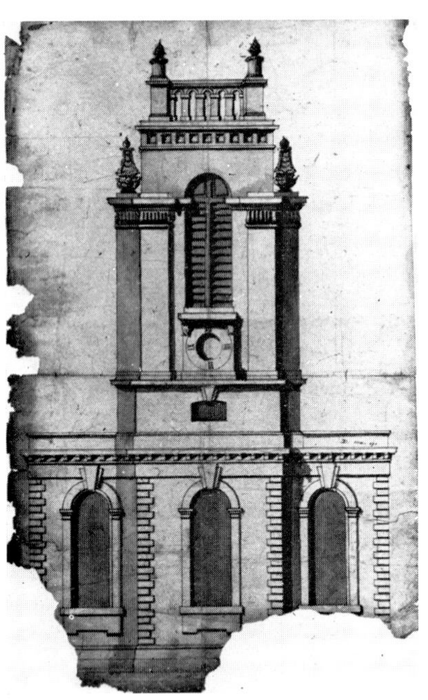

70 Design for a church, *c.*1712–14. *Victoria and Albert Museum.*

71 Blenheim Palace. Kitchen Court arcade.

72 Inigo Jones. Old St Paul's. *Detail of engraving by Wenceslas Hollar.*

73 Blenheim Palace. Kitchen Court tower.

74 Blenheim. The Bridge. Engraving by H. Terasson. *Bodleian Library.*

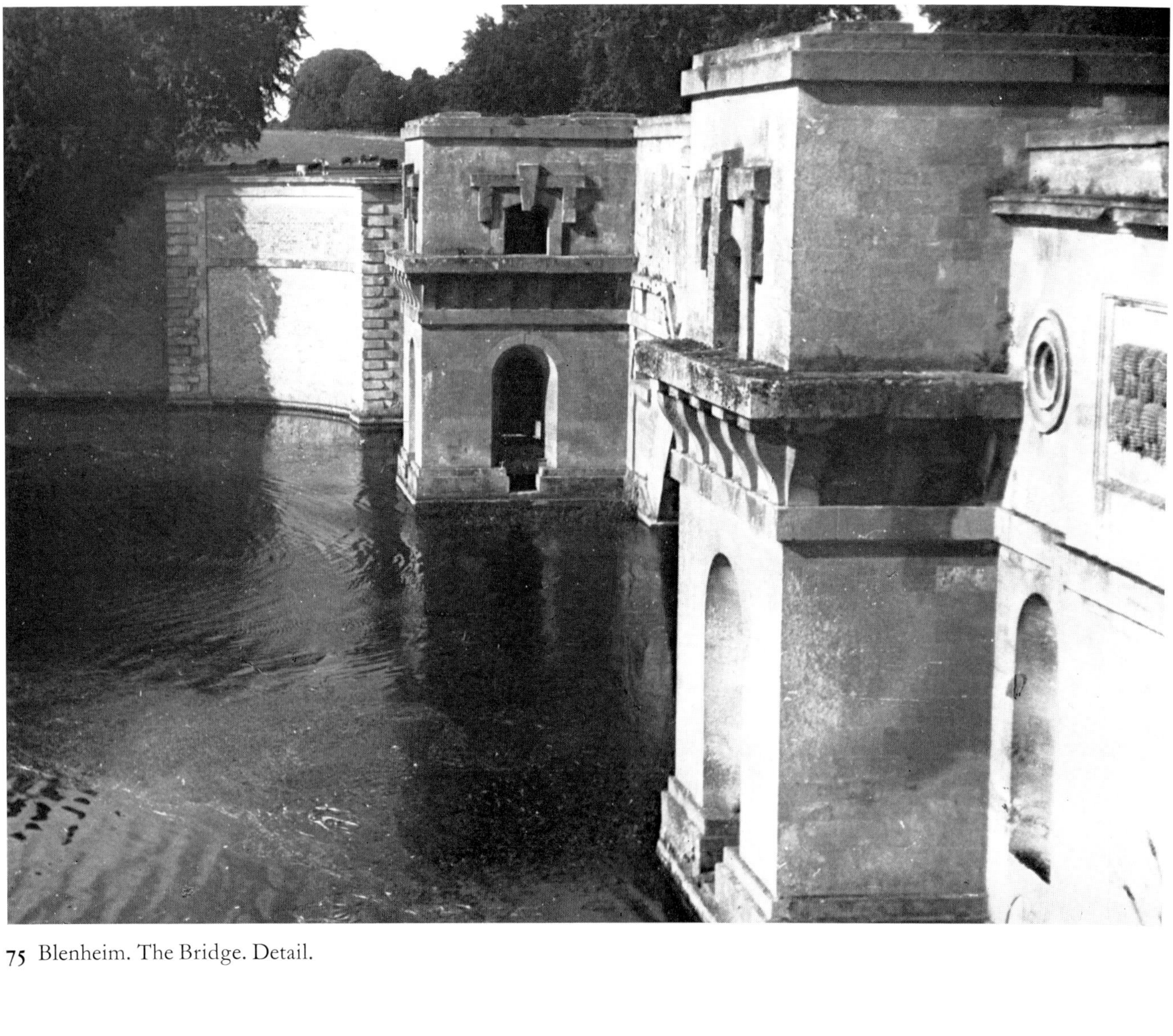

75 Blenheim. The Bridge. Detail.

76 Blenheim. The Bridge.

77 Hawksmoor. Blenheim Palace. Hensington Gate piers.

78 Blenheim Palace. The Hall.

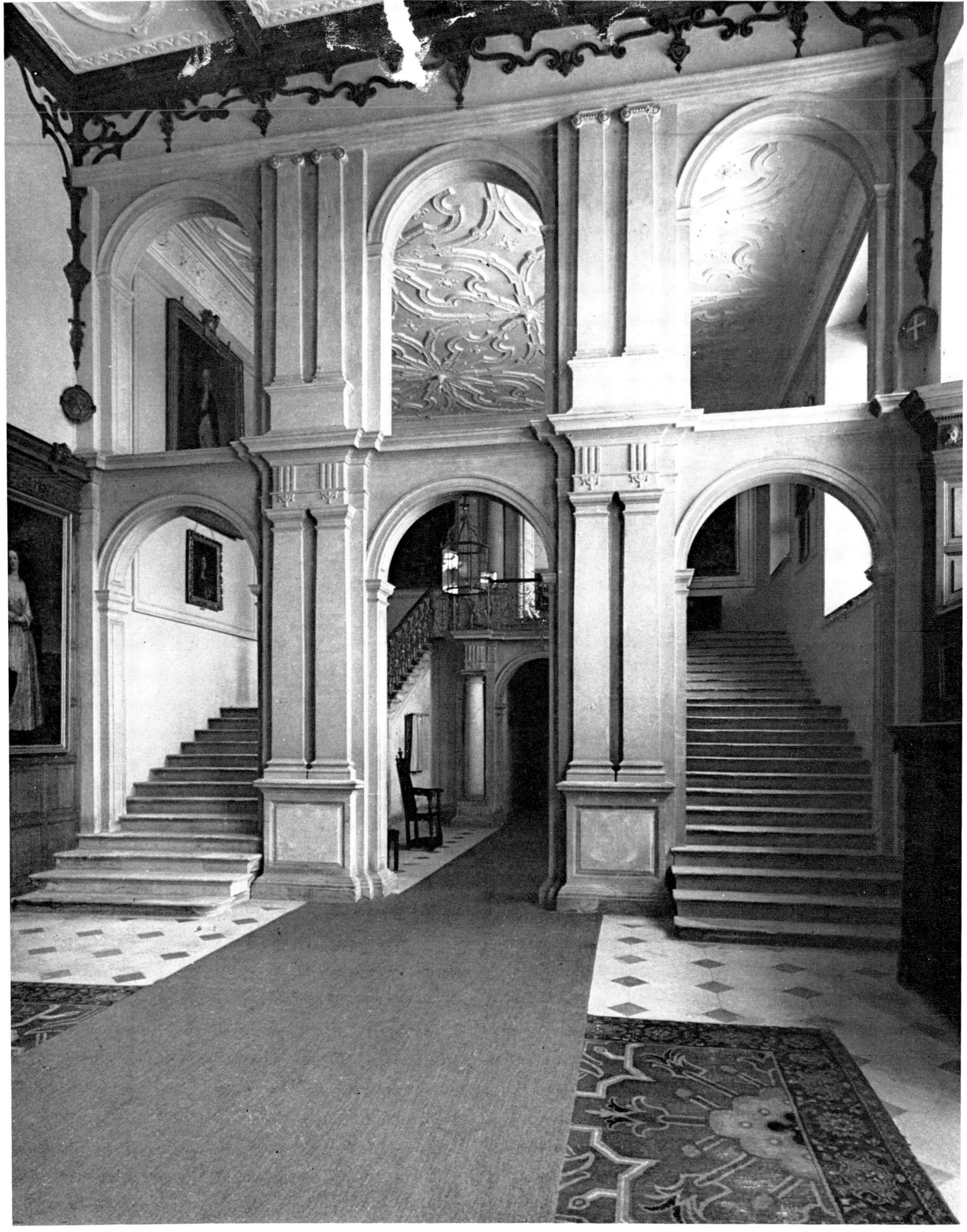

79 Audley End, Essex. Staircase and screen, *c.*1708.

80 Blenheim Palace. The Saloon. Doorcase.

81 Blenheim Palace. The Hall.

82 Hawksmoor and Grinling Gibbons. Project for the Saloon at Blenheim. *Bodleian Library.*

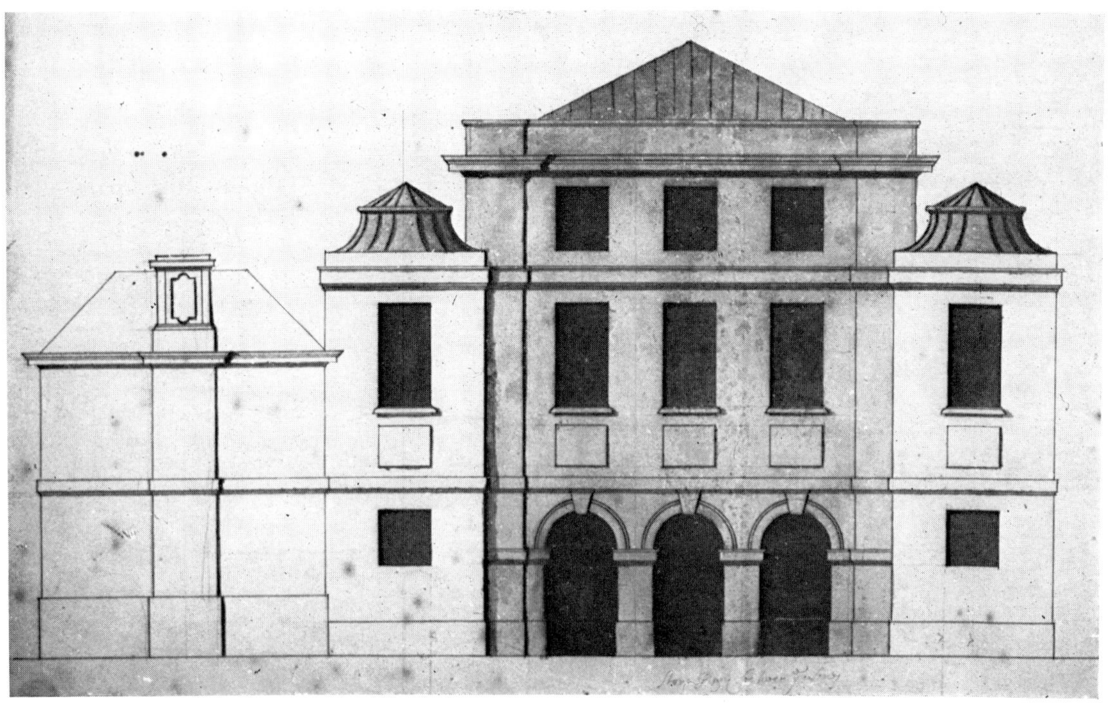

83 Hawksmoor. Design for Christ's Hospital Writing School, 1692. *All Souls, Oxford.*

84 Blenheim Palace. The Hall. Capital.

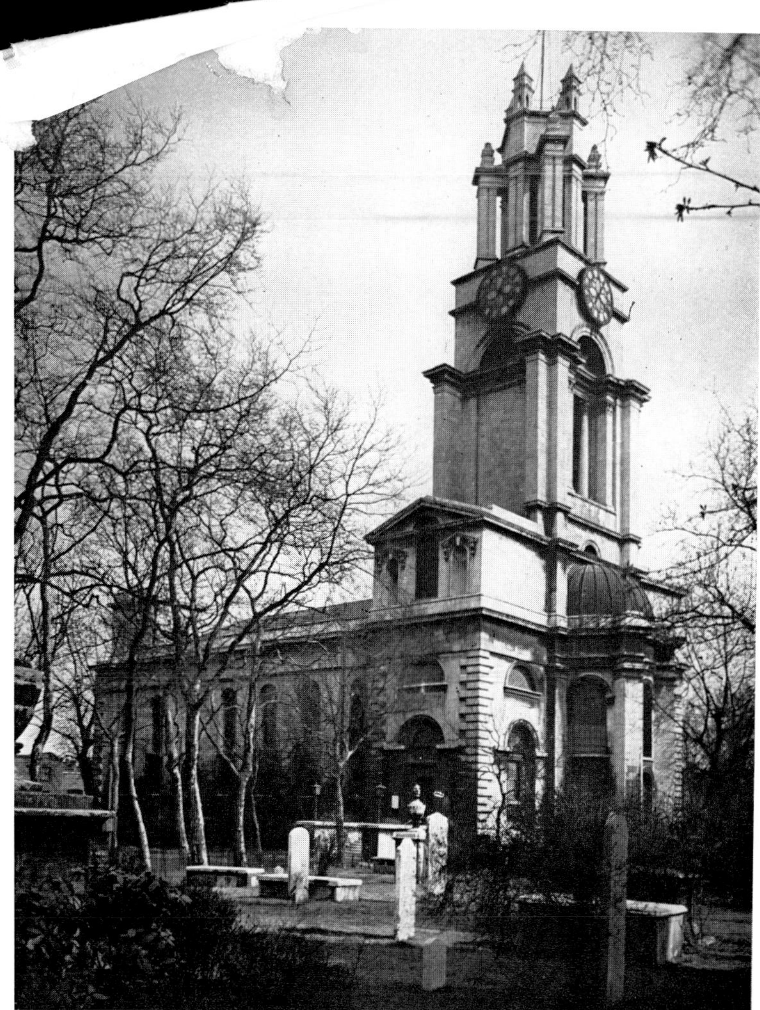

85 Hawksmoor. St Anne, Limehouse, 1714–29.

86 Eastbury, Dorset. First design, *c.*1715. *Victoria and Albert Museum.*

87 Kings Weston, Glos. Staircase.

88 Kings Weston. East front, *c.*1710–14.

89 Kings Weston. Loggia north-west of the house, *c.*1718.

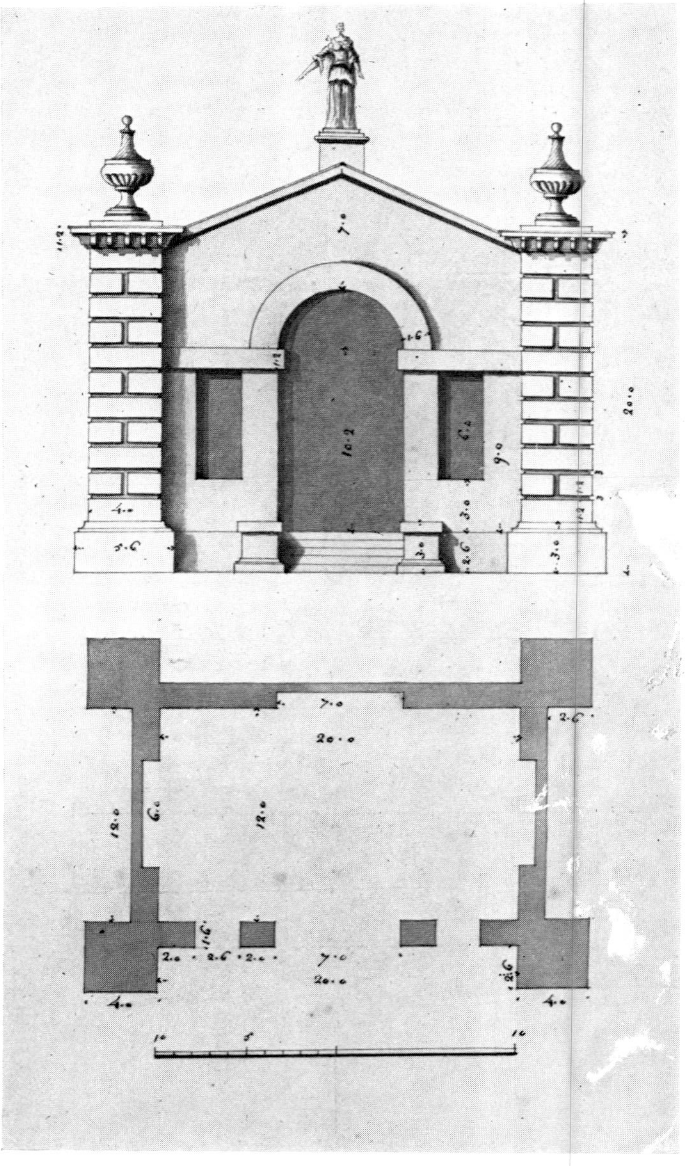

90 Design for a summer-house for the Duke of Newcastle, *c.*1724. *British Museum.*

91 Kings Weston. South front.

92 Design for a house for the Bertie family, *c.*1710. *Lincolnshire Record Office.*

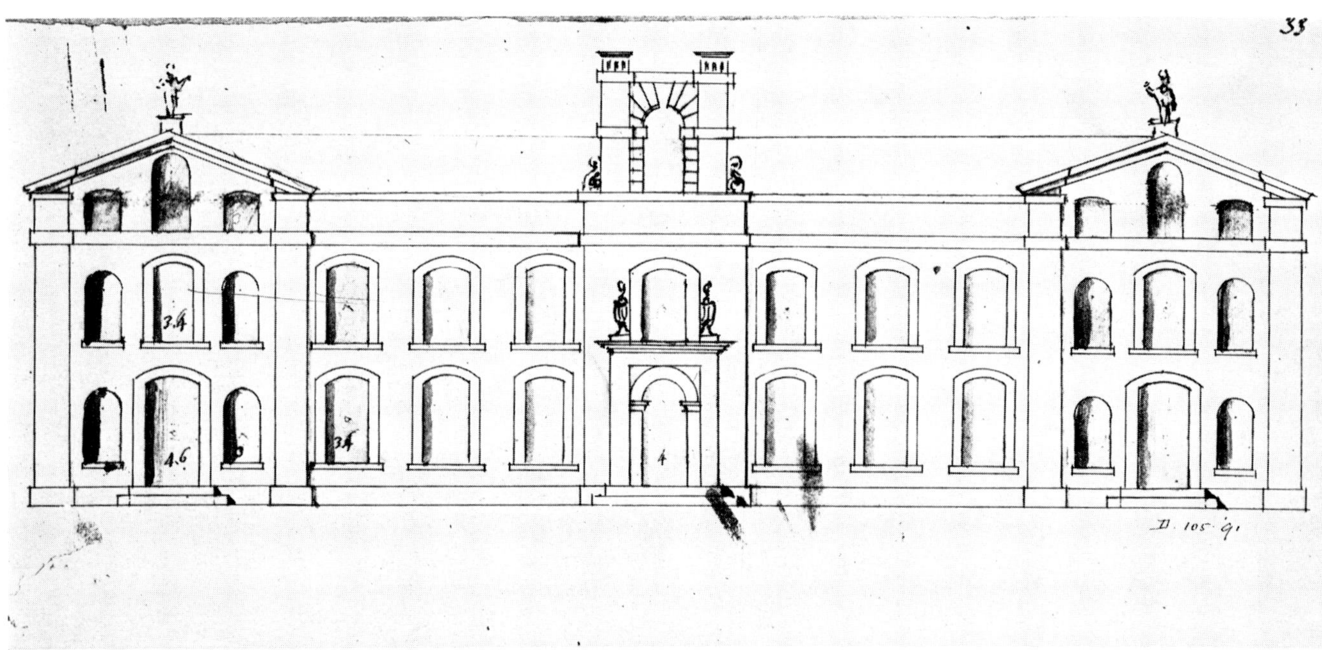

93 Design for Glympton, Oxon., *c.*1705–10. *Victoria and Albert Museum.*

94 Design for a house for the Bertie family. *Lincolnshire Record Office.*

a Scale of 60 Feet
Extends 231
The North Prospect of Cholmondeley Hall in Cheshire. The Seat of the Rt. Honble. The Earl of Cholmondeley Treasurer of his Majesty's Houshold.
to whom this Plate is most humbly Inscrib'd.

95 Design for Cholmondeley Castle, Cheshire, *c.*1713. *Vitruvius Britannicus,* II.

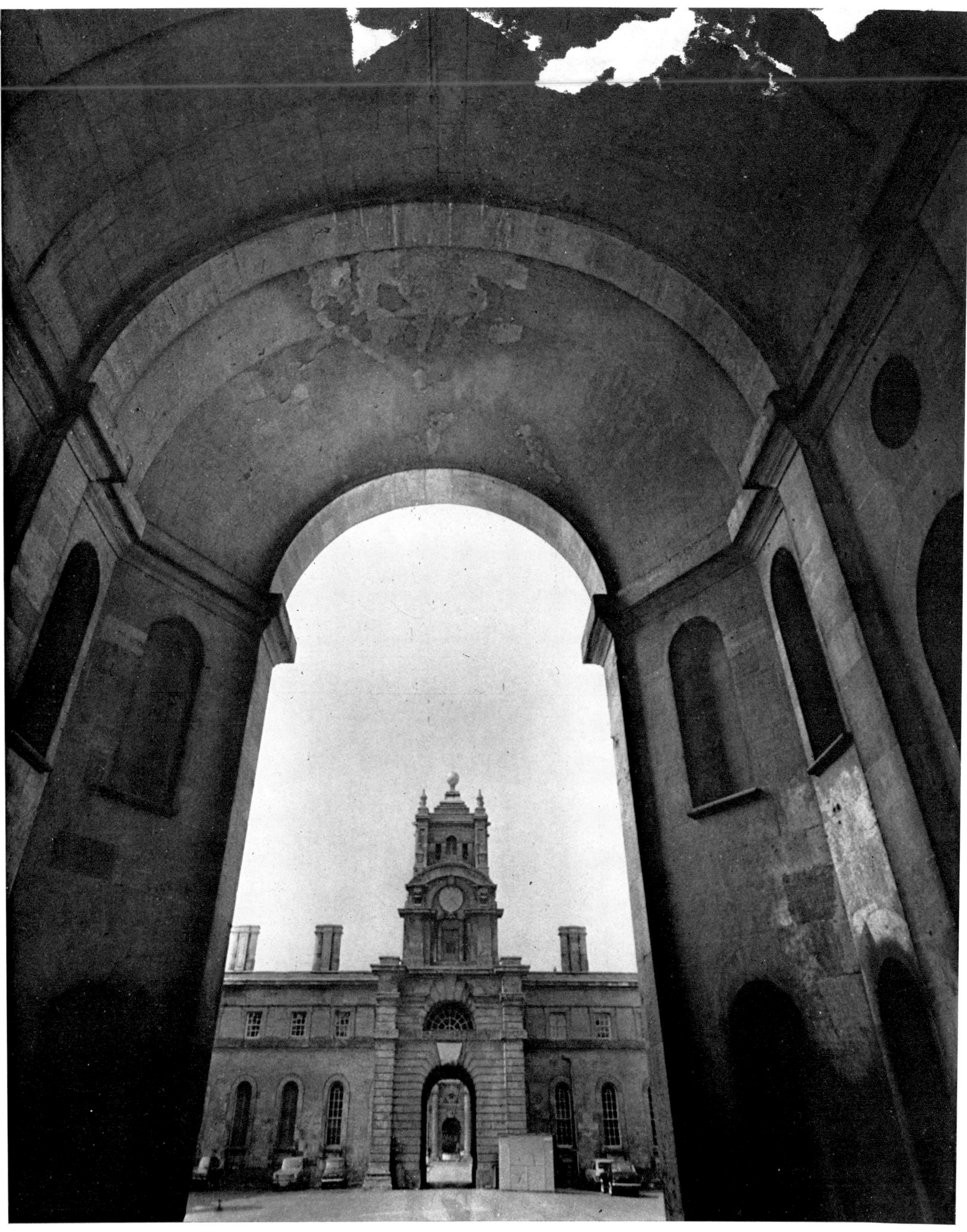

96 Blenheim Palace, East Gate. Interior.

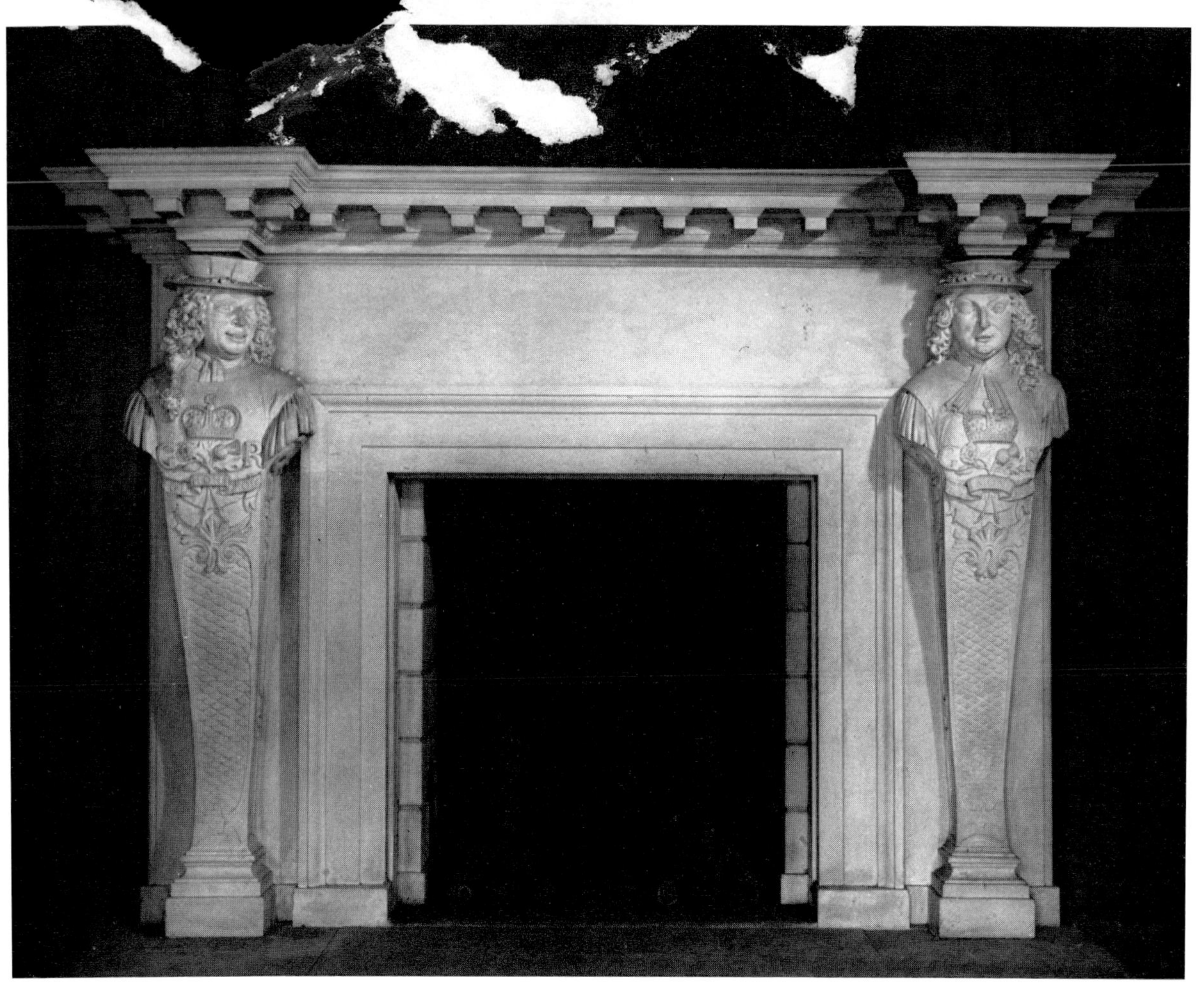

97a Hampton Court. Guard Room. Chimneypiece, 1716.

97b Seaton Delaval. Hall. Chimneypiece.

98 Hampton Court. Prince of Wales's Bedroom. Chimneypiece.

99 Grimsthorpe Castle, Lincs., Hall. Chimneypiece.

100 Hampton Court. Prince of Wales's Drawing-Room. Chimneypiece.

101 Hampton Court. Prince of Wales's Presence-Chamber. Chimneypiece.

102 Vanbrugh Castle, Greenwich. South front. 1718–19.

103 Vanbrugh Castle from the north-east.

104 Gateway to Vanbrugh Fields. Drawing by Paul Sandby.

105 Vanbrugh Castle. Drawing by William Stukeley, 1721. *Society of Antiquaries.*

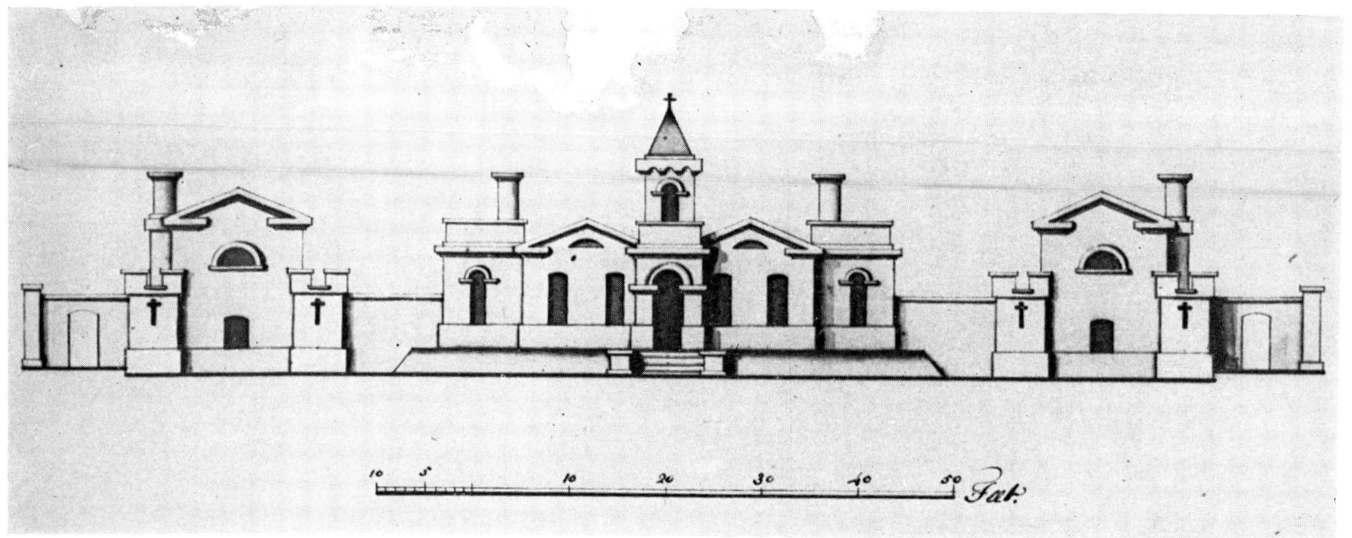

106 The Nunnery, 1719–20, *destroyed*. Elevation. *Elton Hall*.

107 The Nunnery. Drawing by J. C. Buckler, 1823. *British Museum*.

108 Vanbrugh House, 1721–2, *destroyed*. Drawing by William Stukeley. *Bodleian Library*.

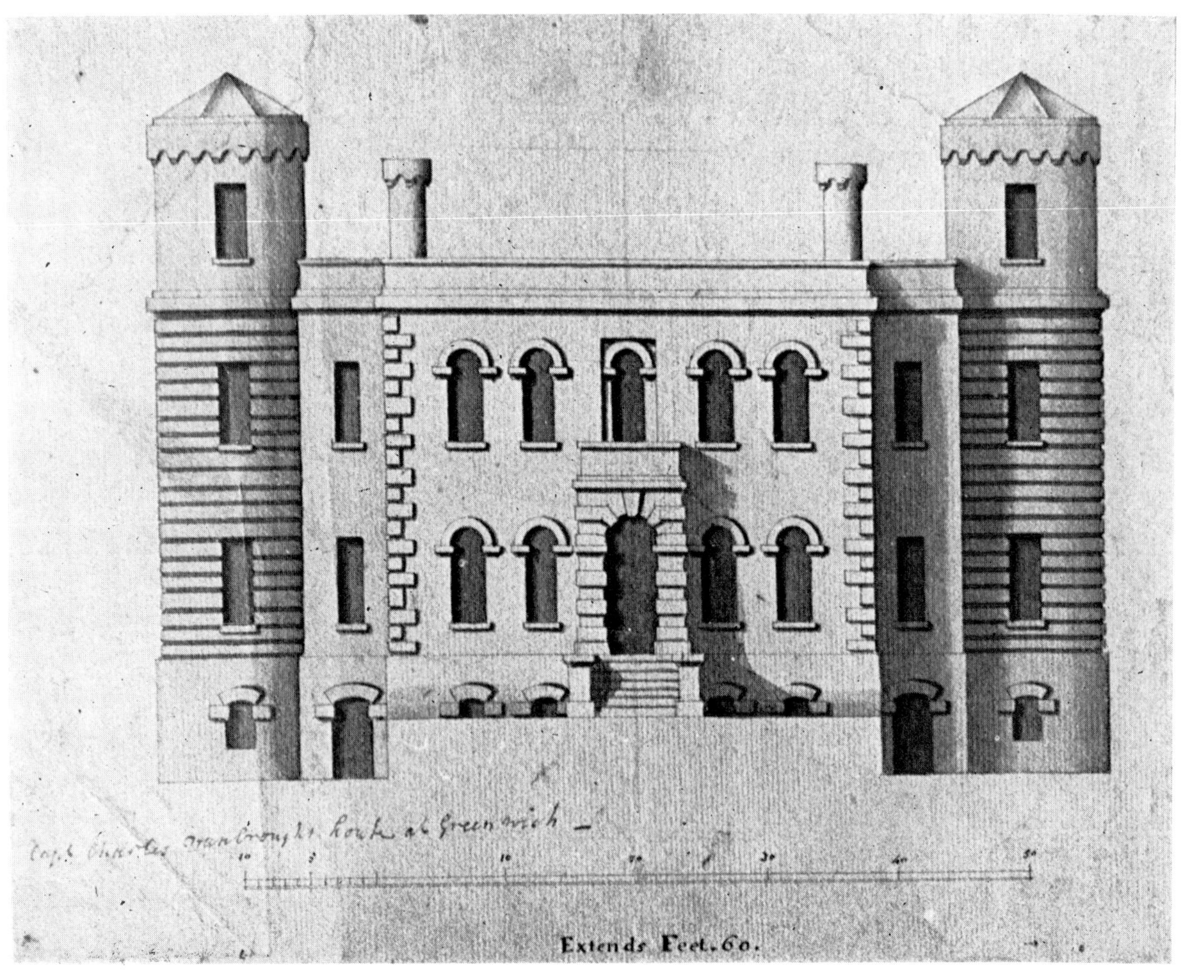

109 Vanbrugh House. Preliminary elevation. *Elton Hall*.

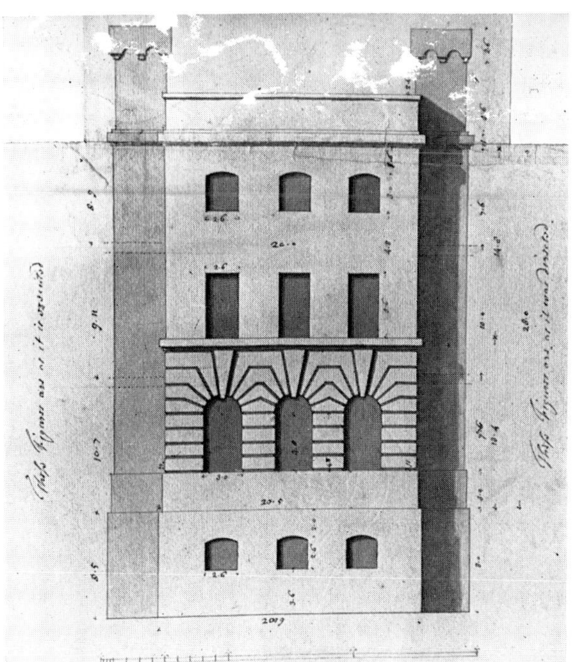

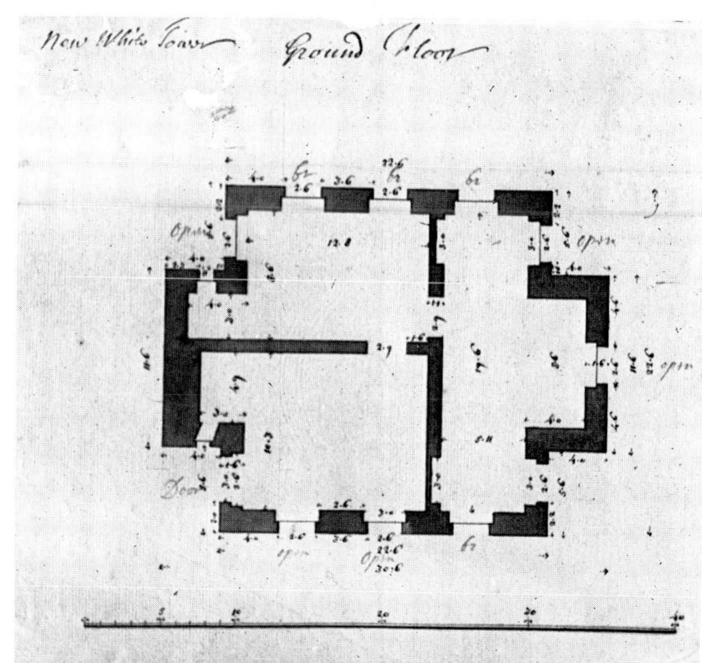

110 The New White Tower, *c.*1722. Elevation and plan. *Elton Hall.*

111 The South White Tower, 1722–4, *destroyed. Martin Collection, London Borough of Greenwich, Local Collection.*

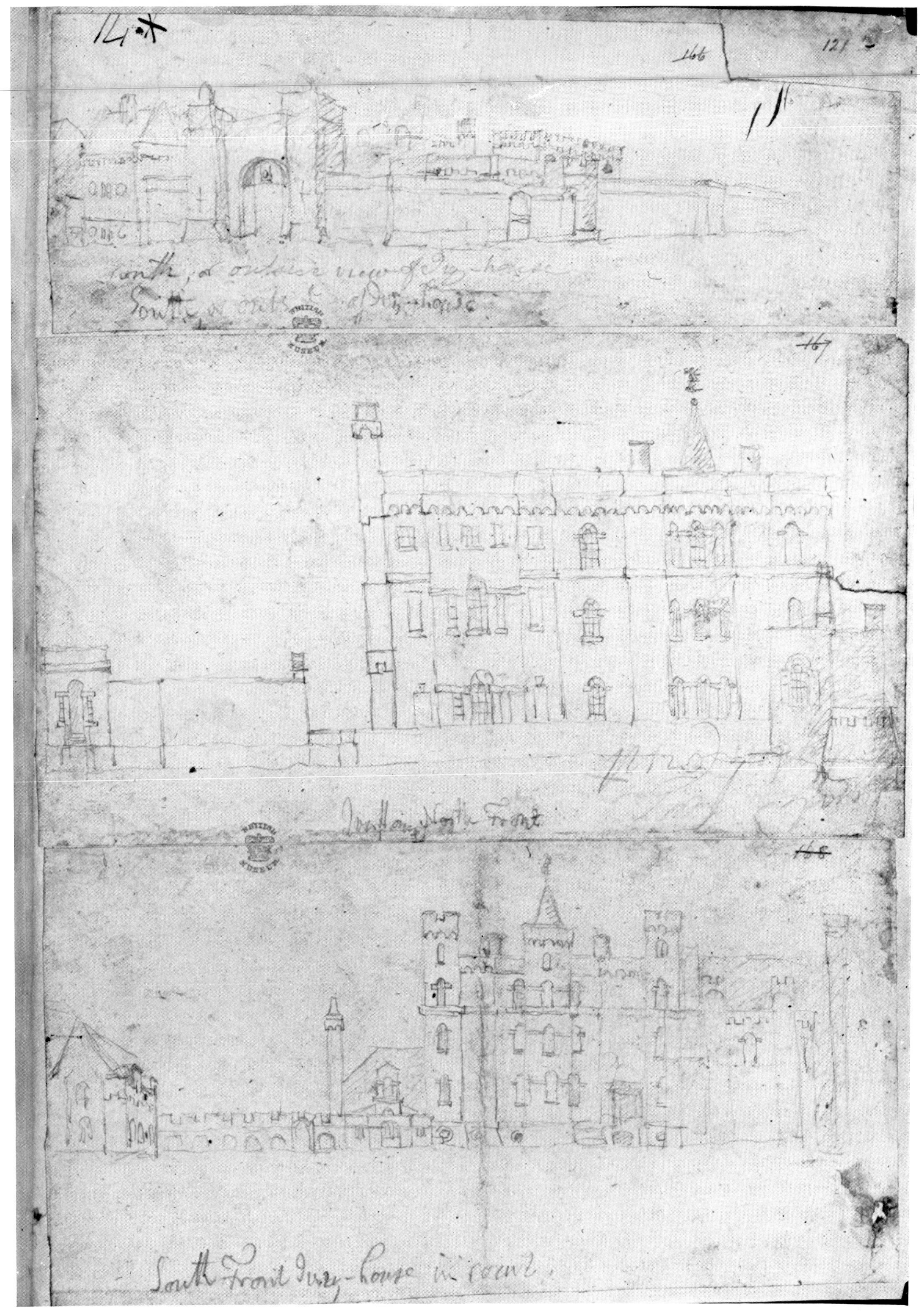

112 Vanbrugh Castle. Drawing by John Carter, 1815. *British Museum*.

113 Vanbrugh Castle. Drawing by J. C. Buckler, 1823. *British Museum.*

114 Vanbrugh Castle from the north-east. Engraving by W. H. Toms after J. Armstrong. *British Museum.*

115 Claremont, Surrey. The Belvedere, 1715. Photographed in 1976.

116 Claremont. View from the roof of the Belvedere in 1962.

117 Swinstead, Lincs. Old Summer House, *c.*1720.

118 Claremont, 1715–20. Drawing by J. F. Rigaud?, *c.*1750. *Royal Library, Windsor Castle.*

119 Seaton Delaval, Northumb., 1720–8. North court.

120 Seaton Delaval. North front.

121 Seaton Delaval. West side.

122 Seaton Delaval. South front.

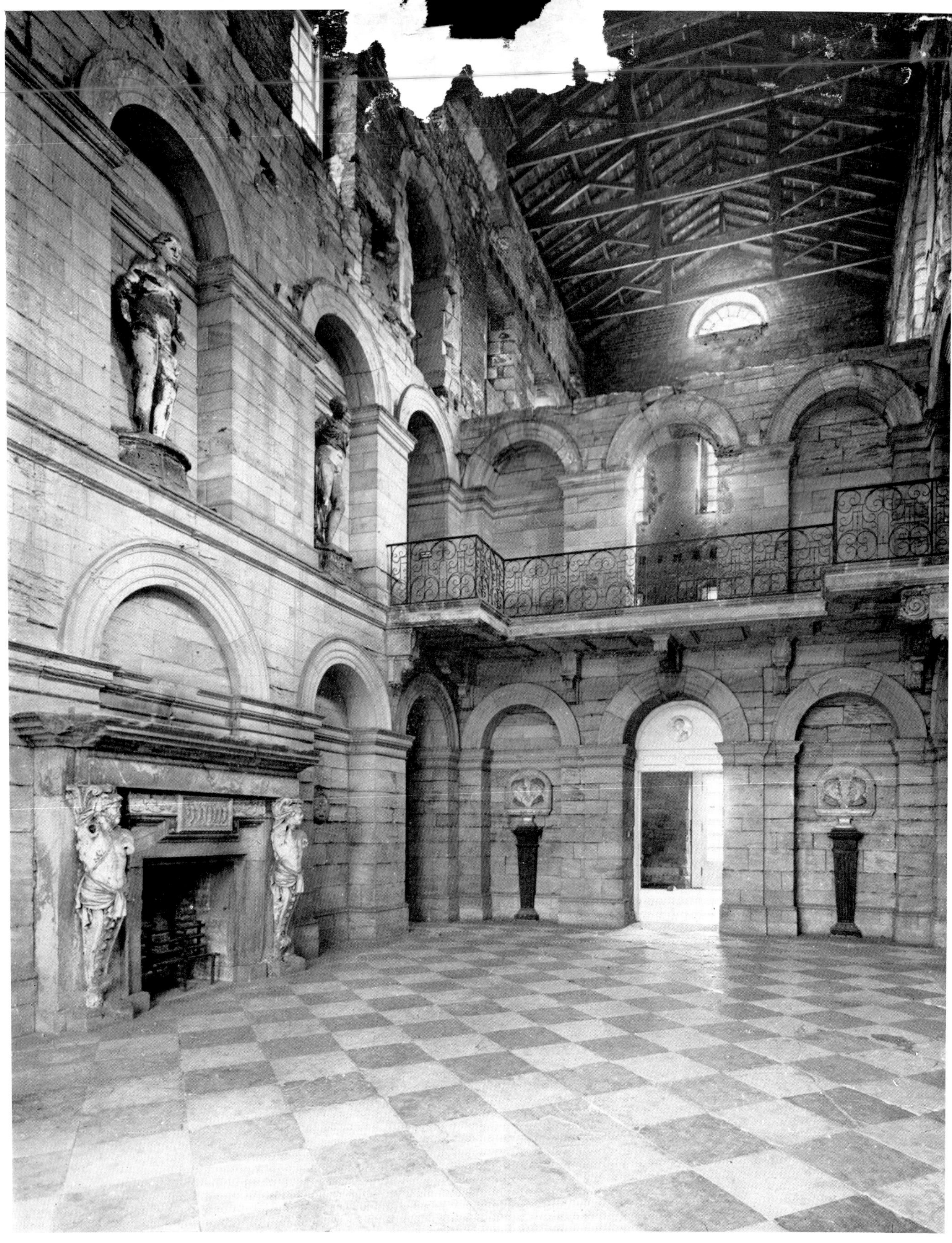

123 Seaton Delaval. The Hall.

124 Castle Howard, Pyramid Gate, 1719.

125 Stowe, Bucks. North portico, *c.*1720.

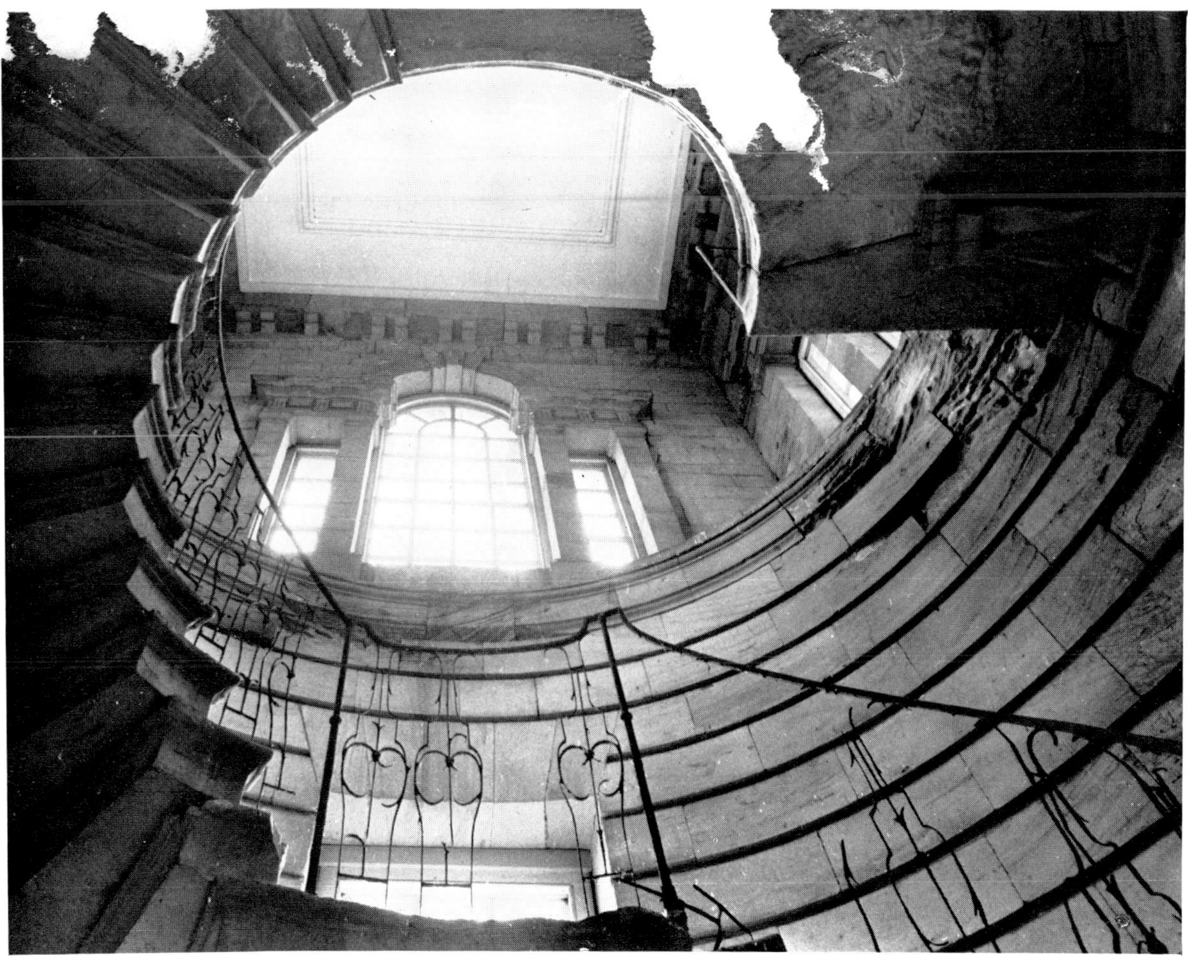

126 Seaton Delaval. Top of west staircase.

127 Lumley Castle, Co. Durham. West front, begun 1722.

128 Duncombe Park, Yorks. Open temple, *c.*1718.

129 Castle Howard. The Temple, 1725–8.

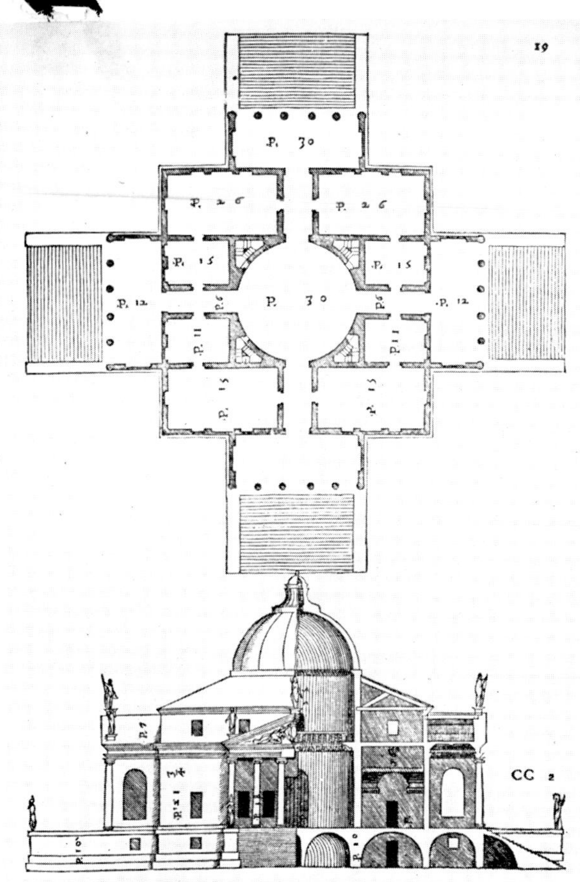

130 Palladio's Rotonda. *Quattro Libri dell' Architettura*, 1570.

131 Castle Howard. The Great Obelisk, 1714.

132 Castle Howard. The Temple. Detail of window-head.

133 Eastbury. First design. Garden front. *Victoria and Albert Museum.*

134 Eastbury. Alternative design. *Worcester College, Oxford.*

135 Eastbury. Gateway to north court.

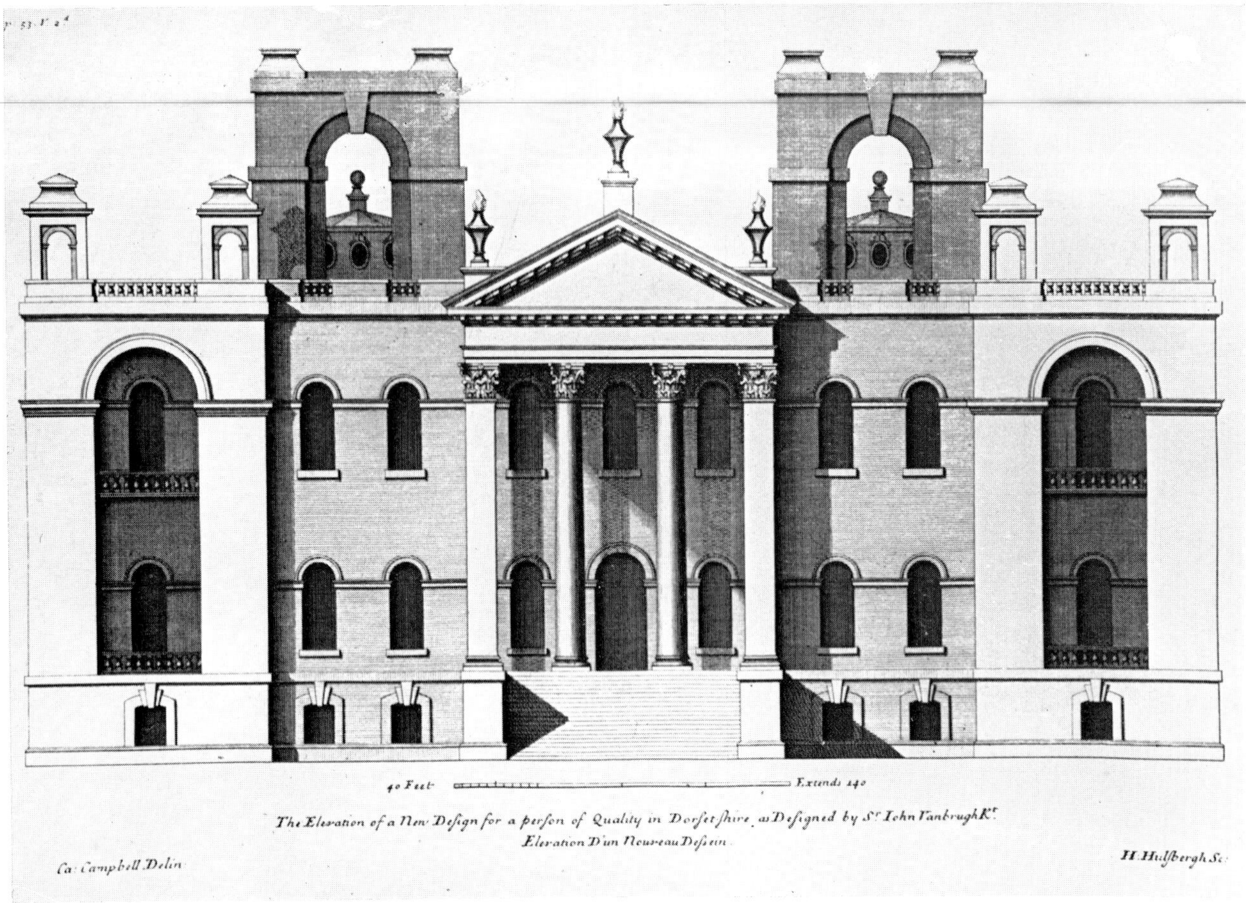

40 Feet
Extends 140
The Elevation of a New Design for a person of Quality in Dorset-shire, as Designed by Sr. John Vanbrugh Kt.
Elevation D'un Nouveau Dessein
Ca: Campbell Delin
H Hulsbergh Sc

136 Eastbury. 'New Design.' Entrance front. *Vitruvius Britannicus*, II.

137 Eastbury. Surviving north wing.

138 Eastbury. 'New Design.' Garden front. *Vitruvius Britannicus*, II.

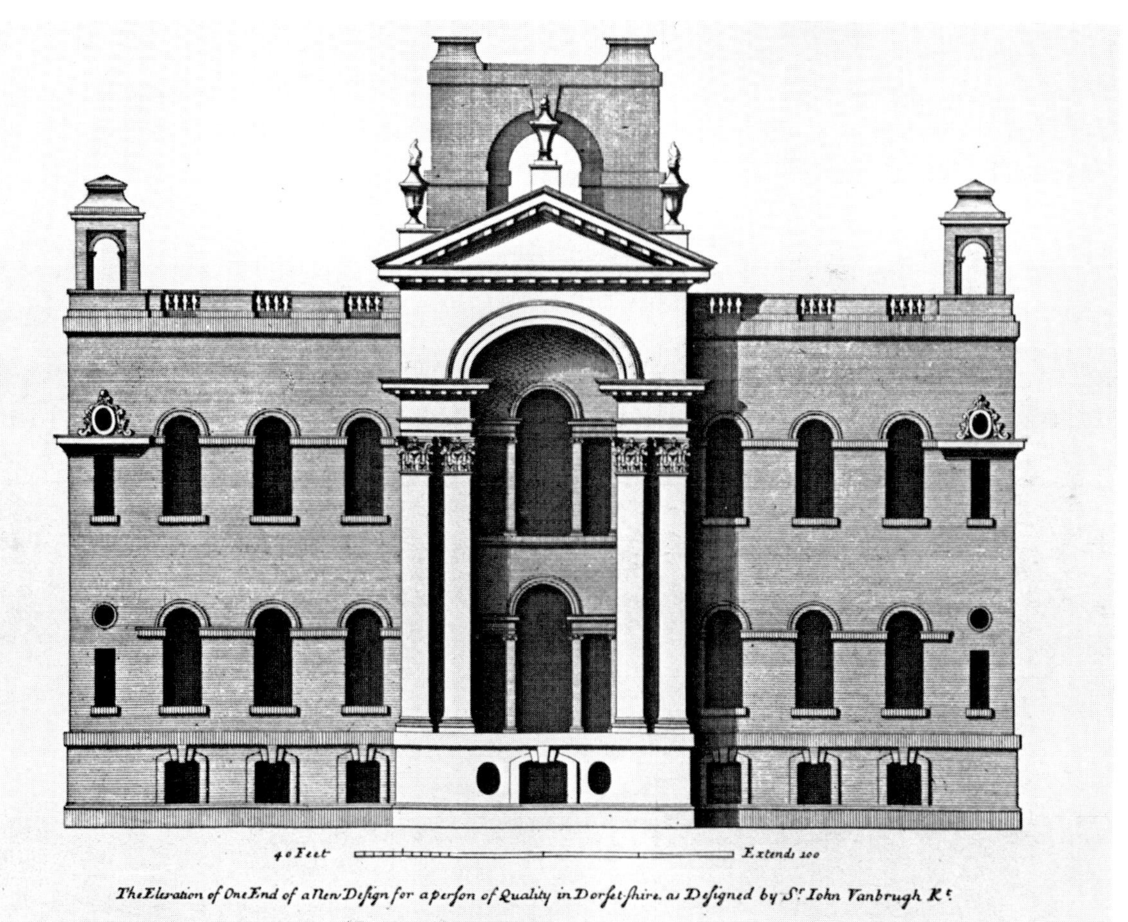

139 Eastbury. 'New Design.' Side elevation. *Vitruvius Britannicus*, II.

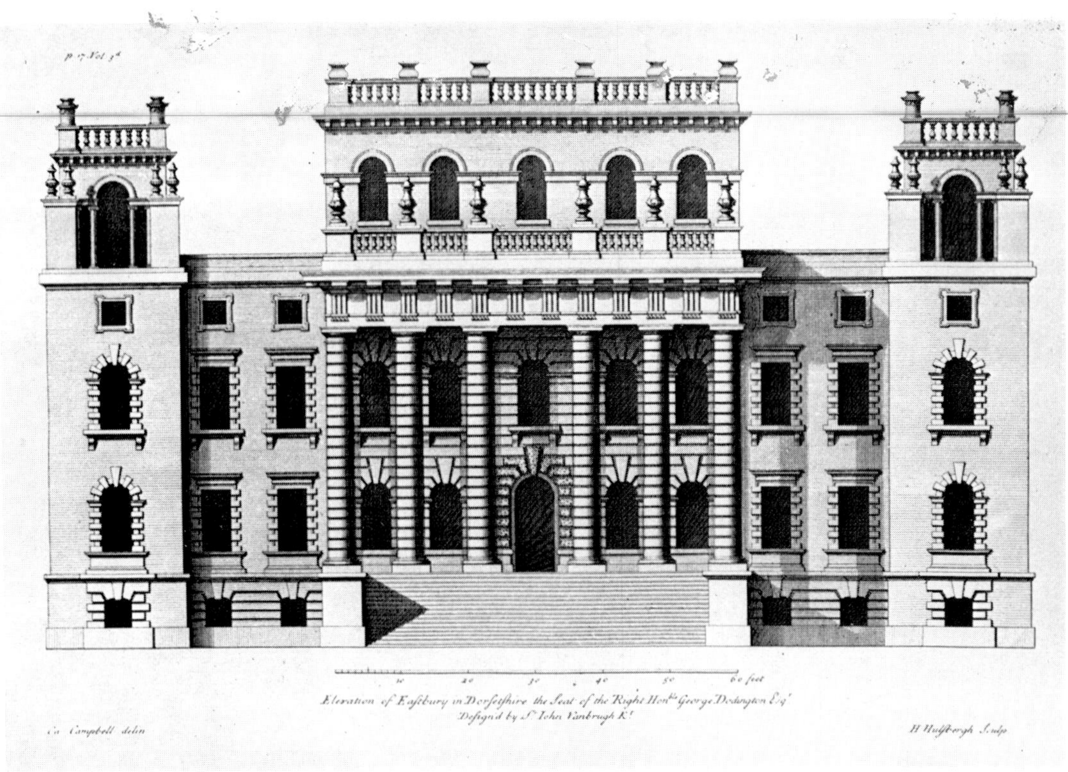

10 20 30 40 50 60 feet
Elevation of Eastbury in Dorsetshire the Seat of the Right Honble George Dodington Esq
Design'd by Sr John Vanbrugh Kt
H Hulsbergh Sculp

140 Eastbury. Final design. Entrance front, *destroyed. Vitruvius Britannicus*, III.

141 Eastbury. The Temple, *destroyed. Vitruvius Britannicus*, III.

142 St James's Palace. The Great Kitchen, 1716–17. J. B. Pyne's *Royal Residences*, 1819.

143 Woolwich. Old Ordnance Board-Room, 1718–20.

144 Devonport. Gun Wharf Terrace, *c.*1720–5.

145 Windsor Park. Pump house, 1718.

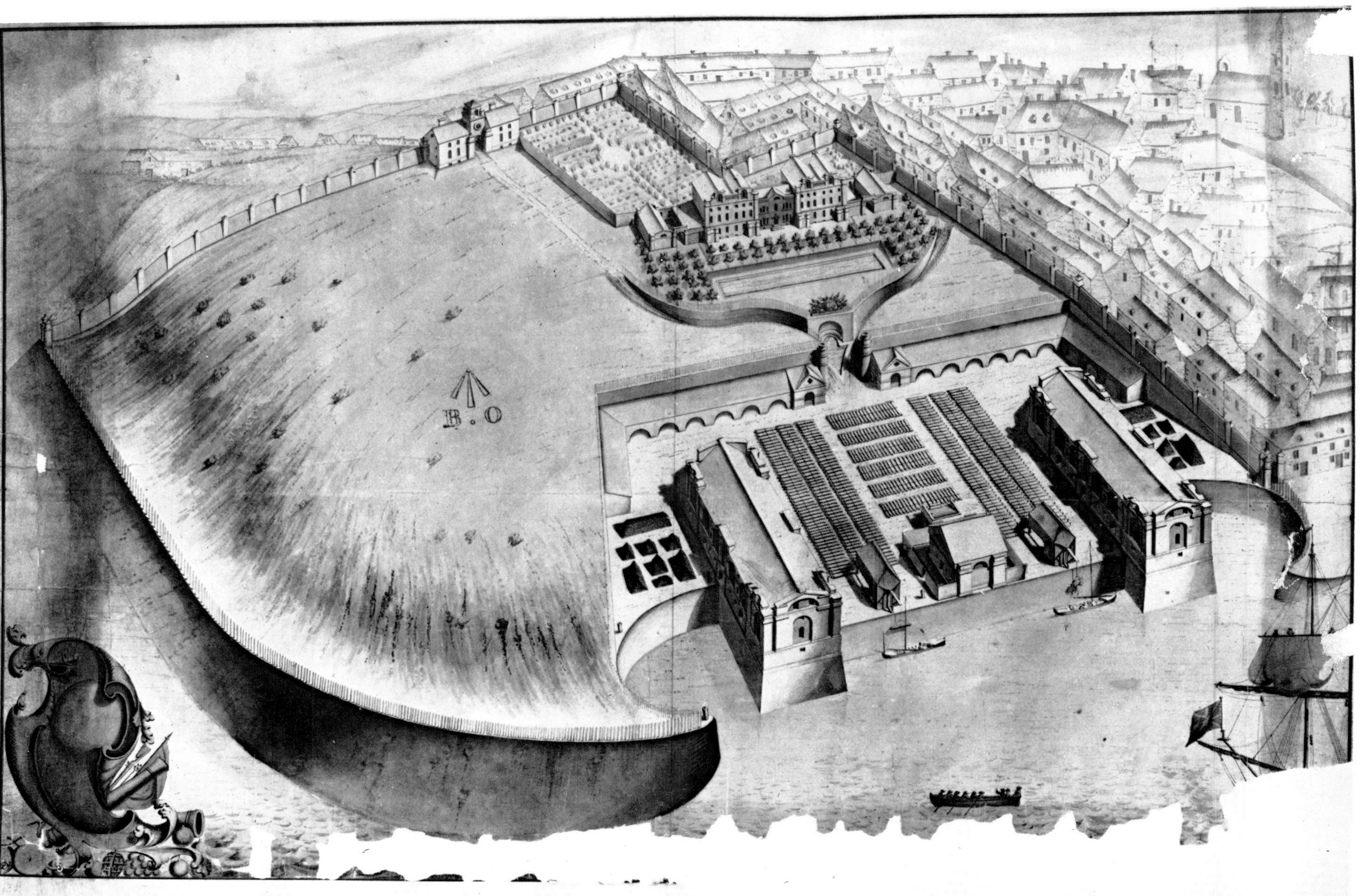

146 Devonport. Gun Wharf, *destroyed. Public Record Office.*

147 Skelbrooke, Yorks. Robin Hood's Well, *c.*1720.

148 Chatham Dockyard. The Great Store, begun 1717.

149 Hanover House, Peckham, *destroyed*. Drawing by J. C. Buckler, *British Museum*.

150 Henry Joynes. Carshalton, Surrey. Water Pavilion, *c.*1725.

151 Grimsthorpe Castle, Lincs., from the north, 1715 ?–26.

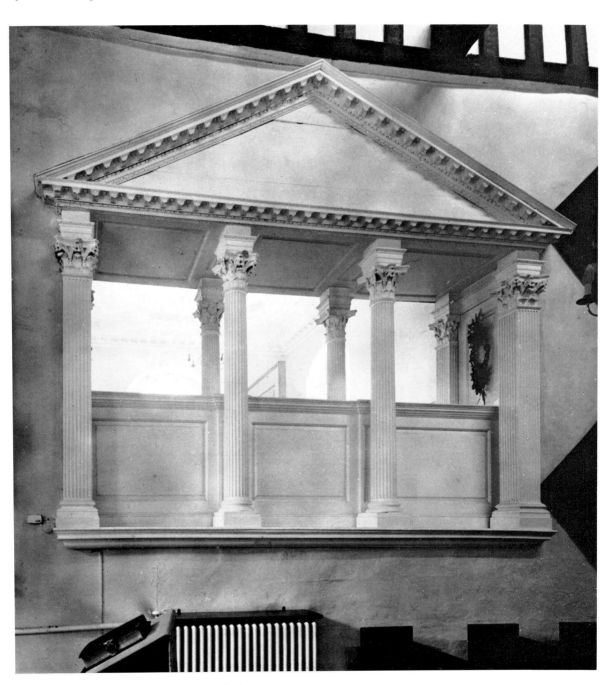

152 Esher Old Church, Surrey, Newcastle Pew, 1723–5.

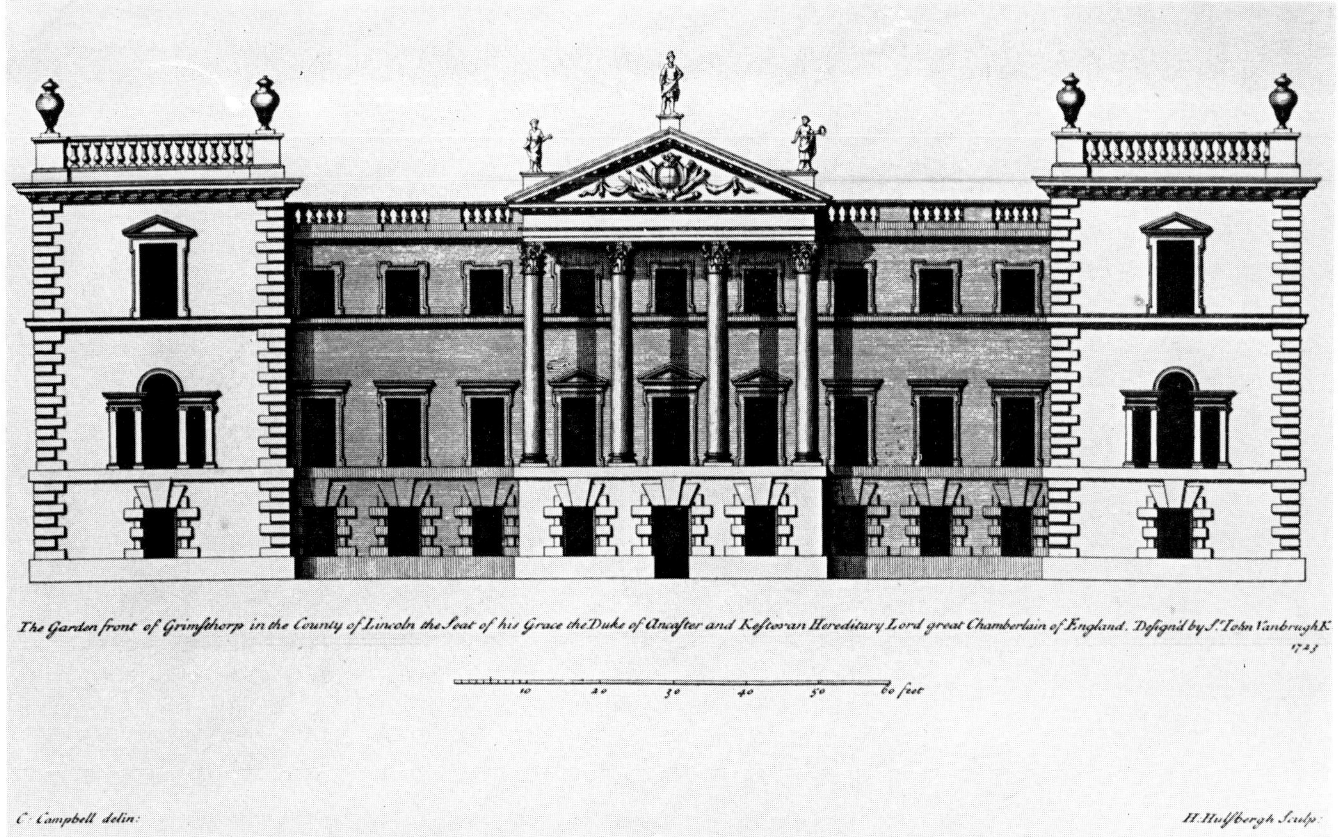

The Garden front of Grimsthorp in the County of Lincoln the Seat of his Grace the Duke of Ancaster and Kesteven Hereditary Lord great Chamberlain of England. Design'd by Sr. John Vanbrugh K.
1723
10 20 30 40 50 60 feet
C: Campbell delin:
H. Hulsbergh Sculp:

153 Grimsthorpe. Project for south front, 1723–4. *Vitruvius Britannicus*, III.

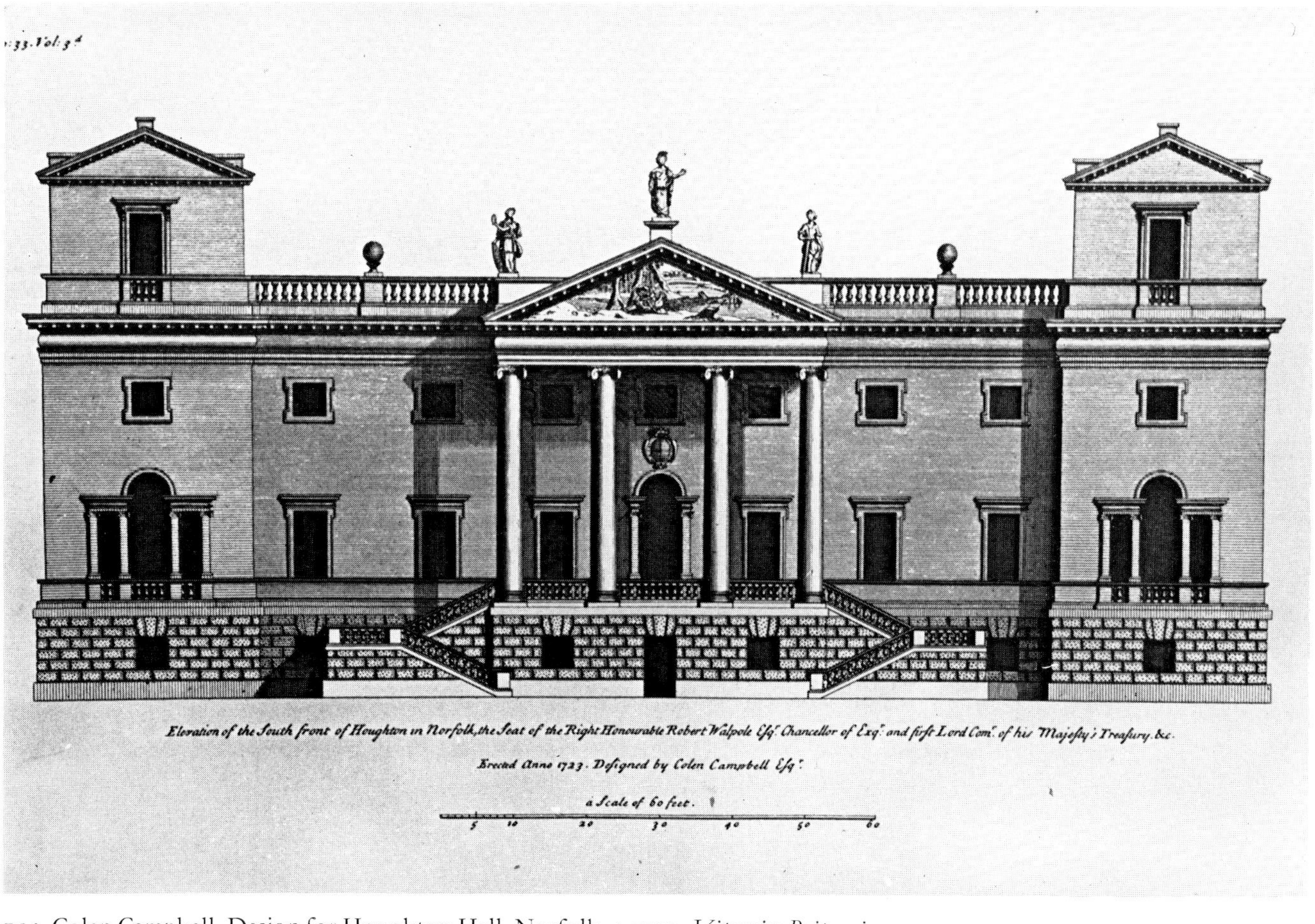

154 Colen Campbell. Design for Houghton Hall, Norfolk, *c.* 1722. *Vitruvius Britannicus*, III.

155 Grimsthorpe. North-east tower.

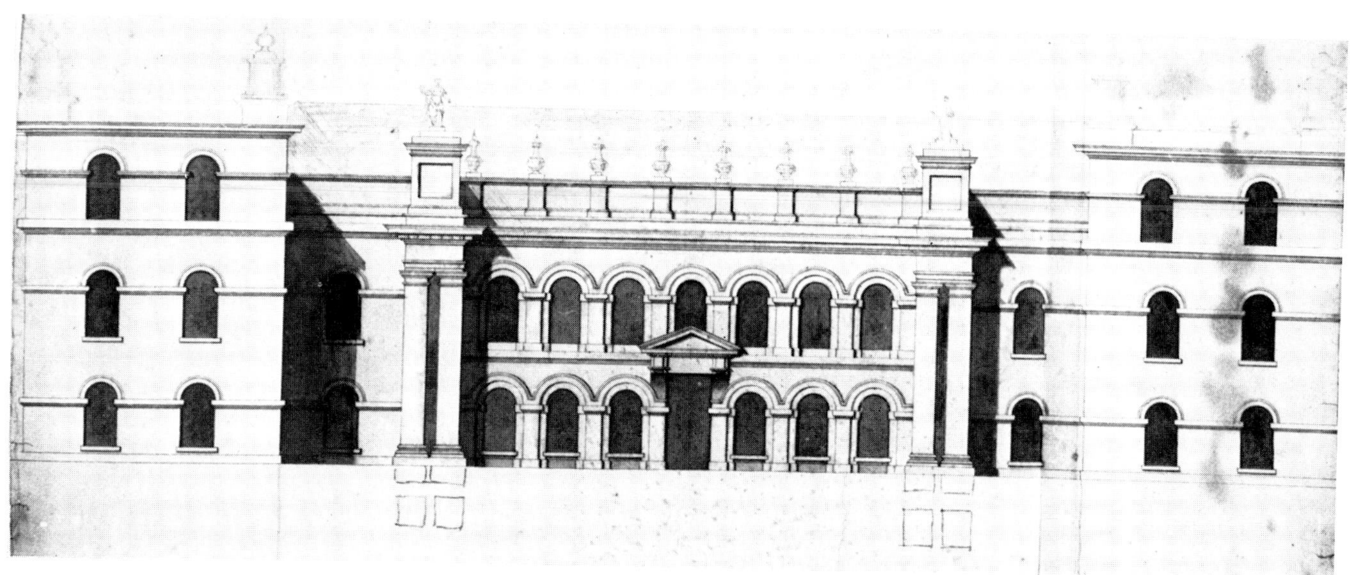

156 Grimsthorpe. Early project for north front, *c.*1715. *Elton Hall.*

157 Grimsthorpe. North front.

158 Grimsthorpe. Staircase arcade.

159 Grimsthorpe. The Hall.

160 Grimsthorpe. Stair gallery doorcase, 1723–6.